Algorithms for Games AI

Algorithms for Games AI

Guest Editors

Wenxin Li
Haifeng Zhang

MDPI

Basel • Beijing • Wuhan • Barcelona • Belgrade • Novi Sad • Cluj • Manchester

Guest Editors

Wenxin Li
Institute for Artificial Intelligence
Peking University
Beijing
China

Haifeng Zhang
Institute of Automation
University of Chinese Academy of Science
Beijing
China

Editorial Office
MDPI AG
Grosspeteranlage 5
4052 Basel, Switzerland

This is a reprint of the Special Issue, published open access by the journal *Algorithms* (ISSN 1999-4893), freely accessible at: https://www.mdpi.com/journal/algorithms/special_issues/Games_AI.

For citation purposes, cite each article independently as indicated on the article page online and as indicated below:

Lastname, A.A.; Lastname, B.B. Article Title. *Journal Name* **Year**, *Volume Number*, Page Range.

ISBN 978-3-7258-4901-7 (Hbk)
ISBN 978-3-7258-4902-4 (PDF)
https://doi.org/10.3390/books978-3-7258-4902-4

Contents

algorithms

MDPI

Editorial

Algorithms for Game AI

Wenxin Li [1,*] and Haifeng Zhang [2]

1 School of Computer Science, Peking University, Beijing 100871, China
2 Institute of Automation, Chinese Academy of Sciences, Beijing 100190, China; haifeng.zhang@ia.ac.cn
* Correspondence: lwx@pku.edu.cn; Tel.: +86-10-62753425

Games have long been benchmarks for AI algorithms and, with the boost of computational power and the application of new algorithms, AI systems have achieved superhuman performance in games for which it was once thought that they could only be mastered by humans due to their high complexity. Since Deep Blue beat professional human players in chess [1], many milestones have been reported in various games, from board games like Go [2–4] and card games like Texas Hold'em [5–7] to video games like StarCraft [8], Dota 2 [9], and HoK [10].

There are two reasons why games are excellent benchmarks for AI algorithms. First, games are born to test and challenge human intelligence—just as children learn about the world by playing with games and toys during their first years of life, the diversity of games can provide a rich context to test different cognitive and decision-making capabilities. For example, board games, with their formalized state representation and perfect information, require searching and planning from the current game state. Card games, with their non-deterministic transition and imperfect information, reveal more sophisticated strategies, such as bluffing and deception, skills that are normally reserved for humans. Video games, with their high-dimensional states and long episodes, require feature extraction, memorization, long-term planning, and multi-agent cooperation and competition. These characteristics make games strong testbeds for the gradual skill progression of AI.

Second, solving complex real-world problems usually requires repeated trial and error, which can be very costly. By simulating or emulating real-world scenarios, games provide a low-cost or even zero-cost platform to validate various algorithms and solutions. In a broad sense, games are not limited to those that people play for entertainment, but any decision-making problems can be modeled and simulated as games, from simple robot control to complex scenarios of resource allocation, scheduling, and routing across various industrial fields. Algorithms proposed and developed to play games are eventually applied to various real-world problems for social benefit in all aspects of life.

This Special Issue entitled "Algorithms for Game AI" covers new and innovative approaches for solving game AI problems. These approaches range from traditional algorithms like planning and searching, to modern algorithms such as deep reinforcement learning. The papers in this Special Issue address both the theoretical and practical challenges of the application of these algorithms.

AI techniques have been implemented in gaming industry with a wide range of applications [11], such as procedure content generation (PCG), where algorithms autonomously create game worlds, levels, and assets to enhance replayability, and AI-driven non-player character (NPC) behavior, simulating human-like decision-making and emotional responses for better engagement. Nevertheless, we mainly focused on the application of building game-playing agents, because of the inherent challenges and the potential for solving real-world decision-making problems. In this field, game AI algorithms can be divided into several categories, such as the following:

- Search algorithms are used for real-time planning. These algorithms are designed to expand a search tree from the game state currently encountered to evaluate future states under different sequences of actions. Some algorithms like A* [12] leverage heuristic functions to guide the selection of unexplored nodes, which evaluate game states based on the domain knowledge of human players. In general, searching more deeply usually yields better policies because it eliminates some errors of value estimation by looking more steps ahead. However, searching more deeply costs more computation, and the search depth is usually, in practice, fixed or decided by iterative deepening to limit the time cost. In multi-agent competitive games, adversarial search algorithms such as Minimax [13] are often used, where the agents must act against opponents and maximize their own benefits. Monte Carlo Tree Search (MCTS) [14] is one of the most popular search algorithms due to its efficiency and robustness with no domain knowledge needed. Many variants of MCTS have been proposed to further improve its efficiency by incorporating upper confidence bounds [15], domain knowledge [16], and parallelization [17].
- Optimization algorithms refine solutions to achieve specific goals, which are used to train agents with parameterized models. Among these, linear programming algorithms optimize objective functions under a set of constraints; evolutionary methods, such as Genetic Algorithms (GA) and Evolutionary Strategies (ES) [18], create a population of individuals where the fitter ones have a higher probability of reproducing and inheriting part of their structures, inspired by the process of natural selection; gradient descent is the foundation of deep learning, which achieves the efficient parameter tuning of modern artificial neural networks. These algorithms train policy models or value models containing prior knowledge before actual gameplay, which can be combined with real-time planning algorithms during the inference phase.
- Supervised learning is a data-driven method to learn patterns and relationships from labeled data. In the context of game AI, the data usually refer to the game states or observations, and the task is to learn a policy model or value model that predicts the action or the estimated value under the current state. These algorithms require a great deal of labeled data in the form of state–action or state–value pairs, usually collected from data on human gameplay or data generated by other game-playing algorithms. In general, there are two types of applications based on the data source. Applying supervised learning on human data can learn implicit human knowledge and store it in policy models or value models. Another type of application, known as policy distillation [19], relies on data generated by other models, which is used to distill a lightweight model from a larger one to improve computational efficiency or to consolidate multiple task-specific policies into a single unified policy.
- Reinforcement learning (RL) studies how agents should take actions in an environment to maximize cumulative rewards over time. Typically, RL models the environment as a Markov Decision Process (MDP), where the transition probability and rewards satisfy the Markov property that they are only related to the current state and action. When the transition model is known, generalized policy iteration, such as value iteration, uses dynamic programming to solve the optimal policy and its value function based on Bellman Equation. However, in most cases, the environment model is unknown, and model-free algorithms are preferable as they learn from experiences by interacting with the environment. There are two kinds of model-free algorithms:
    - Value-based algorithms optimize the policy by approximating the values of states or state–action pairs and selecting better actions based on these values.

There are different ways to update the value function [20]. A Monte Carlo (MC) algorithm updates the value function based on the cumulative rewards towards the end of the episode, while a temporal difference (TD) algorithm updates the value function based on the current reward and the value of the next state in a bootstrapping manner. Algorithms such as DQN [21] use deep neural networks to approximate the state–action value function, which can be applied to games with large state space.

  - Policy-based algorithms directly learn parameterized policies based on gradients of some performance measure using the gradient descent method. For example, REINFORCE [22] samples full episode trajectories with Monte Carlo methods to estimate returns as the loss function. However, such pure policy-based algorithms suffer from high variance, and actor–critic algorithms [23] have been proposed, which use actors to learn parameterized policies and critics to learn value functions, allowing the policy updates to consider the value estimates to reduce the variance. Actor–critic algorithms include DDPG [24], A3C [25], IMPALA [26], TRPO [27], and PPO [28], to name but a few.

- Regret-based algorithms seek to find the Nash equilibrium in games with imperfect information. The basic idea is to choose actions to minimize the regret of not having chosen other actions in previous games. Counterfactual regret minimization (CFR) [29] traverses the game tree for multiple iterations to calculate the cumulative regrets of each state–action pair. Many variants of CFR, such as Discounted CFR [30] and MCCFR [31], have been proposed to improve efficiency by incorporating sampling, discounting, and reweighting techniques. For games with large state space, algorithms such as Deep CFR [32] and DREAM [33] adopt neural networks to approximate the regrets and policies.
- Self-play algorithms are often used in competitive multi-agent environments. In fictitious play (FP) [34], each agent calculates its best response to the opponent's average policies, which has been proven to converge to the Nash equilibrium in theory. When applied to games with large state space, neural fictitious self-play (NFSP) [35] adopts neural networks as the policy model, using reinforcement learning to calculate best responses and supervised learning to learn average policies. Double oracle (DO) [36] starts from a small policy subset, where each agent iteratively calculates the Nash equilibrium under the current strategy set and adds it to the set. Policy-space response oracles (PSRO) [37] provide a unified view of them using a policy pool to train new policies to be added, which has become the common practice of multi-agent RL training.
- Multi-agent RL (MARL) algorithms extend single-agent RL algorithms to multi-agent settings, usually following a training paradigm called centralized training decentralized execution (CTDE). CTDE jointly trains multiple agents in a centralized manner but keeps their independence in execution, which can provide a mechanism of communication to eliminate the problems of unstable dynamics in independent training. For example, value-based algorithms like Value Decomposition Network (VDN) [38] and QMIX [39] are variants of DQN in cooperative multi-agent settings that adopt centralized state-action value functions, using summation and mixing networks to combine individual Q-networks. Multi-agent DDPG (MADDPG) [40] is a policy-based algorithm that generalizes DDPG to multi-agent settings, and many variants of it have been proposed to improve its performance and efficiency.

This Special Issue presents eleven papers covering a wide range of game AI topics, including the quantification of non-transitivity in chess, the expressiveness of level generators in Super Mario Bros, Mahjong as a new game AI benchmark, new MARL algorithms to reduce Q-value bias, surveys of various AI algorithms in cyber defense, energy areas and games, the application of MCTS in Amazons, the application of deep reinforcement learning in autonomous vehicle driving, and the application of transformers in both offline RL and imitation learning. The list of contributions to this Special Issue is as follows:

Contribution 1 [41] examines the issue of cyber defense from the perspective of decision-making and proposes a framework to study the problem characteristics of different cyber defense contexts. The framework identifies four stages in the life cycle of threats—pentest, design, response, and recovery—integrating both the attacker's and defender's perspectives. By analyzing the decision-making scenarios in each of these four stages, this paper presents a comprehensive survey of existing research on the application of reinforcement learning in cyber defense, providing a review of both the problem boundary and current methods.

Contribution 2 [42] measures the degree of non-transitivity in chess and investigates the implications of non-transitivity for population-based self-play algorithms. By measuring both the Nash clusters and the length of the longest transition cycles in the policies from billions of human games, this paper reveals that the strategy space of chess indicates a spinning top geometry where middle-level strategies have longer non-transitive cycles than top-level or worst-performing ones. Further experiments with a fixed-memory fictitious play algorithm, which simulates the behavior of common population-based self-play methods, indicate not only that larger populations are required for training to converge, but that the minimum size of the population is also related to the degree of non-transitivity of the strategy space.

Contribution 3 [43] reviews machine learning algorithms to solve combinatorial optimization problems (COPs) in energy areas. COPs are a class of NP-hard problems used to optimize an objective function within a discrete domain, which have been the focus of traditional game AI research and can be seen across various industrial fields, from resource allocation and scheduling to routing scenarios. This paper focuses on the context of energy areas, including petroleum supply chains, steel making, electric power systems, and wind power. It presents a systematic review of ML algorithms used to solve COPs in these scenarios, including supervised learning (SL), deep learning (DL), reinforcement learning (RL), and recently proposed game theory-based methods. Application of these algorithms are discussed in detail, including recent advances and the challenges and future directions of this field.

Contribution 4 [44] reviews algorithms and paradigms to build high-performance game-playing agents. Many game AI algorithms, from searching and planning to SL, RL, and game theory-based methods are presented as basic components of game AI systems. By summarizing the implementation of recent state-of-the-art game AI systems in various games, which have been achieving superhuman performance, this paper provides a comprehensive comparison of these milestones via decomposing each into its components and relating them to the characteristics of the games to which they are applied. Three types of paradigms are concluded from these milestones, with their scope and limitations discussed in detail. Stemming from these comparisons and analyses, the paper claims that deep reinforcement learning is likely to become a general methodology for game AI as future trends unfold.

Contribution 5 [45] introduces Official International Mahjong as a new benchmark for game AI research. Mahjong presents challenges for AI research due to its multi-agent nature, rich hidden information, and complex scoring rules. This paper presents in detail Mahjong Competition Rules (MCR), a Mahjong variant widely used in competitions due to its complexity, as well as a series of Mahjong AI competitions held in IJCAI, which adopts the duplicate format to reduce variance. By comparing the algorithms and the performance of AI agents in these competitions, the paper shows that supervised learning and reinforcement learning are currently the state-of-the-art methods in this game and perform much better than heuristic methods. While the top AI agents still cannot beat professional human players, this paper claims that this game can be a new benchmark for AI research due to its complexity and popularity.

Contribution 6 [46] explores the application of language models in offline RL, and proposes Action-Translator Transformer (ATT) as the policy model. ATT is built upon the Sequence-to-Sequence (Seq2Seq) model structure used in text translation tasks. Different from Decision Transformer (DT), which predicts next states as well as rewards and actions, ATT only predicts actions to maximize cumulative rewards, given partial trajectories containing states, actions, and rewards. Positional encoding typically used in NLP tasks is also devised to adapt to new input elements of RL. Experiments performed in several Mujoco environments show that ATT performs better than other offline RL algorithms such as DT.

Contribution 7 [47] discusses the issue of Q-value overestimation in MADDPG, and proposes two variants to reduce estimation bias, called Multi-Agent Mutual Twin Delayed Deep Deterministic Policy Gradient (M2ATD3) and Multi-Agent Softmax Twin Delayed Deep Deterministic Policy Gradient (MASTD3). Both methods introduce a second Q-network for each agent and incorporate either the minimum or maximum value of two Q-values to reduce bias in the opposite direction. MASTD3 further extends the Softmax Bellman operation to multi-agent settings by fixing others' actions and only changing its own actions. Experiments on two multi-agent environments, Particles and Tank, show some performance improvement and Q-value bias reduction compared to baseline methods such as MATD3.

Contribution 8 [48] investigates the quality of PCG and specifically evaluates the expressive range of three level generators for Super Mario Bros (SMB) under different algorithms, including Genetic Algorithms (GA), Generative Adversarial Networks (GAN), and Markov Chains (MC). By defining nine metrics for each SMB level covering different types of characteristics, this paper visualizes the expressive ranges based on the metric distribution of generated levels and concludes that GA and MC have a much wider expressive range than GAN. The practice of expressive range analysis (ERA) presented in this paper can help game developers to recognize potential problems early in the PCG process to guarantee high-quality game content.

Contribution 9 [49] explores the application of the MCTS algorithm in Amazons, and proposes MG-PEO, a combination of several optimization strategies called "Move Groups" and "Parallel Evaluation", to improve performance and efficiency. Move groups is a method used to divide a move into two parts, which can largely reduce the branching factor of the game tree and focus the visited nodes of MCTS more on promising subtrees. Parallel evaluation uses multiple threads to speed up the evaluation of leaf nodes. A technique called "Shallow Rollout" is also used to expand the small, fixed depth of nodes and apply the evaluation function to them. Ablation experiments show that MG-PEO agents achieve higher win rate than vanilla MCTS agents, indicating the effectiveness of the proposed optimization strategies.

Contribution 10 [50] explores the application of vision transformer (ViT) to imitate the strategy of human Go players. While AlphaGo has achieved superhuman performance in Go, it often comes up with moves beyond human players' comprehension. This paper adopts supervised learning to train a policy network with vision transformer as its backbone architecture, which achieves professional-level play while mimicking the decision-making of human players. Experiments show that this ViT model achieves higher accuracy than models based on convolutional neural networks (CNNs).

Contribution 11 [51] develops a vehicle driving game and explores the application of different reinforcement learning, including PPO and SAC [52], to train autonomous driving agents. By designing a series of tasks with rising complexity as a curriculum, the agent can gradually learn to navigate through multiple targets within lane boundaries without running into obstacles. Rewards are carefully designed in each task for effective and robust driving. Experiments show that though SAC agents learn faster in early phase, PPO agents achieve better performance and adaptability than SAC, shedding light on the applications of autonomous systems in real-world scenarios.

Finally, as the Guest Editor, it was my pleasure to work with the editorial staff of *Algorithms* to prepare this Special Issue.

Funding: This research received no external funding.

Conflicts of Interest: The author declares no conflicts of interest, since her co-authored paper in this Special Issue has been externally reviewed and accepted.

List of Contributions:

1. Wang, W.; Sun, D.; Jiang, F.; Chen, X.; Zhu, C. Research and Challenges of Reinforcement Learning in Cyber Defense Decision-Making for Intranet Security. *Algorithms* **2022**, *15*, 134. https://doi.org/10.3390/a15040134.
2. Sanjaya, R.; Wang, J.; Yang, Y. Measuring the Non-Transitivity in Chess. *Algorithms* **2022**, *15*, 152. https://doi.org/10.3390/a15050152.
3. Yang, X.; Wang, Z.; Zhang, H.; Ma, N.; Yang, N.; Liu, H.; Zhang, H.; Yang, L. A Review: Machine Learning for Combinatorial Optimization Problems in Energy Areas. *Algorithms* **2022**, *15*, 205. https://doi.org/10.3390/a15060205.
4. Lu, Y.; Li, W. Techniques and Paradigms in Modern Game AI Systems. *Algorithms* **2022**, *15*, 282. https://doi.org/10.3390/a15080282.
5. Lu, Y.; Li, W.; Li, W. Official International Mahjong: A New Playground for AI Research. *Algorithms* **2023**, *16*, 235. https://doi.org/10.3390/a16050235.
6. Li, Z.; Chen, X.; Fu, J.; Xie, N.; Zhao, T. Reducing Q-Value Estimation Bias via Mutual Estimation and Softmax Operation in MADRL. *Algorithms* **2024**, *17*, 36. https://doi.org/10.3390/a17010036.
7. Li, J.; Xie, N.; Zhao, T. Optimizing Reinforcement Learning Using a Generative Action-Translator Transformer. *Algorithms* **2024**, *17*, 37. https://doi.org/10.3390/a17010037.
8. Schaa, H.; Barriga, N.A. Evaluating the Expressive Range of Super Mario Bros Level Generators. *Algorithms* **2024**, *17*, 307. https://doi.org/10.3390/a17070307.
9. Zhang, L.; Zou, H.; Zhu, Y. An Efficient Optimization of the Monte Carlo Tree Search Algorithm for Amazons. *Algorithms* **2024**, *17*, 334. https://doi.org/10.3390/a17080334.
10. Hsieh, Y.-H.; Kao, C.-C.; Yuan, S.-M. Imitating Human Go Players via Vision Transformer. *Algorithms* **2025**, *18*, 61. https://doi.org/10.3390/a18020061.
11. Penelas, G.; Barbosa, L.; Reis, A.; Barroso, J.; Pinto, T. Machine Learning for Decision Support and Automation in Games: A Study on Vehicle Optimal Path. *Algorithms* **2025**, *18*, 106. https://doi.org/10.3390/a18020106.

References

1. Campbell, M.; Hoane, A.J., Jr.; Hsu, F.H. Deep blue. *Artif. Intell.* **2002**, *134*, 57–83. [CrossRef]
2. Silver, D.; Huang, A.; Maddison, C.J.; Guez, A.; Sifre, L.; Van Den Driessche, G.; Schrittwieser, J.; Antonoglou, I.; Panneershelvam, V.; Lanctot, M.; et al. Mastering the game of Go with deep neural networks and tree search. *Nature* **2016**, *529*, 484–489. [CrossRef]
3. Silver, D.; Schrittwieser, J.; Simonyan, K.; Antonoglou, I.; Huang, A.; Guez, A.; Hubert, T.; Baker, L.; Lai, M.; Bolton, A.; et al. Mastering the game of go without human knowledge. *Nature* **2017**, *550*, 354–359. [CrossRef]
4. Silver, D.; Hubert, T.; Schrittwieser, J.; Antonoglou, I.; Lai, M.; Guez, A.; Lanctot, M.; Sifre, L.; Kumaran, D.; Graepel, T.; et al. A general reinforcement learning algorithm that masters chess, shogi, and Go through self-play. *Science* **2018**, *362*, 1140–1144. [CrossRef] [PubMed]
5. Moravčík, M.; Schmid, M.; Burch, N.; Lisý, V.; Morrill, D.; Bard, N.; Davis, T.; Waugh, K.; Johanson, M.; Bowling, M. Deepstack: Expert-level artificial intelligence in heads-up no-limit poker. *Science* **2017**, *356*, 508–513. [CrossRef] [PubMed]

6. Brown, N.; Sandholm, T. Superhuman AI for heads-up no-limit poker: Libratus beats top professionals. *Science* **2018**, *359*, 418–424. [CrossRef]
7. Brown, N.; Sandholm, T. Superhuman AI for multiplayer poker. *Science* **2019**, *365*, 885–890. [CrossRef]
8. Vinyals, O.; Babuschkin, I.; Chung, J.; Mathieu, M.; Jaderberg, M.; Czarnecki, W.M.; Dudzik, A.; Huang, A.; Georgiev, P.; Powell, R.; et al. Alphastar: Mastering the real-time strategy game starcraft ii. *Deep. Blog* **2019**, *2*, 20.
9. Berner, C.; Brockman, G.; Chan, B.; Cheung, V.; Dębiak, P.; Dennison, C.; Farhi, D.; Fischer, Q.; Hashme, S.; Hesse, C.; et al. Dota 2 with large scale deep reinforcement learning. *arXiv* **2019**, arXiv:1912.06680.
10. Ye, D.; Chen, G.; Zhang, W.; Chen, S.; Yuan, B.; Liu, B.; Chen, J.; Liu, Z.; Qiu, F.; Yu, H.; et al. Towards playing full moba games with deep reinforcement learning. *Adv. Neural Inf. Process. Syst.* **2020**, *33*, 621–632.
11. Xia, B.; Ye, X.; Abuassba, A.O. Recent research on ai in games. In Proceedings of the 2020 International Wireless Communications and Mobile Computing (IWCMC), Limassol, Cyprus, 15–19 June 2020; pp. 505–510.
12. Hart, P.E.; Nilsson, N.J.; Raphael, B. A formal basis for the heuristic determination of minimum cost paths. *IEEE Trans. Syst. Sci. Cybern.* **1968**, *4*, 100–107. [CrossRef]
13. Stockman, G.C. A minimax algorithm better than alpha-beta? *Artif. Intell.* **1979**, *12*, 179–196. [CrossRef]
14. Browne, C.B.; Powley, E.; Whitehouse, D.; Lucas, S.M.; Cowling, P.I.; Rohlfshagen, P.; Tavener, S.; Perez, D.; Samothrakis, S.; Colton, S. A survey of monte carlo tree search methods. *IEEE Trans. Comput. Intell. AI Games* **2012**, *4*, 1–43. [CrossRef]
15. Kocsis, L.; Szepesvári, C. Bandit based monte-carlo planning. In Proceedings of the European Conference on Machine Learning, Berlin, Germany, 18–22 September 2006; Springer: Berlin/Heidelberg, Germany, 2006; pp. 282–293.
16. Gelly, S.; Silver, D. Combining online and offline knowledge in UCT. In Proceedings of the 24th International Conference on Machine Learning, Corvallis, OR, USA, 20–24 June 2007; pp. 273–280.
17. Chaslot, G.M.B.; Winands, M.H.; van Den Herik, H.J. Parallel monte-carlo tree search. In Proceedings of the Computers and Games: 6th International Conference, CG 2008, Proceedings 6, Beijing, China, 29 September–1 October 2008; Springer: Berlin/Heidelberg, Germany, 2008; pp. 60–71.
18. Rechenberg, I. Evolutionsstrategien. In Proceedings of the Simulationsmethoden in der Medizin und Biologie: Workshop, Hannover, Germany, 29 September–1 October 1977; Springer: Berlin/Heidelberg, Germany, 1978; pp. 83–114.
19. Rusu, A.A.; Colmenarejo, S.G.; Gulcehre, C.; Desjardins, G.; Kirkpatrick, J.; Pascanu, R.; Mnih, V.; Kavukcuoglu, K.; Hadsell, R. Policy distillation. *arXiv* **2015**, arXiv:1511.06295.
20. Sutton, R.S.; Barto, A.G. *Reinforcement Learning: An Introduction*; MIT Press: Cambridge, MA, USA, 1998; Volume 1, pp. 9–11.
21. Mnih, V.; Kavukcuoglu, K.; Silver, D.; Graves, A.; Antonoglou, I.; Wierstra, D.; Riedmiller, M. Playing atari with deep reinforcement learning. *arXiv* **2013**, arXiv:1312.5602.
22. Williams, R.J. Simple statistical gradient-following algorithms for connectionist reinforcement learning. *Mach. Learn.* **1992**, *8*, 229–256. [CrossRef]
23. Konda, V.; Tsitsiklis, J. Actor-critic algorithms. In Proceedings of the Neural Information Processing Systems, Denver, CO, USA, 29 November–4 December 1999; pp. 1008–1014.
24. Lillicrap, T.P.; Hunt, J.J.; Pritzel, A.; Heess, N.; Erez, T.; Tassa, Y.; Silver, D.; Wierstra, D. Continuous control with deep reinforcement learning. *arXiv* **2015**, arXiv:1509.02971.
25. Mnih, V.; Badia, A.P.; Mirza, M.; Graves, A.; Lillicrap, T.P.; Harley, T.; Silver, D.; Kavukcuoglu, K. Asynchronous methods for deep reinforcement learning. In Proceedings of the International Conference on Machine Learning, PmLR, New York, NY, USA, 19–24 June 2006; pp. 1928–1937.
26. Espeholt, L.; Soyer, H.; Munos, R.; Simonyan, K.; Mnih, V.; Ward, T.; Doron, Y.; Firoiu, V.; Harley, T.; Dunning, I.; et al. Impala: Scalable distributed deep-rl with importance weighted actor-learner architectures. In Proceedings of the International Conference on Machine Learning, PMLR, Stockholm, Sweden, 10–15 July 2018; pp. 1407–1416.
27. Schulman, J.; Levine, S.; Abbeel, P.; Jordan, M.; Moritz, P. Trust region policy optimization. In Proceedings of the International Conference on Machine Learning, PMLR, Lille, France, 6–11 July 2015; pp. 1889–1897.
28. Schulman, J.; Wolski, F.; Dhariwal, P.; Radford, A.; Klimov, O. Proximal policy optimization algorithms. *arXiv* **2017**, arXiv:1707.06347.
29. Zinkevich, M.; Johanson, M.; Bowling, M.; Piccione, C. Regret minimization in games with incomplete information. In Proceedings of the Neural Information Processing Systems, Vancouver, BC, Canada, 3–6 December 2007; pp. 1729–1736.
30. Brown, N.; Sandholm, T. Solving imperfect-information games via discounted regret minimization. In Proceedings of the AAAI Conference on Artificial Intelligence, Honolulu, HI, USA, 27 January–1 February 2019; Volume 33, pp. 1829–1836.
31. Lanctot, M.; Waugh, K.; Zinkevich, M.; Bowling, M. Monte Carlo sampling for regret minimization in extensive games. In Proceedings of the Neural Information Processing Systems, Vancouver, BC, Canada, 7–10 December 2009; pp. 1078–1086.
32. Brown, N.; Lerer, A.; Gross, S.; Sandholm, T. Deep counterfactual regret minimization. In Proceedings of the International Conference on Machine Learning, PMLR, Long Beach, CA, USA, 9–15 June 2019; pp. 793–802.

33. Steinberger, E.; Lerer, A.; Brown, N. Dream: Deep regret minimization with advantage baselines and model-free learning. *arXiv* **2020**, arXiv:2006.10410.
34. Heinrich, J.; Lanctot, M.; Silver, D. Fictitious self-play in extensive-form games. In Proceedings of the International Conference on Machine Learning, PMLR, Lille, France, 6–11 July 2015; pp. 805–813.
35. Heinrich, J.; Silver, D. Deep reinforcement learning from self-play in imperfect-information games. *arXiv* **2016**, arXiv:1603.01121.
36. McMahan, H.B.; Gordon, G.J.; Blum, A. Planning in the presence of cost functions controlled by an adversary. In Proceedings of the 20th International Conference on Machine Learning (ICML-03), Washington, DC, USA, 21–24 August 2003; pp. 536–543.
37. Lanctot, M.; Zambaldi, V.; Gruslys, A.; Lazaridou, A.; Tuyls, K.; Perolat, J.; Silver, D.; Graepel, T. A unified game-theoretic approach to multiagent reinforcement learning. In Proceedings of the Neural Information Processing Systems, Long Beach, CA, USA, 4–9 December 2017; pp. 4190–4203.
38. Sunehag, P.; Lever, G.; Gruslys, A.; Czarnecki, W.M.; Zambaldi, V.; Jaderberg, M.; Lanctot, M.; Sonnerat, N.; Leibo, J.Z.; Tuyls, K.; et al. Value-decomposition networks for cooperative multi-agent learning. *arXiv* **2017**, arXiv:1706.05296.
39. Rashid, T.; Samvelyan, M.; De Witt, C.S.; Farquhar, G.; Foerster, J.; Whiteson, S. Monotonic value function factorisation for deep multi-agent reinforcement learning. *J. Mach. Learn. Res.* **2020**, *21*, 1–51.
40. Lowe, R.; Wu, Y.I.; Tamar, A.; Harb, J.; Pieter Abbeel, O.; Mordatch, I. Multi-agent actor-critic for mixed cooperative-competitive environments. In Proceedings of the Neural Information Processing Systems, Long Beach, CA, USA, 4–9 December 2017; pp. 6379–6390.
41. Wang, W.; Sun, D.; Jiang, F.; Chen, X.; Zhu, C. Research and Challenges of Reinforcement Learning in Cyber Defense Decision-Making for Intranet Security. *Algorithms* **2022**, *15*, 134. [CrossRef]
42. Sanjaya, R.; Wang, J.; Yang, Y. Measuring the Non-Transitivity in Chess. *Algorithms* **2022**, *15*, 152. [CrossRef]
43. Yang, X.; Wang, Z.; Zhang, H.; Ma, N.; Yang, N.; Liu, H.; Zhang, H.; Yang, L. A Review: Machine Learning for Combinatorial Optimization Problems in Energy Areas. *Algorithms* **2022**, *15*, 205. [CrossRef]
44. Lu, Y.; Li, W. Techniques and Paradigms in Modern Game AI Systems. *Algorithms* **2022**, *15*, 282. [CrossRef]
45. Lu, Y.; Li, W.; Li, W. Official International Mahjong: A New Playground for AI Research. *Algorithms* **2023**, *16*, 235. [CrossRef]
46. Li, Z.; Chen, X.; Fu, J.; Xie, N.; Zhao, T. Reducing Q-Value Estimation Bias via Mutual Estimation and Softmax Operation in MADRL. *Algorithms* **2024**, *17*, 36. [CrossRef]
47. Li, J.; Xie, N.; Zhao, T. Optimizing Reinforcement Learning Using a Generative Action-Translator Transformer. *Algorithms* **2024**, *17*, 37. [CrossRef]
48. Schaa, H.; Barriga, N.A. Evaluating the Expressive Range of Super Mario Bros Level Generators. *Algorithms* **2024**, *17*, 307. [CrossRef]
49. Zhang, L.; Zou, H.; Zhu, Y. An Efficient Optimization of the Monte Carlo Tree Search Algorithm for Amazons. *Algorithms* **2024**, *17*, 334. [CrossRef]
50. Hsieh, Y.-H.; Kao, C.-C.; Yuan, S.-M. Imitating Human Go Players via Vision Transformer. *Algorithms* **2025**, *18*, 61. [CrossRef]
51. Penelas, G.; Barbosa, L.; Reis, A.; Barroso, J.; Pinto, T. Machine Learning for Decision Support and Automation in Games: A Study on Vehicle Optimal Path. *Algorithms* **2025**, *18*, 106. [CrossRef]
52. Haarnoja, T.; Zhou, A.; Abbeel, P.; Levine, S. Soft Actor-Critic: Off-Policy Maximum Entropy Deep Reinforcement Learning with a Stochastic Actor. In Proceedings of the 35th International Conference on Machine Learning, Stockholmsmässan, Stockholm, Sweden, 10–15 July 2018; pp. 1856–1865.

algorithms

MDPI

Review

A Review: Machine Learning for Combinatorial Optimization Problems in Energy Areas

Xinyi Yang [1], Ziyi Wang [2], Hengxi Zhang [3], Nan Ma [1], Ning Yang [2,*], Hualin Liu [1], Haifeng Zhang [2] and Lei Yang [1]

1 Key Laboratory of Oil & Gas Business Chain Optimization, CNPC, Petrochina Planning and Engineering Institute, Beijing 100083, China; yangxy234@petrochina.com.cn (X.Y.); manan2013@petrochina.com.cn (N.M.); liuhualin08@petrochina.com.cn (H.L.); yang_lei@petrochina.com.cn (L.Y.)
2 Institute of Automation, Chinese Academy of Sciences, Beijing 100190, China; wangziyi2021@ia.ac.cn (Z.W.); haifeng.zhang@ia.ac.cn (H.Z.)
3 Tsinghua-Berkeley Shenzhen Institute, Tsinghua University, Shenzhen 518055, China; zhanghx20@mails.tsinghua.edu.cn
* Correspondence: ning.yang@ia.ac.cn; Tel.: +86-1305-150-9251

Abstract: Combinatorial optimization problems (COPs) are a class of NP-hard problems with great practical significance. Traditional approaches for COPs suffer from high computational time and reliance on expert knowledge, and machine learning (ML) methods, as powerful tools have been used to overcome these problems. In this review, the COPs in energy areas with a series of modern ML approaches, i.e., the interdisciplinary areas of COPs, ML and energy areas, are mainly investigated. Recent works on solving COPs using ML are sorted out firstly by methods which include supervised learning (SL), deep learning (DL), reinforcement learning (RL) and recently proposed game theoretic methods, and then problems where the timeline of the improvements for some fundamental COPs is the layout. Practical applications of ML methods in the energy areas, including the petroleum supply chain, steel-making, electric power system and wind power, are summarized for the first time, and challenges in this field are analyzed.

Keywords: combinatorial optimization problem; machine learning; supervised learning; reinforcement learning; game theory; refinery scheduling; steel-making; electric power system; wind power

1. Introduction

The optimization problem in energy areas has always been a hot topic with the development of the various types of industries over the past decades. Due to the natural mathematical similarities between energy models and COPs, many energy problems can be regarded as COPs. To figure out the above issues, an increasing amount of individuals and groups have begun to employ the multi-agent system framework, such as game theory, and intelligent learning approaches, such as machine learning methods, considering their satisfactory solution and implementation flexibility. In this work, we specifically concentrate on the interdisciplinary part among COP, ML, game theory and energy areas presented as Figure 1.

COP is the sub-field of the optimization problems and can be seen almost everywhere in the resource allocation, scheduling, and routing scenarios over the industrial fields. The task of COPs is to search and find the maximum or minimum of an objective function with a discrete domain rather than a continuous space [1–3]. In other words, the objective of COP, in mathematics, is to seek an optimal object combination from a collection of objects, in which the solution is either a discrete set or can be simplified to a discrete set [4]. Basically, a COP is established as either a maximization problem or a minimization one, just depending on the specific scenarios of given objective functions. In algorithmic, maximization and minimization problems, they are treated equivalently in consideration of the same computational logic.

Meanwhile, in consideration of the abundant COP characteristics in energy scenarios, people have started to treat various industrial energy issues, such as crude oil scheduling, pipeline scheduling, electricity scheduling, and steel making, as well as other energy issues, as COPs. For instance, the task of crude oil scheduling is to utilize limited production equipment for oil manufacturing to achieve a certain objective, such as maximizing profits or minimizing cost [5–9]. A general pipeline operation can be presented as pumping a certain amount of product into the pipeline at the starting point while receiving the same volume of product at the other end of the pipeline [10]. For multi-product pipeline problems, delivery planning and production injection are two essential tasks in real pipeline operations [11,12]. The electricity scheduling aims to improve efficiency, reliability and security through automation and modern communication technologies, which are generally based on the optimization of the whole electricity system [13–16]. Steel making continues to be of high concern around the world since steel is a metal that is widely in usage in the construction of roads, bridges, railways, and other infrastructures, and even a tiny optimization of the manufacturing process will lead to a huge decrease in cost [17]. Any of the manufacturing, such as casting [18], charge calculation and melt [19], and emission [20].

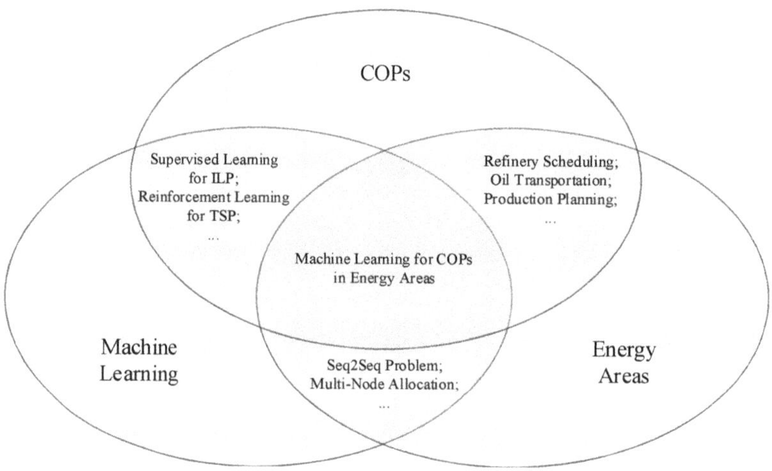

Figure 1. The interdisciplinary areas of COP, ML and energy areas.

Furthermore, there are numerous COPs in energy scenarios where many energy nodes are involved and modeled as different decision makers to optimize the operation efficiency of the whole energy system. Herein, game theory is a general framework that facilitates the comprehension of decision making in cooperative and competitive situations where agents have their own beliefs [21]. According to the type of information and the behaviors of players in the game environment, games can be generally grouped into four categories. First, static game with complete information. A static game is a simultaneous-move game where players must take action at the same time. With complete information, each player in the game has access to so-called common knowledge, including payoff functions and strategies as well as utility functions. The objective for each player is to formulate their strategies and maximize their benefits based on common knowledge. A famous example is the prisoner's dilemma. It introduces a situation where two individuals act for their own best interests and explores the corresponding decision-making policy taken by both [22,23]. Besides, Cournot competition is another instance conceptually similar to the prisoner's dilemma. This game model describes a dual-industry competition scenario where the product output is the competition objective for both industries, and independent decisions are required to be made by them both simultaneously to compete against each other [24,25]. Second, static game with incomplete information. As opposed to the game with complete information, a game with incomplete information, also known as a Bayesian game, describes such situations where players possess only partial information about other players. For maximizing the benefits or minimizing the penalties of their own, each player needs to form the behavior expectations of others to support their own decision making. A typical instance is called matching pennies. This is a zero-sum game in which two players place a penny on the table at the same time and the profit depends on whether the pennies match [26,27]. Auction is another example of a game with an incomplete information, in which each bidder is required to make a decision only with the utility function of his own, without knowing other bidders' willingness toward the good. The third class is the dynamic game with complete information. On the other hand, the move mechanism in dynamic games is sequential in contrast to the static games. Players act one by one and adjust the strategies accordingly to achieve the objectives on their own. The Stackelberg game is a game formulation that belongs to this category. It is a strategic game, where a leader and a follower move sequentially and compete for quantity [28]. Dynamic game with incomplete information is the forth class. Correspondingly, a dynamic game with incomplete information presents a game scenario in which players sequentially make actions without full information about others to maximize their payoffs. Many primary game models take this form. In the model of job market signaling [29], workers and employers both seek the one that matches their expectations. The employers generally offer the workers a competitive salary equivalent to their expected ability. Another instance is initial public offerings [30], where the owner of a firm and a set of potential investors are modeled as players. The objective of the firm owner is to decide what fraction to sell to the potential investors and how much while the investors need to decide whether to take or refuse. In addition, games can also be generally classified into cooperative and non-cooperative, i.e., competitive games according to the interests of players in the game.

Under the framework of game theory, ML methods can be hopefully designed to help players or agents in the game environment to effectively form and update their strategies or policies. ML is a method for autonomous data analyzing [31], which is a branch of artificial intelligence. The idea behind it is that the system with a learning algorithm inside can learn from data and hence reinforce its experience in recognizing patterns and making decisions on its own. With the naturally interdisciplinary characteristics of both above, people have begun to investigate further a series of ML learning approaches which integrate both their merits and may hopefully enhance the decision-making strategy of the intelligent system. According to the signal feature of the learning environment, we generally divide all ML methods into three categories: supervised learning, unsupervised learning and reinforcement learning. The objective of supervised learning methods is to establish a mathematical mapping relationship of a collection of data that maps the inputs to the expected outputs [32]. As opposed to supervised learning, the data that unsupervised learning approaches take only contain the inputs. Their goal is to seek underlying structures in the data and present them, such as the clustering of distinguishable data [33–35]. Reinforcement learning (RL) is a reward-oriented learning approach, where agents are required to continuously explore the environment and maximize its accumulative reward [36–39]. Moreover, since abundant RL scenarios involve the participation of more than one single agent, an increasing amount of studies has been implemented in recent years, which has directly led to the development of multi-agent RL (MARL). In addition, the agents in the multi-agent system not only interact with the environment, but have to deal with those actions of other agents, which can be treated as a part of the environment, and therefore the equilibrium points in the system must be considered [40,41]. This is where the principles of game theory emerge. With the development of relevant game theory and ML methods, more and more individuals and institutes have started to integrate both of them on industrial issues, such as device-to-device (D2D) communication using the Stackelberg game and MARL method [42], anti-jamming for internet of satellites through the deep RL approach and Stackelberg game [43], moving target defense using MARL in Bayesian Stackelberg Markov games [40], etc.

In this work, we mainly survey the COPs in energy areas, using a series of modern ML approaches, i.e., the interdisciplinary areas of COPs, ML and energy areas. We first list the categories of the classical COPs, such as the traveling salesman problem (TSP), maximum independent set (MIS) and minimum spanning tree (MST), etc., then investigate the ML techniques that can effectively address the above COPs, where the SL, DL and RL, as well as game-theoretic approaches, are mainly concerned due to their unique abilities. The research works of COPs in energy areas with ML methods are specifically studied afterwards. We mainly survey the petroleum supply chain, steel-making, electric power system, and wind power, which are currently popular applications in energy fields since the resource consumption is fairly high and even a little optimization can help save numerous costs. Finally, we also find some important deficiencies when investigating the above materials, and the challenges of this cross area are also summarized. On the one hand, we hopefully notice that game theory can be appropriately integrated into ML, DL and RL methods for handling the COPs in consideration of the typical issues, such as accuracy, efficiency, and scalability. On the other hand, the applications in energy areas are frequently represented in a complicated manner since the objective functions are often formulated as NP-hard problems with a great many constraints. The learning methods above can probably be a category of promising technique in dealing with these issues.

In addition, the contents are analyzed as follows. The search identified 274 documents containing the theoretical conclusions of various algorithms and the results of applicable approaches. Background information contains relevant knowledge in COPs [44–54], deep learning [55–61] and reinforcement learning [36,62–68]. Supervised learning, reinforcement learning and game theoretic methods are introduced in learning methods, where supervised learning includes methods of B&B [69–74], sequence to vector [57,75–77], GNN [78–82] and end-to-end architecture [83,84]. A few sources are relevant to reinforcement learning [85–88], and different types of games were demonstrated [89–92]. Another aspect mentioned was classic COPs [71,72,84,85,93–97], where ILP, MIS, MC, MVC and TSP were introduced. The rest of the literature references demonstrate application. The aspects contain petroleum supply chain [10,11,98–107], steel-making [108–111], electric power system [112–119], and wind power [120–123]. The aforementioned references were mostly searched from Google Scholar with related key words, such as "optimization", "combinatorial optimization problem", "machine learning", "supervised learning", "reinforcement learning", "game theory", "refinery scheduling", "steel-making", "electric power system", "wind power", etc.

The rest of this review is organized as follows. In Section 2, we introduce the background of combinatorial optimization problems and several popular approaches of ML in addressing this kind of issue over the past years. The sub-fields of combinatorial optimization problems and more details of these ML methods are further discussed in Section 3. In Section 4, we concentrate on some specific applications in energy field and investigate how the ML algorithms are applied to these issues. In Section 5, we summarize the challenges over these energy applications in which the ML methods are deployed. Then, some conclusions are drawn in facing the development of the ML theory in Section 6.

2. Background

In this section, we present a basic overview of COPs and the corresponding ML learning approaches for resolving them. Several primary COPs and corresponding applications are first reviewed. Then we investigate the attention mechanism and graphic neural networks (GNNs) as well as their typical categories and implementations. Moreover, since both of them can also be regarded as the policy network of RL agents, we further study how this framework is deployed and how it works. At the end of this section, we concentrate on RL and MARL approaches, in which the related game theories are considered a natural combination to improve the performance of the agents in specific scenarios.

2.1. Combinatorial Optimization Problem

The optimization problem can be viewed in terms of a decision problem, in which the total value of current solutions is mathematically evaluated by the objective function established in advance. Through a series of decisions, the task is to search and find the optimal value among different solutions. Typical COPs can be summarized as follows:

2.1.1. Traveling Salesman Problem

We herein would like to take the visit of cities as an example. The objective of the traveling salesman problem (TSP) is to seek the shortest possible path that allows the salesman to visit each city only once and returns to the origin city given the city list and connection distances between any two city nodes. TSP is utilized as a basic formulation for many optimization approaches, such as vehicle routing [44], scheduling [45], path planning [46], logistics [47], DNA sequencing [48] and the computing system [49]. In these applications, the city nodes in the graph represent, for instance, customers, soldering points, or DNA fragments, and each city pair or the distance represents the traveling time duration or cost, or the measurement between DNA fragments. Corresponding algorithms for coping with TSP include reinforcement learning [50], simulated annealing [51], genetic algorithm [52], ant colony [53], tabu search [54], or some mixed ones [124–126].

2.1.2. Maximum Independent Set

Maximum independent set (MIS) is a typical central problem in distributed graph algorithms, also known as the maximal stable set, which is an independent set that does not belong to any other independent sets. That is to say, an independent vertex set of a graph is a subset of the vertices such that no two vertices in the subset indicate an edge of this graph. Given a vertex cover of a graph, all vertices not in the cover define an independent vertex set. In addition, a MIS is also a dominating set in the graph, and each independent dominating set must be maximally independent. Many meaningful applications can be mathematically established as MIS problems, such as the communication system [127,128], computational system and graph coloring problem [129]. For handling MIS problems, some early researchers in studying graphs proposed some interesting algorithms [130–132]. Afterwards, more individuals and groups started to deploy a series of approaches with higher efficiency, such as the ML method [133], small messages rather than large messages [134], local search [135] and exact algorithm [136].

2.1.3. Minimum Spanning Tree

For an edge-weighted undirected graph, a minimum spanning tree (MST) is a tree that connects all vertices while not having any cycles and has a minimum total edge weight. That is, the sum of edge weights is supposed to be as small as possible for a spanning tree. There are many applications related to the MST problem. The direct ones consist of communication networks [137], transportation networks [138], water supply networks [139], and electrical grids [140]. Other practical cases based on MST include COVID-19 pandemic transmission forecasting [141], clustering [142], constructing trees for broadcasting [143], image registration and segmentation [144], circuit design [145] and emotion recognition [146]. There do exist several primary algorithms, namely, classic algorithm and faster algorithm; however, in consideration that such MST-like models will facilitate the development of multifarious industrial areas, more and more individuals have turned to design a variety of intuitive algorithms to figure out such issues, such as reinforcement learning [147], genetic algorithm [148] and fast parallel algorithm [149].

2.1.4. Maximum Cut Problem

The maximum cut (MC) problem is to find a cut such that the amount of edges between two complementary sets in a graph is as large as possible. The applications of the max-cut problem include theoretical physics [150–152], very large scale integration (VLSI) design [153,154], and the protein-folding problem [155,156], Accordingly, various approaches and algorithms, such as eigenvalues [157], randomized heuristics [158], harmony search and genetic algorithm [159], and scatter search [160] have been proposed to address this problem over the past decades.

2.1.5. Bin Packing Problem

The bin packing problem (BPP) is one of the most classical COPs, where a series of items with different sizes are required to be packed into a series of bins with positive integer capacities such that the number of bins used is minimized. Generally, there are two types of BPPs: online BPP, and offline BPP. The online BPP considers a situation in which the items keep appearing in a given order and they need to be placed inside the bins one by one, while the latter one concerns modifying the given list of items. BPP has many variations, such as 2D packing [161], 3D packing [162], linear packing [163], packing by weight [164], packing by cost [165], and so on. Such problems have arisen in resource allocation with an increasing frequency over the past years, such as edge computing [166], cloud storage [167], parcel delivery [168], aircraft maintenance task allocation [169] and product transportation [170]. For the online version, there are a diverse set of online algorithms designed for BPP. Single-class algorithms consist of next fit [171], next-k-fit [172], first-fit [173], best-fit [174] and worst-fit [175]. Refined algorithms include harmonic-k [176] and refined-harmonic [177]. On the other side, the offline algorithm is able to observe all the items before beginning to place them into bins. Multiplicative approximation is the simplest approach utilized by the offline algorithm. The members in this family are first-fit-decreasing [178], next-fit-decreasing [179] and modified first-fit-decreasing [178]. Additive approximation [180] and exact algorithms [181] are also widely mentioned in solving BPPs.

2.2. *Deep Learning*

Deep learning (DL) is a member of ML methods, where multiple layers of artificial neurons or neural networks (NNs) are structured to learn the representation of data [55]. The structures of NNs can be quite fruitful, such as deep neural networks (DNNs), convolutional neural networks (CNNs), recurrent neural networks (RNNs), attention mechanism, graph neural networks (GNNs), etc. In this work, we mainly concentrate on attention mechanism and GNNs in consideration of the natural connection between COPs and these two techniques.

2.2.1. Attention Mechanism

Some COPs are typical sequence-to-sequence (Seq2Seq) [56] problems, (for example, TSP), which require an encoder to map the input sequence into a d-dimensional space, and then use a decoder to map it to the output sequence, and the sequences are usually long (due to large problem size) and variable in length. With the rapid development of DNNs in the ML approach over the past years, people have started to realize that conventional encoders, such as RNNs, fail to utilize the information of previous segments in a relatively long sequence. Thus, a novel technique that mimics cognitive attention, namely attention mechanism, was proposed afterwards.

The idea behind is that the network should devote more attention to those smaller but more important parts of the input data. It was first used to deal with the Seq2Seq model, especially for neural machine translation [57]. Then the encoder–decoder architecture was widely known. The decoder utilizes the most relevant segments of the input sequence, which are encoded as a fixed-length vector by the encoder in a flexible manner to obtain the variable-length target consequence [58].

Nevertheless, the decoder here can just partially obtain the information from the input sequence. This would probably cause trouble, especially for those long or complicated sequences in which the dimensionality of the representation ingredient is constrained to be the same as for shorter or simpler sequences. Afterward, the proposal of self-attention and transformer models [59] revolutionized the implementation of attention by dispensing recurrence and convolutions used in RNNs [60] and CNNs [61], respectively, and relying solely on a self-attention mechanism alternatively.

(1) Additive Attention

Additive attention, proposed by Dzmitry Bahdanau [57] and therefore regarded as Bahdanau attention, is the first type of attention. The objective of this type of attention is to enhance the performance of the Seq2Seq model especially in machine translation tasks through aligning the decoder with the relevant inputs and correspondingly employing the attention mechanism. The method in this work, on the other hand, replaces the fixed-length vector with a variable-length one, to improve the translation performance of the basic encoder–decoder model. With time passing by, this method has been implemented more and more often due to its high performance, such as automatic music transcription [182], Fastformer [183], classification [184] and image search [185].

(2) Pointer Networks

Considering those problems, such as sequence sorting, where the sequence size is variable, and diverse COPs cannot be figured out by conventional Seq2Seq and neural turing machines [186], the pointer network was proposed by Vinyals et al. [76] to learn the conditional probability of an output sequence and hence to resolve variable-sized output problems. The attention is utilized as the pointer for choosing a member of the input sequence as the output. Pointer networks can be widely employed in dependency parsing [187], code completion [188], dialogue context generation [189], etc.

(3) Multiplicative Attention

Multiplicative attention is also referred to as Luong attention, proposed by Thang Luong [190]. This attention mechanism was established based on the additive attention mechanism. The differences are as follows: First, the way that the alignment score is calculated; And secondly, the position at which the attention mechanism is introduced in the decoder. The overall architecture of the attention decoder is distinguishable from multiplicative attention since the context vector is leveraged only after the RNN has produced the output for that time step. There are various applications that can be supported by this attention mechanism, such as aspect category and sentiment detection [191], time series forecasting [192], and the prediction of air pollutant concentration [193]. As COPs usually have variable sequence sizes (e.g., when solving TSP formulated as a sequence-to-sequence structure, the number of cites to go is variable, forming a variable input size), pointer networks are used most frequently.

2.2.2. Graphic Neural Networks

Graph structures are common in COPs, so we need to encode graphs reasonably. In addition, the graph-structured representation is more suitable for some COPs than sequence representation. For instance, the permutation invariant property in the TSP cannot be characterized in the sequence representation. GNNs belong to the category of NNs and are widely utilized in DL methods [55], especially in those scenarios where the data are expressed by graph structures. Considering the representation superiority of graph data, people have begun to leverage the characteristics of graphs to design various types of ingenious GNN structures through integrating other techniques, such as graph convolutional networks [194], graph attention networks [195], and graph recurrent networks [196] over different applications, which range from node-type, edge-type, to graph-type predictive assignments. In general, GNNs are customarily employed to resolve those issues in which the graph-structured data are represented. Five typical problem categories are listed as follows.

(1) Graph Classification Problem

Fundamentally, the goal of graph classification is to divide the whole graph into domains with disparate features. In other words, the entire graph is required to be separated into different segments in this classification scenario. There are numerous applications of this classification, such as document categorizing [197], social recommendation [198], protein function prediction [199], etc.

(2) Graph Grouping Problem

Graph grouping is a class of grouping methods, the task of which is to put together graph data that have similar features [200]. There are also two sub-fields of graph grouping. The first is node clustering, which is based on density. High edge weight or long edge distance corresponds to high density. On the other hand, the graphs are regarded as objects and, hence, grouped based on similarity.

(3) Node Classification Problem

For node classification cases, the nodes in the graph are used to represent the label of samples. The objective of this task is to decide which label each node belongs to via checking their neighbor labels. With each node being tagged a specific label, all nodes in this graph system can be grouped into different classifications. The training approach in this type of case is a semi-supervised learning method [201], where only a portion of nodes in the graph are tagged.

(4) Link Prediction Problem

To predict whether or not two nodes in a graph exist a link is the research objective of this scenario. This function is widely investigated in a recommendation system consisting of friend recommendation [202], movie recommendation [203] and commerce recommendation [204]. Some COPs are well structured and can be reflected in these typical problems, e.g., MIS can be regarded as a node classification problem with two categories representing whether a node is included in MIS. For more COPs, abundant works are reshaping the graph to using GNNs.

2.3. *Reinforcement Learning*

Many COP environments involve more than one node or executor and can therefore be considered for inclusion in the game theory framework due to their advantage in figuring out multi-player problems. Meanwhile, RL is a reward-oriented approach to help improve the performance of the player or agent. At this point, the two aforementioned techniques are naturally integrated to address COPs.

2.3.1. Single-Agent Reinforcement Learning

RL, especially single-agent RL, is a human-like learning method in which the agent acts like a human and is trained to obtain the expected objective through a series of positive or negative rewards across time [36]. During the learning phase, the RL agent is required to continuously observe the environment and take actions based on its perceptions and rewards offered by the environment. This learning mode makes the agent gradually collect experience and perform better by reinforcing those good behaviors while abandoning the bad ones. In general, RL methods are grouped into two categories, i.e., the model-based RL [62] and the model-free one [63].

In model-based learning approach, the system is able to utilize the predictive model, which is not available in a model-free algorithm, and execute sequential decision making [64]. In contrast to the large amounts of interaction required in the model-free learning, a transparent advantage of model-based learning is the usage of predictive comprehension over the environment model [65].

On the other hand, the model-free algorithm is more flexible since it does not need any prior information about the environment system. All the agents supposed to do is to explore and learn. The model-free algorithm consists of value-based learning and policy-based learning.

Furthermore, Sarsa [66] and Q-learning [67] are the most fundamental online and offline policy learning approaches in value-based learning, respectively. Policy-based learning includes the actor–critic method [68] and the trust region policy optimization (TRPO) method [205], where the policy gradient is implemented, and a continuous strategy is available.

2.3.2. Multi-Agent Reinforcement Learning

Multi-agent RL (MARL) is a sub-field of RL that is becoming increasingly relevant and is extremely impressive. Considering that there exist more than one agent in the systems over enormous applications, such as communication networks [206,207], cyber–physical systems [208,209], financial activities [210,211], and social communities [212], research individuals and groups have started to transfer single-agent RL (SARL) models to the MARL ones. An obvious distinction between SARL and MARL is the number of agents in the environment. Hence, the research objective on MARL is to investigate how multiple agents are going to interact with each other in a common system and how this system evolves [213]. Specifically, the goal of each agent in this multi-agent system is, by treating other agents as part of the environment, to constantly optimize its policy for maximizing the expected long-term rewards.

According to the types of agents, MARL can be generally divided into homogeneous MARL [214], where all agents in the system are homogeneous and able to play an interchangeable role, and heterogeneous MARL [215], in which agents possess different action space and state space.

2.3.3. Multi-Agent Reinforcement Learning with Game Theory

Since the agents in MARL are continuously interacting with the environment and other agents, some interaction modes can be identified and classified, such as cooperative, competitive, or a mix of both. From this moment, researchers have started to integrate MARL with game theory in consideration that game theory is such a study of mathematical models of strategic interactions among rational agents.

(1) Cooperative MARL [216]

In cooperative scenarios, agents are designated as collaborators to achieve the goal of the common system while interacting with the environment. A series of coordination settings, such as sharing sensing information, sharing the same reward function or sharing the policies, are widely investigated and studied [217]. The corresponding applications include rescue operations [218], cooperative exploration [219], resource allocation [220], etc.

(2) Competitive MARL [221]

In those situations with competitive settings, the interests of agents are in conflict. In other words, the more that one or a portion of agents earn, the more others lose, which is also known as a zero-sum game [222]. There are numerous MARL cases with competitive settings that have been studied over the past years, such as Atari games [223], pricing strategies in electronic market [224], sports game [225], etc. Notably, the computational complexities for figuring out two-player and multi-player zero-sum games are quite distinguishable.

(3) Mixed MARL [226]

Mixed MARL is a combination of fully cooperative and fully competitive situations. That is, both cooperative and competitive behaviors are going to appear in this setting, which therefore makes this type of learning architecture notoriously challenging and burdensome to handle [213]. Compared to the above two scenarios, mixed MARL seems not to be so popular due to its complicated optimization procedure and computational process in finding stationary Nash or a related equilibrium. Multi-player poker game [227] and multi-player online battle arenas, such as DOTA 2 [228] and StarCraft 2 [229], are several classical applications using mixed settings, in which human-level or superhuman-level is achieved.

3. Learning to Solve COPs

Recent works for solving COPs with ML methods are presented systematically in this section. Firstly, they are categorized based on the ML approach: supervised learning, reinforcement learning, and game theoretic methods, basically presented according to the years that they were proposed. Then, the categorization is based on fundamental problems in COPs, including integer programming (ILP), MIS, maximum clique (MC), MVC, and TSP. Figure 2 shows an overview of how ML methods are applied to solve all kinds of fundamental COPs.

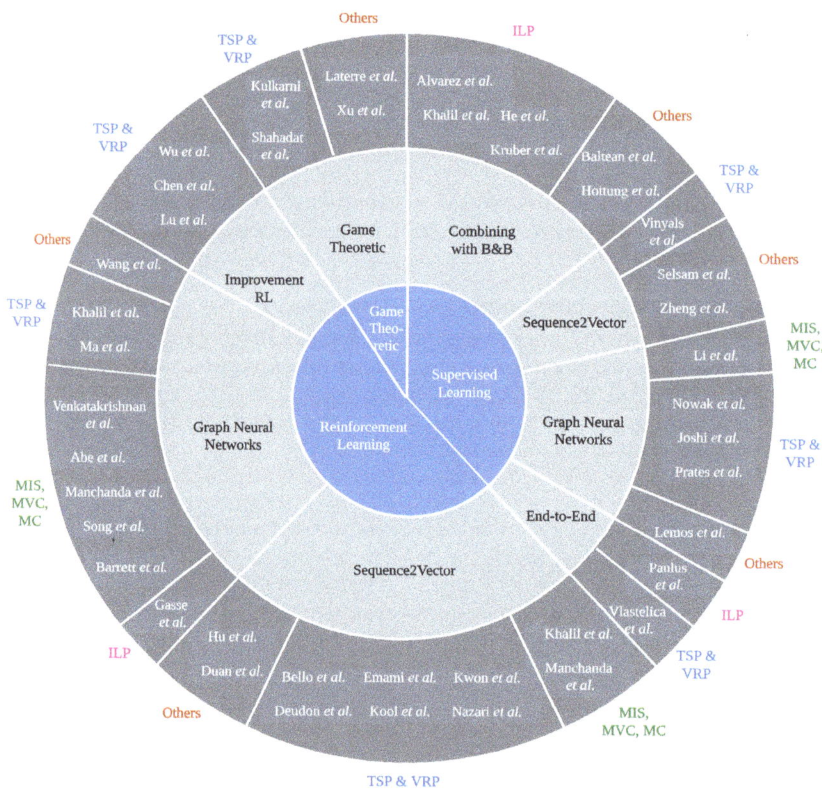

Figure 2. ML methods for COPs. Recent works are categorized firstly based on the ML approach and then the fundamental problems in COPs.

3.1. Methods

3.1.1. Supervised Learning

Combining with Branch and Bound

Traditional approaches for COPs have the same challenges: high computational complexity and dependence on expert knowledge. There have been rich works studying how to replace some components of traditional approaches with supervised learning methods to respond to those challenges. Most of them focus on a classical algorithm called branch and bound (B&B) [69], which is broadly applied for ILP-formed COPs. Table 1 summarizes them.

Alvarez et al. [70] proposed to approximate the scoring strategy of strong branching (SB) with supervised learning for solving mixed ILP problems. Similarly, He et al. [71] proposed to speed up the traditional B&B method with imitation learning. He et al. clearly formulated B&B search as a sequential decision-making process and learned the node selection (prioritizing) policy as well as a node-pruning policy using DAgger. Compared to traditional approaches, this method learns problem-solving patterns from experience, which speeds up the future process. Meanwhile, the sequential decision-making process takes the effects on the future into account when choosing actions. It may be also treated as a simple reinforcement learning approach since it involves the concept of learning from demonstration, but essentially, it directly fits the policy with collected data, which is more like a kind of supervised learning.

Moreover, Khali et al. [72] proposed to solve the scoring problem of SB as a learning-to-rank problem as opposed to a regression or classification problem, and enabled an on-the-fly solver, where the transition from traditional to ML approaches is seamless. That is, instead of learning a policy offline as [70,71], Khali et al. proposed a three-phased online method for a given mixed ILP problem. Firstly, SB is used as the branching strategy for a limited number of nodes. Then, the dataset collected in phase iis fed into a learning-to-rank algorithm. At last, the learned model replaces SB for branching until termination.

Table 1. Supervised learning approaches combining with traditional algorithms, such as branch and bound.

Reference	Year	Advantage or Novelty
Alvarez et al. [70]	2014	approximated SB with supervised learning
He et al. [71]	2014	formulated B&B as sequential decision-making process and learned it with imitation learning
Khali et al. [72]	2016	solved the scoring problem of SB with a learning-to-rank algorithm, online algorithm
Baltean et al. [73]	2018	used supervised learning to select quadratic semi-definite outer approximation of cutting planes
Hottung et al. [74]	2020	learned the container pre-marshaling problem (CPMP)

Baltean et al. [73] applied the above idea to the selection of quadratic semi-definite outer approximation of cutting planes. They used NNs to learn cut selection offline, thereby reducing the computational complexity during testing. Hottung et al. [74] applied the idea for the container pre-marshaling problem (CPMP) (the Container Pre-Marshaling Problem is concerned with the re-ordering of containers in container terminals during off-peak times so that containers can be quickly retrieved when the port is busy), using DNNs to learn the branching strategy and predict bounding bounds.

Sequence2Vector

Sequence-to-sequence is a typical structure of COPs. To deal with those problems, encoders are needed to obtain the vector-form embeddings. Early encoders are RNNs, such as LSTM [75], which can cope with the relationship between an element in the sequence and the previous elements, but RNNs tend to "forget" the information of previous elements when sequences are long. Bahdanau et al. [57] proposed an attention mechanism to solve the problem of long-range dependencies. By calculating the similarity between two elements, the importance of the previous elements is decided, and the mixed information of the sequence is obtained. That is, the decoder can obtain the information of all states from the encoder instead of the current state. Based on the attention mechanism, Vinyals et al. [76] proposed pointer network (Ptr-Net), which solved the problem that the length of the output sequence depends on the input sequence and became a milestone breakthrough in solving COPs. The main idea of Ptr-Net is to point to each element of the input sequence instead of the mixed information and to obtain the probability distribution over the elements of the input sequence.

Vinyals et al. [76] applied Ptr-Net for the convex hull problem, Delaunay Triangulation, and small-scale planar TSP problems, obtaining higher accuracy than LSTM and LSTM with attention.

Zheng et al. [77] then applied Ptr-Net for the permutation flow shop scheduling problem (PFSP) (the Permutation Flow-shop Scheduling Problem involves the determination of the order of processing of n jobs on m machines). They showed that the average relative percentage deviation (ARPD) of Ptr-Net is better than the LSTM and LSTM with attention. They also found that the element order of the input sequence has some impact on the results.

Graph Neural Networks

Another typical form of COPs is graph based, which characterized the permutation-invariant property of nodes. GNNs [78–80] are a commonly used architecture to encode the input of the graph structure. The input is a vector representing a node or an edge, then the information of nodes and edges is integrated according to the local neighbor structure of the graph, which is used for updating the embedding after. Works related to this approach are summarized in Table 2.

Table 2. Supervised learning methods using graph neural networks.

Reference	Year	Advantage or Novelty
Nowak et al. [81]	2017	encode source and target graphs
Joshi et al. [82]	2017	just encode source graph
Selsam et al. [230]	2018	model SAT as an undirected graph
Li et al. [231]	2018	solve SAT, MIS, MVC and MC with GNNs
Lemos et al. [232]	2019	solve graph coloring problem (GCP) with GNNs
Prates et al. [233]	2019	solve problems involving numerical information

Nowak et al. [81] discussed how to apply GNN [78] to the quadratic assignment problem (QAP) (examples of matching and TSP are given). For two graphs, A and B with the same number of nodes, GNN is used to encode them into two normalized adjacency matrices, E_1 and E_2, respectively, and then the loss related to E_1 and E_2 is calculated for autoregressive learning. For the TSP problem, A and B are the input graph and the ground truth TSP cycle. Finally, the solution is generated by the adjacency matrix obtained from the input graph with beam search.

Instead of using the one-shot autoregressive method as [81], Joshi et al. [82] only used Graph ConvNet to obtain the adjacency probability matrix from the input TSP graph, and then directly calculated the loss related to ground-truth TSP cycle. During the test, Joshi et al. tried three kinds of search methods and compared them: greedy search (greedily selecting the next node from its neighbors with the highest probability), beam search (expanding the b most probable edge connections among the node's neighbors), and beam search with shortest tour heuristic (selecting the shortest tour among the set of b complete tours as the final solution at the end of beam search). Experiments show that for TSP problems with a fixed number of nodes, the quality of the solution outperforms previous DL approaches.

Selsam et al. [230] solved the satisfiability (SAT) problem with GNNs [78,234]. Due to the permutation invariance and negation invariance properties of SAT, Selsam et al. modeled SAT as an undirected graph with one node for every literal and clause, one edge between each literal and clause, and one edge between literal and complementary literal. Then, the message-passing method [235] is used to update the embedding of each node, and the resulting embeddings are fed into MLP to obtain the literals' votes, which are then used to calculate the loss with the true label. The model parameters of [230] are independent of the problem size due to two aggregation operators: to form the incoming message by summing the messages of one node's neighbors, and to form the logit probability by calculating the mean of literal votes.

Similar to [230], Lemos et al. [232] solved the graph coloring problem (GCP) (the graph coloring problem (GCP): does a graph G accept a C-coloring?) with GNNs [78,80,232]. They took the vertex-to-color adjacency matrix as input, and finally used MLP to obtain the logit probability and calculated the loss with true labels.

Selsam et al. [230] and Lemos et al. [232] successfully solved some NP-hard problems involving symbolic relationships (e.g., whether an edge is connected), and Prates et al. [233] further applied GNNs [79] to solve the NP-hard problems involving numerical information (in this paper, they focused on a variant of TSP: does graph G admit a Hamiltonian path with cost $< C$?). In order to encode the weights of edges, Prates et al. used a vertex-edge adjacency matrix as input, and represented an edge using the concatenation of weight and C, which is a 2-d vector $\in \mathrm{R}^2$. Then, similar to [230,232], the refined edge embeddings are fed into an MLP to compute the logit probability.

Li et al. [231] solved four NP-hard problems with GCN [236,237]: SAT, MIS, MVC and MC. Taking MIS as an example, the graph is presented by an $N \times N$ binary adjacency matrix, and then mapped to an N-dimensional real-valued vector through GCN, indicating how likely each vertex is to belong to the MIS. Finally, the solution is obtained from this real-valued vector. A basic method to obtain it is greedy search using the vector as the heuristic function. However, Li et al. pointed out that this search method can become confused when there are multiple optimal solutions for the same graph. Therefore, a further improvement is using GCN to generate multiple probability maps, which is integrated into the tree search procedure (breadth-first account for the diversity of solutions).

End-to-End Architecture

Some recent works focus on how to integrate combinatorial building blocks into neural network architectures as layers so that combinatorial optimization solvers can be embedded into NNs as black boxes, enabling end-to-end optimization.

Vlastelica et al. [83] and Paulus et al. [84] proposed such approaches to integrate ILP solvers. The NN-based solver takes the parameters of the ILP (objective function weight c, constraint parameters A and b) as network weights, inputs an integer solution y, outputs the value of the objective function, and computes loss with the given optimal value. Paulus et al. [84] addressed two main difficulties in achieving the end-to-end optimization: (1) the value of objective function in integer programming is piece-wise and thus non-differentiable; (2) the constraints of ILP are not necessarily active. Vlastelica et al. [83] used the continuous interpolation method to solve the differentiating problem of the objective function weight c and applied this solver for three graph-structure problems: shortest path problem, min-cost problem and TSP. Paulus et al. [84] implemented the differentiation of c as well as A and b using gradient surrogate methods, and conducted experiments on the weighted set cover problem, KNAPSACK, and keypoint matching problem.

3.1.2. Reinforcement Learning

Parameterization of Policy Network

As pointed out by Bello et al. [85], training strategies for COPs with supervised learning require a large number of labels, while the optimal labels for many COPs are not easy to obtain. However, it is relatively easy to evaluate the quality of a given solution. Therefore, Bello et al. proposed to use evaluation as a reward feedback in an RL paradigm to solve the labeling problem, which is another milestone work. More other works follow the same structure and shape the parameterization of the policy network as shown in Table 3, which is the similar concept of an encoder in supervised learning.

Table 3. Works on policy network of reinforcement learning.

Reference	Year	Advantage or Novelty
Bello et al. [85]	2016	used evaluation as reward feedback in RL paradigm
Hu et al. [238]	2017	solved the 3D BPP problem using RL
Nazari et al. [239]	2018	the properties of the input sequence is not static
Khalil et al. [95]	2017	formulated partial solutions as decision sequence
Venkatakrishnan et al. [240]	2018	improved scalability on larger testing graph than training set
Manchanda et al. [241]	2020	billion-sized graphs
Song	2020	combined information from both graph-based representation and ILP-form representation

Bello et al. [85] modeled the 2D Euclidean TSP problem as a sequential decision problem. At each step, a distribution over the next city to visit in the tour is output by the policy, which forms the travel strategy by the chain rule at the terminal step, and the objective is to shorten the travel distance. The policy model is based on Ptr-Net proposed by Vinyals et al. [76] without glimpse, which reads the state s (the city sequence, one city at a time), encodes it as a d-dimensional embedding with an LSTM, and decodes it with an LSTM to obtain the action (the distribution of the next city). Bello et al. used the travel distance to indicate the reward and train the policy with an actor–critic method.

Hu et al. [238] applied [85] to the 3D BPP problem to learn the order of packing items into bins, and proved that it outperforms the well-designed heuristic approach.

A major limitation of [85] is that it assumes the problem is static over time, thus it cannot be used to solve problems, such as VRP, where the properties of the input sequence keep changing. To solve this problem, Nazari et al. [239] proposed a new policy model which leaves out the encoder RNN. They dealt with the static elements and dynamic elements in the input separately, that is, the embeddings of the static elements are input to the RNN decoder and then input to an attention mechanism with glimpses similar to Ptr-Net together with the embeddings of the dynamic elements. Finally, the probability vector of the next destination is output.

For another typical form of CO problem-graph structure, Khalil et al. [95] proposed a training method combining GNNs with reinforcement learning to remove the dependence on sample labels, called S2V-DQN. Khalil et al. presented a partial solution as an ordered list S (a decision-making sequence). At each time step, a node is greedily selected to join S so that the evaluation value Q is maximized. The embedding of each node in list S is obtained by Structure2Vec [242] according to its graph structure (the properties of the node and its neighbor), and Q depends on the embeddings of the candidate nodes and the embedding of the whole graph. Parameters are trained using n-step Q-learning and fitted Q-iteration. Khalil et al. tested S2V-DQN on MVC, MC, and 2-D TSP, showing its applicability to multiple different problems, graph types, and graph sizes.

Venkatakrishnan et al. [240] focused on the scalability of methods on graph structure problem: can a graph neural network trained at a certain scale perform well on orders-of-magnitude larger graphs [240]? To address this problem, Venkatakrishnan et al. proposed G2S-RNN. Instead of mapping the graph structure to a fixed-length vector to obtain the embeddings of the vertices, G2S-RNN uses a discrete-time dynamical system to process the graph structure. The nodes' embeddings are updated by multiple rounds of convolution, and finally, the entire time-series vector is used as the embedding of the graph, which makes the embeddings' length variable (related to the number of convolution layers). Then, Seq2Vec takes the embedding as input to obtain the vector representation of each node, and Q-learning is used to update the policy.

Manchanda et al. [241] focused on larger graph structures. They tested [95] on MC and show that S2V-DQN fails on graphs beyond 2000 nodes. Based on the observation that, although the graph may be large, only a small percentage of the nodes are likely to contribute to the solution set [241], Manchanda et al. proposed a two-stage method called GCOMB, which uses supervised learning to prune poor nodes and learns the node's embedding with GCN, and searches for solutions on good nodes with Q-learning. The experiment results show that the efficiency is successfully improved on billion-sized graphs.

Song et al. [243] proposed CoPiEr which uses information from both graph-based representation and ILP-form representation. The trajectories are generated by algorithms using two kinds of representations, respectively, following an exchange between two trajectories. Specifically, two trajectories are evaluated by the reward function, and the one with a higher reward is used as a demonstration for the algorithm based on the other trajectory.

Reinforcing Methods

Some works pay more attention to improving the optimization process rather than designing the policy network, which is shown in Table 4.

Table 4. Works on reinforcing methods of reinforcement learning.

Reference	Year	Advantage or Novelty
Deudon et al. [86]	2018	enhanced the framework with 2-opt
Emami et al. [87]	2018	learned permutation instead of decision sequences point by point
Kool et al. [88]	2018	re-designed the baseline of REINFORCE algorithm as the cost of a solution from the policy defined by the best model
Ma et al. [244]	2019	solved COPs with constraints
Abe et al. [245]	2019	used CombOpt inspired by AlphaGo Zero to replace Q-learning
Barrett	2020	explored the solution space during test time
Kwon et al. [246]	2020	handled equally optimal solutions

Based on Bello et al. [85], Deudon et al. [86] proposed a policy network with only attention mechanism and enhanced the framework with 2-opt. Instead of using LSTM, the decoder maps three last sampled actions (visited cities) to a vector, and 2-opt is used to improve the output solution.

The previous idea of using reinforcement learning to solve COPs is usually to generate decision sequences point by point, which is a greedy heuristic. On the contrary, Emami et al. [87] proposed the Sinkhorn policy gradient (SPG) algorithm to learn permutation so that in addition to TSP-type problems, it can also solve other issues, for example, maximum weight matching. The state of SPG is a permutation instance of size N, and the action is an $N \times N$ permutation matrix. To use a deterministic policy gradient method, such as DDPG, Emami et al. used Sinkhorn layers to approximate the permutation matrix and added a term to the critic loss to de-bias the policy gradient.

Kool et al. [88] improved [85] on two aspects: (1) They used an attention mechanism instead of LSTM for encoding, which introduces invariance to the node input order and enables parallel computation. (2) They designed the baseline of REINFORCE algorithm as the cost of a solution from the policy defined by the best model, which is similar to self-play that improves itself by comparing with the previous solutions.

Ma et al. [244] focused on COPs with constraints, for example, TSP with time window (TSPTW), and proposed to solve them using hierarchical RL. Ma et al. compared two hierarchical structures: one is that the lower layer is to make the solution satisfy the feasible region constraints, and the higher layer is to optimize the objective function; the other is that the lower layer is to optimize the solution of an unconstrained TSP, and the higher layer is to give an instance of TSP with constraints. They proved that in the TSP experiment the first structure is better. Ma et al. also proposed graph pointer network (GPN), which uses LSTM to encode a graph with context provided by GNN to obtain more transferable representations.

Abe et al. [245] addressed the problem that previous methods obtained poor empirical performance on some graphs due to the limited exploration space of the Q-learning method. They proposed CombOpt inspired by AlphaGo Zero to replace Q-learning. While the original AlphaGo Zero is designed for two-player games with a terminal state of win/lose/draw, Abe et al. modeled the state value of AlphaGo by "how likely the player is going to win", and extended it to COPs by a reward normalization technique relating to "how good it is compared to random actions".

Barrett et al. [247] addressed the necessity of exploration of the solution space during test time since many COPs are too complex to learn only through training. They designed a reward structure to motivate the agent to find better solutions when testing by adding or removing a node. This method is complementary to many training methods.

Kwon et al. [246] addressed the problem that for some COPs with equally optimal solutions, previous works always learn one of them, which is a biased strategy. They pointed out that previous works are sensitive to the selection of the first node, thus they used the idea of entropy maximization to improve exploration. In addition, they proposed a new baseline for policy gradient to avoid local minima.

Improvement RL

The previous works usually use NNs to generate COP solutions in one shot. Despite the efficiency, there is always a certain gap from the optimal in such methods. Another type of work learns the improvement heuristic, which improves an initial solution iteratively.

Chen et al. [97] proposed a method of making incremental improvement until convergence by locally rewriting feasible strategies, called NeuRewriter. Chen et al. modeled the rewriting process as MDP, where the state is the partial solution, the action is the desired local region and the associated rewriting rule. They trained the policy with the advantaged actor–critic algorithm and applied NeuRewriter to three problems—expression simplification, online job scheduling, and vehicle routing problems (VRP)—where NeuRewriter performs better than strong heuristics.

Wu et al. [248] proposed to use deep RL to automatically improve an initial solution based on neighborhood search. The architecture is based on self-attention, where the action is a node pair for pairwise local operators. Learning with the actor–critic algorithm, the model generates a probability matrix for each pair.

Lu et al. [249] proposed a new framework to improve heuristic methods with reinforcement learning for capacitated vehicle routing problems (CVRP). They divided heuristic operators into two classes, improvement operators and perturbation operators. According to each state, a certain class of operators is selected first, and then a specific operator is selected within the class. Specifically, given recent solutions, the method for selecting a class is a threshold-based rule. If a local minimum is reached, the perturbation operator is activated to generate a new solution, otherwise, the improvement operator is activated. They used reinforcement learning to select the specific improvement operator, where the problem, solution, and running history are used as the features of the state, and different operators are used as actions. Lu et al. designed two kinds of rewards: one is +1 if the solution is improved, otherwise −1, and the other is to take the total distance achieved by the problem instance during the first improvement iteration as a baseline.

3.1.3. Game Theoretic Methods

Single-Player Game

Some COPs are modeled as reinforcement learning problems, in which the idea of single-player games and self-play can be applied.

Laterre et al. [89] used the concept of self-play on 2D and 3D BPP problems and proposed the ranked reward algorithm. When applying MCTs to solve a BPP problem modeled as MDP, the reward for all non-terminal states is usually set to 0 and for the terminal state, is obtained according to the quality of the solution. Laterre et al. reshaped the reward function by storing the agent's recent performance against which new solutions are compared, earning the reward related to whether or not it outperformed itself. In this approach, ranked reward reproduces the benefits of self-play for single-player games, removes the requirement of training data, and obtains a well-suited adversary. Experiments show that it outperforms ranked-free strategies on BPP problems.

Xu et al. [250] proposed a method to transform certain COPs into Zermelo games to use self-play-based neural MCTS. The Zermelo game is a two-player, finite information game with perfect information. During the game, two players alternate actions, and finally one wins and one loses. Xu et al. modeled a type of COP (the highest safe rung (HSR) problem (Highest safe rung (HSR): consider throwing jars from a specific rung of a ladder where the jars could either break or not. If a jar is unbroken during a test, it can be used next time. The highest safe rung is a rung that for any test performed above it, the jar will break.)) as a Zermelo game, mainly using its recursive property. The state–space convergence and solution quality of the algorithm prove to be good, but it faces the common time-consuming problem of the neural MCTS algorithm.

Drori et al. [90] modeled some COPs of choosing edges over graphs as a single-player game, represented by a decision tree. Drori et al. used the graph attention network to encode the line-graph variant of the original graph, and then used the attention mechanism to select actions (add/remove an edge). Finally, they updated the network weights through the evaluation oracle of the leaf nodes, where perfect information game theory proved that a similar mechanism could approximately converge to an optimal policy. Drori et al. conducted experiments on four problems of minimum spanning tree, shortest path, TSP, and VRP, and demonstrated linear running times with good optimality gaps.

Competitive Game

Shahadat et al. [91] regarded each strategy of the TSP problem as a player and iteratively updated them through competition and reinforcement to obtain the optimal strategy. Specifically, Shahadat et al. first randomly initialized some strategies, each of which has a payoff equal to 0. In each round of iteration, for the player X_i, an opponent player X_j is chosen to compare; if X_j wins, then X_i imitates the strategy of X_j (copy some sequence from the opponent) to update itself, and rewards the winning player according to probabilistic utility theory, otherwise, X_i updates itself according to the current global best player and the local best player (the strongest strategy that X_i has explored).

If the update does not exceed its previous performance, the strategy of X_i is updated again with a local search strategy 2-opt.

Cooperative Game

In tasks involving cooperation among multiple agents, the concept of equilibrium and communication in game theory tends to lead to good solution quality.

Kulkarni et al. [92] proposed to use probability collectives to solve the small-scale multi-depot multiple traveling salesmen problem (MDMTSP). This method is a kind of cooperative approach, and the main idea is to treat each salesman as an agent, and each route as a strategy that forms an agent's strategy set. In each iteration, each agent independently updates the probability distribution over its own strategy set to select a specific action that has the highest probability of optimizing its own utility (private utility) until the probability distribution can no longer be changed (to reach Nash equilibrium). As a cooperative approach, the private utility is allocated by the global utility, so the global objective is optimized in each iteration, too. In order to deal with the problem of node-repeated-selection in TSP, Kulkarni et al. also used heuristic methods, including node insertion and elimination, and neighboring and node swapping. This method solves the MDMTSP of 3 depots, 3 vehicles, and 15 nodes in a short time, but Kulkarni et al. also pointed out that it can only solve small-scale problems with few constraints.

3.2. Problems

In this section, the historical solution process of classical COPs are concerned, focusing on the change of methods and the data scale of the experiments, so as to guide application to practical problems. It can also reflect how the ML algorithms proposed in recent years move the field forward. Some problem-specific solutions not mentioned in Section 3.1 are added.

3.2.1. Integer Linear Programming

ILP is a general form for many discrete COPs and is of great practical significance. Table 5 presents ML methods proposed in recent years to solve the ILPs.

To solve MILP problems, B&B is a common approach, which builds an optimization tree and selects variables for branching at each step, and prunes according to the results of LP-relaxation. In the branching stage, strong branching (SB) gives the score of candidate nodes to guide the selection. Alvarez et al. [70] proposed to treat the scoring stage of SB as a regression problem and used supervised learning for fitting to solve binary MILP problems. The method effectively improves operation efficiency. He et al. [71] formally modeled the decision process of B&B as MDP, and treated node selection and node pruning as classification problems. They set the label of expand and prune according to whether the node is optimal, and then used the imitation learning method to deal with the problem of imperfect information. On larger-scale problems, the method of He et al. further reduces the computational time and the gap with the optimal solution on MILP problems. Khalil et al. [72] further regarded the SB scoring problem as a learning-to-rank problem where nodes are labeled by binary ranking, that is, nodes with scores close to the highest score are ranked higher than others. The ranking strategy is learned by supervised learning methods. In addition, the method proposed by Khalil et al. seamlessly transfers the branching strategy from the SB- to ML-based method when applied to a given problem, instead of learning the strategy offline. Gasse et al. [93] also formulated B&B as MDP and learned the policy by behavioral cloning. They treated the binary tree as a bipartite graph and used GCNN to encode the state to improve the generalization ability of the algorithm on test instances.

The work of Kruber et al. [251] concerned the issue of the decomposition of MIPs. A MIP problem can be decomposed in many ways, and some of them can well reflect the structure of the original model for which the MIP can be reformulated to an easier form to solve, while some decompositions are not suitable. Kruber et al. proposed to use supervised learning to train a classifier to decide whether a given decomposition of MIP is worth continuing to be reformulated. Kruber et al. tested the classifier on both structured instances (such as set covering, BPP, VRP, etc.) and unstructured instances with a total of 1619 decompositions.

Table 5. Methods for ILPs.

Method	Reference	Year	Description	Scale
SL	Alvarez [70]	2014	learning SB scoring decisions on binary MILP	hundreds variables, 100 constraints
	He [71]	2014	using Dagger to learn binary branching and pruning policy on MILP	200–1000 variables, 100–500 constraints
	Khalil [72]	2016	learning ranking policy derived by SB, on-the-fly learning	50,000 and 500,000 nodes
	Kruber [251]	2017	to decide whether a decomposition of MIP is suitable	–
	Gasse [93]	2019	using GCNN to encode the bipartite graph	–
	Paulus [84]	2021	an end-to-end trainable architecture to learn constraints and cost terms of ILP	1–8 variables, 2–16 constraints
RL	Tang [94]	2020	learning to cut plane with RL on IP	variables × constraints = 200, 1000, 5000

Paulus et al. [84] directly used the mathematical gradient substitution method to enable the loss between the objective function and the optimal objective function to be passed to the parameters c of cost function and the parameters A and b of the constraints, thereby realizing an end-to-end black-box solver. Paulus et al. showed high accuracy of this method on very small-scale ILP problems.

Tang et al. [94] used reinforcement learning to improve the cutting plane method (specifically, Gomory's method [252]) for solving IPs. Tang et al. modeled the process of selecting cutting planes as an MDP, where the state is the current feasible region and the reward is the change in the value of the objective function between episodes. In order to deal with the problem that the policy is independent of the order of the constraint parameters and the input length is variable, Tang et al. used the attention network and LSTM, respectively. In the experiment, Tang et al. considered problems of three scales with the number of variables, and the number of constraints being about 200, 1000, and 5000.

3.2.2. MIS, MVC, MC

MIS, MC, and MIS problems are COPs over graphs and are equivalent problems mathematically, thus, the methods for these problems are similar. Table 6 represents the surveyed works on this problem.

Table 6. Methods for MIS, MC, MVC.

Method	Reference	Year	Problem	Description	Scale (Vertice)
SL	Li [231]	2018	MIS, MC, MVC	using GCN to generate multiple probability maps and doing tree-search on them	1000–100,000
RL	Khalil [95]	2017	MC, MVC	using S2V-DQN to select desired node once a time	50–2000
	Venka-takrish-nan [240]	2018	MIS, MC, MVC	using Graph2Seq to handle variable graph size trained by Q-learning	25–3200
	Abe [245]	2019	MC, MVC	using CombOpt to solve the problem of limited exploration space	100–5000
	Barrett [247]	2020	MC	using ECO-DQN to improve the solution during test time	20–500
	Song [243]	2020	MVC	co-training algorithms with graph-based and ILP-based representa-tions	100–500
	Manch-anda [241]	2020	MC, MVC	learning to prune poor nodes in order to generalize to larger graph	50 K–65 M
	Karal-ias [96]	2020	MC	traing GNN in unsuper-vised way by constructing a differen-tiable loss function	up to 1500

With the development of deep networks, GNNs are widely used to solve problems based on graph structures, including COPs. Khalil et al. [95] used GNNs to solve MC and MVC firstly. As described in Section 3.1.2, they proposed to select the desired node once a time, using the Structre2Vector network to embed nodes that are learned by Q-learning, and tested this method on graphs with 50–2000 nodes. Li et al. [231] regarded the output of GCN as an n-dimension real-valued probability map. Instead of converting the probability map to the discrete solution directly, they proposed to generate multiple maps and used a breadth-first tree search to obtain the complete solution. They showed that this method generalized well on graphs with 1000 nodes to 100,000 nodes and 10 million edges. Venkatakrishnan et al. [240] proposed Graph2Seq-RNN based on [95], which uses a discrete-time dynamical system to deal with the graph and enables the network to perform well on graphs with different sizes from the trained one. Experiments are performed on graphs with 25–3200 vertices and various edge probabilities, notably, the policy is trained on graphs of size 15 and edge probability 0.15. Abe et al. [245] proposed CombOpt to solve the problem of limited exploration space in the Q-learning method, which uses a reward normalization technique relating to comparison with random actions. The training set includes graphs with 40–50 nodes for MC and 80–100 nodes for other problems, and the testing set includes graphs of various sizes from 100 to 5000. Manchanda et al. [241] extended the method of [95,231] to graphs with 50 K to 65 M nodes with up to 1.8 B edges by learning to prune poor nodes that have little contribution to the solution set. Karalias et al. [96] proposed a principle method to construct the differentiable loss function from discrete problems, and trained a GNN to minimize this loss function in an unsupervised way, following selecting a node according to the vector output by GNN.

Rather than improve the training process, Barrett et al. [247] focused on improving the solution during test time. They proposed ECO-DQN with a reward structure to guide exploration, that is, adding or removing a node from the solution. They tested this method on graphs with 20–500 vertices and showed that it beat S2V-DQN in most cases.

Song et al. [243] used both graph-based and ILP-based representations of COPs. They solved a problem with two algorithms based on two kinds of representation separately and exchanged the information between two solutions. Experiments were performed on graphs of sizes 100–500 and showed good generalizing ability and solution quality.

3.2.3. Traveling Salesman Problems

Due to the natural structure of the TSP, it is easy to treat the strategy as a decision sequence, where nodes are selected one by one and form a route. There are two ways to deal with the input structure: a sequence or a graph. Generally, the graph representation characterizes the structure better since the order of depots in input has the property of being permutation invariant. Recent works on this problem are presented in Table 7.

The first attempt to apply the sequence-to-sequence model into COPs is made by Vinyals et al. [76]. They proposed Ptr-Net based on the attention mechanism, which enables a variable length of input and is trained with supervised learning. Nodes are selected according to the probability distribution over candidate nodes set as output by Ptr-Net. They tested it on small-scale TSPs with fewer than 50 nodes and found that Ptr-Net seems to break for 40 nodes and beyond. Bello et al. [85] improved [76] by learning the probability distribution with REINFORCE, removing the reliance on training data. Active search was used to construct the final solution. Experiments were performed on TSP20, 50, and 100. Refs. [86–88,239,246] used similar architecture based on S2S. Emami et al. [87] proposed to learn the permutation matrix of nodes instead of the probability sequence using the Sinkhorn policy gradient and test it on TSP-20, obtaining better performance. Kwon et al. [246] proposed POMO to solve the problem that equivalent optimal solutions are unequally selected by previous methods.

To solve problems such as VRP where the input status changes over time, Nazari et al. [239] proposed a variant of [85] which embeds the static elements and dynamic elements in the input separately. Experiments suggest this method can obtain better results than classical heuristics.

Nowak et al. [81] proposed to apply GNN to COPs. It is trained in a supervised such way that the loss between the bedded origin graph and target graph with the same number of nodes is calculated. Nowak et al. tested the method on TSP20 and mentioned a performance gap with Ptr-Net [76]. Khalil et al. [95] further proposed S2V-DQN to remove training data, as described in Section 3.1.2. Joshi et al. [253] improved [81] by replacing the self-regression approach and compared different search methods. Prates et al. [233] focused on COPs with numerical information (in this case, TSP with cost constraints) and proposed to embed edges with weights and constraints and trained the GNNs with labels. Ma et al. [244] also focused on COPs with constraints and proposed to use the graph pointer network and hierarchical RL architecture, where two levels aim at optimization and making solutions feasible, respectively.

Table 7. Methods for TSP.

Problem	Method	Reference	Year	Description	Scale
TSP	S2V	Vinyals [76]	2015	Ptr-Net	<50
		Bello [85]	2016	Ptr-Net + REINFORCE	20, 50, 100
		Deudon [86]	2018	attention+REIN-FORCE+2-opt	20, 50, 100
		Emami [87]	2018	attention+Sinkhorn Policy Gradient	20
		Kool [88]	2019	Transformer+REIN-FORCE with baseline relating to the best model so far	20, 50, 100
		Kwon [246]	2020	attention+REINFORCE	20, 50, 100
	G2V	Nowak [81]	2017	GNNs	20
		Khalil [95]	2017	GNNs + Q-learning, S2V-DQN	50–2000
		Joshi [253]	2019	GCNs + beam search	20, 50, 100
		Prates [233]	2019	GNNs, message passing	20–40
		Ma [244]	2019	Graph pointer Net-work+hierarchical RL	250, 500, 750, 1000
	improve-ment RL	Wu [248]	2021	transformer+AC	20, 50, 100
	end-to-end	Vlaste-lica [83]	2020	an end-to-end trainable architecture to learn cost terms of ILP	5, 10, 20, 40
	game	Kulkar-ni [92]	2009	Probability Collectives	3 depots, 3 vehicles
		Shaha-dat [91]	2021	competitive game among strategies	-

Table 7. *Cont.*

Problem	Method	Reference	Year	Description	Scale
VRP	S2V	Nazari [239]	2018	RNN + attention + policy gradient	10, 20, 50, 100 customers, 20, 30, 40, 50 vehicle capacity
		Kwon [246]	2020	attention + REIN-FORCE	20, 50, 100
	improve-ment RL	Chen [97]	2019	using NeuRewriter to find a local region and the associated rewriting rule	20, 50, 100
		Lu [249]	2020	use RL to choose operators	20, 50, 100
		Wu [248]	2021	transformer + AC	20, 50, 100

Some RL improvement methods are proposed to solve TSP. Chen et al. [97] proposed NeuRewriter to learn region-picking and rule-picking policies and improved a feasible solution by locally rewriting. They tested NeuRewriter on Capacitated VPR of sizes 20, 50, and 100. Lu et al. [249] proposed to use RL to choose heuristic improvement operators, and the other class of operators, namely perturbation operators, was used to avoid the local optimum. Wu et al. [248] proposed an attention mechanism-based architecture to choose a node pair for pairwise local operators without human guidance, which outperforms other deep models on TSP and CVRP instances.

Game theoretic methods have also been applied in TSPs. Kulkarni et al. [92] proposed to solve MTSPs using probability collectives, where agents try to maximize their own utility, which is assigned by a global utility independently. They obtained good solutions in a short time on small-scale MTSPs. Shahadat et al. [91] created a competitive game among strategies over TSPs. At each step, two strategies were compared, and the winner was used as a demonstration to the loser.

4. Applications in Energy Field

This section mainly focuses on applications in problems in the energy field [254]. Applications in several aspects were surveyed, including petroleum supply chain, steel-making, electric power system, and wind power. The results of the review are reported, respectively, as follows.

4.1. Petroleum Supply Chain

Three scenarios of the petroleum supply chain were focused on: refinery production planning, crude oil scheduling, and oil transportation, each of which plays a significant role in the supply chain by a sequence of operation processes. Then a brief review of progress on application to solutions of the aforementioned problems in the petroleum supply chain was presented, for these processes are major concerns of worldwide petroleum supply systems. Table 8 gives a brief summary of applications surveyed.

Table 8. Application in petroleum supply chain.

Senario	Problem	Reference	Year	Approach
Refinery Production Planning	refinery product profits	[99]	2007	stochastic algorithm
	strategic refinery production planning	[98]	2017	Cournot oligopoly-type game
	refinery operation problem	[100]	2017	Cournot oligopoly model
	gasoline industry investment	[101]	2020	three-phase Stackelberg game
Refinery Scheduling	refinery production and operation	[105]	2009	DP + mixed genetic
	crude oil scheduling	[104]	2010	fuzzy and chance-constrained programming
	refinery planning and crude oil operation scheduling	[255]	2011	Lagrangian decomposition
	scheduling refinery problem	[256]	2011	logic-expressed heuristic rules
	oil-refinery scheduling	[102]	2015	heuristic algorithm
	refinery crude oil scheduling	[257]	2020	line-up competition algorithm
	crude oil operation scheduling	[258]	2020	NSGA-III
	crude oil supply problem	[259]	2020	MILP clustering
	tank blending and scheduling	[260]	2020	discretization-based algorithm
	oil blending and processing optimization	[261]	2020	discrete-time-presented multi-periodic MILP model
	crude oil refinery operation	[262]	2020	unit-specific event-based time representation
Oil Transportation	refinery product profits	[99]	2007	stochastic algorithm
	long-term multi-product pipeline scheduling	[10]	2014	MILP-based continuous-time approach
	multi-product treelike pipeline scheduling	[12]	2015	continuous-time MILP
	long-distance pipeline transportation	[263]	2015	outer-approximation-based iterative algorithm
	crude oil pipeline scheduling	[264]	2016	two-stage stochastic algorithm
	pipeline scheduling	[11]	2017	SM + ACO
	fuel replenishment problem	[107]	2020	adaptive large neighborhood search
	refined oil pipeline transportation	[265]	2020	parallel computation + heuristic rules + adaptive search
	refined oil transportation	[266]	2021	improved variable neighborhood search

4.1.1. Refinery Production Planning

Refinery production planning is the precondition of all the operations, as it defines the number of end products to be produced and predicts the total profits of the whole production process. The ML model based on game theory was investigated to deal with refinery production planning problems.

Tominac et al. [98] presented a structure based on game theory according to a Cournot oligopoly-type game to solve strategic refinery production planning problem, as the model involves multiple refineries and markets. The results show rational and robust decisions and are mutual best responses in the competitive planning game. Ravinger [99] built a Cournot oligopoly model embedding a stochastic algorithm to cope with product profits problem for refineries. This model with an oligopolistic market structure takes into account key characteristics of refineries and yields a solution concerning investment decisions under demand shock. Tominac [100] also constructed a Cournot oligopoly model for refinery operation problems in multiple markets competition, which is an optimal strategic production planning problem. The model takes into account both economic objectives and process constraints to tackle such MILP. On the aspect of economy, Babaei et al. [101] used a three-phase Stackelberg game theory approach based on a multi-agent method to analyze the gasoline industry investment by the government under massive consumption and shortage of production in developing countries. The results show that profit is maximized for investors under the management of production volume.

From producing point of view, the ML approach based on game theory regards each refinery as a single rational agent, where each considers both their profits and integrated profits in the game to achieve Nash equilibrium. Therefore, with cooperation, i.e., transporting products to each other refinery, the whole supply system maximizes profit. However, transportation costs cannot be easily considered in this game model since none of the agents would be willing to take the risk. Therefore, dealing with transportation costs in the ML approach based on game theory would be another challenge.

4.1.2. Refinery Scheduling

Refinery scheduling is a significant production operation in the upstream petroleum supply chain in which many complex chemical sub-operations are involved, including crude oil unloading, crude oil mixing, production unit operation, products blending, and refined oil distribution [102]. These scheduling optimization problems are stochastically uncertain and have multiple constraints and objective functions [103]. It is difficult to optimize the model with such complexity, not to mention large-scale scheduling problems. Therefore, different models and algorithms with built-in ML mechanisms were surveyed, where each approach either simplifies the model or reduces the time of solving.

Crude oil scheduling sometimes can involve uncertain conditions, especially when dealing with product demands or ship arrival time at the terminal. To solve crude oil scheduling problems under uncertain conditions, Wang et al. [104] developed a two-stage robust model which transforms fuzzy programming and chance-constrained programming into deterministic counterpart problems at the first stage and proposes the second stage based on the scenario. The experiment shows that the feasible rate raised from 32% to 97% compared to the approach proposed by Cal et al. Li et al. [105] suggested a hybrid mechanism combining DP and mixed genetics to improve the general DP algorithm, which is computationally expensive to solve the model with inequality constraints. The algorithm successfully solves multi-stage production and operation DP problems in refineries under uncertain market demand and yields an adaptive and effective solution.

Among all the literature works investigated, many applications of heuristic aim to simplify the model and thus make the algorithm computationally cheaper to obtain the optimization. Shah et al. [102] proposed a heuristic algorithm based on a decomposed network to solve the oil-refinery problem. The authors decomposed the problem into two separate scheduling problems and generated multiple integer cuts at the end of each iteration, which significantly reduces the computational time due to fewer iterations being needed.

Similarly, A MIP model integrating logic-expressed heuristic rules was reported by Li [256] to simplify the model of the scheduling refinery problem as well as to improve the efficiency of the solution without losing optimization guaranteed. Yue et al. [257] first proposed a heuristic rule of the oil transport sequence. Then an asynchronous continuous-time CO model based on a line-up competition algorithm was built to transform the original refinery crude oil scheduling problem (RCSP), a MINLP, into a CO problem that makes it easier to obtain the optimal solution, and then solve it within a relatively short computational time. The total cost of scheduling, the objective function, is proved to reduce by 2.1% compared to other approaches mentioned. To solve the crude oil operation scheduling problem for refineries, which is a multi-objective optimization problem, an NSGA-III based method was proposed by Hou et al. [258]. As a meta-heuristic algorithm, NSGA-III improves population diversity by adaptively updating reference points compared to NSGA-II.

There are some sources involving the use of other techniques. Assis et al. [259] presented a MILP clustering mechanism to cope with the operational management of the crude oil supply (OMCOS) problem consisting of the scheduling of vessel traveling between a terminal and platforms. The authors used the clustering solution as a pre-step to simplify operations and reduce the total number of vessel routes. Beach et al. [260] proposed a discretization-based algorithm which can approximate non-convex mixed-integer quadratically constrained programming (MIQCP) as a MILP. To solve the tank blending and scheduling problem, the authors combined the algorithm with a rolling horizon approach, which is evaluated to be supportive of using industrial datasets. Li [261] reported a discrete-time-presented multi-periodic MILP model for oil blending and processing optimization problem. Shown by numerical results, this formulation is computationally effective, as it reduces solving time. Mouret et al. [255] proposed an approach involving Lagrangian decomposition to solve refinery planning and crude oil operation scheduling integration, which is a large-scale MINLP. The authors introduced a hybrid dual problem to update Lagrange multipliers and then solve each problem separately. Bayu et al. [262] reported a unit-specific event-based time representation based on the state task network (STN), an extension of a previous benchmark given by Yadav and Shaik, to solve crude oil refinery operation involving desalting. The proposed model makes it possible to inform the decision maker of resources consumed, such as wash water and sludge.

To conclude this section, the built-in ML algorithm could help simplify the COP model or reduce the solving time with certain architecture constructed. Yet not every part of the production process was considered for refinery scheduling, i.e., the omitted elements, such as dependence on uncertain parameters and uncertainties under non-linear constraints, would cause the results to be different.

4.1.3. Oil Transportation

Now it is time to focus on the intermediate operation that connects upstream and downstream of the petroleum supply chain: oil transportation. The oil transportation system consists of several methods among crude oil fields, refineries, storage terminals, and sales companies: pipeline, trucks, railway, and tankers [106]. The determination is made with respect to different factors, such as distance, oil type, cost, etc. In this section, applications to problems concerning pipeline scheduling were mainly investigated.

Oil transportation through pipeline usually involves multi-product scheduling problems. Mostafaei et al. [10] introduced a MILP-based continuous-time approach for the long-term multi-product pipeline scheduling problem, which is a MINLP. Compared to work performed by Cafaro et al., the formulation proposed by Mostafaei et al. allows 25% less total operation cost. Focusing on the same topic, Mostafaei et al. [12] also presented their work of a continuous-time MILP to address the scheduling of multi-product treelike pipeline scheduling consisting of a single refinery and several downstream depots. The proposed model is proved to be significantly more computationally efficient. Like Mostafaei et al., who focused on pipeline scheduling between a single refinery and multiple terminals, Zhang et al. [11] also concentrated on multiple pump stations, which is a crucial structure for long-distance pipelines. The authors presented a hybrid computational approach embedding SM into ACO. Therefore, with such an architecture, two sub-models are more interactive than other multi-step models in previous literary works.

Now, the reader may look at other approaches. Oliveira et al. [264] presented a two-stage stochastic MILP model to determine the scheduling of pipeline-transported oil and sequence of ships at the terminal, which is a system with supply uncertainty. Zhang et al. [263] developed a continuous-time scheduling model embedding an outer-approximation-based iterative algorithm to tackle the long-distance pipeline transportation problem. Gao et al. [266] proposed an improved variable neighborhood search algorithm (IVNS) for scheduling refined oil transportation with multiple trips and due times. To improve local optimization ability, a greedy strategy is built based on the initial solution obtained by the forwarding insertion heuristic. Therefore, the results converge faster without losing the quality of the solution. Wang et al. [107] constructed an adaptive large neighborhood search (ALNS) heuristic to cope with the fuel-replenishment problem (FRP), a VRP with multiple deliveries, trips, and compartments, where different products are involved. Wang [265] proposed an improved simulated annealing (ISA) algorithm incorporating parallel computation, heuristic rules, and adaptive search to tackle refined oil pipeline transportation problems in order to optimize computation and special constraints. To simplify the structure, the author presented an approach that separates one pipeline transportation scheduling problem into initial-station input scheduling and sub-problems of distribution scheduling at each station along the pipeline. The resulting scheduling plan was proved to be efficient and effective applying to a real instance. Based on previous research of a petroleum products distribution system, where an object-oriented Petri nets (OOPN) framework is proposed, Li et al. [267] presented a queue theory to improve the safety of the existing model, for the OOPN model only shows boundedness and no deadlock without evidence of safety. The improved model was shown to be effective.

So far, the references surveyed in this section were all focused on treelike pipelines with multiple destinations, i.e., the models were built on a single refinery concerning several terminals, while in reality, the pipeline for oil transportation would be more like a complicated network. With such complexity, whether the current algorithm would still be competent is worth questioning.

4.2. Steel-Making

The scheduling problem in steel making is another complicated combinatorial problem in the industrial field. Like petroleum refinery scheduling, steel-making scheduling also involves numerous chemical operations and materials blending. Table 9 gives a brief summary of the applications surveyed.

To deal with dynamic uncertainty involved in steel-making workshops, Lin et al. [108] introduced a deep RL-based algorithm to the crane scheduling problem. Then a DQN algorithm was built into the crane action value network model. The resulting scheduling showed that the task completes faster using this model, thus improving efficiency. Zhou [109] proposed an improved gray wolf optimization algorithm based on a deep deterministic strategy gradient algorithm (DDPG-GWO) to deal with problems such as the local optimum and poor stability of the solution without using the gray wolf algorithm. DDPG can help train the agents, thus avoiding the above problems. It is proven that DDPG-GWO can obtain a more accurate solution in less computational time. Jia [110] aimed at solving batch machine scheduling problems and presented a batch optimization algorithm based on Ptr-Net, which is trained by RL. To improve the performance of Ptr-Net, a hybrid genetic algorithm is introduced, due to its capability for global search. As a crucial link during the steel-making process, the operation and scheduling problem of steel-making and continuous casting has complicated constraints with uncertainty. To realize intelligent optimization, Ma et al. [111] discussed an integrated framework based on ML with rolling optimization algorithm and rule mining.

There were not enough clues to show the application of the algorithm based on game theory that was used in steel making. Most of the references surveyed were relevant to the ML-based algorithm with modification to approaches to solve COPs.

Table 9. Application in steel making.

Problem	Reference	Year	Approach
crane scheduling problem	[108]	2021	deep RL-based algorithm + DQN
scheduling of steelmaking and continuous casting	[109]	2021	DDPG-GWO
batch machine scheduling	[110]	2021	Ptr-Net
steel-making operation and scheduling	[111]	2022	integrated framework + ML

4.3. *Electric Power System*

The scheduling problem in electric power systems is another industrial field that draws attention. Similar to the petroleum supply chain, the electric system is also a multivariate non-linear system with high uncertainty and complexity. Nevertheless, unlike liquid or gas-formed petroleum products, this power cannot be stored due to the special physical feature of electricity. Therefore, solving such a system requires more consideration and is thus more complicated [268]. Table 10 gives a brief summary of the applications surveyed.

ML-based approaches were first surveyed to solve CO scheduling problems in the electric system. Yan et al. [112] proposed an improved Ptr-Net combining the deep RL algorithm to obtain end-to-end self-learning calculation for the topology control strategy of distribution network fault recovery. Dong et al. [113] constructed an optimization dispatch model based on the RL framework using the Markov decision process. Then the model was trained by the AC algorithm and deep deterministic policy gradient algorithm. Then the system was divided into multiple agents concerning data interaction, and the optimization model was transformed into an MARL model. Compared to the SARL algorithm, the training process can converge more stably. Aiming at transient voltage stability in energy internet (EI), Cao et al. [114] proposed a deep RL algorithm based on CNN to improve decision-making optimization to balance the power supply–demand. This algorithm has a more accurate prediction compared to conventional ML algorithms, and it also satisfies the expectation of system stability. Zhang et al. [115] focused on hybrid energy coordinated control optimization problems for hybrid energy storage systems. The authors designed a deep RL framework embedding a neural network model to solve the formulated decision-making problem. Li et al. [116] focused on the scheduling problem of charging stations to predict the power supply capacity required and conduct a neural network mapping model based on DL. Experiments show the capability of dealing with the sizing problem of station charging capacity. Huang et al. [117] suggested a hybrid approach based on the original differential evolution (DE) algorithm, combining the ant system to tackle the optimal reactive power dispatch (ORPD) problem. Having been tested on a real system, the approach can achieve lower power losses during transmission with better results and performance compared to previous methods. Yuce et al. [118] aimed at optimizing the smart scheduling of energy-consuming devices, utilizing artificial neural network/genetic algorithm (ANN-GA). The best performance was found in a Levenverg–Marquardt-based learning algorithm with which the maximized use of renewable sources and reduced energy demand were achieved. With a great interest in generation expansion planning, Huang et al. [119] presented an investment planning model embedding a double-layer optimization construction and three types of agents built with the Q-learning algorithm and GA, considering a change in electricity price and generation cost. The model is effective and was practicably proved by two real-world instances.

Now, research on models that involve game theory are concentrated. This ML approach considers the perspective of the economic market and treats each decision maker as an individual agent. The objective is usually the total profit. To improve the efficiency of the energy system, Sheikhi et al. [269] proposed a model based on cloud computing (CC) framework that modifies the classic energy hub (EH) to support managing communication between utility companies and smart energy hubs (S.E. hub). The approach is applied for users to obtain demand side management (DSM) while the Nash equilibrium is achieved by a subgradient optimization algorithm. Fan et al. [270] drew their interest in energy hub and studied the multi-neighbor cooperative economic scheduling problem, where EHs compose a community to exchange energy with each other to minimize operational cost. The authors built a model of a bargaining, cooperative game for this management problem and found the Nash equilibrium to ensure optimal operations. Peng et al. [271] built a bottom-up inter-regional transaction model for electricity pricing mechanism. The results quantitatively showed the relationship between the retailers' behavior and benefit and cost of electricity under the certain economic assumption. Chen et al. [272] proposed a mechanism based on the Stachelberg game for demand response (DR) scheduling optimization problems with load uncertainty. The authors took into account the users' optimal consumption as well as the price of electricity to model the interaction between the service provider and users for the smart grid. The results reached a balanced demand versus supply. For the same interest, Li et al. [273] also reported an optimization framework based on the Stachelberg game to deal with scheduling of the DR energy system, setting profits of the integrated energy operator (IEO) as the objective. The game was built into a MINLP formulation and solved with an introduced sequence operation theory. The results were verified to be applicable by real-world instances.

More widely used ML approaches are shown in this section on the aspect of management, where each energy hub is considered an agent bargaining with each other. Unlike the petroleum supply chain, the electric power system has a shorter supply chain, and the problem is closer to the market.

Table 10. Application in electric power system.

Problem	Reference	Year	Approach
energy-consuming device optimization	[118]	2000	ANN-GA
optimal reactive power dispatch	[117]	2012	DE + ant system
DR scheduling optimization	[272]	2012	Stachelberg-ML mechanism
energy system efficiency	[269]	2015	CC
generation expansion planning	[119]	2016	Q-learning + GA

Table 10. *Cont.*

Problem	Reference	Year	Approach
charging stations scheduling	[116]	2017	NN + DL
multi-neighbor cooperative economic scheduling	[270]	2018	bargaining cooperative game
electricity pricing	[271]	2018	bottom-up inter-regional transaction model
power supply-demand	[114]	2019	RL + CNN
hybrid energy storage	[115]	2019	RL + NN
distribution network fault recovery	[112]	2021	improved Ptr-Net
optimization dispatch	[113]	2021	AC + deep deterministic policy gradient algorithm
DR energy system	[273]	2021	Stachelberg-ML optimization

4.4. Wind Power

The scheduling problem in wind power is another issue that people are concerned about in the energy field that involves the application of game theory to solve combinatorial problems. Table 11 gives a brief summary of applications surveyed.

Marden et al. [120] focused on energy production optimization problems in wind farms and suggested a model-free distributed learning strategy, an algorithm without building a model of interaction between wind turbines based on game theory and cooperative control. This learning strategy was demonstrated to achieve maximum energy production. Quan et al. [121] proposed a non-parametric neural network-based prediction intervals (PIs) with a built-in Monte Carlo simulation method for wind power prediction problems. The stochastic security-constrained unit commitment (SCUC) model was then solved by a heuristic genetic algorithm and the model was presented to be robust. Mei et al. [122] proposed a min-max game model for the static reserve capacity planning problem with large-scale integration of wind power. The authors then introduced a two-stage relaxation algorithm to cope with the min-max game. The application showed robustness and efficiency. Liu et al. [123] analyzed the capacity planning model based on cooperative game theory in a low-carbon economy and presented an improved strategy for the union of wind-farm and grid companies. The model built a balanced and reasonable profit separating mechanism.

Not many references were surveyed for wind power field. The presented results showed an application of ML approaches with game theory, considering wind turbines as independent agents, similar to that in an electric power system.

Table 11. Application in wind power.

Problem	Reference	Year	Approach
energy production optimization	[120]	2013	model-free distributed learning
wind power prediction	[121]	2014	non-parametric NN
static reserve capacity planning	[122]	2014	two-stage relaxation
capacity planning	[123]	2015	cooperative game theory

5. Challenge

5.1. Developing Game Theoretic Learning Methods

There are three main challenges to solving COPs: (1) Accuracy—the policy space of a COP is always huge and hard to explore. For large-scale COPs, the optimal solution is even unknown. Therefore, it is hard to find the best optimization direction, escape from the local optimal, and bound the optimization gap. (2) Efficiency—solving a COP has been proved to be NP-hard, and all algorithms seek to solve it in considerable time. (3) Scalability—despite having the same structure, when the data or scale of a COP is changed, the solution distribution can be totally different.

Game theory has been widely used to solve complex optimization problems, and been integrated into ML, especially RL. Single-player algorithms (e.g., self-play) can improve the policy by beating an opponent, which is a useful way to improve the accuracy, and multi-player algorithms (e.g., centralized training decentralized execution methods) realize cooperation when agents make decisions independently, which may be used to solve complex COPs that include several independent components whose policies are changeable, improving scalability. However, as summarized in Section 3, more than half of the current methods use RL to update the policy, while few use the idea of game theory.

5.2. Challenge of Application in Energy Field

Given three scenarios in the petroleum supply chain to illustrate the application of the learning approach for COPs, it is undeniable that COPs in the petroleum supply chain are significantly complicated, where each scenario requires a different approach.

Refinery production planning involves strategic decisions of each refinery, considering both productions of other refineries and the demand of the market. This scenario is considered a multi-player game, and ML approaches based on game theory are widely used, where each refinery is seen as a single agent (player) competing or cooperating in the game, considering both their own profits and integrated profits in the game to achieve Nash equilibrium. Yet most of the ML approaches using game theory are applied to the aspect of market taking profits as the objective, although cases may differ in the real production process. Hence, more ML methods on the aspect of industrial production are to be investigated. Refinery scheduling is a more micro scenario which focuses on operations inside a single refinery where complex chemical sub-operations are involved. Since no player is involved in this scenario, no learning approach based on game theory is used when solving the problems. Rather, traditional COP frameworks, such as MILP and MINLP with machine learning improvement, such as heuristic algorithm, are more often utilized. Oil transportation including crude oil transportation and refined oil transportation is a classic programming problem that many industrial fields are facing. Problems of transporting through pipeline are mainly surveyed. Again, no learning approaches based on game theory are used due to lack of players in this scenario, and the traditional COP frameworks' embedding approaches, such as the stochastic algorithm, are introduced.

Steel making has a similar production operational process to refinery scheduling, and hence they utilize the same scheduling problems and approaches. Traditional COP frameworks are widely used with the RL-based algorithm introduced for improvement.

Through investigation, two points of view and corresponding methods to solve scheduling problems in electric power system were discovered. ML-based learning approaches aim at solving CO scheduling problems concentrating on operation, which is similar to approaches for refinery scheduling. On the other hand, ML methods using game theory consider each energy hub as an agent deciding with decentralization. Neither approach provides the decision maker with solutions as the blueprint for the whole system, i.e., the methods emphasize the single stage or partial process in the operation instead of having a macro view. Plus, ML methods based on game theory build the model on the aspect of the economic market rather than industrial production, which may generate application problems.

Not many applications for wind power were surveyed. The existing studies build models concerning power generated from and stored in the wind farm. Further investigation in this field is needed, and more surveys of the wind power system are to be conducted.

Many applications of learning methods are utilized to simplify the model from MINLP to MIP, thus reducing the computational cost. However, such simplification may yield problems, such as poor generalization, low accuracy, limited scalability, expensive computation, etc. For instance, an easily computed algorithm achieving a lower gap to the objective may not be able to establish accurate solutions [71], and an adaptive approach for a specific large-scale problem may propose too strong assumptions a priori and thus have poor generalization [10]. With the growing complexity and scale of problems in the energy field, more attention should be paid to uncertainty, which makes the simplification of the models more difficult.

5.3. Application Gap

How to apply new methods in reality is always a big challenge. As investigated in Section 4, plenty of problems in the real world are formulated as ILP or MIP, which are traditionally solved by B&B and other heuristic algorithms. However, from Figure 2, we can see that general or specific ML-based algorithms for ILP lack attention.

We believe there are several reasons for this phenomenon. Firstly, ILP is more difficult to be solved using machine learning methods than structured problems, such as TSP and MIS. In machine learning areas, natural language processing and computer vision have developed rapidly in recent years, whose structures are the sequence and the graph, respectively. Therefore, strong machine learning algorithms are proposed to solve problems with those two structures and can be applied in COPs conveniently. ILP, as a traditional optimization problem with constraints, is more about logic and mathematics than recognition and neural. Secondly, ILP is well solved by some traditional solvers (e.g., Gurobi, and SCIP), and thus is hard to beat. Although traditional solvers are stable, they depend on large amounts of data and experience and are not very useful for new situations in the application. Last but not least, there are few real-world datasets for researchers since large-scale COPs are usually faced by businesses that are private or state owned.

6. Conclusions

This paper investigates ML methods based on game theory to solve COPs in energy fields.

Section 2 is the introduction of the background of combinatorial optimization problems and several popular approaches of ML in addressing this kind of issue over the past years. COPs can be stated as minimization or maximization problems associated with the given objective function(s). A few classical COPs are mentioned, including the traveling salesman problem, minimum spanning tree problem, and knapsack problem, following which several methods are presented: attention mechanisms can handle problems of fixed-length vectors with limited access to input information in neural networks; GNNs which belong to DL methods are designed for graph-expressed data structure; RL can be applied for models involving strategic interactions among rational agents.

Sub-fields of COPs and more details of these ML methods are further discussed in Section 3. The approaches can cover the shortage of traditional methods for COPs: SL improves the computational performance of traditional approaches; reinforcement learning evaluates the quality of a given solution to avoid the difficulty of obtaining labels in SL; and game theory can be applied to problems modeled as RL. The applications on corresponding COPs are demonstrated chronologically.

Section 3 concentrates on some specific applications in energy field and investigates how the ML algorithms are applied to these issues. Although algorithms based on game theory have been applied in energy fields, there still exists space for further exploration. Among three scenarios of the petroleum supply chain, only refinery production planning involves the application of approaches with game theory, while no clue of game is found in the background of refinery scheduling and oil transportation. The review of steel-making also shows no discovery of application on game theory, as the operation is rather similar to that of petroleum production. There are more widely used ML approaches in the electric system and wind power on the aspect of management, where each energy hub or wind turbine is considered as an agent bargaining with each other.

Section 5 is the summary of the challenges over these energy application in which the ML methods are deployed. Consequently, the existing COPs in energy fields can be solved by applying ML algorithm under certain conditions, and there still exists space for learning methods to develop and apply to a wider range of problems.

Future Work

According to the investigation, great efforts have been made by introducing ML approaches to overcome the high computational complexity of traditional approaches for COPs. In the energy field, there exist large-scale COPs that can be studied by ML methods. However, current researchers still face the challenge of balancing poor generalization, low accuracy, limited scalability, expensive computation, etc. To overcome these challenges, some possible ideas for future working direction are as follows.

1. Further investigation of the application of approaches based on game theory to tackle systematic problems is of vital significance. Currently, there are limited applications in petroleum supply chain. Refineries can be modeled as rational independent agents, while it is possible to model oil fields, pipelines, or transportation tasks as agents as well. Building such a system by approaches based on game theory in which each scene in the petroleum supply chain is a game dependent on each other is worth expecting.
2. Studies on a systematic framework to handle the increasing uncertainty in CO scheduling problems in the energy field are worth investigating. With the development of complexity caused by uncertainty in real-world problems, the algorithms also need to consider adapting to the trend.
3. It is worth studying the application of ML approaches to COPs without the framework of a traditional COP solver. Subtle modification may not be able to fully demonstrate the strengths of ML algorithms. By resolving the problem of complexity due to the large scale, ML algorithms may have better performance on COPs.

Author Contributions: Conceptualization, N.M., N.Y. and H.L.; Data curation, X.Y.; Formal analysis, X.Y. and Z.W.; Funding acquisition, H.L. and L.Y.; Investigation, X.Y., Z.W. and H.Z. (Hengxi Zhang); Methodology, N.Y.; Project administration, N.M. and N.Y.; Resources, N.M., H.L. and L.Y.; Software, H.Z. (Haifeng Zhang); Supervision, N.M., N.Y., H.L., H.Z. (Haifeng Zhang) and L.Y.; Validation, X.Y.; Visualization, X.Y. and H.Z. (Hengxi Zhang); Writing—original draft, X.Y., Z.W. and H.Z. (Hengxi Zhang); Writing—review & editing, N.M., N.Y and H.Z. (Haifeng Zhang) All authors have read and agreed to the published version of the manuscript.

Funding: This research received no external funding.

Institutional Review Board Statement: Not applicable.

Informed Consent Statement: Not applicable.

Data Availability Statement: Not applicable.

Conflicts of Interest: The authors declare no conflict of interest.

References

1. Korte, B.H.; Vygen, J.; Korte, B.; Vygen, J. *Combinatorial Optimization*; Springer: Berlin/Heidelberg, Germany, 2011; Volume 1.
2. Schrijver, A. On the history of combinatorial optimization (till 1960). *Handbooks Oper. Res. Manag. Sci.* **2005**, *12*, 1–68.
3. Papadimitriou, C.H.; Steiglitz, K. *Combinatorial Optimization: Algorithms and Complexity*; Courier Corporation: North Chelmsford, MA, USA, 1998.
4. Schrijver, A. *Combinatorial Optimization: Polyhedra and Efficiency*; Springer: Berlin/Heidelberg, Germany, 2003; Volume 24.
5. Panda, D.; Ramteke, M. Preventive crude oil scheduling under demand uncertainty using structure adapted genetic algorithm. *Appl. Energy* **2019**, *235*, 68–82. [CrossRef]
6. Yang, H.; Bernal, D.E.; Franzoi, R.E.; Engineer, F.G.; Kwon, K.; Lee, S.; Grossmann, I.E. Integration of crude-oil scheduling and refinery planning by Lagrangean Decomposition. *Comput. Chem. Eng.* **2020**, *138*, 106812. [CrossRef]
7. Qin, H.; Han, Z. Crude-oil scheduling network in smart field under cyber-physical system. *IEEE Access* **2019**, *7*, 91703–91719. [CrossRef]
8. Panda, D.; Ramteke, M. Dynamic hybrid scheduling of crude oil using structure adapted genetic algorithm for uncertainty of tank unavailability. *Chem. Eng. Res. Des.* **2020**, *159*, 78–91. [CrossRef]
9. Fragkogios, A.; Saharidis, G.K. Modeling and solution approaches for crude oil scheduling in a refinery. In *Energy Management—Collective and Computational Intelligence with Theory and Applicat*; Springer: Berlin/Heidelberg, Germany, 2018; pp. 251–275.
10. Mostafaei, H.; Ghaffari Hadigheh, A. A general modeling framework for the long-term scheduling of multiproduct pipelines with delivery constraints. *Ind. Eng. Chem. Res.* **2014**, *53*, 7029–7042. [CrossRef]
11. Zhang, H.; Liang, Y.; Liao, Q.; Wu, M.; Yan, X. A hybrid computational approach for detailed scheduling of products in a pipeline with multiple pump stations. *Energy* **2017**, *119*, 612–628. [CrossRef]
12. Mostafaei, H.; Castro, P.M.; Ghaffari-Hadigheh, A. A novel monolithic MILP framework for lot-sizing and scheduling of multi-product treelike pipeline networks. *Ind. Eng. Chem. Res.* **2015**, *54*, 9202–9221. [CrossRef]
13. Li, S.; Yang, J.; Song, W.; Chen, A. A real-time electricity scheduling for residential home energy management. *IEEE Internet Things J.* **2018**, *6*, 2602–2611. [CrossRef]
14. Yang, J.; Liu, J.; Fang, Z.; Liu, W. Electricity scheduling strategy for home energy management system with renewable energy and battery storage: A case study. *IET Renew. Power Gener.* **2018**, *12*, 639–648. [CrossRef]
15. Li, S.; Yang, J.; Fang, J.; Liu, Z.; Zhang, H. Electricity scheduling optimisation based on energy cloud for residential microgrids. *IET Renew. Power Gener.* **2019**, *13*, 1105–1114. [CrossRef]
16. Deng, Z.; Liu, C.; Zhu, Z. Inter-hours rolling scheduling of behind-the-meter storage operating systems using electricity price forecasting based on deep convolutional neural network. *Int. Elect. Power Energy Syst.* **2021**, *125*, 106499. [CrossRef]
17. Griffin, P.W.; Hammond, G.P. The prospects for green steel making in a net-zero economy: A UK perspective. *Glob. Transit.* **2021**, *3*, 72–86. [CrossRef]
18. Song, G.W.; Tama, B.A.; Park, J.; Hwang, J.Y.; Bang, J.; Park, S.J.; Lee, S. Temperature Control Optimization in a Steel-Making Continuous Casting Process Using a Multimodal Deep Learning Approach. *Steel Res. Int.* **2019**, *90*, 1900321. [CrossRef]
19. Adetunji, O.; Seidu, S.O. Simulation and Techno-Economic Performance of a Novel Charge Calculation and Melt Optimization Planning Model for Steel Making. *J. Miner. Mater. Charact. Eng.* **2020**, *8*, 277–300. [CrossRef]
20. Ren, L.; Zhou, S.; Peng, T.; Ou, X. A review of CO_2 emissions reduction technologies and low-carbon development in the iron and steel industry focusing on China. *Renew. Sustain. Energy Rev.* **2021**, *143*, 110846. [CrossRef]
21. Osborne, M.J.; Rubinstein, A. *A Course in Game Theory*; MIT Press: Cambridge, MA, USA. 1994.
22. Zhu, P.; Wang, X.; Jia, D.; Guo, Y.; Li, S.; Chu, C. Investigating the co-evolution of node reputation and edge-strategy in prisoner's dilemma game. *Appl. Math. Comput.* **2020**, *386*, 125474. [CrossRef]
23. Shen, C.; Chu, C.; Shi, L.; Perc, M.; Wang, Z. Aspiration-based coevolution of link weight promotes cooperation in the spatial prisoner's dilemma game. *R. Soc. Open Sci.* **2018**, *5*, 180199. [CrossRef]
24. Bian, J.; Lai, K.K.; Hua, Z.; Zhao, X.; Zhou, G. Bertrand vs. Cournot competition in distribution channels with upstream collusion. *Int. J. Prod. Econ.* **2018**, *204*, 278–289. [CrossRef]
25. Lundin, E.; Tangerås, T.P. Cournot competition in wholesale electricity markets: The Nordic power exchange, Nord Pool. *Int. J. Ind. Organ.* **2020**, *68*, 102536. [CrossRef]
26. Dyson, B.J.; Musgrave, C.; Rowe, C.; Sandhur, R. Behavioural and neural interactions between objective and subjective performance in a Matching Pennies game. *Int. J. Psychophysiol.* **2020**, *147*, 128–136. [CrossRef] [PubMed]
27. Dolgova, T.; Bartsev, S. Neural networks playing "matching pennies" with each other: Reproducibility of game dynamics. In *IOP Conference Series: Materials Science and Engineering*; IOP Publishing: Bristol, UK, 2019; Volume 537, p. 42002.
28. Fiez, T.; Chasnov, B.; Ratliff, L. Implicit learning dynamics in stackelberg games: Equilibria characterization, convergence analysis, and empirical study. In Proceedings of the International Conference on Machine Learning, Virtual, 13–18 July 2020; pp. 3133–3144.

29. Jacobsen, H.J.; Jensen, M.; Sloth, B. Evolutionary learning in signalling games. *Games Econ. Behav.* **2001**, *34*, 34–63. [CrossRef]
30. Allen, F.; Morris, S. Game theory models in finance. In *Game Theory and Business Applications*; Springer: Berlin/Heidelberg, Germany, 2014; pp. 17–41.
31. Jordan, M.I.; Mitchell, T.M. Machine learning: Trends, perspectives, and prospects. *Science* **2015**, *349*, 255–260. [CrossRef]
32. Cunningham, P.; Cord, M.; Delany, S.J. Supervised learning. In *Machine Learning Techniques for Multimedia*; Springer: Berlin/Heidelberg, Germany, 2008; pp. 21–49.
33. Barlow, H.B. Unsupervised learning. *Neural Comput.* **1989**, *1*, 295–311. [CrossRef]
34. Ghahramani, Z. Unsupervised learning. In *Summer School on Machine Learning*; Springer: Berlin/Heidelberg, Germany, 2003; pp. 72–112.
35. Hastie, T.; Tibshirani, R.; Friedman, J. Unsupervised learning. In *The Elements of Statistical Learning*; Springer: Berlin/Heidelberg, Germany, 2009; pp. 485–585.
36. Kaelbling, L.P.; Littman, M.L.; Moore, A.W. Reinforcement learning: A survey. *J. Artif. Intell. Res.* **1996**, *4*, 237–285. [CrossRef]
37. Wiering, M.A.; Van Otterlo, M. Reinforcement learning. *Adapt. Learn. Optim.* **2012**, *12*, 729.
38. Li, Y. Deep reinforcement learning: An overview. *arXiv* **2017**, arXiv:1701.07274.
39. Mnih, V.; Kavukcuoglu, K.; Silver, D.; Graves, A.; Antonoglou, I.; Wierstra, D.; Riedmiller, M. Playing atari with deep reinforcement learning. *arXiv* **2013**, arXiv:1312.5602.
40. Sengupta, S.; Kambhampati, S. Multi-agent reinforcement learning in bayesian stackelberg markov games for adaptive moving target defense. *arXiv* **2020**, arXiv:2007.10457.
41. Zheng, L.; Fiez, T.; Alumbaugh, Z.; Chasnov, B.; Ratliff, L.J. Stackelberg actor-critic: Game-theoretic reinforcement learning algorithms. *arXiv* **2021**, arXiv:2109.12286.
42. Shi, D.; Li, L.; Ohtsuki, T.; Pan, M.; Han, Z.; Poor, V. Make Smart Decisions Faster: Deciding D2D Resource Allocation via Stackelberg Game Guided Multi-Agent Deep Reinforcement Learning. *IEEE Trans. Mob. Comput.* **2021**. [CrossRef]
43. Han, C.; Huo, L.; Tong, X.; Wang, H.; Liu, X. Spatial anti-jamming scheme for internet of satellites based on the deep reinforcement learning and Stackelberg game. *IEEE Trans. Veh. Technol.* **2020**, *69*, 5331–5342. [CrossRef]
44. Modares, A.; Somhom, S.; Enkawa, T. A self-organizing neural network approach for multiple traveling salesman and vehicle routing problems. *Int. Trans. Oper. Res.* **1999**, *6*, 591–606. [CrossRef]
45. Fagerholt, K.; Christiansen, M. A travelling salesman problem with allocation, time window and precedence constraints—An application to ship scheduling. *Int. Trans. Oper. Res.* **2000**, *7*, 231–244. [CrossRef]
46. Debnath, D.; Hawary, A. Adapting travelling salesmen problem for real-time UAS path planning using genetic algorithm. In *Intelligent Manufacturing and Mechatronics*; Springer: Berlin/Heidelberg, Germany, 2021; pp. 151–163.
47. Filip, E.; Otakar, M. The travelling salesman problem and its application in logistic practice. *WSEAS Trans. Bus. Econ.* **2011**, *8*, 163–173.
48. Wang, P.; Sanin, C.; Szczerbicki, E. Evolutionary algorithm and decisional DNA for multiple travelling salesman problem. *Neurocomputing* **2015**, *150*, 50–57. [CrossRef]
49. Uchida, A.; Ito, Y.; Nakano, K. Accelerating ant colony optimisation for the travelling salesman problem on the GPU. *Int. J. Parallel Emergent Distrib. Syst.* **2014**, *29*, 401–420. [CrossRef]
50. Zhang, R.; Prokhorchuk, A.; Dauwels, J. Deep reinforcement learning for traveling salesman problem with time windows and rejections. In Proceedings of the 2020 International Joint Conference on Neural Networks (IJCNN), Glasgow, UK, 19–24 July 2020; pp. 1–8.
51. Zhang, Y.; Han, X.; Dong, Y.; Xie, J.; Xie, G.; Xu, X. A novel state transition simulated annealing algorithm for the multiple traveling salesmen problem. *J. Supercomput.* **2021**, *77*, 11827–11852. [CrossRef]
52. Larranaga, P.; Kuijpers, C.M.H.; Murga, R.H.; Inza, I.; Dizdarevic, S. Genetic algorithms for the travelling salesman problem: A review of representations and operators. *Artif. Intell. Rev.* **1999**, *13*, 129–170. [CrossRef]
53. Dorigo, M.; Gambardella, L.M. Ant colonies for the travelling salesman problem. *Biosystems* **1997**, *43*, 73–81. [CrossRef]
54. Gendreau, M.; Laporte, G.; Semet, F. A tabu search heuristic for the undirected selective travelling salesman problem. *Eur. J. Oper. Res.* **1998**, *106*, 539–545. [CrossRef]
55. LeCun, Y.; Bengio, Y.; Hinton, G. Deep learning. *Nature* **2015**, *521*, 436–444. [CrossRef] [PubMed]
56. Sutskever, I.; Vinyals, O.; Le, Q.V. Sequence to sequence learning with neural networks. *Adv. Neural Inform. Process. Syst.* **2014**, *27*, 1–9.
57. Bahdanau, D.; Cho, K.; Bengio, Y. Neural machine translation by jointly learning to align and translate. *arXiv* **2014**, arXiv:1409.0473.
58. Cho, K.; Van Merrienboer, B.; Bahdanau, D.; Bengio, Y. On the properties of neural machine translation: Encoder-decoder approaches. *arXiv* **2014**, arXiv:1409.1259.
59. Vaswani, A.; Shazeer, N.; Parmar, N.; Uszkoreit, J.; Jones, L.; Gomez, A.N.; Kaiser, Ł.; Polosukhin, I. Attention is all you need. *Adv. Neural Inform. Process. Syst.* **2017**, *30*, 1–15.
60. Zaremba, W.; Sutskever, I.; Vinyals, O. Recurrent neural network regularization. *arXiv* **2014**, arXiv:1409.2329.
61. Yamashita, R.; Nishio, M.; Do, R.K.G.; Togashi, K. Convolutional neural networks: An overview and application in radiology. *Insights Imaging* **2018**, *9*, 611–629. [CrossRef]
62. Deisenroth, M.; Rasmussen, C.E. PILCO: A model-based and data-efficient approach to policy search. In Proceedings of the 28th International Conference on Machine Learning (ICML-11), Bellevue, WA, USA, 28 June–2 July 2011; pp. 465–472.

63. Çalışır, S.; Pehlivanoğlu, M.K. Model-free reinforcement learning algorithms: A survey. In Proceedings of the 2019 27th Signal Processing and Communications Applications Conference (SIU), Sivas, Turkey, 24–26 April 2019; pp. 1–4.
64. Moerland, T.M.; Broekens, J.; Jonker, C.M. Model-based reinforcement learning: A survey. *arXiv* **2020**, arXiv:2006.16712.
65. Kaiser, L.; Babaeizadeh, M.; Milos, P.; Osinski, B.; Campbell, R.H.; Czechowski, K.; Erhan, D.; Finn, C.; Kozakowski, P.; Levine, S.; et al. Model-based reinforcement learning for atari. *arXiv* **2019**, arXiv:1903.00374.
66. Zhao, D.; Wang, H.; Shao, K.; Zhu, Y. Deep reinforcement learning with experience replay based on SARSA. In Proceedings of the 2016 IEEE Symposium Series on Computational Intelligence (SSCI), Athens, Greece, 6–9 December 2016; pp. 1–6.
67. Watkins, C.J.; Dayan, P. Q-learning. *Mach. Learn.* **1992**, *8*, 279–292. [CrossRef]
68. Konda, V.; Tsitsiklis, J. Actor-critic algorithms. In Proceedings of the Advances in Neural Information Processing Systems 12 (NIPS 1999), Denver, CO, USA, 29 November–4 December 1999.
69. Land, A.H.; Doig, A.G. An automatic method for solving discrete programming problems. In *50 Years of Integer Programming 1958–2008*; Springer: Berlin/Heidelberg, Germany, 2010; pp. 105–132.
70. Alvarez, A.M.; Louveaux, Q.; Wehenkel, L. A Supervised Machine Learning Approach to Variable Branching in Branch-and-Bound. In ecml. 2014. Available online: https://orbi.uliege.be/handle/2268/167559 (accessed on 1 May 2022).
71. He, H.; Daume, H., III; Eisner, J.M. Learning to search in branch and bound algorithms. In Proceedings of the Advances in Neural Information Processing Systems 27 (NIPS 2014), Montreal, QC, Canada, 8–13 December 2014.
72. Khalil, E.; Le Bodic, P.; Song, L.; Nemhauser, G.; Dilkina, B. Learning to branch in mixed integer programming. In Proceedings of the AAAI Conference on Artificial Intelligence, Phoenix, AZ, USA, 12–17 February 2016; Volume 30.
73. Baltean-Lugojan, R.; Bonami, P.; Misener, R.; Tramontani, A. *Selecting Cutting Planes for Quadratic Semidefinite Outer-Approximation via Trained Neural Networks*; Technical Report; CPLEX Optimization, IBM: New York, NY, USA, 2018.
74. Hottung, A.; Tanaka, S.; Tierney, K. Deep learning assisted heuristic tree search for the container pre-marshalling problem. *Comput. Oper. Res.* **2020**, *113*, 104781. [CrossRef]
75. Hochreiter, S.; Schmidhuber, J. Long short-term memory. *Neural Comput.* **1997**, *9*, 1735–1780. [CrossRef] [PubMed]
76. Vinyals, O.; Fortunato, M.; Jaitly, N. Pointer networks. In Proceedings of the Advances in Neural Information Processing Systems 28 (NIPS 2015), Montreal, QC, Canada, 7–12 December 2015.
77. Zheng, P.; Zuo, L.; Wang, J.; Zhang, J. Pointer networks for solving the permutation flow shop scheduling problem. In Proceedings of the 48th International Conference on Computers & Industrial Engineering (CIE48), Auckland, New Zealand, 2–5 December 2018; pp. 2–5.
78. Scarselli, F.; Gori, M.; Tsoi, A.C.; Hagenbuchner, M.; Monfardini, G. The graph neural network model. *IEEE Trans. Neural Netw.* **2008**, *20*, 61–80. [CrossRef] [PubMed]
79. Battaglia, P.W.; Hamrick, J.B.; Bapst, V.; Sanchez-Gonzalez, A.; Zambaldi, V.; Malinowski, M.; Tacchetti, A.; Raposo, D.; Santoro, A.; Faulkner, R.; et al. Relational inductive biases, deep learning, and graph networks. *arXiv* **2018**, arXiv:1806.01261.
80. Gori, M.; Monfardini, G.; Scarselli, F. A new model for learning in graph domains. In Proceedings of the 2005 IEEE International Joint Conference on Neural Networks, Montreal, QC, Canada, 31 July–4 August 2005; Volume 2, pp. 729–734.
81. Nowak, A.; Villar, S.; Bandeira, A.S.; Bruna, J. A note on learning algorithms for quadratic assignment with graph neural networks. In Proceedings of the 34th International Conference on Machine Learning (ICML), Sydney, Australia, 6–11 August 2017; Volume 1050, p. 22.
82. Bresson, X.; Laurent, T. Residual gated graph convnets. *arXiv* **2017**, arXiv:1711.07553.
83. Vlastelica, M.; Paulus, A.; Musil, V.; Martius, G.; Rolínek, M. Differentiation of blackbox combinatorial solvers. *arXiv* **2019**, arXiv:1912.02175.
84. Paulus, A.; Rolínek, M.; Musil, V.; Amos, B.; Martius, G. Comboptnet: Fit the right np-hard problem by learning integer programming constraints. In Proceedings of the International Conference on Machine Learning, Virtual, 18–24 July 2021; pp. 8443–8453.
85. Bello, I.; Pham, H.; Le, Q.V.; Norouzi, M.; Bengio, S. Neural combinatorial optimization with reinforcement learning. *arXiv* **2016**, arXiv:1611.09940.
86. Deudon, M.; Cournut, P.; Lacoste, A.; Adulyasak, Y.; Rousseau, L.M. Learning heuristics for the tsp by policy gradient. In Proceedings of the International Conference on the Integration of Constraint Programming, Artificial Intelligence, and Operations Research, Vienna, Austria, 21–24 September 2018; Springer: Berlin/Heidelberg, Germany, 2018; pp. 170–181.
87. Emami, P.; Ranka, S. Learning permutations with sinkhorn policy gradient. *arXiv* **2018**, arXiv:1805.07010.
88. Kool, W.; Van Hoof, H.; Welling, M. Attention, learn to solve routing problems! *arXiv* **2018**, arXiv:1803.08475.
89. Laterre, A.; Fu, Y.; Jabri, M.K.; Cohen, A.S.; Kas, D.; Hajjar, K.; Dahl, T.S.; Kerkeni, A.; Beguir, K. Ranked reward: Enabling self-play reinforcement learning for combinatorial optimization. *arXiv* **2018**, arXiv:1807.01672.
90. Drori, I.; Kharkar, A.; Sickinger, W.R.; Kates, B.; Ma, Q.; Ge, S.; Dolev, E.; Dietrich, B.; Williamson, D.P.; Udell, M. Learning to solve combinatorial optimization problems on real-world graphs in linear time. In Proceedings of the 2020 19th IEEE International Conference on Machine Learning and Applications (ICMLA), Virtual, 14–17 December 2020; pp. 19–24.
91. Shahadat, A.S.B.; Ayon, S.I.; Khatun, M.R. SSGTA: A novel swap sequence based Ggame theory algorithm for traveling salesman problem. In Proceedings of the 2021 24th International Conference on Computer and Information Technology (ICCIT), Dalian, China, 5–7 May 2021; pp. 1–5.

92. Kulkarni, A.J.; Tai, K. Probability collectives: A multi-agent approach for solving combinatorial optimization problems. *Appl. Soft Comput.* **2010**, *10*, 759–771. [CrossRef]
93. Gasse, M.; Chételat, D.; Ferroni, N.; Charlin, L.; Lodi, A. Exact combinatorial optimization with graph convolutional neural networks. In Proceedings of the Advances in Neural Information Processing Systems 32, Vancouver, BC, Canada, 8–14 December 2019.
94. Tang, Y.; Agrawal, S.; Faenza, Y. Reinforcement learning for integer programming: Learning to cut. In Proceedings of the International Conference on Machine Learning, Virtual, 13–18 July 2020; pp. 9367–9376.
95. Khalil, E.; Dai, H.; Zhang, Y.; Dilkina, B.; Song, L. Learning combinatorial optimization algorithms over graphs. In Proceedings of the Advances in Neural Information Processing Systems 30, Long Beach, CA, USA, 4–9 December 2017.
96. Karalias, N.; Loukas, A. Erdos goes neural: An unsupervised learning framework for combinatorial optimization on graphs. *Adv. Neural Inform. Process. Syst.* **2020**, *33*, 6659–6672.
97. Chen, X.; Tian, Y. Learning to perform local rewriting for combinatorial optimization. In Proceedings of the Advances in Neural Information Processing Systems 32, Vancouver, BC, Canada, 8–14 December 2019.
98. Tominac, P.; Mahalec, V. A game theoretic framework for petroleum refinery strategic production planning. *Aiche J.* **2017**, *63*, 2751–2763. [CrossRef]
99. Ravinger, F. Analyzing Oil Refinery Investment Decisions: A Game Theoretic Approach. Ph.D. Thesis, Central European University, Vienna, Austria, 2007.
100. Tominac, P.A. Game Theoretic Approaches to Petroleum Refinery Production Planning—A Justification for the Enterprise Level Optimization of Production Planning. Ph.D. Thesis, McMaster University, Hamilton, ON, Canada, 2017.
101. Babaei, M.; Asgarian, F.; Jamali, M.B.; Rasti-Barzoki, M.; Piran, M.J. A game theoretic approach for pricing petroleum and determining investors' production volume with the consideration of government and intermediate producers. *Sustain. Energy Technol. Assess.* **2020**, *42*, 100825. [CrossRef]
102. Shah, N.K.; Sahay, N.; Ierapetritou, M.G. Efficient decomposition approach for large-scale refinery scheduling. *Ind. Eng. Chem. Res.* **2015**, *54*, 9964–9991. [CrossRef]
103. Liang, Y.; Liao, Q.; Zhang, H.; Nie, S.; Yan, X.; Ma, J. Research progress on production scheduling optimization of refi nery. *Oil Gas Storage Transp.* **2017**, *36*, 646–650.
104. Wang, J.; Rong, G. Robust Optimization Model for Crude Oil Scheduling under Uncertainty. *Ind. Eng. Chem. Res.* **2010**, *49*, 1737–1748. [CrossRef]
105. Li, S.; Su, D. Establishment and solution of refinery multi-stage production scheduling model based on dynamic programming. *Control Inst. Chem. Ind.* **2009**, *36*, 6.
106. Cheng, L.; Duran, M.A. Logistics for world-wide crude oil transportation using discrete event simulation and optimal control. *Comput. Chem. Eng.* **2004**, *28*, 897–911. [CrossRef]
107. Wang, L.; Kinable, J.; Woensel, T.V. The fuel replenishment problem: A split-delivery multi-compartment vehicle routing problem with multiple trips. *Comput. Oper. Res.* **2020**, *118*, 104904. [CrossRef]
108. Lin, S.; Xu, A.; Liu, C.; Kai, F.; Li, J. Crane scheduling method in steelmaking workshop based on deep reinforcement learning. *China Metall.* **2021**, *31*, 7.
109. Zhou, Y. Application Research of Improved Gray Wolf Optimization Algorithm in Optimal Scheduling of Ateelmaking and Continuous Casting. Ph.D. Thesis, Qingdao University of Science and Technology, Qingdao, China, 2021.
110. Jia, C. Deep Reinforcement Learning for Batch Machine Scheduling Problem with Non-Identical Job Sizes. Ph.D. Thesis, Hefei University of Technology, Heifei, China, 2021.
111. Ma, Y.; Liu, X.; Jiang, S. Machine Learning-Based Scheduling Approach for Steelmaking-Continuous Casting Production. *Metall. Ind. Autom.* **2022**, *46*, 2.
112. Yan, D.; Peng, G.; Gao, H.; Chen, S.; Zhou, Y. Research on distribution network topology control based on deep reinforcement learning combinatorial optimization. *Power Syst. Technol.* **2021**, 1–9. [CrossRef]
113. Dong, L.; Liu, Y.; Qiao, J.; Wang, X.; Wang, C.; Pu, T. Optimal dispatch of combined heat and power system based on multi-agent deep reinforcement learning. *Power Syst. Technol.* **2021**, *45*, 9.
114. Cao, J.; Zhang, W.; Xiao, Z.; Hua, H. Reactive Power Optimization for Transient Voltage Stability in Energy Internet via Deep Reinforcement Learning Approach. *Energies* **2019**, *12*, 1556. [CrossRef]
115. Zhang, Z.; Qiu, C.; Zhang, D.; Xu, S.; He, X. A Coordinated Control Method for Hybrid Energy Storage System in Microgrid Based on Deep Reinforcement Learning. *Power Syst. Technol.* **2019**, *6*, 1914–1921. [CrossRef]
116. Li, Z.; Hou, X.; Liu, Y.; Sun, H.; Zhu, Z.; Long, Y.; Xu, T. A capacity planning method of charging station based on depth learning. *Power Syst. Prot. Control* **2017**, *45*, 67–73.
117. Huang, C.M.; Huang, Y.C. Combined Differential Evolution Algorithm and Ant System for Optimal Reactive Power Dispatch. *Energy Procedia* **2012**, *14*, 1238–1243. [CrossRef]
118. Yuce, B.; Rezgui, Y.; Mourshed, M. ANN-GA smart appliance scheduling for optimised energy management in the domestic sector. *Energy Build.* **2016**, *111*, 311–325. [CrossRef]
119. Huang, X.; Guo, R. A multi-agent model of generation expansion planning in electricity market. *Power Syst. Prot. Control* **2016**. Available online: http://en.cnki.com.cn/Article_en/CJFDTOTAL-JDQW201624001.htm (accessed on 1 May 2022).

120. Marden, J.R.; Ruben, S.D.; Pao, L.Y. A model-free approach to wind farm control using game theoretic methods. *IEEE Trans. Control Syst. Technol.* **2013**, *21*, 1207–1214. [CrossRef]
121. Quan, H.; Srinivasan, D.; Khosravi, A. Incorporating wind power forecast uncertainties into stochastic unit commitment using neural network-based prediction intervals. *IEEE Trans. Neural Netw. Learn. Syst.* **2014**, *26*, 2123–2135. [CrossRef] [PubMed]
122. Mei, S.; Zhang, D.; Wang, Y.; Liu, F.; Wei, W. Robust optimization of static reserve planning with large-scale integration of wind power: A game theoretic approach. *IEEE Trans. Sustain. Energy* **2014**, *5*, 535–545. [CrossRef]
123. Liu, W.; Ling, Y.; Zhao, T. Cooperative game based capacity planning model for wind power in low-carbon economy. *Autom. Electr. Power Syst.* **2015**, *39*, 68–74.
124. Kuçukoglu, I.; Dewil, R.; Cattrysse, D. Hybrid simulated annealing and tabu search method for the electric travelling salesman problem with time windows and mixed charging rates. *Expert Syst. Appl.* **2019**, *134*, 279–303. [CrossRef]
125. Zhou, A.H.; Zhu, L.P.; Hu, B.; Deng, S.; Song, Y.; Qiu, H.; Pan, S. Traveling-salesman-problem algorithm based on simulated annealing and gene-expression programming. *Information* **2018**, *10*, 7. [CrossRef]
126. Dewantoro R.W.; Sihombing, P. The combination of ant colony optimization (ACO) and tabu search (TS) algorithm to solve the traveling salesman problem (TSP). In Proceedings of the 2019 3rd International Conference on Electrical, Telecommunication and Computer Engineering (ELTICOM), Medan, Indonesia, 16–17 September 2019; pp. 160–164.
127. Arapoglu, O.; Akram, V.K.; Dagdeviren, O. An energy-efficient, self-stabilizing and distributed algorithm for maximal independent set construction in wireless sensor networks. *Comput. Stand. Interfaces* **2019**, *62*, 32–42. [CrossRef]
128. Kose, A.; Ozbek, B. Resource allocation for underlaying device-to-device communications using maximal independent sets and knapsack algorithm. In Proceedings of the 2018 IEEE 29th Annual International Symposium on Personal, Indoor and Mobile Radio Communications (PIMRC), Bologna, Italy, 9–12 September 2018; pp. 1–5.
129. López-Ramírez, C.; Gómez, J.E.G.; Luna, G.D.I. Building a Maximal Independent Set for the Vertex-coloring Problem on Planar Graphs. *Electron. Notes Theor. Comput. Sci.* **2020**, *354*, 75–89. [CrossRef]
130. Tarjan, R.E.; Trojanowski, A.E. Finding a maximum independent set. *SIAM J. Comput.* **1977**, *6*, 537–546. [CrossRef]
131. Feo, T.A.; Resende, M.G.; Smith, S.H. A greedy randomized adaptive search procedure for maximum independent set. *Oper. Res.* **1994**, *42*, 860–878. [CrossRef]
132. Berman, P.; Furer, M. Approximating maximum independent set. In Proceedings of the Fifth Annual ACM-SIAM Symposium on Discrete Algorithms, Arlington, VA, USA, 23–25 January 1994; Volume 70, p. 365.
133. Reba, K.; Guid, M.; Rozman, K.; Janežič, D.; Konc, J. Exact Maximum Clique Algorithm for Different Graph Types Using Machine Learning. *Mathematics* **2021**, *10*, 97. [CrossRef]
134. Ghaffari, M. Distributed maximal independent set using small messages. In Proceedings of the Thirtieth Annual ACM-SIAM Symposium on Discrete Algorithms, San Diego, CA, USA, 6–9 January 2019; pp. 805–820.
135. Andrade, D.V.; Resende, M.G.; Werneck, R.F. Fast local search for the maximum independent set problem. *J. Heuristics* **2012**, *18*, 525–547. [CrossRef]
136. Xiao, M.; Nagamochi, H. Exact algorithms for maximum independent set. *Inform. Comput.* **2017**, *255*, 126–146. [CrossRef]
137. Zetina, C.A.; Contreras, I.; Fernandez, E.; Luna-Mota, C. Solving the optimum communication spanning tree problem. *Eur. Oper. Res.* **2019**, *273*, 108–117. [CrossRef]
138. Akpan, N.; Iwok, I. A minimum spanning tree approach of solving a transportation problem. *Int. J. Math. Stat. Invent.* **2017**, *5*, 9–18.
139. Bartolín, H.; Martínez, F.; Cortés, J.A. Topological GIS-based analysis of a water distribution network model. Applications of the minimum spanning tree. In Proceedings of the Computing and Control for the Water Industry, Exeter, UK, 5–7 September 2005.
140. Liao, X.Q.; Su, T.; Ma, L. Application of neutrosophic minimum spanning tree in electrical power distribution network. *CAAI Trans. Intell. Technol.* **2020**, *5*, 99–105. [CrossRef]
141. Dong, M.; Zhang, X.; Yang, K.; Liu, R.; Chen, P. Forecasting the COVID-19 transmission in Italy based on the minimum spanning tree of dynamic region network. *PeerJ* **2021**, *9*, e11603. [CrossRef]
142. Kireyeu, V. Cluster dynamics studied with the phase-space minimum spanning tree approach. *Phys. Rev. C* **2021**, *103*, 54905. [CrossRef]
143. Mashreghi, A.; King, V. Broadcast and minimum spanning tree with o (m) messages in the asynchronous CONGEST model. *Distrib. Comput.* **2021**, *34*, 283–299. [CrossRef]
144. Jin, Y.; Zhao, H.; Gu, F.; Bu, P.; Na, M. A spatial minimum spanning tree filter. *Meas. Sci. Technol.* **2020**, *32*, 15204. [CrossRef]
145. Ochs, K.; Michaelis, D.; Solan, E. Wave digital emulation of a memristive circuit to find the minimum spanning tree. In Proceedings of the 2019 IEEE 62nd International Midwest Symposium on Circuits and Systems (MWSCAS), Dallas, TX, USA, 4–7 August 2019; pp. 351–354.
146. Farashi, S.; Khosrowabadi, R. EEG based emotion recognition using minimum spanning tree. *Phys. Eng. Sci. Med.* **2020**, *43*, 985–996. [CrossRef] [PubMed]
147. Dong, W.; Wang, J.; Wang, C.; Qi, Z.; Ding, Z. Graphical Minimax Game and Off-Policy Reinforcement Learning for Heterogeneous MASs with Spanning Tree Condition. *Guid. Navig. Control* **2021**, *1*, 2150011. [CrossRef]
148. Dey, A.; Son, L.H.; Pal, A.; Long, H.V. Fuzzy minimum spanning tree with interval type 2 fuzzy arc length: Formulation and a new genetic algorithm. *Soft Comput.* **2020**, *24*, 3963–3974. [CrossRef]

149. Wang, Y.; Yu, S.; Gu, Y.; Shun, J. Fast parallel algorithms for euclidean minimum spanning tree and hierarchical spatial clustering. In Proceedings of the 2021 International Conference on Management of Data, Virtual, 20–25 June 2021; pp. 1982–1995.
150. Gyoten, H.; Hiromoto, M.; Sato, T. Area efficient annealing processor for ising model without random number generator. *IEICE Trans. Inform. Syst.* **2018**, *101*, 314–323. [CrossRef]
151. Cook, C.; Zhao, H.; Sato, T.; Hiromoto, M.; Tan, S.X.D. GPU-based ising computing for solving max-cut combinatorial optimization problems. *Integration* **2019**, *69*, 335–344. [CrossRef]
152. Patel, S.; Chen, L.; Canoza, P.; Salahuddin, S. Ising model optimization problems on a FPGA accelerated restricted Boltzmann machine. *arXiv* **2020**, arXiv:2008.04436.
153. Tu, K.N. Recent advances on electromigration in very-large-scale-integration of interconnects. *J. Appl. Phys.* **2003**, *94*, 5451–5473. [CrossRef]
154. Wang, J.; Paesani, S.; Ding, Y.; Santagati, R.; Skrzypczyk, P.; Salavrakos, A.; Tura, J.; Augusiak, R.; Mančinska, L.; Bacco, D.; et al. Multidimensional quantum entanglement with large-scale integrated optics. *Science* **2018**, *360*, 285–291. [CrossRef]
155. Noé, F.; De Fabritiis, G.; Clementi, C. Machine learning for protein folding and dynamics. *Curr. Opin. Struct. Biol.* **2020**, *60*, 77–84. [CrossRef]
156. Rodriguez, A.; Wright, G.; Emrich, S.; Clark, P.L. %MinMax: A versatile tool for calculating and comparing synonymous codon usage and its impact on protein folding. *Protein Sci.* **2018**, *27*, 356–362. [CrossRef]
157. Poljak, S.; Rendl, F. Solving the max-cut problem using eigenvalues. *Discrete Appl. Math.* **1995**, *62*, 249–278. [CrossRef]
158. Festa, P.; Pardalos, P.M.; Resende, M.G.; Ribeiro, C.C. Randomized heuristics for the MAX-CUT problem. *Optim. Methods Softw.* **2002**, *17*, 1033–1058. [CrossRef]
159. Kim, Y.H.; Yoon, Y.; Geem, Z.W. A comparison study of harmony search and genetic algorithm for the max-cut problem. *Swarm Evol. Comput.* **2019**, *44*, 130–135. [CrossRef]
160. Martí, R.; Duarte, A.; Laguna, M. Advanced scatter search for the max-cut problem. *INFORMS J. Comput.* **2009**, *21*, 26–38. [CrossRef]
161. Blum, C.; Schmid, V. Solving the 2D bin packing problem by means of a hybrid evolutionary algorithm. *Procedia Comput. Sci.* **2013**, *18*, 899–908. [CrossRef]
162. Hifi, M.; Kacem, I.; Nègre, S.; Wu, L. A linear programming approach for the three-dimensional bin-packing problem. *Electron. Notes Discret. Math.* **2010**, *36*, 993–1000. [CrossRef]
163. Yu, A.B.; Zou, R.; Standish, N. Modifying the linear packing model for predicting the porosity of nonspherical particle mixtures. *Ind. Eng. Chem. Res.* **1996**, *35*, 3730–3741. [CrossRef]
164. Biro, P.; Manlove, D.F.; Rizzi, R. Maximum weight cycle packing in directed graphs, with application to kidney exchange programs. *Discret. Math. Algorithms Appl.* **2009**, *1*, 499–517. [CrossRef]
165. Epstein, L.; Levin, A. Bin packing with general cost structures. *Math. Program.* **2012**, *132*, 355–391. [CrossRef]
166. Lai, P.; He, Q.; Abdelrazek, M.; Chen, F.; Hosking, J.; Grundy, J.; Yang, Y. Optimal edge user allocation in edge computing with variable sized vector bin packing. In Proceedings of the International Conference on Service-Oriented Computing, Hangzhou, China, 12–15 November 2018; Springer: Berlin/Heidelberg, Germany, 2018; pp. 230–245.
167. Mohiuddin, I.; Almogren, A.; Al Qurishi, M.; Hassan, M.M.; Al Rassan, I.; Fortino, G. Secure distributed adaptive bin packing algorithm for cloud storage. *Future Gener. Comput. Syst.* **2019**, *90*, 307–316. [CrossRef]
168. Baldi, M.M.; Manerba, D.; Perboli, G.; Tadei, R. A generalized bin packing problem for parcel delivery in last-mile logistics. *Eur. J. Oper. Res.* **2019**, *274*, 990–999. [CrossRef]
169. Witteman, M.; Deng, Q.; Santos, B.F. A bin packing approach to solve the aircraft maintenance task allocation problem. *Eur. J. Oper. Res.* **2021**, *294*, 365–376. [CrossRef]
170. Qomi, T.; Hamedi, M.; Tavakkoli-Moghaddam, R. Optimization of Crude Oil Transportation using a Variable Cost and Size Bin Packing Problem (VCSBPP). 2021. Available online: https://www.trijournal.ir/article_121959.html?lang=en (accessed on 1 May 2022).
171. Frenk, J.G.; Galambos, G. Hybrid next-fit algorithm for the two-dimensional rectangle bin-packing problem. *Computing* **1987**, *39*, 201–217. [CrossRef]
172. Mao, W. Tight worst-case performance bounds for next-k-fit bin packing. *SIAM J. Comput.* **1993**, *22*, 46–56. [CrossRef]
173. Xia, B.; Tan, Z. Tighter bounds of the First Fit algorithm for the bin-packing problem. *Discrete Appl. Math.* **2010**, *158*, 1668–1675. [CrossRef]
174. El-Ashmawi, W.H.; Abd Elminaam, D.S. A modified squirrel search algorithm based on improved best fit heuristic and operator strategy for bin packing problem. *Appl. Soft Comput.* **2019**, *82*, 105565. [CrossRef]
175. Dhahbi, S.; Berrima, M.; Al-Yarimi, F.A. Load balancing in cloud computing using worst-fit bin-stretching. *Clust. Comput.* **2021**, *24*, 2867–2881. [CrossRef]
176. Bansal, N.; Han, X.; Iwama, K.; Sviridenko, M.; Zhang, G. A harmonic algorithm for the 3D strip packing problem. *SIAM J. Comput.* **2013**, *42*, 579–592. [CrossRef]
177. Gu, X.; Chen, G.; Xu, Y. Deep performance analysis of refined harmonic bin packing algorithm. *J. Comput. Sci. Technol.* **2002**, *17*, 213–218. [CrossRef]

178. Raj, P.H.; Kumar, P.R.; Jelciana, P.; Rajagopalan, S. Modified first fit decreasing method for load balancing in mobile clouds. In Proceedings of the 2020 4th International Conference on Intelligent Computing and Control Systems (ICICCS), Madurai, India, 13–15 May 2020; pp. 1107–1110.
179. Jin, S.; Liu, M.; Wu, Y.; Xu, Y.; Zhang, J.; Xu, Y. Research of message scheduling for in-vehicle FlexRay network static segment based on next fit decreasing (NFD) algorithm. *Appl. Sci.* **2018**, *8*, 2071. [CrossRef]
180. Coffman, E.G.; Garey, M.R.; Johnson, D.S. Approximation algorithms for bin-packing—An updated survey. In *Algorithm Design for Computer System Design*; Springer: Berlin/Heidelberg, Germany, 1984; pp. 49–106.
181. Labbé, M.; Laporte, G.; Martello, S. An exact algorithm for the dual bin packing problem. *Oper. Res. Lett.* **1995**, *17*, 9–10. [CrossRef]
182. Cheuk, K.W.; Luo, Y.J.; Benetos, E.; Herremans, D. Revisiting the onsets and frames model with additive attention. In Proceedings of the 2021 International Joint Conference on Neural Networks (IJCNN), Shenzhen, China, 18–22 July 2021; pp. 1–8.
183. Wu, C.; Wu, F.; Qi, T.; Huang, Y.; Xie, X. Fastformer: Additive attention can be all you need. *arXiv* **2021**, arXiv:2108.09084.
184. Li, X.; Xu, Q.; Chen, X.; Li, C. Additive Attention for CNN-based Classification. In Proceedings of the 2021 IEEE International Conference on Mechatronics and Automation (ICMA), Takamatsu, Japan, 8–11 August 2021; pp. 55–59.
185. Tian, Y.; Newsam, S.; Boakye, K. Image Search with Text Feedback by Additive Attention Compositional Learning. *arXiv* **2022**, arXiv:2203.03809.
186. Graves, A.; Wayne, G.; Danihelka, I. Neural turing machines. *arXiv* **2014**, arXiv:1410.5401.
187. Ma, X.; Hu, Z.; Liu, J.; Peng, N.; Neubig, G.; Hovy, E. Stack-pointer networks for dependency parsing. *arXiv* **2018**, arXiv:1805.01087.
188. Li, J.; Wang, Y.; Lyu, M.R.; King, I. Code completion with neural attention and pointer networks. *arXiv* **2017**, arXiv:1711.09573.
189. Yavuz, S.; Rastogi, A.; Chao, G.L.; Hakkani-Tur, D. Deepcopy: Grounded response generation with hierarchical pointer networks. *arXiv* **2019**, arXiv:1908.10731.
190. Luong, M.T.; Pham, H.; Manning, C.D. Effective approaches to attention-based neural machine translation. *arXiv* **2015**, arXiv:1508.04025.
191. Trueman, T.E.; Cambria, E. A convolutional stacked bidirectional lstm with a multiplicative attention mechanism for aspect category and sentiment detection. *Cogn. Comput.* **2021**, *13*, 1423–1432.
192. Cui, R.; Wang, J.; Wang, Z. Multiplicative attention mechanism for multi-horizon time series forecasting. In Proceedings of the 2021 International Joint Conference on Neural Networks (IJCNN), Shenzhen, China, 18–22 July 2021; pp. 1–6.
193. Gan, J.; Liu, H.; He, T. Prediction of air pollutant concentration based on luong attention mechanism Seq2Seq model. In Proceedings of the 2021 7th Annual International Conference on Network and Information Systems for Computers (ICNISC), Guiyang, China, 23–25 July 2021; pp. 321–325.
194. Zhang, S.; Tong, H.; Xu, J.; Maciejewski, R. Graph convolutional networks: A comprehensive review. *Comput. Soc. Netw.* **2019**, *6*, 1–23. [CrossRef]
195. Veličković, P.; Cucurull, G.; Casanova, A.; Romero, A.; Lio, P.; Bengio, Y. Graph attention networks. *arXiv* **2017**, arXiv:1710.10903.
196. Bai, L.; Yao, L.; Li, C.; Wang, X.; Wang, C. Adaptive graph convolutional recurrent network for traffic forecasting. *Adv. Neural Inform. Process. Syst.* **2020**, *33*, 17804–17815.
197. Wu, L.; Chen, Y.; Shen, K.; Guo, X.; Gao, H.; Li, S.; Pei, J.; Long, B. Graph neural networks for natural language processing: A survey. *arXiv* **2021**, arXiv:2106.06090.
198. Fan, W.; Ma, Y.; Li, Q.; He, Y.; Zhao, E.; Tang, J.; Yin, D. Graph neural networks for social recommendation. In Proceedings of the World Wide Web Conference, San Francisco, CA, USA, 13–17 May 2019; pp. 417–426.
199. Ioannidis, V.N.; Marques, A.G.; Giannakis, G.B. Graph neural networks for predicting protein functions. In Proceedings of the 2019 IEEE 8th International Workshop on Computational Advances in Multi-Sensor Adaptive Processing (CAMSAP), Guadeloupe, France, 15–18 December 2019; pp. 221–225.
200. Tsitsulin, A.; Palowitch, J.; Perozzi, B.; Muller, E. Graph clustering with graph neural networks. *arXiv* **2020**, arXiv:2006.16904.
201. Abu-El-Haija, S.; Kapoor, A.; Perozzi, B.; Lee, J. N-gcn: Multi-scale graph convolution for semi-supervised node classification. In Uncertainty in Artificial Intelligence. 2020. pp. 841–851. Available online: http://proceedings.mlr.press/v115/abu-el-haija20a.html (accessed on 1 May 2022).
202. Adamic, L.A.; Adar, E. Friends and neighbors on the web. *Soc. Netw.* **2003**, *25*, 211–230. [CrossRef]
203. Koren, Y.; Bell, R.; Volinsky, C. Matrix factorization techniques for recommender systems. *Computer* **2009**, *42*, 30–37. [CrossRef]
204. Schafer, J.B.; Konstan, J.; Riedl, J. Recommender systems in e-commerce. In Proceedings of the 1st ACM Conference on Electronic Commerce, Denver, CO, USA, 3–5 November 1999; pp. 158–166.
205. Schulman, J.; Levine, S.; Abbeel, P.; Jordan, M.; Moritz, P. Trust region policy optimization. In Proceedings of the International Conference on Machine Learning, Lille, France, 6–11 July 2015; pp. 1889–1897.
206. Cortes, J.; Martinez, S.; Karatas, T.; Bullo, F. Coverage control for mobile sensing networks. *IEEE Trans. Robot. Autom.* **2004**, *20*, 243–255. [CrossRef]
207. Choi, J.; Oh, S.; Horowitz, R. Distributed learning and cooperative control for multi-agent systems. *Automatica* **2009**, *45*, 2802–2814. [CrossRef]
208. Adler, J.L.; Blue, V.J. A cooperative multi-agent transportation management and route guidance system. *Transp. Res. Part Emerg. Technol.* **2002**, *10*, 433–454. [CrossRef]

209. Wang, S.; Wan, J.; Zhang, D.; Li, D.; Zhang, C. Towards smart factory for industry 4.0: A self-organized multi-agent system with big data based feedback and coordination. *Comput. Netw.* **2016**, *101*, 158–168. [CrossRef]
210. Lee, J.W.; Zhang, B.T. Stock trading system using reinforcement learning with cooperative agents. In Proceedings of the Nineteenth International Conference on Machine Learning, San Francisco, CA, USA, 8–12 July 2002; pp. 451–458.
211. Lee, J.W.; Park, J.; Jangmin, O.; Lee, J.; Hong, E. A multiagent approach to Q-learning for daily stock trading. *IEEE Trans. Syst. Man Cybern. Part A Syst. Hum.* **2007**, *37*, 864–877. [CrossRef]
212. Castelfranchi, C. The theory of social functions: Challenges for computational social science and multi-agent learning. *Cogn. Syst. Res.* **2001**, *2*, 5–38. [CrossRef]
213. Zhang, K.; Yang, Z.; Başar, T. Multi-agent reinforcement learning: A selective overview of theories and algorithms. In *Handbook of Reinforcement Learning and Control*; Springer: Berlin/Heidelberg, Germany, 2021; pp. 321–384.
214. Rădulescu, R.; Legrand, M.; Efthymiadis, K.; Roijers, D.M.; Nowé, A. Deep multi-agent reinforcement learning in a homogeneous open population. In *Proceedings of the Benelux Conference on Artificial Intelligence, 2018*; Springer: Berlin/Heidelberg, Germany, 2018; pp. 90–105.
215. Yu, Y.; Wang, T.; Liew, S.C. Deep-reinforcement learning multiple access for heterogeneous wireless networks. *IEEE J. Sel. Areas Commun.* **2019**, *37*, 1277–1290. [CrossRef]
216. Gupta, J.K.; Egorov, M.; Kochenderfer, M. Cooperative multi-agent control using deep reinforcement learning. In *Proceedings of the International Conference on Autonomous Agents and Multiagent Systems, 2017*; Springer: Berlin/Heidelberg, Germany, 2017; pp. 66–83.
217. OroojlooyJadid, A.; Hajinezhad, D. A review of cooperative multi-agent deep reinforcement learning. *arXiv* **2019**, arXiv:1908.03963.
218. Liu, Y.; Nejat, G. Multirobot cooperative learning for semiautonomous control in urban search and rescue applications. *J. Field Robot.* **2016**, *33*, 512–536. [CrossRef]
219. Liu, I.J.; Jain, U.; Yeh, R.A.; Schwing, A. Cooperative exploration for multi-agent deep reinforcement learning. In Proceedings of the International Conference on Machine Learning, Online, 18–24 July 2021; pp. 6826–6836.
220. Khan, M.I.; Alam, M.M.; Moullec, Y.L.; Yaacoub, E. Throughput-aware cooperative reinforcement learning for adaptive resource allocation in device-to-device communication. *Future Internet.* **2017**, *9*, 72. [CrossRef]
221. Abramson, M.; Wechsler, H. Competitive reinforcement learning for combinatorial problems. In Proceedings of the International Joint Conference on Neural Networks. Proceedings (Cat. No. 01CH37222), Washington, DC, USA, 15–19 July 2001; Volume 4, pp. 2333–2338.
222. Crawford, V.P. Learning the optimal strategy in a zero-sum game. *Econom. J. Econom. Soc.* **1974**, *42*, 885–891. [CrossRef]
223. McKenzie, M.; Loxley, P.; Billingsley, W.; Wong, S. Competitive reinforcement learning in atari games. In *Proceedings of the Australasian Joint Conference on Artificial Intelligence, 2017*; Springer: Berlin/Heidelberg, Germany, 2017; pp. 14–26.
224. Kutschinski, E.; Uthmann, T.; Polani, D. Learning competitive pricing strategies by multi-agent reinforcement learning. *J. Econ. Dyn. Control* **2003**, *27*, 2207–2218. [CrossRef]
225. Movahedi, Z.; Bastanfard, A. Toward competitive multi-agents in Polo game based on reinforcement learning. *Multimed. Tools Appl.* **2021**, *80*, 26773–26793. [CrossRef]
226. McKee, K.R.; Gemp, I.; McWilliams, B.; Duéñez-Guzmán, E.A.; Hughes, E.; Leibo, J.Z. Social diversity and social preferences in mixed-motive reinforcement learning. *arXiv* **2020**, arXiv:2002.02325.
227. Brown, N.; Sandholm, T. Superhuman AI for multiplayer poker. *Science* **2019**, *365*, 885–890. [CrossRef] [PubMed]
228. Ye, D.; Chen, G.; Zhang, W.; Chen, S.; Yuan, B.; Liu, B.; Chen, J.; Liu, Z.; Qiu, F.; Yu, H.; et al. Towards playing full moba games with deep reinforcement learning. *Adv. Neural Inf. Process. Syst.* **2020**, *33*, 621–632.
229. Vinyals, O.; Babuschkin, I.; Czarnecki, W.M.; Mathieu, M.; Dudzik, A.; Chung, J.; Choi, D.H.; Powell, R.; Ewalds, T.; Georgiev, P.; et al. Grandmaster level in StarCraft II using multi-agent reinforcement learning. *Nature* **2019**, *575*, 350–354. [CrossRef]
230. Selsam, D.; Lamm, M.; B'unz, B.; Liang, P.; de Moura, L.; Dill, D.L. Learning a SAT solver from single-bit supervision. *arXiv* **2018**, arXiv:1802.03685.
231. Li, Z.; Chen, Q.; Koltun, V. Combinatorial optimization with graph convolutional networks and guided tree search. *Adv. Neural Inform. Process. Syst.* **2018**, arXiv:1810.10659.
232. Lemos, H.; Prates, M.; Avelar, P.; Lamb, L. Graph colouring meets deep learning: Effective graph neural network models for combinatorial problems. In Proceedings of the 2019 IEEE 31st International Conference on Tools with Artificial Intelligence (ICTAI), Portland, OR, USA, 4–6 November 2019; pp. 879–885.
233. Prates, M.; Avelar, P.H.; Lemos, H.; Lamb, L.C.; Vardi, M.Y. Learning to solve np-complete problems: A graph neural network for decision tsp. In Proceedings of the AAAI Conference on Artificial Intelligence, Honolulu, HI, USA, 27 January–1 February 2019; Volume 33, pp. 4731–4738.
234. Li, Y.; Tarlow, D.; Brockschmidt, M.; Zemel, R. Gated graph sequence neural networks. *arXiv* **2015**, arXiv:1511.05493.
235. Gilmer, J.; Schoenholz, S.S.; Riley, P.F.; Vinyals, O.; Dahl, G.E. Neural message passing for quantum chemistry. In Proceedings of the International Conference on Machine Learning, Sydney, Australia, 6–11 August 2017; pp. 1263–1272.
236. Defferrard, M.; Bresson, X.; Vandergheynst, P. Convolutional neural networks on graphs with fast localized spectral filtering. *Adv. Neural Inform. Process. Syst.* **2016**, arXiv:1606.09375.
237. Kipf, T.N.; Welling, M. Semi-supervised classification with graph convolutional networks. *arXiv* **2016**, arXiv:1609.02907.

238. Hu, H.; Zhang, X.; Yan, X.; Wang, L.; Xu, Y. Solving a new 3d bin packing problem with deep reinforcement learning method. *arXiv* **2017**, arXiv:1708.05930.
239. Nazari, M.; Oroojlooy, A.; Snyder, L.; Takác, M. Reinforcement learning for solving the vehicle routing problem. *Adv. Neural Inform. Process. Syst.* **2018**, arXiv:1802.04240.
240. Venkatakrishnan, S.B.; Alizadeh, M.; Viswanath, P. Graph2seq: Scalable learning dynamics for graphs. *arXiv* **2018**, arXiv:1802.04948.
241. Manchanda, S.; Mittal, A.; Dhawan, A.; Medya, S.; Ranu, S.; Singh, A. Gcomb: Learning budget-constrained combinatorial algorithms over billion sized graphs. *Adv. Neural Inform. Process. Syst.* **2020**, *33*, 20000–20011.
242. Dai, H.; Dai, B.; Song, L. Discriminative embeddings of latent variable models for structured data. In Proceedings of the International Conference on Machine Learning, New York, NY, USA, 24–26 June 2016; pp. 2702–2711.
243. Song, J.; Lanka, R.; Yue, Y.; Ono, M. Co-Training for Policy Learning. Uncertainty in Artificial Intelligence. 2020; pp. 1191–1201. Available online: https://arxiv.org/abs/1907.04484 (accessed on 1 May 2022).
244. Ma, Q.; Ge, S.; He, D.; Thaker, D.; Drori, I. Combinatorial optimization by graph pointer networks and hierarchical reinforcement learning. *arXiv* **2019**, arXiv:1911.04936.
245. Abe, K.; Xu, Z.; Sato, I.; Sugiyama, M. Solving np-hard problems on graphs with extended alphago zero. *arXiv* **2019**, arXiv:1905.11623.
246. Kwon, Y.D.; Choo, J.; Kim, B.; Yoon, I.; Gwon, Y.; Min, S. Pomo: Policy optimization with multiple optima for reinforcement learning. *Adv. Neural Inform. Process. Syst.* **2020**. *33*, 21188–21198.
247. Barrett, T.; Clements, W.; Foerster, J.; Lvovsky, A. Exploratory combinatorial optimization with reinforcement learning. In Proceedings of the AAAI Conference on Artificial Intelligence, New York, NY, USA, 7–12 February 2020; Volume 34, pp. 3243–3250.
248. Wu, Y.; Song, W.; Cao, Z.; Zhang, J.; Lim, A. Learning Improvement Heuristics for Solving Routing Problems. *IEEE Trans. Neural Netw. Learn. Syst.* **2021**. [CrossRef]
249. Lu, H.; Zhang, X.; Yang, S. A learning-based iterative method for solving vehicle routing problems. In Proceedings of the International Conference on Learning Representations, New Orleans, LA, USA, 6–9 May 2019.
250. Xu, R.; Lieberherr, K. Learning self-game-play agents for combinatorial optimization problems. *arXiv* **2019**, arXiv:1903.03674.
251. Kruber, M.; Lubbecke, M.E.; Parmentier, A. Learning when to use a decomposition. In Proceedings of the International Conference on AI and OR Techniques in Constraint Programming for Combinatorial Optimization Problems, Padova, Italy, 5–8 June 2017; Springer: Berlin/Heidelberg, Germany, 2017; pp. 202–210.
252. Gomory, R. *An Algorithm for the Mixed Integer Problem*; Technical Report; RAND Corp.: Santa Monica, CA, USA, 1960.
253. Joshi, C.K.; Laurent, T.; Bresson, X. An efficient graph convolutional network technique for the travelling salesman problem. *arXiv* **2019**, arXiv:1906.01227.
254. Golmohamadi, H. Operational scheduling of responsive prosumer farms for day-ahead peak shaving by agricultural demand response aggregators. *Int. J. Energy Res.* **2020**, *45*, 938–960. [CrossRef]
255. Mouret, S.; Grossmann, I.E.; Pestiaux, P. A new Lagrangian decomposition approach applied to the integration of refinery planning and crude-oil scheduling. *Comput. Chem. Eng.* **2011**, *35*, 2750–2766. [CrossRef]
256. Li, M. Modeling Method Research on Refinery Process Production Shceduling. Ph.D. Thesis, Shandong University, Jinan, China, 2011.
257. Yue, X.; Wang, H.; Zhang, Y.; Shi, B. Optimization of refinery crude oil scheduling based on heuristic rules. *Comput. Appl. Chem.* **2020**, *2*, 147–154.
258. Hou, Y.; Wu, N.Q.; Li, Z.W.; Zhang, Y.; Zhu, Q.H. Many-Objective Optimization for Scheduling of Crude Oil Operations based on NSGA-III with Consideration of Energy Efficiency. *Swarm Evol. Comput.* **2020**, *57*, 100714. [CrossRef]
259. Assis, L.S.; Camponogara, E.; Grossmann, I.E. A MILP-based clustering strategy for integrating the operational management of crude oil supply. *Comput. Chem. Eng.* **2020**, *145*, 107161. [CrossRef]
260. Beach, B.; Hildebrand, R.; Ellis, K.; Lebreton, B. An Approximate Method for the Optimization of Long-Horizon Tank Blending and Scheduling Operations. *Comput. Chem. Eng.* **2020**, *141*, 106839. [CrossRef]
261. Li, M. Refinery Operations Optimization Integrated Production Process and Gasoline Blending. *J. Phys. Conf. Ser.* **2020**, *1626*, 12111. [CrossRef]
262. Bayu, F.; Shaik, M.A.; Ramteke, M. Scheduling of crude oil refinery operation with desalting as a separate task. *Asia-Pac. J. Chem. Eng.* **2020**, *15*, e2539. [CrossRef]
263. Zhang, S.; Xu, Q. Refinery continuous-time crude scheduling with consideration of long-distance pipeline transportation. *Comput. Chem. Eng.* **2015**, *75*, 74–94. [CrossRef]
264. Oliveira, F.; Nunes, P.M.; Blajberg, R.; Hamacher, S. A framework for crude oil scheduling in an integrated terminal-refinery system under supply uncertainty. *Eur. J. Oper. Res.* **2016**, *252*, 635–645. [CrossRef]
265. Wang, H. Batch Optimization Combined with AI Ideas for Refinery Oil Pipeline Networks. Ph.D. Thesis, China University of Petroleum, Beijing, China, 2020.
266. Gao, H.; Xie, Y.; Ma, J.; Zhang, B. Optimization of refined oil distribution with multiple trips and multiple due time. *Control Decis.* **2021**, 1–10. [CrossRef]
267. Li, M.; Huang, Q.; Zhou, L.; Ni, S. Research on modeling of petroleum products distribution system based on object-oriented Petri nets. *Comput. Eng. Appl.* **2015**, *51*, 55–61.

268. Li, Z.; Su, T.; Zhang, L. Application Analysis and Prospect of Artificial Intelligence Technology in Smart Grid. *Telecom Power Technol.* **2020**, *37*, 2.
269. Sheikhi, A.; Rayati, M.; Bahrami, S.; Ranjbar, A.M.; Sattari, S. A cloud computing framework on demand side management game in smart energy hubs. *Int. J. Elect. Power Energy Syst.* **2015**, *64*, 1007–1016. [CrossRef]
270. Fan, S.; Li, Z.; Wang, J.; Longjian, P.; Ai, Q. Cooperative Economic Scheduling for Multiple Energy Hubs: A Bargaining Game Theoretic Perspective. *IEEE Access* **2018**, *6*, 27777–27789. [CrossRef]
271. Peng, X.; Tao, X. Cooperative game of electricity retailers in China's spot electricity market. *Energy* **2018**, *145*, 152–170. [CrossRef]
272. Chen, J.; Bo, Y.; Guan, X. Optimal demand response scheduling with Stackelberg game approach under load uncertainty for smart grid. In Proceedings of the IEEE Third International Conference on Smart Grid Communications, Tainan, Taiwan, 5–8 November 2012.
273. Li, Y.; Wang, C.; Li, G.; Chen, C. Optimal Scheduling of Integrated Demand Response-Enabled Integrated Energy Systems with Uncertain Renewable Generations: A Stackelberg Game Approach. *Energy Convers. Manag.* **2021**, *235*, 113996. [CrossRef]

algorithms

MDPI

Review

Techniques and Paradigms in Modern Game AI Systems

Yunlong Lu and Wenxin Li *

School of Computer Science, Peking University, Beijing 100871, China; luyunlong@pku.edu.cn
* Correspondence: lwx@pku.edu.cn; Tel.: +86-10-62753425

Abstract: Games have long been benchmarks and test-beds for AI algorithms. With the development of AI techniques and the boost of computational power, modern game AI systems have achieved superhuman performance in many games played by humans. These games have various features and present different challenges to AI research, so the algorithms used in each of these AI systems vary. This survey aims to give a systematic review of the techniques and paradigms used in modern game AI systems. By decomposing each of the recent milestones into basic components and comparing them based on the features of games, we summarize the common paradigms to build game AI systems and their scope and limitations. We claim that deep reinforcement learning is the most general methodology to become a mainstream method for games with higher complexity. We hope this survey can both provide a review of game AI algorithms and bring inspiration to the game AI community for future directions.

Keywords: game AI; supervised learning; reinforcement learning; multi-agent learning

1. Introduction

The ultimate goal of artificial intelligence is to reach human-level on a wide range of tasks. Turing test [1] proposed by Alan Turing in 1950 is the earliest criterion to test a machine's ability to exhibit intelligent behavior as humans, which is controversial because a specially designed AI can meet such standards by targeted imitation or deception instead of real intelligence. However, games are born to test and challenge human intelligence, which can be excellent benchmarks for the cognitive and decision-making abilities of AI systems. The diversity of games has provided a rich context for gradual skill progression in the development of artificial intelligence. AI systems beating professional humans in games with increasing complexity have always been considered milestones of AI technologies.

With the boost of computational power and the application of new algorithms, AI systems have made great strides to play games that were once considered exclusively mastered by humans because of their complexity. Since AlphaGo beat professional human players in Go [2], many milestones have been reported in various games, from board games like Go [2–4] and card games like Texas Hold'em [5–7] to video games like StarCraft [8], Dota 2 [9] and HoK [10]. These AI systems achieve superhuman performance in games with increasing complexity while using a wide range of AI techniques. It seems that different approaches are chosen based on the characteristics of the games, but it is hard to find the pattern of algorithm selection when the algorithms vary in each system.

In this survey, we provide a systematic review of the AI techniques typically used to create game-playing agents and summarize how they are used in recent AI milestones. We show that a typical AI system can be broken into basic components related to specific features or challenges of the games they tackle. By analyzing the choices of the algorithms and the characteristics of the games, we extract three kinds of paradigms to build AI systems for different types of games. The application scope and limitations of each paradigm are further discussed, as an indication of the general method applicable to games of higher complexity, such as real-world sports games.

Some related works also investigate recent milestones of game AI. Risi et al. [11] only gives a general introduction of the categories of games and AI technologies and focuses on the application of these techniques to areas outside of game playing, like content generation and player modeling. Perhaps Yin et al. [12] is the most similar work to us, which also makes the comparison between game AI systems and discusses general paradigms. However, that survey mainly focuses on the different training frameworks in various types of games. It does not summarize the basic algorithms used in these frameworks nor compare them concerning game features. Instead, this survey analyzes the basic algorithmic components used in these milestones and summarizes both the techniques and paradigms based on the features of games.

The rest of this survey is organized as follows. Section 2 discusses the background of AI applications in creating game-playing agents. A brief history of game AI milestones is listed, as well as some typical features of games and the modeling of games in the context of AI algorithms. In Section 3, many game AI algorithms are presented as the basic components of game AI systems, which are categorized based on their mechanics and the game features they tackle. Section 4 summarizes the implementation of recent state-of-the-art game AI systems. Section 5 makes a comprehensive comparison of these milestones by decomposing each of them into components and relating the choices to the characteristics of the games. We further extract the common paradigms of these milestones and discuss the general method of game AI as future trends.

2. Background

Recent years have witnessed remarkable progress in artificial intelligence, with games often serving as benchmarks. While board games have been the focus of AI research since the beginning of this field, the advance in algorithms has drawn attention to increasingly complex games in the last decade, such as card games and video games. These games have features that challenge game AI research, spawning many new algorithms in the last decade. In this section, we first discuss the breakthroughs in the history of AI game playing to show how games are used as AI benchmarks. Then we summarize the key features of the games solved in recent years. Finally, we introduce the modeling of games in the context of AI algorithms as a basis for the AI techniques discussed in the next section.

2.1. Game AI Benchmarks

Since the earliest computer, ENIAC, was invented in 1945, game playing has been an important area in artificial intelligence. In 1951, Christopher Strachey wrote a checkers program, and Dietrich Prinz wrote one for chess [13], which were the earliest AI game-playing programs. Most early research on game AI was focused on classic board games like checkers and chess because they have elementary and highly constrained rules yet great complexity that have challenged humans for hundreds or even thousands of years. AI systems beating professional humans in these games have always been considered as milestones and breakthroughs in AI technologies.

The first of these milestones was TD-Gammon developed by Gerald Tesauro in 1992 [14], a backgammon program to beat professional humans. In 1994, the Chinook Checkers program beat the World Checkers Champion Marion Tinsley [15]. Perhaps the most well-known milestone was IBM's Deep Blue, a Chess program that won against reigning grandmaster Kasparov in 1997 in a very famous and publicized event [16]. The latest milestone in board games was in the game of Go. In 2016 Google Deepmind's AlphaGo program beat Lee Sedol in a five-game match [2], and in 2017 a newer version of AlphaGo won against world champion Ke Jie in a three-game competition [3]. While it is possible to construct more complex board games than Go, no such games are popular for humans.

However, classic board games are relatively easier in game AI due to their discrete turn-based mechanics, highly formalized state representation, and fully-visible information to all players. Researchers have turned to more challenging games like card games and video games in the last decade. These games are much more difficult to solve due to the large state and action space, long time horizon, information asymmetry, and possible cooperation between players. Thanks to the rapid development of computational power and AI techniques, several milestones have been achieved.

Card games often involve randomness in dealing cards and asymmetries of information between different players. In 2015, Bowling and his team solved Heads-Up Limit Hold'em, achieving an approximate optimal solution of the game [17]. Their team further built DeepStack in 2017, a program that beat professional players in Heads-Up No-Limit Hold'em [5]. In 2018 Libratus by Brown's team also won professional players with different techniques from DeepStack [6]. Their team later built Pluribus in 2019, achieving superhuman performance in six-player No-Limit Hold'em [7]. In 2019 Suphx, made by MSRA, beat most of the top human players in Riichi Mahjong [18], and in 2022 JueJong, built by Tencent AI Lab, beat a human champion in two-player Mahjong [19]. There are also efforts to solve Doudizhu, a popular card game in China, including DouZero [20] and PerfectDou [21], but no superhuman performance has yet been reported.

Video games are real-time frame-based games where players receive raw pixel-level input and take actions simultaneously. In 2014 Google DeepMind proposed DQN to play the classic Atari 2600 video games and achieved superhuman performance in some of them [22]. Multi-player Online Battle Arena (MOBA) games are complex video games that involve both cooperation and competition between players. In 2019 AlphaStar, proposed by Google DeepMind, beat professional players in StarCraft, which is the first successful AI system to achieve superhuman performance in MOBA games [8]. The same year, OpenAI built OpenAI Five to play Dota 2 and beat OG, the world champion team. It later defeated 99.4% of human players in a public online arena [9]. In 2020 Tencent AI Lab built JueWu to play Honour of Kings and won 40 of 42 matches against professional teams. It also achieves a 97.7% win rate in large-scale public tests against top players [10].

An important reason why games are excellent benchmarks for AI is that games are created to test and challenge human intelligence. Games with high quality usually act as teachers and can exercise many of our cognitive and decision-making abilities. Just as children learn about the world by playing with games and toys during their first years of life, games provide test-beds for gradual skill progression to test AI algorithms with different capabilities. Unlike narrow benchmarks in other fields of AI, the diversity of games can provide a rich context for AI algorithms. Board games, with their formalized state representation and perfect information, only require searching and planning from the current game state. Card games, with their non-deterministic transition and imperfect information, reveal more sophisticated strategies, such as bluffing and deception, skills that are normally reserved for humans. Video games, with their high-dimensional raw state and long time horizon, require feature extraction, memorization, long-term planning, and possible multi-agent cooperation. These characteristics make games strong benchmarks for the development of AI technology.

2.2. *Game Features*

Since AlphaGo achieved superhuman performance in the game of Go, in recent years, many popular games played by humans that were once considered impossible for AI to conquer have been solved. These games are difficult to solve because some features of them bring diverse challenges and difficulties for AI research. Here we focus on games involved in the milestones discussed in Section 4. Table 1 lists several key features of these games, which play an important role in the selection of techniques used to tackle them.

2.2.1. Real Time

Board games and card games are turn-based games, where players take turns to take action and receive new observations. These games do not have a long time horizon, and a typical episode lasts tens or hundreds of turns. Real-time planning algorithms like tree search is often used in turn-based games because the transition model of the environment is known, and seconds or even minutes of thinking time are permitted. Video games are real-time or frame-based games, where the observation is presented frame by frame at a fixed frequency, and the players can take actions at any frame. Such games have a long time horizon, and an episode can last for thousands of frames. Typical AI systems use direct network inference without planning because the environment model is unknown, and a fast response of actions is required.

Table 1. Features of the games tackled in recent milestones.

Game Types	Name	Players	Real-Time	Imperfect Information	Stochasticity	Cooperation	Heterogeneous
Board games	Go	2	✗	✗	✗	✗	✗
Card games	HUNL	2 or 6	✗	✓	✓	✗	✗
	Riichi Mahjong	4	✗	✓	✓	✗	✗
	1-on-1 Mahjong	2	✗	✓	✓	✗	✗
	Doudizhu	3	✗	✓	✗	✓	✗
Video games	Starcraft	2	✓	✓	✓	✗	✓
	Dota 2	10	✓	✓	✓	✓	✓
	Honour of Kings	10	✓	✓	✓	✓	✓

2.2.2. Imperfect Information

Classic board games are games with perfect information, where each player knows all the information about the current game state. According to Zermelo's theory [23], there exists an optimal solution in deterministic perfect-information games, so the purpose of strong AI is to find or approximate that optimal solution. However, most games are of imperfect information, where each player has hidden information that other players cannot observe. In such games, each player may reason about others' private information according to their past actions before making their own decision, which in turn affects others' belief in his private information. Such recursive reasoning brings uncertainty and complexity to the evaluation of strategies. Instead of an optimal solution, algorithms seek to find some equilibrium, such as Nash equilibrium, in imperfect-information games. Nash equilibrium [24] is a solution concept where each player cannot get a higher payoff if he changes his policy only. It also minimizes the exploitability of each player, which is defined as the scoring points one will lose when faced with the worst opponents.

2.2.3. Stochasticity

In games like Go and Doudizhu, the transition of the environment is deterministic, which means that the same initial state and action sequence will lead to the same episode. In contrast, in most games, random events like dice rolling or card dealing bring stochasticity. It is worth noting that stochasticity does not always lead to imperfect information and vice versa. For example, in Texas Hold'em, the card faced down and dealt to each player introduces hidden information, while the dealing of public cards only introduces stochasticity because all players can observe that. Stochasticity in the transition model brings extra complexity to real-time planning algorithms to explore the branches of chance nodes and higher variance for learning algorithms to converge because the same action sequence may have very different payoff values.

2.2.4. Cooperation

Most board games and card games are zero-sum games that are purely competitive. The player who seeks to maximize his payoff also reduces other players' payoff. An exception is Doudizhu, where two peasants cooperate against one landlord and receive the same payoff. MOBA games are usually team games with cooperation, where the competition happens between two teams of players. Starcraft only involves two players who build facilities and direct an army to fight, which is not a cooperative game. Cooperation brings greater challenges to AI algorithms because mechanisms of communication and credit assignment have to be designed to motivate agents for the same target, and some agents have to sacrifice their own interests for team benefits.

2.2.5. Heterogeneous

In board games and card games, different players are homogeneous agents that share the same state space and action space. Although the strategies may differ for players in different positions, they share the same understanding of the game rules. However, many MOBA games are designed to have heterogeneous agents that have quite different strategies and action space. For example, in Starcraft, each player chooses one of three races with different mechanics. In Dota 2 and Honour of Kings, each player selects a hero from a hero pool with unique skills and game-playing strategies. The setting of heterogeneous agents introduces great complexity for AI algorithms as they need to learn different policies under each race or hero combination.

2.3. Game AI Modeling

As an important field of artificial intelligence, game playing is quite different from other fields like computer vision (CV) and natural language processing (NLP) because it can offer the richest form of human-computer interaction. CV and NLP are usually considered as cognitive intelligence, where computers try to extract useful information from images, texts, and videos to understand and interpret them. However, in the context of game playing, computer agents need to constantly interact with the environment and achieve specific goals through the actions they choose. In this way, game AI belongs to the category of decision intelligence, and this process of interaction between agents and environments is the core of game AI modeling.

In general, when modeling a game, the interaction between agents and the environment is divided into discrete steps. In each step, the agents to act first receive observations from the environment, and each chooses an action. Under these actions, the environment will transit to a new state and present new observations for these agents in the next step. For each agent, the intelligence lies in its policy or strategy, which is a mapping from historical observation sequences to actions to decide what to do at each time step. Such a policy model is the ultimate learning target of all AI systems to play specific games, though many algorithms also learn a value model to evaluate the expected payoff of game states and choose actions to maximize the value.

In the context of reinforcement learning, single-agent games are typically modeled as Markov Decision Processes (MDPs) [25]. In each time step, the environment is in some state, and the agent must choose an action available under the state. The environment responds by moving into a new state and giving the agent a corresponding reward. The transition probability and reward satisfy the Markov property that they are only related to the current state and action. For environments that do not follow the Markov property, the state can be defined as the historical observation sequence which satisfies the property. In games like multi-armed bandits, each game only lasts for one step, and the target is to maximize the expected payoff of each game. For games with a longer time horizon or infinite steps, the agent's target is to maximize its cumulative reward in the future. A decaying factor γ is defined to balance the trade-off between the reward in the next step and future steps.

When it comes to multi-agent settings, things become more complex because different agents can have separate observation spaces, causing information asymmetry. These games are usually modeled as Partially Observable MDP (POMDP), where the observations are distinguished from game states. In addition to the MDP defined on hidden states, there is a mapping from these states to observations for each agent, which describes the emitting probability of observations under each hidden state. Since agents have to infer the current state from historical observation sequences, the Markov property is not satisfied on observations, and the strategy has to be defined on the whole sequence of historical observations and actions.

Game theory pays more attention to the interaction between multiple agents rather than the transition dynamics of the environment, so it models games from a different perspective [26]. The extensive form is a straightforward way to model games in the context of game theory. It models the game as a tree, where each node is a game state and a decision point of a player. Edges from each node represent the available actions of the player to act, and the successor node is the next game state after the action is performed. Each agent's payoff is marked on leaf nodes, representing the end of the game. Information sets are defined as the set of states that an agent cannot distinguish because of hidden information, and policies are defined as mappings from information sets to actions. Another way of formally describing games is normal-form representation, which uses a multi-dimensional matrix to list the policy space of each agent and the payoff under each strategy profile, i.e., the combination of strategies of each agent. This form of representation models a situation where players select complete action plans simultaneously, but suffers from an exponential size of strategy space in games with long time horizons.

Reinforcement learning and the game theory model games as a process of interaction from different perspectives. Reinforcement learning models games as a control problem and seeks to maximize the payoff of individual agents in the interaction with an environment, which is initially designed for single-agent games. However, in multi-agent settings, the strategies of different agents can affect each other, resulting in unstable dynamics of the environment from the perspective of individual agents. Game theory puts more emphasis on the interaction between agents. By directly modeling the game as the payoffs under different action sequences or strategy profiles, such representations better capture the interactive nature of multi-agent games and help analyze different solution concepts instead of a static optimal solution.

3. Game AI Techniques

Many AI techniques have been proposed to build game-playing agents for different games. Figure 1 shows a timeline of different types of techniques and the type of games they tackle. In terms of algorithms, evolutionary methods are one of the earliest ways to create game-playing agents by randomized search and selection in the parameter space. Reinforcement learning models games as control problems and seeks to maximize cumulative rewards of individual agents in the interaction with the environment. Given the transition model of the environment, real-time planning algorithms expand a search tree and calculate the best action when each state is encountered during the gameplay, as an enhancement to the original policy and value model. Regret-based methods deal with multi-agent problems and approximate Nash equilibrium by playing games repeatedly and minimizing the cumulative regrets of each player. Self-play methods are game-theoretic methods to calculate Nash equilibrium in multi-agent games, which in practice can extend RL algorithms to multi-agent settings. Besides, there are also RL algorithms specially designed for multi-agent settings by decomposing value functions [27,28] or following a centralized-training-decentralized-execution (CTDE) framework [29,30].

From the timeline, we can see that in different times of game AI history, the increasing complexity of games has spawned new types of algorithms designed for specific features of games. Earlier methods are focused on single-agent problems and try to find an optimal solution for them. As randomized global optimization algorithms, evolutionary methods can solve small-scale problems but suffer from low performance and inefficiency when the policy space is too large. Reinforcement learning initially deals with problems whose transition models are known, using model-based methods like value iteration and policy iteration. Modern RL algorithms are mostly model-free methods that do not require explicit transition dynamics and directly learn policy or value models through interactions with environments. Traditional planning methods like Minimax and MCTS are designed for games with perfect information, while in the last decade, researchers have turned to more complex games such as card games and video games, which are all games with imperfect information. Real-time planning has been applied to these games using variants of MCTS or new algorithms like continual re-solving. There are also methods specially designed for multi-agent games with imperfect information, like CFR algorithms, self-play schemes, and multi-agent RL algorithms.

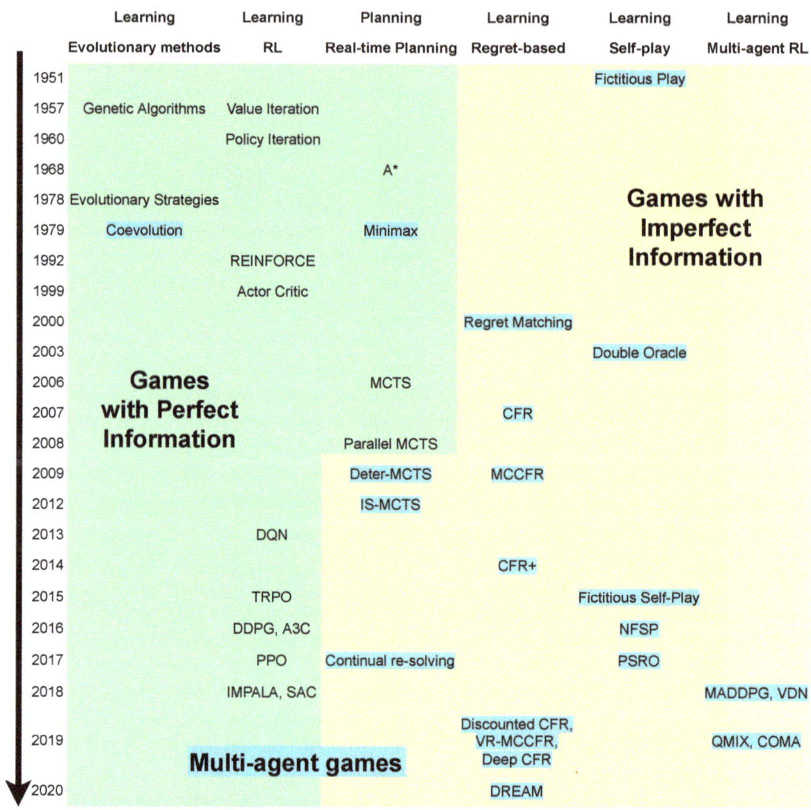

Figure 1. Timeline of different AI techniques to build game-playing agents. Colors indicate the type of games each algorithm tackles, green for games with perfect information, yellow for games with imperfect information, and blue for multi-agent games.

Meanwhile, as the games become more complex, modern game AI systems are no longer application of a single algorithm but a combination of multiple techniques. A typical AI to play a specific game usually involves some 'prior' knowledge, either explicitly incorporated by human experts or learned through pre-training phases. Such knowledge is then used in the game-play, combined with real-time planning and reasoning. This section further categorizes various AI techniques from this perspective. By discussing real-time planning and learning algorithms separately, it would be easier to break modern game AI systems into basic components and compare them thoroughly in the following sections.

3.1. Real-Time Planning

In most cases, the state space of a game is so large that it is difficult to have an optimal strategy for every possible state before the game starts. If the state transition model of the game is known, planning can be done when each specific game state is encountered during the gameplay, as a computation whose output is the selection of a single action under the current state. Such methods are called real-time planning, or decision-time planning, and are most useful in applications where fast responses are not required. For example, in a chess-playing program, seconds or even minutes of thinking time is permitted and can be used for planning, while in a real-time strategy game, low latency for action selection is the priority, and planning is usually not used.

When an evaluation function of game states is available, the simplest form of planning is to choose an action by comparing the values of model-predicted next states for each action. Such planning can look much deeper than one step ahead and expand a search tree to evaluate many future states under different sequences of actions, leading to a more far-sighted agent. These methods are generally called heuristic search. One of the most famous algorithms is A* [31], which uses an evaluation function to guide the selection of unexplored nodes. In general, searching deeper usually yields better policies when the evaluation function is not perfect because it eliminates some errors of value estimation by looking ahead for some steps. However, searching deeper costs more computation, and the search depth is usually fixed or decided by iterative deepening to limit the time cost in practice.

Minimax [32] is a classical real-time planning algorithm in two-player competitive settings and is widely used in board games. The basic assumption is that each player wants to maximize his own values. When expanding the search tree, nodes are divided into max-nodes and min-nodes based on which player is to act. Once the depth limit is reached, an evaluation function on game states is utilized to estimate the value of the first player. Alpha-beta pruning can be further applied in that the value of some subtrees makes no difference to the value of their parent nodes under the min-max mechanism. The Minimax algorithm can be generalized to multiplayer settings, where each node maximizes the value of the player to act, and the evaluation function at leaf nodes returns the values of all players.

Monte-Carlo tree search is another real-time planning algorithm that achieves massive success in board games. It is mainly responsible for the progress achieved in computer Go from a weak amateur level in 2005 to a grandmaster level in 2015 [25]. At each state encountered, the algorithm simulates many trajectories starting from the current state and running to a terminal state. Each simulation first selects a path in the search tree using a tree policy, expands a leaf node, and plays to the end of the episode with a rollout policy. The final score is used to update the state-action value along the path. The main idea is to extend the initial portions of trajectories and focus on those that have received higher evaluations from earlier simulations. Typically, the rollout policy is chosen to be simple to reduce the time cost of each simulation. The tree policy needs to balance exploration and exploitation so that the search is mainly focused on promising trajectories while not missing out on potentially better moves in the unexplored parts. In 2006 Kocsis proposed UCT [33], which applies upper confidence bounds in MCTS to achieve maximum expected payoffs.

There are many variants of MCTS to improve its efficiency and performance. P-UCT [34] combines prior knowledge into MCTS by using default rollout policy and incorporating evaluation function into tree policy. Rapid action value estimation (RAVE) [35] assumes that the value of an action is similar under different states and estimates the value of actions based on all simulations starting from the root state. It allows value estimation to generalize across subtrees to achieve higher efficiency. Parallel MCTS [36] proposes three ways to execute MCTS simulations simultaneously by using the different granularity of parallelization: leaf parallelization runs multiple simulations from the same leaf, root parallelization uses multiple search trees and tree parallelization runs simulations from root node in the same tree. Experiments show that root parallelization achieves not only higher efficiency because the trees are not shared across processes, but also better performance, possibly because using multiple trees can get rid of local minima.

MCTS can also be applied to imperfect-information games. One popular approach is determinization, which has achieved success in games like Bridge [37] and Klondike Solitaire [38]. The main idea is to simply sample states from the current information set and fix the outcomes of future chance events, making instances of deterministic games equivalent to the original one. However, this approach searches a tree of game states that does not truly reveal the imperfect nature of the game and suffers from two problems of strategy fusion and non-locality [39]. Another approach is information set MCTS (IS-MCTS) [40], which searches trees of information sets rather than trees of game states, and can analyze the game structure more directly, reserving the variety of hidden information and stochasticity. Experiments show that IS-MCTS achieves better results than determinization MCTS on imperfect-information games such as Doudizhu [41].

Another real-time planning algorithm for imperfect-information games is called continual re-solving, which has achieved huge success in the game of no-limit Texas Hold'em [5]. It is based on CFR-D, which provides a theoretically sound framework for the decomposition and nested safe subgame solving of imperfect-information games [42]. Traditionally, imperfect-information games have been considered as a generally indivisible whole and cannot be decomposed into subgames to solve, because simply solving a subgame in such games usually produces a subgame strategy that is not part of the equilibrium solution of the whole game. CFR-D uses a player's own range and opponent counterfactual values as constraints of subgame solving to ensure the re-solved subgame strategy is not worse than the previous strategy of the whole game. Here a player's range means the opponent's belief of his private cards, and the counterfactual value is the expected payoff of the current game state, assuming the current payer tries his best to reach this state. Continual re-solving further develops this idea and combines depth-limit search trees with an evaluation function that takes players' ranges as input and produces counterfactual values as outputs. For example, Deepstack trains deep counterfactual value networks in advance and uses continual re-solving as real-time planning algorithms, achieving superhuman performance in no-limit Texas Hold'em.

3.2. *Learning*

Just in the same way that people do not play a new game well when they are just starting, and it takes time to get familiar with the game, most game AI systems also have a training phase to learn some prior knowledge of the game. Such prior knowledge can be stored in models, such as policy models or value models, and is used in the inference phase combined with real-time planning algorithms during actual gameplay. In most cases, this learning phase is the most fundamental part of building a game AI system and is the focus of game AI research. This section discusses various algorithms as building blocks used in modern game AI systems.

3.2.1. Evolutionary Methods

Evolutionary methods [43] are randomized global optimization algorithms inspired by the natural selection process. The basic idea is to create a population of individuals where the fitter ones have a higher probability of reproducing and inheriting part of their structures. Variation operators, including recombination and mutation, are applied to create necessary diversity within the population, and the selective pressure can increase the mean fitness of the whole population over time. This process can be viewed as if evolution is optimizing the fitness function by approaching optimal values closer, making it a strong optimization algorithm in problems where it is hard to find optimal solutions by human experts.

There are several components to specify to define a specific evolutionary algorithm. The first one is the representation or encoding of the solutions. Such encoding can simplify the odd solution space in the problem context into the space of genes so that the variation operators can be mathematically defined. Since one does not know in advance what the optimal solution looks like, it is usually desirable that all possible feasible solutions can be represented under the encoding. Another important component is the fitness function which the population should adapt to improve. In the context of game AI, the solution space usually refers to policy space, and the fitness function is often chosen as the performance of a policy in the game, like the score or payoff it can receive. The implementation of variation operators, parent selection schemes, and survival selection schemes also varies in different evolutionary algorithms.

The most well-known evolutionary algorithm variants are genetic algorithm (GA) and evolutionary strategies (ES) [44]. GA encodes solutions as binary strings and defines variation operators as one-bit flip and crossover of binary strings. The probability of parent selection is proportional to the fitness function, and the spawned children replace all parents immediately. ES encodes solutions as vectors of floating-point values and defines variation operators as Gaussian perturbation and interpolation between vectors. The parents are uniformly selected, and the individuals with the highest fitness function in both parents and children survive.

When applied to multi-agent games, coevolution [45] is a popular evolutionary approach that simulates the interactive nature of the multi-agent settings. The core idea is to define the fitness function as the relative scores received by agents fighting against each other instead of their absolute performance when interacting with the environment. In practice, the algorithm can either use a single population and have individuals challenge each other to evaluate their fitness function or create multiple populations and exploit an arms race, having individuals from different populations battle. It is assumed that such competitive coevolution can improve the fitness of species in a highly interactive environment, just as coevolution does in the natural world. Algorithms involving coevolution have achieved success in many games, including Tic-Tac-Toe [46], Pursuit and Evasion [47], Predator and Prey [48], real-time strategy games like Capture The Flag [49] and Planet Wars [50], and a collectible card game called Hearthstone [51].

3.2.2. Supervised Learning

Supervised learning is a data-driven method to approximate the underlying function between data and their attributes. In the context of game AI, the data usually refers to the game states or observations, and the task is to learn a policy model or value model that predicts the action to choose or the estimated value under the current state. Such algorithms require lots of labeled data in the form of state-action or state-value pairs, usually collected from human data of gameplay or data generated by other game-playing algorithms. Once a policy or value model is trained, it can be used as prior knowledge in the inference stage, combined with some real-time planning algorithms.

In general, supervised learning trains an approximating function by modifying the parameters in the function model. There are many ways to represent such functions, like support vector machines, decision trees, and artificial (deep) neural networks, each with a different algorithm to modify the parameters. Here we focus on the modern approach of neural networks, though in some scenarios, a classic method like decision trees is preferable due to its interpretability. Most modern game AI systems use neural networks to represent policy or value function due to their strong expressivity [52] and adaptation of feature extraction. Variants of neural networks like convolutional neural network (CNN) and recurrent neural network (RNN) are popular due to their ability to extract spatial and temporal features respectively.

The application of supervised learning in modern game AI systems can be divided into three types according to the data source. The most common one is to use human data. Using supervised learning on human data can learn implicit human knowledge and store it in policy models or value models. However, even if the model achieves perfect accuracy on the training set, the generalization error of the model is inevitable, so the level of the model usually cannot surpass the level of the humans it imitates. Besides, models learned from human data are likely to be misled and fall into the traps of human strategy, especially in those complex games where the strategies of professional humans may be far from optimal. Such models are usually used as an initialization [2,8,18] to other learning algorithms like reinforcement learning as a warm start, which can speed up the training during the early phase.

There are two other types of supervised learning applications where the data source is not from human players. One of them is knowledge extraction. Suppose there is a game-playing algorithm that runs too slowly to be used in real-time inference but can be used to generate unlimited data offline; supervised learning can be used to train a model that extracts the implicit knowledge hidden in these data but takes much less time to inference. For example, DeepStack [5] trains three value models at different stages of the NLTH game by supervised learning on data generated by continual re-solving combined with the value model at the next game stage. These models store the knowledge of state value estimation at different game stages and can be used in real-time inference. The other one is knowledge distillation [53], where a lightweight unified model is trained to clone the behavior of another large model. Instead of using the ground-truth label as hard targets in knowledge extraction, knowledge distillation uses probability distribution as soft targets and adopts Shannon entropy as the loss function to reserve the generalization ability of the original model. For example, JueWu [10] uses supervised learning to learn a unified student model from data generated by multiple teacher models with fixed hero combinations, to extract the unified strategy with arbitrary hero combinations in the game Honor of Kings.

3.2.3. Reinforcement Learning

Reinforcement learning is the area of machine learning that studies how agents can take actions in an environment to maximize cumulative rewards. Different from supervised learning where the target is to learn a mapping of labeled data pairs, reinforcement learning deals with control problems and learns how to map situations to actions. Actions are not given as ground truth, but the learner needs to discover which actions can lead to higher future rewards by interacting with the environment and trying them out. The learning focus is usually on the balance of exploration (for potentially better actions) and exploitation (to maximize cumulative rewards). Reinforcement learning has become one of the most popular methods in the field of game AI because learning how to play a game is itself a control problem, which can be directly modeled in the setting of reinforcement learning.

Typically, reinforcement learning models the environment as a Markov Decision Process (MDP). In each time step, the environment is in some state, and the agent must choose an action available under the state. The environment responds by moving into a new state and giving the agent a corresponding reward. The transition probability and reward satisfy the Markov property that they are only related to the current state and action. When the transition model is known, generalized policy iteration uses dynamic programming to solve the optimal policy and its value function, defined as the expected cumulative rewards of states or state-action pairs. One of the most common variants is value iteration, which is based on Bellman Equation that describes the relationship between the policy and value function.

Value iteration is a model-based algorithm because it requires the complete model of MDP. However, in most cases, the environment model is unknown, and model-free algorithms are preferable, which learn from experiences by interacting with the environment. There are two kinds of model-free algorithms, value-based and policy-based. Value-based algorithms optimize the policy by approximating the values of states or state-action pairs and selecting better actions based on these values. For environments with finite state space, the value function can be represented using arrays indexed by states. These kinds of algorithms are called tabular methods [25], and there are different ways to update the value function. Monte Carlo (MC) algorithm updates the value function based on the cumulative rewards towards the end of the episode, while the temporal difference (TD) algorithm updates the value function based on the current reward and the value of the next state in a bootstrapping manner. Monte Carlo algorithm usually suffers from large variance, so algorithms using a TD target such as Q-learning are more preferred in practice. When the state space is too large to fit in memory, function approximation can be used to approximate the value function. For example, DQN [22] is the variant of Q-learning which uses deep neural networks to approximate the state-action value function and achieves success on Atari games.

Policy-based algorithms are another kind of model-free algorithms, which have become increasingly popular due to the development of deep learning. These algorithms directly learn parameterized policies based on gradients of some performance measure using the gradient descent method. One of the earliest works is REINFORCE [54], which samples full episode trajectories with Monte Carlo methods to estimate return as the loss function. However, pure policy-based algorithms suffer from high variance, and actor-critic algorithms [55] have been proposed, which use actors to learn parameterized policies and critics to learn value functions, allowing the policy updates to consider the value estimates to reduce the variance. There are many variants of actor-critic algorithms. Deep deterministic policy gradient (DDPG) [56] addresses the issue of large action space by adding sampled noise to its actor's policy, allowing more exploratory behavior. Asynchronous Advantage Actor-Critic (A3C) [57] is a distributed algorithm where multiple actors running on different threads interact with the environment simultaneously and compute gradients in a local manner. Importance Weighted Actor-Learner Architecture (IMPALA) [58] is another distributed algorithm that uses V-trace to compensate for the gradient error introduced by asynchronous execution. Trust Region Policy Optimization (TRPO) [59] and Proximal Policy Optimization (PPO) [60] are state-of-the-art policy-based algorithms, where policy changes are incorporated into the loss function by adding KL-divergence to the loss or using loss clipping to prevent abrupt changes in policies during training.

3.2.4. Multi-Agent Learning

Learning policies in multi-agent environments are very different from single-agent ones because each agent's behavior can affect other agents' observations, making the environment non-stationary from one agent's perspective. Instead of solving an optimal policy in single-agent settings, multi-agent learning aims to find some equilibrium, such as Nash equilibrium [24], where each player cannot get a higher payoff if he changes his policy. There are many algorithms specially designed for multi-agent learning, and here list some of the most important ones used in modern game AI systems.

Regret matching [61] is a simple and intuitive algorithm to solve the Nash equilibrium of normal-form games. In the algorithm, players choose their actions with probabilities proportional to measures of regret for not having chosen other actions in the past. Counterfactual regret minimization (CFR) [62] extends its application to extensive-form games, which has become a powerful tool to solve imperfect-information games. However, vanilla CFR traverses the whole game tree on each iteration and takes many iterations to converge, making it computationally expensive to solve larger games. Many variants of CFR have been proposed to improve its efficiency. CFR+ [63] and Discounted CFR [64] discount regrets from earlier iterations and reweight iterations in various ways to speed up the training. MCCFR [65] and VR-MCCFR [66] only sample a few paths when traversing the game tree, making them capable of solving games with massive game trees. Some variants utilize state abstraction [67] and function approximation [68] to reduce the time and memory cost. It was not until neural networks were used [69–72] that state abstraction and approximation could be made without human knowledge. Most of these methods with deep learning also take advantage of the ideas in previous variants, including sampling, discounting, and reweighting, resulting in better performance in complex games.

Combining single-agent RL with proper self-play techniques in competitive multi-agent environments can also approach a Nash equilibrium. The earliest algorithm is fictitious play (FP) [73] in two-player zero-sum games, where each agent calculates its best response to the opponent's average policies. Fictitious self play (FSP) [74] extends its application to extensive-form games. Neural FSP (NFSP) [75] adopts neural networks as the policy model to deal with larger games, using reinforcement learning to calculate the best response and supervised learning to learn average policies. Double oracle (DO) [76] only considers a small subset of the policy space, where each agent iteratively calculates the Nash equilibrium under the current strategy set and adds the equilibrium strategy to the set. Policy-space response oracles (PSRO) [77] provides a unified perspective of FSP and DO, using a policy pool to train new policies to be added. In practice, when training RL algorithms, a model pool is usually maintained from which opponents are selected to collect data for training. Different protocols of opponent selection can be used, such as naive self-play that always chooses the latest model, delta-uniform self-play [78] that randomly chooses from recent models, population-based self-play [8,79] that creates different populations for weakness exploitation, and prioritized self-play [9] that chooses opponents according to winning rate.

Centralized Training Decentralized Execution (CTDE) is another popular paradigm in multi-agent learning that jointly trains multiple agents in a centralized manner but keeps their independence in execution. It is proposed to provide a mechanism of communication to eliminate the problems of unstable dynamics in independent training. Value-based algorithms like Value Decomposition Network (VDN) [27] and QMIX [28] are variants of DQN in cooperative multi-agent settings that adopts centralized state-action value functions, using summation and mixing network to combine individual Q-networks. QMIX also introduces the internal state of the environment in the mixing network. Multi-agent DDPG (MADDPG) [29] is a policy-based algorithm that generalizes DDPG to multi-agent settings. Each agent has its own actor and critic network and reward function so it can deal with both competitive and cooperative settings. The critics take observations and actions of other agents as input and are trained in a centralized manner. Counterfactual Multi-agent Policy Gradients (COMA) [30] extends vanilla actor-critic to the setting of Dec-POMDP where all agents share the same reward function. It uses a shared critic network with a counterfactual baseline function to assign credits to different agents.

4. Milestones of Game AI Systems

This section summarizes several important milestones of game AI in recent years. Each of these game AI systems uses different combinations of AI techniques listed in Section 3. The AI systems covered in this section are: AlphaGo series (AlphaGo [2], AlphaGo Zero [3], AlphaZero [4]) in the game of Go, HUNL AI systems (DeepStack [5], Libratus [6], Pluribus [7], AlphaHoldem [80]), Mahjong AI systems (Suphx [18], JueJong [19]), Doudizhu AI systems (DouZero [20], PerfectDou [21]), and AI systems for video games (AlphaStar [8], OpenAI Five [9], JueWu [10]).

4.1. Board Games

Go is a classic board game of much higher complexity than Chess. It is estimated that the game tree of Go has a branching factor of 250 and an average depth of 150, so the state-space complexity is up to 10^{360}. In 2016, Google DeepMind proposed AlphaGo [2], which beat professional human players using a combination of deep learning and tree search. In 2017, a new training framework was proposed to build AlphaGo Zero [3], which does not rely on human data and learns from scratch. The same framework is used to train AlphaZero [4], achieving superhuman performance in Go, Chess, and Shogi.

AlphaGo trains a policy network, a value network, and a rollout policy as prior knowledge. These components are combined with MCTS to select moves in real-time gameplay. The training pipeline consists of three phases. In the first phase, the policy network and the rollout policy are trained using 30 million state-action pairs from matches of professional humans. The policy network is a 13-layer convolutional neural network, while the rollout policy is based on a linear evaluation function of handcraft features, achieving lower accuracy but higher speed than the policy network. In the second phase, the policy network is improved by self-play reinforcement learning. It plays against previous versions of checkpoints and is optimized using policy gradient methods. The improved policy network can achieve an 80% winning rate against the original version. In the third phase, 30 million state-value pairs are collected from self-play matches of the policy network to form a high-quality dataset. A value network of 14 layers is trained on the dataset to learn an evaluation function to estimate the winning rate of board states.

Once the prior knowledge is trained, parallel MCTS is executed in real-time gameplay. The action probability produced by the policy network is used to guide the tree policy. Once reaching a leaf node, the fast rollout policy simulates until the end of the episode. The value of the leaf node is a linear combination of the final payoff and the evaluation of the value network. This scheme of using prior knowledge in MCTS is called APV-MCTS in their work. When running on clusters of 1202 CPUs and 176 GPUs with a thinking time of 5 s per move, AlphaGo achieves an Elo rating of 3140, reaching the level of professional play.

AlphaGo Zero uses a different framework to train a combined policy-value network to predict the actions and values of game states, which is a Resnet [81] that shares the first layers to extract features. A simpler variant of MCTS than AlphaGo is used, where the leaf node of the search tree is evaluated directly using the value network without rollout to the end of the game. The network is trained by reinforcement learning that uses MCTS as the policy improvement operator. Specifically, the training data is generated by the self-play of MCTS agents using the best historical checkpoint. The policy network is trained to approximate the action probability produced by MCTS, and the value network is trained to approximate the final payoff of the game. In other words, through self-play, the policy network is constantly approaching an improved MCTS policy in a supervised manner. After the network is trained on 29 million self-play games for over 40 days, it is combined with MCTS paralleled on 4 TPUs in real-time gameplay, achieving an Elo rating of 5185, much higher than that of the best human player, though it only takes three days of training to surpass old version of AlphaGo.

AlphaZero uses the same training framework as AlphaGo Zero but extends its application to other board games like Chess and Shogi. Data augmentation methods like rotation and reflection used in AlphaGo Zero are not adopted to accommodate a broader class of games. Besides, AlphaGo Zero uses the best checkpoint from all previous iterations to generate self-play data, while AlphaZero maintains the newest checkpoint and updates it continually. AlphaZero achieves state-of-the-art performance on all three games, with the training time of 9 h, 12 h, and 13 days on Chess, Shogi, and Go.

4.2. Card Games

4.2.1. HUNL

Heads-up No-limit Hold'em (HUNL) is a card game involving imperfect information and stochasticity. Two-player HUNL has more than 10^{160} information sets [82], making it impossible to solve by vanilla CFR methods. In 2017 Bowling and his team proposed DeepStack [5], which uses deep learning and continual re-solving to solve HUNL. Brown and his team built Libratus [6] in 2018 and Pluribus [7] in 2019 to solve two-player and six-player HUNL with a different method that combines nested-safe subgame solving with a blueprint strategy on an abstracted game. In 2022 Zhao and his team [80] applied deep reinforcement learning on HUNL, achieving similar results to previous methods.

DeepStack, Libratus, and Pluribus use the same real-time planning technique but give different names as continual re-solving and nested safe subgame solving. The basic idea is to decompose an imperfect information game into the trunk, the first few layers of the game tree, and subgames and solve each subgame when actually encountered in gameplay. By using players' ranges and opponent counterfactual values, as constraints, the re-solved subgame strategy is guaranteed to be not more exploitable when combined with the trunk strategy. The ranges can be updated by Bayes rules at each action and random event when playing, and the opponent counterfactual value is the prior knowledge to be trained and stored in models.

DeepStack trains deep counterfactual value (DCFV) networks to predict counterfactual values of both players given the ranges at each information set. The game of HUNL can be divided into four stages, preflop, flop, turn, and river, and DeepStack trains three DCFV networks at each of the first three stages. In this way, a search tree expanded at any information set can reach one network or the end of the game within a limited depth. By further limiting the action space, the size of such depth-limit sparse look-ahead trees can be brought down to around 10^7 to be solved in seconds. The DCFV networks are trained in reverse order by supervised learning on millions of data pairs generated by randomly initializing ranges at each stage and running continual re-solving with the network in the next stage. In this way, the prior knowledge of counterfactual value prediction in each stage of the game is stored in network models and is combined with continual re-solving in real-time gameplay, beating all 11 professional players in a four-week match.

Instead of dividing the game into stages, Libratus and Pluribus use abstraction to reduce the complexity of HUNL and calculate a blueprint strategy on the abstracted game using MCCFR. Both state abstraction and action abstraction are used to group similar card combinations and limit the choices of betting size. Such blueprint strategy and the subgame values in each abstracted information set are stored in tabular form.

When playing the game in real-time, Libratus always plays according to the blueprint strategy by rounding an off-tree opponent bet size in the first two betting rounds where the abstraction is dense, but will use nested safe subgame solving to re-solve the subgame strategy for off-tree opponent action in the last two betting rounds. To compensate for the error brought by action abstraction in early rounds, Libratus further includes a self-improvement module. Over the 20 days of Brains vs. AI challenge with four professional humans, Libratus analyzes the most frequent bet sizes used in the first betting round by humans and chooses three of them each day to add to and finetune the blueprint strategy overnight, making the abstracted betting sizes of the first round of the blueprint strategy denser. In this way, Libratus gradually fixes its potential weakness of abstraction by leveraging the humans' ability. The competition shows that Libratus can beat professional players by a huge margin of 147 mbb/h.

However, solving to the end of the game in 6-player HUNL is computationally infeasible. When solving the subgames using CFR algorithm, Pluribus assumes that each opponent can only choose among four strategies, the blueprint strategy and its shifted version towards folding, calling, and raising. In each state of the subgame, the opponents always take actions based on the selected strategy, instead of choosing from an abstracted action space in each state as in Libratus. Such an assumption dramatically reduces the size of subgames so that nested safe subgame solving can be performed. Monte Carlo Linear CFR solves large subgames, and vector-based Linear CFR solves small subgames for higher accuracy. Pluribus does not share the self-improvement module with Libratus, probably because of the higher training cost of the blueprint strategy than Libratus. Experiments show that Pluribus achieves superhuman performance when playing with professional humans and is evaluated under AIVAT to reduce variance.

AlphaHoldem uses deep reinforcement learning to train a policy-value network as prior knowledge and only performs one network forwarding at each state in real-time gameplay. The neural network receives a player's observation as input and predicts the action to choose and the estimated value of the state. The training of the network is based on trinal-clip PPO, a variant of the PPO algorithm that adds an upper clipping bound to the importance sampling ratio when the advantage is negative, and a reward clipping to reduce high variance introduced by the stochasticity of the game. During self-play training, the data is collected by having the main agent compete with K-best historical checkpoints to keep both the diversity and quality of the opponent pool. The training takes three days on a server with 8 GPUs and 64 CPUs, generating 6.5 billion samples (2.7 billion hands) of training data. Experiments show that AlphaHoldem performs at a similar level to DeepStack, but with a much faster inference time.

4.2.2. Mahjong

Mahjong is a multiplayer imperfect-information game that is challenging for AI research due to its complex scoring rule and rich hidden information. The average size of information sets is around 10^{48} in Riichi Mahjong and 10^{11} in 1-on-1 Mahjong, which is much larger than that of HUNL (about 10^3). Planning algorithms used in HUNL, like subgame re-solving, are not applicable because of longer game length and difficulty in state abstraction. In 2020 MSRA built Suphx [18] to solve Riichi Mahjong with deep reinforcement learning, outperforming most top human players. In 2022 Tencent AI Lab built JueJong [19] to solve 1-on-1 Mahjong with a combination of CFR and actor-critic framework, beating a human champion.

Suphx trains five policy networks as prior knowledge, which are embedded in a decision flow to be used in real-time gameplay. The training pipeline consists of two phases. In the first phase, five policy networks used in different decision points are trained, each using 4 to 15 million state-action pairs of top human players. All of the five networks use a similar structure to Resnet. In the second phase, only the policy network of the discard model is improved by a variant of the policy gradient algorithm that adds a term of entropy regularization and uses dynamic entropy weight to stabilize the training. The discard model is embedded in the decision flow and always plays against the latest model to collect training data. Since a game of Mahjong consists of multiple rounds, and the strategies vary in different rounds based on cumulative round scores, the reward of each round in RL training is decided by a global reward predictor, which is a recurrent network to predict game rewards after several rounds. This model is trained in advance on state-value pairs of human data using supervised learning. To speed up the training in the imperfect-information setting, Suphx uses a technique called oracle guiding that exposes hidden information as perfect features to the trained model while gradually dropping them out until the oracle agent transits to a normal agent.

In real-time gameplay, Suphx uses the decision flow with five policy networks to choose an action. However, because the initial hand of each round tends to cause different styles of policies, Suphx re-finetunes the policy model at the beginning of each round using parametric Monte-Carlo Policy Adaptation (pMCPA). Specifically, several different trajectories are generated by randomly sampling opponents' hands and running the policy models. The trajectories are used to perform gradient updates to finetune the policy model. Experiments show that Suphx surpasses 99.99% of players in Tenhou and achieves higher stable ranks than professional players.

JueJong trains a policy-value network as prior knowledge and only performs one network forwarding at each state in real-time gameplay. The training of the policy-value network is based on Actor-Critic Hedge (ACH), a practical actor-critic implementation of Neural Weighted CFR that proves to converge to a Nash equilibrium. Specifically, the value network is trained to approximate the final payoff of the game, while the policy network is trained to minimize cumulative counterfactual regrets instead of maximizing cumulative rewards as in typical RL algorithms. The regret is calculated based on the state-action values predicted by the value network under the current state and replaces the advantage function in traditional policy gradient methods to fit in a distributed actor-critic training framework. Only the latest model is used to produce training data in a self-play manner. Experiments show that JueJong is significantly more difficult to exploit than agents trained by other RL algorithms and achieves superhuman performance in head-to-head evaluation with human players.

4.2.3. Doudizhu

Doudizhu is a trendy three-player card game in China that involves imperfect information and cooperation. In the game, two peasants cooperate against one landlord and receive the same payoff. It is estimated that the average size of information sets in Doudizhu is around 10^{23} [83], and the hidden information makes it challenging to learn cooperative behavior. Besides, Doudizhu has a large discrete action space that cannot be easily abstracted. In 2021 DouZero [20] used deep reinforcement learning to solve Doudizhu from scratch, ranking first in the Botzone leaderboard [84] among 344 AI agents. In 2022 PerfectDou [21] proposed perfect information distillation and outperformed DouZero, with much higher training efficiency. Neither AI systems are evaluated by competing with top human players, so no superhuman performance is reported yet.

DouZero trains three value networks as prior knowledge to predict the state-action value for three positions. Since there is no policy network, it chooses the action with the highest value in real-time gameplay. The neural network is a fully connected network that receives the encoding of a state and an action and predicts the expected payoffs under the current state. The state does not include the hidden information of other players, and the reward is simply the final score of the game. The training uses Monte Carlo value targets instead of bootstrapping TD targets to speed up convergence, and the self-play of the latest model generates the training data. Trained from scratch with 4 GPUs and 48 CPUs, DouZero beats DeltaDou in 10 days, one of the best Doudizhu agents before DouZero.

PerfectDou trains a policy-value network as prior knowledge and only performs one network forwarding at each state in real-time gameplay. The training is based on distributed PPO, a variant of IMPALA that uses GAE value targets as in PPO instead of V-trace. The actor network only takes each player's imperfect observation as input, while the critic network has access to the hidden information of other players. PerfectDou calls this scheme perfect-training-imperfect-execution (PTIE), or perfect information distillation, which can reduce the variance caused by imperfect information. An oracle reward is designed as the relative speed to empty one's hand between peasants and the landlord, which is a dense signal and is added to speed up the training in the early phase. As in DouZero, the training data is generated by the self-play of the latest model. Experiments show that PerfectDou achieves not only better performance than DouZero, but also higher efficiency of 10 times fewer training samples. PerfectDou beats some skilled human players in their evaluation, but no professional players are invited to the experiment.

4.3. Video Games

StarCraft, Dota 2, and Honour of Kings (HoK) are multiplayer online video games that are popular and played by millions of people, with human competitions held each season. These games are very complex and difficult to solve by AI algorithms because of the huge state and action space, the imperfect information of game states, cooperation between agents, the balance between long-term targets and short-term benefits, and heterogeneous agents involving different policies. In 2019 DeepMind applies distributed deep reinforcement learning to StarCraft and proposes AlphaStar [8], beating professional human players. In the same year, OpenAI Five [9] beats OG, the world champion team in Dota 2, also based on distributed DRL with huge computational power. In 2020 Tencent AI Lab proposed JueWu [10], which achieves superhuman performance on HoK while not limiting the hero pool as OpenAI Five does.

All of these AI systems are trained under a distributed actor-critic training framework. In this framework, multiple actors distributed in different machines asynchronously interact with the environment to collect training data and send them to a centralized replay buffer, and a learner, which may have multiple GPUs and be distributed on multiple machines, samples data from the buffer to train the neural network. A model pool is also maintained to save historical checkpoints or different populations of agent to sample opponents for the training. Policy-value networks are trained as prior knowledge and are used to produce action in real-time gameplay without any planning algorithms.

The training pipeline of AlphaStar consists of two phases. In the first phase, supervised learning is used to train initial model parameters from a dataset consisting of 971,000 games played by the top 22% players. Since there are three races with different mechanisms in StarCraft, three distinct models are trained. In the second phase, these models are improved by distributed reinforcement learning, which combines multiple techniques of TD(λ) [85], V-trace [58] and upgoing policy update (UPGO) [8]. Specifically, the policy network is updated using the loss function of clipped importance sampling, while the value network is updated using TD(λ). UPGO is a new method proposed by AlphaStar which updates the policy from partial trajectories with better-than-expected returns by bootstrapping when the behavior policy takes a worse-than-average action. In this way, the policy always moves towards better trajectories.

To prevent models from sticking to the local optimal in self-play training, AlphaStar trains three kinds of populations of agents: the main agents, the main exploiters, and the league exploiters, each containing checkpoints of past versions. Specifically, the main agents train against all past agents as well as themselves and are constantly improved over time. The main exploiters only train against the main agents to exploit their weakness, and the league exploiters train against all past agents. Main exploiters and league exploiters are re-initialized when adding new checkpoints to the population. Using population-based self-play, AlphaStar overcomes the problem of non-transitivity in strategies, making the main agents hard to exploit.

OpenAI Five trains the policy-value network using distributed PPO. Instead of population-based self-play, OpenAI Five uses heuristic self-play where the main agent plays against the latest policy for 80% of games and the past checkpoints for 20% of games to generate training data. During the 10-month training, many restarts and reverts happen when the environment or the model's architecture changes. OpenAI Five proposes a collection of tools called continual transfer via surgery to avoid training the model from scratch at every restart. The basic idea is to ensure the new policy implements the same mapping from observation to action probability despite the changes in observation space or network structure so that the training can be smoothly restored.

In the game of Dota 2 and HoK, two teams select five heroes in turn from a hero pool before playing the game to battle. Such a drafting process can be considered a separate game to provide initial configurations of the main game. To prevent an exponential number of hero combinations, OpenAI Five limits the hero pool to 17 heroes (yielding around 4.9 million combinations) and uses randomly selected lineups in the training phase. The winning rate of a fixed lineup can be estimated using the predicted score at the first few frames of the game. During real-time game-play, a drafting program uses the minimax algorithm to pick the hero that maximizes the winning rate under the worst case of opponent hero selection. Further experiments show that including more heroes in training is likely to cause degraded performance and much slower training speed.

JueWu introduces the idea of curriculum learning to deal with exponential numbers of hero combinations and extends to a hero pool of 40 heroes. The training pipeline consists of three phases. In the first phase, several fixed lineups with a balanced winning rate are selected based on a vast amount of human data, and one teacher model is trained for each lineup. In the second phase, a student model is trained by supervised learning to learn the general behavior of those teacher models under different hero lineups. This process of knowledge distillation uses action probabilities as soft targets and adopts Shannon entropy as the loss function. The student model is further improved in the third phase by reinforcement learning under randomly selected lineups to generalize to arbitrary hero combinations. The RL algorithm used is dual-clip PPO which adds an upper clipping bound to the importance sampling ratio when the advantage is negative to reduce variance. JueWu uses the same heuristic self-play scheme with OpenAI Five, which plays against 80% of the latest and 20% of past models to prevent strategy collapse. In real-time gameplay, MCTS instead of minimax is used in drafting because a complete search tree is too large to explore with 40 heroes. A win-rate predictor is trained in advance by supervised learning on match datasets from self-play training. The winning rate of leaf nodes in MCTS is predicted by this small model rather than using the complete model as in OpenAI Five to speed up the inference.

5. Paradigms and Trends

Different AI systems designed for various games use diverse combinations of AI techniques, and it is difficult to find a universal pattern if we only study each in isolation. To thoroughly compare these AI systems and analyze the reasons for their success, this survey breaks each of them into basic components and categorizes these techniques based on the problems they tackle, which are directly related to the characteristics of the games. By comparing the basic techniques used in these AI systems, we discuss the following questions in this section: (1) Are there any paradigms capable of solving different types of games in these systems? (2) How do different game features affect the selection of techniques used to tackle them? (3) Which paradigm will become the general solution of game AI, and which games will likely be addressed in the future?

5.1. Common Paradigms

Table 2 shows an overview of the main components of each game AI system. These AI systems learn some prior knowledge in an offline training phase and use that knowledge in real-time inference. The prior knowledge is policy or value models stored in neural networks or tabular forms. The training usually involves reinforcement learning for policy/value improvement and supervised learning from human data as model initialization. When the environment model is known, the prior knowledge can be combined with real-time planning algorithms to conduct a tree search to produce better policies. In general, there are three kinds of paradigms used in these milestones.

5.1.1. AlphaGo Series

AlphaGo, AlphaGo Zero, and AlphaZero follow a common paradigm to solve classic board games, where the policy and value models are trained and combined with MCTS in real-time gameplay. While AlphaGo uses supervised learning and policy gradient to train the networks, AlphaGo Zero and AlphaZero adopt MCTS as policy improvement operators in the RL training. MCTS is heavily used both as planning and learning algorithms for two reasons. First, MCTS can be used here because these classic board games are all perfect-information games where the environment model is known, and a fast response of actions is not required. Second, board games like Go, Chess, and Shogi have such large state space that a perfect policy or value model is infeasible, but a relatively small time horizon that real-time planning algorithms like MCTS can improve the performance of an imperfect model by a large margin. The feasibility and superiority of the MCTS application are the keys to the success of the AlphaGo series in perfect-information games.

However, this paradigm is limited to perfect-information games because there are some limitations to the use of MCTS. First, an explicit environment model is required to predict the next state under current action. Second, the action space should be discrete and limited so that the branching factor of the search tree is under control. Third, MCTS only expands trees with limited depth and is inefficient to bootstrap values from the end of the episode to the early stages of the game when the time horizon is long. Though MuZero [86] overcomes the first limitation by training an additional representative model to simulate the environment and achieves success on Atari 2600 video games, the latter two limitations make it unable to apply to games with imperfect information or long time horizons.

Table 2. The main components of AI system milestones.

<table>
<tr><th>AI System</th><th>Prior Knowledge</th><th>Training Pipeline</th><th>Inference</th><th>RL Algorithm</th></tr>
<tr><td>AlphaGo</td><td>policy network
rollout policy
value network</td><td>SL + RL
SL
SL</td><td rowspan="3">MCTS + NN</td><td>PG</td></tr>
<tr><td>AlphaGo Zero</td><td rowspan="2">policy-value network</td><td rowspan="2">RL</td><td rowspan="2">MCTS-RL</td></tr>
<tr><td>AlphaZero</td></tr>
<tr><td>DeepStack</td><td>DCFV network</td><td>SL</td><td>Continual re-solving + NN</td><td rowspan="3">N/A</td></tr>
<tr><td>Libratus</td><td rowspan="2">blueprint strategy</td><td rowspan="2">Abstraction + MCCFR</td><td rowspan="2">Nested-safe subgame solving</td></tr>
<tr><td>Pluribus</td></tr>
<tr><td>AlphaHoldem</td><td>policy-value network</td><td>RL</td><td>NN</td><td>Trinal-clip PPO</td></tr>
<tr><td>Suphx</td><td>policy networks
global reward predictor</td><td>SL + RL
SL</td><td>pMCPA finetune + NN</td><td>PG with entropy</td></tr>
<tr><td>JueJong</td><td>policy-value network</td><td>RL</td><td>NN</td><td>ACH</td></tr>
<tr><td>DouZero</td><td>value network</td><td>RL</td><td>One-step greedy + NN</td><td>DMC</td></tr>
<tr><td>PerfectDou</td><td>policy-value network</td><td>RL</td><td>NN</td><td>PPO</td></tr>
<tr><td>AlphaStar</td><td>policy-value network</td><td>SL+RL</td><td>NN</td><td>UPGO</td></tr>
<tr><td>OpenAI Five</td><td>policy-value network</td><td>RL</td><td>Minimax drafting
NN</td><td>PPO</td></tr>
<tr><td>JueWu</td><td>policy-value network
drafting value network</td><td>RL+SL+RL
SL</td><td>MCTS drafting
NN</td><td>Dual-clip PPO</td></tr>
</table>

5.1.2. CFR Series

DeepStack, Libratus, and Pluribus follow a unique paradigm to solve HUNL by CFR algorithms. The core of these systems is to simplify the original game by abstraction and use nested safe subgame solving for real-time planning. Specifically, DeepStack decomposes HUNL into stages and trains value networks at each stage, which is combined with depth-limit sparse look-ahead trees to re-solve subgame policies. In this way, DeepStack always calculates real-time responses to opponent off-tree actions but suffers from approximation error of the value networks. Libratus and Pluribus directly apply abstraction to the whole game and compute a tabular blueprint strategy and the corresponding counterfactual values. Subgame policies are later re-solved based on the value of blueprint strategies. Such abstraction can introduce error when rounding off-tree betting size to the course-grained blueprint strategy but is more robust when the opponent mistakenly chooses an action far from optimal, which could cause unprecedented ranges and value estimation in DeepStack.

However, this paradigm is only a success limited to HUNL, and no further works successfully apply it to larger imperfect-information games. The reason lies in the compromise of computational cost and approximation error. Specifically, the computational cost under this paradigm comes from the CFR iterations both in the training and inference stages, and experiments show that a large number of CFR iterations are needed to produce a high-quality solution [5]. The blueprint strategies are in tabular forms, which are also limited by the available memory resources. Meanwhile, the process of subgame solving expands a search tree of limited depth and branching factor, so more abstraction is needed in larger games. Pluribus uses a very strong assumption that each player can only choose among four strategies to bring down the size of search trees, which introduces large errors in finding optimal policies. In fact, HUNL is relatively small in imperfect-information games considering its average size of information sets and the short time horizon. It can be concluded that the CFR-based paradigm is not scalable to larger games. It achieves superhuman performance on HUNL mainly because of the limited complexity of the game and suboptimality of human strategies.

5.1.3. DRL Series

All other AI systems in Table 2 follow a common paradigm of distributed deep reinforcement learning. Policy-value networks are trained as prior knowledge and directly used to produce actions in real-time inference without any planning algorithm. This paradigm is more general as it does not require a model of the environment. The networks are trained under a distributed actor-critic framework using algorithms like PPO or its variants to be easily scaled to an arbitrary amount of computational resources. Suphx and AlphaStar also use supervised learning to train initial models from human data to speed up the RL training. The training data is generated by playing the main agent against opponents sampled from a model pool to enrich policy diversity and prevent strategy collapse.

Though these AI systems all follow the same paradigm, there are some differences in the choices of each component related to the characteristics of the specific games they tackle. For example, in Riichi Mahjong, one full match consists of several rounds, and the strategies vary in each round, which is different from other games where each match is independent and does not affect the other. To deal with this issue, Suphx [18] trains an extra recurrent network as a global reward predictor to shape the reward of each match. AlphaHoldem [80] suffers from the large variance introduced by the stochasticity of HUNL and uses a variant of PPO with additional clipping to stabilize the training process. JueJong [19] seeks to find a policy with lower exploitability to approximate the Nash equilibrium, so the CFR-based ACH algorithm is used as the RL algorithm instead of PPO to minimize the cumulative regrets of the trained strategy. JueWu [10] deals with a large hero pool with so many hero combinations that a drafting value network is needed to assist the MCTS for fast value prediction.

5.2. Techniques for Game Features

In addition to common paradigms, we also notice that different techniques are selected for some common game features in these milestones. As is shown in Table 3, we make a detailed comparison of these AI systems from the following perspective: the self-play scheme used in multi-agent settings, the methods to deal with imperfect information, and the algorithms to learn policies for heterogeneous agents.

Table 3. The selected techniques for common game features in AI system milestones.

<table>
<tr><th>AI System</th><th>Self-Play Scheme</th><th>Imperfect Information</th><th>Heterogeneous Agents</th></tr>
<tr><td>AlphaGo</td><td>Uniform Random</td><td rowspan="3">N/A</td><td rowspan="11">N/A</td></tr>
<tr><td>AlphaGo Zero</td><td>Best</td></tr>
<tr><td>AlphaZero</td><td>Latest</td></tr>
<tr><td>DeepStack</td><td rowspan="3">N/A</td><td rowspan="3">CFR</td></tr>
<tr><td>Libratus</td></tr>
<tr><td>Pluribus</td></tr>
<tr><td>AlphaHoldem</td><td>K-Best</td><td>No use</td></tr>
<tr><td>Suphx</td><td>Latest</td><td>Oracle Guiding</td></tr>
<tr><td>JueJong</td><td>Latest</td><td>ACH</td></tr>
<tr><td>DouZero</td><td>Latest</td><td>No use</td></tr>
<tr><td>PerfectDou</td><td>Latest</td><td>PID</td></tr>
<tr><td>AlphaStar</td><td>Population</td><td>PID</td><td>Population</td></tr>
<tr><td>OpenAI Five</td><td>Heuristic</td><td>No use</td><td>Random</td></tr>
<tr><td>JueWu</td><td>Heuristic</td><td>PID</td><td>Knowledge Distillation</td></tr>
</table>

5.2.1. Self-Play Scheme

In multi-agent settings, directly applying single-agent RL algorithms to train agents independently is not guaranteed to converge because most games exhibit non-transitive behavior. For example, in the Rock-Paper-Scissor game, rock beats scissor and scissor beats paper, but rock could not beat paper, forming a cyclic sub-structure of the policy space. Previous works suggest that real-world games look like spinning tops [87], where relatively weak strategies tend to form longer circles. So a population of agents is necessary for the self-play in multi-agent training to learn policies with lower exploitability. In practice, several self-play schemes are used in these AI systems.

AlphaZero, Suphx, JueJong, DouZero, and PerfectDou use naive self-play, the simplest form of self-play that only chooses the latest model as the opponent. AlphaGo randomly samples opponents from historical checkpoints for more diversity. OpenAI Five and JueWu use a heuristic scheme that samples 80% of the latest model and 20% of historical models to put more weight on the latest model. AlphaGo Zero uses the best of the historical models for self-play to generate training data of high quality. AlphaHoldem chooses the K-best models to keep both the diversity and quality of the opponent pool. Most of the self-play schemes chosen in these milestones are for no specific reasons, except for PerfectDou, which proves by experiments that K-best self-play performs better than other self-play techniques.

5.2.2. Imperfect Information

Learning a Nash equilibrium in imperfect-information games is more difficult because the hidden information of other players is not included in the current observation and has to be inferred from other players' past actions. CFR-based algorithms generally consider the game as an indivisible whole and minimize the cumulative regrets at each information set to approach a Nash equilibrium. DeepStack, Libratus, and Pluribus combine variants of CFR algorithms with decomposition and abstraction to handle HUNL, which has too many information sets to be solved by vanilla CFR. JueJong proposed Actor-Critic Hedge to solve 1-on-1 Mahjong in a distributed RL framework, which is also based on CFR.

However, RL algorithms learn policies as mappings from observations to actions by interacting with the environment and optimizing the expected cumulative rewards, which can be of high variance in imperfect information settings. Two methods are proposed to reduce the variance and stabilize the training. Suphx uses oracle guiding to handle imperfect information by first exposing the hidden information to the policy and value network to train an oracle agent while gradually dropping them out until the oracle agent transits to a normal agent. However, this way of continual training is still unstable and requires additional tricks to converge [18]. PerfectDou, AlphaStar, and JueWu use perfect information distillation (PID), which exposes the hidden information to the centralized value network to reduce variance, while the policy network does not rely on hidden information in real-time inference. Theoretical analysis shows that PID is a more natural way to handle imperfect information and can generalize to larger games [88].

5.2.3. Heterogeneous Agents

MOBA games are usually designed to have heterogeneous agents with quite different mechanics and strategies. Such games provide another challenge for AI research since an AI system has to train different models for each kind of agent or a unified model which can generalize to distinct policies under different settings. There are three races of agents in StarCraft with different mechanics, so AlphaStar trains separate models for them by creating distinct populations of main agents, main exploiters, and league exploiters for each race. However, in games like Dota 2 and HoK, the number of heterogeneous agents called heroes is large, and there is an exponential number of hero combinations in the 5-versus-5 setting. OpenAI Five trains a unified model to control different heroes by limiting its application to 17 heroes and randomly sampling hero combinations for each game during the training. It suffers from a slow convergence speed and is hard to extend to more heroes, as shown in their further experiments with 25 heroes.

JueWu proposes a new training paradigm under the setting of MOBA games by noticing that many heroes can be classified into several positions with similar strategies for each position, and most of the hero combinations are improper and not preferred by human players. JueWu chooses some typical hero combinations based on human data and trains a separate teacher model for each combination. Knowledge distillation is then used to train a student model to learn the general strategy under different hero combinations by imitating the behavior of teacher models. Such a student model is further trained under random hero combinations to generalize to arbitrary settings. This idea of curriculum learning that learns general behavior from specific settings is the key to the scalability of JueWu, which achieves superhuman performance with a hero pool of 40 heroes.

5.3. Future Trends

As Sutton said [89], "The biggest lesson that can be read from 70 years of AI research is that general methods that leverage computation are ultimately the most effective". So what is the general paradigm in the field of game AI? As is discussed in this section, there are three kinds of paradigms used in these milestones. AlphaGo series and CFR series take advantage of tree search, either MCTS or nested safe subgame solving, and cannot scale to larger games with continuous action space or long time horizons. DRL series train models by advanced self-play with distributed deep reinforcement learning, which is the most general and promising paradigm for three reasons. First, deep neural networks can approximate arbitrary mappings from observations to actions as the policy model and are not restricted to games with finite state or action space. Second, advanced self-play schemes can be adopted to approach a Nash equilibrium with minimal exploitability under multi-agent settings by creating populations of diverse agents as opponents. Third, distributed asynchronous actor-critic training framework like IMPALA is easily scaled to an arbitrary amount of computational resources so that this paradigm is highly scalable to games of higher complexity once more computational resources are available, which is guaranteed by Moore's law [90], or its generalized version of continued exponentially falling of computational cost.

As researchers turn to games with higher complexity, we believe that real-world games, especially sports games, will become the next popular AI benchmarks because of their higher complexity and the inspirations that AI strategies can bring to humans. For example, Gran Turismo is a racing game that precisely reproduces the non-linear control challenges of real race cars, in which a superhuman AI trained by DRL [91] gives inspiration to a professional player and improve his performance. Another example is Google Research Football Environment [92], a football simulator to provide a real-world multiplayer sports game as a challenge for AI research. Previous works [93] have shown that with enough computational power, agents trained by DRL can create a self-supervised auto-curriculum and learn complex emergent behaviors of human-relevant skills without any human guidance. By applying the DRL-based training paradigm to real-world games such as football, it is expected that human-relevant skills can be learned from scratch and inspire humans with new tactics or even innovate the field when AI surpasses human performance.

6. Conclusions

Though AI systems have reached superhuman performance in many complex games in recent years, diverse techniques are used in each of them, and it is hard to see both the key to their success and their limitations. This survey aims to give a detailed analysis of the techniques and paradigms used in modern game AI systems in light of game features. We first summarize the common features in various games and show their challenges to AI research. By systematically reviewing the AI techniques typically used to create game-playing agents, we find that in different times of game AI history, the invention of new algorithms is mainly driven by the increasing complexity of new game features, and many of these algorithms are designed to tackle specific features. Since modern game AI systems are composed of multiple techniques, we propose a novel framework to break these systems into basic algorithmic components and compare them based on the game features. By analyzing the choices of these components and the game features, we extract three common paradigms to build AI systems for different games. Based on the mechanics of these paradigms and the features in modern games, we conclude that deep reinforcement learning is the most general and scalable paradigm to train strong AIs in games with higher complexity. We hope this survey can provide a comprehensive review of modern game AI systems and the basic techniques involved, to inspire researchers to build AI systems for larger games, such as real-world sports games.

Author Contributions: Writing—original draft preparation, Y.L.; Writing—review and editing, W.L. All authors have read and agreed to the published version of the manuscript.

Funding: This research was funded by Science and Technology Innovation 2030—"The New Generation of Artificial Intelligence" Major Project No.2018AAA0100901, China, and by Project No.2020BD003 supported by PKU-Baidu Fund.

Institutional Review Board Statement: Not applicable.

Informed Consent Statement: Not applicable.

Data Availability Statement: Not applicable.

Conflicts of Interest: The authors declare no conflict of interest. The funders had no role in the design of the study; in the collection, analyses, or interpretation of data; in the writing of the manuscript, or in the decision to publish the results.

References

1. Turing, A.M. Computing machinery and intelligence. In *Parsing the Turing Test*; Springer: Berlin/Heidelberg, Germany, 2009; pp. 23–65.
2. Silver, D.; Huang, A.; Maddison, C.J.; Guez, A.; Sifre, L.; Van Den Driessche, G.; Schrittwieser, J.; Antonoglou, I.; Panneershelvam, V.; Lanctot, M.; et al. Mastering the game of Go with deep neural networks and tree search. *Nature* **2016**, *529*, 484–489. [CrossRef]
3. Silver, D.; Schrittwieser, J.; Simonyan, K.; Antonoglou, I.; Huang, A.; Guez, A.; Hubert, T.; Baker, L.; Lai, M.; Bolton, A.; et al. Mastering the game of go without human knowledge. *Nature* **2017**, *550*, 354–359. [CrossRef]
4. Silver, D.; Hubert, T.; Schrittwieser, J.; Antonoglou, I.; Lai, M.; Guez, A.; Lanctot, M.; Sifre, L.; Kumaran, D.; Graepel, T.; et al. A general reinforcement learning algorithm that masters chess, shogi, and Go through self-play. *Science* **2018**, *362*, 1140–1144. [CrossRef]
5. Moravčík, M.; Schmid, M.; Burch, N.; Lisý, V.; Morrill, D.; Bard, N.; Davis, T.; Waugh, K.; Johanson, M.; Bowling, M. Deepstack: Expert-level artificial intelligence in heads-up no-limit poker. *Science* **2017**, *356*, 508–513. [CrossRef]
6. Brown, N.; Sandholm, T. Superhuman AI for heads-up no-limit poker: Libratus beats top professionals. *Science* **2018**, *359*, 418–424. [CrossRef]
7. Brown, N.; Sandholm, T. Superhuman AI for multiplayer poker. *Science* **2019**, *365*, 885–890. [CrossRef]
8. Vinyals, O.; Babuschkin, I.; Chung, J.; Mathieu, M.; Jaderberg, M.; Czarnecki, W.M.; Dudzik, A.; Huang, A.; Georgiev, P.; Powell, R.; et al. Alphastar: Mastering the real-time strategy game starcraft ii. *DeepMind Blog* **2019**, *2*. Available online: https://www.deepmind.com/blog/alphastar-mastering-the-real-time-strategy-game-starcraft-ii (accessed on 8 August 2022).
9. Berner, C.; Brockman, G.; Chan, B.; Cheung, V.; Debiak, P.; Dennison, C.; Farhi, D.; Fischer, Q.; Hashme, S.; Hesse, C.; et al. Dota 2 with large scale deep reinforcement learning. *arXiv* **2019**, arXiv:1912.06680.
10. Ye, D.; Chen, G.; Zhang, W.; Chen, S.; Yuan, B.; Liu, B.; Chen, J.; Liu, Z.; Qiu, F.; Yu, H.; et al. Towards playing full moba games with deep reinforcement learning. *Adv. Neural Inf. Process. Syst.* **2020**, *33*, 621–632.
11. Risi, S.; Preuss, M. From chess and atari to starcraft and beyond: How game ai is driving the world of ai. *KI-Künstliche Intell.* **2020**, *34*, 7–17. [CrossRef]
12. Yin, Q.; Yang, J.; Ni, W.; Liang, B.; Huang, K. AI in Games: Techniques, Challenges and Opportunities. *arXiv* **2021**, arXiv:2111.07631.
13. Copeland, B.J. The Modern History of Computing. Available online: https://plato.stanford.edu/entries/computing-history/ (accessed on 10 August 2022).
14. Tesauro, G. Temporal difference learning and TD-Gammon. *Commun. ACM* **1995**, *38*, 58–68. [CrossRef]
15. Schaeffer, J.; Lake, R.; Lu, P.; Bryant, M. Chinook the world man-machine checkers champion. *AI Mag.* **1996**, *17*, 21–21.
16. Campbell, M.; Hoane, A.J., Jr.; Hsu, F.h. Deep blue. *Artif. Intell.* **2002**, *134*, 57–83. [CrossRef]
17. Bowling, M.; Burch, N.; Johanson, M.; Tammelin, O. Heads-up limit hold'em poker is solved. *Science* **2015**, *347*, 145–149. [CrossRef]

18. Li, J.; Koyamada, S.; Ye, Q.; Liu, G.; Wang, C.; Yang, R.; Zhao, L.; Qin, T.; Liu, T.Y.; Hon, H.W. Suphx: Mastering mahjong with deep reinforcement learning. *arXiv* **2020**, arXiv:2003.13590.
19. Fu, H.; Liu, W.; Wu, S.; Wang, Y.; Yang, T.; Li, K.; Xing, J.; Li, B.; Ma, B.; Fu, Q.; et al. Actor-Critic Policy Optimization in a Large-Scale Imperfect-Information Game. In Proceedings of the International Conference on Learning Representations, Virtual Event, 3–7 May 2021.
20. Zha, D.; Xie, J.; Ma, W.; Zhang, S.; Lian, X.; Hu, X.; Liu, J. Douzero: Mastering doudizhu with self-play deep reinforcement learning. In Proceedings of the International Conference on Machine Learning, Virtual Event, 18–24 July 2021; pp. 12333–12344.
21. Guan, Y.; Liu, M.; Hong, W.; Zhang, W.; Fang, F.; Zeng, G.; Lin, Y. PerfectDou: Dominating DouDizhu with Perfect Information Distillation. *arXiv* **2022**, arXiv:2203.16406.
22. Mnih, V.; Kavukcuoglu, K.; Silver, D.; Graves, A.; Antonoglou, I.; Wierstra, D.; Riedmiller, M. Playing atari with deep reinforcement learning. *arXiv* **2013**, arXiv:1312.5602.
23. Schwalbe, U.; Walker, P. Zermelo and the early history of game theory. *Games Econ. Behav.* **2001**, *34*, 123–137. [CrossRef]
24. Osborne, M.J.; Rubinstein, A. *A Course in Game Theory*; MIT Press: Cambridge, MA, USA, 1994.
25. Sutton, R.S.; Barto, A.G. *Reinforcement Learning: An Introduction*; MIT Press: Cambridge, MA, USA, 2018.
26. Watson, J. *Strategy: An Introduction to Game Theory*; WW Norton: New York, NY, USA, 2002; Volume 139.
27. Sunehag, P.; Lever, G.; Gruslys, A.; Czarnecki, W.M.; Zambaldi, V.; Jaderberg, M.; Lanctot, M.; Sonnerat, N.; Leibo, J.Z.; Tuyls, K.; et al. Value-decomposition networks for cooperative multi-agent learning. *arXiv* **2017**, arXiv:1706.05296.
28. Rashid, T.; Samvelyan, M.; Schroeder, C.; Farquhar, G.; Foerster, J.; Whiteson, S. Qmix: Monotonic value function factorisation for deep multi-agent reinforcement learning. In Proceedings of the International Conference on Machine Learning, PMLR, Stockholm, Sweden, 10–15 July 2018; pp. 4295–4304.
29. Lowe, R.; Wu, Y.I.; Tamar, A.; Harb, J.; Pieter Abbeel, O.; Mordatch, I. Multi-agent actor-critic for mixed cooperative-competitive environments. *Adv. Neural Inf. Process. Syst.* **2017**, *30*, 6382–6393.
30. Foerster, J.; Farquhar, G.; Afouras, T.; Nardelli, N.; Whiteson, S. Counterfactual multi-agent policy gradients. In Proceedings of the AAAI Conference on Artificial Intelligence, New Orleans, LA, USA, 2–7 February 2018; Volume 32. .
31. Hart, P.; Nilsson, N.; Raphael, B. A formal basis for the heuristic determination of minimum cost paths. *IEEE Trans. Syst. Sci. Cybern.* **1968**, *4*, 100–107. [CrossRef]
32. Stockman, G. A minimax algorithm better than alpha-beta? *Artif. Intell.* **1979**, *12*, 179–196. [CrossRef]
33. Kocsis, L.; Szepesvári, C. Bandit based monte-carlo planning. In Proceedings of the European Conference on Machine Learning, Berlin, Germany, 18–22 September 2006; pp. 282–293.
34. Gelly, S.; Silver, D. Combining online and offline knowledge in UCT. In Proceedings of the 24th International Conference on Machine Learning, Corvalis, OR, USA, 20–24 June 2007; pp. 273–280.
35. Gelly, S.; Silver, D. Monte-Carlo tree search and rapid action value estimation in computer Go. *Artif. Intell.* **2011**, *175*, 1856–1875. [CrossRef]
36. Chaslot, G.M.B.; Winands, M.H.; Herik, H. Parallel monte-carlo tree search. In Proceedings of the International Conference on Computers and Games, Beijing, China, 29 September–1 October 2008; pp. 60–71.
37. Ginsberg, M.L. GIB: Imperfect information in a computationally challenging game. *J. Artif. Intell. Res.* **2001**, *14*, 303–358. [CrossRef]
38. Bjarnason, R.; Fern, A.; Tadepalli, P. Lower bounding Klondike solitaire with Monte-Carlo planning. In Proceedings of the Nineteenth International Conference on Automated Planning and Scheduling, Thessaloniki, Greece, 19–23 September 2009.
39. Frank, I.; Basin, D. Search in games with incomplete information: A case study using bridge card play. *Artif. Intell.* **1998**, *100*, 87–123. [CrossRef]
40. Cowling, P.I.; Powley, E.J.; Whitehouse, D. Information set monte carlo tree search. *IEEE Trans. Comput. Intell. Games* **2012**, *4*, 120–143. [CrossRef]
41. Whitehouse, D.; Powley, E.J.; Cowling, P.I. Determinization and information set Monte Carlo tree search for the card game Dou Di Zhu. In Proceedings of the 2011 IEEE Conference on Computational Intelligence and Games (CIG'11), Seoul, Korea, 31 August 2011–3 September 2011; pp. 87–94.
42. Burch, N. Time and Space: Why Imperfect Information Games Are Hard. Available online: https://era.library.ualberta.ca/items/db44409f-b373-427d-be83-cace67d33c41 (accessed on 10 August 2022).
43. Eiben, A.E.; Smith, J.E. *Introduction to Evolutionary Computing*; Springer: Berlin/Heidelberg, Germany, 2003; Volume 53.
44. Rechenberg, I. Evolutionsstrategien. In *Simulationsmethoden in der Medizin und Biologie*; Springer: Berlin/Heidelberg, Germany, 1978; pp. 83–114.
45. Dawkins, R.; Krebs, J.R. Arms races between and within species. *Proc. R. Soc. Lond. Ser. B Biol. Sci.* **1979**, *205*, 489–511.
46. Angeline, P.; Pollack J. Competitive Environments Evolve Better Solutions for Complex Tasks. In Proceedings of the 5th International Conference on Genetic Algorithms, San Francisco, CA, USA, 1 June 1993; pp. 264–270.
47. Reynolds, C.W. Competition, coevolution and the game of tag. In Proceedings of the Fourth International Workshop on the Synthesis and Simulation of Living Systems, Boston, Massachusetts, USA, 6–8. July 1994; pp. 59–69.
48. Sims, K. Evolving 3D morphology and behavior by competition. *Artif. Life* **1994**, *1*, 353–372. [CrossRef]
49. Smith, G.; Avery, P.; Houmanfar, R.; Louis, S. Using co-evolved rts opponents to teach spatial tactics. In Proceedings of the 2010 IEEE Conference on Computational Intelligence and Games, Copenhagen, Denmark, 18–21 August 2010; pp. 146–153.

50. Fernández-Ares, A.; García-Sánchez, P.; Mora, A.M.; Castillo, P.A.; Merelo, J. There can be only one: Evolving RTS bots via joust selection. In Proceedings of the European Conference on the Applications of Evolutionary Computation, Porto, Portugal, 30 March–1 April 2016; pp. 541–557.
51. García-Sánchez, P.; Tonda, A.; Fernández-Leiva, A.J.; Cotta, C. Optimizing hearthstone agents using an evolutionary algorithm. *Knowl.-Based Syst.* **2020**, *188*, 105032. [CrossRef]
52. Hornik, K.; Stinchcombe, M.; White, H. Multilayer feedforward networks are universal approximators. *Neural Netw.* **1989**, *2*, 359–366. [CrossRef]
53. Hinton, G.; Vinyals, O.; Dean, J. Distilling the knowledge in a neural network. *arXiv* **2015**, arXiv:1503.02531.
54. Williams, R.J. Simple statistical gradient-following algorithms for connectionist reinforcement learning. *Mach. Learn.* **1992**, *8*, 229–256. [CrossRef]
55. Konda, V.; Tsitsiklis, J. Actor-critic algorithms. In Proceedings of the Advances in Neural Information Processing Systems 12 (NIPS 1999), Denver, CO, USA, 29 November–4 December 1999; Volume 12.
56. Lillicrap, T.P.; Hunt, J.J.; Pritzel, A.; Heess, N.; Erez, T.; Tassa, Y.; Silver, D.; Wierstra, D. Continuous control with deep reinforcement learning. *arXiv* **2015**, arXiv:1509.02971.
57. Mnih, V.; Badia, A.P.; Mirza, M.; Graves, A.; Lillicrap, T.; Harley, T.; Silver, D.; Kavukcuoglu, K. Asynchronous methods for deep reinforcement learning. In Proceedings of the International Conference on Machine Learning, PMLR, New York, NY, USA, 20–22 June 2016; pp. 1928–1937.
58. Espeholt, L.; Soyer, H.; Munos, R.; Simonyan, K.; Mnih, V.; Ward, T.; Doron, Y.; Firoiu, V.; Harley, T.; Dunning, I.; et al. Impala: Scalable distributed deep-rl with importance weighted actor-learner architectures. In Proceedings of the International Conference on Machine Learning. PMLR, Stockholm, Sweden, 10–15 July 2018; pp. 1407–1416.
59. Schulman, J.; Levine, S.; Abbeel, P.; Jordan, M.; Moritz, P. Trust region policy optimization. In Proceedings of the International Conference on Machine Learning, PMLR, Lille, France, 7–9 July 2015; pp. 1889–1897.
60. Schulman, J.; Wolski, F.; Dhariwal, P.; Radford, A.; Klimov, O. Proximal policy optimization algorithms. *arXiv* **2017**, arXiv:1707.06347.
61. Hart, S.; Mas-Colell, A. A simple adaptive procedure leading to correlated equilibrium. *Econometrica* **2000**, *68*, 1127–1150. [CrossRef]
62. Zinkevich, M.; Johanson, M.; Bowling, M.; Piccione, C. Regret minimization in games with incomplete information. *Adv. Neural Inf. Process. Syst.* **2007**, *20*, 1729–1736.
63. Tammelin, O. Solving large imperfect information games using CFR+. *arXiv* **2014**, arXiv:1407.5042.
64. Brown, N.; Sandholm, T. Solving imperfect-information games via discounted regret minimization. In Proceedings of the Proceedings of the AAAI Conference on Artificial Intelligence, Honolulu, HI, USA, 27 January–1 February 2019; Volume 33, pp. 1829–1836.
65. Lanctot, M.; Waugh, K.; Zinkevich, M.; Bowling, M.H. Monte Carlo Sampling for Regret Minimization in Extensive Games. In Proceedings of the NIPS, Vancouver, BC, Canada, 6–11 December 2009; pp. 1078–1086.
66. Schmid, M.; Burch, N.; Lanctot, M.; Moravcik, M.; Kadlec, R.; Bowling, M. Variance reduction in monte carlo counterfactual regret minimization (VR-MCCFR) for extensive form games using baselines. In Proceedings of the AAAI Conference on Artificial Intelligence, Honolulu, HI, USA, 27 January–1 February 2019; Volume 33, pp. 2157–2164.
67. Waugh, K.; Schnizlein, D.; Bowling, M.H.; Szafron, D. Abstraction pathologies in extensive games. In Proceedings of the AAMAS, Budapest, Hungary, 10–15 May 2009; pp. 781–788.
68. Waugh, K.; Morrill, D.; Bagnell, J.A.; Bowling, M. Solving games with functional regret estimation. In Proceedings of the Twenty-Ninth AAAI Conference on Artificial Intelligence, Austin, TX, USA, 25–30 January 2015.
69. Brown, N.; Lerer, A.; Gross, S.; Sandholm, T. Deep counterfactual regret minimization. In Proceedings of the International Conference on Machine Learning, PMLR, Long Beach, CA, USA, 9–15 June 2019; pp. 793–802.
70. Li, H.; Hu, K.; Ge, Z.; Jiang, T.; Qi, Y.; Song, L. Double neural counterfactual regret minimization. *arXiv* **2018**, arXiv:1812.10607.
71. Steinberger, E. Single deep counterfactual regret minimization. *arXiv* **2019**, arXiv:1901.07621.
72. Steinberger, E.; Lerer, A.; Brown, N. DREAM: Deep regret minimization with advantage baselines and model-free learning. *arXiv* **2020**, arXiv:2006.10410.
73. Brown, G.W. Iterative solution of games by fictitious play. *Act. Anal. Prod. Alloc.* **1951**, *13*, 374–376.
74. Heinrich, J.; Lanctot, M.; Silver, D. Fictitious self-play in extensive-form games. In Proceedings of the International Conference on Machine Learning, PMLR, Lille, France, 7–9 July 2015; pp. 805–813.
75. Heinrich, J.; Silver, D. Deep reinforcement learning from self-play in imperfect-information games. *arXiv* **2016**, arXiv:1603.01121.
76. McMahan, H.B.; Gordon, G.J.; Blum, A. Planning in the presence of cost functions controlled by an adversary. In Proceedings of the 20th International Conference on Machine Learning (ICML-03), Washington, DC, USA, 21–24 August 2003; pp. 536–543.
77. Lanctot, M.; Zambaldi, V.; Gruslys, A.; Lazaridou, A.; Tuyls, K.; Pérolat, J.; Silver, D.; Graepel, T. A unified game-theoretic approach to multiagent reinforcement learning. *Adv. Neural Inf. Process. Syst.* **2017**, *30*, 4193–4206.
78. Bansal, T.; Pachocki, J.; Sidor, S.; Sutskever, I.; Mordatch, I. Emergent complexity via multi-agent competition. *arXiv* **2017**, arXiv:1710.03748.
79. Jaderberg, M.; Dalibard, V.; Osindero, S.; Czarnecki, W.M.; Donahue, J.; Razavi, A.; Vinyals, O.; Green, T.; Dunning, I.; Simonyan, K.; et al. Population based training of neural networks. *arXiv* **2017**, arXiv:1711.09846.

80. Zhao, E.; Yan, R.; Li, J.; Li, K.; Xing, J. AlphaHoldem: High-Performance Artificial Intelligence for Heads-Up No-Limit Texas Hold'em from End-to-End Reinforcement Learning. In Proceedings of the AAAI Conference on Artificial Intelligence, Virtual Event, 22 February–1 March 2022; Volume 36, pp. 4689–4697.
81. He, K.; Zhang, X.; Ren, S.; Sun, J. Deep residual learning for image recognition. In Proceedings of the IEEE Conference on Computer Vision and Pattern Recognition, Las Vegas, NV, USA, 27–30 June 2016; pp. 770–778.
82. Johanson, M. Measuring the size of large no-limit poker games. *arXiv* **2013**, arXiv:1302.7008.
83. Zha, D.; Lai, K.H.; Cao, Y.; Huang, S.; Wei, R.; Guo, J.; Hu, X. Rlcard: A toolkit for reinforcement learning in card games. *arXiv* **2019**, arXiv:1910.04376.
84. Zhou, H.; Zhang, H.; Zhou, Y.; Wang, X.; Li, W. Botzone: An online multi-agent competitive platform for ai education. In Proceedings of the 23rd Annual ACM Conference on Innovation and Technology in Computer Science Education, Larnaca, Cyprus, 2–4 July 2018; pp. 33–38.
85. Sutton, R.S. Learning to predict by the methods of temporal differences. *Mach. Learn.* **1988**, *3*, 9–44. [CrossRef]
86. Schrittwieser, J.; Antonoglou, I.; Hubert, T.; Simonyan, K.; Sifre, L.; Schmitt, S.; Guez, A.; Lockhart, E.; Hassabis, D.; Graepel, T.; et al. Mastering atari, go, chess and shogi by planning with a learned model. *Nature* **2020**, *588*, 604–609. [CrossRef]
87. Czarnecki, W.M.; Gidel, G.; Tracey, B.; Tuyls, K.; Omidshafiei, S.; Balduzzi, D.; Jaderberg, M. Real world games look like spinning tops. *Adv. Neural Inf. Process. Syst.* **2020**, *33*, 17443–17454.
88. Lyu, X.; Baisero, A.; Xiao, Y.; Amato, C. A Deeper Understanding of State-Based Critics in Multi-Agent Reinforcement Learning. *arXiv* **2022**, arXiv:2201.01221.
89. Sutton, R. The bitter lesson. *Incomplete Ideas* **2019**, *13*, 12.
90. Schaller, R.R. Moore's law: Past, present and future. *IEEE Spectr.* **1997**, *34*, 52–59. [CrossRef]
91. Wurman, P.R.; Barrett, S.; Kawamoto, K.; MacGlashan, J.; Subramanian, K.; Walsh, T.J.; Capobianco, R.; Devlic, A.; Eckert, F.; Fuchs, F.; et al. Outracing champion Gran Turismo drivers with deep reinforcement learning. *Nature* **2022**, *602*, 223–228. [CrossRef]
92. Kurach, K.; Raichuk, A.; Stańczyk, P.; Zając, M.; Bachem, O.; Espeholt, L.; Riquelme, C.; Vincent, D.; Michalski, M.; Bousquet, O.; et al. Google research football: A novel reinforcement learning environment. *arXiv* **2019**, arXiv:1907.11180.
93. Baker, B.; Kanitscheider, I.; Markov, T.; Wu, Y.; Powell, G.; McGrew, B.; Mordatch, I. Emergent tool use from multi-agent autocurricula. *arXiv* **2019**, arXiv:1909.07528.

algorithms

MDPI

Article

Research and Challenges of Reinforcement Learning in Cyber Defense Decision-Making for Intranet Security

Wenhao Wang [1], Dingyuanhao Sun [2], Feng Jiang [2], Xingguo Chen [2] and Cheng Zhu [1,*]

[1] Science and Technology on Information Systems Engineering Laboratory, National University of Defense Technology, Changsha 410073, China; wangwenhao11@nudt.edu.cn

[2] Jiangsu Key Laboratory of Big Data Security & Intelligent Processing, Nanjing University of Posts and Telecommunications, Nanjing 210023, China; 1021041203@njupt.edu.cn (D.S.); 1320047710@njupt.edu.cn (F.J.); chenxg@njupt.edu.cn (X.C.)

* Correspondence: zhucheng@nudt.edu.cn

Abstract: In recent years, cyber attacks have shown diversified, purposeful, and organized characteristics, which pose significant challenges to cyber defense decision-making on internal networks. Due to the continuous confrontation between attackers and defenders, only using data-based statistical or supervised learning methods cannot cope with increasingly severe security threats. It is urgent to rethink network defense from the perspective of decision-making, and prepare for every possible situation. Reinforcement learning has made great breakthroughs in addressing complicated decision-making problems. We propose a framework that defines four modules based on the life cycle of threats: pentest, design, response, recovery. Our aims are to clarify the problem boundary of network defense decision-making problems, to study the problem characteristics in different contexts, to compare the strengths and weaknesses of existing research, and to identify promising challenges for future work. Our work provides a systematic view for understanding and solving decision-making problems in the application of reinforcement learning to cyber defense.

Keywords: reinforcement learning; intelligent decision-making model; cyber defense; decision-making framework

1. Introduction

The openness and security in cyberspace have always been conflicting issues. Enterprises, governments and schools hope to provide convenient services. At the same time, nobody wants their confidential data stored and the key systems in the internal network to be controlled by malicious cyber attackers. On 26 May 2021, the National Computer Network Emergency Response Technical Team of China (CNCERT) pointed out that multiple attacks continued to increase during the Coronavirus Disease 2019 (COVID-19) pandemic [1]. As the most threatening form of attack to large organizations or enterprises, Advanced Persistent Threat (APT) attacks compromised the mail servers of some local government departments by sending phishing emails related to COVID-19, which want to obtain more classified intelligence in the internal network. Apart from APT, the ransomware attacks are on the rise in 2020. A large number of corporate networks have been attacked, resulting in serious economic losses. From the analysis of ransomware, it can be seen that technical means of ransomware are constantly escalating and the selection of targets is becoming smarter. The above trends all indicate that cyber attacks on intranet security are becoming more targeted and organized.

(1) Targeted: On one hand, the development of attack techniques has enriched the existing attack surface. Experienced attackers who are able to integrate collected information and knowledge to choose appropriate actions in a task-oriented manner. Therefore, isolated defense technology no longer works in these cases, security experts need to make decisions under different threat situations, which requires more precise objectives.

(2) Organized: In order to obtain the continuous attack effect, the attacker will constantly look for vulnerabilities, and carry out more intelligent attacks by coordinating the attack resources. To fight against the attacker, it is also necessary for the defender to allocate defense resources to deal with both known and unknown threats.

These changes make intranet security increasingly challenging. Due to the continuous upgrading of attack techniques and tools, the traditional data mining based on data, machine learning, deep learning or statistical methods [2–6] cannot solve the problem of how to adapt to changes of cyber attacks, which require a new approach from the perspective of decision-making. Reinforcement learning (RL) algorithms are a popular paradigm for solving decision-making problems under complex interactions. Combined with the powerful expression mechanism of deep learning, it can effectively solve decision-making problems in a large state space. It has been successfully applied to games [7–9], chess [10,11], robots [12,13] and other fields, showing its advantages to help human decision-making. Figure 1 shows the number of relevant literature from 2016 to 2021. It can be seen that applications of reinforcement learning to cyber decision-making has drawn much attention from academia.

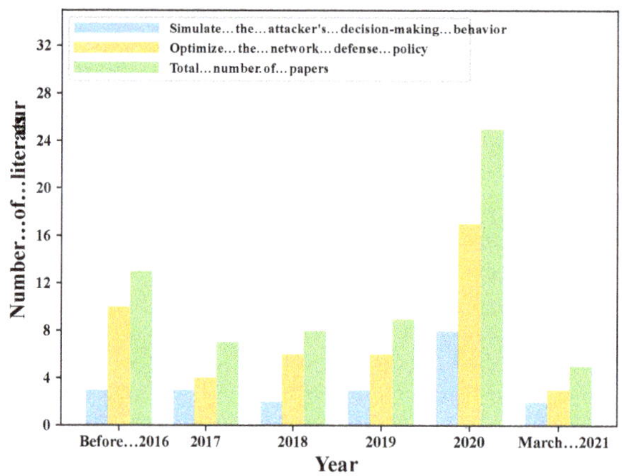

Figure 1. Research trend of cyber defense decision-making based on reinforcement learning.

However, how reinforcement learning can be used to address issues in cyber defense decision-making remains unclear. The researchers group applications of reinforcement learning in cybersecurity into DRL-based security methods for cyber-physical systems, autonomous intrusion detection techniques, and multiagent DRL-based game theory simulations [14], but do not specify how these different classifications are used to support cyber defense decision-making tasks. We extend this perspective, and focus on cyber defense decision-making for the internal network from both the attacker's and defender's perspective. The problem is analyzed from three aspects: problem characteristics, decision-making models and reinforcement learning algorithms. The characteristics of the problem are the basis of decision-making models and reinforcement learning algorithms, and determine the specific decision-making models to be used. Based on the selected models, reinforcement learning algorithms are applied to solve the problem. The major contents presented in this study are shown in Figure 2. In this survey, we make the following contributions:

(1) A new framework PDRR (Pentest Design Response Recovery) was proposed to distinguish different cyber defense decision-making tasks. The framework aimed to demarcate the boundaries of the problems, which can help researchers better understand the cyber defense decision-making problem;

(2) Based on the proposed framework, the existing research literature was summarized from the perspectives of the attack and defender respectively. We first discussed the

problem characteristics from different perspectives, and then categorized literature according to the type of problem and the adopted decision-making model, and finally compared the problem characteristics, strategies, tasks, advantages and disadvantages used in different literature.

(3) After summarizing the existing literature, we analyzed the future direction and challenges from the perspectives of reinforcement learning algorithms and cyber defense decision-making tasks respectively. The purpose of this discussion is to help researchers understand the cyber defense decision-making task more clearly, and to promote the applications of reinforcement learning algorithms to this task.

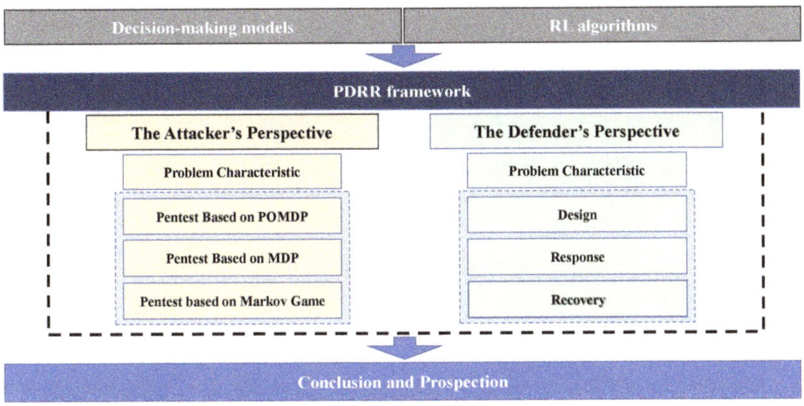

Figure 2. The structure of this paper.

The rest of this paper is organized as follows. First, we introduce the research background in Section 2. We present a framework of network defense decision-making in Section 3. In Sections 4 and 5, we summarize and compare the existing reinforcement learning research on network defense decision-making. After a summary of current works, the future research directions and challenges are pointed out in Section 6. Finally, Section 7 is the conclusion of the whole paper.

2. Research Background

In this section, we provide a brief overview of decision-making models and RL algorithms. The decision-making model abstracts interactions between decision makers and the environment, and the RL algorithm looks for optimal policies under different problem scenarios.

2.1. Decision-Making Models

In a decision-making task, an agent perceives states (or observations) from the environment and takes an action. The environment transfers to a new state (or observation) and feeds back to the agent for a reward. This interaction process between the agent and the environment will keep going or end when it reaches the end state. In this process, the agent learns an optimal policy to maximize the accumulated reward. The decision-making model has a variety of formal abstractions, in which the most classic one is the Markov Decision Process (MDP) [15]. Beyond that, the most commonly used intelligent decision-making models for cyber defense decision-making tasks include (1) Markov Game which is extended from one agent to multiple agents [16]; (2) a Partially Observable Markov Decision Process (POMDP) [17–19] which is obtained from a fully observable state to a partially observable state.

MDP: Only one agent exists in a decision-making task, and the environment satisfies the Markov property, which means that the change of state depends only on the current state and action, instead of the historical state and action. An MDP involves a quadruple

$\langle S, A, R, T\rangle$, where S indicates the status space, and A indicates the executable action space $R : s, a, s' \in S \times A \times S \rightarrow r = R(s, a, s') \in \mathbb{R}$ is a bounded reward function, and $T : S \times A \times S \rightarrow [0, 1]$ is a probability function of state transition, which satisfies the $\forall s, a$, $\sum_{s' \in S} T(s, a, s') = 1$. With its interacting with the Environment, the Agent will learn and optimize a policy $\pi : S \times A \rightarrow [0, 1]$, which is made to maximize the cumulative rewards over the long term $Return = \mathbb{E}_\pi\left[\sum_{t=0}^{\infty} \gamma^t r_t\right]$, where $\gamma \in (0, 1]$ indicates the discount rate, t indicates the discrete time step, and $r_t = R(s_t, a_t, s_{t+1})$ indicates the Rewards for t time, $a_t \sim \pi(s_t, a_t)$.

Markov Game: It is a quintuple consisting of agents:$\langle N, S, \{A_i\}_{i=1}^n, \{R_i\}_{i=1}^n, T\rangle$. Among them, N represent the set of agents, n represent the quantity of agents, and A_i represents the action space of the agent i. If $A = A_1 \times A_2 \cdots \times A_n$ is the joint action space for all agents, then $R_i : S \times A \times S \rightarrow \mathbb{R}$ is the reward function for the Agent i. $R_i(s, \vec{a}, s')$ indicates the reward for Agent i fed back by the Environment after all agents take a joint action $\vec{a}$ on the state S, and $T(s, \vec{a}, s')$ represents the probability that the Environment moves from the state s to the subsequent state s' through the joint action $\vec{a}$.

POMDP: In this process, an Agent cannot obtain the true state of the Environment, but can only observe a part of the state or the state after interference. This is called observation. POMDP is a six-tuple $\langle S, A, R, T, \Omega, O\rangle$, where $\langle S, A, R, T\rangle$ constitute a potential MDP, Ω indicates the limited set of Observations available to an Agent, and the Observation function $O : S \times A \times \Omega \rightarrow [0, 1]$ indicates that the Observation o is obtained according to the Probability $O(o|s', a)$ on the subsequent state s' after the action a is adopted on the state s, and the reward $R(s, a, s')$ is also obtained.

In addition, according to the time of the Agent's decision-making from discrete time step to continuous retention time, the Semi-Markov Decision Process (SMDP) [20,21], Continuous-time Markov Decision Process (CTMDP) [22–24] and other decision-making models can also be applied.

2.2. RL Algorithms

The basic decision-making model of RL is MDP. When the state and action space is small, RL assigns a value to each state or state-action pair, where $V^\pi(s)$ denotes the value of state s.

$$V^\pi(s) \doteq \mathbb{E}_\pi\left[\sum_{t=0}^{\infty} \gamma^t r_t | s_0 = s\right], \tag{1}$$

$Q^\pi(s, a)$ denotes the value of state-action pair (s, a).

$$Q^\pi(s, a) \doteq \mathbb{E}_\pi\left[\sum_{t=0}^{\infty} \gamma^t r_t | s_0 = s, a_0 = a\right]. \tag{2}$$

By definition, the Bellman equation is obtained:

$$V^\pi(s) = \mathbb{E}_\pi\left[R(s, a, s') + \gamma V^\pi(s')\right]. \tag{3}$$

Taking the state value function as an example, the Bellman equation can be defined by Equation (4).

$$\begin{aligned} V^\pi(s) &= \mathbb{E}_\pi\left[\sum_{t=0}^{\infty} \gamma^t r_t | s_0 = s\right] \\ &= \mathbb{E}_\pi\left[R(s, a, s') + \gamma \sum_{t=0}^{\infty} \gamma^t r_t | s_0 = s\right] \\ &= \mathbb{E}_\pi\left[R(s, a, s') + \gamma V^\pi(s')\right]. \end{aligned} \tag{4}$$

The optimal strategy π^* satisfies $\forall s \in S$, $V^*(s) = \max_\pi V^\pi(s)$, where V^* is the optimal value function, which satisfies Bellman's optimal equation.

$$V^*(s) = \max_a \mathbb{E}\Big[R(s,a,s') + \gamma V^*(s')\Big]. \tag{5}$$

Define the Bellman optimal operator $\mathbb{T} : \mathbb{R}^{|S|} \to \mathbb{R}^{|S|}$.

$$\mathbb{T}V(s) \doteq \max_a \mathbb{E}\Big[R(s,a,s') + \gamma V(s')\Big]. \tag{6}$$

The key step of the value iteration algorithm can be obtained: $V_{n+1} = \mathbb{T}V_n$. Synthesizing the multi-step Bellman evaluation operator $\mathbb{T}^\pi$, the operator $\mathbb{T}^{\lambda,\pi}$ that satisfies the compression map can be obtained in $\mathbb{T}^{\lambda,\pi}V \doteq (1-\lambda)\sum_{i=0}^{\infty}\lambda^i(\mathbb{T}^\pi)^{i+1}V$, and thus get the λ-policy iteration algorithm.

Therefore, policies can be expressed based on value functions, or can be defined directly. We summarize related RL algorithms based on tabular values, value function evaluation, and policy evaluation.

RL Algorithms Based on Tabular Values: Policy Iteration and its improved algorithm continue to repeat the two stages of Policy Evaluation and Policy Improvement until the optimal Policy and the optimal value function [25] is converged and obtained. However, the original Policy Iteration algorithm requires the value function to converge to the optimal solution for each Policy Evaluation before making a Policy Improvement. In the process of Policy Evaluation, the Value Iteration algorithm performs only one time of Iteration. When the state space is large, it takes a long time to scan all states. In this case, Asynchronous Value Iteration improves efficiency by iterating only one sample of the state space at a time. In the stage of Policy Evaluation, an optimal solution can be approximated more quickly with λ-Policy Iteration synthesizing all the multi-step Bellman evaluation operators and doing only one iteration; While Q-learning uses Bellman's optimal operator, which is $\max_a \mathbb{E}[R(s,a,s') + \gamma V(s')] \approx \max_a[R(s,a,s') + \gamma V(s')]$, to approximate the optimal value function and perform learning control. This Policy is characterized by the difference between behavioral policy and learning policy, falling into the off-policy learning.

RL Algorithms Based on Value Function Evaluation: Large-scale or continuous states and actions caused the curse of dimensionality, making the tabular value based RL algorithms ineffective. However, the ways to solve these this curse include: (i) to reduce the state and action space; (ii) to estimate the value function V or Policy by using parameters far smaller than the number of states and actions. The state and action space is mapped by function to a set of parameter dimensions that are much smaller than the size of the state and action space. The models of function estimation are usually divided into linear model, kernel method, decision-making tree, neural network, deep neural network etc. DQN [7] is a Q-learning method using deep neural network as value function estimator. By correcting the over-estimation in Q-learning (such as Double Q-learning) [26], Double-DQN [27], Averaged-DQN [28], MellowMaxDQN [29] based on the MellowMax operator [30], SoftMaxDQN [31] based on the SoftMax algorithm, and the soft greedy method based on Rankmax [32] were proposed successively.

RL Algorithms Based on Policy Evaluation: Unlike the Policy based on the representation of value function, RL based on Policy Evaluation explicitly defines the parameterized policy $\pi(a|s,\theta)$, and constantly optimizes the parameter θ by using the policy gradient ascent method according to the policy evaluation function for the parameter $J(\theta)$. The gradient of the policy is $\nabla J(\theta) \propto \sum_s \mu(s) \sum_a q_\pi(s,a) \nabla \pi(a|s,\theta)$. By using the random gradient ascent method and replacing $q_\pi(s,a)$ with Monte Carlo evaluation, the REINFORCE algorithm is obtained [33]. I the value function of state is updated by the Bootstrap method, the Actor-Critic algorithm is obtained [34]. To solve the continuous action space problem, the stochastic policy gradient algorithm can be used if the probability distribution is used as the policy function [15]. If the value function of action is used to adjust the policy directly to ensure that the choice of action is unique in the same state, the deep deterministic policy gradient (DDPG) is obtained [35,36]. The asynchronous execution of multiple simulation processes by using the multi-threading function of CPU can effectively break the correlation of training samples and obtain the Asynchronous Advantage act-critic framework

(A3C) [37]. According to the KL divergence between the old and the new policies, the learning steps are adjusted adaptively to ensure a stable policy optimization process, and then the Trust Region Policy Optimization (TRPO) algorithm can be obtained [38]. By using the proximal optimization algorithm based on the first-order optimization, the PPO (Proximal Policy Optimization) algorithm with greater stability can be obtained [39].

3. PDRR—A Framework for Recognizing Cyber Defense Decision-Making

The type of task determines how reinforcement learning algorithms are used. In an intranet network, the attacker plans to explore the network environment and get closer to the target node, who hopes to avoid being detected by defenders. Faced with the "ghostly" attacker, the defender should make good use of the defend resource to prepare for all possible situations. These different situations will determine the suitability of decision-making models and reinforcement learning algorithms. An example of the internal attack–defense is shown in Figure 3.

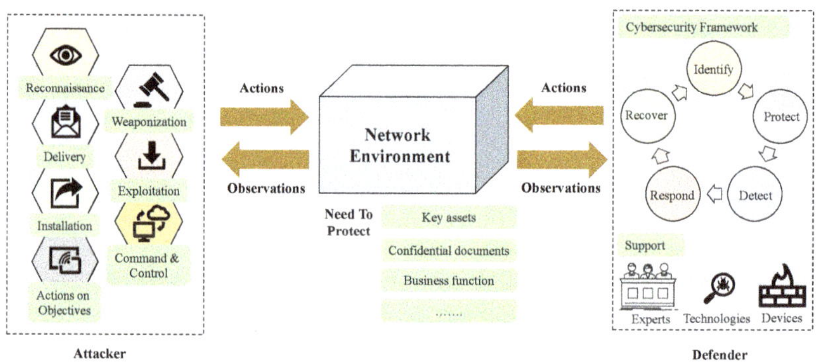

Figure 3. An example of the internal attack–defense.

Therefore, we propose the PDRR framework to distinguish different cyber defense decision-making tasks. The PDDR framework dynamic make decisions over the life cycle of threats, and integrates the perspectives of both attack and defense, which includes four modules, as shown in Figure 4.

Pentest: Pentest, also known as penetration test, attack planning, risk assessment, or vulnerability assessment, is a method to identify potential risks by simulating the decision-making process of attackers. The purpose of the test is not only to find a single vulnerability in the target network, but to form a series of attack chains (multi-step attacks) to reach the target node. The path from the starting node to the target node is called the attack path.

Design: Design is the decision-making task made by defenders to optimize the deployment of defense resources and design defense mechanisms before cyber attacks occur. The defense resources could be the experts, the number of security devices or the deployment location.

Response: Response in the process requires defenders to be able to identify, analyze, and deal with threats. In the real world, defenders often need to analyze a great number of real-time traffic data to prevent or detect threats.

Recovery: Recovery after the event refers to the decision-making mechanism that takes effect after the attack has occurred, to restore business function or minimize loss as soon as possible.

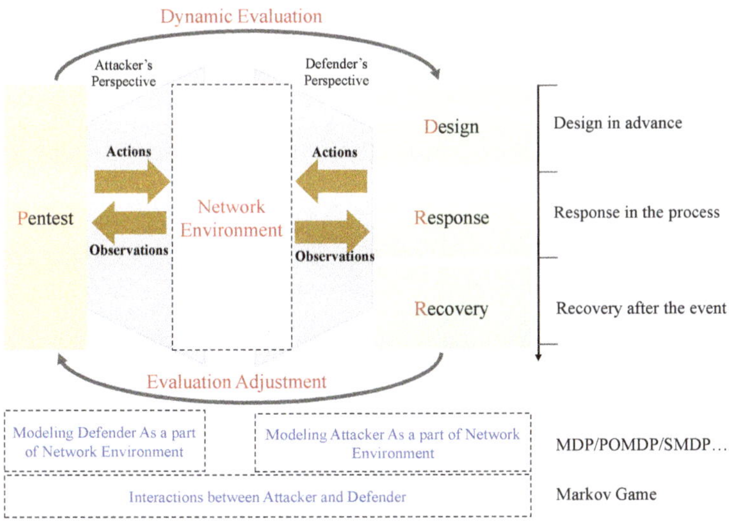

Figure 4. The PDRR framework.

The PDRR framework describes cyber defense decision-making at different stages of threats in an interactive form, forming a dynamic cyclic process. The "Pentest" task identify network defense from an attacker's perspective, dynamically evaluating potential risks by simulating the attacker's behaviors, where the attacker's observations include connectable hosts, exploitable vulnerabilities, currently privileged nodes and so on, and the attacker's actions are usually to obtain network informations and attack the selected nodes based on these informations, such as exploiting vulnerabilities, using passwords to log in to the host and so on. The "Design", "Response" and "Recovery" tasks, recognize the cyber defense at stages from the defender's perspective. Take the "Response" task for example, the defender's observations include detecting whether hosts in the network are attacked, whether there are abnormal behaviors, and whether vulnerabilities are patched and so on. While the defender's actions include reimaging hosts, patching vulnerabilities, and blocking subnets.

In addition to understanding cyber defense decisions as a whole, the biggest benefit of this is that the appropriate decision model can be selected based on the task. As the purpose of cyber defense decision-making at various stages is different, some factors can be selectively ignored or weakened when the conditions are not met. For example, when evaluating a Design module, the consequence is needed rather than the process. Depending on whether the adversary or the environment is considered, single-agent or multi-agent reinforcement learning algorithms can be selected. In terms of single agent's decision-making, the attacker or the defender shall be considered as part of dynamic network environment. Considering that attack and defense agents can interact according to certain strategies, the model should be constructed as a Markov Game.

4. Survey from the Attacker's Perspective

This section focuses on sorting out representative literature about the "Pentest" task, which is from the attacker's perspective. First, problem characteristics are discussed and, secondly, we summarized and compared the problem characteristics, decision-making model, policy and description of related research.

4.1. Problem Characteristics

In a "Pentest" task, we identify possible risks from the attacker's perspective. The attacker needs to find a feasible attack path to the target node in an unknown dynamic network environment, its objective function is usually to find the random shortest path to the target node, which is the default objective function of this section. However, in order to verify the performance of the algorithm, different objective functions are also designed.

Dynamic network environment is composed of static configurations and dynamic behaviors. Static configurations refer to network topology, installed softwares, vulnerabilities, accounts and so on. Dynamic behaviors mainly refer to behaviors of three different roles, the attacker, defender and normal user. These different behaviors can change the state of the environment, which bring uncertainty to the decision-making process [40]. In this paper, the uncertainty in the task can be divided into four parts.

Unknown environment: Due to the fact that the attack process takes place in a non-cooperative network environment, the agent needs to obtain information (such as to find the host can be connected, to figure out whether the vulnerability can be exploited and so on) by exploring the environment. Based on the information, the agent chooses appropriate actions to complete the exploration of the environment.

Partial observability: Since the attacker agent is in a non-cooperative environment, after the agent taking actions, it often cannot judge whether received observations are real states of the system, and can only maintain a certain degree of confidence. In this case, the attacker needs to constantly update its belief in the state of the environment based on the obtained information, and then select appropriate actions.

Competitive environment: Security devices and security experts are the biggest hindrances to the intrusion process. In order to clear the foothold to prevent critical systems from being controlled by the attacker, the defender take countermeasures include restarting computers, shutting down hosts, installing patches, and blocking subnets. Consequently, this will affect the decision-making process of the attacker.

Non-competitive environment: Normal users play a third role in a network environment besides the attacker and the defender. They may perform operations such as restarting hosts, establishing connections between two hosts, and installing new softwares. These actions still cause uncertainty in the decision-making process.

4.2. Related Work

When the attacker treats the defense and ordinary users as part of the environment, the attacker decision-making model can be modeled by MDP, POMDP and other models. If the attack agent and the defense agent are regarded as competitors, the Markov Game can be used to model the interaction between them. In early stage, the "Pentest" is mainly solved by the planning-based method. With continuous and deep research on the reinforcement learning method, more and more researchers use reinforcement learning to solve this problem. Table 1 summarizes representative research work in this direction in recent years.

Table 1. Survey from the attacker's perspective.

Type	Ref	U	P	C	N	Policy	Description
POMDP	[41]	✓	✓	×	×	SARSOP [42]	(1) Introduce beliefs to reflect uncertainty; (2) Excessive computational complexity.
	[43]	✓	✓	×	×	Improved SARSOP	(1) Introduce network structure to reduce complexity; (2) Not applicable when structure changes.
	[44]	✓	×	×	×	Improved RL	Introduce the network information gain to evaluate actions.
	[45]	✓	✓	✓	×	Improved Bayesian RL	Introduce the information decay factor to reflect the influence of the adversary.
	[46]	✓	✓	×	×	Improved GIP [47]	(1) Path coverage exceeds that of human in small networks; (2) Computational cost exceeds that of human on medium LANs.
MDP	[40]	✓	×	×	×	-	Modeling as deterministic planning.
	[48]	✓	×	×	×	Q-learning, Deep Q-learning	(1) Build a system to simulate attack; (2) Ignore the defender and normal user.
	[49]	✓	×	×	×	DQN with WA [50]	(1) Introduce "WA" to reduce action space; (2) Use graph embedding method to abstract state; (3) Low-dimensional vectors lacks interpretability.
	[51]	✓	×	×	×	RNN	The RNN algorithm can also work well when the environment changes.
	[52]	✓	×	×	×	A2C, Q-Learning, SARSA	(1) The A2C algorithm performs better than other algorithms. (2) State representation lacks interpretability.
	[53]	✓	×	×	×	DQN, PPO	(1) The stability and generalization are disscussed for the first time. (2) Current algorithms have poor generalization performance.
Markov Game	[54]	✓	×	✓	✓	Planning-based	Design dynamic network configurations to compare attack and defense interactions.
	[55]	✓	×	✓	×	Strategy sets	(1) The adaptability of algorithms to the adversary is verified. (2) The task is far from real world.
	[56]	✓	×	✓	✓	Q-learning, DQN, XCS [57]	(1) Designed a attack-defense multi-agent system. (2) Different action usages are not discussed.
	[58]	✓	×	✓	×	DQN	(1) Verify the algorithm's applicability. (2) The defined model is difficult to scale.

Note: U indicates "Unknown environment", P indicates "Partial observability", C indicates "Competitive environment" and N indicates "Non-competitive environment".

Pentest based on POMDP: The POMDP uses the "belief" to reflect uncertainty in attack decision-making. Sarraute et al. [41] first introduce POMDP to simulate "Pentest" task, the goal of the task is to find the shortest path to the target node. Due to the high complexity of POMDP algorithms, algorithms can only work in the environment of two hosts. In order to reduce the computational complexity, Sarraute et al. use decomposition and approximation to abstract network attack at four different levels [43]. The algorithm decomposes the network into a tree of biconnected components, then gradually calculates the cost of attacking subnets in each component, hosts in each subnet, and each individual host. Although this method reduces complexity, it ignores the consequences of possible changes in the network environment.

Due to the limited complexity of planning algorithms, some researchers began to use reinforcement learning algorithms to solve this problem. Zhou et al. introduce the network information gain to as the signal for evaluating actions' reward [44]. The information gain is equal to $H(P) = \sum_{j=1}^{|p|}(p_j \log p_j + (1 - p_j)\log(1 - p_j))$, where P_j represents the vector of operating system, open service, port, and protection mechanism probability distribution before (after) taking actions. Experiments showed that RL algorithms with information gain are more effective than other algorithms at finding attack paths.

In addition to considering an "unknown environment", Jonathon et al. also took into account the influence of the opponent, and proposed an information decay factor to represent the observation of the attacker [59]. The author used the Bernoulli process to model the defender's behaviors, and verified that the Bayesian Reinforcement Learning (BRL) algorithms combined with the information decay factor is significantly better than the baseline algorithm in terms of winning rate and reward.

Ghanem built an automated penetration testing system called "IAPTS" to solve the problem of automated Pentest in large network environments [46]. The system preprocesses the original data, and obtains the evaluations by constructing POMDP model to use PERSEUS [15], GIP [47] and PEGASUS [60] algorithms in combination, and then made it available to human experts. The experiments are carried out in small and medium networks. Experimental results showed that the improved GIP algorithm performed better than manual experts on small networks, but the computational cost was higher on medium LANs, requiring more in-depth research on the algorithm.

Pentest Based on MDP: Through existing research, it can be seen that when using POMDP to model the attack decision-making process, due to the computational complexity of algorithms, the scale of applicable scenarios is limited. Therefore, more and more researchers choose to model the "Pentest" task with MDP, where the outcomes of actions are deterministic [40]. This change allows researchers to build the task with more consideration for the similarity of actions to the real world, the changes in the environment, and the presence of the opponent and so on.

Schwartz designed and built a new open-source network attack simulator (NAS) for studying the attack decision-making process [48], and compared different RL algorithms' convergence times. This system promoted the research of reinforcement learning algorithms in the direction of "Pentest", but the abstraction of state space is too simple and lacks consideration of the dynamic environment, so it needs to be further deepened.

Nguyen et al., focused on the problem of large-scale action space reduction [49]. The author combined the DQN algorithm with "Wolpertinger Architecture(WA)" [50] to embed multilevel action. The sensitive machine attacked proportion of the proposed algorithm was obviously better than other algorithms, and was also applicable in the medium and large-scale network. Besides, the graph embedding method is first used to represent the state space, which is worth exploring.

By focusing on how to reduce the number of features represented in the state space and how to approximate the state-action space with a small set of features, Pozdniakov et al. performed the experiment to compare the advantages and disadvantages of three algorithms: Q-learning based on table, RNN with Q-learning and RNN with Q-learning after network configuration changes [51]. The results showed that, compared with Q-learning based on table, RNN with Q-learning can converge faster and respond to the change of environment, showing the potential of model-free learning for automated pentest.

Maeda et al., used the real payloads of attack tools as actions for attack decision-making, and applied A2C, Q-learning and SARSA algorithms to solve the task [52]. The experimental results showed that the A2C algorithm has the best effect in cumulative average reward. However, the defined state representation in the article lacks a certain degree of interpretability.

In order to test the stability and generalization of various DRL algorithms [53], Sultana et al. built five experimental scenarios with different topologies, services, and application configurations based on the Network Attack Simulator (NASim) platform [59]. In the test of stability, the returns of DQN algorithm and PPO were relatively stable. In the test of generalization, when the evaluation network deviates from the training environment, the performance of DQN and PPO algorithms failed to adapt to all experimental scenarios, even worse than the performance of random algorithm in the same environment, which pointed out the possible research directions.

Pentest Based on Markov Game: Markov Game in "Pentest" treats the attacker and the defender as the competing agents and designs a Game model to compare the effectiveness of the two sides's policies. Applebaum et al. systematically modeled dynamic network environment, and used the method of statistical analysis to discuss the winning and losing situations of both players under different environment configurations [54].

Elderman et al., modeled the attack–defense game as zero-sum two-player Markov Game with incomplete information. In the game, agents played in turn-based interactions based on their observations. The attacker tried to reach the target node, while the defender tried to protect the network and stop the attacker. In this process, the decision-making of both sides was influenced by the hidden information [55]. The experiment compared the winning and losing of players using different strategies, and found that neither side can ensure long-term victory under the same strategy.

Niculae built a more realistic multi-agent system, where included the interactions among attackers, defenders and normal users [56]. In the system, ten attack actions, three defense actions and three normal user actions were designed. In addition, attributes such as reliability, duration, noise, and crash probability were added to the attack action to describe the uncertainty of the interaction process. The experiments compared reinforcement learning algorithms such as DQN and Q-learning with rule-based algorithms, results showed that the DQN algorithm had stronger generalization ability, but required a large amount of training time. However, it did not analyze how often the different types of actions designed were used in its algorithm.

Bland et al., used the Petri net as a modeling tool to simulate the attack decision-making process [58]. The author designed several groups of comparative experiments in which static attackers versus dynamic defenders and dynamic attackers versus dynamic defenders. In these comparative experiments, reinforcement learning algorithms using greedy policies improved performance over time, both in achieving player goals and reducing costs. However, using the Petri net requires a detailed definition of the transition between different states, which makes the work less applicable.

5. Survey from the Defender's Perspective

Unlike research from the attacker's perspective, the studies from the defender's perspective needs to consider various situations in the defense decision-making. Based on the PDRR framework, this section reviews research in terms of the three defense phases: Design, Response, and Recovery.

5.1. Problem Characteristics

Although the defender can control the internal network, the agent does not know whether the attack exists and the possible consequences of the attack. Therefore, its decision-making process still has the following challenges.

False Positive Rate: In the abnormal detection process, the detection by the defender will cause a certain false positive rate due to the existence of the anti-detection technology of unknown and known threat samples. This will happen for the high degree of fitting between the existing samples and the malicious samples, or forged signals sent by the attacker to the defense detection algorithm. The existence of a false positive rate will further improve the complexity of learning, leading to the wrong judgment of defense decision.

Local Information Known: Security experts find it difficult to grasp all the information of the network environment in real time due to the dynamic and huge scale of the network environment, though they have the authority to manage the network environment. Therefore, the defender can only manage and maintain the network environment of limited scale, and such local limitation can be alleviated by means of multi-agent cooperative communication, while increasing the difficulty of decision-making.

Constraint of Resources: The attack may be launched at any time using different vulnerable points, and the protection, detection, response and recovery of defense will take up or consume certain resources. Given this, an unrestricted commitment of defense resources is impossible. These resources may be the cost of equipment deployment, or personnel, time and other cost factors. Hence, in a network defense scenario, the defender needs to respond as quickly as possible and cut the cost as much as possible to complete the task.

Table 2 summarizes and compares representative research literature from the defender's perspective. Like the attacker perspective, we also classify these three tasks from the adopted decision-making model, and compared decision-making models, task, strategies used and descriptions of related research.

Table 2. Survey from the defender's perspective.

Type	Model	Ref	F	L	C	Policy	Description
Design	MDP	[61]	×	×	✓	Value Iteration	Dynamic optimization algorithm and manual intervention are combined.
		[62]	✓	×	✓	Q-learning	Proposed a new adaptive control framework.
		[63]	×	✓	✓	Q-learning	Proposed a spoofing resource deploy algorithm without strict constraints on attacker.
	Markov Game	[64]	–	×	✓	Q-learning	An algorithm that can obtain the optimal security configuration in multiple scenarios;
Response	MDP	[65]	✓	×	✓	DDQN, A3C	(1) Design an autonomous defense scenarios and interfere with training process; (2) observation is less limited.
		[66]	✓	✓	×	DQN	(1) The convergence is accelerated by expert artificial reward (2) Limited reward setting.
		[67]	×	×	×	Q-learning	(1) Knowledge graph is used to guide the algorithm design (2) High trust in open source data.
		[68]	–	×	✓	Value Iteration	(1) Introduces a botnet detector based on RL; (2) Action cost not taken into account.
		[69]	–	×	✓	Reward structure	Multi-agent network with collaborative framework and group decision-making.
		[70]	×	×	×	Sarsa	(1) Hierarchical collaborative team learning can extend to large scenarios; (2) Difficult to guarantee convergence.
	Markov Game	[71]	×	✓	✓	Q-learning	(1) Pareto optimization is used to improve Q-learning's efficiency; (2) The attacker takes random actions.
		[72]	×	✓	✓	Q-learning	(1) A defense policy selection simulator is constructed; (2) Random attack actions.
		[73]	✓	✓	×	Q-learning	(1) Respond to attacks with limited information; (2) Rely on expertise to evaluate rewards.
		[74]	✓	✓	✓	MA-ARNE	Solving resource utilization and effective detection of APT with MARL.
	POMDP	[75]	×	✓	✓	Q-learning	POMDP is modeled based on Bayes attack graph.
		[76]	×	✓	✓	Q-learning	(1) The transfer probability is estimated using Thompson sampling; (2) Fixed attack transfer probability.
		[77]	✓	✓	×	Value Iteration	(1) Adaptively adjust the recognition configuration according to the false alarm rate; (2) Cannot face adaptive attackers well.
		[78]	✓	✓	✓	Q-learning	(1) Multi-agent collaboration model based on signal and hierarchy; (2) Cannot guarantee the convergence.
		[79]	✓	✓	✓	Q-learning	(1) A decentralized threat perception model is proposed; (2) Value functions needs expert knowledge.
	SMDP	[80,81]	–	×	✓	Q-learning;	The interaction in the honeypot is modeled as a semi-Markov process.
Recovery	MDP	[82]	–	×	×	DDPG	(1) The continuous numerical method is used to obtain a better real-time recovery policy; (2) Low convergence rate.
		[83]	–	×	×	Q-learning	(1) Proposed an effective strategy based on a realistic power flow model with RL; (2) Low convergence rate.
		[84]	–	×	×	DDPG	Applied reinforcement learning to backup policy.

Note: F indicates "False Positive Rate", O indicates "Local Information Known ", C indicates "Constraint of Resources".

5.2. Design

"Design" task refers to deploying resources or designing mechanisms to deal with different cyber attacks.

The moving target defense (MTD) is proposed to "change the rules of the game" facing with attacks [85]. MTD mainly works to confuse the attacker by constantly shifting the attack surface, increase the attack cost and difficulty, and improve the resilience of the defense system. Ganesan et al. [61] proposed a dynamic stochastic model for scheduling security analysts. The risk can be kept below target levels by coordinating the allocation of staff and sensor resources.

Winterrose et al. [62] has developed a method based on online reinforcement learning to achieve the ideal balance between system security and system performance in a dynamic threat environment. With this method, the best parameters needed to defend against adversaries in the security performance space can be autonomously computed even as the threat changes. However, it usually consumes a lot of energy and resources.

In addition to changing the attack surface, researchers have also countered the attack by deploying network deception devices such as honeypots. Wang et al. [63] used Q-learning-based agents to find the best policy of deploying spoofed resources. The algorithm solves the problem that the static deployment of spoofing resources is easy to identify and bypass. In the actual network experiment, this method can reach the defense success rate of 80%.

Jiang et al. [86] proposed the concept of "moderate security", which means that we should seek a risk-input balance when considering the constraints of resources and other actual conditions. In other words, the limited resources should be used to make a reasonable decision, so the game theory can be used to study the strategies of both players.

A good defense mechanism "Design" should also be found in attack–defense confrontation. Panfili [64] et al. obtained the optimal security configuration by searching Nash Equilibrium of multi-agent attack and defense game. It can minimize the damage caused by an attack, even making it less than the cost of executing the attack policy.

5.3. Response

"Response" task requires the defender to be able to detect abnormal network traffic and take appropriate response measures, especially in response to unknown attacks.

A zero-day vulnerability is a vulnerability that has not been disclosed. Before releasing system patches for zero-day vulnerabilities, how to actively establish a response mechanism during the repair window to deal with unknown cyber attacks is a challenging problem. Sun et al. [71] modeled the network attack and defense as a zero-sum multi-objective game in a simple network topology, and proposed the Q-learning algorithm with pareto optimization for the "Response" task, where helps network security analysis improved significantly. Based on the above research, Sun et al. improved the granularity and authenticity of the network model [72]. A set of defense policy selection simulator was built to the Q-learning algorithm with pareto optimization. However, in the above two studies, the attackers used random actions that did not fit well with real attacks.

Hu et al. [75] modeled the "Response" task as a partially observable Markov decision process on a bayesian attack graph. In the experiments, Q-learning was used to identify cyber attacks, and verified the performance of the algorithm in a small network. However, it is assumed here that the process of responding is phased, making it difficult to detect online. Based on the previous work, Hu et al. proposed a new adaptive network defense mechanism [76]. The task was modeled as a POMDP problem with uncertain state transition, and the state transition probability was estimated by using Thompson sampling. The optimal defense action was obtained based on reinforcement learning without any false positives. Based on the real network attack numerical simulation, the cost-effectiveness of the algorithm was verified. However in the real world, the attack value may change continuously.

Han et al. [65] explored the feasibility of reinforcement learning algorithm for autonomous defense in SDN and the false positive problem of attack. In their experiment, the defense agent used various reinforcement learning methods to learn the best operations to protect critical servers while isolating as few nodes as possible. In addition, in their adversarial training, the attacker can damage the reward and state of the defensive agent, thus causing false positives. Therefore, the reinforcement learning may make sub-optimal or even wrong decisions, which indirectly proves that the adversarial training can reduce such negative effects for the defender.

The false positive rate and defense expenses will increase with the rising number, type and complexity of network attacks. As an attacker will often hide from the network's constant real-time monitoring after successfully entering a network environment, the defender should implement appropriate means to identify and respond to abnormalities in time, formulate corresponding response mechanisms to handle abnormal detection results containing false positive rate. Chung et al. [73] proposed an automatic detection technique to respond to the hostile behavior of suspicious users. This is based on the game model of expert knowledge and uses Q-learning to solve. Experiments based on simulation showed that, when the information of the opponent is limited, the Naive Q-learning can effectively learn the behavior of the opponent and has better performance than other algorithms with limited assumptions. Due to the lack of consistency in security metrics, the damage and reward of attacks were mainly based on the expert knowledge.

Liu [66] studied the interactive reinforcement learning method which was used to improve the adaptability and real-time performance of intrusion detection. Based on the experience replay buffer and Long Short-Term Memory (LSTM) optimization learning, the feedback of network security experts was added in the reward to accelerate convergence. In addition, the expert also reported different rewards based on the difference between true positive and false negative rates. An excellent detection effect was achieved on the NSL-KDD dataset [87].

Sahabandu et al. [74] studied how to weight the resource efficiency and detection effectiveness in dynamic information flow tracking analysis models. Their game model captured the security costs, false positives and missing positives associated with dynamic information flow tracking, and a multi-agent average reward Nash equilibrium algorithm is proposed (MA-ARNE) was proposed, which was able to converge to an average reward Nash equilibrium on the ransomware data set.

Piplai et al. [67] used the prior knowledge represented by the network security knowledge graph to guide the reinforcement learning algorithm to detect the malicious process, and applied the prior knowledge mined from the open text information source describing the malicious network attack to guide the reinforcement learning algorithm to adaptively change parameters to adjust the value function and explore the probability. The simulation experiment proved that such system was better than the basic reinforcement learning system in terms of detecting malicious software.

Modern botnets often operate in a secretive manner, which make it difficult to detect. Venkatesan et al. [68] based on reinforcement learning, detected the presence of botnets by deploying honeypots and detectors in a simulated environment, and performed the comparative experiments with static policies in PeerSim [88]. The results showed that the performance was improved significantly.

Alauthman et al. [77] proposed a detection system combined with reinforcement learning technology, in which, the network traffic reduction technology was mainly used to deal with large-scale network traffic. As a result, the botnet hosts with high accuracy (98.3%) and relatively low false positive rate (0.012%) can be detected, which was better than other detection methods. Dynamic improving system based on reinforcement learning can alleviate the dynamic changes existing in botnets, but it cannot well face the methods of avoiding detection taken by botnet administrators, such as rootkits (A malicious software that can hide itself and files and networks from the host).

In response to different attacks, Honeypot technology is adopted to protect the network. Honeypot technology is an active defense technology which can effectively defend network resources by deceiving attackers to obtain information [89]. Huang et al. [80,81] applied a semi-Markov decision process to characterize the random transitions and linger time of the attackers in the honeypot, and designed a defense scheme where the agent actively interacted with the attacker in the honeypot to increase the attacker's attack cost and collect threat information. According to the numerical results, the proposed adaptive policy can quickly attract attackers to the target honeypot and interact with them for a long enough time to obtain valuable threat information. At the same time, the penetration probability was kept at a low level.

The multi-agent system, a classic model of distributed artificial intelligence, can provide better adaptability and more effective decision-making for cyber defense [90]. Miller and Inoue [69] used the Synergistic and Perceptual Intrusion Detection with reinforcement (SPIDeR) [91] and an agent with its Self-Organizing Map (SOM) to cooperate to detect anomalies. Additionally, decisions were made by the central blackboard system in SPIDeR based on reinforcement learning. SPIDeR showed positive results in 1999 KDD Cup [92].

Malialis [70] also introduced a multi-agent cooperative architecture to build a layered anomaly detection framework, so as to improve the response speed and scalability of intrusion detection, and studied the cooperative team learning of agents. However, similar to the study of Servin et al. [78], the large-scale collaborative learning of distributed agents was difficult to guarantee the convergence.

Liu et al. [79] designed a collaborative network threat perception model (DDI-MDPS) based on decentralized coordination to solve the problems such as high pressure, low fault tolerance, low damage resistance and high construction cost of the static centralized network intrusion detection system (NIDS). In addition, they tested the DDI MDPs model based on the open data CICIDS2017, and the simulation results proved that the interaction between multiple agents enhanced the network threat perception. However, designing value functions for agents to deal with the network threat perception problems in unknown networks largely relies on prior domain knowledge.

5.4. Recovery

"Response" task needs the defender to be able to take measures to restore network functionality after cyber attacks have occurred.

In the case of unavoidable exceptions or damages, the defender should take adequate measures to restore the normal operation of the network in time and minimize the impact caused by attacks. For critical power infrastructure, the system can quickly recover by using reinforcement learning technology after detecting and removing the invasion [93]. A malicious attacker can trip all transmission lines to block power transmission as long as it takes control of a substation. As a result, asynchrony will emerge between the separated regions interconnected by these transmission lines.

Wei et al. [82], proposed a recovery policy for how to properly choose the reclosing time, which uses a deep reinforcement learning framework, so as to reclose the tripped transmission lines at the optimal reclosing time. This policy was given with adaptability and real-time decision-making ability to uncertain network attack scenarios. Numerical results showed that the policy proposed can greatly minimize the impact of network attacks in different scenarios.

Wu et al. [83] modeled the cascade failure and recovery process in the power system as MDP and used Q-learning to identify the optimal line sequence recovery sequence. The recovery performance of this method was proven to be better than that of the baseline heuristic recovery policy in IEEE57 simulation systems.

Debus et al. modeled the threat model and decision-making problem mathematically for the traditional network defense methods, and transformed the problem of finding the best backup policy into a reinforcement learning problem [84]. The storage device updating scheme based on the proposed algorithm can achieve or even exceed the performance of the existing scheme. In addition, thanks to the function approximation property of the policy network, the algorithm not only provides a fixed set of update rules and steps, but also can deal with the deviation from the planned scheme and dynamically adjust the backup scheme back to the best route.

6. Open Directions and Challenges

According to existing literature, It can be seen that most of the work still remains on how to apply reinforcement learning algorithms. Therefore, this paper makes an outlook from both reinforcement learning and cyber defense decision-making perspectives.

6.1. Challenges in Reinforcement Learning Algorithms

In terms of existing studies on reinforcement learning, reinforcement learning algorithms are too simple to solve the real problems in cyber defense decision-making. Therefore, the reinforcement learning research in network defense decision-making still needs to overcome the following challenges:

Appropriate Objective Function and Optimization Method: Different from supervised learning, there is no unified optimal goal because the reinforcement learning has no labels. Objective functions are designed in terms of stability, convergence rate and accuracy of value function. However, what kind of objective function is more suitable for the policy solution of network attack and defense decision-making task needs to be further studied. In addition, the optimization methods such as batch gradient descent, random gradient descent, least squares, Kalman filtering, Gauss process optimization, proximal optimization, Newton method etc. should be further discussed given the objective function.

Value Functions and Policy Gradients: Both reinforcement learning algorithms are based on the value function and policy gradient ascending algorithm which directly defines a policy exist in many network attack and defense decision-making tasks. Reinforcement learning algorithms based on a value function are usually used in discrete action space, while policy gradient based reinforcement learning algorithms are usually used in continuous action space. However, how to define a policy for a specific task should be considered carefully [15].

Sparse Reward Challenge: In network attack and defense decision-making tasks, rewards are usually sparse. Sparse reward is one of the important factors affecting the convergence rate of reinforcement learning. Using reward shaping to make sparse rewards denser can effectively improve the convergence rate of learning, one of whose cores is to satisfy policy invariance [94]. There is another scheme, where the decision-making behavioral data of experts are collected and the techniques such as inverse reinforcement learning are used to reverse the reward function [95,96].

Non-stationary Challenges: Reinforcement learning assumes that the environment is stationary: Time-independent uncertainty. However, in the network attack and defense game, the following two situations lead to nonstationary environment:

(1) Environmental uncertainty may be time-varying [97], for example, the network topology disturbed by uncertain factors (abnormal shutdown, etc.) may lead to the failure of nodes;

(2) The competitive game between attacking and defending agents causes the environment to respond to different action pairs.

Such a nonstationary environment will seriously affect the convergence of reinforcement learning algorithm. Therefore, it is necessary to conduct context detection, track potential changes [98], predict [99], and construct a model to accommodate it, such as meta-reinforcement learning [100] and worst case idea [101] etc.

Non-Ergodicity Challenges: Reinforcement learning assumes that the environment satisfies Ergodicity, also known as Ergodicity of each state, which means that the probability of each state is non-zero and converges to a definite value. However, in the network attack and defense game, this ergodicity is broken, causing that some nodes in the topology are broken at a very low possibility. This brings a strong challenge to reinforcement learning. Given this, how to design a stable and efficient reinforcement learning under the assumption of non-ergodicity is much needed, such as using utility function based on a value function [102–104].

6.2. Challenges in Cyber Defense Decision-Making

Network defense decision-making requires in-depth study of problem characteristics in combination with real scenarios, so as to provide a basis for more convenient simulation experiments and theoretical analysis, as well as better evaluation of defense decision-making effects. The challenges in network defense decision-making are as follows.

Task model: In order to accurately characterize the characteristics of cyber attack and defense interactions, the researchers proposed FilpIt [105,106], Hide-and- Seek [107–110], two-person zero-sum game [55] and other task models to analyze the decision-making behavior of both attacker and defender. The above models have abstracted the characteristics of network attack and defense, such as concealability and dynamics, but it is still difficult to provide guidance for the decision-making process due to the theoretical reasons as follows: (1) The design of environment, action and state of the existing models is abstract and lacks the mapping with the real world. (2) Most network attack and defense games are abstracted as two-person zero-sum games, whose design of reward and ending mechanism cannot accurately reflect the decision-making preferences of both attacker and defender. Therefore, to conduct a more in-depth analysis on the characteristics of attack and defense game in actual task scenarios such as Pentesting and virus infection is necessary.

Table 3. Comparison of Current Network Training and Testing Platform.

Network Implementation	Model	Literature	Convenience	Fidelity	Expansibility
Network Simulation	MulVAL [111]	[112–115]	Middle	Low	Low
	Petri net [116]	[58]	Low	High	High
	NS3 [117]	[118]	Middle	High	Middle
	Mininet [119]	[65]	Middle	Middle	Middle
Testing platform	NASim [59]	[48]	High	Middle	High
	CyberBattleSim [120]	-	High	Middle	High

Simulation platform: Previous studies mainly verify the effectiveness of network attack and defense decision-making algorithm by MulVAL [111], NS3 [117], Petri net [116] real data playback or using virtual machine network. In Table 3, the relevant work of the existing training and testing platform is summarized, which is divided into three indexes of high, middle and low to measure the convenience, fidelity and expansibility of each network training and testing platform.

(1) Convenience: How easy the platform is to use, which is evaluated on the basis of the size of the package, the platform on which it is running, the language in which it is compiled, and how it is installed.
(2) Fidelity: Closeness to the real world, which is mainly evaluated from action design, network environment, evaluation indexes, etc.
(3) Expansibility: The difficulty of secondary development, which is evaluated based on the open source degree of the platform and the difficulty of the experiment of researchers.

Obviously, using NS3, real data playback and other methods to build the training test environment will bring a lot of unnecessary details in terms of decision-making, such as raw data preprocessing or traffic packet parsing. As a result, the processing complexity of the algorithm is increased. However, Petri net or MulVAL and other methods to build the training testing environment need a lot of pre-defined work, which is difficult to reflect the dynamic of network attack and defense. Therefore, it has become a current development trend for researchers to use multi-agent methods to build training and testing platforms for attack and defense, such as the Network Attack Simulator [59] by Schwartz and CyberBattleSim [120] by Microsoft. However, these training test platforms are still developing, which are difficult to define and expand the elements of attacking and defending actions, states and tasks flexibly. So, to further develop diversified training environments to meet the needs of decision-making algorithm is required.

Best response strategy: In single-agent reinforcement learning, an agent repeatedly interacts with the environment to optimize its policies until there is no way to provide further performance (as measured by rewards or other metrics). However, the attacker in the process of defense may have more than one policy; the defender therefore shall comprehensively consider different policies, different starting points, and even different attackers with different capabilities, so as to make the optimal response as far as possible. In this case, empirical game analysis and reinforcement learning [121] shall be used to find the optimal defense response policy in the policy space.

State representation: The state of the decision-making process needs to consider elements such as network topology, vulnerabilities, and accounts, and Network topology is a natural graph structure. Therefore, graph neural networks, graph convolutional deep neural networks [122,123] and graph deep neural networks [124,125] can be used to effectively represent the state and observation of network attack and defense decision-making processes. However, only little literature [50] discusses the use of graph embedding method, more in-depth research should be performed on how to better represent the multidimensional characteristics in the attack and defense decision-making and analyze the differences between different representation methods.

Centralized control and distributed control: In the existing research on network attack and defense decision-making, most of them adopt distributed cooperative mode to control multiple agents for intrusion detection and anomaly detection. However, large-scale collaborative learning of distributed agents was difficult to guarantee the convergence [69,70,78]. Furthermore, the hostile behavior has gradually taken on the purposeful, organizational characteristics in the current network attack and defense decision-making environment. Therefore, the most important work in the next stage is to study a set of centralized control learning methods, and multiple agents are controlled to make unified decisions at the same time, in order to respond to the hostile behavior with clear goals and organizational discipline.

7. Conclusions

Internet technology is the foundation of cyberspace, while network security is an inevitable problem in the development of cyberspace. Reinforcement learning, as a new technology, has been used by many researchers to solve the cyber defense decision-making problem. In this paper, based on the summary of intelligent decision-making models and reinforcement learning technology, representative literature is summarized and contrasted from perspectives of the attacker and the defender, respectively. The former focuses on the uncertain process of attack decision-making, and the latter focuses on addressing the various scenarios that cyber defenses may face.

This paper is prepared to sort out the technology and application of reinforcement learning in the field of network attack and defense decision-making, and provide ideas for further research on network attack and defense decision-making by systematically analyzing the advantages and disadvantages of existing research. At the end of the paper, the challenges of reinforcement learning and network defense decision-making are summarized. It can be seen that reinforcement learning shows the potential to solve cyber defense decision-making problems, but the task models, platforms and algorithms still need further research to promote this direction.

Author Contributions: Conceptualization, W.W.; investigation, D.S. and F.J.; methodology, W.W.; resources, X.C.; writing—original draft, W.W.; writing—review & editing, C.Z. All authors have read and agreed to the published version of the manuscript.

Funding: Supported by National Natural Science Foundation of China, General Program, 71571186.

Institutional Review Board Statement: Not applicable.

Informed Consent Statement: Not applicable.

Data Availability Statement: Not applicable.

Conflicts of Interest: The authors declare no conflict of interest.

References

1. CNCERT. The Overview of Chinese's Internet Security Situation in 2020. 2021. Available online: https://www.cert.org.cn/publish/main/46/index.html (accessed on 13 March 2022).
2. Buczak, A.L.; Guven, E. A survey of data mining and machine learning methods for cyber security intrusion detection. *IEEE Commun. Surv. Tutor.* **2015**, *18*, 1153–1176. [CrossRef]
3. Masduki, B.W.; Ramli, K.; Saputra, F.A.; Sugiarto, D. Study on implementation of machine learning methods combination for improving attacks detection accuracy on Intrusion Detection System (IDS). In Proceedings of the 2015 International Conference on Quality in Research (QiR), Lombok, Indonesia, 10–13 August 2015; pp. 56–64.
4. Li, J.H. Cyber security meets artificial intelligence: A survey. *Front. Inf. Technol. Electron. Eng.* **2018**, *19*, 1462–1474. [CrossRef]
5. Xin, Y.; Kong, L.; Liu, Z.; Chen, Y.; Li, Y.; Zhu, H.; Gao, M.; Hou, H.; Wang, C. Machine learning and deep learning methods for cybersecurity. *IEEE Access* **2018**, *6*, 35365–35381. [CrossRef]
6. Dasgupta, D.; Akhtar, Z.; Sen, S. Machine learning in cybersecurity: A comprehensive survey. *J. Def. Model. Simul.* **2020**. [CrossRef]
7. Mnih, V.; Kavukcuoglu, K.; Silver, D.; Graves, A.; Antonoglou, I.; Wierstra, D.; Riedmiller, M. Playing atari with deep reinforcement learning. *arXiv* **2013**, arXiv:1312.5602.
8. Vinyals, O.; Babuschkin, I.; Czarnecki, W.M.; Mathieu, M.; Dudzik, A.; Chung, J.; Choi, D.H.; Powell, R.; Ewalds, T.; Georgiev, P.; et al. Grandmaster level in StarCraft II using multi-agent reinforcement learning. *Nature* **2019**, *575*, 350–354. [CrossRef]
9. Berner, C.; Brockman, G.; Chan, B.; Cheung, V.; Dębiak, P.; Dennison, C.; Farhi, D.; Fischer, Q.; Hashme, S.; Hesse, C.; et al. Dota 2 with large scale deep reinforcement learning. *arXiv* **2019**, arXiv:1912.06680.
10. Silver, D.; Huang, A.; Maddison, C.J.; Guez, A.; Sifre, L.; Van Den Driessche, G.; Schrittwieser, J.; Antonoglou, I.; Panneershelvam, V.; Lanctot, M.; et al. Mastering the game of Go with deep neural networks and tree search. *Nature* **2016**, *529*, 484–489. [CrossRef]
11. Silver, D.; Schrittwieser, J.; Simonyan, K.; Antonoglou, I.; Huang, A.; Guez, A.; Hubert, T.; Baker, L.; Lai, M.; Bolton, A.; et al. Mastering the game of go without human knowledge. *Nature* **2017**, *550*, 354–359. [CrossRef]
12. Gu, S.; Holly, E.; Lillicrap, T.; Levine, S. Deep reinforcement learning for robotic manipulation with asynchronous off-policy updates. In Proceedings of the 2017 IEEE International Conference on Robotics and Automation (ICRA), Singapore, 29 May–3 June 2017; pp. 3389–3396.
13. Zha, D.; Xie, J.; Ma, W.; Zhang, S.; Lian, X.; Hu, X.; Liu, J. DouZero: Mastering DouDizhu with Self-Play Deep Reinforcement Learning. *arXiv* **2021**, arXiv:2106.06135.
14. Nguyen, T.T.; Reddi, V.J. Deep reinforcement learning for cyber security. *IEEE Trans. Neural Netw. Learn. Syst.* **2019**. [CrossRef]
15. Sutton, R.S.; Barto, A.G. *Reinforcement Learning: An Introduction*, 2nd ed.; The MIT Press: Cambridge, MA, USA, 2018.
16. Littman, M.L. Markov games as a framework for multi-agent reinforcement learning. In *Machine Learning Proceedings 1994*; Elsevier: Burlington, MA, USA, 1994; pp. 157–163.
17. Murphy, K.P. A Survey of POMDP Solution Techniques. *Environment* **2000**, *2*, X3.
18. Ross, S.; Pineau, J.; Paquet, S.; Chaib-Draa, B. Online planning algorithms for POMDPs. *J. Artif. Intell. Res.* **2008**, *32*, 663–704. [CrossRef]
19. Warrington, A.; Lavington, J.W.; Scibior, A.; Schmidt, M.; Wood, F. Robust asymmetric learning in pomdps. In Proceedings of the International Conference on Machine Learning, Virtual, 18–24 July 2021; pp. 11013–11023.
20. Huang, Y.; Guo, X.; Song, X. Performance analysis for controlled semi-Markov systems with application to maintenance. *J. Optim. Theory Appl.* **2011**, *150*, 395–415. [CrossRef]
21. Huang, Y.; Guo, X.; Li, Z. Minimum risk probability for finite horizon semi-Markov decision processes. *J. Math. Anal. Appl.* **2013**, *402*, 378–391. [CrossRef]
22. Piunovskiy, A.; Zhang, Y. *Continuous-Time Markov Decision Processes*; Springer: Cham, Switzerland, 2020.
23. Guo, X.; Liao, Z.W. Risk-sensitive discounted continuous-time Markov decision processes with unbounded rates. *SIAM J. Control Optim.* **2019**, *57*, 3857–3883. [CrossRef]
24. Zhang, Y. Continuous-time Markov decision processes with exponential utility. *SIAM J. Control Optim.* **2017**, *55*, 2636–2660. [CrossRef]
25. Bertsekas, D.; Tsitsiklis, J.N. *Neuro-Dynamic Programming*; Athena Scientific: Belmont, MA, USA, 1996.
26. Hasselt, H.V. Double Q-learning. In *Proceedings of the 23rd International Conference on Neural Information Processing Systems*; Curran Associates Inc.: Red Hook, NY, USA, 2010; Volume 2, pp. 2613–2621.
27. Hasselt, H.V.; Guez, A.; Silver, D. Deep reinforcement learning with double Q-Learning. In Proceedings of the Thirtieth AAAI Conference on Artificial Intelligence, Phoenix, AZ, USA, 12–17 February 2016; pp. 2094–2100.
28. Anschel, O.; Baram, N.; Shimkin, N. Averaged-dqn: Variance reduction and stabilization for deep reinforcement learning. In Proceedings of the 34th International Conference on Machine Learning, Sydney, Australia, 6–11 August 2017; Volume 70, pp. 176–185.

29. Kim, S.; Asadi, K.; Littman, M.; Konidaris, G. Removing the target network from deep Q-networks with the Mellowmax operator. In Proceedings of the 18th International Conference on Autonomous Agents and MultiAgent Systems, Montreal, QC, Canada, 13–17 May 2019; pp. 2060–2062.
30. Asadi, K.; Littman, M.L. An alternative softmax operator for reinforcement learning. In Proceedings of the International Conference on Machine Learning, Sydney, Australia, 6–11 August 2017; pp. 243–252.
31. Song, Z.; Parr, R.; Carin, L. Revisiting the softmax bellman operator: New benefits and new perspective. In Proceedings of the International Conference on Machine Learning, Long Beach, CA, USA, 18–23 January 2019; pp. 5916–5925.
32. Kong, W.; Krichene, W.; Mayoraz, N.; Rendle, S.; Zhang, L. Rankmax: An Adaptive Projection Alternative to the Softmax Function. *Adv. Neural Inf. Process. Syst.* **2020**, *33*, 633–643.
33. Williams, R.J. Simple statistical gradient-following algorithms for connectionist reinforcement learning. *Mach. Learn.* **1992**, *8*, 229–256. [CrossRef]
34. Greensmith, E.; Bartlett, P.L.; Baxter, J. Variance reduction techniques for gradient estimates in reinforcement learning. *J. Mach. Learn. Res.* **2004**, *5*, 1471–1530.
35. Silver, D.; Lever, G.; Heess, N.; Degris, T.; Wierstra, D.; Riedmiller, M. Deterministic policy gradient algorithms. In Proceedings of the International Conference on Machine Learning, Beijing, China, 21–26 June 2014; pp. 387–395.
36. Chou, P.W.; Maturana, D.; Scherer, S. Improving stochastic policy gradients in continuous control with deep reinforcement learning using the beta distribution. In Proceedings of the International Conference on Machine Learning, Sydney, Australia, 6–11 August 2017; pp. 834–843.
37. Mnih, V.; Badia, A.P.; Mirza, M.; Graves, A.; Lillicrap, T.; Harley, T.; Silver, D.; Kavukcuoglu, K. Asynchronous methods for deep reinforcement learning. In Proceedings of the International Conference on Machine Learning, New York, NY, USA, 20–22 June 2016; pp. 1928–1937.
38. Schulman, J.; Levine, S.; Abbeel, P.; Jordan, M.; Moritz, P. Trust region policy optimization. In Proceedings of the International Conference on Machine Learning, Lille, France, 6–11 July 2015; pp. 1889–1897.
39. Schulman, J.; Wolski, F.; Dhariwal, P.; Radford, A.; Klimov, O. Proximal Policy Optimization Algorithms. *arXiv* **2017**, arXiv:1707.06347.
40. Hoffmann, J. Simulated Penetration Testing: From "Dijkstr" to "Turing Test++". In Proceedings of the Twenty-Fifth International Conference on Automated Planning and Scheduling, Jerusalem, Israel, 7–11 June 2015; pp. 364–372.
41. Sarraute, C.; Buffet, O.; Hoffmann, J. Penetration Testing==POMDP Solving? *arXiv* **2013**, arXiv:1306.4714.
42. Brock, O.; Trinkle, J.; Ramos, F. SARSOP: Efficient Point-Based POMDP Planning by Approximating Optimally Reachable Belief Spaces. In *Robotics: Science and Systems IV*; MIT Press: Cambridge, MA, USA, 2008. [CrossRef]
43. Sarraute, C.; Buffet, O.; Hoffmann, J. POMDPs make better hackers: Accounting for uncertainty in penetration testing. In Proceedings of the Twenty-Sixth AAAI Conference on Artificial Intelligence, Toronto, ON, Canada, 22–26 July 2012; pp. 1816–1824.
44. Zhou, T.Y.; Zang, Y.C.; Zhu, J.H.; Wang, Q.X. NIG-AP: A new method for automated penetration testing. *Front. Inf. Technol. Electron. Eng.* **2019**, *20*, 1277–1288. [CrossRef]
45. Schwartz, J.; Kurniawati, H.; El-Mahassni, E. POMDP+ Information-Decay: Incorporating Defender's Behaviour in Autonomous Penetration Testing. In Proceedings of the International Conference on Automated Planning and Scheduling, Nancy, France, 14–19 June 2020; Volume 30, pp. 235–243.
46. Ghanem, M.C.; Chen, T.M. Reinforcement learning for efficient network penetration testing. *Information* **2020**, *11*, 6. [CrossRef]
47. Walraven, E.; Spaan, M.T. Point-based value iteration for finite-horizon POMDPs. *J. Artif. Intell. Res.* **2019**, *65*, 307–341. [CrossRef]
48. Schwartz, J.; Kurniawati, H. Autonomous penetration testing using reinforcement learning. *arXiv* **2019**, arXiv:1905.05965.
49. Nguyen, H.V.; Nguyen, H.N.; Uehara, T. Multiple Level Action Embedding for Penetration Testing. In Proceedings of the 4th International Conference on Future Networks and Distributed Systems (ICFNDS), St. Petersburg, Russia, 26–27 November 2020; pp. 1–9.
50. Dulac-Arnold, G.; Evans, R.; van Hasselt, H.; Sunehag, P.; Lillicrap, T.; Hunt, J.; Mann, T.; Weber, T.; Degris, T.; Coppin, B. Deep reinforcement learning in large discrete action spaces. *arXiv* **2015**, arXiv:1512.07679.
51. Pozdniakov, K.; Alonso, E.; Stankovic, V.; Tam, K.; Jones, K. Smart security audit: Reinforcement learning with a deep neural network approximator. In Proceedings of the 2020 International Conference on Cyber Situational Awareness, Data Analytics and Assessment (CyberSA), Dublin, Ireland, 15–19 June 2020; pp. 1–8.
52. Maeda, R.; Mimura, M. Automating post-exploitation with deep reinforcement learning. *Comput. Secur.* **2021**, *100*, 102108. [CrossRef]
53. Sultana, M.; Taylor, A.; Li, L. Autonomous network cyber offence strategy through deep reinforcement learning. In *Artificial Intelligence and Machine Learning for Multi-Domain Operations Applications III*; International Society for Optics and Photonics: Bellingham, WA, USA, 2021; Volume 11746, p. 1174622.
54. Applebaum, A.; Miller, D.; Strom, B.; Foster, H.; Thomas, C. Analysis of automated adversary emulation techniques. In Proceedings of the Summer Simulation Multi-Conference, Bellevue, WA, USA, 9–12 July 2017; pp. 1–12.
55. Elderman, R.; Pater, L.J.; Thie, A.S.; Drugan, M.M.; Wiering, M.A. Adversarial Reinforcement Learning in a Cyber Security Simulation. In Proceedings of the International Conference on Agents and Artificial Intelligence (ICAART), Porto, Portugal, 24–26 February 2017; pp. 559–566.

56. Niculae, S. Reinforcement Learning vs. Genetic Algorithms in Game-Theoretic Cyber-Security. Ph.D Thesis, University of Bucharest, Bucharest, Romania, 2018.
57. Butz, M.V.; Wilson, S.W. An algorithmic description of XCS. In Proceedings of the International Workshop on Learning Classifier Systems, Cagliari, Italy, 21–23 June 2000; pp. 253–272.
58. Bland, J.A.; Petty, M.D.; Whitaker, T.S.; Maxwell, K.P.; Cantrell, W.A. Machine learning cyberattack and defense strategies. *Comput. Secur.* **2020**, *92*, 101738. [CrossRef]
59. Schwartz, J.; Kurniawatti, H. NASim: Network Attack Simulator. 2019. Available online: https://networkattacksimulator.readthedocs.io/ (accessed on 13 March 2022).
60. Ng, A.Y.; Jordan, M. PEGASUS: A policy search method for large MDPs and POMDPs. In Proceedings of the Sixteenth Conference on Uncertainty in Artificial Intelligence, San Francisco, CA, USA, 30 June–3 July 2000; pp. 406–415.
61. Ganesan, R.; Jajodia, S.; Shah, A.; Cam, H. Dynamic scheduling of cybersecurity analysts for minimizing risk using reinforcement learning. *ACM Trans. Intell. Syst. Technol. (TIST)* **2016**, *8*, 1–21. [CrossRef]
62. Winterrose, M.L.; Carter, K.M.; Wagner, N.; Streilein, W.W. Balancing security and performance for agility in dynamic threat environments. In Proceedings of the 2016 46th Annual IEEE/IFIP International Conference on Dependable Systems and Networks (DSN), Toulouse, France, 28 June–1 July 2016; pp. 607–617.
63. Wang, S.; Pei, Q.; Wang, J.; Tang, G.; Zhang, Y.; Liu, X. An intelligent deployment policy for deception resources based on reinforcement learning. *IEEE Access* **2020**, *8*, 35792–35804. [CrossRef]
64. Panfili, M.; Giuseppi, A.; Fiaschetti, A.; Al-Jibreen, H.B.; Pietrabissa, A.; Priscoli, F.D. A game-theoretical approach to cyber-security of critical infrastructures based on multi-agent reinforcement learning. In Proceedings of the 2018 26th Mediterranean Conference on Control and Automation (MED), Zadar, Croatia, 19–22 June 2018; pp. 460–465.
65. Han, Y.; Rubinstein, B.I.; Abraham, T.; Alpcan, T.; De Vel, O.; Erfani, S.; Hubczenko, D.; Leckie, C.; Montague, P. Reinforcement learning for autonomous defence in software-defined networking. In Proceedings of the International Conference on Decision and Game Theory for Security, Seattle, WA, USA, 29–31 October 2018; pp. 145–165.
66. Liu, Z. Reinforcement-Learning Based Network Intrusion Detection with Human Interaction in the Loop. In Proceedings of the International Conference on Security, Privacy and Anonymity in Computation, Communication and Storage, Nanjing, China, 18–20 December 2020; pp. 131–144.
67. Piplai, A.; Ranade, P.; Kotal, A.; Mittal, S.; Narayanan, S.N.; Joshi, A. Using Knowledge Graphs and Reinforcement Learning for Malware Analysis. In Proceedings of the 4th International Workshop on Big Data Analytics for Cyber Intelligence and Defense, IEEE International Conference on Big Data, Atlanta, GA, USA, 10–13 December 2020.
68. Venkatesan, S.; Albanese, M.; Shah, A.; Ganesan, R.; Jajodia, S. Detecting stealthy botnets in a resource-constrained environment using reinforcement learning. In Proceedings of the 2017 Workshop on Moving Target Defense, Dallas, TX, USA, 30 October 2017; pp. 75–85.
69. Miller, P.; Inoue, A. Collaborative intrusion detection system. In Proceedings of the 22nd International Conference of the North American Fuzzy Information Processing Society, NAFIPS 2003, Chicago, IL, USA, 24–26 July 2003; pp. 519–524.
70. Malialis, K. Distributed Reinforcement Learning for Network Intrusion Response. Ph.D. Thesis, University of York, York, UK, 2014.
71. Sun, Y.; Xiong, W.; Yao, Z.; Moniz, K.; Zahir, A. Network defense strategy selection with reinforcement learning and pareto optimization. *Appl. Sci.* **2017**, *7*, 1138. [CrossRef]
72. Sun, Y.; Li, Y.; Xiong, W.; Yao, Z.; Moniz, K.; Zahir, A. Pareto optimal solutions for network defense strategy selection simulator in multi-objective reinforcement learning. *Appl. Sci.* **2018**, *8*, 136. [CrossRef]
73. Chung, K.; Kamhoua, C.A.; Kwiat, K.A.; Kalbarczyk, Z.T.; Iyer, R.K. Game theory with learning for cyber security monitoring. In Proceedings of the 2016 IEEE 17th International Symposium on High Assurance Systems Engineering (HASE), Orlando, FL, USA, 7–9 January 2016; pp. 1–8.
74. Sahabandu, D.; Moothedath, S.; Allen, J.; Bushnell, L.; Lee, W.; Poovendran, R. A Multi-Agent Reinforcement Learning Approach for Dynamic Information Flow Tracking Games for Advanced Persistent Threats. *arXiv* **2020**, arXiv:2007.00076.
75. Hu, Z.; Zhu, M.; Liu, P. Online algorithms for adaptive cyber defense on bayesian attack graphs. In Proceedings of the 2017 Workshop on Moving Target Defense, Dallas, TX, USA, 30 October 2017; pp. 99–109.
76. Hu, Z.; Zhu, M.; Liu, P. Adaptive Cyber Defense Against Multi-Stage Attacks Using Learning-Based POMDP. *ACM Trans. Priv. Secur. (TOPS)* **2020**, *24*, 1–25. [CrossRef]
77. Alauthman, M.; Aslam, N.; Al-Kasassbeh, M.; Khan, S.; Al-Qerem, A.; Choo, K.K.R. An efficient reinforcement learning-based Botnet detection approach. *J. Netw. Comput. Appl.* **2020**, *150*, 102479. [CrossRef]
78. Servin, A.; Kudenko, D. Multi-agent reinforcement learning for intrusion detection. In *Adaptive Agents and Multi-Agent Systems III. Adaptation and Multi-Agent Learning*; Springer: Berlin/Heidelberg, Germany, 2005; pp. 211–223.
79. Liu, M.; Ma, L.; Li, C.; Li, R. Fortified Network Security Perception: A Decentralized Multiagent Coordination Perspective. In Proceedings of the 2020 IEEE 3rd International Conference on Electronics Technology (ICET), Chengdu, China, 8–12 May 2020; pp. 746–750.
80. Huang, L.; Zhu, Q. Adaptive honeypot engagement through reinforcement learning of semi-markov decision processes. In Proceedings of the International Conference on Decision and Game Theory for Security, Stockholm, Sweden, 30 October–1 November 2019; pp. 196–216.

81. Huang, L.; Zhu, Q. Strategic Learning for Active, Adaptive, and Autonomous Cyber Defense. In *Adaptive Autonomous Secure Cyber Systems*; Springer: Cham, Switzerland, 2020; pp. 205–230.
82. Wei, F.; Wan, Z.; He, H. Cyber-attack recovery strategy for smart grid based on deep reinforcement learning. *IEEE Trans. Smart Grid* **2019**, *11*, 2476–2486. [CrossRef]
83. Wu, J.; Fang, B.; Fang, J.; Chen, X.; Chi, K.T. Sequential topology recovery of complex power systems based on reinforcement learning. *Phys. A Stat. Mech. Its Appl.* **2019**, *535*, 122487. [CrossRef]
84. Debus, P.; Müller, N.; Böttinger, K. Deep Reinforcement Learning for Backup Strategies against Adversaries. *arXiv* **2021**, arXiv:2102.06632.
85. Jajodia, S.; Ghosh, A.K.; Swarup, V.; Wang, C.; Wang, X.S. *Moving Target Defense: Creating Asymmetric Uncertainty for Cyber Threats*; Springer Science & Business Media: New York, NY, USA, 2011.
86. Jiang, W.; Fang, B.X.; Tian, Z.H.; Zhang, H.L. Evaluating network security and optimal active defense based on attack-defense game model. *Chin. J. Comput.* **2009**, *32*, 817–827. [CrossRef]
87. Tavallaee, M.; Bagheri, E.; Lu, W.; Ghorbani, A.A. A detailed analysis of the KDD CUP 99 data set. In Proceedings of the 2009 IEEE Symposium on Computational Intelligence for Security and Defense Applications, Ottawa, ON, Canada, 8–10 July 2009; pp. 1–6.
88. Montresor, A.; Jelasity, M. PeerSim: A scalable P2P simulator. In Proceedings of the 2009 IEEE Ninth International Conference on Peer-to-Peer Computing, Seattle, WA, USA, 9–11 September 2009; pp. 99–100.
89. Leyi, S.; Yang, L.; Mengfei, M. Latest research progress of honeypot technology. *J. Electron. Inf. Technol.* **2019**, *41*, 498–508.
90. Xuan, P.; Lesser, V.; Zilberstein, S. Communication decisions in multi-agent cooperation: Model and experiments. In Proceedings of the Fifth International Conference on Autonomous Agents, Montreal, QC, Canada, 28 May–1 June 2001; pp. 616–623.
91. Miller, P.; Mill, J.L.; Inoue, A. Synergistic Perceptual Intrusion Detection with Reinforcement Learning (SPIDER). In Proceedings of the Fourteenth Midwest Artificial Intelligence and Cognitive Sciences Conference (MAICS 2003), Cincinnati, OH, USA, 12–13 April 2003; pp. 102–108.
92. Archive, U.K. KDD Cup 1999 Data. 1999. Available online: http://kdd.ics.uci.edu/databases/kddcup99/kddcup99.html (accessed on 13 March 2022).
93. Singh, N.K.; Mahajan, V. Smart grid: Cyber attack identification and recovery approach. In Proceedings of the 2019 2nd International Conference on Innovations in Electronics, Signal Processing and Communication (IESC), Shillong, Indian, 1–2 March 2019; pp. 1–5.
94. Ng, A.Y.; Harada, D.; Russell, S. Policy invariance under reward transformations: Theory and application to reward shaping. In Proceedings of the 16th International Conference on Machine Learning, Bled, Slovenia, 27–30 June 1999; pp. 278–287.
95. Zhifei, S.; Er, M.J. A survey of inverse reinforcement learning techniques. *Int. J. Intell. Comput. Cybern.* **2012**, *5*, 293–311. [CrossRef]
96. Arora, S.; Doshi, P. A survey of inverse reinforcement learning: Challenges, methods and progress. *Artif. Intell.* **2021**, *297*, 103500. [CrossRef]
97. Ditzler, G.; Roveri, M.; Alippi, C.; Polikar, R. Learning in nonstationary environments: A survey. *IEEE Comput. Intell. Mag.* **2015**, *10*, 12–25. [CrossRef]
98. Padakandla, S.; Prabuchandran, K.; Bhatnagar, S. Reinforcement learning algorithm for non-stationary environments. *Appl. Intell.* **2020**, *50*, 3590–3606. [CrossRef]
99. Marinescu, A.; Dusparic, I.; Clarke, S. Prediction-based multi-agent reinforcement learning in inherently non-stationary environments. *ACM Trans. Auton. Adapt. Syst. (TAAS)* **2017**, *12*, 1–23. [CrossRef]
100. Al-Shedivat, M.; Bansal, T.; Burda, Y.; Sutskever, I.; Mordatch, I.; Abbeel, P. Continuous Adaptation via Meta-Learning in Nonstationary and Competitive Environments. In Proceedings of the International Conference on Learning Representations, Vancouver, BC, Canada, 30 April–3 May 2018.
101. Lecarpentier, E.; Rachelson, E. Non-Stationary Markov Decision Processes a Worst-Case Approach using Model-Based Reinforcement Learning. In Proceedings of the 33rd Conference on Neural Information Processing Systems (NeurIPS 2019), Vancouver, BC, Canada, 8–14 December 2019; pp. 1–18.
102. Peters, O. The ergodicity problem in economics. *Nat. Phys.* **2019**, *15*, 1216–1221. [CrossRef]
103. Moreira, C.; Tiwari, P.; Pandey, H.M.; Bruza, P.; Wichert, A. Quantum-like influence diagrams for decision-making. *Neural Netw.* **2020**, *132*, 190–210. [CrossRef]
104. Doctor, J.N.; Wakker, P.P.; Wang, T.V. Economists's views on the ergodicity problem. *Nat. Phys.* **2020**, *16*, 1168–1168. [CrossRef]
105. Bowers, K.D.; Van Dijk, M.; Griffin, R.; Juels, A.; Oprea, A.; Rivest, R.L.; Triandopoulos, N. Defending against the unknown enemy: Applying FlipIt to system security. In Proceedings of the International Conference on Decision and Game Theory for Security, Budapest, Hungary, 5–6 November 2012; pp. 248–263.
106. Laszka, A.; Horvath, G.; Felegyhazi, M.; Buttyán, L. FlipThem: Modeling targeted attacks with FlipIt for multiple resources. In Proceedings of the International Conference on Decision and Game Theory for Security, Los Angeles, CA, USA, 6–7 November 2014; pp. 175–194.
107. Chapman, M.; Tyson, G.; McBurney, P.; Luck, M.; Parsons, S. Playing hide-and-seek: An abstract game for cyber security. In Proceedings of the 1st International Workshop on Agents and CyberSecurity, Paris, France, 6 May 2014; pp. 1–8.

108. Tandon, A.; Karlapalem, K. Medusa: Towards Simulating a Multi-Agent Hide-and-Seek Game. In Proceedings of the 27th International Joint Conference on Artificial Intelligence and the 23rd European Conference on Artificial Intelligence, Stockholm, Sweden, 13–19 July 2018; pp. 5871–5873.
109. Pandey, S.; Kühn, R. A random walk perspective on hide-and-seek games. *J. Phys. A Math. Theor.* **2019**, *52*, 085001. [CrossRef]
110. Tandon, A.; Karlapalem, K. Agent Strategies for the Hide-and-Seek Game. Ph.D. Thesis, International Institute of Information Technology Hyderabad, Hyderabad, India, 2020.
111. Ou, X.; Govindavajhala, S.; Appel, A.W. MulVAL: A Logic-based Network Security Analyzer. In *USENIX Security Symposium*; USENIX: Baltimore, MD, USA, 2005; Volume 8, pp. 113–128.
112. Durkota, K.; Lisý, V.; Kiekintveld, C.; Bošanský, B.; Pěchouček, M. Case studies of network defense with attack graph games. *IEEE Intell. Syst.* **2016**, *31*, 24–30. [CrossRef]
113. Yichao, Z.; Tianyang, Z.; Xiaoyue, G.; Qingxian, W. An improved attack path discovery algorithm through compact graph planning. *IEEE Access* **2019**, *7*, 59346–59356. [CrossRef]
114. Chowdhary, A.; Huang, D.; Mahendran, J.S.; Romo, D.; Deng, Y.; Sabur, A. Autonomous security analysis and penetration testing. In Proceedings of the 2020 16th International Conference on Mobility, Sensing and Networking (MSN), Tokyo, Japan, 17–19 December 2020; pp. 508–515.
115. Hu, Z.; Beuran, R.; Tan, Y. Automated Penetration Testing Using Deep Reinforcement Learning. In Proceedings of the 2020 IEEE European Symposium on Security and Privacy Workshops (EuroS&PW), Genoa, Italy, 7–11 September 2020; pp. 2–10.
116. Petri, C. Kommunikation Mit Automaten. Ph.D. Thesis, University of Hamburg, Hamburg, Germany, 1962.
117. Riley, G.F.; Henderson, T.R. The ns-3 network simulator. In *Modeling and Tools for Network Simulation*; Springer: Berlin/Heidelberg, Germany, 2010; pp. 15–34.
118. Otoum, S.; Kantarci, B.; Mouftah, H. A comparative study of ai-based intrusion detection techniques in critical infrastructures. *ACM Trans. Internet Technol. (TOIT)* **2021**, *21*, 1–22. [CrossRef]
119. Team, M. Mininet An Instant Virtual Network on Your Laptop (or other PC). 2012. Available online: http://mininet.org/ (accessed on 13 March 2022).
120. Team, M.D.R. CyberBattleSim. Created by Christian Seifert, Michael Betser, William Blum, James Bono, Kate Farris, Emily Goren, Justin Grana, Kristian Holsheimer, Brandon Marken, Joshua Neil, Nicole Nichols, Jugal Parikh, Haoran Wei. 2021. Available online: https://github.com/microsoft/cyberbattlesim (accessed on 13 March 2022).
121. Lanctot, M.; Zambaldi, V.; Gruslys, A.; Lazaridou, A.; Tuyls, K.; Pérolat, J.; Silver, D.; Graepel, T. A unified game-theoretic approach to multiagent reinforcement learning. In Proceedings of the 31st International Conference on Neural Information Processing Systems, Long Beach, CA, USA, 4–9 December 2017; pp. 4193–4206.
122. Kipf, T.N.; Welling, M. Semi-supervised classification with graph convolutional networks. *arXiv* **2016**, arXiv:1609.02907.
123. Wu, F.; Souza, A.; Zhang, T.; Fifty, C.; Yu, T.; Weinberger, K. Simplifying graph convolutional networks. In Proceedings of the International Conference on Machine Learning, Long Beach, CA, USA, 9–15 June 2019; pp. 6861–6871.
124. Scarselli, F.; Gori, M.; Tsoi, A.C.; Hagenbuchner, M.; Monfardini, G. The graph neural network model. *IEEE Trans. Neural Netw.* **2008**, *20*, 61–80. [CrossRef]
125. Xu, K.; Hu, W.; Leskovec, J.; Jegelka, S. How Powerful are Graph Neural Networks? In Proceedings of the International Conference on Learning Representations, Vancouver, BC, Canada, 30 April–3 May 2018.

algorithms

MDPI

Article

Measuring the Non-Transitivity in Chess

Ricky Sanjaya [1], Jun Wang [1] and Yaodong Yang [2,*]

[1] Department of Computer Science, University College London, London WC1E 6EA, UK; ucabrs5@ucl.ac.uk (R.S.); jun.wang@ucl.ac.uk (J.W.)
[2] Institute for Artificial Intelligence, Peking University, Beijing 100191, China
* Correspondence: yaodong.yang@pku.edu.cn

Abstract: In this paper, we quantify the non-transitivity in chess using human game data. Specifically, we perform non-transitivity quantification in two ways—Nash clustering and counting the number of rock–paper–scissor cycles—on over one billion matches from the Lichess and FICS databases. Our findings indicate that the strategy space of real-world chess strategies has a spinning top geometry and that there exists a strong connection between the degree of non-transitivity and the progression of a chess player's rating. Particularly, high degrees of non-transitivity tend to prevent human players from making progress in their Elo ratings. We also investigate the implications of non-transitivity for population-based training methods. By considering *fixed-memory fictitious play* as a proxy, we conclude that maintaining large and diverse populations of strategies is imperative to training effective AI agents for solving chess.

Keywords: game theory; multi-agent AI; non-transitivity quantification

1. Introduction

Since the mid-1960s, computer scientists have referred to chess as the *Drosophila* of AI [1]: similar to the role of the fruit fly in genetics studies, chess provides an accessible, familiar, and relatively simple test bed that nonetheless can be used to produce much knowledge about other complex environments. As a result, chess has been used as a benchmark for the development of AI for decades. The earliest attempt dates back to Shannon's interest in 1950 [2]. Over the past few decades, remarkable progress has been made in developing AIs that can demonstrate super-human performance in chess, including IBM DeepBlue [3] and AlphaZero [4]. Despite the algorithmic achievements made in AI chess playing, we still have limited knowledge about the geometric landscape of the strategy space of chess. Tied to the strategic geometry are the concepts of *transitivity* and *non-transitivity* [5]. Transitivity refers to how one strategy is better than other strategies. In transitive games, if strategy A beats strategy B and B beats C, then A beats C. On the other hand, non-transitive games are games where there exists a loop of winning strategies. For example, strategy A beats strategy B and B beats C, but A loses to C. One of the simplest purely non-transitive games is rock–paper–scissors. However, games in the real world are far more complex; their strategy spaces often have both transitive and non-transitive components.

Based on the strategies generated by AIs, researchers have hypothesised that the majority of real-world games possess a strategy space with a spinning top geometry. In such a geometry (see Figure 1a), the radial axis represents the non-transitivity degree and the upright axis represents the transitivity degree. The middle region of the transitive dimension is accompanied by a highly non-transitive dimension, which gradually diminishes as the skill level either grows towards the Nash equilibrium [6] or degrades to the worst-performing strategies.

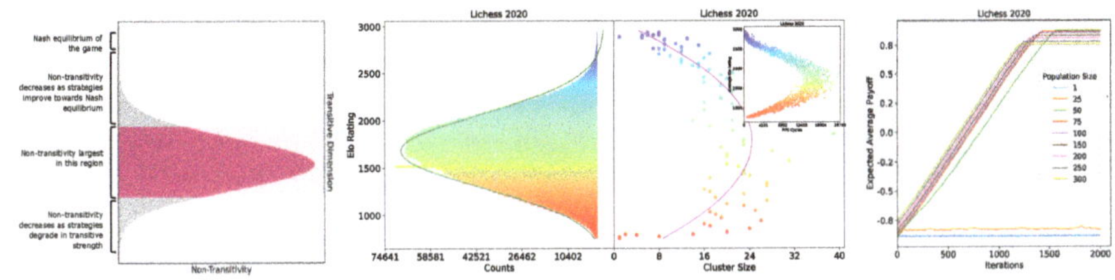

(a) (b) (c)

Figure 1. We justify the spinning top hypothesis represented by (**a**), which states that many real-world games—including chess—possess a strategy space with a spinning top geometry, where the radial axis represents the non-transitivity degree (e.g., A beats B, B beats C, and C beats A) and the upright axis represents the transitivity degree (e.g., A beats B, B beats C, and A beats C). We studied the geometric properties of chess based on one billion game records from human players. (**b**) shows the comparison between the histogram of Elo ratings (i.e., the transitivity degree) in Lichess 2020 (left) and the degree of non-transitivity at each Elo level (right), where the non-transitivity is measured by both the size of the Nash clusters and the number of rock–paper–scissor cycles (top-right corner). A skewed-normal curve is fitted to illustrate the non-transitivity profile, which verifies the spinning top hypothesis in (**a**). Specifically, the middle region of the transitive dimension is accompanied by a large degree of non-transitivity, which gradually diminishes as skill evolves towards high Elo ratings (upward) or degrades (downward). Notably, the peak of the Elo histogram lies between 1300 and 1700, a range where most human players get stuck. Furthermore, the peak of the non-transitivity curve coincides with the peak of the Elo histogram; this indicates a strong relationship between the difficulty of playing chess and the degree of non-transitivity. Our discovered geometry has important implications for learning. For example, our findings provide guidance to improve the Elo ratings of human players, especially in stages with high degrees of non-transitivity (e.g., by dedicating more efforts to learning diverse opening tactics). In (**c**), we show the performances of population-based training methods with different population sizes. A phase change in performance occurs when the population size increases; this justifies the necessity of maintaining large and diverse populations when training AI agents to solve chess.

While the idea of non-transitivity is intuitive, quantifying it remains an open challenge. An early attempt has been made to quantify non-transitivity [5], based on which the spinning top hypothesis was proposed. However, their sampled strategies were all artificial, in the sense that they only studied strategies that were generated by various algorithmic AI models. While one can argue that both artificial and human strategies are sampled from the same strategy space, they could have completely different inherent play styles; for example, [7] has shown that the Stockfish AI [8] performed poorly in mimicking the play style of weak human players, despite being depth-limited to mimic those players. Therefore, there is no guarantee that the conclusions from [5] would apply to human strategies. Consequently, the geometric profile of the strategy space of chess is still unclear, which directly motivated us to investigate and quantify the degree of non-transitivity in human strategies.

Aside from its popularity historically, chess is one of the most popular classical games today. It provides the largest number of well-maintained human game records of any type, which are publicly available from various sources. These databases include Lichess [9], which contains games played since 2013, and the Free Internet Chess Server (FICS), which contains games played since 1999 [10]. In this paper, by studying over one billion records of human games on Lichess and FICS, we measure the non-transitivity of chess games, and investigate the potential implications for training effective AI agents and for human skill progression. Specifically, we performed two forms of non-transitivity measurement: Nash clustering and counting the number of rock–paper–scissor (RPS) cycles. Our findings indicated that the strategy space occupied by real-world chess strategies demonstrates a spinning top geometry. More importantly, there exists a strong connection between the degree of non-transitivity and the progression of a chess player's rating. In particular, high degrees of non-transitivity tend to prevent human players from making progress on their Elo rating, whereas progression is easier at the level of ratings where the degree of non-transitivity is lower. We also investigated the implication of the degree of non-transitivity on population-based training methods. By considering *fixed-memory Fictitious Play* as a proxy, we concluded that maintaining a large and diverse population [11] of strategies is imperative to train effective AI agents in solving chess, which also matched the empirical findings that have been observed based on artificial strategies [5].

In summary, the main contributions of this paper are as follows:

- We perform non-transitivity quantification in two ways (i.e., Nash Clustering and counting rock–paper–scissor cycles) on over one billion human games collected from Lichess and FICS. We found that the strategy space occupied by real-world chess strategies exhibited a spinning top geometry.
- We propose several algorithms to tackle the challenges of working with real-world data. These include a two-staged sampling algorithm to sample from a large amount of data, and an algorithm to convert real-world chess games into a Normal Form game payoff matrix.
- We propose mappings between different chess player rating systems, in order to allow our results to be translated between these rating systems.
- We investigate the implications of non-transitivity on population-based training methods, and propose a fixed-memory Fictitious Play algorithm to illustrate these implications. We find that it is not only crucial to maintain a relatively large population of agents/strategies for training to converge, but that the minimum population size is related to the degree of non-transitivity of the strategy space.
- We investigate potential links between the degree of non-transitivity and the progression of a human chess player's skill. We found that, at ratings where the degree of non-transitivity is high, progression is harder, and vice versa.

The remainder of this paper is organized as follows: Section 2 provides a brief overview of the works related to this paper. Section 3 provides some background on Game Theory, followed by theoretical formulations and experimental procedures to quantify non-transitivity, as well as to study its implications for training AI agents and human skill progression. Section 4 presents the results of these experiments and the conclusions drawn from them. Section 5 presents our concluding remarks and several suggestions for future work.

2. Related Works

Our work is most related to that of [5], who proposed the Game of Skill geometry (i.e., the spinning top hypothesis), in which the strategy space of real-world games resembles a spinning top in two dimensions, where the vertical axis represents the transitive strength and the horizontal axis represents the degree of non-transitivity. This hypothesis has empirically been verified for several real-world games, such as Hex, Go, Tic-Tac-Toe, and Starcraft. The approach taken by [5] was to sample strategies uniformly along the transitive strength, where the strategies are generated by first running solution algorithms such as the Minimax Algorithm with Alpha-Beta pruning [12] and Monte-Carlo Tree Search (MCTS) [13]. Sampling strategies uniformly in terms of transitive strength is then conducted by varying the depth up to which Minimax is performed, or by varying the number of simulations for MCTS. For Starcraft, sampling strategies have been carried out by using the agents from the training of the AlphaStar AI [14]. However, such sampling of strategies means that the empirical verification is performed on artificial strategies, and some works have suggested an inherent difference in the play style of AI and humans. For example, [7] have shown that Stockfish AI [8] performed poorly in mimicking the play style of human players, despite being depth-limited to mimic such players. This motivated us to perform similar investigations, but using human strategies.

This paper is focused on non-transitivity quantification in real-world chess strategies. However, chess players are rated primarily using the Elo rating system, which is only valid for the pool of players being considered, and many variants of this system have been implemented around the world. The two most-used implementations are those of the Fédération Internationale des Échecs (FIDE) [15] and the United States Chess Federation (USCF) [16]. In its most basic implementation, the Elo rating system consists of two steps: assigning initial ratings to players and updating these ratings after matches. USCF and FIDE determine a player's starting rating by taking into account multiple factors, including the age of the player and their ratings in other systems [17,18]. However, the specific rules used to determine the starting rating differs between the two organisations. Furthermore, the update rules also differ significantly. These are defined in the handbook of each organisation [17,18]. On the other hand, online chess platforms, such as Lichess and the FICS, which are the data sources used in this paper, typically use a refined implementation of the Elo rating system; namely, the Glicko [19] system for FICS, and Glicko-2 [20] for Lichess. These systems typically set a fixed starting rating, and then include the computation of a rating deviation for Glicko while updating the player rating after matches. Glicko-2 includes the rating deviation and rating volatility, both of which represent the reliability of the player's current rating.

3. Theoretical Formulations and Methods

Some notations used in this paper are provided in the following. For any positive integer k, $[k]$ denotes the set $\{1, ..., k\}$, and Δ_k denotes the set of all probability vectors with k elements. For any set A and some function f, $\{f(a)\}_{a \in A}$ denotes the set constructed by applying f to each element of A. Furthermore, for any set $A = \{A_1, ..., A_{|A|}\}$, $\{s_i\}_{i \in A}$ denotes $\{s_{A_1}, ..., s_{A_{|A|}}\}$. Moreover, for some integer k, $\{s_i\}_{i=1}^{k}$ denotes $\{s_1, ..., s_k\}$. $\mathbb{N}_1$ denotes the set $\{1, 2, ...\}$; that is, the natural numbers starting from 1. For a set $A = \{A_1, ..., A_{|A|}\}$, the notation A_{-j} denotes A without the jth element (i.e., $A_{-j} = \{A_i\}_{i \in [|A|], i \neq j}$). Hence, $A = \{A_j, A_{-j}\}\ \forall j \in [|A|]$. Furthermore, we use $I[a > b]$ for $a, b \in \mathbb{R}$ to denote the indicator function, where $I[a > b] = 1$ if $a > b$ and 0 otherwise. Finally, for any integers m and k where $k \leq m$, let $\mathbf{e_k^m}$ denote a vector of length m, where the vector is all zeroes, but with a single 1 at the kth element. Likewise, $\mathbf{0}_k$ and $\mathbf{1}_k$ denote the vector of zeroes and ones of length k, respectively.

3.1. Game Theory Preliminaries

Definition 1. *A game consists of a tuple of (n, S, M), where:*

- *$n \in \mathbb{N}_1$ denotes the number of players;*
- *$S = \prod_{i=1}^{n} S_i$ denotes the joint strategy space of the game, where S_i is the strategy space of the ith, $i \in [n]$. A strategy space is the set of strategies a player can adopt;*
- *$M = \{M_i\}_{i=1}^{n}$, where $M_i : S \to \mathbb{R}$ is the payoff function for the ith player. A payoff function maps the outcome of a game resulting from a joint strategy to a real value, representing the payoff received by that player.*

3.1.1. Normal Form (NF) Games

In NF games, every player takes a single action simultaneously. Such games are fully defined by a payoff matrix $\boldsymbol{\mathcal{M}}$, where

$$\boldsymbol{\mathcal{M}}_{d_1, d_2, ..., d_n} = \{M_1(a_1, a_2, ..., a_n), ..., M_n(a_1, a_2, ..., a_n)\},$$

with $a_k \in A_k$, $d_k \in [|A_k|]$, $k \in [n]$, A_k denoting the action space of the kth player, and d_k denoting the index corresponding to a_k. $\boldsymbol{\mathcal{M}}$ fully specifies an NF game as it contains all the components of a game by Definition 1. In an NF game, the strategy adopted by a player is the single action taken by that player. Therefore, the action space A_k is equivalent to the strategy space S_k for $k \in [n]$.

An NF game is zero-sum when $\sum_{z \in \mathcal{M}_{d_1,...,d_n}} z = 0$ for $d_k \in [|A_k|]$, $k \in [n]$. For two-player zero-sum NF games, the entries of $\mathcal{M}$ can, therefore, be represented by a single number, as the payoff of one player is the negative of the other. Additionally, if the game is symmetric (i.e., both players have identical strategy spaces), then the matrix $\mathcal{M}$ is skew-symmetric.

A well-known solution concept that describes the equilibrium of NF games is the Nash Equilibrium (NE) [6,21]. Let $\mathbf{p_i}(s)$, where $s \in S_i$, $\mathbf{p_i} \in \Delta_{|S_i|}$, and $i \in [n]$, denote the probability of player i playing the pure strategy s according to probability vector $\mathbf{p_i}$. Additionally, let $p = \{\mathbf{p_1}, ..., \mathbf{p_n}\}$, and $p[j : \mathbf{k}]$ denote changing the jth element in p to the probability vector $\mathbf{k}$, where $\mathbf{k} \in \Delta_{|S_j|}$.

Definition 2. *The set of distributions p^*, where $p^* = \{\mathbf{p_1^*}, ..., \mathbf{p_n^*}\}$ and $\mathbf{p_i^*} \in \Delta_{|S_i|}$ $\forall i \in [n]$, is an NE if $\sum_{s \in S} p^*(s) M_i(s) \geq \sum_{s \in S} p^*[i : \mathbf{e_k^{|S_i|}}](s) M_i(s)$ $\forall i \in [n]$, $k \in [|S_i|]$, where $p^*(s) = \prod_{j \in [n]} \mathbf{p_j^*}(s_j)$ and $s = \{s_1, ..., s_n\}$, $s_i \in S_i$ $\forall i \in [n]$.*

Definition 2 implies that, under an NE, no player can increase their expected payoff by unilaterally deviating to a pure strategy. While such an NE always exists [6], it might not be unique. To guarantee the uniqueness of the obtained NE, we apply the maximum entropy condition when solving for the NE. The maximum-entropy NE has been proven to be unique [22].

Theorem 1. *Any two-player zero-sum symmetric game always has a unique maximum entropy NE, given by $\{\mathbf{p}^*, \mathbf{p}^*\}$ where $\mathbf{p}^* \in \Delta_{|S_g|}$, where S_g is the strategy space for each of the two players [22].*

As a consequence of Theorem 1, finding the maximum entropy NE of a two-player zero-sum symmetric game amounts to solving the Linear Programming (LP) problem shown in Equation (1):

$$\begin{aligned} \mathbf{p}^* = \arg\max_{\mathbf{p}} & \sum_{j \in [|S_g|]} -\mathbf{p}_j \log \mathbf{p}_j \\ \text{s. t.} \quad & \mathcal{M}\mathbf{p} \leq \mathbf{0}_{|S_g|} \\ & \mathbf{p} \geq \mathbf{0}_{|S_g|} \\ & \mathbf{1}_{|S_g|}^{\top} \mathbf{p} = 1, \end{aligned} \quad (1)$$

where $\mathcal{M}$ is the skew-symmetric payoff matrix of the first player.

3.1.2. Extensive Form (EF) Games

EF games [23] model situations where participants take actions sequentially and interactions happen over more than one step. We consider the case of perfect information, where every player has knowledge of all the other player's actions, and a finite horizon, where interactions between participants end in a finite number of steps (denoted as K). In EF games, an action refers to a single choice of move from some player at some stage of the game. Therefore, the term action space is used to define the actions available to a player at a certain stage of the game.

Definition 3. *A history at stage k, h_k, is defined as $h_k = \{a_1, ..., a_{k-1}\}$, where $a_j = \{a_j^1, ..., a_j^n\}$ for $j \in [k-1]$. a_j is the action profile at stage j, denoting the actions taken by all players at that stage.*

The action space of player i at stage k is, therefore, a function of the history at that stage (i.e., $A_i(h_k)$ for $k \in [K], i \in [n]$), as the actions available to a player depend on how the game goes.

Definition 4. *Let H_k be the set of all possible histories at stage k. Let $A_i(H_k) = \bigcup_{h_k \in H_k} A_i(h_k)$ be the collection of actions available to player i at stage k from all possible histories at that stage. Let the mapping $s_i^k : H_k \to A_i(H_k)$ be a mapping from any history at stage k (i.e., h_k) to an action available at that stage due to h_k; that is, $s_i^k(h_k) \in A_i(h_k)\ \forall h_k \in H_k$. A strategy of player i is defined as $s_i = \bigcup_{k \in [K]} s_i^k$, $s_i \in S_i$, where S_i is the strategy space of player i.*

In EF games, behavioural strategies are defined as a contingency plan for any possible history at any stage of the game. According to Kuhn's theorem [24], for perfect recall EF games, each behavioural strategy has a realisation-equivalent mixed strategy. Finally, the payoff function of an EF game is defined as the mapping of every terminal history (i.e., the history at stage $K+1$) to a sequence of n real numbers, denoting the payoffs of each player (i.e., $M_i : H_{K+1} \to R$ for $i \in [n]$, where H_{K+1} is the set of all terminal histories). However, any terminal history is produced by at least one joint strategy adopted by all players. Therefore, the payoff of a player is also a mapping from the joint strategy space to a real number, consistent with Definition 1.

An EF game can be converted into an NF game. When viewing an EF game as an NF game, the "actions" of a player in the corresponding NF game would be the strategies of that player in the original EF game. Therefore, an n-player EF game would have a corresponding $\mathcal{M}$ matrix of n dimensions, where the ith dimension is of length $|S_i|$. The entries of this matrix correspond to a sequence of n real numbers, representing the payoff of each player as a consequence of playing the corresponding joint strategies.

3.2. Elo Rating

The Elo Rating system is a rating system devised by Arpad Elo [25]. It is a measure of a participant's performance, relative to others within a pool of players. The main idea behind Elo rating is that, given two players A and B, the system assigns a numerical rating to each of them (i.e., r_A and r_B, where $r_A, r_B \in \mathbb{R}^+$), such that the winning probability of A against B (i.e. $p(A > B)$) can be approximated by:

$$p(A > B) \approx \frac{1}{1 + \exp(-k(r_A - r_B))} = \sigma(k(r_A - r_B)), \tag{2}$$

where $k \in \mathbb{R}^+, \sigma(x) = 1/1 + \exp(-x)$.

3.3. Non-Transitivity Quantification

We employed two methods to quantify the degree of non-transitivity; namely, by counting strategic cycles of length three, and by measuring the size of Nash Clusters obtained in Nash Clustering [5]. Both methods require formulating chess as an NF game (i.e., using a single payoff matrix). Furthermore, Nash Clustering also requires the payoff matrix to be zero-sum and skew-symmetric. Section 3.3.1 outlines the techniques employed for construction of the payoff matrix.

3.3.1. Payoff Matrix Construction

The raw data for the experiments were game data stored in Portable Game Notation (PGN) format [26], obtained from two sources. The primary source was the Lichess [9] database, which contains games played from 2013 until 2021. The second data set was sourced from the FICS [10] database, and we used games from 2019, as it contained the highest number of games. Figure 2 shows an example of a chess game recorded in PGN format. Altogether, we collected over one billion match data records from human players. In order to process such a large amount of data, we introduced several novel procedures to turn the match records into payoff matrices.

The first processing step was to extract the required attributes from the data of every game. These include the outcome of the game (to create the payoff matrix) and the Elo ratings of both players (as a measure of transitive strength).

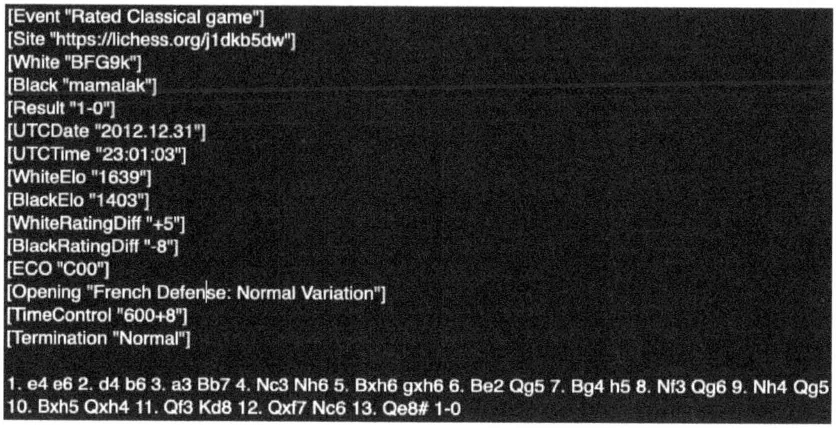

```
[Event "Rated Classical game"]
[Site "https://lichess.org/j1dkb5dw"]
[White "BFG9k"]
[Black "mamalak"]
[Result "1-0"]
[UTCDate "2012.12.31"]
[UTCTime "23:01:03"]
[WhiteElo "1639"]
[BlackElo "1403"]
[WhiteRatingDiff "+5"]
[BlackRatingDiff "-8"]
[ECO "C00"]
[Opening "French Defense: Normal Variation"]
[TimeControl "600+8"]
[Termination "Normal"]

1. e4 e6 2. d4 b6 3. a3 Bb7 4. Nc3 Nh6 5. Bxh6 gxh6 6. Be2 Qg5 7. Bg4 h5 8. Nf3 Qg6 9. Nh4 Qg5
10. Bxh5 Qxh4 11. Qf3 Kd8 12. Qxf7 Nc6 13. Qe8# 1-0
```

Figure 2. Lichess PGN format.

The second step concerned the number of games taken from the whole Lichess database. As of 2021, the Lichess database contains a total of more than 2 billion games hosted from 2013. Therefore, sampling was required. Games were sampled uniformly across every month and year, where the number of games sampled every month was 120,000 as, for January of 2013, the database contains only a little more than 120,000 games. To avoid the influence of having a different number of points from each month, the number of games sampled per month was, thus, kept constant. In earlier years, sampling uniformly across a month was trivial, as games from an entire month could be loaded into a single data structure. However, for months in later years, the number of games in any given month could reach as many as 10 million. Therefore, a two-stage sampling method was required, as shown in Algorithm 1.

Algorithm 1: Two-Stage Uniform Sampling.

Inputs: Set of m objects, i.e., $U = \{U_1, ..., U_m\}$, number of objects to sample $d \in \mathbb{N}_1$;
Divide U into k chunks $H_1, ..., H_k$, each of size h (i.e., $h \times k = m, h, k \in \mathbb{N}_1$), where $H_i \cap H_j = \emptyset \; \forall i \neq j, i, j \in [k], \bigcup_{j \in [k]} H_j = U$;
Initialize $G = []$;
for $i \in [k]$ **do**
  Sample d objects uniformly from H_i, forming t;
  Append all elements in t to G;
end
Sample d objects uniformly from G, forming F;
Output F as the set of d objects sampled uniformly from U.

Algorithm 1 can be proven to sample uniformly from U; that is, the probability of any object in U being sampled into F is $\frac{d}{m}$. The proof is given in Appendix C. Note that, for FICS, the number of games in every month was relatively small, such that the database could be sampled directly.

The third processing step concerned discretisation of the whole strategy space to create a skew-symmetric payoff matrix representing the symmetric NF game. For this purpose, a single game outcome should represent the two participants playing two matches, with both participants playing black and white pieces once. We refer to such match-up as a two-way match-up. A single strategy, in the naïve sense, would thus be a combination of one contingency plan (as defined in Definition 4) if the player plays the white pieces with another one where the same player plays the black pieces. However, such a naïve interpretation of strategy would result in a very large strategy space. Therefore, we discretised the strategy space along the transitive dimension. As we used human games, we utilised the Elo rating of the corresponding players to measure the transitive strength. Therefore, given a pair of Elo ratings g_1 and g_2, the game where the white player is of rating g_1 and the black player is of rating g_2, and then another game where the black player is of rating g_1 and the white player is of rating g_2, corresponds to a single two-way match-up. Discretisation was conducted by binning the Elo ratings such that, given two bins a and b, any two-way match-up where one player's rating falls into a and the other player's rating falls into b was treated as a two-way match-up between a and b. The resulting payoff matrix of an NF game is, thus, the outcomes of all two-way match-ups between every possible pair of bins. As two-way match-ups were considered, the resulting payoff matrices were skew-symmetric.

However, when searching for the corresponding two-way match-up between two bins of rating in the data set, there could either be multiple games or no games corresponding to this match-up. Consider a match-up between one bin $a = [a_1, a_2]$ and another bin $b = [b_1, b_2]$. To fill in the corresponding entry of the matrix, a representative score for each case is first calculated. Let $rs_{a,b}$ denote the representative score for the match-up where the white player's rating is within a and the black player's rating is within b, and $rs_{b,a}$ denote the other direction. For the sake of argument, consider finding $rs_{a,b}$. As games are found for bin a against b, scores must be expressed from the perspective of a. The convention used in this paper is 1, 0, and -1 for a win, draw, and loss, respectively. This convention ensures that the entries of the resulting payoff matrix are skew-symmetric. In the case where there are multiple games where the white player's rating falls in a and black player's rating falls in b, the representative score is then taken to be the average score from all these games. On the other hand, if there are no such games, the representative score is taken to be the expected score predicted from the Elo rating; that is,

$$\mathbb{E}_s[a > b] = 2p(a > b) - 1, \tag{3}$$

where $\mathbb{E}_s[a > b]$ is the expected score of bin a against bin b, and $p(a > b)$ is computed using Equation (2), by setting k as $\frac{\ln(10)}{400}$, $r_a = \frac{a_1+a_2}{2}$, and $r_b = \frac{b_1+b_2}{2}$. As this score is predicted using the Elo rating, it is indifferent towards whether the player is playing black or white pieces. After computing the representative score for both cases, the corresponding entry in the payoff matrix for the two-way match-up between bin a and b is simply the average of the representative score of both cases (i.e., $\frac{rs_{a,b}+rs_{b,a}}{2}$). The payoff matrix construction procedure is summarised in Algorithm 2.

In Algorithm 2, $D[W \in b_i, B \in b_j]$ collects all games in D where the white player's rating W is $b_i^L \leq W \leq b_i^H$ and the black player's rating B is $b_j^L \leq B \leq b_j^H$. $\text{Av}(D_{W,B})$ averages game scores from the perspective of the white player (i.e., the score is 1, 0, -1 if the white player wins, draws, or losses, respectively). Finally, in computing $p(i > j)$ following Equation (2), r_i and r_j in the equation follow from the r_i and r_j computed in the previous line in the algorithm.

Algorithm 2: Chess Payoff Matrix Construction.

```
Inputs: Data set of games D, set of m tuples B = {b_1, ..., b_m};
Initialise M as an m × m matrix of zeroes;
for i ∈ [m] do
    for j ∈ [m] do
        if i ≥ j then
            continue;
        else
            D_{W,B} = D[W ∈ b_i, B ∈ b_j];
            if D_{W,B} = ∅ then
                r_i, r_j = (b_i^L + b_i^H)/2, (b_j^L + b_j^H)/2;
                E_{W,B} = 2p(i > j) − 1;
            else
                E_{W,B} = Av(D_{W,B});
            end
            D_{B,W} = D[B ∈ b_i, W ∈ b_j];
            if D_{B,W} = ∅ then
                r_i, r_j = (b_i^L + b_i^H)/2, (b_j^L + b_j^H)/2;
                E_{B,W} = 2p(i > j) − 1;
            else
                E_{B,W} = Av(D_{B,W});
            end
            M_{i,j}, M_{j,i} = (E_{W,B} + E_{B,W})/2, −(E_{W,B} + E_{B,W})/2;
        end
    end
end
Output M as the payoff matrix;
```

3.3.2. Nash Clustering

Having constructed the payoff matrix in Section 3.3.1, we can now proceed with non-transitivity quantification. The first method of quantifying non-transitivity is through Nash Clustering [5]. Nash Clustering is derived from the layered game geometry, which states that the strategy space of a game can be clustered into an ordered list of layers such that any strategy in preceding layers is strictly better than any strategy in the succeeding layers. A game where the strategy space can be clustered in this way is known as a layered finite game of skill.

Definition 5. *A two-player zero-sum symmetric game is defined as a k-layered finite game of skill if the strategy space of each player S_g can be factored into k layers L_i $\forall i \in [k]$, where $\bigcup_{i\in[k]} L_i = S_g$, $L_i \cap L_j = \emptyset$ $\forall i \neq j, i,j \in [k]$, such that $M_1(s_1, s_2) > 0$ $\forall s_1 \in L_i, s_2 \in L_j, \forall i,j \in [k], i < j$ and $\exists z \in \mathbb{N}_1$ satisfying $\forall i < z, |L_i| \leq |L_{i+1}|, \forall i \geq z, |L_i| \geq |L_{i+1}|$.*

A consequence of Definition 5 is that strategies in preceding layers would have a higher win-rate than those in succeeding layers. For any strategy $s \in S_g$, the corresponding win-rate $TS(s)$ is

$$TS(s) = \frac{1}{|S_g| - 1} \sum_{z \in S_g} I[M_1(s,z) > 0]. \tag{4}$$

Therefore, if we define the transitive strength of a layer to be the average win-rate of the strategies within that layer, the transitive strength of the layers would be ordered in descending order. Hence, intuitively, one can see the k-layered finite game of skill geometry as separating the transitive and non-transitive components of the strategy space. The non-transitivity is contained within each layer, whereas the transitivity variation happens across layers. It is, thus, intuitive to use the layer sizes as a measure of non-transitivity.

Furthermore, in Definition 5, the layer size increases monotonically up to a certain layer, from which it then decreases monotonically. Thus, when the transitive strength of each layer is plotted against its size, a two-dimensional spinning top structure would be observed if the change in size is strictly monotonic and $k > 2$. It is also for this reason that [5] named this geometry the spinning top geometry.

For every finite game, while there always exists $k \geq 1$ for which the game is a k-layered finite game of skill, a value of $k > 1$ does not always exist for any game; furthermore, the layered geometry is not useful if $k = 1$. Therefore, a relaxation to the k-layered geometry is required. In this alternative, a layer is only required to be "overall better" than the succeeding layers; however, it is not necessary that every strategy in a given layer beats every strategy in any succeeding layers. Such a layer structure was obtained through Nash Clustering.

Let $\text{Nash}(\boldsymbol{\mathcal{M}}|X)$, where $X \subset S_g$, denote the symmetric NE of a two-player zero-sum symmetric game, in which both players are restricted to only the strategies in X, and $\boldsymbol{\mathcal{M}}$ is the payoff matrix from the perspective of player 1. Furthermore, let $\text{supp}(\text{Nash}(\boldsymbol{\mathcal{M}}|X))$ denote the set of pure strategies that are in support of the symmetric NE. Finally, let the set notation $A \backslash B$ denote the set A excluding the elements that are in set B.

Definition 6. *Nash Clustering of a finite two-player zero-sum symmetric game produces a set of clusters C, defined as*

$$C = \{C_j : j \in \mathbb{N}_1, C_j \neq \varnothing\}, \ \textit{where}$$
$$C_0 = \varnothing, \ C_i = supp\Big(Nash(\boldsymbol{\mathcal{M}}|S_g \backslash \bigcup_{k=0}^{i-1} C_k)\Big), \ \forall i \geq 1. \tag{5}$$

Furthermore, to ensure that the Nash Clustering procedure is unique, we use the maximum entropy NE in Equation 1. Following Nash Clustering, the measure of non-transitivity would, thus, be the size or number of strategies in each cluster.

We then applied the Relative Population Performance (RPP) [27] to determine whether a layer or cluster is overall better than another cluster. Given two Nash clusters C_i and C_j, C_i is overall better or wins against C_j if $\text{RPP}(C_i, C_j) > 0$. When using the RPP as a relative cluster performance measure, the requirement that any given cluster is overall better than any succeeding clusters proves to hold [5]. Following this, one can then use the fraction of clusters beaten, or win-rate, defined in Equation 6, as the measure of transitive strength of each cluster:

$$TS(C_a) = \frac{1}{|C| - 1} \sum_{C_i \in C} I\Big[\text{RPP}(C_a, C_i) > 0\Big], \tag{6}$$

where I is the indicator function. We refer to the above win-rate as the RPP win-rate. Using the RPP win-rate as the measure of transitive strength of a Nash cluster guarantees that the transitive strength of Nash clusters are arranged in descending order.

Theorem 2. *Let C be the Nash Clustering of a two-player zero-sum symmetric game. Then, $TS(C_i) > TS(C_j) \ \forall i < j, C_i, C_j \in C$.*

Proof. Let C be the Nash Clustering of a two-player zero-sum symmetric game. Let $C_i, C_j \in C$ where $i < j, i, j \in [|C|]$. Let $n_i = \sum_{c \in C} I[\text{RPP}(C_i, c) > 0]$ and $n_j = \sum_{c \in C} I[\text{RPP}(C_j, c) > 0]$. Using the fact that $\text{RPP}(C_i, C_j) \geq 0 \ \forall i \leq j, C_i, C_j \in C$, as proven in [5], $n_i = |C| - i$ and $n_j = |C| - j$. As $i < j$, therefore, $n_j < n_i$ and since $TS(C_i) = \frac{n_i}{|C|-1}$ and $TS(C_j) = \frac{n_j}{|C|-1}$, then $TS(C_i) > TS(C_j)$. □

However, working with real data allowed us to use an alternative measure of transitive strength. We used the average Elo rating in Equation (2) of the pure strategies inside each

Nash cluster to measure the transitive strength of the cluster. Specifically, given the payoff matrix from Section 3.3.1, each pure strategy corresponds to an Elo rating bin, and the transitive strength of a Nash cluster is therefore taken to be the average Elo rating of the bins inside that cluster. Let $C_k \in C$ be a Nash cluster, c_k be the integer indices of the pure strategies in support of C_k, and $B = \{b_1, ..., b_m\}$ be the bins used when constructing the payoff matrix, where each bin b_i has lower and upper bounds (b_i^L, b_i^H), such that the bins corresponding to C_k are $\{b_j\}_{j \in c_k}$. The average Elo rating of the Nash cluster C_k is defined as

$$TS_{\text{Elo}}(C_k) = \frac{1}{|C_k|} \sum_{j \in c_k} \frac{b_j^L + b_j^H}{2}. \tag{7}$$

Given the average Elo rating against the cluster size for every Nash cluster, the final step would be to fit a curve to illustrate the spinning top geometry. For this purpose, we fitted an affine-transformed skewed normal distribution by minimising the Mean Squared Error (MSE). This completed the procedure of Nash Clustering using the average Elo rating as the measure of transitive strength.

In addition to using the average Elo rating, we also investigated the use of win-rates as a measure of transitive strength, as defined in Equation (6). However, instead of using the RPP to define the relative performance between clusters, we used a more efficient metric that achieves the same result when applied to Nash clusters. We refer to this metric as the Nash Population Performance (NPP).

Definition 7. *Let $C = \{C_1, ..., C_{|C|}\}$ be the Nash Clustering of a two-player zero-sum symmetric game with payoff matrix $\mathcal{M}$. $NPP(C_i, C_j) = \mathbf{p_i}^\top \mathcal{M} \mathbf{p_j}$, where $\mathbf{p_k} = Nash(\mathcal{M} | \bigcup_{r=k}^{|C|} C_r$ for $k \in [|C|]$ and $C_i, C_j \in C$.*

Using NPP also satisfies the requirement that any cluster is overall better than the succeeding clusters.

Theorem 3. *Let C be the Nash Clustering of a two-player zero-sum symmetric game. Then, $NPP(C_i, C_j) \geq 0 \; \forall i \leq j,\, C_i, C_j \in C$, and $NPP(C_i, C_j) \leq 0 \; \forall i > j,\, C_i, C_j \in C$.*

The proof of Theorem 3 is given in Appendix C.

Theorem 3 suggests that applying the NPP to compute Equation (6) instead of the RPP would result in an identical win-rate for any Nash cluster, and the descending win-rate guarantee is preserved. Using the NPP is more efficient as, in Definition 7, $\mathbf{p_k}$ for any Nash cluster is the corresponding NE solved during Nash Clustering to obtain that cluster; however, this means that the NPP is more suitable as a relative performance measure of Nash clusters, but less so for general population of strategies. For the latter, the RPP would be more suitable.

3.3.3. Rock–Paper–Scissor Cycles

Intuitively, a possible second method to quantify non-transitivity is to measure the length of the longest cycle in the strategy space, as this stems directly from the definition of non-transitivity. A cycle is defined as the sequence of strategies that starts and ends with the same strategy, where any strategy beats the immediate subsequent strategy in the sequence. However, calculating the length of the longest cycle in a directed graph is well-known to be NP-hard [28]. Therefore, we used the number of cycles of length three (i.e., rock–paper–scissor or RPS cycles) passing through every pure strategy as a proxy to quantify non-transitivity.

To obtain the number of RPS cycles passing through each pure strategy, an adjacency matrix is first formed from the payoff matrix. Letting the payoff matrix from Section 3.3.1 be $\mathcal{M}$, the adjacency matrix $\mathcal{A}$ can be written as $\{\mathcal{A}_{i,j}\}_{i,j=1}^{|S_g|}$, where $\mathcal{A}_{i,j} = 1$ if $\mathcal{M}_{i,j} > 0$, and 0 otherwise.

Theorem 4. *For an adjacency matrix $\boldsymbol{\mathcal{A}}$ where $\boldsymbol{\mathcal{A}}_{i,j} = 1$ if there exists a directed path from node n_i to node n_j, the number of paths of length k that start from node n_i and end on node n_j is given by $(\boldsymbol{\mathcal{A}}^k)_{i,j}$, where the length is defined as the number of edges.*

The proof of Theorem 4 can be found in Appendix C. By Theorem 4, the number of RPS cycles passing through a strategy can thus be found by taking the diagonal of $\boldsymbol{\mathcal{A}}^3$. Note that this does not apply to cycles with length of more than three, as the diagonal element of $\boldsymbol{\mathcal{A}}^n$ would include cycles with repeated nodes.

Finally, the measures of transitive strength used in this method are identical to those applied in Section 3.3.2, but applied to single strategies instead of clusters. This, therefore, completes the quantification of non-transitivity by counting RPS Cycles.

3.4. Relationships between Existing Rating Systems

As mentioned in Section 2, there are various chess player rating systems throughout the world, each of which is only valid for the pool of players over which the system is defined. As we used game data from Lichess and FICS to perform non-transitivity quantification, the results are therefore not directly applicable to different rating systems, such as USCF and FIDE. An investigation into the mappings between these rating systems is, thus, required.

We conducted a short experiment to obtain mappings between the rating systems of Lichess, USCF, and FIDE. The data set for this experiment was obtained from Chess-Goals [29], which consisted of player ratings from four sites: Chess.com [30], FIDE, USCF, and Lichess.

To investigate the mappings, we created three plots representing the mappings between pairs of rating systems: Lichess to USCF, Lichess to FIDE, and USCF to FIDE. A linear model was then fitted for each plot by MSE minimisation.

3.5. Implications of Non-Transitivity on Learning

Based on the discovered geometry, we also investigated the impact of non-transitivity on multi-agent reinforcement learning (MARL) [31]. Specifically, we designed experiments to verify the influence of non-transitivity on a particular type of MARL algorithm: Population-based learning [32–35]. This is a technique that underpins much of the existing empirical success in developing game AIs [36,37]. In fact, for simulated strategies [5], it has been found that, if the spinning top geometry exists in a strategy space, then the larger the non-transitivity of the game, in terms of layer size (for a k-layered geometry) or Nash cluster size (for Nash Clustering), the larger the population size required for methods such as fixed-memory Fictitious Play to converge. We attempted to verify whether the above conclusion still holds when real-world data are used instead. Furthermore, observing the above convergence trend with respect to the starting population size provides even stronger evidence for the existence of the spinning top geometry in the strategy space of real-world chess.

As a proxy for a population-based training method, fixed-memory Fictitious Play starts with a population (or set) of pure strategies P^0, of fixed size k. The starting pure strategies in P^0 are chosen to be the k weakest pure strategies, based on the win-rate against other pure strategies, as shown in Equation (4). At every iteration t of the fictitious play, the oldest pure strategy in the population P^{t-1} is replaced with a pure strategy that is not in P^{t-1}. The replacement strategy is required to beat all the strategies in the current population on average; that is, suppose that π is the replacement strategy at iteration t. Then, it is required that $\sum_{s \in P^{t-1}} M(\pi, s) > 0$. If there are multiple strategies satisfying this condition, then the selected strategy is the one with the lowest win-rate (i.e., $\pi = \arg\min_{s \in S_a} TS(s)$, where $S_a = \{s \in S_g \backslash P^{t-1}, \sum_{r \in P^{t-1}} M(s, r) > 0\}$).

To measure the performance at every iteration of the fictitious play, we used the expected average payoff of the population at that iteration. Suppose that, at any iteration t, the probability allocation over the population P^t, which is of size k, is $\mathbf{p^t}$. Given the payoff matrix $\mathcal{M}$ of size $m \times m$, the performance of the population P^t, $WR(P^t)$, is written as:

$$WR(P^t) = \sum_{i \in [k]} \frac{\mathbf{p^t}_i}{m} \sum_{j \in [m]} M(P_i^t, S_j), \tag{8}$$

where S_j is the pure strategy corresponding to the jth column of $\mathcal{M}$. The complete fixed-memory Fictitious Play is summarised in Algorithm 3.

Algorithm 3: Fixed-Memory Fictitious Play.

Inputs: $m \times m$ payoff matrix $\mathcal{M}$, $k \in \mathbb{N}_1$ representing the fixed population size, $n \in \mathbb{N}_1$ representing the number of rounds of fictitious play;
Initialise $w = []$, $t_l = []$, $it = 0$;
for $i \in [m]$ **do**
  $v = 0$;
  for $j \in [m]$ **do**
    if $\mathcal{M}[i,j] > 0$ **then**
      $v \leftarrow vs. + 1$;
  end
  $v \leftarrow \frac{v}{m-1}$; Append v to t_l;
end
$ids = \text{argsort}(t_l)$; $pop\_id = ids[: k]$;
$wr = \text{compute win rate}(pop\_id, \mathcal{M})$; Append wr to w; $it \leftarrow it + 1$;
while $it < n$ **do**
  $t_k = []$;
  for $i \in [m]$ **do**
    if $i \notin pop\_id$ **then**
      $v = 0$;
      for $j \in [m]$ **do**
        $v \leftarrow vs. + \mathcal{M}[i,j]$;
      end
      if $v > 0$ **then**
        Append i to t_k;
  end
  $ws = \text{argsort}(t_l[t_k])[0]$; $\pi = t_k[ws]$;
  Remove 1st element of pop_id and append π to pop_id;
  $wr = \text{compute win rate}(pop\_id, \mathcal{M})$; Append wr to w; $it \leftarrow it + 1$;
end
Output w as the list of training performance at every time-step.

In Algorithm 3, for any list a and b where b contains integers, the notation $a[b]$ means taking all elements in a at index positions denoted by the elements in b, in the order that the integers are arranged in b. Furthermore, argsort(a) returns a list of indices d, such that $a[d]$ is a sorted in ascending order. Additionally, "compute win rate" in Algorithm 3 is the function described in Algorithm 4. In this function, for any $m \times m$ matrix M, the notation M_b means taking all rows and columns of M only at positions indicated by the elements in b. Finally, size(a) returns the number of elements in the list a.

Algorithm 4 is used to compute the training performance of a population of k strategies at every round of fictitious play, following Equation (8). The convergence of fixed-memory Fictitious Play in Algorithm 3 is not dependent on the metric used to measure performance at every round, as convergence of the fictitious play means there are no more valid replacement strategies (i.e., $S_a = \emptyset$). Hence, we chose to use Algorithm 4 to measure the performance at every step, due to its simplicity.

Algorithm 4: Compute Win Rate.

Inputs: $m \times m$ payoff matrix $\mathcal{M}$ and pop_id being a list of k integers representing indices corresponding to the strategies in the population;
Initialise $res = 0$;
$k = \text{size}(pop\_id)$;
$p = []$;
for $i \in [k]$ **do**
  Append $\frac{1}{k}$ to p;
end
for $i \in [k]$ **do**
  $v = 0$;
  for $j \in [m]$ **do**
    $id = pop\_id[i]$;
    $v \leftarrow vs. + \mathcal{M}[id, j]$;
  end
  $v \leftarrow \frac{v}{m}$;
  $res \leftarrow res + vs. \times p[i]$;
end
Output res as the computed win-rate of the population of strategies.

3.6. Link to Human Skill Progression

In Section 3.5, we hypothesised that non-transitivity has implications on the performance improvement of AI agents during training. On the other hand, one of the most common issue faced by human chess players is the phenomenon of becoming stuck at a certain Elo rating [38–40]. Having performed experiments using real data, we also investigated whether non-transitivity has implications for a human player's skill or rating progression. In particular, we investigated whether a link exists between the non-transitivity of the strategy space of real-world chess to the phenomenon of players getting stuck at certain Elo ratings. This was conducted by comparing the histogram of player ratings every year using the data from Section 3.3.1, with the corresponding Nash Clustering plot.

3.7. Algorithm Hyperparameter Considerations

Algorithms 2 and 3, introduced in Sections 3.3.1 and 3.5, respectively, contain hyperparameters, and the choice of values for these hyperparameters merits further discussion.

In Algorithm 2, the hyperparameter is the size of the payoff matrix m. The time complexity of Algorithm 2 with respect to the payoff matrix dimension m is $\mathcal{O}(m^2)$. Therefore, having a large payoff matrix would severely slow down the payoff matrix construction. However, using a small payoff matrix would result in more data being unused. Algorithm 2 constructs a payoff matrix that is skew-symmetric and, so, the diagonal of the payoff matrix is be 0. As m gets smaller, the bin widths get wider and, thus, a wider range of Elo ratings are absorbed into a single bin. As a result, the non-diagonal elements of the matrix would correspond to two-way match-ups between two players with a more significant difference in Elo ratings, which is less likely to be present in the actual data, as players are typically matched with other players having similar Elo ratings. Therefore, a majority of the non-diagonal elements of the matrix will be filled using the Elo formula in Equation (3), instead of real data, which effectively turns the game into a purely transitive Elo game [5]. This leads to us not being able to observe the spinning top geometry in the strategy space occupied by real-world strategies. In our experiments, we used an m of 1500, as this was sufficiently large to demonstrate the existence of the spinning top geometry, while keeping the payoff matrix construction reasonably fast.

In Algorithm 3, the hyperparameters are the population size k and the number of rounds n. The time complexity of Algorithm 3 is more affected by the number of rounds n, on the order of $\mathcal{O}(n)$. While it grows slower than the time complexity of Algorithm 2 with respect to m, it is still desirable to keep n relatively small, as fixed-memory Fictitious Play would have to be carried out for a number of population sizes. However, n should be large enough to demonstrate the convergence behaviour of the training process, if any. From our experiments, we found that 2000 rounds were sufficient for this purpose. The choice of population sizes is elaborated more in Section 4.3.

4. Results and Discussions

4.1. Non-Transitivity Quantification

Following Sections 3.3.2 and 3.3.3, non-transitivity quantification was carried out on Lichess game data from 2013 to 2020, and FICS 2019 data, using the average Elo rating as a measure of transitive strength, and the Nash Cluster size and number of RPS cycles as measures of non-transitivity. The results are as shown in Figure 3.

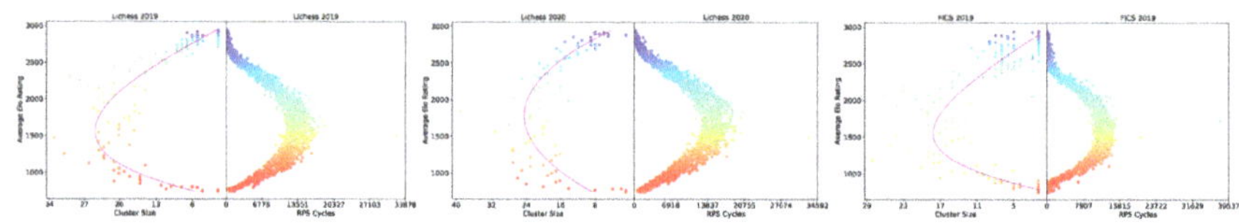

(a) (b) (c)

Figure 3. Nash Clustering (left of each plot) and RPS Cycles (right of each plot) on Lichess 2019 (**a**), Lichess 2020 (**b**), and FICS 2019 (**c**). See Figure A1 in Appendix A for the full version of the results, which include Lichess 2013–2020 and FICS 2019.

Figures 3 and A1 illustrate that the spinning top geometry was observed in both Nash Clustering and RPS Cycles plots, for all of the considered years. Furthermore, both the Nash cluster size and number of RPS cycles peaked at a similar Elo rating range (1300–1700) for all of the years. This provides comprehensive evidence that the strategies adopted in real-world games do not vary throughout the years or from one online platform to another, and that the non-transitivity of real-world strategies is highest in the Elo rating range of 1300–1700.

Furthermore, as stated in Sections 3.3.2 and 3.3.3, we also performed the above non-transitivity quantifications using win-rates as a measure of transitive strength, as it provides stronger evidence for the existence of the spinning top geometry should this geometry persist. The results are shown in Figure 4.

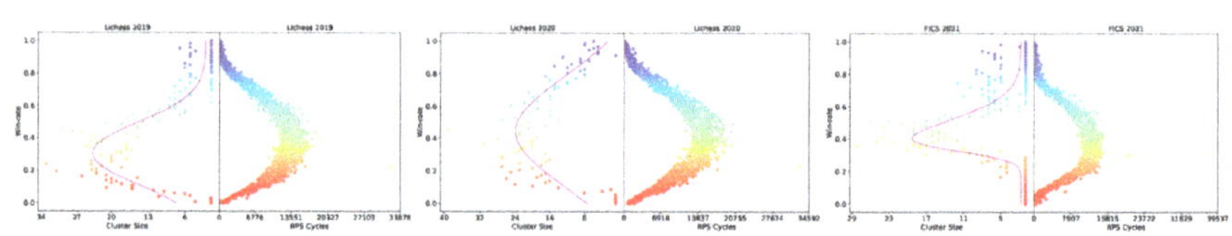

(a) (b) (c)

Figure 4. Nash Clustering (left of each plot) and RPS Cycles (right of each plot) on Lichess 2019 (**a**), Lichess 2020 (**b**), and FICS 2019 (**c**) with win-rate as a measure of transitive strength. See Figure A2 in Appendix B for the full version of the results, which include Lichess 2013–2020 and FICS 2019.

Despite using a different measure of transitive strength in Figures 4 and A2, the results show that the spinning top geometry still persisted for all the years. Not only does this provide stronger evidence for the existence of a spinning top geometry within the real-world strategy space of chess, it also indicates that measuring non-transitivity using both Nash Clustering and RPS Cycles is agnostic towards the measure of transitive strength used.

4.2. Relationships between Existing Rating Systems

Following Section 3.4, we fitted three Linear Regression models representing the mappings between three rating systems discussed in that section; namely, Lichess, USCF, and FIDE rating systems. The results are shown in Figure 5.

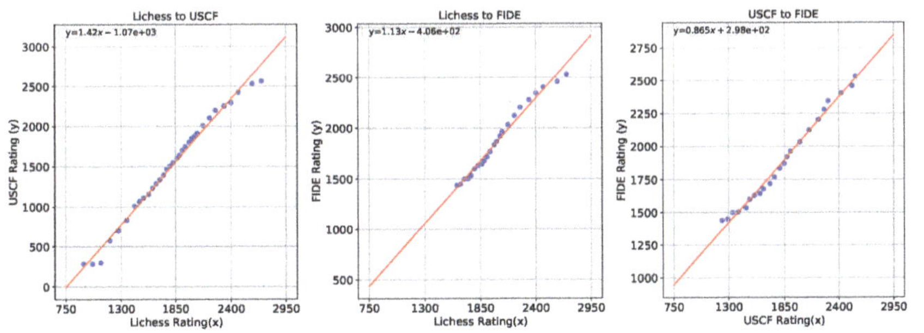

Figure 5. Chess Rating Mappings between Lichess, USCF, and FIDE.

Figure 5 shows that the relationships between Lichess, USCF, and FIDE ratings were largely linear and monotonically increasing, and that the linear models fit the data sufficiently well. As the mappings between the rating systems were monotonically increasing, the spinning top geometry observed in Figure 3 is expected to still hold when mapped to USCF or FIDE rating systems. This is as the relative ordering of the Nash clusters or pure strategies based on Elo rating will be preserved. Therefore, our results are directly applicable to different rating systems.

4.3. Implications of Non-Transitivity on Learning

Following Section 3.5, we conducted fixed-memory Fictitious Play, as described in Algorithm 3, using payoff matrices constructed following Section 3.3.1. Fictitious Play was carried out with population sizes of 1, 25, 50, 75, 100, 150, 200, 250, and 300, in order to demonstrate the effect of non-transitivity, in terms of Nash Cluster sizes, on the minimum population size needed for training to converge. These values were chosen by comparing the games in [5] with similar Nash Cluster sizes. Figures 3 and A1 show that the largest Nash cluster sizes were in the range of 25 to slightly above 50. In [5], the game Hex 3×3 [41] had similar Nash cluster sizes, with the largest size being slightly less than 50. For this game, [5] used population sizes of 1, 25, 50, 75, 100, 150, 200, 250, and 300; thus, we used these values in our experiments as well. The results are shown in Figure 6.

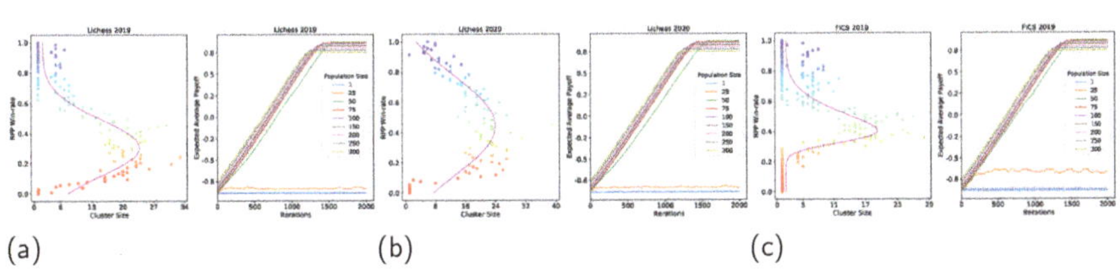

Figure 6. (Left of each plot) Nash Clustering using the RPP win-rate as a measure of transitive strength on Lichess 2019 (**a**), 2020 (**b**), and FICS 2019 (**c**). (Right of each plot) Fixed-Memory Fictitious Play on Lichess 2019 (**a**), Lichess 2020 (**b**), and FICS 2019 (**c**). See Figure A2 in Appendix B and Figure A1 in Appendix A for full versions of the results for Nash Clustering with the RPP win-rate and fixed-memory Fictitious Play, respectively.

Figures 6 and A1 show that the training process converged for all cases, provided that the population size was 50 or above. This is because the Nash cluster sizes are never much larger than 50 and, therefore, a population size of 50 ensures good coverage of the Nash clusters at any transitive strength. Such convergence behaviour also provides additional evidence that the spinning top geometry is present in the strategy space of real-world chess.

It should be noted, however, that the minimum population size needed for training to converge does not always correspond to the largest Nash cluster size, for which there are two contributing factors. The first factor is that covering a full Nash cluster (i.e., having a full Nash cluster in the population at some iteration) only guarantees the replacement strategy at that iteration to be from a cluster of greater transitive strength than the covered cluster. There are no guarantees that this causes subsequent iterations to cover Nash clusters of increasing transitive strength. The second factor is that the convergence guarantee is with respect to the k-layered game of skill geometry defined in Definition 5. As Nash Clustering is a relaxation of this geometry, covering a full Nash cluster does not guarantee that the minimal population size requirement will be satisfied.

4.4. Link to Human Skill Progression

Following Section 3.6, we plotted the histogram of player ratings alongside the corresponding Nash Clustering plots for comparison. The results are shown in Figure 7.

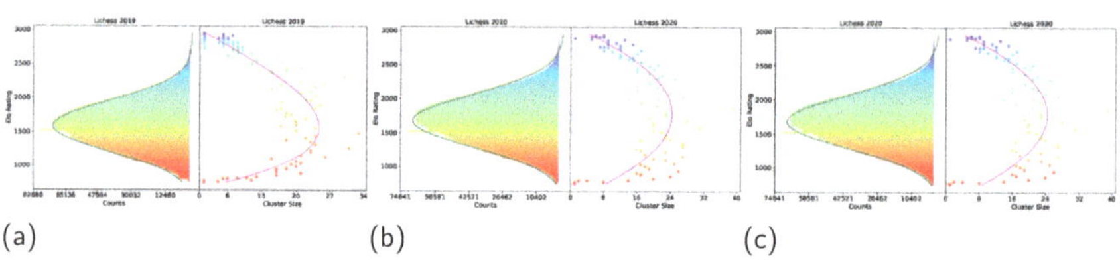

Figure 7. (Left of each plot) Histogram of Player Elo Ratings and (Right of each plot) Nash Clustering on Lichess 2019 (**a**), Lichess 2020 (**b**), and FICS 2019 (**c**). See Figure A1 in Appendix A for the full version of the results.

Figures 7 and A1 shows that the peaks of the histograms and the bulk of the data consistently fell in the 1300–1700 Elo rating range, which matches with the range of Elo ratings in which players tend to get stuck, as stated in [38–40], suggesting that players tend to get stuck in this range. Furthermore, the peaks of the histograms coincided with the peak of the fitted skewed normal curve on the Nash Clustering plots. This implies that high non-transitivity in the 1300 to 1700 rating range is one potential cause of players getting stuck in this range.

A plausible explanation is that, in the 1300–1700 Elo rating range, there exist a lot of RPS cycles (as can be seen from Figure 3), which means there exist a large number of counter-strategies. Therefore, to improve from this Elo rating range, players need to learn how to win against many strategies; for example, by dedicating more effort toward learning diverse opening tactics. Otherwise, their play-style may be at risk of being countered by some strategies at that level. This is in contrast to ratings where non-transitivity is low. With a lower number of counter-strategies, it is arguably easier to improve, as there are relatively fewer strategies to adapt towards.

5. Conclusions and Future Work

The goal of this paper was to measure the non-transitivity of chess games and investigate the potential implications for training effective AI agents, as well as those for human skill progression. Our work is novel in the sense that we, for the first time, profiled the geometry of the strategy space based on real-world data from human players. This, in turn, prompted the discovery of the spinning top geometry, which has only been previously observed for AI-generated strategies; more importantly, we uncovered the relationship between the degree of non-transitivity and the progression of human skill in playing chess. Additionally, the discovered relationship also indicates that, in order to overcome the non-transitivity in the strategy space, it is imperative to maintain large population sizes when applying population-based methods in training AIs. Throughout our analysis, we managed to tackle several practical challenges. For example, despite the variation in Elo rating systems for chess, we introduced effective mappings between those rating systems, which enables direct translation of our findings across different rating systems.

Finally, there are several avenues for possible improvements, which we leave for future work:

- In Section 3.3.1, missing data between match-ups of bins are filled using Elo formulas; that is, Equations (2) and (3). However, the Lichess ratings use the Glicko-2 system [20], which has a slightly different win probability formula that also considers the rating deviation and volatility of the rating. Therefore, a possible improvement would be to additionally collect the rating deviation and volatility of the players in every game, and apply the Glicko-2 predictive formula to compute the win probability, instead of Equation (2).
- Non-transitivity analysis could also be carried out using other online chess platforms, such as Chess.com [30], in order to provide more comprehensive evidence on the spinning top geometry of the real-world strategy space. Furthermore, the non-transitivity analysis could also be carried out using real-world data on other, more complex, zero-sum games, such as Go, DOTA and StarCraft.
- Other links between non-transitivity and human progression can be investigated. One possible method would be to monitor player rating progression from the start of their progress to when they achieve a sufficiently high rating in a chess platform, such as Lichess. Their rating progression can then be compared to the non-transitivity at that rating and in that year. However, player rating progression is typically not available on online chess platforms and, thus, would require monitoring player progress over an extended period of time.

Author Contributions: Conceptualization, R.S.; methodology, R.S.; software, R.S.; validation, R.S.; formal analysis, R.S.; investigation, R.S.; resources, R.S.; data curation, R.S.; writing—original draft preparation, R.S.; writing—review and editing, R.S. and Y.Y.; supervision, Y.Y. and J.W.; project administration, Y.Y. and W.J. All authors have read and agreed to the published version of the manuscript.

Funding: This research received no external funding.

Institutional Review Board Statement: Not applicable

Informed Consent Statement: Not applicable

Data Availability Statement: The python codes to replicate the experiments in this paper are available at https://anonymous.4open.science/r/MSc-Thesis-8543 (accessed on 13 March 2022). `README.md` contains all the instructions to run the codes. Finally, the data sets can be downloaded from https://database.lichess.org/ (accessed on 13 March 2022) for Lichess and https://www.ficsgames.org/ (accessed on 13 March 2022) for FICS.

Conflicts of Interest: The authors declare no conflict of interest.

Appendix A. Additional Results

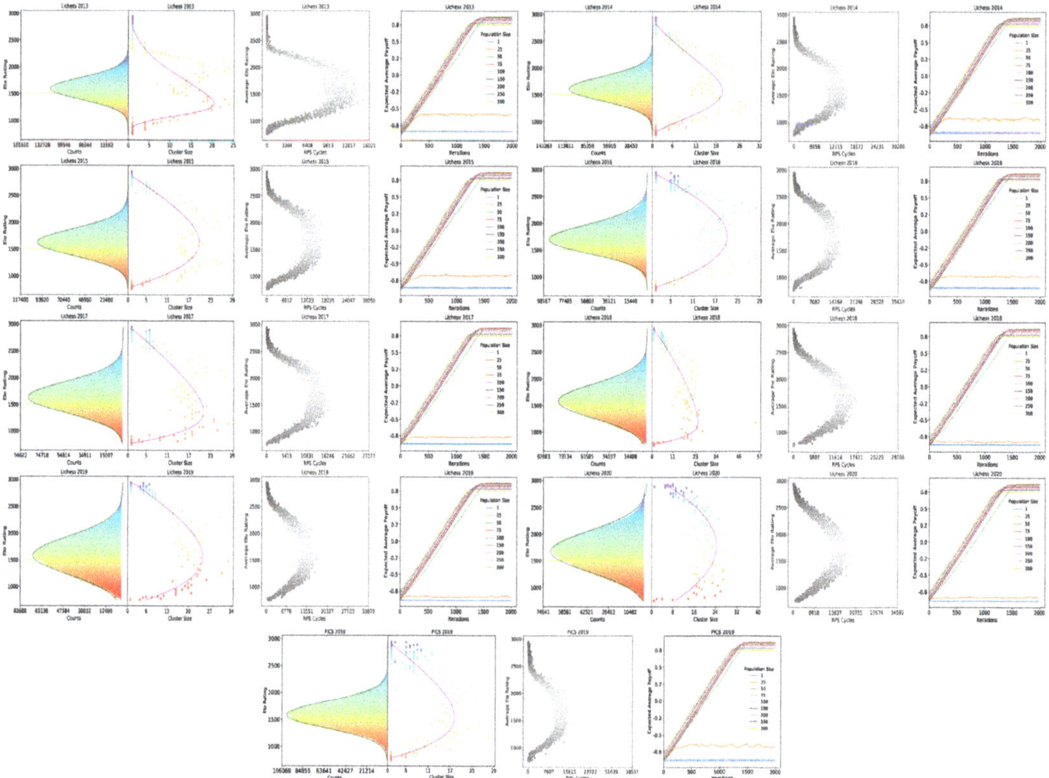

Figure A1. Histogram of player Elo ratings (first of each plot), Nash Clustering (second of each plot), RPS Cycles (third of each plot), and fixed-memory Fictitious Play (fourth of each plot) on Lichess 2013–2020 and FICS 2019 data.

Appendix B. Additional Results with Alternative Measure of Transitive Strength

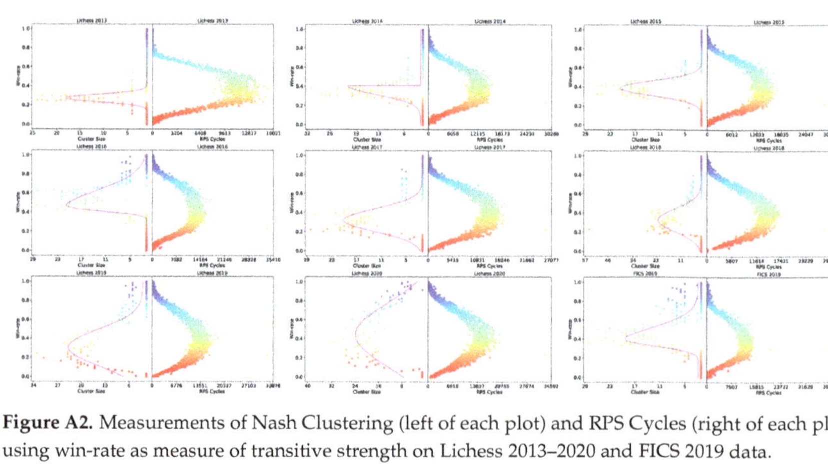

Figure A2. Measurements of Nash Clustering (left of each plot) and RPS Cycles (right of each plot) using win-rate as measure of transitive strength on Lichess 2013–2020 and FICS 2019 data.

Appendix C. Theorem Proofs

Theorem A1. *With Algorithm 1, the probability of any object in M being sampled into F is* $\frac{d}{m}$.

Proof. For any object in U to end up in F, they must first get picked into G. As $H_i \cap H_j = \emptyset$ $\forall i,j \in [k]$, $i \neq j$, the probability that any object is sampled into G is $\frac{{}^{h-1}C_{d-1}}{{}^{h}C_d} = \frac{d}{h}$. Then, given that they are in G, they must get sampled into F. The probability that this happens is $\frac{{}^{d\times k-1}C_{d-1}}{{}^{d\times k}C_d} = \frac{1}{k}$. Hence, the probability that any object from U gets sampled into F is $\frac{d}{h\times k} = \frac{d}{m}$. □

Theorem A2. *Let C be the Nash Clustering of a two-player zero-sum symmetric game. Then,* $NPP(C_i, C_j) \geq 0 \; \forall i \leq j, C_i, C_j \in C$ *and* $NPP(C_i, C_j) \leq 0 \; \forall i > j, C_i, C_j \in C$.

Proof. Let C be the Nash Clustering of a two-player zero-sum symmetric game with a payoff matrix of $\boldsymbol{\mathcal{M}}$ and strategy space S_g for each of the two players. For any $k \in [|C|]$, let $\mathbf{p_k}$ be the NE solved to obtain the kth cluster; that is, $\mathbf{p_k} = \text{Nash}(\boldsymbol{\mathcal{M}} | \bigcup_{i=k}^{|C|} C_i)$, where $\mathbf{p_k} \in \Delta_{|C|}$. As $\mathbf{p_k}$ is restricted to exclude $\bigcup_{i=1}^{k-1} C_i$, therefore, $\mathbf{p_k}$ would be all zeroes at the positions corresponding to all pure strategies $s \in \bigcup_{i=1}^{k-1} C_i$. Let $X_k = \bigcup_{i=1}^{k-1} C_i$ and $\boldsymbol{\mathcal{M}}_{-X_k}$ be the payoff matrix of the game, but excluding the rows and columns that corresponds to the pure strategies in X_k. Additionally, let $\mathbf{p_k}^{X_k}$ denote the vector $\mathbf{p_k}$ but removing all entries at positions corresponding to the pure strategies in X_k. Hence, $\boldsymbol{\mathcal{M}}_{-X_k} \in \mathbb{R}^{|S_g \setminus X_k| \times |S_g \setminus X_k|}$ and $\mathbf{p_k}^{X_k} \in \Delta_{|S_g \setminus X_k|}$. Furthermore, it is also true that $\mathbf{p}^\top \boldsymbol{\mathcal{M}} \mathbf{p} = (\mathbf{p}^{X_k})^\top \boldsymbol{\mathcal{M}}_{-X_k} \mathbf{p}^{X_k}$ for any $\mathbf{p} \in \Delta_{|S_g|}$, provided that the entries of $\mathbf{p}$ at positions corresponding to pure strategies in X_k are zeroes.

By definition of NE in [42], we have that $(\mathbf{p_k}^{X_k})^\top \boldsymbol{\mathcal{M}}_{-X_k} \mathbf{p_k}^{X_k} \leq (\mathbf{p_k}^{X_k})^\top \boldsymbol{\mathcal{M}}_{-X_k} \mathbf{p}' \; \forall \mathbf{p}' \in \Delta_{|S_g \setminus X_k|}$ and $(\mathbf{p_k}^{X_k})^\top \boldsymbol{\mathcal{M}}_{-X_k} \mathbf{p_k}^{X_k} \geq \mathbf{p}'^\top \boldsymbol{\mathcal{M}}_{-X_k} \mathbf{p_k}^{X_k} \; \forall \mathbf{p}' \in \Delta_{|S_g \setminus X_k|}$. Now, consider two clusters C_i and C_j, where $i < j$ and $C_i, C_j \in C$. By the first definition of NE earlier, $(\mathbf{p_i}^{X_i})^\top \boldsymbol{\mathcal{M}}_{-X_i} \mathbf{p_i}^{X_i} \leq (\mathbf{p_i}^{X_i})^\top \boldsymbol{\mathcal{M}}_{-X_i} \mathbf{p}' \; \forall \mathbf{p}' \in \Delta_{|S_g \setminus X_i|}$, which implies $(\mathbf{p_i}^{X_i})^\top \boldsymbol{\mathcal{M}}_{-X_i} \mathbf{p_i}^{X_i} \leq (\mathbf{p_i}^{X_i})^\top \boldsymbol{\mathcal{M}}_{-X_i} \mathbf{p_j}^{X_i}$ and, thus, equivalently $\mathbf{p_i}^\top \boldsymbol{\mathcal{M}} \mathbf{p_i} \leq \mathbf{p_i}^\top \boldsymbol{\mathcal{M}} \mathbf{p_j}$. Then, by the properties of skew-symmetric matrices, $\mathbf{p_i}^\top \boldsymbol{\mathcal{M}} \mathbf{p_i} = 0$ and, hence, $\mathbf{p_i}^\top \boldsymbol{\mathcal{M}} \mathbf{p_j} \geq 0$; that is, $\text{NPP}(C_i, C_j) \geq 0$. Furthermore, by the second definition of NE earlier, $(\mathbf{p_i}^{X_i})^\top \boldsymbol{\mathcal{M}}_{-X_i} \mathbf{p_i}^{X_i} \geq \mathbf{p}'^\top \boldsymbol{\mathcal{M}}_{-X_i} \mathbf{p_i}^{X_i} \; \forall \mathbf{p}' \in \Delta_{|S_g \setminus X_i|}$, which implies $(\mathbf{p_i}^{X_i})^\top \boldsymbol{\mathcal{M}}_{-X_i} \mathbf{p_i}^{X_i} \geq (\mathbf{p_j}^{X_i})^\top \boldsymbol{\mathcal{M}}_{-X_i} \mathbf{p_i}^{X_i}$ and, thus, equivalently $\mathbf{p_i}^\top \boldsymbol{\mathcal{M}} \mathbf{p_i} \geq \mathbf{p_j}^\top \boldsymbol{\mathcal{M}} \mathbf{p_i}$. Finally, using the property of skew-symmetric matrices again, $\mathbf{p_j}^T \boldsymbol{\mathcal{M}} \mathbf{p_i} \leq 0$; that is, $\text{NPP}(C_j, C_i) \leq 0$. □

Theorem A3. *For an adjacency matrix* $\boldsymbol{\mathcal{A}}$ *where* $\boldsymbol{\mathcal{A}}_{i,j} = 1$, *if there exists a directed path from node* n_i *to node* n_j, *the number of paths of length k that starts from node* n_i *and ends on node* n_j *is given by* $(\boldsymbol{\mathcal{A}}^k)_{i,j}$, *where the length is defined as the number of edges in that path.*

Proof. By induction, the base case is when $k = 1$. A path from node n_i to node n_j of length 1 is simply a direct edge connecting n_i to n_j. The presence of such an edge is indicated by $\boldsymbol{\mathcal{A}}_{i,j}$, which follows from the definition of adjacency matrix, thereby proving the base case. The inductive step is then to prove that if $(\boldsymbol{\mathcal{A}}^k)_{i,j}$ is the number of paths of length k from node n_i to n_j for some $k \in \mathbb{N}_1$, then $(\boldsymbol{\mathcal{A}}^{k+1})_{i,j}$ is the number of paths of length $k+1$ from node n_i to n_j. This follows from matrix multiplication. Let $\boldsymbol{\mathcal{R}} = \boldsymbol{\mathcal{A}}^{k+1} = \boldsymbol{\mathcal{A}}^k \boldsymbol{\mathcal{A}}$. Then, $\boldsymbol{\mathcal{R}}_{i,j} = \sum_{r=1}^{|S_g|} \boldsymbol{\mathcal{A}}^k_{i,r} \boldsymbol{\mathcal{A}}_{r,j}$. The inner multiplicative term of the sum will only be non-zero if both $\boldsymbol{\mathcal{A}}^k_{i,r}$ and $\boldsymbol{\mathcal{A}}_{r,j}$ are non-zero, indicating that there exists a path of length k from node n_i to some node n_r and, then, a direct edge from that node n_r to n_j. This forms a path of length $k+1$ from node n_i to n_j. Therefore, $\boldsymbol{\mathcal{R}}_{i,j}$ counts the number of paths of length $k+1$ from node n_i to n_j, proving the inductive hypothesis. □

References

1. Ensmenger, N. Is chess the drosophila of artificial intelligence? A social history of an algorithm. *Soc. Stud. Sci.* **2012**, *42*, 5–30. [CrossRef] [PubMed]
2. Shannon, C.E. XXII. Programming a computer for playing chess. *Lond. Edinb. Dublin Philos. Mag. J. Sci.* **1950**, *41*, 256–275. [CrossRef]
3. Campbell, M.; Hoane, A.J., Jr.; Hsu, F.h. Deep blue. *Artif. Intell.* **2002**, *134*, 57–83. [CrossRef]
4. Silver, D.; Hubert, T.; Schrittwieser, J.; Antonoglou, I.; Lai, M.; Guez, A.; Lanctot, M.; Sifre, L.; Kumaran, D.; Graepel, T.; et al. Mastering chess and shogi by self-play with a general reinforcement learning algorithm. *arXiv* **2017**, arXiv:1712.01815.
5. Czarnecki, W.M.; Gidel, G.; Tracey, B.; Tuyls, K.; Omidshafiei, S.; Balduzzi, D.; Jaderberg, M. Real World Games Look Like Spinning Tops. In Proceedings of the Advances in Neural Information Processing Systems, Vancouver, BC, Canada, 6–12 December 2020.
6. Nash, J. Non-cooperative games. *Ann. Math.* **1951**, *54*, 286–295. [CrossRef]
7. McIlroy-Young, R.; Sen, S.; Kleinberg, J.; Anderson, A. Aligning Superhuman AI with Human Behavior: Chess as a Model System. In Proceedings of the Proceedings of the 26th ACM SIGKDD International Conference on Knowledge Discovery & Data Mining, Virtual Event, CA, USA, 6–10 July 2020; pp. 1677–1687.
8. Romstad, T.; Costalba, M.; Kiiski, J.; Linscott, G. Stockfish: A strong open source chess engine. 2017. *Open Source*. Available online: https://stockfishchess.org (accessed on 18 August 2021).
9. Lichess. About lichess.org. Available online: https://lichess.org/about (accessed on 16 August 2021).
10. FICS. FICS Free Internet Chess Server. Available online: https://www.freechess.org/ (accessed on 16 August 2021).
11. Yang, Y.; Luo, J.; Wen, Y.; Slumbers, O.; Graves, D.; Bou Ammar, H.; Wang, J.; Taylor, M.E. Diverse Auto-Curriculum is Critical for Successful Real-World Multiagent Learning Systems. In Proceedings of the 20th International Conference on Autonomous Agents and MultiAgent Systems, London, UK, 3–7 May 2021; pp. 51–56.
12. Russell, S.; Norvig, P. *Artificial Intelligence: A Modern Approach*; Prentice Hall: Englewood Cliffs, NJ, USA, 2002 .
13. Chaslot, G.; Bakkes, S.; Szita, I.; Spronck, P. Monte-Carlo Tree Search: A New Framework for Game AI. *AIIDE* **2008**, *8*, 216–217.
14. Vinyals, O.; Babuschkin, I.; Czarnecki, W.M.; Mathieu, M.; Dudzik, A.; Chung, J.; Choi, D.H.; Powell, R.; Ewalds, T.; Georgiev, P.; et al. Grandmaster level in StarCraft II using multi-agent reinforcement learning. *Nature* **2019**, *575*, 350–354. [CrossRef] [PubMed]
15. International Chess Federation. FIDE Charter, Art. 1 FIDE—Name, Legal Status and Seat. Available online: https://handbook.fide.com/files/handbook/FIDECharter2020.pdf (accessed on 16 August 2021).
16. United States Chess Federation. About US Chess Federation. Available online: https://new.uschess.org/about (accessed on 16 August 2021).
17. Glickman, M.E.; Doan, T. The US Chess Rating System. 2020. Available online: https://new.uschess.org/sites/default/files/media/documents/the-us-chess-rating-system-revised-september-2020.pdf (accessed on 18 August 2021).
18. International Chess Federation. FIDE Handbook, B. Permanent Commissions/02. FIDE Rating Regulations (Qualification Commission)/FIDE Rating Regulations Effective from 1 July 2017 (with Amendments Effective from 1 February 2021)/. Available online: https://handbook.fide.com/chapter/B022017 (accessed on 20 August 2021).
19. Glickman, M.E. *The Glicko System*; Boston University: Boston, MA, USA,1995; Volume 16, pp. 16–17.
20. Glickman, M.E. *Example of the Glicko-2 System*; Boston University: Boston, MA, USA, 2012; pp. 1–6.
21. Deng, X.; Li, Y.; Mguni, D.H.; Wang, J.; Yang, Y. On the Complexity of Computing Markov Perfect Equilibrium in General-Sum Stochastic Games. *arXiv* **2021**, arXiv:2109.01795.
22. Balduzzi, D.; Tuyls, K.; Pérolat, J.; Graepel, T. Re-evaluating evaluation. In *Proceedings of the NeurIPS*; Neural Information Processing Systems Foundation, Inc.: Montréal, QC, Canada, 2018; pp. 3272–3283.
23. Hart, S. Games in extensive and strategic forms. In *Handbook of Game Theory with Economic Applications*; Elsevier: Amsterdam, The Netherlands, 1992; Volume 1, pp. 19–40.
24. Kuhn, H.W. Extensive games. In *Lectures on the Theory of Games (AM-37)*; Princeton University Press: Princeton, NJ, USA, 2009; pp. 59–80.
25. Elo, A.E. *The Rating of Chessplayers, Past and Present*; Arco Pub.: Nagoya, Japan, 1978.
26. Edwards, S.J. Standard Portable Game Notation Specification and Implementation Guide. 1994. Available online: http://www.saremba.de/chessgml/standards/pgn/pgncomplete.htm (accessed on 10 August 2021).
27. Balduzzi, D.; Garnelo, M.; Bachrach, Y.; Czarnecki, W.; Perolat, J.; Jaderberg, M.; Graepel, T. Open-ended learning in symmetric zero-sum games. In Proceedings of the International Conference on Machine Learning. PMLR, Long Beach, CA, USA, 9–15 June 2019; pp. 434–443.
28. Björklund, A.; Husfeldt, T.; Khanna, S. Approximating longest directed paths and cycles. In Proceedings of the International Colloquium on Automata, Languages, and Programming, Turku, Finland, 12–16 July 2004; pp. 222–233.
29. *ChessGoals Rating Comparison Database*; 2021. Available online: https://chessgoals.com/rating-comparison/
30. Chess.com. About Chess.com. Available online: https://www.chess.com/about (accessed on 16 August 2021).
31. Yang, Y.; Wang, J. An Overview of Multi-Agent Reinforcement Learning from Game Theoretical Perspective. *arXiv* **2020**, arXiv:2011.00583.

32. Lanctot, M.; Zambaldi, V.; Gruslys, A.; Lazaridou, A.; Tuyls, K.; Pérolat, J.; Silver, D.; Graepel, T. A unified game-theoretic approach to multiagent reinforcement learning. In Proceedings of the 31st International Conference on Neural Information Processing Systems, Long Beach, CA, USA, 4–9 December 2017; pp. 4193–4206.
33. Perez-Nieves, N.; Yang, Y.; Slumbers, O.; Mguni, D.H.; Wen, Y.; Wang, J. Modelling Behavioural Diversity for Learning in Open-Ended Games. In Proceedings of the International Conference on Machine Learning. PMLR, Virtual, 18–24 July 2021; pp. 8514–8524.
34. Liu, X.; Jia, H.; Wen, Y.; Yang, Y.; Hu, Y.; Chen, Y.; Fan, C.; Hu, Z. Unifying Behavioral and Response Diversity for Open-ended Learning in Zero-sum Games. *arXiv* **2021**, arXiv:2106.04958.
35. Dinh, L.C.; Yang, Y.; Tian, Z.; Nieves, N.P.; Slumbers, O.; Mguni, D.H.; Ammar, H.B.; Wang, J. Online Double Oracle. *arXiv* **2021**, arXiv:2103.07780.
36. Zhou, M.; Wan, Z.; Wang, H.; Wen, M.; Wu, R.; Wen, Y.; Yang, Y.; Zhang, W.; Wang, J. MALib: A Parallel Framework for Population-based Multi-agent Reinforcement Learning. *arXiv* **2021**, arXiv:2106.07551.
37. Lanctot, M.; Lockhart, E.; Lespiau, J.B.; Zambaldi, V.; Upadhyay, S.; Pérolat, J.; Srinivasan, S.; Timbers, F.; Tuyls, K.; Omidshafiei, S.; et al. OpenSpiel: A framework for reinforcement learning in games. *arXiv* **2019**, arXiv:1908.09453.
38. Chess.com. *Stuck at the Same Rating for a Long Time*; 2019.
39. Lichess. *My Friends Are Stuck at 1500–1600 How Long Will it Take Them to Get Up to 1700*; 2021. Available online: https://www.chess.com/forum/view/general/stuck-at-the-same-rating-for-a-long-time-1 (accessed on 13 March 2022).
40. Lichess. *Stuck at 1600 Rating*; 2021. Available online: https://lichess.org/forum/general-chess-discussion/stuck-at-1600-rating (accessed on 13 March 2022).
41. Hayward, R.B.; Toft, B. *Hex, Inside and Out: The Full Story*; CRC Press: Boca Raton, FL, USA, 2019.
42. Daskalakis, C. Two-Player Zero-Sum Games and Linear Programming. 2011. Available online: http://people.csail.mit.edu/costis/6896sp10/lec2.pdf (accessed on 21 August 2021).

algorithms

MDPI

Article

Official International Mahjong: A New Playground for AI Research

Yunlong Lu [1], Wenxin Li [1,*] and Wenlong Li [2]

[1] School of Computer Science, Peking University, Beijing 100871, China
[2] Mahjong International League, 1002 Lausanne, Switzerland
* Correspondence: lwx@pku.edu.cn; Tel.: +86-10-62753425

Abstract: Games have long been benchmarks and testbeds for AI research. In recent years, with the development of new algorithms and the boost in computational power, many popular games played by humans have been solved by AI systems. Mahjong is one of the most popular games played in China and has been spread worldwide, which presents challenges for AI research due to its multi-agent nature, rich hidden information, and complex scoring rules, but it has been somehow overlooked in the community of game AI research. In 2020 and 2022, we held two AI competitions of Official International Mahjong, the standard variant of Mahjong rules, in conjunction with a top-tier AI conference called IJCAI. We are the first to adopt the duplicate format in evaluating Mahjong AI agents to mitigate the high variance in this game. By comparing the algorithms and performance of AI agents in the competitions, we conclude that supervised learning and reinforcement learning are the current state-of-the-art methods in this game and perform much better than heuristic methods based on human knowledge. We also held a human-versus-AI competition and found that the top AI agent still could not beat professional human players. We claim that this game can be a new benchmark for AI research due to its complexity and popularity among people.

Keywords: game AI; supervised learning; reinforcement learning; AI competition; Mahjong

1. Introduction

Games are born to test and challenge human intelligence and have always been benchmarks and testbeds throughout the history of artificial intelligence. Board games such as checkers [1] and chess [2] were the first to be solved by AI algorithms in the last century. With the boost in computational power and the application of new algorithms, in the last decade, AI systems have achieved superhuman performance in many games that once, only humans were believed to be able to master, from board games such as Go [3–5] and card games such as Texas Hold'em [6–8] to video games such as StarCraft [9], Dota 2 [10], and HoK [11]. These games are all popular among humans, with various annual and seasonal competitions held all over the world. Such popularity has spurred the academic community to put effort into them and develop new algorithms to solve them.

Mahjong is one of the most popular games played in China and has spread worldwide since the early 20th century. Originating from China and with a long history dating back to the 12th century, many regional variants of Mahjong have been developed and are widely played in almost every region of China. It is estimated to have 600 million players all over the world. However, there are so many regional variants in rules that most of the Mahjong communities focus on different regional variants, and there is no competition that covers a majority of players to have enough impact. Because of this, the game has been overlooked by the community of AI research.

Mahjong is a four-player tile-based game with complex scoring rules and rich hidden information, which presents several challenges to AI research. The complexity of the game is much higher than that of Texas Hold'em when measured by the average size of information sets. Unlike most of the other card games such as poker and bridge, the goal of Mahjong is to form various scoring patterns from the tiles, while other games usually involve a single target such as making a bigger hand or emptying the hand as quickly as possible. Mahjong tiles are equal in their strength, which is different from poker, where cards are ranked from two to Ace and players can have a clear value judgement. The strategy of Mahjong involves choosing between multiple target patterns based on the similarity between the current hand and various patterns, which is hard to estimate but relies more on the aesthetic feeling of the tile combinations. The result of the game is also affected by luck, causing high variance when solved by AI algorithms.

Official International Mahjong is one of the three variants recognized and standardized by the Mahjong International League (MIL) as a set of competition rules called the Mahjong Competition Rules (MCR). This variant consists of 81 different scoring patterns, much larger than other variants, to emphasize the strategic thinking and calculation ability of players. The other two variants are Riichi Competition Rules (RCR) from Japanese Mahjong and Sichuan Bloody Rules (SBR) from Sichuan Mahjong. SBR is dominated by luck instead of strategies and is not suitable for AI research. RCR features a unique set of rules and encourages a more conservative style of play. It has fewer scoring patterns and is easier than MCR, and has been preliminarily solved by the AI system named Suphx built by MSRA [12]. Among those variants, Official International Mahjong is the most suitable variant as a playground for AI algorithms because of the complexity in its scoring rules and the emphasis on strategies instead of luck.

As an effort to promote Official International Mahjong in AI research, we held two Mahjong AI competitions in conjunction with the International Joint Conference on Artificial Intelligence (IJCAI) in 2020 and 2022. Dozens of teams participated in the competitions and used a variety of algorithms to build their agents. These algorithms include heuristic methods based on human knowledge and methods based on deep learning, such as supervised learning and reinforcement learning. The results of the competitions showed that the agents trained by supervised learning and reinforcement learning turned out to perform better than those with heuristic methods. A human-versus-AI competition was also held after the first Mahjong AI competition to challenge professional human players with one of the top AIs. The result showed that the AI agent was still far behind the top human players.

These competitions mark the beginning of Official International Mahjong as a new playground for AI research. While the best AI agents in the competitions still cannot beat the best human players, we believe that AI systems built by new algorithms with more computational power will eventually achieve superhuman performance in this game as long as this game draws enough attention from the community of AI research, which is achieved by more AI competitions. To conclude, our contributions are as follows.

- We are the first to hold AI competitions of Official International Mahjong. We provide the judge program that implements the rules of this Mahjong variant and open source libraries to calculate scoring patterns. We also build match datasets from both humans and top AI agents for further research.
- We innovatively adopt the duplicate format in the evaluation of AI agents to reduce the high variance introduced by the randomness of the game, which is commonly used in top-level human competitions but rarely used in AI competitions.
- We promote Official International Mahjong as a challenge and benchmark for AI research. We summarize the algorithms of AI agents in the two AI competitions and conclude that modern game AI algorithms based on deep learning are the current state-of-the-art methods. We claim that more powerful algorithms are needed to beat professional human players in this game.

The rest of this paper is organized as follows. Section 2 discusses the background of games as benchmarks and testbeds for AI research. An overview of game AI algorithms and a brief introduction to Mahjong are also presented. Section 3 presents a detailed description of the rules of Official International Mahjong. Section 4 introduces the two AI competitions and the human-versus-AI competition we have held of this game, including the platform and our novel competition format. Section 5 summarizes the algorithms used in the AI agents submitted by the competitors.

2. Background

2.1. AI and Games

The goal of artificial intelligence is to reach human levels in a variety of tasks. But how can we measure the intelligence level of AI systems against humans? Turing test [13] may be the earliest criterion to test the intelligent behavior of AI systems, but it has been controversial, as more and more AI systems have managed to pass the test by targeted imitation or deception without real intelligence. However, games are created to test and challenge human intelligence, making them excellent benchmarks and testbeds for the evolution of AI. The diversity of games provides a rich context for gradual skill progression to test a wide range of AI systems' abilities. From Deep Blue to AlphaGo, AI systems beating professional players in games with increasing complexity have always been considered major milestones and breakthroughs in the development of AI technologies.

The earliest research on game AI focused on classic board games such as checkers [1], chess [2], and Go [3]. These games are relatively simpler to solve by AI algorithms due to their discrete turn-based mechanics, highly formalized state representation, and fully visible information to all players. However, these games almost exclusively test the strength of different strategies and are not fun enough to be very popular among humans. Nowadays, popular games played by humans are often much more complex, involving randomness and luck to introduce fun, imperfect information between players to introduce deduction and deception, or more complex game elements and multi-player team battles to improve playability. The increasing complexity and diversity of games bring new challenges for AI research, thus promoting the invention of new algorithms to solve them.

In the last decade, AI systems have achieved superhuman performance in many popular games played by humans, thanks to the advances in AI techniques and the boost in computational power. These games include card games such as Texas Hold'em [6–8], which is the most popular card game played in America, and multi-player video games such as StarCraft [9] and Dota 2 [10], which have well-established e-sports events popular all over the world. One important reason these games draw attention to AI research is that these games are famous enough to form communities of players who organize annual or seasonal tournaments both for human players and for AI programs. For example, the World Series of Pokers (WSOP) [14] is a series of poker tournaments held annually since 1970, where over half of the events are variants of Texas Hold'em. Meanwhile, as an effort to develop a system to compare poker agents, the Annual Computer Poker Competition (ACPC) [15] has been held annually since 2006 in conjunction with top-tier AI conferences such as AAAI and IJCAI. ACPC began with only five competitors in the first year but attracted dozens of teams from many countries several years later. Such tournaments provide AI researchers with great platforms to compare and improve their AI agents until more and more powerful agents finally beat professional human players, marking that the game has finally been solved by AI.

2.2. Game AI Algorithms

Many AI algorithms have been proposed to build game-playing agents for different games. These algorithms can be divided into three categories [16]. Heuristic methods, also called expert systems, rely heavily on human knowledge, which is the most straightforward way to build a game AI system from scratch. Real-time planning algorithms compute the action to take when each specific game state is actually encountered during gameplay, usually by expanding a search tree from the current state, and are widely used in board games such as chess and Go, where fast responses are not required. Learning algorithms train models in advance to store policies or value functions in the form of model parameters, which are later used in real-time gameplay. Supervised learning and reinforcement learning are the most common learning algorithms in the field of game AI.

There are three basic ways of using explicit human knowledge in heuristic methods. The first way is to incorporate human knowledge in feature extraction. Strategy-related features can be calculated from the raw features of the game state based on the understanding of human players to guide the selection of better actions. The second way is to provide explicit rule-based policies, usually written in an 'if-else' manner. Such policies are formally modeled by decision trees, where each internal nodes are conditions about the game state to choose a child node, and each leaf node is an action label. Some decision trees also have chance nodes, where child nodes are selected based on probabilities. The third way is to create an evaluation function based on human knowledge, to estimate the preference of human players on game states. Such evaluation functions can be further combined with real-time planning algorithms to select the action that potentially leads to better states in the following steps.

In most cases, the state space of a game is so large that it is difficult to have an optimal strategy before the game starts. Real-time planning algorithms can compute the action at each game state in real-time gameplay if the state transition model of the game is known. When an evaluation function of game states is available, the simplest form of planning is to choose an action by comparing the values of the model-predicted next states for each action. Such planning can look much deeper than one step ahead and expand a search tree to evaluate many future states under different sequences of actions, leading to a more far-sighted agent. One of the most famous algorithms is A* [17], which uses an evaluation function to guide the selection of unexplored nodes in the search tree. Minimax [18] is another classical real-time planning algorithm in two-player competitive settings and is widely used in board games, based on the assumption that each player wants to maximize their own payoffs. Monte-Carlo tree search (MCTS) simulates many trajectories starting from the current state and running to a terminal state, and updates the state-action value along the path based on the final score, which is then used to yield better trajectories. This algorithm has achieved huge success in two-player board games and accounts mostly for the progress achieved in computer Go from a weak amateur level in 2005 to a grandmaster level in 2015 [19].

The model trained by learning algorithms is the most fundamental part of building a game AI system and is the focus of game AI research. Supervised learning learns a policy or value model that predicts the action to choose or the estimated value under the current state. It requires lots of labeled data in the form of state–action or state–value pairs, usually collected from human gameplay data or data generated by other game-playing algorithms. Reinforcement learning (RL) models the environment as a Markov Decision Process (MDP) and discovers which actions can lead to higher future rewards by interacting with the environment and trying them out. Traditional RL algorithms deal with single-agent settings and can be divided into value-based methods and policy-based methods, depending on whether they only learn value models or learn policy models as well. PPO is probably the most popular RL algorithm because it empirically has a more stable training process compared to other algorithms, and is widely used in most of the game AI milestones achieved in recent years, such as AlphaStar and OpenAI Five. When combined with proper self-play techniques, single-agent RL algorithms are proved to approach a Nash equilibrium in competitive multi-agent environments [20–22]. In practice, a model pool is usually maintained from which opponents are selected to collect data for training, which has become a general paradigm for applying RL algorithms to multi-agent games.

2.3. Mahjong

Mahjong is a game almost as popular in China as Texas Hold'em in America; however, it has not attracted much attention from the community of game AI research. This game and its regional variants are widely played all over the world and estimated to have 600 million players in total, according to an internal report of the Mahjong International League. It is worth noting that Mahjong should not be confused with Mahjong Solitaire [23], which is a single-player picture-matching game using the same set of tiles. Instead, four-player Mahjong is similar to a Western card game called rummy, using tiles to form patterns instead of cards.

There are many regional variants of Mahjong rules, and here, we present a brief introduction of the basic rules. Mahjong is played with a basic set of 144 tiles with Chinese characters and symbols, though many regional variations may omit some of the tiles. Usually, each player begins with 13 tiles which are not shown to other players. Players draw and discard tiles in turn until they complete a winning hand with a 14th tile. The basic type of winning hand consists of four melds and a pair, while there exist winning hands with several special patterns. Most of the regional variations have some basic rules in common, including the order of play, how a tile is drawn and discarded, how a tile can be robbed from another player, and the basic kinds of melds allowed. Different variations differ mainly on the criteria for legal melds and winning hands, and they can have very different scoring systems and some additional rules. In general, the game of Mahjong requires skill and strategy, as well as a decent amount of luck to win, making it entertaining enough to have many players all over the world.

Among those various regional variants of Mahjong rules, only three of them are recognized and standardized for Mahjong competition by the Mahjong International League, a non-profit organization aiming to promote Mahjong as a mind sport throughout the world. These three variants are recognized mainly because of their popularity and the different emphasis in their strategies. The first of them is Official International Mahjong, founded by the General Administration of Sport in China in July of 1998, known as Mahjong Competition Rules (MCR), which includes a large variety of scoring rules to emphasize strategy and calculation ability, and is widely adopted for Mahjong competition. The second is Riichi Competition Rules (RCR) from Riichi Mahjong, or Japanese Mahjong. This variant features a unique set of rules such as Riichi and the use of dora, encouraging a more conservative style of play. The third is Sichuan Bloody Rules (SBR) from Bloody Mahjong, or Sichuan Mahjong, because this variant is fast-paced and dominated by luck.

From the perspective of game AI, Mahjong presents several challenges for AI algorithms. First, as a four-player game, multi-agent AI algorithms are required to solve it because both competition and cooperation exist between different agents. Second, the private tiles of each agent are not exposed to other agents, and players have to deduce other players' hands by their discarded tiles, making it a game with rich hidden information. The complexity of imperfect-information games can be measured by information sets, defined as the game states that each player cannot distinguish from their own observations [24]. Figure 1 shows the number and average size of information sets of Mahjong. The average size of information sets in Mahjong is much larger than that of Texas Hold'em and another card game popular in China called DouDizhu, making it difficult to solve by CFR-based algorithms, which have achieved success in variants of Texas Hold'em. Last, randomness and luck also contribute to the results of the game, causing high variance and instability in convergence when applying learning algorithms.

Unlike other popular card games such as bridge, Texas Hold'em, and Doudizhu, which also have imperfect information and have been testbeds for AI research, the rules and strategies of Mahjong are unique in the following ways. First, in most card games, each card has a different strength, usually ranking from two to Ace (A). Higher cards can beat lower cards so that each hand can have a clear value judgment in the eyes of players. However, there is no such concept of "strength" of individual tiles in Mahjong, and each Mahjong tile is equal in its role in forming various patterns. The value judgment of each hand is based on the similarity between the current hand and different scoring patterns, which is dominated by the aesthetic feeling of the tile combinations. Second, the strategies of Mahjong involve making the choice between multiple targets of patterns, especially in Official International Mahjong with 81 different scoring patterns, while other card games usually have a single target such as making a bigger hand than others or emptying the hand as soon as possible. These factors make it harder to acquire an optimal strategy in Mahjong, and even professional players can have quite different value judgments and strategies with the same hand.

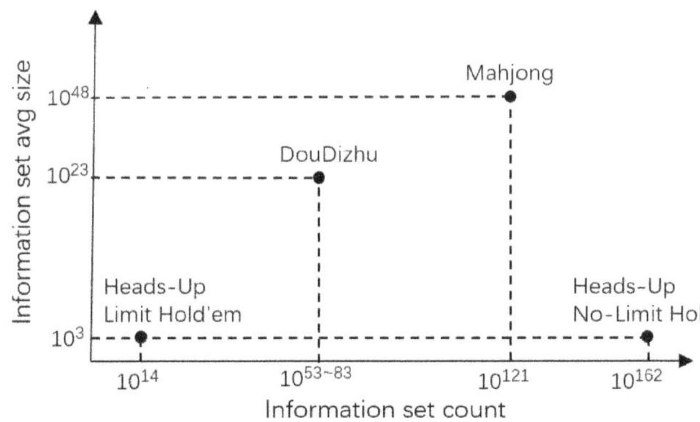

Figure 1. The number and average size of information sets of some imperfect-information games.

3. Official International Mahjong

As the official variant of Mahjong rules widely used in Mahjong competitions, Official International Mahjong is a better playground for AI research than other Mahjong variants for two reasons. First, unlike most of the regional variants such as SBR where luck dominates the result of the game, Official International Mahjong involves a moderate amount of luck, but mostly strategies and skills. Second, Official International Mahjong has a complex scoring rule with 81 different scoring patterns, many more than in other variants, including RCR. In fact, Official International Mahjong integrates most of the scoring patterns among various regional variants, requiring more sophisticated strategies for human players and indicating higher complexity for AI algorithms. This section introduces the rules of Official International Mahjong in detail.

Official International Mahjong is played with a full set of 144 Mahjong tiles split into 3 categories: suited tiles, honored tiles, and flower tiles, as shown in Table 1. Suited tiles are divided into three suits: Characters, Bamboos, and Dots, each numbered from one to nine. There are 4 identical copies of each tile, totaling 108 suited tiles. Honor tiles are divided into two sets: wind tiles of four directions and dragon tiles of three colors. Like suited tiles, each tile has 4 identical copies, totaling 28 honor tiles. The remaining eight tiles are special flower tiles, each with an artistic rendering of one plant or season, which play a unique role in the mechanics of the game.

When playing the game, four players sit down at their respective positions around the table in the shape of an inverted compass: east is the dealer, the right of the dealer is south, across is west, and the left is north. The position of each player is called their "seat wind". A full match usually consists of four rounds, each representing a "prevailing wind", starting with east. Four games are played each round, with players shifting their seat winds. The seat wind and prevailing wind are important because they affect the scoring of the game, which is further discussed in Appendix A.

When a game starts, all of the tiles are randomly shuffled and stacked as two layers before each player to form a square wall. Tiles are drawn from a specific breaking position of the wall so that the tile wall decreases clockwise, and that position is usually decided by dice rolling. At the start of each game, 13 initial tiles are drawn by each player in a specific order, as shown in Figure 2. Then, players draw and discard one tile in turn in counterclockwise order until some player declares a winning hand, or no one wins before the tile wall runs out, ending in a tie.

This regular order of play can be interrupted in four cases. In the first case, whenever a player draws a flower tile, it should be exposed and put aside. The player has to draw the last tile of the wall as a replacement so that they still have 14 tiles before they discard any tile. This also happens when dealing the initial 13 tiles, and can happen successively in a player's turn if they draw another flower tile as the replacement.

Table 1. A full set of 144 Mahjong tiles consists of 108 suited tiles, 28 honor tiles, and 8 flower tiles.

Suited Tiles		Numbers								
		One	Two	Three	Four	Five	Six	Seven	Eight	Nine
Suits	Characters									
	Bamboos	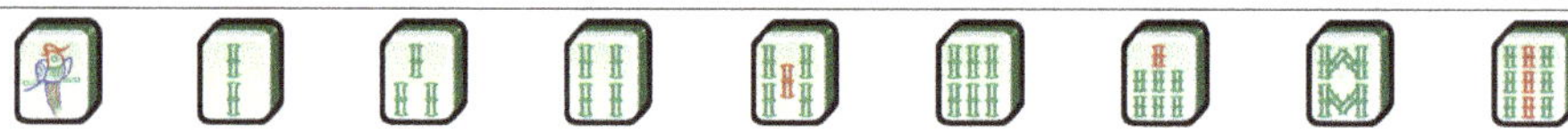								
	Dots									
Honor tiles	Winds				Dragons					
	East	South	West	North	Red	Green	White			

Flower tiles	Plants				Seasons					
	Plum blossom	Orchid	Daisy	Bamboo	Spring	Summer	Fall	Winter		
	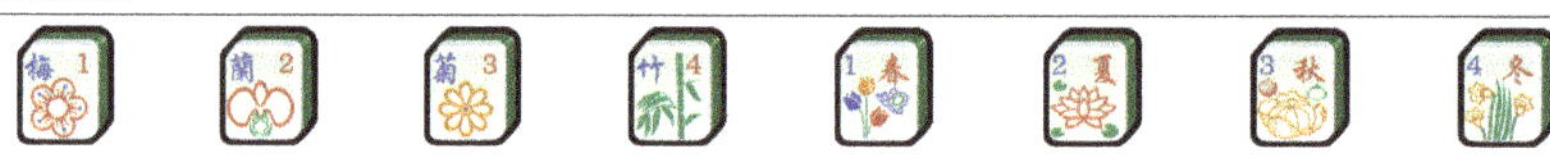									

In the second case, when a player discards a tile, any other player may steal the tile to complete a meld. Melds are groups of tiles within players' hands, which are essential components to form a winning hand. There are three kinds of melds: pungs, kongs, and chows. A pung is three identical tiles, either suited tiles or honor tiles. A kong is four identical tiles, but only counts as a set of three tiles. A chow is three suited tiles of the same suit in a consecutive numerical sequence. When a meld is formed by stealing another player's discard, it is put aside and exposed to all players; otherwise, it remains concealed. A player can only steal a tile from the player left to them to form a chow, but from any player to form a pung or a kong. If multiple players try to steal the same discard, the priority of pung and kong is higher than that of chow. After the player steals the tile to complete a pung or a chow, they become the next player to discard a tile because there are currently 14 tiles in their hand. However, since a kong only counts as three tiles, the player who steals a tile to complete a kong has to draw another tile from the end of the wall before they discard their tile.

In the third case, a player can also declare a kong upon drawing a tile. There are two different ways to complete such kongs. In the first case, the player can declare a concealed kong if they hold four identical tiles in their hand, which do not necessarily include the tile they just drew. These four tiles are put aside but remain concealed from other players. In the second case, if the player has an exposed pung and holds the fourth tile, they can promote the pung to a kong by adding the fourth tile. In both cases, the player has to draw another tile from the end of the wall before they discard their tile.

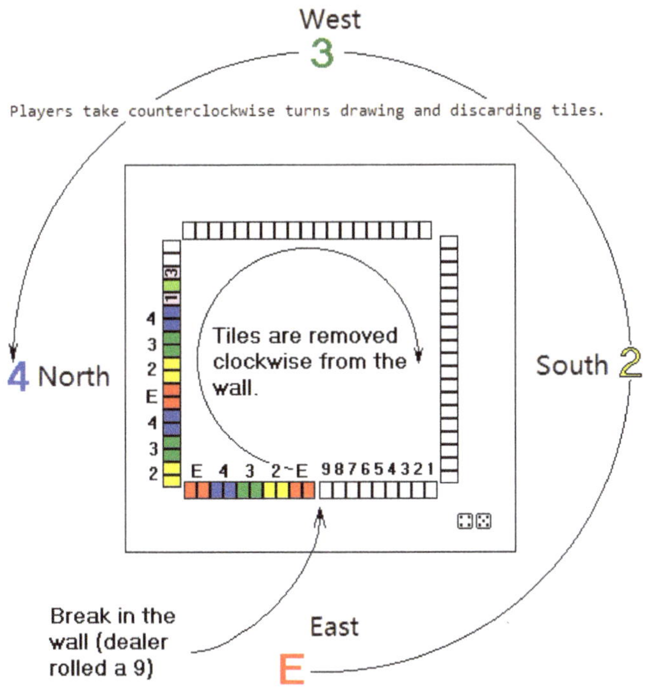

Figure 2. The seat positions of players and the initial configuration of the two-layer tile wall. The tile wall decreases clockwise from a breaking point, and the colors indicate the order of dealing the initial 13 tiles of each player. Then, players draw and discard tiles in counterclockwise order. Image modified from [25].

In the fourth case, a player can declare a winning hand and end the game. All their tiles are then exposed to others for a validity check. A winning hand consists of 14 tiles. Since players always have 13 tiles in their hand during play (flower tiles are not counted), they must win by either drawing a tile or seizing another player's discarded tile, making a 14-tile winning hand. There is a special case when another player adds a fourth tile to promote a pung to a kong; a player can rob it if they can make a winning hand with it.

A winning hand has to satisfy specific patterns. The basic form of a winning hand consists of four melds, either exposed or concealed, and a pair of identical tiles called the eye. The hand is then compared to a variety of scoring patterns to count a so-called "*fan*" value. There are 81 different scoring patterns in total, and the detailed list can be found in Appendix A. Each matched pattern is worth some *fans*, and they are summed up as the *fan* value of this hand. A player can only win when their hand is worth no less than eight *fans*. There are also some special forms of winning hands, which match scoring patterns without four melds and an eye. All forms of winning patterns are listed in Table 2. The final scores of each player depend on the winner's *fan* value and the provider of the 14th winning tile. Specifically, if the winner makes a winning hand of x *fans* by drawing a tile themselves, they receive $8 + x$ points from the other three players. Instead, if the 14th winning tile comes from another player, either discarded or added to the promoted pung, the winning player receives $8 + x$ points from the provider of this tile, and only 8 points from the other two players.

Table 2. Five forms of winning patterns in Official International Mahjong. A hand of basic winning pattern has to meet eight *fans* to win, while other patterns are worth more than eight *fans* themselves.

Winning Patterns	Explanation with an Example
Basic pattern	Four melds and a pair, with *fan* value no less than 8.
	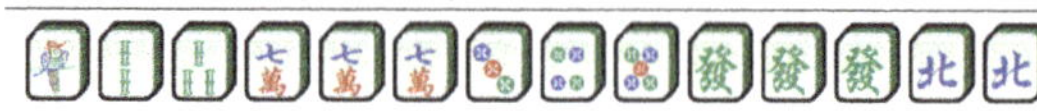
Thirteen orphans	1 and 9 of each suit, one of each wind, one of each dragon, and one duplicate tile of any.
	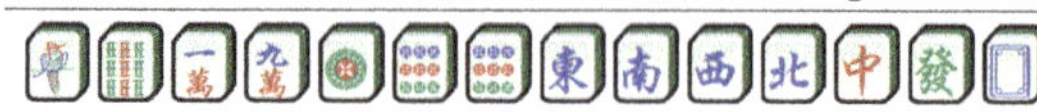
Seven pairs	A hand with seven pairs.
	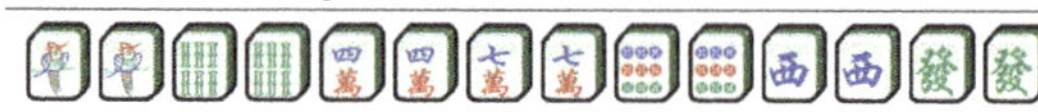
Honors and knitted tiles	A hand of 14 tiles from these 16 tiles: number 1, 4, 7 of one suit; number 2, 5, 8 of second suit; number 3, 6, 9 of third suit; and all honor tiles.
	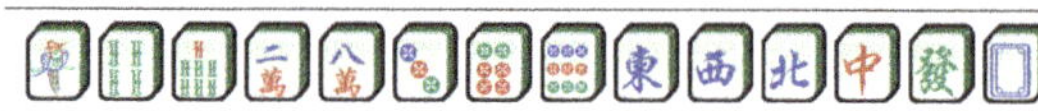
Knitted Straight	Number 1, 4, 7 of one suit, number 2, 5, 8 of second suit, number 3, 6, 9 of third suit, plus a meld and a pair.
	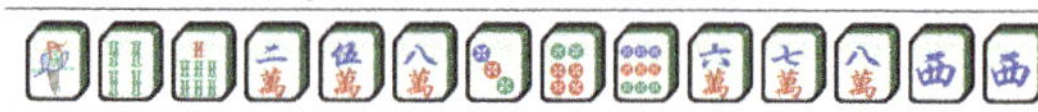

Since a full match of Mahjong consists of four rounds with different prevailing winds and each round is composed of four games with different seating positions, the final ranking of players depends on the total scores of all sixteen games. Although the scoring of each game is zero-sum, where players are strictly competitive with each other, it is common to cooperate with some players based on the cumulative scores to secure one's final ranking and adopt some different strategies, especially in the last few games of a match.

4. AI Competitions

In an effort to unlock the potential of modern game AI algorithms in Official International Mahjong and promote it as a playground for AI research, we held two AI competitions in 2020 and 2022 in conjunction with the International Joint Conference on Artificial Intelligence (IJCAI). Dozens of teams from universities and companies participated in the competitions, and they contributed their wisdom and submitted their AI programs to play Mahjong with a variety of algorithms. We adopted the duplicate format in these competitions under the guidance of the Mahjong International League, which greatly reduces the variance in the evaluation of AI agents. We also organized a human-versus-AI competition in the beginning of 2021, where two professional human players were invited to challenge the top AIs from the AI competition in 2020. This section presents an introduction of these competitions.

4.1. Botzone

Both Mahjong AI competitions were held based on Botzone [26], an online multi-agent competitive platform built by our lab. The platform is designed to provide a universal interface to evaluate AI agents in different programming languages in a variety of games, including traditional board games such as Gomoku, Ataxx, chess, and Go, card games such as DouDizhu and Mahjong, and modified versions of Atari games such as Pac-Man and Tank. Users can upload their programs to the platform, called bots, which can play against any other bots of the same game as long as they follow the input–output protocol specified by the platform. The platform also supports games between human players and bots, or only human players.

Apart from creating isolated games to evaluate the performance of agents, Botzone has an Elo ranking system that constantly runs games between randomly selected agents and calculates the real-time Elo scores of each bot, maintaining a ladder list of each game. Additionally, Botzone also supports creating groups to hold individual tournaments, with multiple rounds of games played between a fixed set of agents under predefined formats. This tournament system to evaluate AI agents makes Botzone a strong platform to support both AI research and education. Over the years, dozens of courses have used this platform to hold competitions in their course project to write AI agents for various games. The platform has so far accumulated more than 160 thousand AI agents in over 40 games, with more than 50 million games played.

4.2. Competition Format

As a competition to evaluate the performance of multiple agents, it is important that the final ranking can reveal the actual strength of different agents. However, Mahjong is a four-player imperfect-information game with a high degree of randomness in dealing tiles, making it hard to design the competition format with an accurate ranking. In both Mahjong AI competitions, we applied a combination of Swiss rounds and the duplicate format as the competition format, which reduces the variance in individual games as much as possible. The illustration of the format is shown in Figure 3.

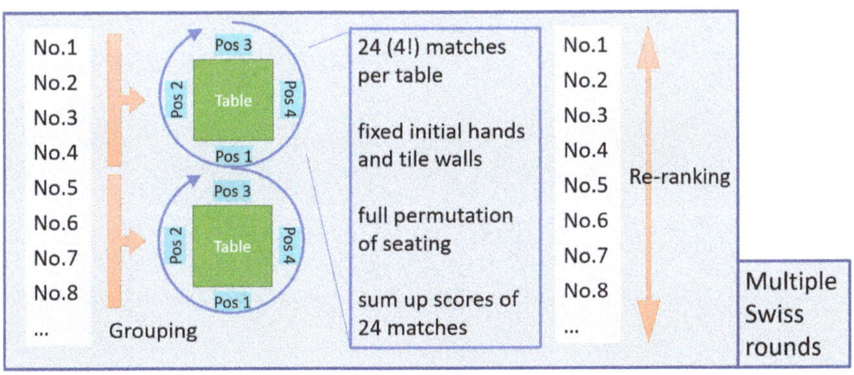

Figure 3. The competition format of Mahjong AI competitions, a combination of a Swiss-round system and duplicate format.

Duplicate format is a popular technique to mitigate the factor of luck and reduce variance in games. It was initially applied in the game of bridge and was later used heavily in poker competitions, including ACPC. The basic idea is to play multiple games with players taking different seats while keeping the same outcomes of all random events in each game, including the cards or tiles dealt throughout the game. In two-player games such as Heads-Up No-Limit Hold'em (HUNL), each game is played twice with the same set of cards for each seat, but with different player seating. This can significantly mitigate the factor of luck because even if a player has a good hand and wins the game, their opponent will eventually have the same hand in another game. However, Mahjong is a four-player game where not only the tiles dealt to each player contribute to the result of the game, but the order of players in drawing and discarding the tile also matters. When applying duplicate format to Mahjong, the public tile wall has to be split into four parts for each seat, and each player draws tiles only from their own part, including their initial hands. The same tile wall is used for a total of 24 games, where the players change their seats in all possible permutations. The scores of these games are summed up as the score of one "duplicate game". In this way, not only is the factor of luck from the tile wall mitigated, but the influence of each player to other players such as stealing tiles can also be reduced. It is worth noting that though Suphx built by MSRA is reported to beat top human players in Riichi Mahjong, no duplicate format was used in the evaluation, and their results may suffer from high variance.

As Mahjong is a four-player game, competition formats such as round robin cannot be applied because there are too many possible combinations of players. Instead, the competitions use Swiss round as the high-level format, with each round pitting the closest-ranked players against each other. The initial ranking of players is randomly decided before the first round. In each round, four players are grouped to play 24 games of duplicate format. The raw scores of each game are summed up to decide the rankings of each player in this "duplicate game" to assign ranking points of 4, 3, 2, or 1 to each player. The players are then re-ranked by their accumulated ranking points. The typical Swiss-round format has a relatively small number of rounds, usually the logarithm of the number of players. However, considering the randomness and imperfect information in Mahjong, it takes hundreds of Swiss rounds to achieve a stable ranking of players, especially when they are close in level of play.

Additionally, to further mitigate the factor of luck and reduce the variance in each game, the flower tiles in Mahjong, i.e., plant tiles and season tiles, are excluded in both Mahjong AI competitions and the human-versus-AI competition, because flower tiles only affect the final scores of each player after someone makes a winning hand, and are not involved in the strategy of either discarding or melding. The design of flower tiles makes it a random perturbation term in the accurate evaluation of agents, though it can bring fun to human players as a factor of luck. In conclusion, the competition format of both Mahjong AI competitions combined Swiss rounds, duplicate format, and the exclusion of flower tiles to make the ranking as accurate as possible.

4.3. Mahjong AI Competition

We held two Mahjong AI competitions in 2020 and 2022. Both of them were divided into 3 rounds: the qualification round to determine the top 16, the elimination round to determine the top 4, and the final round to determine the champion. The participants need to upload their bots before the qualification round and the elimination round, while the final round uses the same bots as the elimination round.

The first Mahjong AI competition [27] was held in conjunction with IJCAI 2020, which was postponed in the second year as a virtual conference due to the COVID-19 pandemic. Thirty-seven teams submitted their agents in the qualification round on 31 November, where three tournaments were held in a week, each running six Swiss rounds and each round comprising four "duplicate games" of twenty-four matches. The results of the three tournaments were weighted proportionally to calculate the ranking of the qualification round. The top 16 teams joined the elimination round on 1 January 2021, which comprised a single tournament of 96 Swiss rounds, each comrising 4×24 games in duplicate format. The final round was held later, with 128 Swiss rounds, to provide a more accurate ranking of the top four agents. We organized a symposium during the IJCAI 2020 session, and the top 16 teams all made oral presentations to discuss their methods. Some of the teams also submitted papers to introduce their algorithms in detail.

The second Mahjong AI competition [28] had a similar schedule to the first one, and was held as a competition session at IJCAI 2022. The qualification round was on 22 May, the elimination round was on 3 July, and the final round was on 4 July. The competition format was slightly different from the competition in the first year. First, only one tournament was held in the qualification round instead of three. Second, each Swiss round consisted of only 1 duplicate game with 24 games of the same till wall, but more Swiss rounds were used to ensure that each agent still played hundreds of duplicate games or thousands of individual games in total. Most of the top 16 teams gave their presentations to introduce their algorithms in the symposium held on 28 July during the session at IJCAI 2022. The schedules of both competitions are summarized in Table 3, and the list of winning teams can be found on the homepages of the competitions.

Table 3. Summary of the schedule of the two Mahjong AI competitions.

Year	Qualification Round			Elimination Round			Final Round			Dataset
	Time	Teams	Rounds	Time	Teams	Rounds	Time	Teams	Rounds	
2020–2021	31 November	37	$3 \times 6 \times 4$	1 January	16	96×4	6 January	4	128×4	Human data
2022	22 May	25	128	3 July	16	128	4 July	4	512	AI data

Since Official International Mahjong has a complex scoring system involving 81 scoring patterns and some principles regarding whether each pattern is counted in various cases, it is very difficult and error-prone for the competitors to write code to calculate scores when playing the game. We provided an open source library [29] to calculate the *fan* value of each hand, with two versions in Python and C++. Additionaly, we built two Mahjong datasets for the competitors to use in these competitions. Specifically, the dataset provided in the first competition consists of about half a million matches of human players from an online Mahjong game platform, which belongs to another variant of Mahjong with different scoring rules, but shares the same basic rules and some of the most common scoring patterns. The dataset provided in the second competition consists of over 98 thousand self-play matches generated on Botzone by the top agents of the first competition, which has much higher quality than the previous dataset in the strength of strategies. Many teams used the provided dataset for algorithms based on machine learning, which is further discussed in Section 5.

4.4. Human-versus-AI Competition

The human-versus-AI competition was held on 30 January 2021, shortly after the final round of the first Mahjong AI competition. We invited two professional human players to the competition to compete against AI programs. The human players were Wenlong Li, the winner of the Japan MCR Championship (2016) who is ranked in the top three of the MIL master points system (2022), and Zhangfei Zhang, the winner of the China MCR Championship (2010). The AI program was called Kima, which was the agent ranked third in the first Mahjong AI competition.

We also adopted the duplicate format in this competition, where multiple games are played with the same tile wall but different player seatings. However, the application of duplicate format to competitions with human players is different from that with AI players, because a human player can memorize the tile wall if the same tile wall is used for multiple games. Instead, the competitors sat in the same position at different tables and were faced with the same tile wall, while the other three players on each table were another AI program as a fixed baseline player, which was chosen as the agent ranked fourth place. A total of 16 games were played in the competition, with a full round of prevalent and seat winds of the competitors. The scores of each player were summed up to decide the final ranking. This competition format can mitigate the factor of luck introduced by both the tile wall and the opponents, since the tile wall and the opponents of each player are all the same.

The competition results are shown in Table 4. Due to the use of the duplicate format to control variance, three competitors achieved the same score in about half of the games, but the two human players tended to perform better than the AI programs in the remaining games, resulting in a huge difference in the total scores between the human players and the AI agents. In an interview after the competition, Li claimed that the AI agent was still not flexible enough to handle some cases. It can be concluded that the AI ranked third place in the first Mahjong AI competition is still a far cry from professional human players, and Official International Mahjong can be a good benchmark and testbed for AI research, calling for more powerful algorithms.

Table 4. The scores of each game in the human-versus-AI competition.

Player	East Wind				South Wind				West Wind				North Wind				Total
Li	−22	32	51	−19	54	99	−8	−17	34	−8	34	−8	34	−27	−8	−16	205
Zhang	−22	60	54	−19	54	−8	−8	−30	37	33	66	−8	35	−16	−8	−16	204
Kima (AI)	−22	60	−8	−19	54	−8	−8	−28	−8	−8	66	−8	35	−8	−8	−16	66

5. AI Algorithms

This section summarizes the algorithms used in the AI agents in the two Mahjong AI competitions based on the presentations given by the competitors. Though the details of the algorithms vary, they can be divided into three categories: heuristic methods, supervised learning, and reinforcement learning. An overview of the methods of the top 16 agents in both competitions is illustrated in Figure 4.

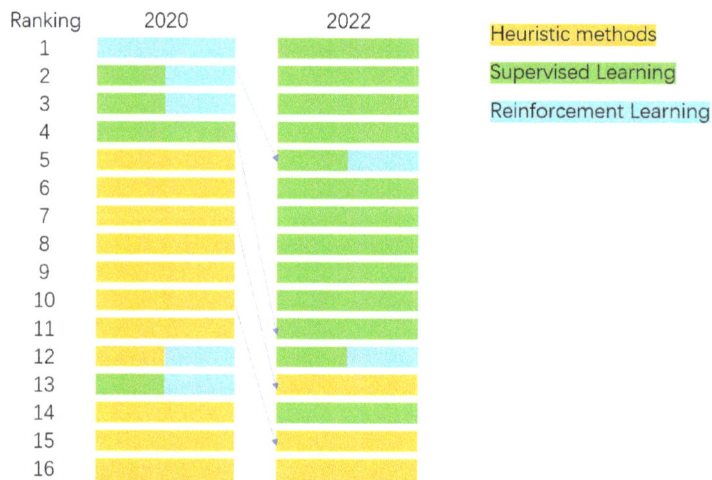

Figure 4. The category of algorithms used in the top sixteen agents in the two Mahjong AI competitions. The arrows indicate that the agents were uploaded by the same team who participated in both competitions.

5.1. Heuristic Methods

Most of the teams in the first competition built their AI agents with heuristic methods, which rely heavily on human knowledge. For a human player, the goal of Mahjong is to make a winning hand as soon as possible by choosing the right tile to discard and stealing other players' discarded tiles to make melds when necessary. The minimal number of tiles to replace from the current hand to a winning pattern is defined as the "shanten" value, which is an important concept in the strategies of humans to measure their distance from winning. Some heuristic methods simply calculate the current shanten value by expanding a search tree, trying all possible tiles it can replace until it forms a winning pattern. Upon finding the shortest path to a winning pattern, the agent just keeps the useful tiles and discards a tile from those to be replaced until the shanten value drops to zero, waiting for the 14th tile to win. However, such shanten values only reflect the distance between the current hand and a winning pattern, but the *fan* value of the winning pattern may not be enough to win; that value must be no less than eight. Since the *fan* value depends on a wide variety of scoring patterns that not only describe the tiles in the hand, but also the exposed or concealed state of each meld and some properties of the 14th tile, including these states in the search tree would make it too large to be traversed in limited time.

Instead, human players not only try to reduce the shanten value but also think about the scoring patterns they want to make in advance. Since there are five different winning patterns in Official International Mahjong, and the strategies differ when making different patterns, some heuristic methods try to decide on a pattern to make based on the current hand and move to the pattern according to detailed strategies. These methods usually choose the pattern according to predefined rules based on the experience of human players. For example, human players tend to make the "Seven Pairs" pattern if there are five pairs in the current hand, and make the "Thirteen Orphans" pattern if there are no less than 11 terminal tiles and honor tiles. Some AI agents even consider dozens of scoring patterns as targets, choosing the target based on predefined conditions, and use different strategies for each pattern, making a complex behavior tree.

After deciding which winning pattern or scoring pattern to make, more heuristics can be applied based on the targeted pattern. Some of the AI agents calculate the winning probability by the probability of occurrence of each tile based on visible information. The action is chosen based on a combination of reducing shanten values and maximizing the winning probability. All of these rely heavily on human expertise. Learning-based models can also be embedded in the behavior tree as the detailed strategies for some patterns. For example, the AI agent ranked 12th in the first competition integrates a model learned by reinforcement learning into a behavior tree as the detailed strategy of the basic winning pattern, while the other patterns use heuristic strategies.

In conclusion, heuristic methods rely heavily on human experience and simulate the way human players play the game. Search-based algorithms are used to calculate the shanten value or approximate the winning probability to guide the choice of actions. Most of them also use predefined rules to decide the target pattern to make, forming a behavior tree with more detailed strategies embedded to handle each targeted pattern. The performance of these agents is mainly restricted by the strength of human heuristics, and the behavior trees designed by better human players tend to be more complex and have better performance.

5.2. Supervised Learning

Supervised learning was also widely used, especially in the second Mahjong AI competition, probably because of the availability of high-quality datasets. The basic idea of supervised learning is to train a policy model to predict the action to choose under the current observation from the match dataset in advance, and directly use the model to compute an action during the gameplay. Since the policy model is learned directly to clone the behavior in the match dataset, the performance of the model depends on the quality of the dataset. Despite the low quality of the dataset provided in the first competition, which consists of matches of human players of different levels in another Mahjong variant, agents trained by supervised learning still outperform those using heuristic methods, indicating the huge potential of deep learning algorithms on this game. More participants turned to supervised learning in the second competition, making up most of the top 16 agents.

The supervised models of different teams differ mainly in three components: the design of the features, the design of the network model, and the data preprocessing scheme. Most teams designed the features as all visible information from the current player, including the current hand, the exposed melds and their types for each player, the discarded tiles of each player, the prevalent wind and the seat wind, and the number of unseen tiles. Some teams missed some of the features or caused information loss by combining some of the features, such as ignoring the order of the discarded tiles. Meanwhile, these features were encoded differently as tensors by different teams. The most basic method is to treat all of these features as vectors and stack fully connected layers as the network model. While such encoding can retain all useful information, it overlooks the spatial relationship between the Mahjong tiles, since most of the scoring patterns involve special patterns of tiles such as pungs and shifted chows. Suphx [12], an AI system built by MSRA to play Riichi Mahjong, encodes the hand as 4 channels of images of 34×1, and uses 1-dimensional convolutional neural networks (CNN) to extract high-level features from the multi-channel images. Inspired by and improved from the design of Suphx, many teams in the competition encoded the tiles as 4 channels of images of 4×9 to better capture the spatial relationship between suited tiles of the same number. The encoding of both schemes is illustrated in Figure 5.

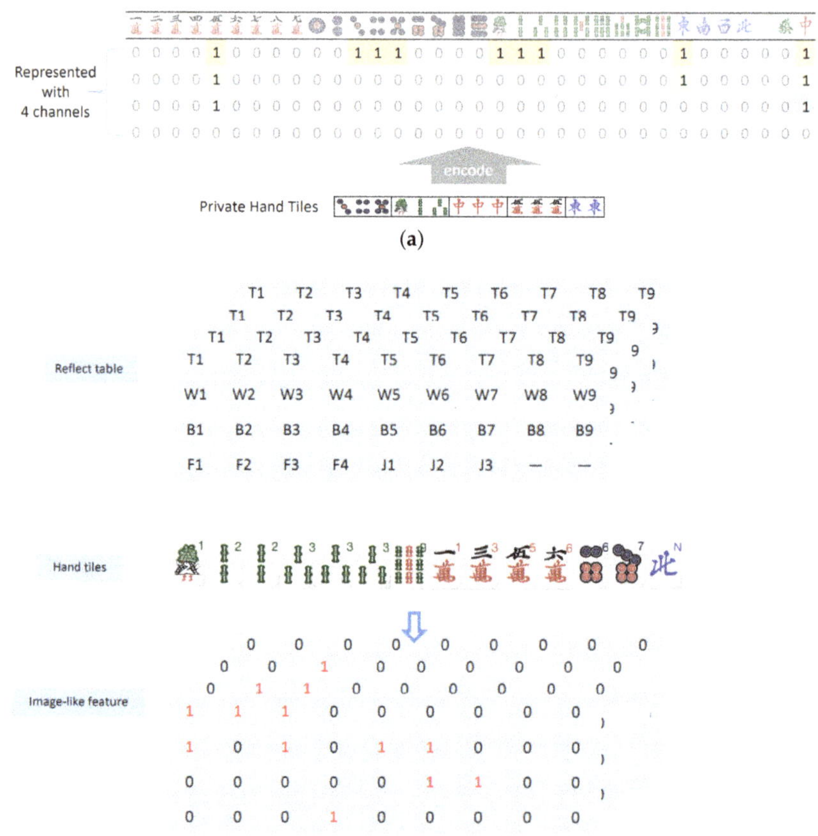

Figure 5. The encoding of features in Suphx and some AI agents submitted by the competitors. (**a**) Tiles encoded as 4 channels of images of 34×1. Image from [12]. (**b**) Tiles encoded as 4 channels of images of 4×9. Image from [30].

While the designs of features differ in most of the AI agents using supervised learning, the action space of different agents is quite similar, including winning, discarding, and different types of melding. Most of the teams used variants of CNN as the network model to predict the action, a method that is widely used in the field of computer vision to extract features from images due to its strong capability to capture spatial patterns. Specifically, the agents in the first Mahjong AI competition mainly use Resnet [31] as the CNN model, while other variants of CNN such as ResNeXt [32] can also be seen in the agents submitted in the second competition. These variants of CNN adopt deeper layers by adding shortcut connections, or use kernels with more complex structures to increase the ability to extract high-level features.

Before training the network, the given dataset of matches is first preprocessed into millions of state–action pairs. The schemes of data preprocessing of these teams are also different from each other. Some teams simply took all of the actions made by each player and the corresponding observation of the player as the states in these matches. A few teams only used the state–action pair of the winning player of each match, based on the assumption that the winner's strategy was better than that of the other players, especially for the dataset of human matches provided in the first competition. Some teams also applied data augmentation, based on the fact that some tiles are symmetric in their roles to form scoring patterns. For example, three types of suits can be exchanged arbitrarily, and the suited tiles of numbers one to nine can also be reversed as nine to one without breaking most of the scoring patterns, except for some rare patterns such as "All Green" and "Reversible Tiles". Different wind tiles and dragon tiles can also be exchanged as long as the prevailing wind and the seat wind change correspondingly. This augmentation can significantly increase the amount of data and improve the generalization ability of the network model.

5.3. Reinforcement Learning

The top three teams in the first Mahjong AI competition all used reinforcement learning (RL) to train their agents. Different from supervised learning which requires a large amount of game data to clone the behavior of the other players, RL deals with control problems and learns how to choose the right action to lead to higher future payoffs by interacting with other players and trying the actions out. Traditional reinforcement learning models the environment as a Markov Decision Process (MDP) and can only deal with single-agent problems. When combined with proper self-play schemes, it has been proved [22,33] that single-agent RL algorithms can approach a Nash equilibrium in competitive multi-agent environments, and in recent years, such algorithms have achieved good performance in various multi-agent games such as StarCraft [9], Dota 2 [10], and Texas Hold'em [34].

All of the top three teams used a similar paradigm of reinforcement learning, combining the algorithm of Proximal Policy Optimization (PPO), a distributed actor–critic training framework, and the self-play of the latest model to collect training data. PPO [35] is a policy-based RL algorithm which is more stable than other algorithms, such as REINFORCE [36] and A3C [37], because it clips the ratio of action probabilities between new models and old models. The network model is a joint policy–value network consisting of a CNN-based backbone to extract features, a policy branch to predict the actions, and a value branch to provide the estimated expected payoff under the current observation. The distributed training framework consists of a learner, a replay buffer, and many actors distributed across multiple machines, as shown in Figure 6. The actors use the latest model to generate self-play matches and store those data in the replay buffer. The learner samples data from the replay buffer to update the current model and broadcast the latest parameters to each actor. This distributed training framework can be easily scaled to an arbitrary amount of computational resources. Since reinforcement learning requires a large amount of data generated by self-play matches, especially in games with high variance such as Mahjong, which involves randomness in dealing tiles, the quality of models depends mainly on the computational resources used. In fact, the top three teams in the first competition were all from the industrial community, and hundreds of CPU cores were used in their training, in spite of the fact that they also adopted various tricks to stabilize the training.

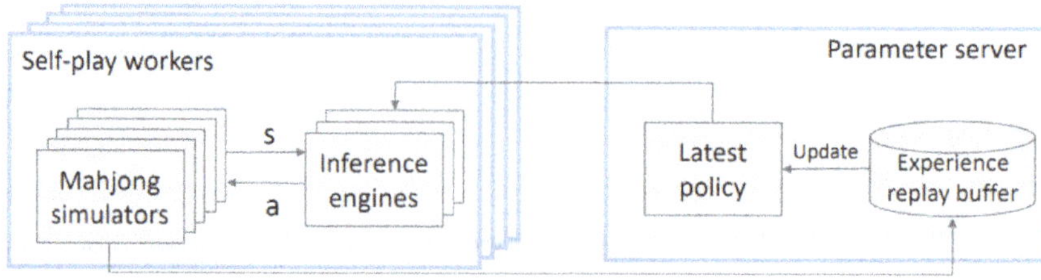

Figure 6. The distributed actor–critic training framework used by the competitors.

Though these teams shared a similar training paradigm, there were also some differences in their RL implementations. Some teams used supervised learning to train an initial model from the given datasets or matches generated by heuristic methods in advance, and ran reinforcement learning based on the initial model to speed up the training in the early phase. The agent ranked first in the first competition further adopted the technique of reward shaping and perfect information distillation. Specifically, they did not directly use the final score of the game as the reward, as other teams did, but clipped it to a smaller range to mitigate the randomness and high variance and stabilize the training. Perfect information distillation [38] is another technique to deal with games with imperfect information. While the policy network only takes the observation of the current player as the input, the value network also takes invisible information such as other players' hands and the remaining tile walls as the input to better predict the value of the current game state.

6. Conclusions

Throughout the history of AI research, games have always been benchmarks and testbeds because they provide a rich context to test a wide range of abilities of AI systems. The most popular games played by humans have undoubtedly promoted the development of AI algorithms, in that AI systems achieving superhuman performance in these games have always been considered milestones of AI technologies. Mahjong, one of the most popular games played in China, presents challenges to AI research due to its complex scoring rules and rich hidden information, but it has been overlooked by the community of AI research because there are too many regional variants to form a joint community of players. This paper provides a detailed description of the rules of Official International Mahjong, the variant used in most official competitions due to its complex scoring rules and the emphasis on strategies. By holding two AI competitions under our novel competition format, which combines Swiss rounds and the duplicate format to reduce variance, and comparing the methods of the top teams, we promote this game as a new benchmark for AI research and summarizing the state-of-the-art algorithms on this game. We conclude that supervised learning and reinforcement learning perform better than heuristic methods based on human knowledge. We also held a human-versus-AI competition, which showed that the top AI agent still cannot beat professional human players. We believe that this game can be a new playground for game AI research and promote the development of multi-agent AI algorithms in the setting of imperfect information. As Mahjong is a popular game among humans, the strategies of AI agents in playing the game can also bring inspiration to human players, because even professional players can have quite different strategies in some situations.

Author Contributions: Resources, W.L. (Wenlong Li); Writing—original draft preparation, Y.L.; Writing—review and editing, W.L. (Wenxin Li). All authors have read and agreed to the published version of the manuscript.

Funding: This research was funded by Science and Technology Innovation 2030—"The New 34 Generation of Artificial Intelligence" Major Project No.2018AAA0100901, China, and by Project No.2020BD003 supported by PKU-Baidu Fund.

Institutional Review Board Statement: Not applicable.

Informed Consent Statement: Not applicable.

Data Availability Statement: The data presented in this study are available on request from the corresponding author. The data are not publicly available due to privacy restrictions.

Conflicts of Interest: The authors declare no conflict of interest. The funders had no role in the design of the study; in the collection, analyses, or interpretation of data; in the writing of the manuscript; or in the decision to publish the results.

Appendix A. Scoring system in Official International Mahjong

This section describes the scoring system in Official International Mahjong in detail, including the scoring principles and the full list of scoring patterns.

Appendix A.1. Scoring Principles

There are 81 different scoring patterns in Official International Mahjong, many more than those in other variants. When a player declares a winning hand, it is compared to all of these patterns, and several patterns may match or even occur more than once. Most of the patterns specify part or even all of the tiles in the hand, but there are also some patterns describing how the winning hand is completed, i.e., the property of the winning tile. Each scoring pattern is worth a *fan* value, and the player only wins when their hand is worth more than eight *fans*. When counting the *fan* value of a winning hand, the basic rule is to sum up the *fan* values of all matched patterns. However, in many cases, the matched patterns may overlap in their descriptions of the hand, and some patterns are not counted in. The following principles are followed when choosing the right patterns to sum up.

- The Non-Repeat Principle: When a scoring pattern is inevitably implied or included by another pattern, the pattern with a lower *fan* value is not counted.
- The Non-Separation Principle: After combining some melds to match a scoring pattern, these melds cannot be separated and rearranged to match another pattern.
- The Non-Identical Principle: Once a meld has been used to match a scoring pattern, the player is not allowed to use the same meld together with other melds to match the same pattern.
- The High-versus-Low Principle: When there are multiple ways to break the hand to match different sets of scoring patterns, the way with the highest total *fan* value is chosen.
- The Account-Once Principle: When a player has combined some melds to match a scoring pattern, they can only combine any remaining melds once with a meld that has already been used to match other patterns.

Appendix A.2. Scoring Patterns

All of the scoring patterns are listed below, grouped by their corresponding *fan* value. A pattern with higher *fan* value tends to be more difficult to obtain.

Patterns worth 88 *fans*

(1) Big Four Winds: A hand with pungs or kongs of all four winds.
Implied patterns are not counted: "Big Three Winds", "All Pungs", "Seat Wind", "Prevalent Wind", "Pungs of Terminals or Honors".

Example: 

(2) Big Three Dragons: A hand with pungs or kongs of all three dragons.
Implied patterns are not counted: "Dragon Pung", "Two Dragon Pungs".

Example: 

(3) All Green: A hand consisting of only green tiles, i.e., .
Implied patterns are not counted: "Half Flush".

Example: 

(4) Nine Gates: First collect 13 number tiles 1112345678999 of one suit with no exposed melds. The 14th tile can be any tile of the same suit.

Implied patterns are not counted: "Full Flush", "Fully Concealed Hand", "Concealed Hand", "No Honors".

Example: 

(5) Four Kongs: A hand with four kongs, regardless of whether they are exposed or concealed.

Implied patterns are not counted: "Melded Kong", "Concealed Kong", "Two Melded Kongs", "Two Concealed Kongs", "Three Kongs", "All Pungs", and "Single Wait".

Example: 

(6) Seven Shifted Pairs: A hand of seven pairs in the same suit with consecutive numbers.

Implied patterns are not counted: "Seven Pairs", "Full Flush", "Fully Concealed Hand", "Single Wait".

Example: 

(7) Thirteen Orphans: One of each terminal tile (number one and nine of each suit), one of each honor tile, plus one duplicate tile of any of those thirteen tiles.

Implied patterns are not counted: "All Types", "Fully Concealed Hand", "Concealed Hand", "Single Wait".

Example: 

Patterns worth 64 *fans*

(8) All Terminals: A hand consisting of only terminal tiles, i.e., number 1 or 9 of each suit.

Implied patterns are not counted: "No Honours", "Pung of Terminals or Honors", "Mixed Double Pung", "All Pungs".

Example: 

(9) Little Four Winds: A hand with melds of three winds and a pair of the other wind.

Implied patterns are not counted: "Big Three Winds", "Pung of Terminals or Honors".

Example: 

(10) Little Three Dragons: A hand with melds of two dragons and a pair of the other dragon.

Implied patterns are not counted: "Two Dragon Pungs" and "Dragon Pung".

Example: 

(11) All Honors: A hand consisting of only honor tiles.

Implied patterns are not counted: "All Pungs", "Pung of Terminals or Honors".

Example: 

(12) Four Concealed Pungs: A hand with four concealed pungs or kongs.

Implied patterns are not counted: "All Pungs", "Three Concealed Pungs", "Two Concealed Pungs", "Fully Concealed Hand", "Concealed Hand".

(13) Pure Terminal Chows: A hand with two chows of number 1, 2, 3, two chows of number 7, 8, 9, and a pair of number 5, all in the same suit, i.e., 12312378978955 in one suit. It is not treated as seven pairs, even if all chows are concealed.

Implied patterns are not counted: "Full Flush", "All Chows".

Example: 

Patterns worth 48 *fans*

(14) Quadruple Chow: A hand with four identical chows.

Implied patterns are not counted: "Pure Triple Chow", "Pure Double Chow", "Tile Hog".

Example: 

(15) Four Pure Shifted Pungs: A hand with four pungs or kongs in the same suit with consecutive numbers.

Implied patterns are not counted: "Pure Shifted Pungs", "All Pungs".

Example: 

Patterns worth 32 *fans*

(16) Four Pure Shifted Chows: A hand with four successive chows in the same suit with a fixed interval of either one or two, but not a combination of both.

Implied patterns are not counted: "Pure Shifted Chows".

Example: 

(17) Three Kongs: A hand with three kongs, regardless of whether they are exposed or concealed.

Implied patterns are not counted: "Melded Kong", "Concealed Kong", "Two Melded Kongs", "Two Concealed Kongs".

Example: 

(18) All Terminals and Honors: A hand consisting of only terminal (number 1 or 9 of each suit) and honor tiles.

Implied patterns are not counted: "Pung of Terminals or Honors", "All Pungs".

Example: 

Patterns worth 24 *fans*

(19) Seven Pairs: A hand with seven pairs. Four identical tiles can be treated as two pairs, in which case "Tile Hog" is counted.

Implied patterns are not counted: "Fully Concealed Hand", "Concealed Hand", "Single Wait".

Example: 

(20) Greater Honors and Knitted Tiles: A hand consisting of one of each honor tile, and seven tiles out of a knitted straight. A knitted straight is made up of number 1, 4, 7 of one suit, number 2, 5, 8 of second suit, and number 3, 6, 9 of a third suit.

Implied patterns are not counted: "Lesser Honors and Knitted Tiles", "All Types", "Fully Concealed Hand", "Concealed Hand".

Example: 

(21) All Even Pungs: A hand consisting of four pungs or kongs and a pair, where all tiles are suited tiles of even numbers.

Implied patterns are not counted: "All Pungs", "All Simples".

Example: 

(22) Full Flush: A hand consisting of only suited tiles of the same suit.

Implied patterns are not counted: "No Honors".

Example: 

(23) Pure Triple Chow: A hand with three identical chows.

Implied patterns are not counted: "Pure Double Chow".

Example: 

(24) Pure Shifted Pungs: A hand with three pungs or kongs in the same suit with consecutive numbers.

Example: 

(25) Upper Tiles: A hand consisting of only suited tiles of number 7, 8, and 9.

Implied patterns are not counted: "Upper Four", "No Honors".

Example: 

(26) Middle Tiles: A hand consisting of only suited tiles of number 4, 5, and 6.

Implied patterns are not counted: "All Simples", "No Honors".

Example: 

(27) Lower Tiles: A hand consisting of only suited tiles of number 1, 2, and 3.

Implied patterns are not counted: "Lower Four", "No Honors".

Example: 

Patterns worth 16 *fans*

(28) Pure Straight: A hand with three chows in the same suit of numbers 1, 2, 3; 4, 5, 6; 7, 8, 9.

Example: 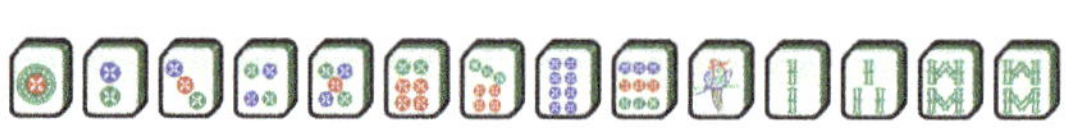

(29) Three-Suited Terminal Chows: A hand with two chows of number 1, 2, 3 and 7, 8, 9 in one suit, another two chows of the same number in a second suit, and a pair of number 5 in a third suit.

Implied patterns are not counted: "All Chows", "Two Terminal Chows", "Mixed Double Chow", "No Honors".

Example: 

(30) Pure Shifted Chows: A hand with three successive chows in the same suit with a fixed interval of either one or two, but not a combination of both.

Example: 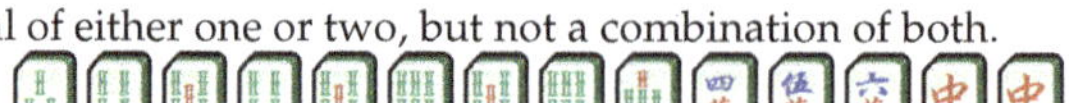

(31) All Fives: A hand with suited tiles of number five in all four melds and the pair. Implied patterns are not counted: "All Simples".

Example: 

(32) Triple Pung: A hand with three pungs or kongs in different suits with the same number.

Example: 

(33) Three Concealed Pungs: A hand with three concealed pungs or kongs.

Patterns worth 12 *fans*

(34) Lesser Honors and Knitted Tiles: A hand consisting of 14 tiles from these 16 tiles: number 1, 4, 7 of one suit; number 2, 5, 8 of a second suit; number 3, 6, 9 of a third suit; and all honor tiles.

Implied patterns are not counted: "All Types", "Fully Concealed Hand", "Concealed Hand".

Example: 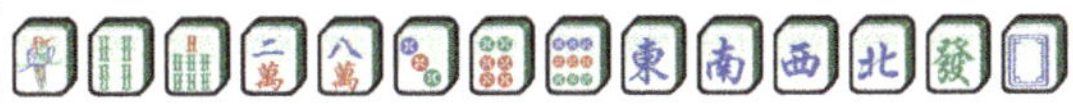

(35) Knitted Straight: A hand consisting of number 1, 4, 7 of one suit, number 2, 5, 8 of a second suit, and number 3, 6, 9 of a third suit, plus a meld and a pair.

Example: 

(36) Upper Four: A hand consisting of only suited tiles of number 6, 7, 8, and 9. Implied patterns are not counted: "No Honors".

Example: 

(37) Lower Four: A hand consisting of only suited tiles of number 1, 2, 3, and 4. Implied patterns are not counted: "No Honors".

Example: 

(38) Big Three Winds: A hand with three pungs or kongs of wind tiles.

Example: 

Patterns worth 8 *fans*

(39) Mixed Straight: A hand with three chows of numbers 1, 2, 3; 4, 5, 6; 7, 8, 9 in different suits.

Example: 

(40) Reversible Tiles: A hand consisting of only tiles whose shape is point-symmetric regardless of colors. Available tiles are 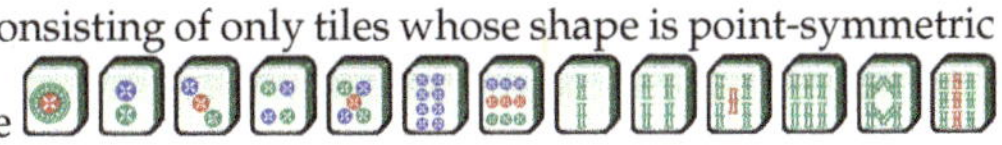 .

Implied patterns are not counted: "One Voided Suit".

Example: 

(41) Mixed Triple Chow: A hand with three chows in different suits with the same numbers.

Implied patterns are not counted: "Mixed Double Chow".

Example: 

(42) Mixed Shifted Pungs: A hand with three pungs or kongs in different suits with consecutive numbers.

Example: 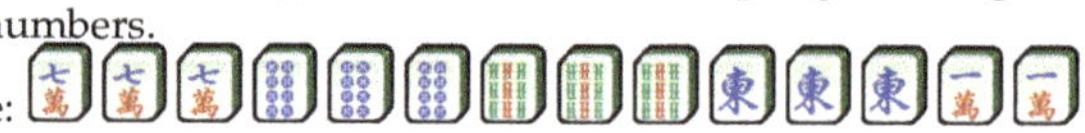

(43) Chicken Hand: A hand which would otherwise be worth of zero *fans*, with flower tiles not included.

Example: 

(44) Last Tile Draw: The winning hand is completed by drawing the last tile of the wall.

Implied patterns are not counted: "Self Drawn".

(45) Last Tile Claim: The winning hand is completed by seizing a tile from another player when the tile wall is empty.

(46) Out With Replacement Tile: The winning hand is completed when drawing a tile right after making a concealed kong or a promoted kong.

Implied patterns are not counted: "Self Drawn".

(47) Robbing the Kong: The winning hand is completed by robbing the tile which another player adds to an exposed pung to form a kong.

Implied patterns are not counted: "Last Tile".

Patterns worth 6 *fans*

(48) All Pungs: A hand with four pungs or kongs, regardless of whether they are exposed or concealed.

Example: 

(49) Half Flush: A hand consisting of only honor tiles and suited tiles of one suit.

Example: 

(50) Mixed Shifted Chows: A hand with three consecutive chows in different suits, each shifted up one number from the one before it.

Example: 

(51) All Types: A hand containing tiles of all three suits, wind tiles and dragon tiles.

Example: 

(52) Melded Hand: Every meld and pair in the hand must be completed by tiles from other players, which means that all melds must be exposed, and one tile of the pair is the 14th winning tile from other players.

Implied patterns are not counted: "Single Wait".

(53) Two Concealed Kongs: A hand with two concealed kongs.
Implied patterns are not counted: "Concealed Kong".

(54) Two Dragon Pungs: A hand with two pungs or kongs of dragon tiles.
Implied patterns are not counted: "Dragon Pung".

Patterns worth 4 *fan*s

(55) Outside Hand: A hand with terminals (number 1 or 9 of suited tiles) and honor tiles in every meld and the pair.

(56) Fully Concealed Hand: A hand with no tiles from other players, which means that all melds must be concealed, and the winning tile is drawn by the winner.

(57) Two Melded Kongs: A hand with two exposed kongs.

(58) Last Tile: The winning tile is the last tile of the same tile that has not been revealed to all players, which means three of the same tile has been exposed in melds or discarded on the table.

Patterns worth 2 *fan*s

(59) Dragon Pung: A hand with a pung or kong of dragon tiles. This pattern can be counted more than once if there are multiple melds meeting this requirement.
Implied patterns are not counted: "Pung of Terminals or Honors".

(60) Prevalent Wind: A hand with a pung or kong of the prevalent wind of this game.
Implied patterns are not counted: "Pung of Terminals or Honors".

(61) Seat Wind: A hand with a pung or kong of the seat wind of the current player.
Implied patterns are not counted: "Pung of Terminals or Honors".

(62) Concealed Hand: A hand with no tiles from other players except the winning tile, which means that all melds must be concealed, while the winning tile is seized from other players.

(63) All Chows: A hand with four chows and a pair of suited tiles.

(64) Tile Hog: A hand with four identical tiles without forming a kong. This pattern can be counted more than once if there are multiple tiles meeting this requirement.

(65) Mixed Double Pung: A hand with two pungs or kongs in different suits with the same number. This pattern can be counted more than once if there are multiple melds meeting this requirement.

(66) Two Concealed Pungs: A hand with two concealed pungs or kongs.

(67) Concealed Kong: A hand with a concealed kong.

(68) All Simples: A hand with no terminal tiles (number 1 or 9 of suited tiles) and honor tiles.

Patterns worth 1 *fan*

(69) Pure Double Chow: A hand with two identical chows. This pattern can be counted more than once if there are multiple melds meeting this requirement.

(70) Mixed Double Chow: A hand with two chows in different suits with the same number. This pattern can be counted more than once if there are multiple melds meeting this requirement.

(71) Short Straight: A hand with two chows in the same suit with successive numbers, like 234 and 567. This pattern can be counted more than once if there are multiple melds meeting this requirement.

(72) Two Terminal Chows: A hand with two chows in the same suit with numbers 1, 2, 3 and 7, 8, 9. This pattern can be counted more than once if there are multiple melds meeting this requirement.

(73) Pung of Terminals or Honors: A hand with a pung or kong of terminal tiles (number 1 or 9 of suited tiles) or honor tiles. This pattern can be counted more than once if there are multiple melds meeting this requirement.

(74) Melded Kong: A hand with one exposed kong.

(75) One Voided Suit: A hand with exactly two of the three suits of tiles.

(76) No Honors: A hand with no honor tiles.

(77) Edge Wait: The winning tile must be a suited tile of number 3 to complete a chow of 1, 2, 3, or number 7 to complete a chow of 7, 8, 9. This pattern is not counted if there exists multiple tiles to complete a winning pattern.

(78) Closed Wait: The winning tile must be a suited tile to complete a chow as the middle number. This pattern is not counted if there exists multiple tiles to complete a winning pattern.

(79) Single Wait: The winning tile must be the tile to complete a pair. This pattern is not counted if there exists multiple tiles to complete a winning pattern.

(80) Self Drawn: The winning tile must be drawn by the winner.

(81) Flower Tile: Each flower tile is worth of one *fan*. However, the *fan* value of flower tiles cannot be counted to meet the winning criteria of 8 *fans*. It is only given as a bonus if the player actually wins by no less than eight *fans* without flower tiles.

References

1. Schaeffer, J.; Lake, R.; Lu, P.; Bryant, M. Chinook the world man-machine checkers champion. *AI Mag.* **1996**, *17*, 21.
2. Campbell, M.; Hoane, A.J., Jr.; Hsu, F.h. Deep blue. *Artif. Intell.* **2002**, *134*, 57–83. [CrossRef]
3. Silver, D.; Huang, A.; Maddison, C.J.; Guez, A.; Sifre, L.; Van Den Driessche, G.; Schrittwieser, J.; Antonoglou, I.; Panneershelvam, V.; Lanctot, M.; et al. Mastering the game of Go with deep neural networks and tree search. *Nature* **2016**, *529*, 484–489. [CrossRef] [PubMed]
4. Silver, D.; Schrittwieser, J.; Simonyan, K.; Antonoglou, I.; Huang, A.; Guez, A.; Hubert, T.; Baker, L.; Lai, M.; Bolton, A.; et al. Mastering the game of go without human knowledge. *Nature* **2017**, *550*, 354–359. [CrossRef] [PubMed]
5. Silver, D.; Hubert, T.; Schrittwieser, J.; Antonoglou, I.; Lai, M.; Guez, A.; Lanctot, M.; Sifre, L.; Kumaran, D.; Graepel, T.; et al. A general reinforcement learning algorithm that masters chess, shogi, and Go through self-play. *Science* **2018**, *362*, 1140–1144. [CrossRef]
6. Moravčík, M.; Schmid, M.; Burch, N.; Lisý, V.; Morrill, D.; Bard, N.; Davis, T.; Waugh, K.; Johanson, M.; Bowling, M. Deepstack: Expert-level artificial intelligence in heads-up no-limit poker. *Science* **2017**, *356*, 508–513. [CrossRef]
7. Brown, N.; Sandholm, T. Superhuman AI for heads-up no-limit poker: Libratus beats top professionals. *Science* **2018**, *359*, 418–424. [CrossRef]

8. Brown, N.; Sandholm, T. Superhuman AI for multiplayer poker. *Science* **2019**, *365*, 885–890. [CrossRef]
9. Vinyals, O.; Babuschkin, I.; Chung, J.; Mathieu, M.; Jaderberg, M.; Czarnecki, W.M.; Dudzik, A.; Huang, A.; Georgiev, P.; Powell, R.; et al. Alphastar: Mastering the real-time strategy game starcraft ii. *DeepMind Blog* **2019**, *2*.
10. Berner, C.; Brockman, G.; Chan, B.; Cheung, V.; Debiak, P.; Dennison, C.; Farhi, D.; Fischer, Q.; Hashme, S.; Hesse, C.; et al. Dota 2 with large scale deep reinforcement learning. *arXiv* **2019**, arXiv:1912.06680.
11. Ye, D.; Chen, G.; Zhang, W.; Chen, S.; Yuan, B.; Liu, B.; Chen, J.; Liu, Z.; Qiu, F.; Yu, H.; et al. Towards playing full moba games with deep reinforcement learning. *ADvances Neural Inf. Process. Syst.* **2020**, *33*, 621–632.
12. Li, J.; Koyamada, S.; Ye, Q.; Liu, G.; Wang, C.; Yang, R.; Zhao, L.; Qin, T.; Liu, T.Y.; Hon, H.W. Suphx: Mastering mahjong with deep reinforcement learning. *arXiv* **2020**, arXiv:2003.13590.
13. Copeland, B.J. The Modern History of Computing. Available online: https://plato.stanford.edu/entries/computing-history/ (accessed on 28 April 2023).
14. Wikipedia. World Series of Poker—Wikipedia, The Free Encyclopedia. 2023. Available online: http://en.wikipedia.org/w/index.php?title=World%20Series%20of%20Poker&oldid=1133483344 (accessed on 8 February 2023).
15. Bard, N.; Hawkin, J.; Rubin, J.; Zinkevich, M. The annual computer poker competition. *AI Mag.* **2013**, *34*, 112. [CrossRef]
16. Lu, Y.; Li, W. Techniques and Paradigms in Modern Game AI Systems. *Algorithms* **2022**, *15*, 282. [CrossRef]
17. Hart, P.E.; Nilsson, N.J.; Raphael, B. A formal basis for the heuristic determination of minimum cost paths. *IEEE Trans. Syst. Sci. Cybern.* **1968**, *4*, 100–107. [CrossRef]
18. Stockman, G.C. A minimax algorithm better than alpha-beta? *Artif. Intell.* **1979**, *12*, 179–196. [CrossRef]
19. Sutton, R.S.; Barto, A.G. *Reinforcement Learning: An Introduction*; MIT Press: Cambridge, MA, USA, 2018.
20. Heinrich, J.; Lanctot, M.; Silver, D. Fictitious self-play in extensive-form games. In Proceedings of the International Conference on Machine Learning. PMLR, Lille, France, 7–9 July 2015; pp. 805–813.
21. McMahan, H.B.; Gordon, G.J.; Blum, A. Planning in the presence of cost functions controlled by an adversary. In Proceedings of the 20th International Conference on Machine Learning (ICML-03), Washington, DC, USA, 21–24 August 2003; pp. 536–543.
22. Lanctot, M.; Zambaldi, V.; Gruslys, A.; Lazaridou, A.; Tuyls, K.; Pérolat, J.; Silver, D.; Graepel, T. A unified game-theoretic approach to multiagent reinforcement learning. *Adv. Neural Inf. Process. Syst.* **2017**, *30*, 4193–4206.
23. Wikipedia. Mahjong solitaire—Wikipedia, The Free Encyclopedia. 2023. Available online: http://en.wikipedia.org/w/index.php?title=Mahjong%20solitaire&oldid=1129612325 (accessed on 8 February 2023).
24. Osborne, M.J.; Rubinstein, A. *A Course in Game Theory*; MIT Press: Cambridge, MA, USA, 1994.
25. Sloper, T. FAQ 10: Simplified Rules for Mah-Jongg—sloperama.com. Available online: https://sloperama.com/mjfaq/mjfaq10.html (accessed on 8 February 2023).
26. Zhou, H.; Zhang, H.; Zhou, Y.; Wang, X.; Li, W. Botzone: An online multi-agent competitive platform for ai education. In Proceedings of the 23rd Annual ACM Conference on Innovation and Technology in Computer Science Education, Larnaca, Cyprus, 2–4 July 2018; pp. 33–38.
27. IJCAI 2020 Mahjong AI Competition—botzone.org.cn. Available online: https://botzone.org.cn/static/gamecontest2020a.html (accessed on 8 February 2023).
28. IJCAI 2022 Mahjong AI Competition—botzone.org.cn. Available online: https://botzone.org.cn/static/gamecontest2022a.html (accessed on 8 February 2023).
29. GitHub—ailab-pku/PyMahjongGB: Python Fan Calculator for Chinese Standard Mahjong—github.com. Available online: https://github.com/ailab-pku/PyMahjongGB (accessed on 8 February 2023).
30. Yata. SuperJong. Available online: https://botzone.org.cn/static/IJCAI2020MahjongPPT/03-SuperJong-yata.pdf (accessed on 8 February 2023).
31. He, K.; Zhang, X.; Ren, S.; Sun, J. Deep residual learning for image recognition. In Proceedings of the IEEE Conference on Computer Vision and Pattern Recognition, Las Vegas, NV, USA, 27–30 June 2016; pp. 770–778.
32. Xie, S.; Girshick, R.; Dollár, P.; Tu, Z.; He, K. Aggregated residual transformations for deep neural networks. In Proceedings of the IEEE Conference on Computer Vision and Pattern Recognition, Honolulu, HI, USA, 21–26 July 2017; pp. 1492–1500.
33. Heinrich, J.; Silver, D. Deep reinforcement learning from self-play in imperfect-information games. *arXiv* **2016**, arXiv:1603.01121.
34. Zhao, E.; Yan, R.; Li, J.; Li, K.; Xing, J. AlphaHoldem: High-Performance Artificial Intelligence for Heads-Up No-Limit Texas Hold'em from End-to-End Reinforcement Learning. In Proceedings of the AAAI Conference on Artificial Intelligence, Virtual Event, 22 February–1 March 2022; Volume 36, pp. 4689–4697.
35. Schulman, J.; Wolski, F.; Dhariwal, P.; Radford, A.; Klimov, O. Proximal policy optimization algorithms. *arXiv* **2017**, arXiv:1707.06347.
36. Williams, R.J. Simple statistical gradient-following algorithms for connectionist reinforcement learning. *Mach. Learn.* **1992**, *8*, 229–256. [CrossRef]

37. Mnih, V.; Badia, A.P.; Mirza, M.; Graves, A.; Lillicrap, T.; Harley, T.; Silver, D.; Kavukcuoglu, K. Asynchronous methods for deep reinforcement learning. In Proceedings of the International Conference on Machine Learning, PMLR, New York City, NY, USA, 19–24 June 2016; pp. 1928–1937.
38. Guan, Y.; Liu, M.; Hong, W.; Zhang, W.; Fang, F.; Zeng, G.; Lin, Y. PerfectDou: Dominating DouDizhu with Perfect Information Distillation. *arXiv* **2022**, arXiv:2203.16406.

algorithms

MDPI

Article

Reducing Q-Value Estimation Bias via Mutual Estimation and Softmax Operation in MADRL

Zheng Li [1], Xinkai Chen [1], Jiaqing Fu [1], Ning Xie [1,*] and Tingting Zhao [2,3]

[1] Center for Future Media, the School of Computer Science and Engineering, and Yibin Park, University of Electronic Science and Technology of China, Chengdu 611731, China; 202152080128@std.uestc.edu.cn (Z.L.); 202152011708@std.uestc.edu.cn (X.C.); 17713626261@163.com (J.F.)

[2] School of Computer Science and Technology, Tianjin University of Science and Technology, Tianjin 300457, China; tingting@tust.edu.cn

[3] RIKEN Center for Advanced Intelligence Project (AIP), Tokyo 103-0027, Japan

* Correspondence: xiening@uestc.edu.cn or seanxiening@gmail.com; Tel.: +86-1779-640-6627

Abstract: With the development of electronic game technology, the content of electronic games presents a larger number of units, richer unit attributes, more complex game mechanisms, and more diverse team strategies. Multi-agent deep reinforcement learning shines brightly in this type of team electronic game, achieving results that surpass professional human players. Reinforcement learning algorithms based on Q-value estimation often suffer from Q-value overestimation, which may seriously affect the performance of AI in multi-agent scenarios. We propose a multi-agent mutual evaluation method and a multi-agent softmax method to reduce the estimation bias of Q values in multi-agent scenarios, and have tested them in both the particle multi-agent environment and the multi-agent tank environment we constructed. The multi-agent tank environment we have built has achieved a good balance between experimental verification efficiency and multi-agent game task simulation. It can be easily extended for different multi-agent cooperation or competition tasks. We hope that it can be promoted in the research of multi-agent deep reinforcement learning.

Keywords: reinforcement learning; game AI; multi-agent Q-network mutual estimation; softmax bellman operation; reinforcement learning environment

1. Introduction

The emergence and development of Artificial Intelligence in various key domains has intrinsic ties with games. The earliest AI program was a draughts game written by Christopher Strachey in 1951. It successfully ran for the first time on the Ferranti Mark I universal electronic computer at the University of Manchester in the UK. Impressed and influenced by Strachey and Turing, Arthur Samuel took on the draughts project's key points initiated by Strachey in 1952 and expanded it considerably over the years, allowing the program to learn from experience. As one of the earliest cases of Artificial Intelligence search technology, these advancements enabled the program to win a match against a former draughts champion from Connecticut, USA. Samuel's experiments and accumulation in the game technology field helped him propose the concept of machine learning in 1959.

In March 2016, Google's Deep Mind developed the Alpha Go system, defeating the then human world champion of Go, Lee Sedol, thus creating a global sensation. The Go board is composed of 19 horizontal lines and 19 vertical lines, with a total of 19 × 19 = 361 intersections. Each intersection on the Go board has three possibilities: a black stone, a white stone, or empty. Therefore, Go has a staggering number of possible positions: 3 to the power of 361. Each turn in Go has 250 possibilities, and a game can last up to 150 turns. As a result, the computational complexity of Go is 250 to the power of 150, which is approximately 10 to the power of 170. However, the observable number of atoms in the entire universe is only 10 to the power of 80. This clearly demonstrates the complexity and variability of the game of Go. In principle, AlphaGo uses a modified version of the Monte Carlo algorithm, but more importantly, it enhances its learning effect by leveraging deep reinforcement learning [1].

Reinforcement learning is a machine learning method that utilizes sequence information consisting of actions from agents, states from the environment, and rewards through interaction between agents and the environment [2]. The Q function is a fundamental concept in reinforcement learning, which can output the value of action a in state s. Learning an accurate Q function can help policy functions update in the correct direction. Due to the influence of updated formulas, inflexible function estimation methods, and noise, the Q function often has bias in estimating the true Q value [3,4]. The deviation in Q-value estimation may lead to the algorithm converging to a suboptimal policy, resulting in a decrease in algorithm performance.

Bright possibilities also exist for the application of deep reinforcement learning in multi-agent systems like drone formation control, cooperative-control multi-robots, and traffic vehicle control, all of which can significantly improve collective gains and enhance the quality of human life. Multi-agent reinforcement learning can be seen as the expansion of single-agent reinforcement learning algorithms in a multi-agent scenario. The migration of policy gradient algorithms based on Q-function learning to multi-agent scenarios will bring more severe impact due to the bias in Q-function estimation. The bias in the estimation of the Q-function will increase the variance of the network gradient and affect the update process of the policy network. In a multi-agent environment, with the increase in agents, the difficulty of updating the policy network in the correct direction increases exponentially, so such a bias will bring greater difficulties to policy learning in multi-agent scenarios.

This article primarily revolves around the research of the Q-value estimation bias problem in Multi-Agent Deep Reinforcement Learning, and constructs a new multi-agent experimental environment. The detailed research objectives are as follows:

1. The method of combining multiple Q networks to reduce the Q-value estimation bias is further studied, according to the feature of all agents having the same structured Q network in the architecture of centralized training with distributed execution in multi-agent systems. In this research objective, we aim not to increase the network parameters of the model, but to alleviate the problem of Q-value underestimation caused by dual Q networks by organizing multi-agent systems.

2. The method of using softmax operation to reduce Q-value estimation bias is further studied, and the softmax operation method is applied to multi-agent algorithms. This research aims to utilize the characteristics of softmax to reduce the overestimation bias of Q-value, and to simplify the action space used for computation in multi-agent systems, thereby reducing computational load.

3. For scientific research on multi-agent reinforcement learning, we have developed the multi-agent tank environment of the University of Electronic Science and Technology of China (UESTC-tank). This is a tank simulation game environment with multiple units and scenes, which can generate cooperative, adversarial, and mixed task scenarios. It can achieve competitions of player vs. player, player vs. AI, AI vs. AI types, and collect battle data for model training. It can support unit editing, map editing, and rule editing, and has good scalability. We tested our proposed algorithm on UESTC-tank and achieved good experimental results.

The rest of this paper is arranged as follows: Firstly, we introduced the research context in Section 2. Then, in Sections 3 and 4, we introduced the multi-agent twin-delayed deep deterministic policy gradient and multi-agent soft-maximization twin-delayed deep deterministic policy gradient algorithms. In Sections 5 and 6, we introduced the multi-agent particle environment and multi-agent tank environment, conducted experiments, and analyzed the results. After summarizing our work so far, Section 7 provides limitations and conclusions of the paper.

2. Research Background

2.1. Deep Reinforcement Learning

Reinforcement learning can be modeled as an agent is faced with a sequential decision making problem. At time t, the agent observes state s_t from the environment, and adopts action a_t based on its policy. Due to the interaction of the agent, the environment transitions from state s_t to the next state $s_t + 1$ and returns a reward r to the agent. If the environment transitions to a termination state, we call it the end of an episode. The goal of reinforcement learning is to enable agents to learn an optimal policy to obtain the maximum cumulative reward (called return) from the entire episode.

Reinforcement learning algorithms can be classified into policy function-based [5] and value function-based [6]. A common value function is the action value function, also known as the Q function, which inputs the current state of the environment and the action taken by the agent, and outputs an estimate of the expected return for that state–action pair. When the agent learns the optimal Q function, the optimal policy can be to select the action that can maximize the output value of the optimal Q-function in any state. In deep reinforcement learning, we use deep neural networks to fit the policy function, value function, and Q function, hence also known as policy networks, value networks, and Q networks.

2.2. Deep Q-Learning Algorithms

Mnih and others [6] were the first to integrate deep learning and traditional reinforcement learning algorithm, thus proposing the DQN algorithm. This pioneering piece of work marked the first end-to-end deep reinforcement learning algorithm using only Atari game pixel data and game scores for reinforcement learning state information. Finally, the trained network could output action-value functions or Q-values for each action. From this, the decision with the highest corresponding Q-value is selected. The entire structure of the DQN algorithm is shown in Figure 1.

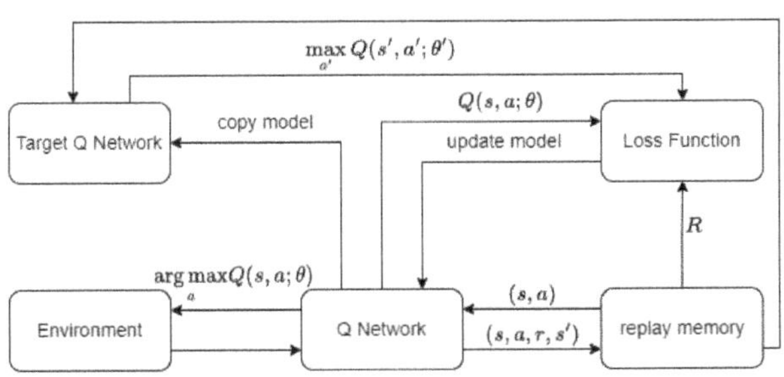

Figure 1. DQN Algorithm Flowchart. DQN uses deep neural networks to fit the Q function, selects the action that maximizes the Q value through a ε-greedy policy, interacts with the environment, and stores the obtained samples in replay memory. DQN continuously extracts samples from replay memory, performs gradient descent based on the loss function, and updates the parameters of the Q-network. The parameters of the Q-network are periodically copied to the target Q-network, which participates in the calculation of the loss function and makes Q-learning more stable.

The DQN algorithm introduces the experience replay mechanism, which stores the sample tuple (s, a, r, s') of the agent at each time step into an experience replay pool. During reinforcement learning training, a batch of samples is sampled from the experience replay pool and the neural network is updated using gradient descent. The use of experience replay mechanism greatly improves the data utilization of reinforcement learning algorithms and to some extent reduces the correlation between training data and sequences.

Another important contribution of the DQN algorithm is the concept of the target network, which achieves stable value estimation. The target value y for updating the Q network by computing the loss function is represented as:

$$y = r + \gamma \max_{\hat{a}} Q_{\theta'}(s', \hat{a}) \tag{1}$$

where $Q_{\theta'}$ represents the target network. γ is a discount factor ($0 < \gamma < 1$), used to give a preference for rewards reaped sooner in time. $\hat{a}$ is the action that allows the Q function to take the maximum value. The structure of the target network is the same as the Q network, but its parameters are only copied from the Q network every certain number of iterations.

The Q network updates its parameters in each round by minimizing the loss function defined in Equation (2):

$$L(\theta) = E_{(s,a,r,s')}\left[(y - Q_\theta(s,a))^2\right] \tag{2}$$

E represents mathematical expectation, which is calculated using Monte Carlo estimation method in practice, taking the average value of batch samples to estimate. The neural network is updated to make the Q network approximate the target value y, which essentially applies the Bellman equation. The use of target network helps improve the stability of the algorithm, and experiments have shown that NPC controlled by DQN algorithm can reach the level of professional players in many Atari games.

The DDPG [7] algorithm can be seen as a combination of Deterministic Policy Gradient (DPG) algorithm and deep neural networks, and it can also be seen as an extension of DQN algorithm in a continuous action space. It can solve the problem of the DQN algorithm's inability to directly apply to continuous action space, but there is still the problem of overestimation of Q values. The DDPG algorithm simultaneously establishes a Q network (critic) and a policy network (actor) [8]. The Q network is the same as the DQN algorithm, updated using a temporal difference method. The policy network utilizes the estimation of the Q network and is updated using policy gradient method.

In the deep deterministic policy gradient algorithm, the policy network is a deterministic policy function represented as $\pi_\phi(s)$, with the learning parameters represented as ϕ. Each action is directly computed by $a = \pi_\phi(s)$, without sampling from a random policy.

2.3. Estimation Bias of Q-Learning Algorithms

When an agent executes action a in state s, the environment will transition to state s' and return an immediate reward r. In the standard deep Q-learning algorithm, we update the Q-function using Equation (1). When using neural networks and other tools as function approximators to handle complex problems, there can be errors in the estimation of Q values, which means:

$$Q(s', \hat{a}) = Q^*(s', \hat{a}) + Y_{s'}^{\hat{a}} \tag{3}$$

where $Y_{s'}^{\hat{a}}$ is a zero-mean noise term, Q^* is a Q function that can output the real Q value, or the optimal Q function.

However, when using the maximum operation to select actions, there can be errors between the estimated Q values and the real Q values. The error is represented as Z_S:

$$Z_S \overset{\text{def}}{=} \gamma\left(\max_{\hat{a}} Q(s', \hat{a}) - \max_{\hat{a}} Q^*(s', \hat{a})\right) \tag{4}$$

Considering the noise term $Y_{s'}^{\hat{a}}$, some Q values may be underestimated, while others may be overestimated. The maximization operation always selects the maximum Q value for each state, which makes the algorithm overly sensitive to the high estimated Q values of the corresponding actions. In this case, the noise term causes $\mathbb{E}[Z_S] > 0$, resulting in the problem of overestimation of Q values.

The TD3 [9] algorithm introduces clipped Double Q-Learning on the basis of the DDPG algorithm, by establishing two Q networks $Q_{\theta_1}, Q_{\theta_2}$ to estimate the value of the next state, and using the minimum estimated Q-value of two target networks to calculate the Bellman equation:

$$y = r + \gamma \min_{i=1,2} Q_{\theta'_i}(s', \pi_\phi(s')) \tag{5}$$

where y is the update target for Q_{θ_1} and Q_{θ_2}, and π_ϕ is the policy network.

Using clipped Double Q-Learning, the value estimation of target networks will not bring excessive estimation errors to the Q-Learning target. However, this update rule may cause underestimation. Unlike actions with overestimated Q values, actions with underestimated Q values will not be explicitly updated.

Here is proof of the underestimation of the clipped Double Q-Learning, the two outputs values (Q_1 and Q_2) of the Q network, and that Q_i^* is the real Q value. The errors brought by the fitting of the two networks can be defined as:

$$Y^i = Q_i(s', \pi_\phi(s')) - Q^*(s', \pi_\phi(s')) \tag{6}$$

Assuming errors Y^1 and Y^2 are two independent random variables with nontrivial zero-mean distributions, the minimization operation of the TD3 algorithm introduces an error. The error denoted as D is as follows:

$$D = r + \gamma \min_{\mathrm{i}=1,2} Q_i(s', \pi_\phi(s')) - (r + \gamma Q^*(s', \pi_\phi(s'))) = \gamma \min\left(Y^1, Y^2\right) \tag{7}$$

where r is the reward and γ is the discount factor. Let Z be minimum value between Y^1, Y^2, and we have:

$$\mathrm{E[Z]} = \mathrm{E}[Y^1] + \mathrm{E}[Y^2] - \mathrm{E}[|Y^1 - Y^2|]/2 \tag{8}$$

Obviously, there is $E(Y^1) = 0$, $E(Y^2) = 0$ and $\mathrm{E}[|Y^1 - Y^2|] \leq 0$. Therefore, we can deduce that $E(D) \leq 0$, which means that the clipped Double Q-Learning usually has underestimation.

Specifically, in order to have a more intuitive perception of underestimation, we can assume that the error follows an independent and uniform distribution in the range $[-\varepsilon, \varepsilon]$. Since the estimated Q values and the true Q values have error Y^i that follows a uniform distribution, the probability density function and the probability distribution are represented by $f(\mathrm{x})$ and $P(Y^i > \mathrm{x})$, respectively:

$$\begin{gathered} f(x) = \begin{cases} \frac{1}{2\varepsilon}, & x \in [-\varepsilon, \varepsilon] \\ 0, & x \in \text{ else} \end{cases} \\ P\left(Y^i > \mathrm{x}\right) = \begin{cases} 1, & x \leq -\varepsilon \\ \frac{\varepsilon - x}{2\varepsilon}, & x \in (-\varepsilon, \varepsilon) \\ 0, & x \geq \varepsilon \end{cases} \end{gathered} \tag{9}$$

Also, since Y^1 and Y^2 are independent, it follows that:

$$\begin{aligned} P\left(\min\left(Y^1, Y^2\right) > \mathrm{x}\right) &= \prod_{i=1,2} P\left(Y^i > \mathrm{x}\right) \\ &= \begin{cases} 1, & x \leq -\varepsilon \\ \left(\frac{\varepsilon - x}{2\varepsilon}\right)^2, & x \in (-\varepsilon, \varepsilon) \\ 0, & x \geq \varepsilon \end{cases} \end{aligned} \tag{10}$$

Let Z be the minimum value between Y^1, Y^2. The probability density function and cumulative distribution function of Z are represented as $f_Z(\mathrm{x})$ and $F_Z(\mathrm{x})$, respectively:

$$\begin{gathered} f_Z(\mathrm{x}) = \begin{cases} \frac{\varepsilon - x}{2\varepsilon^2}, & x \in [-\varepsilon, \varepsilon] \\ 0, & x \in \text{ else} \end{cases} \\ F_Z(\mathrm{x}) = \begin{cases} 0, & x \leq -\varepsilon \\ 1 - \left(\frac{\varepsilon - x}{2\varepsilon}\right)^2, & x \in (-\varepsilon, \varepsilon) \\ 1, & x \geq \varepsilon \end{cases} \end{gathered} \tag{11}$$

Therefore, the expected value of Z can be calculated as follows:

$$E[Z] = \int_{-\varepsilon}^{\varepsilon} x f_Z(x) dx = \int_{-\varepsilon}^{\varepsilon} x \left(\frac{\varepsilon - x}{2\varepsilon^2} \right) dx = -\frac{1}{3}\varepsilon \tag{12}$$

Thus, it has been theoretically proven that the Q network update in the TD3 algorithm will result in an underestimation error for the true Q values.

2.4. Multi-Agent Twin Delayed Deep Deterministic Policy Gradient (Matd3)

The training modes of multi-agent deep reinforcement learning include Decentralized Training Decentralized Execution (DTDE), Centralized Training Centralized Execution (CTCE), and Centralized Training Decentralized Execution (CTDE), as shown in Figure 2.

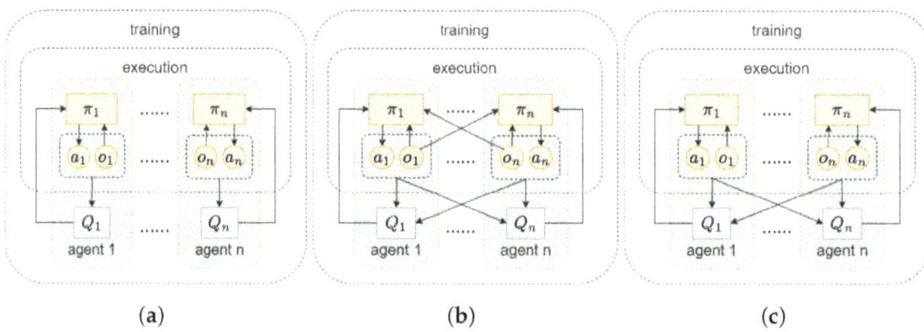

Figure 2. Multi-agent reinforcement learning training modes: (**a**) DTDE, each agent i makes decisions based on its own observation information, and each agent is relatively independent, with no information sharing between agents; (**b**) CTCE, which receives observation information from all agents through a centralized policy function and outputs the joint probability distribution of all agent action spaces; (**c**) CTDE, during the execution process of agents, each agent inputs its own local observation information into the policy function and outputs the probability distribution of the action space. However, during the training process, the agent can obtain additional information from other agents.

The MATD3 [10] algorithm extends the single-agent TD3 algorithm to a multi-agent environment, adopting the centralized training decentralized execution reinforcement learning framework. During the behavior execution process of the agents, each agent inputs their local observation information into the policy network, outputs deterministic actions, and during the training process, the agents can obtain additional information from other agents to evaluate their own actions.

The problem of Q network estimation bias will have a more severe impact when transferring policy gradient algorithms with Q-functions to a multi-agent scene, because the estimation bias of the Q network can increase the variance of the neural network gradient and affect the update process of the policy network neural network. In a multi-agent environment, as the number of agents increases, the difficulty of updating the policy function in the correct direction increases exponentially. The MATD3 algorithm simply extends the TD3 algorithm to a multi-agent environment, and there are still problems with the underestimation of Q values. In a multi-agent environment, this bias will have a greater impact on the agent's strategy learning.

3. Multi-Agent Mutual Twin Delayed Deep Deterministic Policy Gradient (M2ATD3)

In multi-agent scenarios, single Q network algorithms such as Multi-Agent Deep Deterministic Policy Gradient (MADDPG) have problems of overestimation. However, twin Q network's MATD3 algorithm, while resolving the overestimation of Q value, inevitably leads to underestimation. The Multi-Agent Three Delayed Deep Deterministic Policy Gradient (MATHD3) algorithm is proposed to create a third Q network. The overestimated results from it, and the underestimated results from the minimization of the first two Q networks, are added together by adjusting the weight hyperparameter α, and an unbiased estimate of the actual Q value can be obtained. In multi-agent algorithms, we denote the observation received at runtime by agent i as o_i, and the full state information as s, from which the observations o_i are derived. The Q network update target y_i of the MATHD3 algorithm is as follows:

$$y_i = r_i + \gamma\alpha \min_{j=1,2} Q^{\pi'}_{i,j}(s', a'_1, \cdots, a'_n) + \gamma(1-\alpha)Q^{\pi'}_{i,3}(s', a'_1, \cdots, a'_n) \tag{13}$$

where a'_i is obtained by adding noise ϵ to the output of the target policy network $\pi_{\phi'_i}$ of agent i based on its observation o'_i, that is: $a'_i = \pi_{\phi'_i}(o'_i) + \epsilon$.

While the MATHD3 algorithm effectively reduces bias in Q value estimates, it requires introducing a new Q network, leading to an increase in model parameters and increased model training difficulty.

Psychological studies show that humans exhibit overconfidence, typically estimating themselves beyond their actual abilities [11]. Introducing external evaluations can mitigate this phenomenon. Weinstein suggests that people are unrealistically optimistic because they focus on factors that improve their own chances of achieving desirable outcomes and fail to realize that others may have just as many factors in their favor [12]. Inspired by this, we propose the Multi-Agent Mutual Twin Delayed Deep Deterministic Policy Gradient (M2ATD3) algorithm. The training mode of M2ATD3 algorithm is shown in Figure 3.

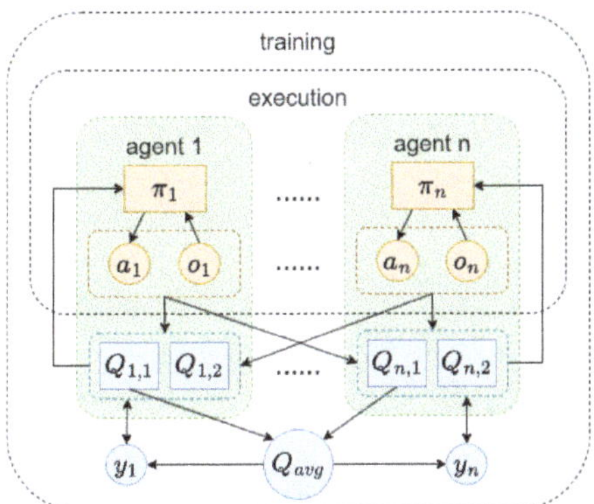

Figure 3. The training mode of M2ATD3. In this figure, rectangles represent networks, circles represent values, and dashed boxes represent sets or processes. Under the CTDE framework, each agent, equipped with Q networks of the same structure, can obtain shared information and make estimates of the current action-state value. The Q network of other agents can act as external critics, estimating the Q value of agent i and taking the average, denoted as the Q_{avg}. Agent i obtains the update objective y_i of the Q network through weighted sum of $\min(Q_{i,1}, Q_{i,2})$ and Q_{avg}.

Single Q networks, affected by noise, always overestimate Q values. Averaging the estimated Q values from each agent's Q network results in a slightly overestimated mutual Q value estimate. The mutual estimate of the Q value and the minimum value of two Q network estimates for agent i are weighted together to obtain the Q network update target y_i of the M2ATD3 algorithm:

$$\begin{aligned} Q^{\pi'}_{avg}(s', a'_1, \cdots, a'_n) &= \frac{1}{n} \sum_{i=1,\cdots,n} Q^{\pi'}_{i,1}(s', a'_1, \cdots, a'_n) \\ y_i = r_i + \gamma\alpha \min_{j=1,2} Q^{\pi'}_{i,j}(s', a'_1, \cdots, a'_n) &+ \gamma(1-\alpha)Q^{\pi'}_{avg}(s', a'_1, \cdots, a'_n) \end{aligned} \tag{14}$$

The mutual estimate of the Q value is overestimated, and the minimization of the twin Q network will lead to underestimation. By adjusting the weight hyperparameter α, in theory, an unbiased estimate of the true Q value of agent i can be obtained. The M2ATD3 algorithm reduces the Q value estimation bias without needing to introduce a new Q network. Moreover, the operation of taking the average of Q value estimates can also reduce the variance of Q value estimate errors [13], making the training process more stable.

We have maintained the delayed policy updates used in the TD3 algorithm. The TD3 algorithm proposes that the policy network should be updated at a lower frequency than the value network, to first minimize error before introducing a policy update. This method requires updating the policy and target networks only after a fixed number of updates d to the critic.

The M2ATD3 algorithm pseudo code can be found in Algorithm 1.

Algorithm 1 Multi-Agent Mutual Twin Delayed Deep Deterministic policy gradient

initialize Replay buffer D and network parameters
for t = 1 to T **do**
  Select action $a_i \sim \pi_i(o_i) + \epsilon$
  Execute action $a = (a_1, \cdots, a_n)$ and get reward r_i, transition to next state s'
  Store the state transition tuple $(s, a, r_1, \cdots r_N, s')$ into D
  $s \leftarrow s'$
  for agent i = 1 to N **do**
    A sample batch of size S is sampled from $D\left(s^b, a^b, r^b, s'^b\right)$
    $Q^{\pi'}_{avg} = \frac{1}{n}\sum_{i=1,\cdots,n} Q^{\pi'}_{i,1}\left(s'^b, a_1, \cdots, a_n\right)\Big|_{a_k=\pi'_k(o'^b_k)+\epsilon}$
    $y^b = r^b_i + \gamma\alpha \min_{j=1,2} Q^{\pi'}_{i,j}\left(s'^b, a_1, \cdots, a_n\right)\Big|_{a_k=\pi'_k(o'^b_k)+\epsilon} + \gamma(1-\alpha)Q^{\pi'}_{avg}$
    Minimize the loss of two Q-functions, j = 1,2:
    $L(\theta_j) = \frac{1}{S}\sum_b\left(Q^{\pi}_{i,j}\left(s^b, a^b_1, \cdots, a^b_n\right) - y^b\right)^2$
    if t mod d = 0 (d is the policy delay update parameter) **then**
      update π_i:
      $\nabla_{\phi_i} J \approx \frac{1}{S}\sum_b \nabla_\phi \pi_{\phi_i}\left(o^b_i\right)\nabla_{a_i} Q^{\pi}_{i,1}\left(s^b, a^b_1, \cdots, \pi_{\phi_i}\left(o^b_i\right), \cdots, a^b_n\right)$
      Update target network:
      $\theta' \leftarrow \tau\theta + (1-\tau)\theta'$
      $\phi' \leftarrow \tau\phi + (1-\tau)\phi'$
      where τ is the proportion of target network soft updates
    end if
  end for
end for

4. Multi-Agent Softmax Twin Delayed Deep Deterministic Policy Gradient (MASTD3)

4.1. Theory Related to Softmax Bellman Operation

The standard Bellman operator is defined as:

$$\mathcal{T}Q(s,a) = R(s,a) + \gamma\sum_{s'} P(s' \mid s,a) \max_{a'} Q(s',a') \tag{15}$$

We define the softmax Bellman operation symbol as:

$$\mathcal{T}_{\text{soft}}\, Q(s,a) = R(s,a) + \gamma\sum_{s'} P(s' \mid s,a) \frac{\exp(\tau Q(s',a'))}{\sum_{\bar{a}} \exp(\tau Q(s',\bar{a}))} Q(s',a') \tag{16}$$

The optimal action-value function $Q^*(s, a)$ outputs the maximum cumulative return that can be obtained after choosing action a at state s. Q^* is the fixed point of the standard Bellman operator $\mathcal{T}Q$; that is, starting from any starting Q_0, we have:

$$\lim_{k\to\infty} \mathcal{T}^k Q_0 = Q^* \tag{17}$$

However, due to the noise of the function approximator, the maximization operation of the standard Bellman operator always selects the maximum Q value for each state. This makes the algorithm exceptionally sensitive to the overestimated Q value of the action, and the overestimated Q value will be explicitly updated, which leads the Q value to the overestimation problem.

Softmax operation is generally considered to result in suboptimal action-value function and interfere with the convergence of the Bellman operator. Zhao Song et al. [14] proved that the softmax Bellman operator can quickly converge to the standard Bellman operator, and for any(s,a), when k approaches positive infinity, the difference between $\mathcal{T}_{\text{soft}}^{k}\,\mathcal{Q}_0(\text{ s,a})$ and $\mathcal{Q}^*(\text{ s,a})$ is bounded:

$$\begin{aligned}
\limsup_{k\to\infty} \mathcal{T}_{\text{soft}}^{k}\,\mathcal{Q}_0(\text{ s,a}) &\le \mathcal{Q}^*(\text{ s,a}) \\
\liminf_{k\to\infty} \mathcal{T}_{\text{soft}}^{k}\,\mathcal{Q}_0(\text{ s,a}) &\ge \mathcal{Q}^*(\text{ s,a}) - \frac{\gamma(m-1)}{(1-\gamma)}\max\left\{\frac{1}{\tau+2},\frac{2Q_{\max}}{1+\exp(\tau)}\right\}
\end{aligned} \tag{18}$$

Through experiments, Zhao Song et al. discovered that the combination of softmax Bellman operator and Deep Q Network yields better results than the Double Q-learning algorithm. They proved that the softmax Bellman operator can reduce the high estimation bias of Q value and believe this is the key reason for the superior performance of this method.

4.2. Multi-Agent Softmax Operation

The method of utilizing softmax operator to reduce overestimation of Q value can also be applied in multi-agent deep reinforcement learning algorithms. However, as the number of agents increases, the action space of the task will increase exponentially. It is impractical to simply apply the softmax operator to every possible combination of multi-agent joint actions, and the estimated Q value given by the Q network for the joint action, which is rarely sampled, is unreliable.

Ling Pan and others proposed an approximate softmax operator in Regularized Softmax Deep Multi-Agent Q-Learning (RES) [15]. Firstly, find the joint action $\hat{a} = \max_{\hat{a}} Q_{tot}(s,a)$ that makes the joint Q value the greatest. For the agent i, fix the actions of other agents $\hat{a}_{-i}$ and only change the action of the agent a to obtain the corresponding action subset $A_i = \{(a_i,\hat{a}_{-i}) \mid a_i \in A\}$. The approximate action space $\widehat{A} = A_1 \cup \cdots \cup A_n$ is obtained by combining the action subsets of all agents. The approximate softmax operator used in the RES algorithm is to use this approximate action space rather than the complete action space for Q value softmax operation calculation. Ling Pan and others proved that the difference brought by the calculation using the approximate action space and the complete action space is bounded, and because the approximate softmax operator reduces the dependence on unreliable joint Q values, this method performs better than the softmax operator using the complete action space.

Inspired by the Softmax Deep Double Deterministic Policy Gradients (SD3) [16] and RES, this paper applies the softmax operator to multi-agent algorithms and proposes the MASTD3 algorithm. Firstly, the MASTD3 algorithm further reduces the action space used for Q value softmax operation calculation in the choice of action space.

Suppose there are N agents in a multi-agent task, each agent action space is of size K, the complete action space includes all permutations and combinations of the actions, and the softmax operation requires computing K to the power of N Q values. The approximate action space proposed in the RES algorithm, while traversing the action space of a single agent, will fix the optimal action of the other agents, and then merge each agent's sub action space as the approximate action space, the softmax operation needs to calculate K times N Q values. This article believes, within the structure of the MASTD3 algorithm, the Q network of the agent i can make a reliable estimate of the $(s,a)\mid_{a\in A_i}$ state–action pair, but the estimate of the $(s,a)\mid_{a\in A_{-i}}$ state–action pair formed through changes in the actions of other agents is not accurate. Therefore, in the simple softmax operator proposed in this article, when agent i performs the softmax operation calculation on the Q value, only the sub-action space A_i containing all of its own actions, while the actions of other agents are fixed, is considered, and each agent only needs to calculate Q values K times:

$$\mathrm{softmax}_{\tau,i}(Q_i(s,\cdot)) = \sum_{a \in A_i} \frac{\exp(\tau Q(s,a))}{\sum_{a' \in A_i} \exp(\tau Q(s,a'))} Q_i(s,a) \tag{19}$$

where τ is the temperature parameter in the softmax operation, controls the level of exploration versus exploitation in decision-making.

The softmax operator will lead to underestimation of the Q value, and the high estimate Q value obtained by using the twin Q network maximization operation to perform the softmax operation can alleviate the impact of underestimation. Therefore, the Q network update target y_i of the MASTD3 algorithm is as follows:

$$\begin{aligned} A_i' &= \{(a_i', \pi(s_{-i}')) \mid a_i' \in A\}, \\ y_i &= r_i + \gamma\, \mathrm{softmax}_{\tau,i}\left(\max_{j=1,2} Q_{i,j}^{\pi}(s', a') \mid a' \in A_i'\right) \end{aligned} \tag{20}$$

5. The Multi-Agent Particle Environment Experiment

The multi-agent particle environment was used as the experimental environment in this study, proposed by Lowe et al. [17], and used for the verification of MADDPG algorithm. The multi-agent particle environment is a recognized multi-agent reinforcement learning environment [10,14,17], including different tasks, covering competition, cooperation, and communication scenarios in multi-agent problems. The particle environment is composed of a two-dimensional continuous state space, in which agents move to fulfill specific tasks. The state information includes the agent's coordinates, direction, speed, etc. The shape of the agent is spherical, and actual collision between agents is simulated through rigid body collision. Figure 4 displays the cooperative communication task and the cooperative navigation task for the particle experiment.

Cooperative communication task: This task involves two types of cooperative agents who play the roles of speaker and listener, respectively, and there are three landmarks with different colors in the environment. In each round of the game, the listener's objective is to reach the designated color landmark, and the reward obtained is inversely proportional to the distance from the correct landmark. The listener can obtain the relative position and color information of the landmarks, but they cannot identify the target landmark on their own. The observation information for the speaker is the color information of the target landmark, and they send messages at every moment to help the listener reach the designated landmark.

Cooperative navigation task: This task involves N cooperative types of agents and N landmarks. The aim of the task is for the N agents to move to different N landmarks, respectively, while at the same time avoiding collisions with other agents. Each agent's observation information comprises its own and the landmarks' relative position information and the relative position information with other agents. The reward function is calculated based on the closeness of each agent to its landmark—the closer it is, the higher the reward. Additionally, each agent actually occupies a certain physical volume and will be punished when it collides with other agents.

Under the multi-agent particle environment, the M2ATD3 algorithm proposed in this paper was compared with the MASTD3 algorithm, the previous MATD3 algorithm, and the MADDPG algorithm. Below is a presentation of the hyperparameter settings for this study. To ensure the fairness of the experiment, general parameters were set uniformly, learning rate $\alpha = 0.01$, batch sample size $N = 1024$. All algorithms share the same neural network structure, i.e., two fully connected layers with a width of 64 serving as the hidden layer of the policy network and Q network. The activation function of the neural network used Rectified Linear Units (Relu), and all experiments employed Adam as the optimizer of the neural network.

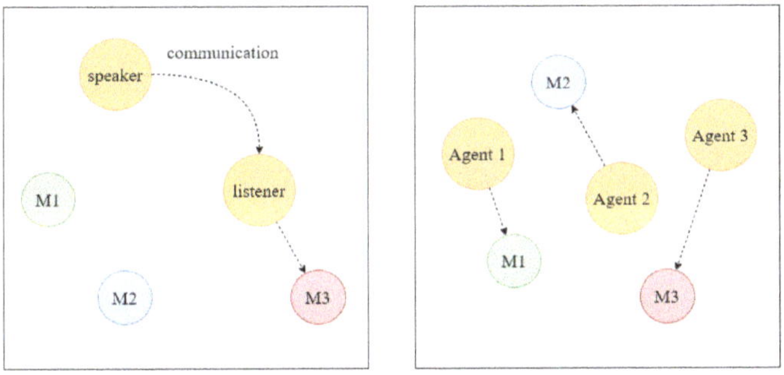

(a) (b)

Figure 4. The Multi-Agent Particle Environment: (**a**) Cooperation Communication Task. In this example, the speaker needs to inform the listener that the target landmark is red landmark M3, and the listener needs to approach the correct landmark based on the speaker's information. (**b**) Cooperation Navigation Task. In this example, agent 1 needs to approach green landmark M1, agent 2 needs to approach blue landmark M2, agent 3 needs to approach red landmark M3, and they should try to avoid colliding with each other while moving.

5.1. Q Value Estimation Bias Experiment

This article conducted a Q-value estimation bias experiment based on a cooperative navigation task in the particulate environment. By sampling from the experience replay pool to obtain samples of actions, states, and reward information to calculate the real Q-value and the estimated Q-value. In state s and action a, the average of 200 rounds of 100 steps' cumulative rewards calculation is taken as the estimated value of the real Q-value. The comparison of the approximate value obtained through the Q network output with the real Q-value can reflect the situation of Q-function estimation bias of different algorithms.

As shown in Figure 5, the lines marked with crosses represent the Q-value estimated by the neural network, and the lines marked with triangles represent the real Q-value. In the MADDPG algorithm, the blue line with the triangle logo's Q-value is higher than the orange line, implying that the MADDPG algorithm has an over-estimation, which is more apparent in the early training; under the MATD3 algorithm, the blue line with the triangle logo's Q-value is lower than the orange line, indicating that the MATD3 algorithm actually has an under-estimation. Under the M2ATD3, MASTD3, and other algorithms, the blue line with the triangle logo's Q-value is lower than the orange line, which means that M2ATD3, MASTD3, and other algorithms actually have an under-estimation, and the degree of underestimation is similar to that of the MATD3 algorithm, and it can be observed that the real Q-value of MATD3, M2ATD3, MASTD3, and other algorithms are higher than the real Q-value of the MADDPG algorithm, reflecting from the side that these three kinds of algorithms' policies are better.

The Q-value estimation bias comparative experiment can qualitatively reflect whether different algorithms have overestimation or underestimation. However, due to the complexity, randomness, and instability of multi-agent games, it is difficult to accurately calculate the true Q-values. Therefore, it is difficult for us to reliably compare the degree of Q-value underestimation of MATD3, M2ATD3, and MASTD3 algorithms, and further research is needed through performance experiments.

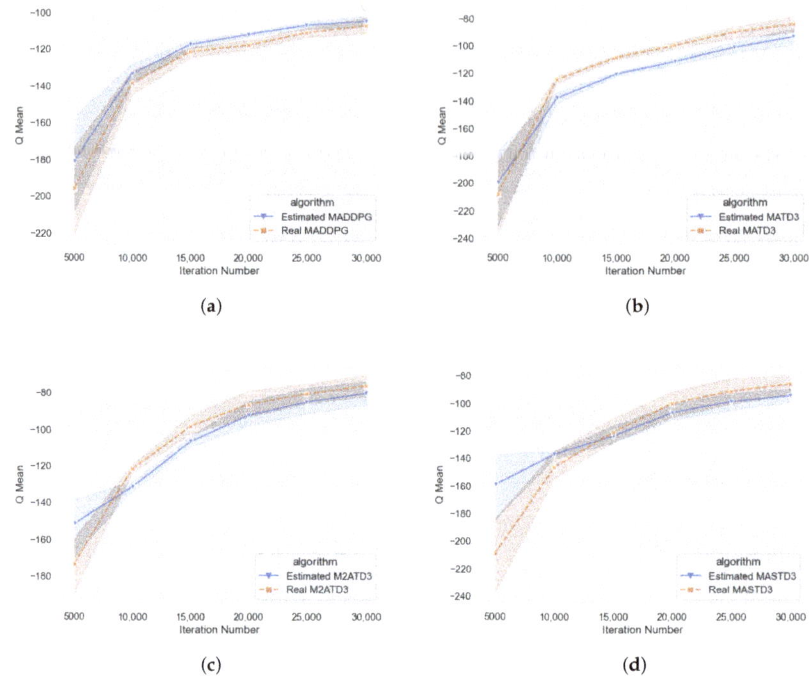

Figure 5. Q-value estimation bias comparative experiment based on cooperative navigation task in MPE. The Q-values estimated by the Q-network and the true Q-values are shown. The results are averaged across 5 runs and 95% CIs of the mean are shown for the estimated values. (**a**) DDPG, (**b**) MATD3, (**c**) M2ATD3, (**d**) MASTD3.

5.2. Algorithm Performance Experiment

In this section, the M2ATD3 algorithm and the MASTD3 algorithm are verified with the cooperative communication task and the cooperative navigation task in the particulate environment, and compared with the MADDPG algorithm and the MATD3 algorithm. All the experiments were trained for 60,000 steps. The experiment results are as shown in Figure 6.

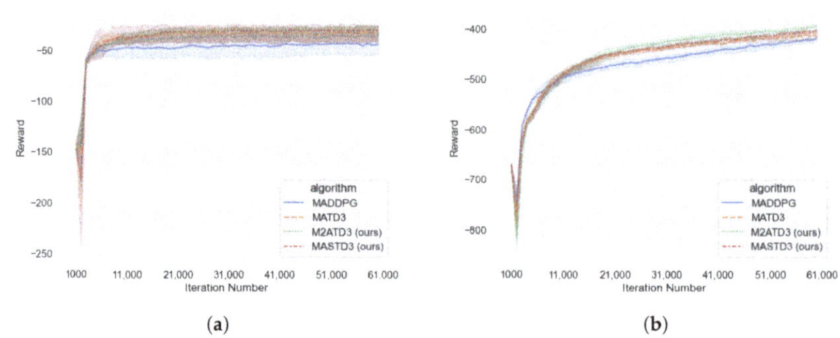

Figure 6. Comparative experiments using different Q-based multi-agent algorithms in MPE. Shown is the mean episodic reward over the last 1000 episodes, shaded areas are the 95% confidence intervals of the mean, averaged across 20 trials. (**a**) Cooperative Communication Task, (**b**) Cooperative Navigation Task.

As shown in Figure 6, in the Cooperative Communication Task and the Cooperative Navigation Task, the performance of the MATD3 algorithm is superior to the MADDPG algorithm, and both the M2ATD3 algorithm and the MASTD3 algorithm have achieved higher total rewards than the MATD3 algorithm.

As shown in Equation (14), hyperparameters α determine the proportion of the clipped double Q value to the average Q value when calculating the updated target value y_i, and select the appropriate hyperparameter α being able to balance the impact of underestimation of clipped double Q and overestimation of average Q.

As shown in Figure 7, in the cooperative communication task and the cooperative navigation task, the M2ATD3 algorithm receives lower rewards when the α is set to 0.2 or 0.8, indicating that the low estimation of Q value caused by the clipped Double Q-Learning or the high estimation of Q value caused by the average Q value estimates will have a negative impact on the algorithm. However, the M2ATD3 algorithm receives the highest reward when the α is set to 0.5, indicating that by balancing the two Q-value estimation methods, reducing the bias in Q-value estimation can improve the performance of the algorithm.

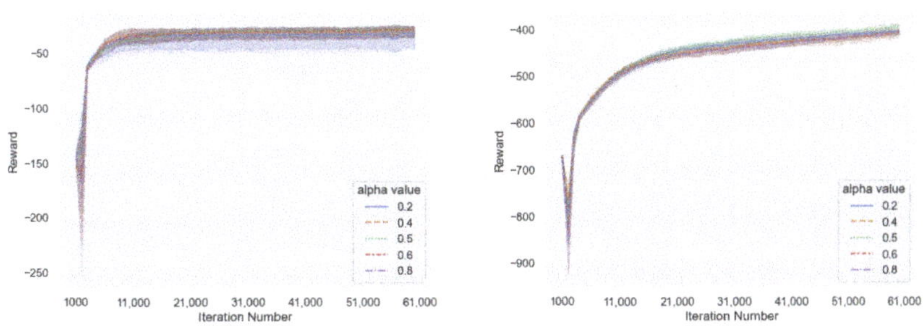

(a) (b)

Figure 7. Comparative experiments using different hyperparameter α value on the M2ATD3 algorithm in MPE. Shown is the mean episodic reward over the last 1000 episodes, shaded areas are the 95% confidence intervals of the mean, averaged across 20 trials. (**a**) Cooperative Communication Task, (**b**) Cooperative Navigation Task.

6. Multi-Agent Tank Environment

Games have long been benchmarks and testbeds for AI research. Yunlong Lu et al. [18] held two AI competitions of Official International Mahjong, and claim that Mahjong can be a new benchmark for AI research. In order to further investigate the performance of M2ATD3 and MASTD3 algorithms, we searched for existing reinforcement learning game environments. The Atari gaming environment [19] is rich in content, but it is mainly a single-agent gaming environment; StarCraft [20] and Honor of Kings [21] are multi-agent environments, but the game state space is too large, the game randomness is too much, and the game running mechanism is protected. This places high demands on training resources and makes it difficult to set specific challenge scenarios according to research needs. Therefore, this paper referred to the classic "Tank Battle" game content and developed a multi-agent tank environment and its multi-agent reinforcement learning framework based on pygame and pytorch. This experimental environment can reflect the performance of different algorithms in real games, with suitable training scales, and can easily create different types of challenge scenarios according to research needs.

6.1. Introduction to the Multi-Agent Tank Environment

The Multi-agent Tank Environment is a game that simulates a tank battle scenario. As shown in Figure 8, the environment is divided into two types: the scoring task and the battle task. In the scoring task, the goal is for the AI-controlled tanks to collide with as many scoring points as possible within a certain number of steps. In the battle task, the two teams of tanks win by firing bullets to destroy enemy tanks or the enemy base.

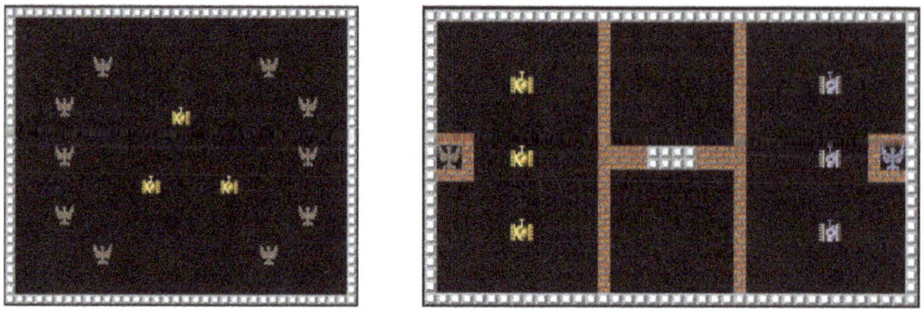

(**a**) (**b**)

Figure 8. Multi-agent Tank Environment. (**a**) Scoring task, (**b**) battle task.

Common units in the game include: tanks, which have a certain amount of hit points (HP). When hit by a bullet, the tank will lose HP, and when the HP drops to 0, it is considered destroyed. Tanks can move and shoot. The shooting action will fire a bullet in the current direction of the tank. The bullet will be destroyed when it collides with an object or flies out of the map boundary. Bases also have a certain amount of HP. When hit by a bullet, the base will lose HP, and when the HP drops to 0, it is considered destroyed. The base cannot move. There are brick walls that can be destroyed by bullets, and stone walls that cannot be destroyed by bullets. The game map can be created and edited using xlsx format files.

Each agent in the game can obtain local observations, which include unit features and image features. The unit features are given in the order of friendly base, friendly tank, enemy base, and enemy tank, including each unit's survival, HP, absolute position, relative position, orientation, etc. These features are normalized. The image features use a six-channel binary image to represent whether there are stone walls, brick walls, friendly units, enemy units, friendly bullets, and enemy bullets within a 25 × 25 range near the agent. If the corresponding unit exists, the value is assigned to 1; if not, the value is assigned to 0. By using the six-channel binary image, the agent's complete nearby situation can be depicted. Figure 9 shows an example of graphical features of multi-agent tank environments. If the positions where the channel value is 1 are drawn as the channel index, and the positions where the value is 0 are not drawn, a complete image feature can be drawn as shown in Figure 9b.

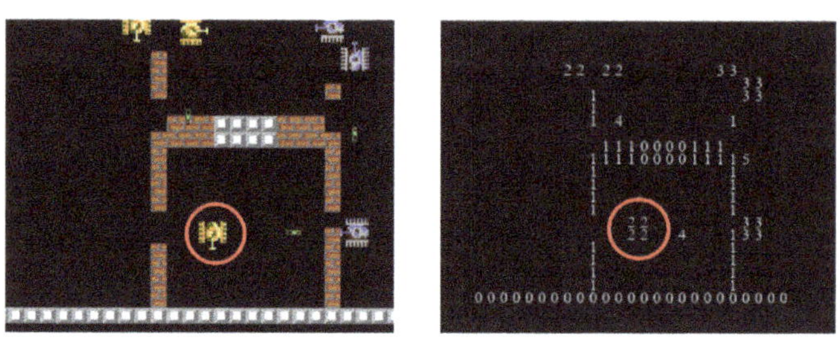

(**a**) (**b**)

Figure 9. Example of image features in Multi-agent Tank Environment. (**a**) Original image, (**b**) image features. Draw the positions with a value of 1 for each channel as the channel index, and do not draw the positions with a value of 0 to obtain a diagram of 6 channel combinations.

The deterministic policy of the reinforcement learning algorithm enables the agent to make decisions in a continuous action space, which is more intuitive in video games. For the deterministic policy of the reinforcement learning algorithm, we design the agent's action space as shown in Figure 10. We received inspiration from the way characters are controlled by the joystick in video games to design our action space for moving, as shown in Figure 10a, where we use a 2D action to control the tank's movement. Each movement action ranges from −1 to 1, corresponding to the joystick's movement from left to right or from bottom to top. We determine the direction of the tank's movement based on the maximum absolute value of the action in the horizontal or vertical direction. If the absolute value of the action in both the horizontal and vertical directions is less than 0.3, which is analogous to the joystick being in the blind area, the tank will not move. Similarly, we use a 1D action to control the tank's shooting, as shown in Figure 10b. The shooting action ranges from −1 to 1. When the value of the shooting action is greater than 0, the tank will shoot; otherwise, it will not shoot. The tank itself has a shooting cooldown. During the shooting cooldown, even if the agent issues a shooting action, the tank still cannot fire.

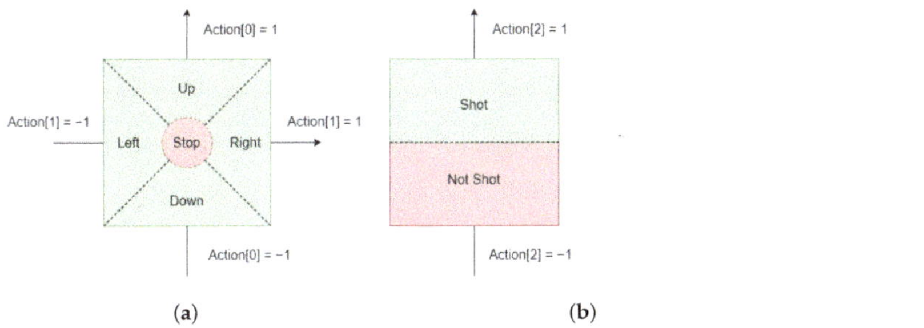

Figure 10. Example of action space in Multi-agent Tank Environment. (**a**) Move action, (**b**) shot action.

6.2. Multi-Agent Tank Environment Experiment

The process of deep reinforcement learning training using the Multi-agent Tank Environment is as follows: First, a corresponding model is created for each agent based on the selected algorithm. The model obtains actions through the policy network and interacts with the Multi-agent Tank Environment. The sequence samples obtained from the interaction are sent to the sample pool. When the samples stored in the sample pool reach a certain number, the training of the policy network and Q network of the model will start, and the model parameters will be updated at certain step intervals.

All algorithms in the experiment use the same neural network structure. A two-layer full connection layer with a width of 64 is used to process the unit features, and a convolutional neural network (CNN) is used to process the image features. The processed unit features and image features are concatenated and used as the input of the policy network and Q network. A two-layer full connection layer with a width of 64 is used as the hidden layer of the policy network and Q network. The network structure is shown in Figure 11.

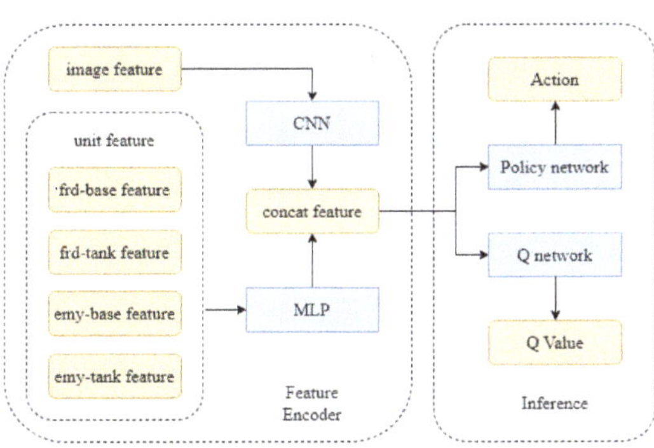

Figure 11. Neural network structure diagram of the Multi-agent Tank Environment experiment.

We conducted an experiment on the performance of multi-agent deep reinforcement learning algorithms in the scoring task. This task requires the AI to control three tanks to collide with as many scoring points as possible within 500 steps. There are a total of 10 optional scoring point birth positions on the map, and three positions are randomly selected each time to create scoring points. After the tank collides with a scoring point, the tank will receive a reward of +2, and a new scoring point will be created at a random other birth position. Since the reward for colliding with a scoring point is a sparse reward, we also set a dense reward according to the change in the distance from the tank to the nearest scoring point. In addition, in order to reduce the ineffective samples of the tank still moving towards the wall after colliding with the wall, we set an action mask, and set the action value in the direction of the wall to 0. The action mask effectively improves the efficiency of training.

The hyperparameters of the scoring task experiment are set as follows: learning rate $\alpha = 0.0005$, discount factor $\gamma = 0.95$, batch sample size N = 512. All algorithms use the same neural network structure, with the hidden layers of the policy network and Q network using two full connection layers with a width of 128. Training is conducted every 5000 steps using the current model to complete 20 evaluation rounds, and the average value of the evaluation round rewards is calculated. A total of 120,000 steps are trained, and the results are shown in Figure 12.

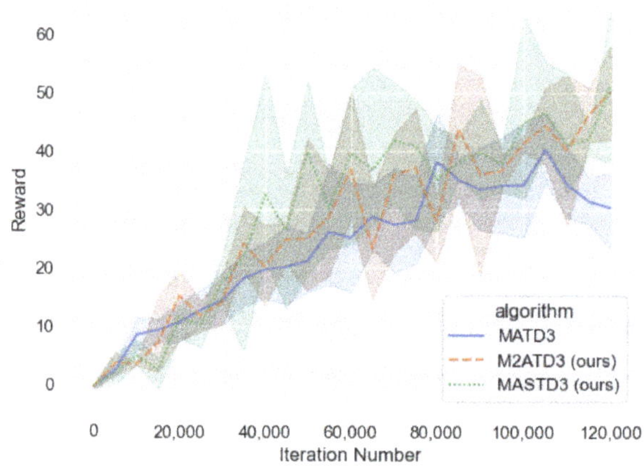

Figure 12. Comparative experiments using different Q-based multi-agent algorithms in the scoring task of UESTC-tank. Shown is the mean episodic reward over the last 50 evaluation episodes, shaded areas are the 95% confidence intervals of the mean, averaged across 20 trials.

- The performance of the M2ATD3 algorithm and MASTD3 algorithm is better than that of the MATD3 algorithm, and they can achieve higher rewards than the MATD3 algorithm.

7. Limitations and Conclusions

7.1. Limitations

As the policy function of the agent is even more difficult to update in the correct gradient direction in the multi-agent scenario, the bias in the Q-function estimation in the multi-agent scenario can have a greater impact on policy learning compared to the single-agent scenario. Therefore, studying the bias in Q-function estimation in multi-agent scenarios is very meaningful. The M2ATD3 and MASTD3 algorithms presented in this study reduce the bias in Q-function estimation, but both algorithms have certain limitations in their application scenarios. In the M2ATD3 algorithm, each agent should have similar functions to ensure the reliability of the joint Q-value, while the application of MASTD3 in continuous action space tasks has not been deeply explored. Expanding the application scenarios of these two methods to reduce Q-function estimation bias is a direction worth further study. In addition, the unit types and task types provided by the multi-agent tank environment are relatively simple, and the content of this environment can be further enriched, providing a good experimental environment for more experiments, such as multi-agent algorithm experiments, agent cooperation with human players experiments, and so on.

7.2. Conclusions

This paper primarily studies the Q-learning of agents based on deep reinforcement learning in multi-agent scenarios, and explores methods to reduce Q-value estimation bias in multi-agent scenarios, from multi-agent reinforcement learning algorithm theory to practical model deployment.

In the theory of multi-agent reinforcement learning algorithms, the focus is on solving the bias problem of the Q-function estimation of the MADDPG algorithm and its derivative algorithm, MATD3. In the MADDPG algorithm, the Q-function evaluates the policy function, so an unbiased estimation of the Q-function helps to learn better agent strategies. This research empirically demonstrates that the MADDPG algorithm overestimates the Q-function, while the MATD3 algorithm underestimates the Q-function, and theoretically proves that bias in the MATD3 algorithm. This is followed by the introduction of the M2ATD3 and MASTD3 algorithms presented in this study to solve this problem. The M2ATD3 algorithm combines the overestimation of the Q-value brought about by the joint estimation and the underestimation brought about by the minimization operation to reduce the bias in the Q-function estimation. The MASTD3 algorithm reduces the bias in Q-function estimation by combining softmax operation with maximization operation. The two algorithms have been tested in the multi-agent particle environment and the multi-agent tank environment, proving that they can indeed solve the estimation bias problem and that agents can learn better strategies to obtain higher rewards.

In the practice of multi-agent reinforcement learning, we constructed the UESTC-tank environment. This is a tank simulation game environment with multiple units and scenes, which can generate cooperative, adversarial, and mixed mission scenarios. We focused on its scalability when building the environment, so it can support unit editing, map editing, and rule editing. We hope it can become an open and effective benchmark in the field of multi-agent reinforcement learning.

Author Contributions: All authors contributed to the study conception and design. Methodology, software, validation, investigation, data analysis, and model verification: Z.L.; Investigation, resources, data curation, visualization, writing—review and editing, X.C.; Methodology, investigation, writing—original draft preparation, J.F.; Supervision, project administration, funding acquisition: N.X. and T.Z. All authors have read and agreed to the published version of the manuscript.

Funding: This work was supported by the National Key R&D Program of China (Grant No. 2022YFB3104600), and by Chengdu Science and Technology Project (2019-YF08-00285-GX), and by the National Natural Science Foundation of China under Grant No. 61976156, and by Intelligent Terminal Key Laboratory of SiChuan Province under Grant SCITLAB-30005.

Institutional Review Board Statement: Not applicable.

Informed Consent Statement: Not applicable.

Data Availability Statement: Dataset available on request from the authors.

Conflicts of Interest: The authors declare no conflicts of interest. The funders had no role in the design of the study; in the collection, analyses, or interpretation of data; in the writing of the manuscript; or in the decision to publish the results.

References

1. Silver, D.; Huang, A.; Maddison, C.J.; Guez, A.; Sifre, L.; Van Den Driessche, G.; Schrittwieser, J.; Antonoglou, I.; Panneershelvam, V.; Lanctot, M.; et al. Mastering the game of go with deep neural networks and tree search. *Nature* **2016**, *529*, 484–489. [CrossRef] [PubMed]
2. Sutton, R.S.; Barto, A.G. *Reinforcement Learning: An Introduction*; MIT Press: Cambridge, MA, USA, 1998.
3. Hasselt, H. Double Q-learning. *Adv. Neural Inf. Process. Syst.* **2010**, *23*, 2613–2621.
4. van Hasselt, H. Insight in Reinforcement Learning. Formal Analysis and Empirical Evaluation of Temporal-Difference Algorithms. Ph.D. Thesis, Utrecht University, Utrecht, The Netherlands, 2011; ISBN 978-90-39354964.
5. Schulman, J.; Wolski, F.; Dhariwal, P.; Radford, A.; Klimov, O. Proximal policy optimization algorithms. *arXiv* **2017**, arXiv:1707.06347.
6. Mnih, V.; Kavukcuoglu, K.; Silver, D.; Graves, A.; Antonoglou, I.; Wierstra, D.; Riedmiller, M. Playing atari with deep reinforcement learning. *arXiv* **2013**, arXiv:1312.5602.
7. Lillicrap, T.P.; Hunt, J.J.; Pritzel, A.; Heess, N.; Erez, T.; Tassa, Y.; Silver, D.; Wierstra, D. Continuous control with deep reinforcement learning. *arXiv* **2015**, arXiv:1509.02971.
8. Mnih, V.; Badia, A.P.; Mirza, M.; Graves, A.; Lillicrap, T.; Harley, T.; Silver, D.; Kavukcuoglu, K. Asynchronous methods for deep reinforcement learning. In Proceedings of the International Conference on Machine Learning, New York, NY, USA, 20–22 June 2016; PMLR; pp. 1928–1937.
9. Fujimoto, S.; Hoof, H.; Meger, D. Addressing function approximation error in actor-critic methods. In Proceedings of the International Conference on Machine Learning, Stockholm, Sweden, 10–15 July 2018; pp. 1587–1596.
10. Ackermann, J.; Gabler, V.; Osa, T.; Sugiyama, M. Reducing Overestimation Bias in Multi-Agent Domains Using Double Centralized Critics. *arXiv* **2019**, arXiv:1910.01465.
11. Polivy, J.; Herman, C.P. If at First You don't Succeed: False Hopes of Self-change. *Am. Psychol.* **2002**, *57*, 677–689. [CrossRef] [PubMed]
12. Weinstein, N.D. Unrealistic optimism about future life events. *J. Personal. Soc. Psychol.* **1980**, *39*, 806–820. [CrossRef]
13. Anschel, O.; Baram, N.; Shimkin, N. Averaged-DQN: Variance Reduction and Stabilization for Deep Reinforcement Learning. In Proceedings of the International Conference on Machine Learning, Mountain View, CA, USA, 13–15 November 2017; pp. 176–185.
14. Song, Z.; Parr, R.; Carin, L. Revisiting the softmax bellman operator: New benefits and new perspective. In Proceedings of the International Conference on Machine Learning, Long Beach, CA, USA, 10–15 June 2019; pp. 5916–5925.
15. Pan, L.; Rashid, T.; Peng, B.; Huang, L.; Whiteson, S. Regularized softmax deep multi-agent q-learning. *Adv. Neural Inf. Process. Syst.* **2021**, *34*, 1365–1377.
16. Pan, L.; Cai, Q.; Huang, L. Softmax deep double deterministic policy gradients. *Adv. Neural Inf. Process. Syst.* **2020**, *33*, 11767–11777.
17. Lowe, R.; Wu, Y.I.; Tamar, A.; Harb, J.; Pieter Abbeel, O.; Mordatch, I. Multi-agent actor-critic for mixed cooperative-competitive environments. *Adv. Neural Inf. Process. Syst.* **2017**, *30*, 6379–6390.
18. Lu, Y.; Li, W.; Li, W. Official International Mahjong: A New Playground for AI Research. *Algorithms* **2023**, *16*, 235. [CrossRef]
19. Bellemare, M.G.; Naddaf, Y.; Veness, J.; Bowling, M. The arcade learning environment: An evaluation platform for general agents. *J. Artif. Intell. Res.* **2013**, *47*, 253–279. [CrossRef]
20. Vinyals, O.; Ewalds, T.; Bartunov, S.; Georgiev, P.; Vezhnevets, A.S.; Yeo, M.; Makhzani, A.; Küttler, H.; Agapiou, J.; Schrittwieser, J.; et al. Starcraft ii: A new challenge for reinforcement learning. *arXiv* **2017**, arXiv:1708.04782.
21. Wei, H.; Chen, J.; Ji, X.; Qin, H.; Deng, M.; Li, S.; Wang, L.; Zhang, W.; Yu, Y.; Linc, L.; et al. Honor of kings arena: An environment for generalization in competitive reinforcement learning. *Adv. Neural Inf. Process. Syst.* **2022**, *35*, 11881–11892.

algorithms

MDPI

Article

Optimizing Reinforcement Learning Using a Generative Action-Translator Transformer

Jiaming Li [1], Ning Xie [1,*] and Tingting Zhao [2,3]

[1] Center for Future Media, School of Computer Science and Engineering, and Yibin Park, University of Electronic Science and Technology of China, Chengdu 611731, China; 202122080124@std.uestc.edu.cn

[2] College of Artificial Intelligence, Tianjin University of Science and Technology, Tianjin 300457, China; tingting@tust.edu.cn

[3] RIKEN Center for Advanced Intelligence Project (AIP), Tokyo 103-0027, Japan

* Correspondence: xiening@uestc.edu.cn or seanxiening@gmail.com; Tel.: +86-1779-640-6627

Abstract: In recent years, with the rapid advancements in Natural Language Processing (NLP) technologies, large models have become widespread. Traditional reinforcement learning algorithms have also started experimenting with language models to optimize training. However, they still fundamentally rely on the Markov Decision Process (MDP) for reinforcement learning, and do not fully exploit the advantages of language models for dealing with long sequences of problems. The Decision Transformer (DT) introduced in 2021 is the initial effort to completely transform the reinforcement learning problem into a challenge within the NLP domain. It attempts to use text generation techniques to create reinforcement learning trajectories, addressing the issue of finding optimal trajectories. However, the article places the training trajectory data of reinforcement learning directly into a basic language model for training. Its aim is to predict the entire trajectory, encompassing state and reward information. This approach deviates from the reinforcement learning training objective of finding the optimal action. Furthermore, it generates redundant information in the output, impacting the final training effectiveness of the agent. This paper proposes a more reasonable network model structure, the Action-Translator Transformer (ATT), to predict only the next action of the agent. This makes the language model more interpretable for the reinforcement learning problem. We test our model in simulated gaming scenarios and compare it with current mainstream methods in the offline reinforcement learning field. Based on the presented experimental results, our model demonstrates superior performance. We hope that introducing this model will inspire new ideas and solutions for combining language models and reinforcement learning, providing fresh perspectives for offline reinforcement learning research.

Keywords: machine learning; reinforcement learning; Transformer; action prediction; Action-Translator Transformer

1. Introduction

In recent years, with the continuous development and progress in the field of artificial intelligence, AI has achieved remarkable success in many areas, even surpassing human performance in scenarios such as board games and electronic games [1]. In the field of reinforcement learning, offline reinforcement learning is a crucial research area. Unlike online reinforcement learning, which requires the training process to occur in a real environment or a simulated one, offline reinforcement learning relies solely on historical offline datasets. This allows the training of policy or value functions for complex environments that are either difficult to model or entail high execution costs without the need for environment simulation. However, current algorithms based on offline reinforcement learning are mostly built on the theoretical foundation of traditional MDP and suffer from the problem of distribution shift [2], where the training policy differs from the behavior policy.

With the continuous development in the field of NLP from BERT [3] to GPT-3 [4] and the latest ChatGPT [5], interdisciplinary integration has become increasingly common. NLP models and algorithms are being experimented with in the field of reinforcement learning. The classic NLP model Transformer has been integrated into reinforcement learning algorithms, as the nature of reinforcement learning itself involves causal sequences that require the transmission of historical information for training the next step. Although early models like Long Short Term Memory (LSTM) [6] and Gate Recurrent Unit (GRU) [7] have been used in reinforcement learning, the Transformer [8], with its powerful memory function, is now being embedded into reinforcement learning. However, due to the peculiarities of Transformer model training, it requires substantial data and computational resources. Current research on the combination of Transformer and reinforcement learning primarily focuses on integrating the Transformer into the training process of traditional reinforcement learning algorithms and addressing the issue of mismatch. Based on this, the proposed algorithms include GTrXL [9] and CoBERL [10]. However, this simple integration has not only failed to address the existing problems in traditional reinforcement learning, but has also introduced new issues, such as unstable Transformer training and the need for extensive datasets.

With the introduction of the Decision Transformer (DT) [11] algorithm, a new domain has been opened up in the training of reinforcement learning. The underlying framework of the original reinforcement learning training, namely the Markov decision process, is abandoned. Instead, the language model is directly employed as the training framework for reinforcement learning, and the training process is conducted based on the GPT model. This aims to find the optimal trajectory and solve the reinforcement learning problem. Since language models often need to be built on large data sets for training [12], this model method can only be applied to the field of offline reinforcement learning. Because of its simple structure and being suitable for text generation tasks, the GPT model has excellent performance in the optimal trajectory generation of reinforcement learning. However, the model also has unreasonable aspects, leading to a lack of interpretability in the model. During the training process of DT, the entire offline trajectory is used directly as the training data input for GPT, serving as historical information to predict the optimal action at the next time step. However, when the DT model outputs this optimal action, it also includes the next time step's state and reward information in the output. State and reward information change automatically during the reinforcement learning training process in conjunction with the action, and should not be considered as model outputs to calculate the loss function. Additionally, these extra outputs increase the training difficulty of the model because the performance of a language model itself depends on the length of the input sequence. Introducing unnecessary input–output pairs will reduce the training effectiveness of the model. We will provide a detailed introduction to DT in the related work and validate its shortcomings.

In order to explore more possibilities for combining language models with reinforcement learning and enhance the adaptability of the model to the reinforcement learning training process, this paper proposes a novel intelligent agent training model based on a text translation model in the context of training game AI in offline reinforcement learning. The main contributions of this paper are as follows:

- A novel sequence-decision-based reinforcement learning method: We introduce the ATT network model, which is built upon the Sequence to Sequence model structure used in text translation tasks. It predicts actions based on observable scene information, utilizes the Transformer model to identify trajectories with the maximum reward return in different game environments, and is the first to employ the translation task framework to align with the reinforcement learning task.
- Encoding form adapted for text translation models: We devise a unique encoding form based on the original elements of reinforcement learning (state, action, reward) and introduce positional information to tailor it for the language model's training process.

- Based on a review of the existing literature, we analyze future development directions and challenges from the perspectives of reinforcement learning algorithms and other tasks in the field of natural language processing. The purpose of this discussion is to help researchers better comprehend the key aspects of combining reinforcement learning with large models and encourage the application of more language models in reinforcement learning tasks.

The structure of the subsequent sections of this paper is as follows: In Section 2, we will introduce the relevant background knowledge and theoretical system of reinforcement learning and natural language processing. We will briefly highlight algorithms that perform well in the combined field. In Section 3, our focus will be on introducing the ATT model, covering the problems it addresses, details of the method design, model architecture, and the training and inference processes. In Section 4, we will conduct specific verifications of ATT experiments, including an introduction to the experimental environment and an analysis of the experimental results. In Section 5, based on a summary of existing methods and the proposed method in this paper, we will discuss future research directions and challenges of combining reinforcement learning with NLP.

2. Background

From the initial proposal of the Markov theoretical system, based on Bellman's optimal equation, various methods have been suggested to tackle the reinforcement learning problem. With the advent of deep learning, Convolutional Neural Networks (CNN) found application across diverse fields. Simultaneously, reinforcement learning capitalized on the neural network's capacity for processing high-dimensional problems. It mapped some of the original complex multi-dimensional problems onto neural networks, leading to the development of highly efficient deep reinforcement learning algorithms. In recent years, NLP models have experienced rapid development, prompting an increasing number of researchers to explore the potential combination of language modeling with reinforcement learning. In this section, we will briefly introduce the relevant theoretical foundations of reinforcement learning and natural language processing. Concurrently, we will outline various attempts made by researchers to integrate the two fields. Finally, we will introduce the Decision Transformer, a highly successful model that combines NLP and RL. This model will serve as a key point of comparison, and we will explain its relevant structure and theory to facilitate understanding of the subsequent improvements made in this paper.

2.1. Markov Decision Process (MDP)

Reinforcement learning centers around the sequential decision-making process in the interaction between an agent (as the subject) and the environment (as the object). In a specific environment, there exists an agent capable of perceiving the current environmental information and generating actions based on this information. These actions lead to changes in the observed environmental information for the agent and, simultaneously, a reward signal is provided to the agent when the environmental state undergoes a change. This process continues until the agent ceases its actions or the environment reaches a terminal state. The objective of reinforcement learning is to train the agent's action policy, enabling it to attain the maximum cumulative reward during interaction with the environment [13]. MDP is a classical model for intelligent decision-making. Its core theory posits that if the future state of a state is independent of its past state, i.e., it depends solely on the present state, then this state possesses the Markov property. We define the information involved in this process as follows:

- S: a finite set of states, where s_i represents the state at step i.
- A: a finite set of actions, where a_i represents the action at step i.
- $P_{s,a}$: the probability of state transition, which denotes the probability of transitioning to other states given the action a in the current state s.
- R: the immediate or expected reward obtained from the state transition.
- γ: the discount factor that adjusts the influence of future rewards on the current state.

Thus, MDP can be represented as a quintuple:

$$M = (S, A, P_{s,a}, R, \gamma) \tag{1}$$

Due to the existence of the reward value R, the action a chosen by the agent is no longer random, but is aimed at obtaining the maximum cumulative reward. The state transition in this system is determined by both the current state s_t and the action taken a_t, the next state s_{t+1} is determined by the transition probability model $P(s_{t+1}|s_t, a_t)$, and the reward value r_t obtained at the current time is also determined by the probability distribution $P(r_t|s_t, a_t)$.

2.2. Reinforcement Learning Algorithms

Currently, mainstream reinforcement learning algorithms train agents based on modeling the environment with MDP. When agents need to make actions interacting with the environment, they either follow the current policy or use the current value function. In deep reinforcement learning, policies and value functions are often parameterized by variables in deep neural networks. Subsequently, gradient-based methods are employed for optimization. Loss is calculated using a loss function, followed by backpropagation to update network parameters until the value or policy function meets the training objectives. Based on the mentioned training approaches, mainstream reinforcement learning methods can be categorized into three major classes: Value-Based, Policy-Based, and Actor-Critic algorithms that simultaneously rely on both policy and value functions.

Value-Based: This method requires us to define a value function. For tasks with a small state space and action space, we can use a tabular form to represent the value function, such as Q-Learning. It optimizes a state-action value table where each data entry represents the immediate reward obtained by taking action a in state s, denoted as $Q(s, a)$. The core update formula is as follows:

$$Q(s_t, a_t) \leftarrow Q(s_t, a_t) + \alpha[r_t + \gamma \max_{a_{t+1}} Q(s_{t+1}, a_{t+1}) - Q(s_t, a_t)] \tag{2}$$

Here, α represents the update step size, and the value function $Q(s_t, a_t)$ is continuously updated through iterations until convergence. Based on the action-value function, the optimal action in a certain state can be selected. In high-dimensional and complex environments, using a table alone is insufficient to represent all states and actions. Therefore, we use neural networks to fit the value function, leading to the birth of the classic deep reinforcement learning algorithm, Deep Q-Network (DQN) [14], which uses parameters θ to approximate the value function. Subsequent Value-Based algorithms mainly focus on further optimizing the direction of reducing errors and improving sample learning efficiency.

Policy-Based: Unlike value-based methods, policy-based methods directly learn parameterized policies π_θ. This allows us to avoid the need to solve the value function for each action in the space. Therefore, this method is suitable for solving problems with high-dimensional or continuous action spaces. It intuitively improves the performance of the policy π_θ in the parameter space through gradient ascent methods and policy iteration updates, achieving the maximization of cumulative rewards. For example, the Policy Gradient (PG) [15] algorithm has the objective function to maximize the expected return by adjusting θ, represented as follows:

$$J(\pi_\theta) = E_{\pi \sim \tau}[R(\tau)] \tag{3}$$

In the above equation, τ represents a complete trajectory from the beginning to the end, π represents the current policy of the agent, and $\pi \sim \tau$ represents the action trajectory of the agent sampled under this policy. For this maximization problem, we use the gradient ascent algorithm to find its maximum value, and the optimization formula for parameter θ is as follows:

$$\theta^* = \theta + \alpha \nabla J(\pi_\theta) \tag{4}$$

The essence of policy-based algorithms lies in determining the gradient of the final return function $J(\pi_\theta)$ with respect to θ, commonly referred to as the policy gradient. This forms the basis for the optimization of various mainstream policy-based algorithms like PPO, TRPO, etc.

Actor-Critic: This approach, which integrates both policy and value, concurrently learns an actor function and a critic function. The actor function serves as the agent's policy function $\pi(\cdot|s)$, determining the action the agent will take in the current state. Meanwhile, the critic function functions as the state value function, providing an assessment of the action taken by the agent [16]. In this context, the Actor network is implemented using the policy gradient algorithm. For the Critic network, the Actor-Critic algorithm adopts the bootstrap method for estimating the Q-value function, and it learns the Critic function by minimizing the temporal-difference error, with the loss function given by:

$$J_Q = (r_t + \gamma Q(s_{t+1}, a_{t+1}) - Q(s_t, a_t))^2 \tag{5}$$

where the action a_{t+1} is obtained by sampling the current policy π_θ in state s_{t+1}. Algorithms arising from the Actor-Critic base such as A3C are also important algorithms in reinforcement learning.

2.3. Transformer

The Transformer was introduced by the Google Brain team in 2017 to address the limitation of parallelizing computations using RNN in NLP. RNN-based models faced inefficiency issues due to their inability to parallelize, making them less effective. The Transformer is a deep learning model built entirely on the self-attention mechanism. In NLP tasks, when dealing with text input data after Tokenization and Embedding processing, RNN structures would require feeding each token individually into the model. This is because RNNs rely on hidden state information passed from the previous input for each subsequent input. However, the attention mechanism in the Transformer allows the entire sequence to be input into the model. It ensures the sequence's order by introducing positional coding information and utilizes masking to facilitate parallel training. The Transformer's increased complexity results in higher accuracy and performance compared to RNN. The basic structure is illustrated in Figure 1:

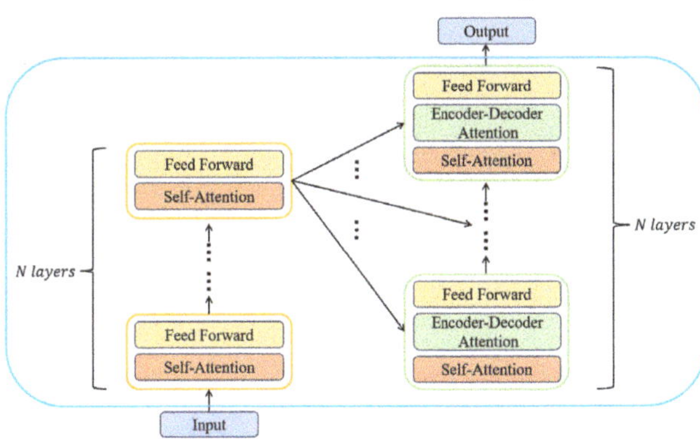

Figure 1. The overall framework of the Transformer model consists mainly of Encoders and Decoders. It is composed of six small Encoder and Decoder structures. The Encoders on the left process contextual text and calculate correlations between texts using the attention mechanism. On the right, the Decoders handle textual correlations for text output. The output form varies depending on the type of task.

Taking the text translation task as an example, during the pre-training stage, the input text data undergoes a series of steps. Firstly, the text is tokenized, breaking it into a sequence of words. Subsequently, the words are vectorized through embedding, where each word is input, and a corresponding vector is output. Before feeding these embedded vectors into the Transformer model, they are further encoded with position-related information. This positional encoding can be manually computed by presetting the positional encoding information. Following this, self-attention is computed for each position, expressing the correlation between different positions by calculating attention values for each position relative to other positions. The underlying principle is that when attention is given to data in the current position, information from other positions is also considered. The attention mechanism regulates the extent to which attention is given to other positions. The formula for calculating self-attention is as follows:

$$Attention(Q, K, V) = softmax(\frac{QK^T}{\sqrt{d_k}})V \tag{6}$$

where Q (Query), K (Key), and V (Value) are obtained by multiplying the encoded matrix by a weight matrix, and d_k is the dimensionality of our data after encoding. The self-attention mechanism allows positions to be interconnected, addressing the challenge of forgetfulness associated with longer sequences in the original LSTM and GRU models.

Another significant factor enabling parallel training in the Transformer is the introduction of the Mask mechanism. In the Decoder side, we input the translated text as a whole, but the Mask restricts the visibility of future words when predicting the word at a specific position. This approach ensures that the model leverages information from preceding words to make predictions for the current position, enhancing its ability to utilize previous context effectively during parallel training. By preventing the model from accessing actual future data during parallel training, this method maintains training effectiveness.

2.4. Transformer in RL

Reinforcement learning provides a mathematical framework for solving sequential decision problems and determining optimal actions through formulas. A persistent challenge in reinforcement learning is sample utilization. Inadequate sample utilization necessitates more training data and increased agent-environment interactions, significantly raising algorithm training overhead. This limitation hampers the agent's ability to learn an effective policy. Researchers have proposed various solutions to address this issue, including the utilization of buffers, autonomous construction of environment models, and more. However, most RL architectures are built upon methods related to supervised learning and semi-supervised learning. In high-dimensional scenarios, CNN serves as a function approximator, while for partially observable environments or situations requiring information retention, RNN processes the feature information.

The Transformer model has garnered considerable attention since its introduction, demonstrating superior performance compared to CNN and RNN. It exhibits excellent capabilities in handling long sequence problems, possesses strong scalability, and has evolved into a prevalent paradigm for numerous supervised learning tasks. Consequently, researchers have initiated efforts to apply the Transformer architecture to the realm of reinforcement learning.

Analogous to the use of neural networks in RL, researchers initially attempted to employ the Transformer as a function approximator in RL algorithms. However, merely substituting Transformer for LSTM in reinforcement learning yielded poorly trained models. Mishra et al. [17] explored the application of Transformer to various simple RL tasks (e.g., Bandit task, tabular version of Markov process) and found that the performance only matched that of the as-you-go policy. The main reasons for this were analyzed as follows:

- The training parameters of Transformer are complex and demand substantial data and computational resources to converge, while RL itself suffers from low sample utilization.

- RL receives state observation information sequentially in chronological order, and the order is not explicitly given but must be learned by Transformer.
- RL algorithms are highly sensitive to the architecture of deep neural networks.

These challenges hinder the effectiveness of Transformer in the original framework of reinforcement learning. In 2019, Parisotto et al. [9] proposed the GTrXL framework, leveraging the capability of Transformer-XL [18] to learn more than a fixed-length dependency without disrupting temporal coherence. The modified structure of GTrXL demonstrated significant improvement over LSTM in environments requiring long-term memory, effectively addressing various long and short-term memory requirements. Simultaneously, this new network structure can be combined with various strategies, rendering Transformer more suitable for the optimization process of reinforcement learning. The GTrXL framework established a baseline for using Transformer in reinforcement learning, prompting the emergence of subsequent approaches that build upon it. For instance, Adaptive Transformer in RL [19] enhances the efficiency of the original framework by increasing the memory size of GTrXL and employing Adaptive Attention Span. Ultimately, it maintains similar performance to the original GTrXL with a notable increase in training speed and a reduction in resource consumption. CoBERL [10], inspired by the self-supervised training task of mask prediction in BERT, combines GTrXL and LSTM using Trainable Gate. It integrates the two-way mask prediction self-supervised task and BERT's comparison learning method, resulting in improved learning outcomes for this combined model.

All the aforementioned approaches operate within the original RL framework, aiming to investigate the adaptability of Transformer in RL and optimize the training setup to mitigate the impact of Transformer's inherent challenges on the training task. Essentially, they continue to address the reinforcement learning problem by solving the value function or the policy network. In the following, we will introduce a novel concept that maximizes the advantages of Transformer in solving sequence problems. This approach discards the traditional RL framework and has shown remarkable results.

2.5. Decision Transformer (DT)

The DT model was introduced in 2021 by Lili [11] and collaborators, pioneering a novel approach to integrating NLP models with reinforcement learning. Previously, the utilization of the Transformer in reinforcement learning primarily involved substituting a portion of the structure within the reinforcement learning algorithm, while the overall training framework still adhered to the principles of MDP. The DT algorithm distinguishes itself from traditional reinforcement learning in that it employs Transformer to directly learn the actions that the intelligent agent should take to achieve the desired reward, rather than focusing on learning strategies or value functions.

To align with the Transformer structure, DT processes the training data differently. For the traditional trajectory $(s_0, a_0, r_0, s_1, a_1, r_1, s_2, \dots, s_t, a_t, r_t, s_{t+1})$, it needs to be transformed into the following format:

$$\tau = (\hat{R}_0, s_0, a_0, \hat{R}_1, s_1, a_1, \dots, \hat{R}_t, s_t, a_t) \tag{7}$$

Here, a and s represent actions and states at a given moment, as in the original definition. However, $\hat{R}$ is not an immediate reward; instead, it represents the cumulative reward that can be earned from the current state to the end of the trajectory (Returns-to-go). This definition enables the conversion of reinforcement learning into a supervised learning form for training. The training framework is illustrated in Figure 2.

We input the encoded sequence data as a token (the row of circles beneath the Embedding layer in Figure 2) into our Transformer. Here, three elements of the same moment $(\hat{R}_t, s_t, a_t)$ share the same positional information since these data come from the same moment. We model the joint distribution of the total return, state, and action trajectories for subsequent trajectories through Transformer. During training, we use a mask to hide the subsequent information of the current moment. This ensures that the Transformer can only use historical trajectories to infer the current action to be executed and output it. The optimization goal is the difference between predicted actions and real actions, using cross-entropy if the action is discrete and mean square error (MSE) if the action is continuous.

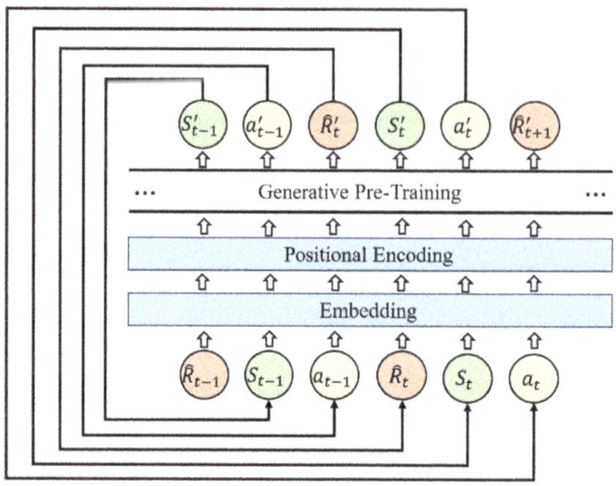

Figure 2. DT structure, which models reinforcement learning using a generative task approach, based on a sequence of inputs $(\hat{R}, s, a)$, with the entire sequence output intact at the output.

After training the network, we input the maximum reward value of the environment as our target reward (a priori knowledge). We then input the network and the current state, performing the derivation to obtain a trajectory that can yield the target reward. The outlined process represents the fundamental flow of the DT structure.

3. Action-Translator Transformer

3.1. Problem Description

The DT algorithm introduces a novel approach to solving reinforcement learning problems using NLP methods. Since the language model utilized demands extensive datasets for training, in online reinforcement learning, the data collected by the sample pool is often insufficient to support the training of the language model. Therefore, this method is primarily applied to offline reinforcement learning scenarios, leveraging a large repository of offline sample data to facilitate model training. In the DT algorithm, the model employed for training follows a GPT structure—a simplified version compared to the original Transformer, consisting of multiple Decoders stacked together. The structure is illustrated in Figure 3.

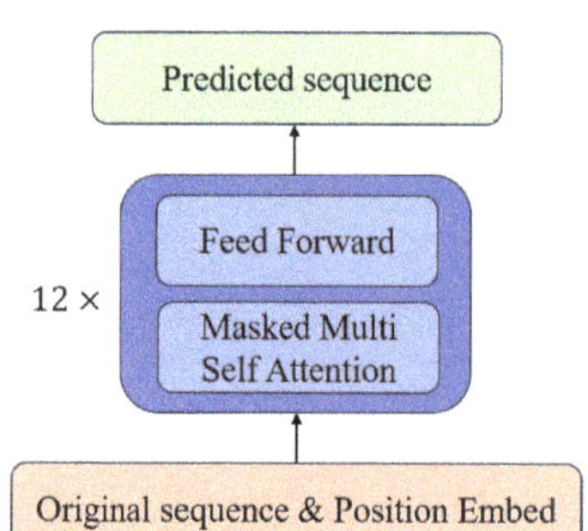

Figure 3. The language model (GPT) used in DT, which contains only one part with respect to Transformer, for the input of a text, predicts that text sequence in its entirety and is suitable for text generation tasks.

The GPT language model adopts a unidirectional structure without a clear distinction between Encoder and Decoder. To accommodate the input into the model, DT processes offline trajectory data into a single trajectory, i.e., a sequence of $(\hat{R}_t, s_t, a_t)$, which is then used for model training after incorporating position encoding information. The training process resembles a text generation task, where the DT predicts the output reward sum $\hat{R}$, state s, and action a simultaneously for the next position based on the preceding sequence. However, considering the spontaneous changes in state transfer and reward feedback information during actions in reinforcement learning environments, treating them as predictive outputs seems unreasonable and redundant. We assess the impact of the model's output on state s and reward sum $\hat{R}$ in optimizing the model by modifying the loss function in the DT optimization process. The two loss functions employed are:

$$L_1 = \frac{1}{n}\sum_{i=0}^{n}(a_i^{'} - a_i)^2 \tag{8}$$

$$L_2 = \frac{1}{n}\sum_{i=0}^{n}[(a_i^{'} - a_i)^2 + (s_i^{'} - s_i)^2 + (\hat{R}_i^{'} - \hat{R}_i)^2] \tag{9}$$

where $a_i^{'}$, $s_i^{'}$ and $\hat{R}_i^{'}$ are our predictions.

We analyze results within the original DT experimental environment, and detailed information about the setup will be provided in Section 4.1. We optimize the DT model using two different loss functions (L_1 and L_2), denoted as DT (L_1) and DT (L_2), respectively. We compare the two DT models using offline datasets of varying qualities (introduced in Section 4.2), calculating the total reward values obtainable from the predicted trajectories of the models after 100k training steps. The results are shown in Table 1.

Table 1. Performance results of DT with different types of loss functions.

Environment	Dataset	DT (L_1)	DT (L_2)
Walker	Medium	74.0	73.1
	Medium-Expert	108.1	108.3
	Medium-Replay	66.6	67.2
Hopper	Medium	67.6	67.0
	Medium-Expert	107.6	108.0
	Medium-Replay	82.7	78.4

Observing the experimental results, we can conclude that incorporating the predicted output of the reward sum $\hat{R}$ and environmental state information s into the loss function does not lead to an improvement in the model's predictions. Despite adapting the GPT structure used by the DT algorithm to the required input data format for training, it still outputs sequence data in the same format as the input, predicting the generation of additional redundant information $(\hat{R}, s)$. For the reinforcement learning task, our primary goal is to obtain the optimal action maximizing the reward for the intelligent agent. In this paper, we will focus on experiments related to this specific problem.

3.2. Model Formulation

3.2.1. Basic Introduction of the Model

We have devised a novel reinforcement learning sequence decision model called the Action-Translator Transformer (ATT) for the task of generating reinforcement learning sequence trajectories. This model leverages existing trajectory data to learn the relationship between the target reward and the trajectory. It learns sequences that lead to the target reward, allowing the generation of corresponding trajectories based on a user-defined target reward value. This approach aims to achieve the maximum target reward in the current environment, completing the reinforcement learning task. Similar to DT, ATT directly models trajectory data and avoids the training instability associated with bootstrapping and iteration, eliminating issues related to MDP-based reinforcement learning errors (refer to Appendix A).

To ensure that our model focuses solely on predicting actions without providing additional environment and reward information, we draw inspiration from the field of NLP, specifically the text translation problem. We conceptualize the training process as a translation task, transforming state and reward information into the corresponding actions. As illustrated in Figure 4, we define a target reward value (the maximum reward value of the environment) based on environment-specific information or prior knowledge. This target reward value, along with the current environment state information, is inputted into our ATT model, which then predicts the action to be performed. After interacting with the environment to update the state and receive instant rewards, we update the historical trajectory information, the current target reward value, and the current state information. This process is repeated, predicting the next action until reaching a termination state or satisfying the target reward. This outlines the fundamental process of using ATT to predict optimal actions and obtain optimal trajectories.

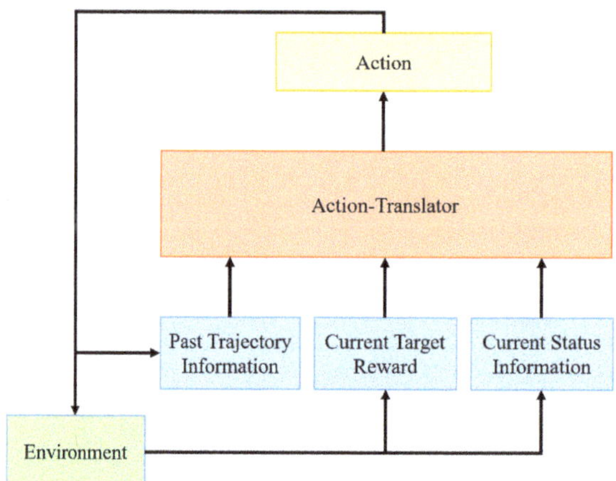

Figure 4. Schematic of the overall framework of the ATT model, abstracting the predicted actions into text translation task solving. The details of the Action-Translator are shown in Figure 5.

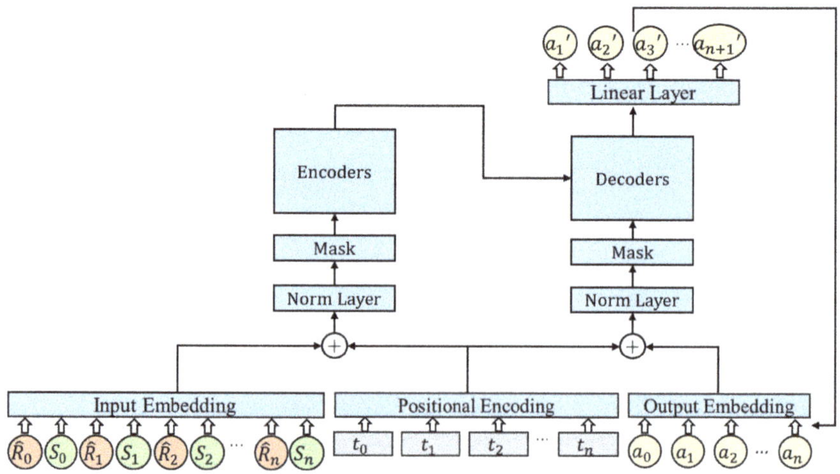

Figure 5. Action-Translator Transformer overall model architecture.

3.2.2. Overall Structure of the Model

To ensure that the model's output consists solely of optimal actions while using the environment and target reward as objective information for training, we leverage text translation task processing. We opt for the Transformer structure, encompassing both the encoder and decoder sides, as illustrated in Figure 5. To establish a connection between the reward information and context, we employ the reward treatment from DT, recalculating immediate rewards in offline data as the total reward obtained from the current moment to the end of the trajectory. Considering our dual-end structure, the intelligent agent observes the target reward value and current environment state information, serving as the input for the encoder side (i.e., as global information for the intelligent agent). The decoder side, responsible for action prediction output, undergoes different input forms during the pre-training and inference phases. The specific processes for training and inference will be detailed below. Moreover, as our model's overall structure is based on the Transformer, a substantial dataset is required to meet the model's training needs, making it primarily suitable for offline reinforcement learning tasks.

Our model follows the Sequence-to-Sequence style, comprising an encoder side and a decoder side. The encoder side consists of six encoders stacked together, receiving the encoded and masked global environment information $(s, \hat{R})$ and inputting the result into our decoder side. The decoder side also comprises six stacked decoders, primarily conducting the action prediction learning process. It accepts the encoded and masked action (a) sequence information and predicts the next action based on the observable action and global environment information input from the encoder side, completing the decision-making process for reinforcement learning. This framework represents the overall structure of the ATT model, adopting the Transformer model architecture format. It is divided into an encoder side and a decoder side, each with its corresponding encoding structure. Data are input into the encoder and decoder sides from the initial encoding module, with the final action prediction output through the linear layer in the decoder side.

3.2.3. Model Details

Target Reward: As we employ offline reinforcement learning data, traditional reinforcement learning sample data are stored in the format of (s_t, a_t, r_t). However, the Transformer model is designed to train sequence data containing contextual information. Therefore, it is necessary to establish a connection between the data and, simultaneously, segment the data into appropriate lengths for the Transformer network to facilitate learning. The representation of offline reinforcement learning trajectory data are shown in the equation below:

$$\tau = (\ldots, s_{t-1}, a_{t-1}, r_{t-1}, s_t, a_t, r_t, s_{t+1}, a_{t+1}, r_{t+1}, \ldots) \tag{10}$$

where s represents the state information at a certain moment, a represents the action information at a certain moment, and r represents the instant reward information at a certain moment. Such trajectory data can only represent the relevant information at each moment, and it cannot be used as the training data for the Transformer model to learn contextual information. Therefore, we need to process the data. We retain the original forms of s and a in the trajectory data, and process r. We represent r in a new form, denoted as $\hat{R}$, calculated as follows:

$$\hat{R}_t = r_t + r_{t+1} + r_{t+2} + \cdots + r_{end} \tag{11}$$

The information represented by $\hat{R}_t$ is the total reward value available from the current moment to the end of the trajectory. This transformation establishes a link between the data at different moments, and the trajectory history data are processed into the following form:

$$\hat{\tau} = (\hat{R}_0, s_0, a_0, \hat{R}_1, s_1, a_1, \ldots, \hat{R}_t, s_t, a_t) \tag{12}$$

Although the Transformer can handle long sequences of text, it is also sensitive to sequence length limitations. Therefore, we need to preprocess the trajectory data into segments of length K that the model can accept. In cases where the original trajectory is shorter than K, we fill the remaining positions with zeros.

Embedding: After processing, the data can meet the training requirements of the Transformer. Following the flow of a text translation task, we need to encode the processed data. We use a fully connected layer to encode the state s, action a, and target reward $\hat{R}$. Utilizing the dual-end structure of the Transformer, we concatenate $\hat{R}$ and s to form a sequence on the encoder side, encoding it as observable environmental information during action translation. On the decoder side, the sequence composed of a is encoded as the predicted output control of our model. We input the real action information as the target prediction into the decoder side, because we employ the Teacher-Forcing training method, a parallel training method of Transformer, which will be explained in detail later. Here, we only introduce the input form. Both the input-side coding layer and the output-side coding layer use a fully connected layer structure, as shown in Figure 6.

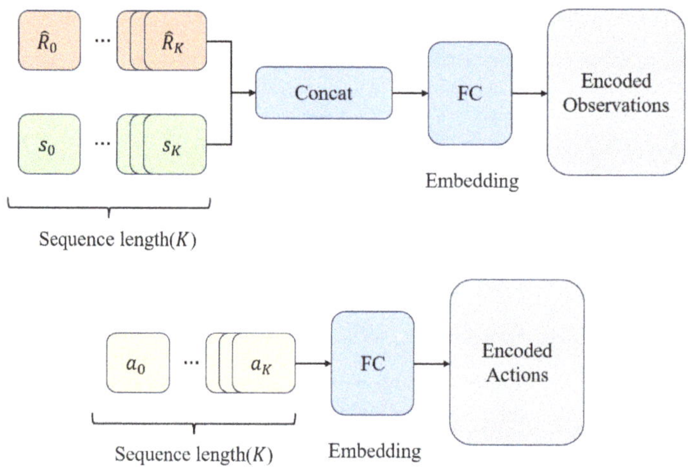

Figure 6. Encoding process of the original input in Encoders and Decoders.

Positional Encoding: During the training process of the Transformer network model, it is essential to introduce positional information to enable the model to perceive the relative positions of elements in the sequence. As our reinforcement learning trajectory data already includes temporal information, i.e., it corresponds to a specific time step, we can directly use the time step as our positional information. Considering a complete trajectory as a timeline, sequentially numbered starting from zero, we input the position encoding function to generate the positional encoding information. Our position encoding method involves creating a coding matrix that maps a certain range of numbers to unique vectors, which serve as the encoded positional information. The network structure details of the encoding part are illustrated in Figure 7. Following the encoding of positional information, we directly sum the position information encoded at each time step with the Encoder Observations and Encoder Actions obtained in the previous step. The objective of this step is to incorporate temporal information into our training data, facilitating the model in learning the causal sequence information of the entire trajectory. This encompasses understanding the distinct state transition relationships between time nodes and changes in reward information.

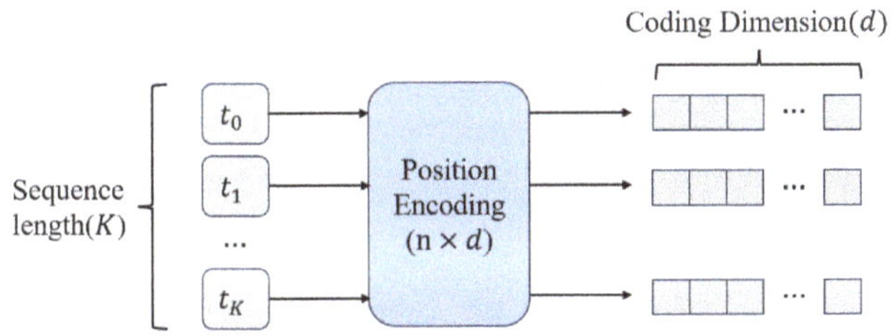

Figure 7. Flowchart of location information encoding.

Mask: After data preprocessing and the introduction of positional information, we obtain the data required to meet the training needs of the Transformer. At this stage, it is essential to consider the distinction between the model during the Training phase and the Inference phase—ensuring consistent contextual data forms. During the Training phase, using offline trajectory data, a complete trajectory is known. Therefore, the inputs on both the encoder and decoder sides are segments extracted from the entire trajectory. However, in the Inference phase of Reinforcement Learning, actions are initiated from a random state, extrapolating trajectory generation, and this process cannot observe global trajectory information. To align the tasks in the Train and Inference phases, and to cater to the lack of global trajectory information in the Inference phase, we need to introduce the Mask mechanism. Masks are applied to both the encoder and decoder sides, taking the form of upper triangular matrices. This ensures that, at a given time point, the intelligent agent can only use information from that specific moment and preceding moments to predict actions.

The input data from both Encoders and Decoders undergo Mask processing, as illustrated in Figure 8. Each sample input transforms into a square matrix, and each row of the matrix has certain information masked out. This masking is crucial for achieving parallel training using the Transformer. In the matrix, each row corresponds to a predicted output, and the predicted value in each row is the first value that has been masked out in the current row. When predicting an action at a specific time, only the real information before that point in time is used. This training approach is known as Teacher-forcing [20], a method effective in avoiding unstable network training and accelerating convergence. Employing this method allows us to simultaneously train predictions for each position in a sample, thus expediting the model's convergence.

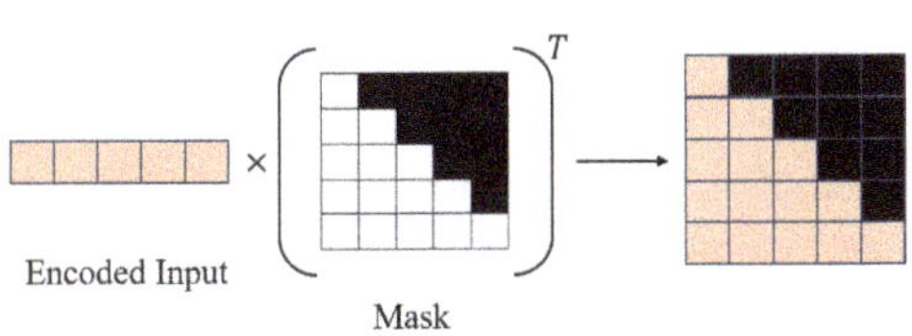

Figure 8. Mask mechanism for vectors.

The incorporation of the Mask mechanism enables our model to undergo parallel training across multi-dimensional matrices for multiple time points, expediting the training process. The training method under the Mask mechanism is shown in Figure 9. Moreover, it facilitates the alignment of task types between the training and testing phases. In the Inference phase, where the complete sequence of future actions is unknown, aligning the tasks ensures that our model performs optimally in prediction scenarios.

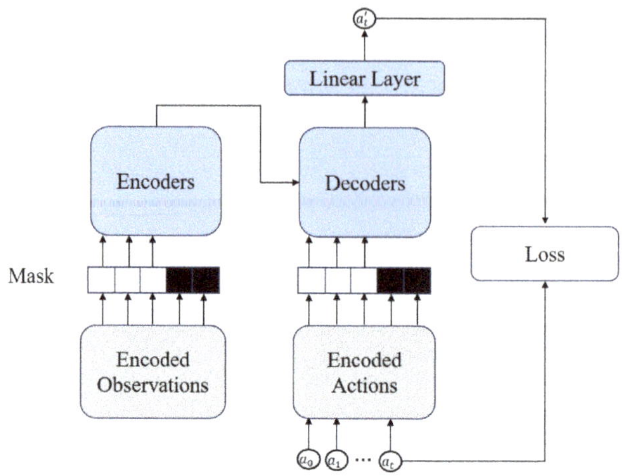

Figure 9. In the Teacher-forcing-based training process, the encoded data undergo Mask processing, marking the data after a specific point in time as invisible. The data input into the subsequent steps contains only the information before that point in time. After the encoding and decoding of the known information, and finally through the linear layer of decoding, we obtain the corresponding time point of the action a_t and the predicted value a_t'. Subsequently, we can optimize the model based on the loss of the action. The details of the loss model are shown in Equation 8.

Encoders–Decoders: The data subjected to Mask processing is subsequently input into the Encoders and Decoders, constituting the standard Transformer structure. Both Encoders and Decoders consist of several small structures stacked together, with the architectural intricacies depicted in Figure 10, following the design outlined by Vaswani et al. [6].

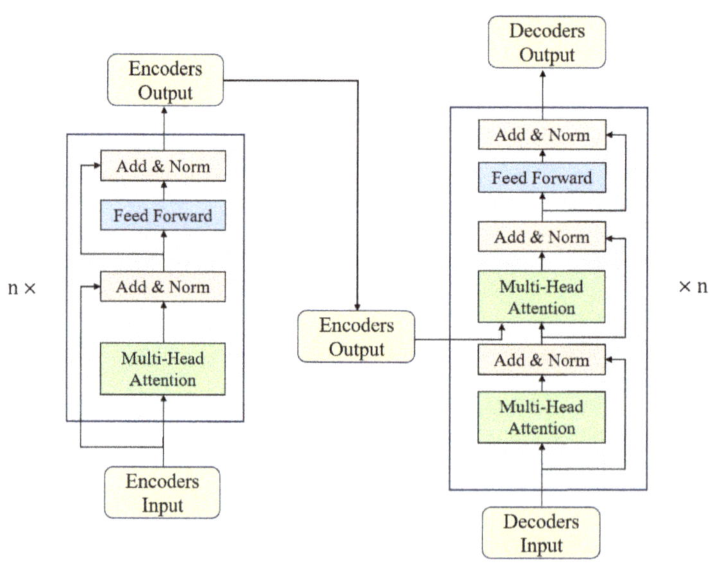

Figure 10. The internal structure of Encoders and Decoders comprises numerous smaller encoder structures. These smaller encoders encompass attention calculations and various network layer structures. The output of the last small encoder is then transmitted to each small decoder to engage in attention calculations within the encoder. Ultimately, the final output is derived from the last small decoder.

Each small Encoder incorporates a Multi-Head Attention calculation, employed to compute the similarity between the current state of the agent's environment and the state in the preceding sequence. Additionally, a Feed Forward component is included, facilitating a linear transformation that maps the data to a high-dimensional space and subsequently to a low-dimensional space, enabling the extraction of more profound features.

In Decoders, unlike in Encoders, two Multi-Head Attention computations take place. In the second computation, the environment feature information from the agent, outputted by the Encoders, serves as both Q and K in the Attention computation. This allows our model to learn the action output based on the environment information.

Action Decoding: After obtaining the data output from the Decoders, we have completed the process of action prediction. The actions at this stage are high-dimensional encoded actions that need to be decoded. In this experiment, we directly use a linear layer to transform the corresponding high-dimensional actions into the dimensions of the intelligent body's actions in the current environment, representing the final output of the predicted actions.

3.2.4. Training and Inference

The whole training process of ATT we can summarize as Algorithm 1.

Algorithm 1 ATT training, optimize network parameters based on offline trajectories

Input: Data set $D = \{(s_t, a_t, r_t)\}$
$\hat{R}_t \leftarrow r_t + r_{t+1} + r_{t+2} + \cdots + r_{end}$
Initialize weight θ, training iterations I, step size η, batch size B, the state embedding matrix $W_s \in \mathbb{R}^{(d_{\hat{R}}+d_s)\times B}$, the action embedding matrix $W_a \in \mathbb{R}^{d_a \times B}$
for $i = 1$ **to** I **do**
    Stack $(\hat{R}, s)$
    Embedding: $(\hat{R}, s)_{emb} \leftarrow W_s \times (\hat{R}, s)$
    Embedding: $a_{emb} \leftarrow W_a \times a$
    Positional Encoding
    $Encoders \leftarrow (\hat{R}, s)_{emb} + P(t)$
    $Decoders \leftarrow a_{emb} + P(t)$
    Masked
    Train
    Output a'
    $loss \leftarrow L(a', a)$
    $\theta \leftarrow \theta + \eta \nabla L(\theta)$
end for
return θ

At the beginning of training, for the offline dataset samples, firstly, r in the sample data are calculated as $\hat{R}$, and the samples are processed to a specific length. After encoding and introducing the position information, they are processed by Mask and then entered into the Transformer for training using the Teacher-forcing method. The prediction of the action a' is then compared with the original input action sequence a to calculate the loss for optimizing the model. The complete pre-training process of ATT is outlined above. The loss function used here is given by Equation (8).

The Inference process of ATT, we can summarize as Algorithm 2.

The Inference of the ATT model is mainly derived using self-regression, where for each prediction, the model's output is used as input for the next prediction. By initializing the model with the necessary information, we continuously utilize the model to predict actions and generate trajectories. Eventually, we obtain the target trajectory based on our initial settings. During this process, the inputs to the model include the cumulative target rewards, where we set the maximum possible reward value $\hat{R}$ (as the ultimate goal of reinforcement learning is to achieve the maximum reward in the current environment) based on prior knowledge or environmental information. The initial state of the environment s is obtained directly by initializing the environment. We initialize the action a on the decoder side and input all this information into the encoder and decoder sides according to the input mode during the training process after padding operation. Specifically, $\hat{R}$ and s are input into the encoder side as global observable information and then passed to the decoder side after going through the Mask and Encoders.

Algorithm 2 ATT inference, generate full trajectories based on target rewards

$Initializeenv()$
Initialize $\hat{R}, s, a, step = 0, length, G = 0$
Padding
while s not equal to end **or** $step<length$ **do**
  Positional Encoding
  $Encoders \leftarrow (\hat{R}, s) + P(t)$
  $Decoders \leftarrow a + P(t)$
  Masked
  Output a_{next}
  $r_{next}, s_{next} \leftarrow env(a_{next})$
  $\hat{R} \leftarrow \hat{R} - r_{next}$
  $G \leftarrow G + r_{next}$
  $step \leftarrow step + 1$
end while
return G

The next action is predicted at the decoder side based on the input historical action information a and the global observable information from the encoder side. After the model outputs the next action a_{next}, we execute a_{next} in the current environment. At this point, our environment changes to s_{next} due to the agent's interaction behavior, and we obtain the instant reward r_{next}. Based on this instant reward, we update the expected reward sum $\hat{R}_t$ and then add the newly obtained $a_{\text{next}}, \hat{R}_{\text{next}}, s_{\text{next}}$ to the existing sequence as the observable data for predicting the next action. This process continues, and eventually, based on our artificially set expected reward sum $\hat{R}$, we obtain a complete trajectory. Through the accumulation of instant rewards r obtained during the process, we can calculate the total reward sum of the trajectory, G, and evaluate the strengths and weaknesses of our model.

4. Experimental Validation

Because both our ATT and DT utilize sequence modeling to address offline reinforcement learning tasks, we will compare them with DT and some classical offline reinforcement learning algorithms in a specific experimental setting to analyze the strengths and weaknesses of our models.

4.1. Experimental Environment

The experiment utilizes the Mujoco [21] simulation environment within the Gym environment. This environment incorporates a comprehensive robot motion engine, providing detailed motion information for each component of the intelligent agent. It encompasses the state information of the agent, along with reward-related settings, making it suitable for training in reinforcement learning tasks. The environment offers a variety of task scenarios, and the experiment specifically involves conducting assessments in the Hopper, Walker2D, and HalfCheetah environments. The experimental scenario is illustrated in Figure 11.

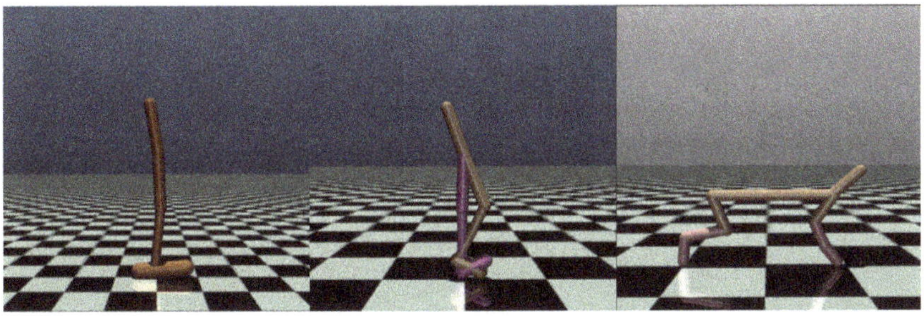

Figure 11. The Hopper, Walker, and HalfCheetah environments represent versatile experimental scenarios within a general-purpose physics engine. This engine is specifically designed to support various domains, including robotics, biomechanics, graphics and animation, machine learning, and other fields requiring precise simulation of articulated structures interacting with their environment.

Hopper: This environment features a single-legged robot with four main body parts: torso, thighs, legs, and feet. The robot's motion involves the control of three joints to execute a jumping maneuver. The state observation encompasses angular velocity, joint angles, and coordinates. The action space is defined by the control values for the three joints, and rewards are provided based on the robot maintaining an upright posture and successfully propelling forward.

Walker: In this environment, the robotic body features two complete legs and is composed of four main components: torso, thighs, legs, and feet. Unlike Hopper, the intelligent body in this scenario has two legs and two feet. The state observation space is similar to that of Hopper, while the action space expands in spatial dimension due to the increased number of joints in the intelligent body. Reward feedback is obtained when the intelligent agent maintains an upright position and successfully propels forward.

HalfCheetah: This environment involves a two-legged robot that exhibits animal-like movements and endeavors to progress within the plane defined by its legs. The state observation space encompasses the angles, angular velocities, and coordinates of the joints. Similarly, the action space includes control information for the joints. Reward feedback is provided when the intelligent agent maintains an appropriate upright posture and moves in the correct direction.

In the second segment of the experiment, we utilized the Maze2D game environment, focusing on a navigation task. The objective of the test is to discover the shortest path to the target point by integrating sub-optimal trajectories with the Offline RL algorithm. This environment comprises three game scenarios: Umaze, Medium, and Large, each featuring a maze structure illustrated in Figure 12. The primary evaluation of the model's performance revolves around its capacity to concatenate sub-optimal trajectories to efficiently find the shortest path to the target point.

Figure 12. Umaze, Medium, and Large three maze environments, Maze2D is a navigation task. The test goal is to find the shortest path to the target point by combining the sub-optimal trajectory with the offline RL algorithm. In the illustration, the green dots represent the current position of the agent, while the red dots indicate the target points that the agent needs to reach.

4.2. Dataset

The dataset utilized in this experiment is sourced from the Python data package D4RL [22]. It encompasses the complete action trajectory of an agent in the Mujoco environment under Gym, incorporating the state information s of the agent at a specific moment in time, the action information a taken by the agent, and the instantaneous rewards r acquired by the agent. The dataset is structured as (s_t, a_t, r_t). Within this package, various trajectory data types are available for the same game environment, originating from diverse data collection methods. For this experiment, the focus is primarily on three data types:

- Medium dataset: A strategy network is trained online using Soft Actor-Critic (SAC), and the training is prematurely terminated to collect 1M samples from this partially trained strategy.
- Medium-replay dataset: Comprising all samples recorded in the replay buffer during training until the policy achieves a "medium" performance level.
- Medium-expert dataset: This dataset introduces a "medium-expert" dataset by blending an equal amount of expert demonstration and sub-optimal data. The latter is generated either by partially trained strategies or by expanding a uniformly randomized strategy.

These three data types offer comprehensive coverage of the domains in which our model is tested, allowing for a thorough evaluation of the model's strengths and weaknesses.

Additionally, for the Maze2D environment, we trained the model using the tracks for the three scenarios stored in the D4RL dataset. The performance is then compared with the CQL and DT algorithms.

4.3. Experimental Results

We compare ATT with DT and several other key offline reinforcement learning algorithms, including CQL [23], BEAR [24], BRAC [25], AWR [26], and BC [27]. Our ATT model focuses on transformational tasks, DT is centered around generative tasks, and CQL is recognized as a top-performing MDP-based RL algorithm. The experiments are conducted in three Mujoco scenarios. For ATT, we configure both the stacked Encoder and Decoder structures with six layers, set the learning rate to 1×10^{-3}, and establish the length of receivable sequences (K) at the encoder and decoder sides to be 20. The sum of target rewards ($\hat{R}$) is determined based on historical trajectory data, with Hopper set to 3600, HalfCheetah to 12,000, and Walker to 5000. After training for $100k$ steps under identical conditions, we compare the effectiveness of various algorithms. To facilitate comparison, we normalize the results using the training results of the SAC algorithm as the expert score and those of a random strategy as the random score. The normalization formula used is as follows:

$$normalized = 100\% \times \frac{score - random}{expert - random} \tag{13}$$

The results of the experiment are shown in Table 2. The results of the DT are referenced from [11], while the results of CQL, BEAR, BRAC-v, AWR, and BC are referenced from [22].

Table 2. Comparison of ATT with other offline reinforcement learning algorithms in Mujoco.

Dataset	Environment	ATT (Ours)	DT	CQL	BEAR	BRAC-v	AWR	BC
Medium-expert	Hopper	109.8	107.6	**111.0**	96.3	0.8	27.1	76.9
	Walker	**110.2**	108.1	98.7	40.1	81.6	53.8	36.6
	HalfCheetah	**88.9**	86.8	62.4	53.4	41.9	52.7	59.5
Medium	Hopper	**68.4**	67.6	58.0	52.1	31.1	35.9	63.9
	Walker	**82.0**	74.0	79.2	59.1	81.1	17.4	77.4
	HalfCheetah	40.3	42.6	44.4	41.7	**46.3**	37.4	43.1
Medium-replay	Hopper	79.3	**82.7**	48.6	33.7	0.6	28.4	27.6
	Walker	**68.7**	66.6	26.7	19.2	0.9	15.5	36.9
	HalfCheetah	36.3	36.6	46.2	38.6	**47.7**	40.3	4.3

The bold numbers in each row represent the best performance in the corresponding environment for that row.

We compare ATT, DT, and CQL in three scenarios of Maze2D to investigate the model's ability to splicing sub-optimal trajectories. The results are shown in Table 3.

Table 3. Comparison of ATT with other offline reinforcement learning algorithms in Maze2D.

Environment	ATT	DT	CQL
Maze2D-umaze	42.2	31.0	**94.7**
Maze2D-medium	13.7	8.2	**41.8**
Maze2D-large	10.2	2.3	**49.6**

The bold numbers in each row represent the best performance in the corresponding environment for that row.

4.4. Discussion

Based on the experimental results, we conclude that our ATT model exhibits comparable performance to DT, outperforming DT in most scenarios and settings. Moreover, ATT surpasses many traditional offline reinforcement learning algorithms, demonstrating an ability to learn trajectories with superior reward payoff values. While CQL, an offline reinforcement learning algorithm based on MDP, maintains a certain advantage, it struggles with low data quality, unlike ATT and DT, which leverage sequence modeling to enhance sample utilization in offline datasets. This allows them to learn effectively, even from suboptimal offline data. These findings highlight the efficacy of using trajectory data for decision-making in offline reinforcement learning. Our transformational modeling approach in ATT yields better results compared to the generative model DT. Notably, ATT places a greater emphasis on action output, separating the sequence of environmental information from the sequence of actions. As a result, our model achieves superior performance in the realization of suboptimal trajectory splicing compared to DT.

5. Conclusions

In our work, we explore a novel application of reinforcement learning in the domain of Natural Language Processing (NLP), specifically focusing on the Text Translation Task. Drawing inspiration from the original work on the Dual-Transformer (DT), we devise a unique approach to data segmentation and encoding, tailoring it to meet the requirements of bipartite training for the Transformer model in the context of offline reinforcement learning. The designed ATT model structure incorporates a comprehensive set of Train and Inference processes, ensuring consistent data distribution across different stages of the task for effective training. By utilizing an input method that considers both the environment and target rewards and predicts action values, our model aligns with the reinforcement learning objective of identifying optimal actions and generally outperforms DT in various tasks.

Given that the combination of language modeling and reinforcement learning is still in its early stages, and NLP is rapidly evolving with the emergence of more efficient models, the potential for RL-NLP integration remains vast. In light of our model's future research direction, we identify key aspects for consideration:

- **Target Reward Setting:** In both ATT and DT, we adopt the supervised learning task training approach, requiring the calculation of a target reward value as the trajectory label for offline dataset training. Fluctuations in experimental results may be attributed to the accurate setting of reward values. Future research should explore methods to precisely set reward values or update them dynamically during training.
- **Efficient Language Model Training:** The language model, serving as the foundational training architecture, demands a substantial amount of datasets for effective training. While reinforcement learning can generate trajectory data through interaction, this method is not applicable to online reinforcement learning due to efficiency concerns. Investigating how to train the language model in an online interactive manner becomes a focal point for future work, expanding the model's usability.
- **Exploration of Different NLP Models:** The field of NLP boasts numerous powerful models, each with distinct characteristics and adaptive capabilities. Future endeavors

can involve experimenting with other high-performing NLP models, aligning them with various reinforcement learning tasks, and further exploring the potential of combining these technologies.

Author Contributions: Methodology, software, validation and writing—original draft preparation, J.L.; writing—review and editing, N.X. and T.Z. All authors have read and agreed to the published version of the manuscript.

Funding: This work was supported by the National Key R&D Program of China (Grant No. 2022YFB3104600), and by Chengdu Science and Technology Project (2019-YF08-00285-GX), and by the National Natural Science Foundation of China under Grant NO. 61976156, and by Intelligent Terminal Key Laboratory of SiChuan Province under Grant SCITLAB-30005.

Data Availability Statement: The dataset used in this study is the publicly available dataset D4RL, which can be found at the following website: https://github.com/Farama-Foundation/D4RL, accessed on 7 January 2024.

Conflicts of Interest: The authors declare no conflicts of interest. The funders had no role in the design of the study; in the collection, analyses, or interpretation of data; in the writing of the manuscript; or in the decision to publish the results.

Appendix A. Error Analysis of Reinforcement Learning Based on MDP

Take DQN, a classical deep reinforcement learning algorithm, as an example. In order to adapt to the training scenario of higher dimensions of reinforcement learning, DQN is an algorithm that introduces neural networks into reinforcement learning. It uses neural networks to approximate fit the value function in reinforcement learning. TD algorithm update goal is:

$$y_t = r_t + \max_a Q(s_{t+1}, a; W) \tag{A1}$$

where r_t is the immediate reward at time t, Q is the action value function, s_{t+1} is the state at the next time, and W is the neural network parameter. The Gradient Descent method is used to update the weight of the neural network:

$$W \leftarrow W - \alpha \cdot (Q(s_t, a_t; W) - y_t) \cdot \frac{\partial Q(s_t, a_t; W)}{\partial W} \tag{A2}$$

where α is the update step. The error in the updating process mainly comes from two aspects: the use of maximization operators and the problems caused by bootstrap.

Appendix A.1. Maximization

For n real numbers: $x_1, x_2, \ldots, x_n$, we add noise with a mean of 0 to these n real numbers to obtain: $Q_1, Q_2, \ldots, Q_n$. Because the mean value of noise is 0, it does not change the mean value:

$$E[mean_i(Q_i)] = E[mean_i(x_i)] \tag{A3}$$

In the above formula, *mean* represents the mean function, and $mean_i(x_i)$ signifies taking the mean of the entire set of x_i. Adding noise with a mean of 0 affects the maximum value of the new real sequence:

$$E[max_i(Q_i)] \geq E[max_i(x_i)] \tag{A4}$$

In the above formula, *max* represents the maximum function, and $max_i(x_i)$ signifies taking the maximum value over the entire set of x_i. For the observed action value: $x(a_1), x(a_2), \ldots, x(a_n)$, the motion value estimate with noise is obtained by DQN: $Q(s_1, a_1; W)$, $Q(s_2, a_2; W), \ldots, Q(s_n, a_n; W)$. We assume that it is an unbiased estimate:

$$mean_a x(a) = mean_a Q(s, a; W) \tag{A5}$$

the following overestimation problem will arise:

$$q = \max_{a} Q(s, a; W) \geq \max_{a} x(a) \tag{A6}$$

Therefore, the TD update method will cause overestimation of the target value and introduce errors.

Appendix A.2. Bootstrapping

Suppose that the DQN algorithm has overestimated the action value, then the action value of $t+1$ moment is overestimated as:

$$Q(s_{t+1}, a; W) \tag{A7}$$

then the optimal action value at time $t+1$ is further overestimated:

$$q_{t+1} = \max_{a} Q(s_{t+1}, a; W) \tag{A8}$$

When the optimal action value at time $t+1$ is used to update the Q network, the overestimation of DQN is further aggravated.

References

1. Lu, Y.; Li, W. Techniques and Paradigms in Modern Game AI Systems. *Algorithms* **2022**, *15*, 282. [CrossRef]
2. Prudencio, R.F.; Maximo, M.R.O.A.; Colombini, E.L. A survey on offline reinforcement learning: Taxonomy, review, and open problems. *IEEE Trans. Neural Netw. Learn. Syst.* **2023**. [CrossRef] [PubMed]
3. Devlin, J.; Chang, M.W.; Lee, K.; Toutanova, K. Bert: Pre-training of deep bidirectional transformers for language understanding. In Proceedings of the 2019 Conference of the North American Chapter of the Association for Computational Linguistics: Human Language Technologies, Minneapolis, MN, USA, 2–7 June 2019; pp. 4171–4186.
4. Brown, T.; Mann, B.; Ryder, N.; Subbiah, M.; Kaplan, J.D.; Dhariwal, P.; Neelakantan, A.; Shyam, P.; Sastry, G.; Askell, A.; et al. Language models are few-shot learners. In Proceedings of the Advances in Neural Information Processing Systems 33, Online, 6–12 December 2020; pp. 1877–1901.
5. OpenAI. GPT-4 Technical Report. *arXiv* **2023**, arXiv:2303.08774.
6. Vaswani, A.; Shazeer, N.; Parmar, N.; Uszkoreit, J.; Jones, L.; Gomez, A.N.; Kaiser, Ł.; Polosukhin, I. Attention is all you need. In Proceedings of the Advances in Neural Information Processing Systems 30, Los Angeles, CA, USA, 4–9 December 2017.
7. Hochreiter, S.; Schmidhuber, J. Long short-term memory. *Neural Comput.* **1997**, *9*, 1735–1780. [CrossRef] [PubMed]
8. Dey, R.; Salem, F.M. Gate-variants of gated recurrent unit (GRU) neural networks. In Proceedings of the 2017 IEEE 60th International Midwest Symposium on Circuits And Systems (MWSCAS), Boston, MA, USA, 6–9 August 2017; pp. 1597–1600.
9. Parisotto, E.; Song, F.; Rae, J.; Pascanu, R.; Gulcehre, C.; Jayakumar, S.; Jaderberg, M.; Kaufman, R.L.; Clark, A.; Noury, S.; et al. Stabilizing transformers for reinforcement learning. In Proceedings of the 37th International Conference on Machine Learning, Online, 13–18 July 2020; pp. 7487–7498.
10. Banino, A.; Badia, A.P.; Walker, J.; Scholtes, T.; Mitrovic, J.; Blundell, C. Coberl: Contrastive bert for reinforcement learning. In Proceedings of the Tenth International Conference on Learning Representations (ICLR), Virtual Event, 25–29 April 2022.
11. Chen, L.; Lu, K.; Rajeswaran, A.; Lee, K.; Grover, A.; Laskin, M.; Abbeel, P.; Srinivas, A.; Mordatch, I. Decision transformer: Reinforcement learning via sequence modeling. In Proceedings of the Advances in Neural Information Processing Systems 34, Online, 6–14 December 2021; pp. 15084–15097.
12. Collobert, R.; Weston, J.; Bottou, L.; Karlen, M.; Kavukcuoglu, K.; Kuksa, P. Natural language processing (almost) from scratch. *J. Mach. Learn. Res.* **2011**, *12*, 2493–2537.
13. Sutton, R.S.; Barto, A.G. *Reinforcement Learning: An Introduction*; MIT Press: Cambridge, MA, USA, 2018.
14. Mnih, V.; Kavukcuoglu, K.; Silver, D.; Graves, A.; Antonoglou, I.; Wierstra, D.; Riedmiller, M. Playing atari with deep reinforcement learning. In Proceedings of the Advances in Neural Information Processing Systems 26, Lake Tahoe, NV, USA, 5–10 December 2013.
15. Sutton, R.S.; McAllester, D.; Singh, S.; Mansour, Y. Policy gradient methods for reinforcement learning with function approximation. In Proceedings of the Advances in Neural Information Processing Systems 12, Denver, CO, USA, 29 November–4 December 1999.
16. Mnih, V.; Badia, A.P.; Mirza, M.; Graves, A.; Lillicrap, T.; Harley, T.; Silver, D.; Kavukcuoglu, K. Asynchronous methods for deep reinforcement learning. In Proceedings of the 33rd International Conference on Machine Learning, New York, NY, USA, 20–22 June 2016; pp. 1928–1937.
17. Mishra, N.; Rohaninejad, M.; Chen, X.; Abbeel, P. A simple neural attentive meta-learner. In Proceedings of the 6th International Conference on Learning Representations (ICLR), Vancouver, BC, Canada, 30 April–3 May 2018.

18. Dai, Z.; Yang, Z.; Yang, Y.; Carbonell, J.; Le, Q.V.; Salakhutdinov, R. Transformer-xl: Attentive language models beyond a fixed-length context. In Proceedings of the 57th Conference of the Association for Computational Linguistics (ACL), Florence, Italy, 28 July–2 August 2019; pp. 2978–2988.
19. Kumar, S.; Parker, J.; Naderian, P. Adaptive transformers in RL. *arXiv* **2020**, arXiv:2004.03761.
20. Goodman, S.; Ding, N.; Soricut, R. TeaForN: Teacher-forcing with n-grams. In Proceedings of the 2020 Conference on Empirical Methods in Natural Language Processing, Online, 16–20 November 2020; pp. 8704–8717.
21. Todorov, E.; Erez, T.; Tassa, Y. Mujoco: A physics engine for model-based control. In Proceedings of the 2012 IEEE/RSJ International Conference on Intelligent Robots and Systems, Vilamoura-Algarve, Portugal, 7–12 October 2012, pp. 5026–5033.
22. Fu, J.; Kumar, A.; Nachum, O.; Tucker, G.; Levine, S. D4rl: Datasets for deep data-driven reinforcement learning. *arXiv* **2020**, arXiv:2004.07219.
23. Kumar, A.; Zhou, A.; Tucker, G.; Levine, S. Conservative q-learning for offline reinforcement learning. In Proceedings of the Advances in Neural Information Processing Systems 33, Online, 6–12 December 2020; pp. 1179–1191.
24. Kumar, A.; Fu, J.; Tucker, G.; Levine, S. Stabilizing off-policy q-learning via bootstrapping error reduction. In Proceedings of the Advances in Neural Information Processing Systems 32, Vancouver, BC, Canada, 8–14 December 2019; pp. 11761–11771.
25. Wu, Y.; Tucker, G.; Nachum, O. Behavior regularized offline reinforcement learning. In Proceedings of the Asian Conference on Machine Learning (ACML 2021), Virtual Event, 17–19 November 2021; pp. 204–219.
26. Peng, X.; Kumar, A.; Zhang, G.; Levine, S. Advantage-weighted regression: Simple and scalable off-policy reinforcement learning. *arXiv* **2019**, arXiv:1910.00177.
27. Torabi, F.; Warnell, G.; Stone, P. Behavioral cloning from observation. In Proceedings of the 27th International Joint Conference on Artificial IntelligenceJuly 2018, Stockholm, Sweden, 13–19 July 2018; pp. 4950–4957.

algorithms

MDPI

Article

Evaluating the Expressive Range of Super Mario Bros Level Generators

Hans Schaa [1] and Nicolas A. Barriga [2,*]

[1] Doctoral Program in Engineering Systems, Faculty of Engineering, Universidad de Talca, Curicó 3340000, Chile; hschaa12@alumnos.utalca.cl

[2] Department of Interactive Visualization and Virtual Reality, Faculty of Engineering, Universidad de Talca, Talca 3460000, Chile

* Correspondence: nbarriga@utalca.cl

Abstract: Procedural Content Generation for video games (PCG) is widely used by today's video game industry to create huge open worlds or enhance replayability. However, there is little scientific evidence that these systems produce high-quality content. In this document, we evaluate three open-source automated level generators for Super Mario Bros in addition to the original levels used for training. These are based on Genetic Algorithms, Generative Adversarial Networks, and Markov Chains. The evaluation was performed through an Expressive Range Analysis (ERA) on 200 levels with nine metrics. The results show how analyzing the algorithms' expressive range can help us evaluate the generators as a preliminary measure to study whether they respond to users' needs. This method allows us to recognize potential problems early in the content generation process, in addition to taking action to guarantee quality content when a generator is used.

Keywords: Procedural Content Generation; evaluation methods; Expressive Range Analysis; platformer; videogames

1. Introduction

Research on Procedural Content Generation for video games consists of studying procedural generation methods that allow the creation of levels for video games automatically through computational algorithms [1]. Currently, these computational algorithms can potentially save money [2], time, and effort in various areas, such as engineering [1], music [3], and art [4]. The total person-hours needed to complete certain activities can be reduced because these AI-driven systems imitate human action to some degree and deliver results as good as those that a game designer could create [5].

Thanks to PCG, companies have adapted their workflows to be more competitive and achieve better results. There are even situations where artists have begun to be replaced by these intelligent systems to create games more quickly and economically while maintaining quality [6]. Nowadays, companies not only settle for the initial release but also add new content to keep their audience captive. We know this strategy as "Downloadable Content" (DLC) [7], where companies offer additional content that is sold separately, allowing them to generate greater profits. PCG can be a powerful tool for creating DLCs and, thus, offering better services to users.

In this article, we carry out a study of the expressiveness of open-source automatic level generators for Super Mario Bros (SMB). These are

1. A Multi-Population Genetic Algorithm [8].
2. A Deep Convolutional Generative Adversarial Network (DCGAN) and Covariance Matrix Adaptation Strategy (CMA-ES) [9].
3. Markov Chains (MCs) (https://github.com/hansschaa/MarkovChains_SMB (accessed on 13 June 2024)).

This article's main contribution is comparing three generative spaces using Expressive Range Analysis (ERA) [10]. Two of the three evaluated implementations are peer-reviewed [8,9], the third is our implementation of Markov Chains, and finally, these are contrasted with the SMB levels used as training data. The levels were analyzed with nine metrics through heat charts and box/whisker graphs. As seen in Figure 1, we used the tiles from the video game Super Tux [11] throughout this article because of its GPL license.

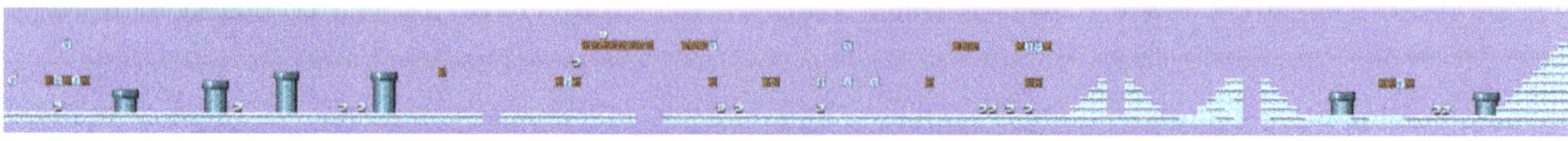

Figure 1. Level 1-1 of Super Mario Bros.

To carry out this study, 200 boards were generated with each generator, and then, for each level, the nine metrics were calculated. Finally, these values are graphed to perform a comparative analysis between generators. The results show that GA and MC have a noticeably wider expressive range than GAN. GA benefits from its exploitation and exploration capacity to find diverse levels, and MC, through the training data, creates levels similar to those that a human can design.

This document is structured as follows: Section 2 briefly presents the technique's state of the art. Then, in Section 3, the implemented algorithms are reported. In Section 4, the experiments carried out and results obtained are presented, and finally, Sections 5 and 6 show the discussion and conclusions, respectively.

2. Background

Creating PCG systems can be an arduous and challenging task; the literature specifies five characteristics that these should exhibit [1]. These are the following:

- **Speed**: How fast can the generator deliver the content [12]? This metric measures the time that PCG systems take to generate content. We can categorize these as methods *online* (the video game has a game loop that allows the generator to create the content at runtime) or *offline* (the video game does not allow the generator to create the content at runtime), so it must be executed outside of the user experience.
- **Reliability**: How faithful is the generator to the configuration imposed on it [13]? Sometimes, we need some features to be strictly adhered to. The generator should only produce content that satisfies the previously configured constraints for games to be solvable.
- **Controllability**: Does the generator allow designers to customize the required content [13]? A highly controllable system will allow greater flexibility and freedom for the designers or engineers using the generator.
- **Expressiveness and diversity**: Does the expressiveness of the generator allow for the generation of diverse and interesting content [14]? PCG systems are required to give rise to content valued by the audience. For example, one could have an Age of Empires map generator, but if they present the same biomes with different dimensions, it could bore the player.
- **Creativity and credibility**: In some cases, it is useful to know that the generator produces content similar to that of humans [15].

Creating a quality generator is not easy, and evaluating it is much less so. People are different in different aspects, be they those of psychology, motor skills, ability, or what amuses them. We relate many of these metrics to a subjective factor where the audience is widely diverse, and we, as researchers and developers, must learn to read that to create ad hoc content for each of them. We can broadly divide evaluation methods into the following four groups:

1. **Static functions**: Static functions are widely used in search-based PCG to guide the search toward quality content. Three types of functions can be observed: direct,

simulation-based, and interactive functions [1]. Some examples could be the number of pushes needed to solve a Sokoban board [5] or the location of resources on a map for strategy video games [16].
2. **Expressive Range Analysis**: The analysis of the algorithms that generate content is quite useful since it allows us to have an early view of the behavior of a generator [10]. However, these methods should never replace the evaluations the target audience can make. Researchers often use heatmaps to position the generated content based on two variables: linearity and lenience.
3. **User testing**: These methods are often expensive and time-consuming. Although they provide first-hand information, they are methods that require many resources to carry them out. Among these, we can find playtesting, Turing tests, Likert surveys, and post-interviews, among others [2].
4. **Bots**: With advances in machine learning and reinforcement learning, creating bots that allow levels to be evaluated automatically has been made possible. This allows evaluation of the content as if a person were playing the experience [17]. For example, bots have been trained with *Reinforcement Learning* (RL) to play PCG levels of Super Mario Bros while simulating the actions of a human and, thus, evaluating their playability [18].

2.1. PCG for Super Mario Bros

Super Mario Bros (SMB) is a widely known platformer video game. Its origin dates back to 1985 in Japan, when it was distributed for the Famicon [19]. Its popularity, simplicity, and documentation, among others, make it an attractive study subject. Below are some key events in the study of SMB.

The generation of SMB levels began with the general study of platformer games [20]. The authors created categories of tile patterns: basic patterns (patterns without repetition), complex patterns (repetition of the same component but with certain changed settings, such as a sequence of platforms with holes of increasing length), compound patterns (alternating between two types of basic patterns), and composite patterns (two components are placed close together in such a way that they require a different type of action or a coordinated action, which would not be necessary for each one individually). Then, they establish a link between the game rhythm that they want to deliver and the music inspired by previous research [21]. They report that although relating music to the design of platformer levels seems somewhat discordant, this depends greatly on the rhythm. When the user must jump over obstacles, they must follow a game rhythm. The design applied to video games of this genre creates a rhythmic sequence based on the placement of enemies and obstacles. These were the bases for several later studies that referred to how to evaluate platformer levels. For example, regarding difficulty, the authors of [22] proposed a metric based on the probability of loss that the player has. For this, they created five types of scenarios where each event (jumping, climbing stairs, dodging bullets) had an associated probability of loss. In the same research on measuring difficulty, evolutionary preference was also used in learning via a simple neural network to assess fun, frustration, and challenge levels [23]. In 2009, the Mario AI Competition began, aiming to create bots to play SMB levels. These have allowed the levels to be evaluated according to their playability, expanding the possible analyses of SMB levels.

2.1.1. PCG Algorithms

Various algorithms have been used to generate SMB levels. With the rise of long short-term memory (LSTM) networks, such algorithms have created playable SMB levels similar to those that a human would build by introducing information about the agent's routes to solve them [24]. Large Language Models (LLMs) have also been used to create levels through different prompts, achieving excellent results [25]; the authors implemented an adjusted GPT2 Large-Scale Language Model, and 88% of the levels were playable. It has also been proven that these architectures can give rise to highly structured content, such as Sokoban levels; the results improve considerably according to the amount of training data provided [26]. The popularity of LLMs is such that a large number of studies showing their potential in video games have been published [27–29]. In the same line as the use of ML, through reinforcement learning, agents capable of designing SMB levels have been created, and then a neural-network-assisted evolutionary algorithm repairs them. The authors assert that their proposed framework can generate infinite playable SMB levels with different degrees of fun and playability [30]. Unlike these black-box models, other level generation systems have also been proposed, such as constructive algorithms [31–33] and search-based algorithms [34–36].

In addition to the aforementioned methods, Markov Chains have been a popular approach for content generation [37]. These are known as a particular example of a Dynamic Bayesian Network (DBN) [38]; they map states through probabilities of transitioning between them. Related to the procedural generation of SMB levels, several works that generally use human-created levels to sample new columns of tiles based on the probability at which they appear can be found [39–41]. Given the stochastic nature of the Markov Chain, there may be a problem in that some levels that are created cannot be playable, which is why hybrid strategies that incorporate search algorithms to join segments of levels have been studied [42].

2.1.2. Expressive Range Analysis

Analyzing the expressive range of algorithms as an early quality assessment measure has been one of the most popular strategies within the scientific community for PCG. The steps of performing an ERA are the following [10]:

1. **Determining the metrics**: The set of metrics to be evaluated must be chosen; they ideally emerge from the generator's point of view since we can control these variables.
2. **Generating the content**: A representative sample of the generator's ability to calculate the previously defined metrics is created.
3. **Visualizing the generative space**: The scores reflect the expressive range of the generator. This can be displayed through heatmaps or histograms to find patterns or gaps.
4. **Analyzing the impacts of the parameters**: Comparisons can now be made by modifying the generator variables and determining their expressiveness.

To carry out an Expressive Range Analysis, most studies select the variables by intuition or simply try to use free-for-all heat graphics. To achieve a greater knowledge of the PCG system implemented, methods to study the characteristics that have the greatest impact on the video game have been created; thus, they are selected in such a way as to carry out the analysis with a much more representative set of the level qualities desired to be evaluated [43]. Graphically, heatmaps and box/whisker graphs have been used to statistically study generative power when creating SMB levels [44]. In another case, categorizations have been proposed for metrics and neural networks to estimate how good the aesthetics are or how complicated a game level is [45].

3. PCG Algorithms Evaluated

3.1. Multi-Population Genetic Algorithm

This is a multi-population genetic algorithm for the procedural generation of SMB levels. The central idea of this algorithm is to evolve terrain, enemies, coins, and blocks independently. Each of these has its own coding and fitness function. When the evolutionary algorithm finishes the specified generations, the best individuals from each population are chosen to build a level. By combining each population to create the level, the algorithm makes sure to position each element in the correct place. For example, enemies are placed on the highest floor tile in each column, and coins are placed at a height defined by the genotype, as are blocks.

3.1.1. Representation

Each of the individuals is encoded as a vector of integers; thus, the level will be represented by the union of these four vectors. Each one follows the following logic:

- **Floor**: The vector for the floor is a vector of the length of the level, where each element takes values between 0 and 15. Each position shows the place on the x-axis where the floor tile will go.
- **Blocks**: The blocks follow a structure similar to that of the vector for the ground. The difference is that each element takes values between 0 and 4 to show the type of block (improvement, coin, solid, destructible). These are placed four spaces above the highest floor tile, so only one block can be placed per column.
- **Enemies**: The vector of enemies has the same definition as the vector of blocks, except that they are located immediately after the ground. Each of its elements can take values between 0 and 3 because of the three types of enemies.
- **Coins**: The vector of coins works the same as that of the ground, where each value shows the height at which they are located.

3.1.2. Fitness Function

The fitness function is the same for everything except the floor. It evaluates this under the concept of entropy [46]. This allows the measurement of the unpredictability of an event, and here, it is used to calculate the unpredictability of the ground. The entropy function is applied to parts of the floor. This decision was made to avoid having a straight floor shape (minimum entropy) or a very stepped one (maximum entropy).

The other level elements use the concept of "dispersion" [47]. Its definition contemplates giving a high dispersion to sets of elements with a high average distance. The goal of the algorithm is to minimize dispersion.

3.2. Deep Convolutional Generative Adversarial Network

GANs are novel neural models capable of delivering interesting content by making use of the corpus of levels stored in the Video Game Level Corpus (VGLC) (https://github.com/TheVGLC/TheVGLC (accessed on 13 June 2024)) to create SMB levels. Although the created GAN produces good content, it can be improved through a Covariance Matrix Adaptation Strategy (CMA-ES) so that, through different aptitude functions, it is possible to discover levels in the latent space that maximize the desired properties.

3.2.1. Process

The applied approach is divided into two phases: the first is the training of the GAN with an SMB level. This is encoded as a multidimensional matrix; there is also a generator that operates on a Gaussian noise vector using this same representation and is trained to create SMB levels. Then, the discriminator is used to discern between the existing and generated levels. When this process is completed, we can understand the GAN as a system that maps from genotype to phenotype, takes a latent vector as an input variable, and generates a tile-level description of SMB. The CMA-ES is then used to search through the latent space for levels with different properties [9].

3.2.2. Training

The algorithm that trains the GAN is called Wasserstein GAN (WGAN) and follows the original DCGAN architecture. It also uses batch normalization in the generator and discriminator after each layer. Unlike the original architecture [48], the study's implementation uses ReLU activation functions in all generator layers, including the output, since this produces better results.

In this phase, each tile is represented by an integer extended to a one-hot encoding vector. So, the inputs for the discriminator are 10 channels of 32×32. For example, in the first channel, if there is a floor, they mark it with 1 and the voids with 0. The dimension of the latent vector input to the generator is 32. When running the evolution, the final dimensional output of $10 \times 32 \times 32$ is cut to $10 \times 20 \times 14$, and each vector in each tile is transformed into an integer using the ArgMax function.

3.3. Markov Chains

For this work, an algorithm that implements Markov Chains was programmed to create an SMB level. As in the previous section, we also used the VGLC. The pseudocode in Algorithm 1 shows the procedure for generating an SMB level with a length of 100. We describe it in more detail below.

1. **ExtractColumns**: We extract columns from the VGLC levels and add them to a vector.
2. **RemoveDuplicates**: The repeated columns are removed. This is essential since the transition matrix will then be calculated with the remaining states.
3. **GetTransitionMtx**: The transition matrix is a matrix or data structure that has, for each column, the columns that are successors, along with the frequency with which the element in question precedes them.
4. **AppendNewColumn**: This function finds the next column based on the transition matrix and adds it to the level structure.
5. **Level construction**: Once the columns that will form the level have been specified, the level can be built and exported to the required format.

Algorithm 1 MC SMB generation pseudocode.

```
levelColumns ← ExtractColumns (file)
levelColumns ← RemoveDuplicates (levelColumns)
TransitionMatrix ← GetTransitionMtx (levelColumns)
seqLength ← int 100
for i ← 1 seqLength n do
    sequence.AppendNewColumn()
end for
```

3.4. Metric Computation

Once the generators were running, software was programmed in Java 17.0.11 to extract the metrics of each level and, thus, be able to perform the ERA. This is public and stored on GitHub (https://github.com/hansschaa/SBM-Expressive-Range-Study (accessed on 13 June 2024)). As seen in Table 1, there are 9 metrics related to the difficulty and level structure.

Table 1. Metrics evaluated for each SMB level.

Metric	Description
Empty Spaces	Percentage of empty spaces.
Negative Spaces	Percentage of spaces that are reachable by Mario.
Interesting elements	Percentage of elements that are not floor or empty places.
Significant Jumps	Number of jumps needed to complete the level, calculated as the numbers of jumps over holes and enemies.
Lenience	This calculation considers the number of enemies and power-ups in the level as a measure of the associated difficulty. Here, we calculated it as the number of enemies multiplied by a factor related to the difficulty of killing those enemies minus the number of power-ups.
Linearity	Linearity of the game level. A completely linear stage means a flat level. This was calculated as the sum of differences between each pair of columns divided by the number of columns.
Enemy Compression (EC)	For a margin "m", we calculate how many enemies surround others within a distance "m", giving rise to a compression measurement. High compression means that there are many groups of enemies.
Density	Quantity of floor tiles mounted on top of others of the same type.
Enemy count	Number of enemies.

The metrics were calculated so that a high value indicates a high presence. For example, a linearity of 1 indicates that the level is very linear.

4. Experiments and Results

We generated 200 boards of 100 tiles for each of the generators to have a large amount of information and, thus, capture their true generative nature (Table 2 shows the symbology used). Then, the levels were imported into the software to calculate their metrics. We normalized these values, considering the maximum and minimum of all resulting values as the upper and lower thresholds, respectively. Finally, to create the charts, we divided them into four files (three for each generator and the original levels) and imported them into a Jupyter notebook (https://github.com/hansschaa/SMB-ERA-Graphs (accessed on 13 June 2024)) to create the heatmaps and box/whisker graphs. Finally, the graphs were analyzed, and we describe each one and compare them.

Table 2. Symbols used for SMB level encoding.

Character	Type
X	Ground and power-up blocks.
-	Empty space.
B	Block in the air.
P	Power-up.
E	Enemy.
S	Enemy Spiny or plant.
C	Coins.

Regarding the format of the levels, the generator based on GA [9] considers a subgroup of the tiles used for the training of the GAN and MC algorithms. We were forced to simplify some game tiles to just one character. For example, 'Q' and 'S' (blocks that Mario can break and an empty question block) from a study that implemented a GAN [9] were now blocks represented only by the character 'B' (block). Likewise, the shapes of the bottom of the pipes are represented only by 'X' (floor) and not with [,], <, >. This logic allows us to unify metrics and make the logical representation of each PCG algorithm comparable.

We also include the original levels used in the MC generator (https://github.com/TheVGLC/TheVGLC/tree/master/Super%20Mario%20Bros/Original (accessed on 13 June 2024)) for an additional point of comparison and analysis. Some final results can be seen in Figure 2. The hyperparameters of the algorithms were extracted from each of the articles [8,9]. Tables 3 and 4 show the hyperparameters for the GA and the GAN, respectively, and the MC-based algorithm only has one hyperparameter called n-level, which is 2.

Table 3. Hyperparameters for the Genetic Algorithm.

Hyperparameter	Value
Population size	250
Chromosome size	100
Mutation probability	0.3
Crossover probability	0.9
Elite size	1
Tournament size	2
Stop criteria	50 gen
Ground entropy	0
Blocks' desired sparseness	1
Enemies' desired sparseness	0.5
Coins' desired sparseness	0.5

Table 4. Hyperparameters for the Generative Adversarial Network.

Hyperparameters	Value
Optimizer	RMSprop
Batch size	32
Learning rate	0.00005
Epochs	5000

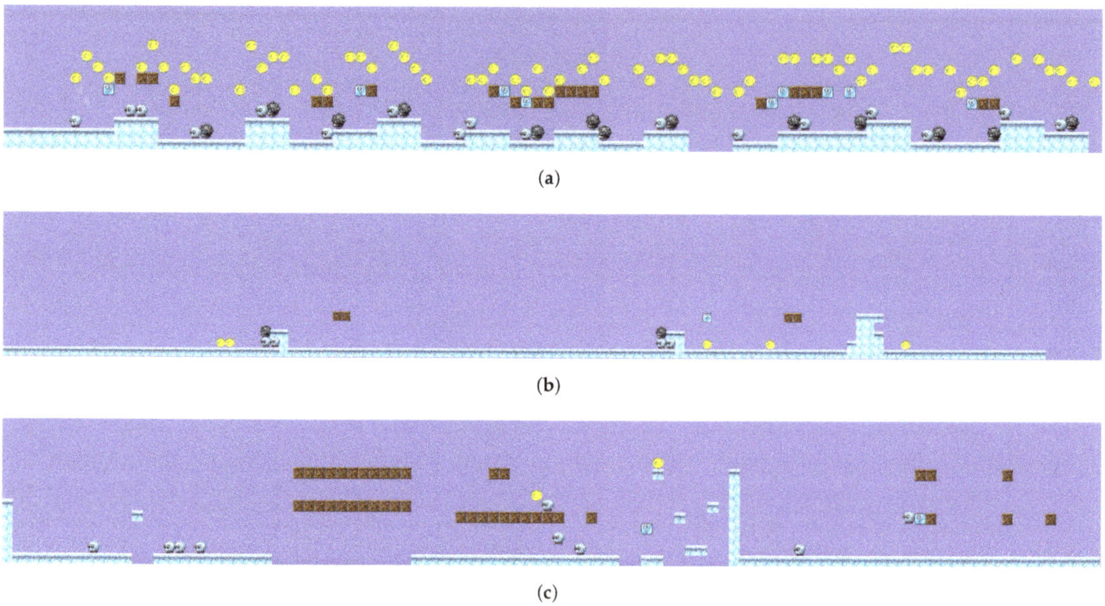

Figure 2. Examples of the levels generated by each generator. Most levels present similarities, for example, in the absence of structures in the GAN generator or the lack of structural verticality in the GA generator. (**a**) Level generated by the GA generator. (**b**) Level generated by the GAN generator. (**c**) Level generated by the MC generator.

Expressive Range

Heatmaps and box/whisker graphs were created to perform a visual reading of the generators. One of the most commonly studied concepts in the generation of video game levels is difficulty. To do this, in Figure 3b, one can see the heatmaps for the three generators and the SMB levels. The GAN produces mostly linear and less diverse levels, while the GA and MC produce semi-linear levels. Regarding lenience, the GAN does not create highly difficult levels in comparison with the GA, which, through the evolutionary method, can build challenging scenarios. The original SMB levels cover a larger area of the generative space with respect to these two metrics; this is very different from the behavior of the other generators, whose respective distributions have a lower variance. Visually, the GAN generator is the most dissimilar. These levels created through Genetic Algorithms and Markov Chains are those that come closest to the characteristics of the original levels. However, a more in-depth analysis must be performed to accurately make this conclusion. Figure 3b,c is also intended to show the degree of difficulty in the generated content. Having enemies too close together can make it difficult to solve the level since the player has a limited jumping height, and rows of enemies can kill them. In this, one can see that the MC generates various configurations on the Y axis, obtaining a wide expressive range regarding the compression of enemies. The GAN obtains poor performance, while the GA concentrates all of the values, giving rise to a low diversity of enemy distribution.

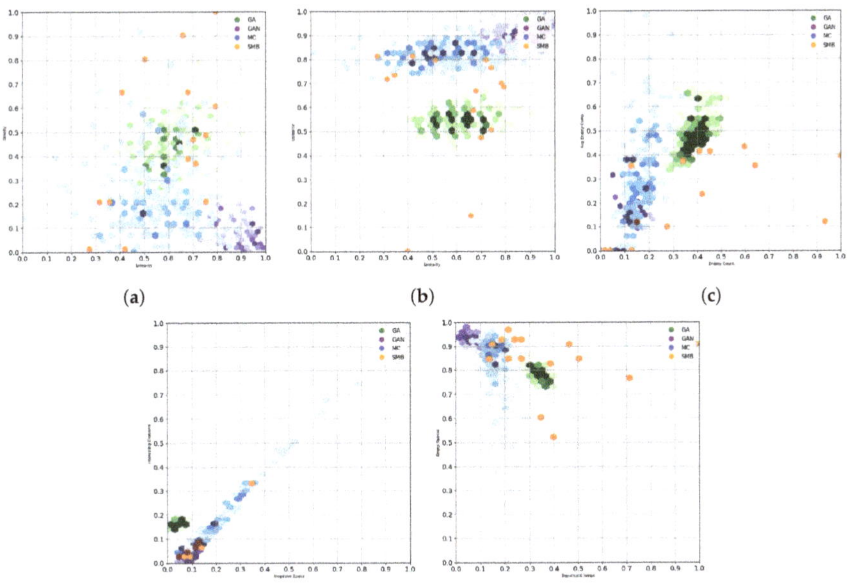

Figure 3. Expressive range of each generator. Each pair of variables was selected to study relevant characteristics. Density, linearity, and negative space represent the complexity of the level's navigation; the lenience, average enemy compression, and enemy count variables refer to the degrees of challenge, and finally, interesting elements correspond to the number of interactive elements (power-ups, coins, enemies) in the level. (**a**) Density vs. linearity. Dense levels with a high linearity can be boring to play. (**b**) Lenience vs. linearity. Lenience and linearity can help us estimate a level's hardness. (**c**) Average EC vs. enemy count. Various enemies can lead to very challenging levels. (**d**) Interesting elements vs. negative space. Much negative space without interesting elements can result in repetitive structures and is far from being a challenge. (**e**) Empty spaces vs. significant jumps. A high number of free spaces can result in more complex situations than those that allow greater navigation of the stage without too many jumps.

The heatmaps in Figure 3a,d are related to the levels' design in appearance and navigation. Figure 3a shows how the GA and MC generators obtain a similar linearity. The GA and MC differ mainly in how the floor tiles are stacked, resulting in denser levels for the GA generator than for the MC. Regarding the GAN, the levels are highly linear with a low density, which results in SMB levels with a low number of columns and complex ground structures. Again, the SMB levels have a wide distribution, as seen on the Y axis, where the density displayed runs along the entire axis. Additionally, the heatmap in Figure 3d shows a limited number of interesting elements with the GA, which produces the greatest number of elements other than soil, but with a low variance in comparison with the MC generator. In this case, there is a similarity in behavior between the original SMB levels and the GAN and MC generators. Still, the MC generator exhibits greater monotony between this pair of variables, covering a larger area of the generative space where its projection is almost linear. Last, Figure 3e shows again how the SMB levels cover a much more uniform space than that of the other generators. This characteristic is desired since a high diversity is needed due to the expressiveness of the algorithms. The three generators distribute their data in a similar way, where the greatest variation with respect to the calculated metrics is given by the MC generator. Curiously, these levels escape the expressive range that the original levels have, since, despite their having been provided as training data, the Markov Chains manage to generate content that has not been seen with respect to the evaluated metrics. This may be caused by the number of columns that the MC considers to create the transition matrix, causing the patterns to be examined locally and not globally, as in the GA and the GAN.

To analyze the generated levels further, we constructed four figures with three box/whisker graphs with normalized data to observe the differences among the generators. The variables studied were the average enemy compression, enemy count, linearity, and lenience. Figure 4d shows how the median of the GA generator is very different from that of the GAN and MC, supporting the idea that this generator creates complex levels concerning difficulty, that is, with high numbers of holes and enemies. This fact is also supported by Figure 4a,b, where it can be seen that the GA obtains levels with many enemies and a high average compression thereof. Figure 4a,c show that the MC generator has a high expressive range when compared to the other generators in terms of linearity and enemy compression, producing diverse levels in terms of structure and difficulty. The data shown by the MC generator are very similar to the original levels, except for Figure 4d, where these seem more challenging.

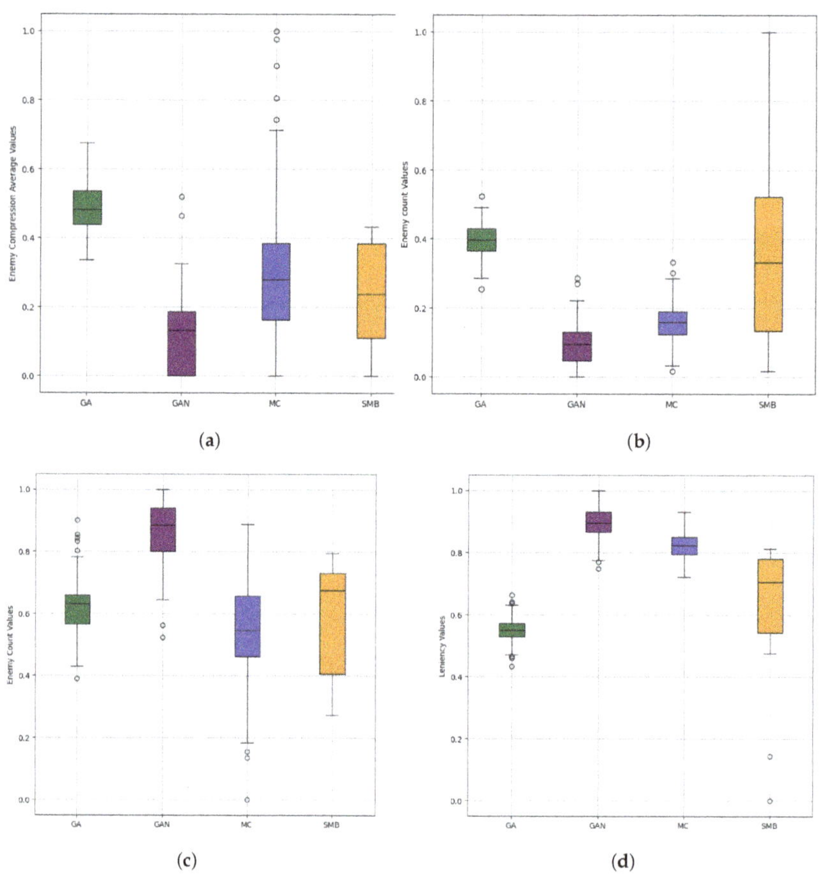

Figure 4. Boxplots for each generator to compare a single variable of interest. Each of these allows us to observe the dispersion of the data achieved by each generator. The description of each of the variables is found in Table 1. (**a**) Average enemy compression. (**b**) Enemy count. (**c**) Linearity. (**d**) Lenience.

5. Discussion

The evaluated generators are different in their approaches, each with its own advantages and disadvantages depending on the implementation. For instance, training data can be fed to machine learning algorithms such as a GAN, and the results depend on the quality of this phase. However, they are fast methods capable of execution at runtime. As can be seen in Figure 5, the GAN sometimes produced incoherent content, which would detract from the user experience. This can be fixed through some constructive algorithms or other generative approaches that consider constraints that make the generated content playable [49].

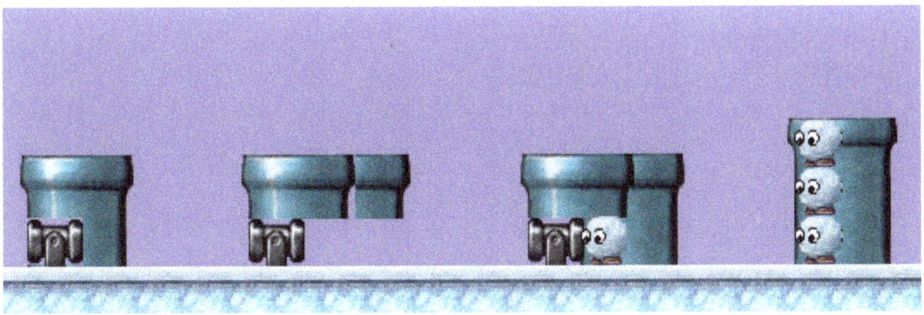

Figure 5. Incoherent results by the GAN generator.

As observed, the MC generator exhibited a wide expressive range in several metrics. This is the one that distributed the evaluated metrics most uniformly within the plot, the other generators showed a reduced generative space that was concentrated in a small range of values, which did not provide much diversity in the final content. GAs are recognized for being highly configurable, debuggable, and controllable, making them one of the most favored methods for generating content. However, while effective, GAs are slow and tend to fall into local optima easily. To address this, the Quality Diversity algorithms [14] aim to deliver a diverse and high-quality set of individuals as a product.

Conducting an ERA early on can help discern whether to use one method over another depending on the practitioner's needs. It is not costly and does not require an extensive programming period for calculating metrics and constructing graphs. However, the question of whether there are heuristics that can bring us closer to human thinking remains. These metrics cannot replace user testing but serve as an initial probe in analyzing procedural content generators for video games.

6. Conclusions

This paper evaluates three automatic level generators for Super Mario Bros and their training data. These are based on Genetic Algorithms, Generative Adversarial Networks, and Markov Chains. We tested 200 levels and 9 metrics, performing an evaluation through an Expressive Range Analysis.

Expressive Range Analysis is useful for the early evaluation stages, as heatmaps allow us to clearly visualize how algorithms exhibit uncertain desired characteristics. We observed how genetic algorithms show a wide expressive range despite their early convergence. The presented example uses four different populations, allowing high locality in the search space and generating diverse content. Markov Chains are efficient due to their simplicity and the speed with which they are executed. It is important to have a large corpus of levels to guarantee greater diversity in the results. However, like ML methods, they are complicated to control. GANs produced good content but were sometimes incoherent, not very diverse, and had a limited expressive range.

In future work, it is necessary to include more generators. There is a research gap regarding evaluating machine-learning-based generators for platform levels. It is necessary to include an evaluation of agents to gain more information about the levels, such as their playability and navigation. Although some levels were played, an automatic method is required to obtain metrics regarding the agent and how it overcomes the game level. It is also interesting to investigate the correlations between the metrics studied and humans' perception, to change them, or to pay attention to those relevant to the study [43]. Also, it would be very useful to carry out a study of the search space that each generator reaches to obtain better-founded conclusions about its generative power.

Author Contributions: Conceptualization, N.A.B. and H.S.; methodology, N.A.B. and H.S.; software, H.S.; validation, N.A.B. and H.S.; formal analysis, N.A.B.; investigation, N.A.B. and H.S.; resources, N.A.B. and H.S.; data curation, H.S.; writing—original draft preparation, H.S.; writing—review and editing, N.A.B. and H.S.; visualization, H.S.; supervision, N.A.B.; project administration, N.A.B. and H.S.; funding acquisition, N.A.B. and H.S. All authors have read and agreed to the published version of the manuscript.

Funding: This research was partially funded by the National Agency for Research and Development (Agencia Nacional de Investigación y Desarrollo, ANID Chile), ANID-Subdirección del Capital Humano/Doctorado Nacional/2023-21230824, and FONDECYT Iniciación grant 11220438.

Data Availability Statement: The dataset is available from the authors upon request.

Conflicts of Interest: The authors declare no conflicts of interest.

Abbreviations

The following abbreviations are used in this manuscript:

PCG	Procedural Content Generation
ERA	Expressive Range Analysis
DLC	Downloadable Content
SMB	Super Mario Bros
DCGAN	Deep Convolutional Generative Adversarial Network
MC	Markov Chain
RL	Reinforcement Learning
LSTM	Long Short-Term Memory
VGLC	Video Game Level Corpus
CMA-ES	Covariance Matrix Adaptation Strategy
WGAN	Wasserstein GAN
ReLU	Rectified Linear Unit
DBN	Dynamic Bayesian Network
LLM	Large Language Model
EC	Enemy Compression

References

1. Shaker, N.; Togelius, J.; Nelson, M.J. *Procedural Content Generation in Games*; Springer: Cham, Switzerland, 2016.
2. Korn, O.; Blatz, M.; Rees, A.; Schaal, J.; Schwind, V.; Görlich, D. Procedural content generation for game props? A study on the effects on user experience. *Comput. Entertain. (CIE)* **2017**, *15*, 1–15. [CrossRef]
3. Scirea, M.; Barros, G.A.; Shaker, N.; Togelius, J. SMUG: Scientific Music Generator. In Proceedings of the ICCC, Park City, UT, USA, 29 June–2 July 2015; pp. 204–211.
4. Gandikota, R.; Brown, N.B. DC-Art-GAN: Stable Procedural Content Generation using DC-GANs for Digital Art. *arXiv* **2022**, arXiv:2209.02847.
5. Schaa, H.; Barriga, N.A. Generating Entertaining Human-Like Sokoban Initial States. In Proceedings of the 2021 40th International Conference of the Chilean Computer Science Society (SCCC), La Serena, Chile, 15–19 November 2021; pp. 1–6.
6. Amato, A. Procedural content generation in the game industry. In *Game Dynamics: Best Practices in Procedural and Dynamic Game Content Generation*; Springer: Cham, Switzerland, 2017; pp. 15–25.
7. Tyni, H.; Sotamaa, O. Extended or exhausted: How console DLC keeps the player on the rail. In Proceedings of the 15th International Academic MindTrek Conference: Envisioning Future Media Environments, Tampere, Finland, 28–30 September 2011; pp. 311–313.
8. Ferreira, L.; Pereira, L.; Toledo, C. A multi-population genetic algorithm for procedural generation of levels for platform games. In Proceedings of the Companion Publication of the 2014 Annual Conference on Genetic and Evolutionary Computation, Vancouver, BC, Canada, 12–16 July 2014; pp. 45–46.
9. Volz, V.; Schrum, J.; Liu, J.; Lucas, S.M.; Smith, A.; Risi, S. Evolving mario levels in the latent space of a deep convolutional generative adversarial network. In Proceedings of the Genetic and Evolutionary Computation Conference, Kyoto, Japan, 15–19 July 2018; pp. 221–228.

10. Smith, G.; Whitehead, J. Analyzing the expressive range of a level generator. In Proceedings of the 2010 Workshop on Procedural Content Generation in Games, Monterey, CA, USA, 18 June 2010; pp. 1–7.
11. The SuperTux Team, SuperTux. Available online: https://www.supertux.org/ (accessed on 10 July 2024).
12. Kerssemakers, M.; Tuxen, J.; Togelius, J.; Yannakakis, G.N. A procedural procedural level generator generator. In Proceedings of the 2012 IEEE Conference on Computational Intelligence and Games (CIG), Granada, Spain, 11–14 September 2012; pp. 335–341.
13. Togelius, J.; Champandard, A.J.; Lanzi, P.L.; Mateas, M.; Paiva, A.; Preuss, M.; Stanley, K.O. Procedural content generation: Goals, challenges and actionable steps. In *Artificial and Computational Intelligence in Games. Dagstuhl Follow-Ups*; Schloss Dagstuhl-Leibniz-Zentrum fuer Informatik: Wadern, Germany, 2013.
14. Gravina, D.; Khalifa, A.; Liapis, A.; Togelius, J.; Yannakakis, G.N. Procedural content generation through quality diversity. In Proceedings of the 2019 IEEE Conference on Games (CoG), London, UK, 20–23 August 2019; pp. 1–8.
15. Craveirinha, R.; Santos, L.; Roque, L. An author-centric approach to procedural content generation. In Proceedings of the Advances in Computer Entertainment: 10th International Conference, ACE 2013, Boekelo, The Netherlands, 12–15 November 2013; Proceedings 10; Springer: Cham, Switzerland, 2013; pp. 14–28.
16. Togelius, J.; Preuss, M.; Yannakakis, G.N. Towards multiobjective procedural map generation. In Proceedings of the 2010 Workshop on Procedural Content Generation in Games, Monterey, CA, USA, 18 June 2010; pp. 1–8.
17. Liu, J.; Snodgrass, S.; Khalifa, A.; Risi, S.; Yannakakis, G.N.; Togelius, J. Deep learning for procedural content generation. *Neural Comput. Appl.* **2021**, *33*, 19–37. [CrossRef]
18. Guzdial, M.; Sturtevant, N.; Li, B. Deep static and dynamic level analysis: A study on infinite mario. In Proceedings of the AAAI Conference on Artificial Intelligence and Interactive Digital Entertainment, Burlingame, CA, USA, 8–12 October 2016; Volume 12, pp. 31–38.
19. Wikipedia. Super Mario Bros. Available online: https://en.wikipedia.org/wiki/Super_Mario (accessed on 27 December 2023).
20. Compton, K.; Mateas, M. Procedural level design for platform games. In Proceedings of the AAAI Conference on Artificial Intelligence and Interactive Digital Entertainment, Burlingame, CA, USA, 8–12 October 2016; Volume 2, pp. 109–111.
21. Iyer, V.; Bilmes, J.; Wright, M.; Wessel, D. A novel representation for rhythmic structure. In Proceedings of the 23rd International Computer Music Conference, Thessaloniki, Greece, 25–30 September 1997; pp. 97–100.
22. Mourato, F.; Santos, M.P.d. Measuring difficulty in platform videogames. In Proceedings of the 4ª Conferência Nacional Interacção Humano-Computador, Aveiro, Portugal, 13–15 October 2010.
23. Pedersen, C.; Togelius, J.; Yannakakis, G.N. Modeling player experience in super mario bros. In Proceedings of the 2009 IEEE Symposium on Computational Intelligence and Games, Milan, Italy, 7–10 September 2009; pp. 132–139.
24. Summerville, A.; Mateas, M. Super mario as a string: Platformer level generation via lstms. *arXiv* **2016**, arXiv:1603.00930.
25. Sudhakaran, S.; González-Duque, M.; Freiberger, M.; Glanois, C.; Najarro, E.; Risi, S. Mariogpt: Open-ended text2level generation through large language models. In Proceedings of the Advances in Neural Information Processing Systems, New Orleans, LA, USA, 10–16 December 2023; Volume 36.
26. Todd, G.; Earle, S.; Nasir, M.U.; Green, M.C.; Togelius, J. Level Generation Through Large Language Models. In Proceedings of the 18th International Conference on the Foundations of Digital Games (FDG 2023), Lisbon, Portugal, 12–14 April 2023. [CrossRef]
27. Gallotta, R.; Todd, G.; Zammit, M.; Earle, S.; Liapis, A.; Togelius, J.; Yannakakis, G.N. Large Language Models and Games: A Survey and Roadmap. *arXiv* **2024**, arXiv:2402.18659.
28. Nasir, M.U.; James, S.; Togelius, J. Word2World: Generating Stories and Worlds through Large Language Models. *arXiv* **2024**, arXiv:2405.06686.
29. Nasir, M.U.; Togelius, J. Practical PCG Through Large Language Models. *arXiv* **2023**, arXiv:2305.18243.
30. Shu, T.; Liu, J.; Yannakakis, G.N. Experience-driven PCG via reinforcement learning: A Super Mario Bros study. In Proceedings of the 2021 IEEE Conference on Games (CoG), Copenhagen, Denmark, 17–20 August 2021; pp. 1–9.
31. Hauck, E.; Aranha, C. Automatic generation of Super Mario levels via graph grammars. In Proceedings of the 2020 IEEE Conference on Games (CoG), Osaka, Japan, 24–27 August 2020; pp. 297–304.
32. Shaker, N.; Yannakakis, G.N.; Togelius, J.; Nicolau, M.; O'neill, M. Evolving personalized content for super mario bros using grammatical evolution. In Proceedings of the AAAI Conference on Artificial Intelligence and Interactive Digital Entertainment, Stanford, CA, USA, 8–12 October 2012; Volume 8, pp. 75–80.
33. Shi, P.; Chen, K. Online level generation in Super Mario Bros via learning constructive primitives. In Proceedings of the 2016 IEEE Conference on Computational Intelligence and Games (CIG), Santorini, Greece, 20–23 September 2016; pp. 1–8.
34. de Pontes, R.G.; Gomes, H.M. Evolutionary procedural content generation for an endless platform game. In Proceedings of the 2020 19th Brazilian Symposium on Computer Games and Digital Entertainment (SBGames), Recife, Brazil, 7–10 November 2020; pp. 80–89.
35. Dahlskog, S.; Togelius, J. Procedural content generation using patterns as objectives. In Proceedings of the European Conference on the Applications of Evolutionary Computation, Granada, Spain, 23–25 April 2014; pp. 325–336.
36. Sarkar, A.; Cooper, S. Procedural content generation using behavior trees (PCGBT). *arXiv* **2021**, arXiv:2107.06638.
37. Snodgrass, S. *Markov Models for Procedural Content Generation*; Drexel University: Philadelphia, PA, USA, 2018.
38. Murphy, K.P. Markov Models. 2007. Available online: https://citeseerx.ist.psu.edu/document?repid=rep1&type=pdf&doi=6c4d1f04f5c5004370f03f2e759e6a4b1115cb8c (accessed on 1 June 2024).

39. Snodgrass, S.; Ontañón, S. A hierarchical approach to generating maps using markov chains. In Proceedings of the AAAI Conference on Artificial Intelligence and Interactive Digital Entertainment, Raleigh, NC, USA, 3–7 October 2014; Volume 10, pp. 59–65.
40. Snodgrass, S.; Ontanon, S. A hierarchical mdmc approach to 2D video game map generation. In Proceedings of the AAAI Conference on Artificial Intelligence and Interactive Digital Entertainment, Santa Cruz, CA, USA, 14–18 November 2015; Volume 11, pp. 205–211.
41. Snodgrass, S.; Ontanón, S. Learning to generate video game maps using markov models. *IEEE Trans. Comput. Intell. AI Games* **2016**, *9*, 410–422. [CrossRef]
42. Biemer, C.F.; Cooper, S. On linking level segments. In Proceedings of the 2022 IEEE Conference on Games (CoG), Beijing, China, 21–24 August 2022; pp. 199–205.
43. Withington, O.; Tokarchuk, L. The Right Variety: Improving Expressive Range Analysis with Metric Selection Methods. In Proceedings of the 18th International Conference on the Foundations of Digital Games, Lisbon, Portugal, 12–14 April 2023; pp. 1–11.
44. Horn, B.; Dahlskog, S.; Shaker, N.; Smith, G.; Togelius, J. A comparative evaluation of procedural level generators in the mario AI framework. In Proceedings of the Foundations of Digital Games 2014, Ft. Lauderdale, FL, USA, 3–7 April 2014; pp. 1–8.
45. Summerville, A.; Mariño, J.R.; Snodgrass, S.; Ontañón, S.; Lelis, L.H. Understanding mario: An evaluation of design metrics for platformers. In Proceedings of the 12th International Conference on the Foundations of Digital Games, Hyannis, MA, USA, 14–17 August 2017; pp. 1–10.
46. Shannon, C.E. A mathematical theory of communication. *Bell Syst. Tech. J.* **1948**, *27*, 379–423. [CrossRef]
47. Cook, M.; Colton, S. Multi-faceted evolution of simple arcade games. In Proceedings of the 2011 IEEE Conference on Computational Intelligence and Games (CIG'11), Seoul, Republic of Korea, 31 August–3 September 2011; pp. 289–296.
48. Arjovsky, M.; Chintala, S.; Bottou, L. Wasserstein generative adversarial networks. In Proceedings of the International Conference on Machine Learning, ICML, Sidney, Australia, 6–1 August 2017; pp. 214–223.
49. Di Liello, L.; Ardino, P.; Gobbi, J.; Morettin, P.; Teso, S.; Passerini, A. Efficient generation of structured objects with constrained adversarial networks. In Proceedings of the Advances in Neural Information Processing Systems, Online, 6–12 December 2020; Volume 33, pp. 14663–14674.

algorithms

MDPI

Article

An Efficient Optimization of the Monte Carlo Tree Search Algorithm for Amazons

Lijun Zhang [1,2], Han Zou [1,2] and Yungang Zhu [1,2,*]

1 College of Computer Science and Technology, Jilin University, Changchun 130012, China; zhanglj2121@mails.jlu.edu.cn (L.Z.); zouhan1221@mails.jlu.edu.cn (H.Z.)
2 Key Laboratory of Symbolic Computation and Knowledge Engineering of Ministry of Education, Jilin University, Changchun 130012, China
* Correspondence: zhuyungang@jlu.edu.cn

Abstract: Amazons is a computerized board game with complex positions that are highly challenging for humans. In this paper, we propose an efficient optimization of the Monte Carlo tree search (MCTS) algorithm for Amazons, fusing the 'Move Groups' strategy and the 'Parallel Evaluation' optimization strategy (MG-PEO). Specifically, we explain the high efficiency of the Move Groups strategy by defining a new criterion: the winning convergence distance. We also highlight the strategy's potential issue of falling into a local optimum and propose that the Parallel Evaluation mechanism can compensate for this shortcoming. Moreover, We conducted rigorous performance analysis and experiments. Performance analysis results indicate that the MCTS algorithm with the Move Groups strategy can improve the playing ability of the Amazons game by 20–30 times compared to the traditional MCTS algorithm. The Parallel Evaluation optimization further enhances the playing ability of the Amazons game by 2–3 times. Experimental results show that the MCTS algorithm with the MG-PEO strategy achieves a 23% higher game-winning rate on average compared to the traditional MCTS algorithm. Additionally, the MG-PEO Amazons program proposed in this paper won first prize in the Amazons Competition at the 2023 China Collegiate Computer Games Championship & National Computer Games Tournament.

Keywords: Amazons; algorithm optimization; Move Groups; Parallel Evaluation

1. Introduction

Amazons is a two-player board game that was introduced by Walter Zamkauskas of Argentina in 1988 [1,2]. It is the designated game for the Olympia computer game programming competition. Due to its complex gameplay, Amazons is very challenging for humans [3], making it a popular subject for computer game competitions and research. The game rules are as follows: The game is played on a 10 × 10 square board. Each player controls four identical pieces called "Amazons". These pieces and arrows follow the same rules as a queen in chess: They can move any number of squares in any direction—horizontal, vertical, or diagonal—but cannot jump over other pieces or arrows. The objective is to restrict the opponent's movement by shooting arrows until none of the opponent's four pieces can move. If, on a player's turn, all four of their pieces are immobilized, that player loses, and the other player wins. Notably, there are no ties in Amazons.

The main challenge of the Amazons game lies in its complexity: Each move offers a vast number of possible choices, typically more than 500 [4,5], and the game can extend for over 80 moves [6,7]. This high level of complexity makes Amazons an excellent experimental sample for testing search strategy algorithms [8,9]. Since its invention, it has garnered significant attention from computer scientists [10] and computer science students [11].

The Monte Carlo method [12] is a computational technique that produces numerical results through repeated random sampling. When integrated with tree search algorithms and suitable evaluation functions, the Monte Carlo tree search (MCTS) algorithm has yielded impressive results in board games with a high-branching factor (such as Go) [13–15], and in real-time strategy games (such as StarCraft [16]). For instance, in 2016, DeepMind's AlphaGo program [17] defeated the Korean world champion of Go, Lee Sedol, with a score of 4:1. In 2018, OpenAI's OpenAI Five program [18] defeated the world champion team in Dota 2 with an overwhelming advantage; both accomplishments are based on the Monte Carlo tree search algorithm.

The 'Move Groups-Parallel Evaluation' optimization strategy (MG-PEO) accommodates the rules of the Amazons board game by subdividing a complete move into two parts: Amazon Movement and Arrow Shot. Both Amazon Movement and Arrow Shot are treated as tree nodes, rather than considering a complete move as a single tree node. This approach is known as the Move Groups strategy in the literature [19]. While this strategy has been applied to the Amazons game [20], it still lacks an objective analysis of its effectiveness. Moreover, there is a widespread belief that this method only possesses advantages without any drawbacks. In this paper, we explain the high efficiency of the Move Groups strategy in Amazons by defining a new criterion: the winning convergence distance. We also identify certain shortcomings of this strategy. To address these, we propose using a Parallel Evaluation mechanism to compensate for the limitations of the Move Groups strategy. Our experimental results demonstrate that MG-PEO is an effective fusion optimization strategy.

The main contributions of this paper are as follows:

- We propose an effective optimization of the Monte Carlo tree search algorithm for the Amazons game: the MG-PEO algorithm optimization, which combines the Move Groups strategy with the Parallel Evaluation strategy.
- We provide a performance analysis of the Move Groups strategy in Amazons. By defining a new criterion, the winning convergence distance, we explained the high efficiency of the strategy. Moreover, we also highlight that this strategy has certain shortcomings. The Move Groups strategy involves refining the rules of the Amazons game and using simulations to assign corresponding value scores to additional layer nodes. By utilizing these value scores (e.g., the Upper Confidence Bound Apply to Tree (UCT) strategy [15]), we can achieve effective pruning to save time. However, the addition of extra layer nodes means that more nodes need to be traversed and evaluated in the worst-case scenario, where pruning has not occurred, potentially leading to increased time-consuming overhead. This overhead is incurred as the algorithm strives to find the local optimal solution.
- We propose using a Parallel Evaluation mechanism to address the potential shortcomings of the Move Groups strategy. By parallelizing the evaluation function for the Amazons game, we aim to accelerate the expansion process of the Monte Carlo tree search and minimize the likelihood of the Move Groups strategy falling into a local optimum.

Additionally, we conducted rigorous performance analysis and game experiments. The performance analysis indicates that—compared to the traditional MCTS algorithm—the MCTS algorithm with the Move Groups strategy can enhance the playing ability of Amazons by 20–30 times, while the Parallel Evaluation optimization component can improve the playing ability of Amazons by 2–3 times. Experimental results demonstrate that—compared to the traditional MCTS algorithm—the MCTS algorithm with the MG-PEO strategy achieves an average 23% increase in the game-winning rate and exhibits stronger playing ability.

The remainder of this paper is structured as follows: In Section 2, we present preliminary information about the Amazons game and discuss its relevance to the MCTS algorithm. In Section 3, we provide a detailed description of the MCTS algorithm with the MG-PEO strategy. In Section 4, we offer performance analyses of the Move Groups strategy and Parallel Evaluation strategy, respectively. Section 5 outlines a series of experiments conducted to verify the efficiency of the MCTS algorithm with the MG-PEO strategy. Finally, conclusions and avenues for future research are summarized in Section 6.

2. Related Work

In this section, we provide an overview of the relevant research that forms the basis of our work. Specifically, we will discuss three key modules in the literature that are relevant to Amazons: historical research on Amazons algorithms, the application of the MCTS algorithm to Amazons, and knowledge about game situation evaluation.

2.1. Amazons Playing Algorithm

The Amazons game has undergone extensive study; its algorithm development can be roughly categorized into three stages. Initially, traditional methods rooted in mathematical theory, such as the minimax search algorithm [21], dominated the field. The second phase saw the emergence of Monte Carlo algorithms, including various variants of the Monte Carlo tree search [19,20,22–24]. In the third stage, deep learning techniques leveraging Amazons game databases came to the forefront [25,26]. Notably, the most representative Amazons program, Invader [27–29], relies on MCTS for prospective exploration, supplemented by neural network training on chess databases, resulting in formidable playing ability in the Amazons game. It can be said that further optimization of Monte Carlo algorithms remains crucial for advancing research on Amazons.

2.2. Monte Carlo Tree Search Algorithm

The development of the Monte Carlo tree search algorithm in Amazons can be roughly divided into two lines of research: algorithm optimization in terms of tree search and algorithm optimization in terms of evaluation functions. In terms of tree search algorithm optimization, researchers have worked on improving search algorithms to improve the performance of Amazons. For example, Guo et al. divided the game into early, middle, and late stages, employing different strategies in each stage [30]. Li et al. applied the UCT algorithm to Amazons [31]; Quan et al. demonstrated the superiority of the UCT algorithm in Amazons [32]. On the other hand, optimizing the evaluation function is also one of the focuses of the research. By optimizing the evaluation function, the current game can be evaluated more accurately and the search algorithm can be guided to make more informed decisions. Lieberum et al. dedicate their research to this aspect [33,34], focusing mainly on improving hyperparameter tuning and designing new evaluation functions. Overall, the Monte Carlo tree search algorithm cannot be improved without any one aspect, and in this paper, our proposed fusion of the Move Groups strategy and the Parallel Evaluation strategy represents a comprehensive consideration of the two historical research focuses. This fusion of the Monte Carlo tree search algorithm is cutting-edge and effective.

2.3. Evaluation Function

At present, almost all search algorithms are faced with a problem: situation evaluation. Good situation evaluation is very important in the Amazons game and can even determine the quality of the game program [33].

Similar to many board games, Amazons can be roughly divided into three stages: opening, middle, and ending, with distinct strategies for each stage. The main indicators of the Amazons evaluation function include territory, position, and mobility, and the importance of these three characteristics varies across different stages. Based on these ideas, Guo et al. [30] proposed a phased evaluation function, as shown in Equation (1):

$$Value = k_1 * t_1 + k_2 * t_2 + k_3 * p_1 + k_4 * p_2 + k_5 * mobility \quad (1)$$

where t_1 and t_2 are territory metric values, which, respectively, represent the evaluation of each side's control over space, based on the QueenMove Method and KingMove Method. p_1 and p_2 are position metric values, reflecting the strategic position of each side's pieces, also based on the QueenMove and KingMove Methods relative to the space. *mobility* is the flexibility evaluation value of both Amazon pieces. k_1, k_2, k_3, k_4, and k_5 are the corresponding weight values. How these values are calculated is described below.

According to the literature [2], calculating territory and position values involves two types of methods: QueenMove and KingMove. QueenMove means that a move can be made as long as there are no obstacles to be crossed in any of the eight directions (the obstacles include pieces and arrows), while KingMove means that the distance of a single move is one, i.e., only one move can be made to a neighboring square. The QueenMove value represents the minimum number of moves a player's four pieces need to reach a given space (i.e., no pieces or arrows); the KingMove value represents the minimum number of moves a player's four pieces need to make to reach a given space. As shown in Figure 1 on the left side, value 2 in the upper-left corner of the upper-left (A, 1) square indicates that the white piece needs at least two moves to reach this space via the QueenMove method, and value 4 in the lower-right corner indicates that the black piece needs four moves. Similarly, values 2 and 7 in the same square in Figure 1 on the right side indicate the situation when the KingMove method is used.

Figure 1. Calculation results of the QueenMove and KingMove methods. The left is the result of the KingMove calculation, and the right is the result of the QueenMove calculation.

Accordingly, we can use the following calculation formula for all the indicators:

t_1 represents the difference in the control of the territory using the QueenMove method. t_2 represents the difference in the control of the territory using the KingMove method. As shown in Equations (2) and (3):

$$t_i = \sum v(B_i, W_i) \tag{2}$$

$$v(B_i, W_i) = \begin{cases} 0, B_i(A) = W_i(A) = \infty \\ k, B_i(A) = W_i(A) \neq \infty \\ 1, B_i(A) < W_i(A) \\ -1, B_i(A) > W_i(A) \end{cases} \tag{3}$$

where B represents black pieces, W represents white pieces, with the subscript 1 indicating the QueenMove method and 2 indicating the KingMove method. A represents empty squares. k represents the preponderance of the leading square, and the value range is greater than -1 and less than 1. When the player with the first move is white, k is greater than 0, otherwise, it is less than 0.

p_1 represents the positions of the two pieces on control space A using the QueenMove method. p_2 represents the positions of the two pieces on control space A using the KingMove method. As shown in Equations (4) and (5):

$$p_1 = 2\Sigma\left(2^{-B_1(A)} - 2^{-W_1(A)}\right) \tag{4}$$

$$p_2 = \sum_{A} \min(1, \max(-1, B_2(A) - W_2(A)/6)) \tag{5}$$

mobility means the flexibility of the pieces. As shown in Equations (6) and (7):

$$mobility = \sum_{w \in \text{white piece}} F(w) - \sum_{b \in \text{black piece}} F(b) \tag{6}$$

$$F(a) = \begin{cases} \text{surrounding spaces}, & \text{a is the space} \\ 0, & \text{a is the obstacle} \\ \sum_{s \subset S_a} \dfrac{F_{space}(s)}{D(a,s)}, & \text{a is an Amazon piece} \end{cases} \tag{7}$$

where F denotes flexibility, S_a denotes the set of spaces that can be reached by a piece using the QueenMove method, and $D(a,s)$ is the minimum number of moves by a to s using the KingMove method.

We retained the hyper-parameterization settings according to the literature [2]; detailed information about each assessment indicator is shown in Table 1.

Table 1. Weight coefficient table.

	Evaluation Metrics	Territory		Position		Mobility
	Evaluation Factor	t_1	t_2	p_1	p_2	*mobility*
	Weight Coefficient	k_1	k_2	k_3	k_4	k_5
Stages	Opening	0.14	0.37	0.13	0.13	0.20
	Middle	0.30	0.25	0.20	0.20	0.05
	Ending	0.80	0.10	0.05	0.05	0.00

Table 1 shows that t_1 gradually increases in importance as the game progresses, starting smaller in the opening, becoming larger in the middle, and reaching its peak in the endgame. This is because as the game progresses, board control becomes more crucial to victory or defeat. t_2 is extremely crucial in the opening phase to ensure the safety of neighboring regions and territorial boundaries, but its role decreases as the game progresses, and it can be almost ignored in the endgame. It reflects the urgency of the initial layout defense and territorial competition. p_1 and p_2 denote piece positions, which mainly play roles in the opening phase when a balanced distribution of pieces is crucial to the subsequent strategic deployment; in the endgame, the pattern of the game has already been determined, and the distribution of pieces is no longer a key point; *mobility* denotes flexibility, which is the most significant in the early stage of the game, as blocking the pieces can be seriously disadvantageous; as the game progresses and the initial layout is established, the distribution of pieces becomes increasingly critical. As the game progresses and the layout is completed, the impact of piece mobility on the game's situation is weakened, so its weight is reduced to negligible in the middle and late game. This reflects the need for strategic flexibility in the early stages of freedom of movement.

3. Research Methodology

In this section, we first describe the overall framework of the MCTS algorithm enhanced with the MG-PEO strategy. We then elaborate on the optimization details, focusing on two aspects: Move Groups and Parallel Evaluation.

3.1. Overall Framework of Algorithm

We propose an MG-PEO algorithm optimization strategy based on the Monte Carlo tree search [22]. As shown in Figure 2, the optimized Monte Carlo tree search algorithm involves iteratively constructing a search tree, creating a new tree each round until the time constraint is reached or the game ends. At this point, the search stops and returns the best-performing root operation (a combination of actions from certain nodes in the second and third layers).

Specifically, the following four steps are performed for each search iteration:

(1) Selection: Starting from the root node, a certain strategy is applied to recursively go down through the tree for expandable node selection. A node is expandable if it represents a non-terminal state and has unvisited children.
(2) Expansion: Expand the tree by adding one (or more) child node(s), depending on the available operations.
(3) Simulation: Run a simulation from a new node to produce results according to the default strategy.
(4) Backpropagation: Back up the simulation results through the selected nodes to update their statistics.

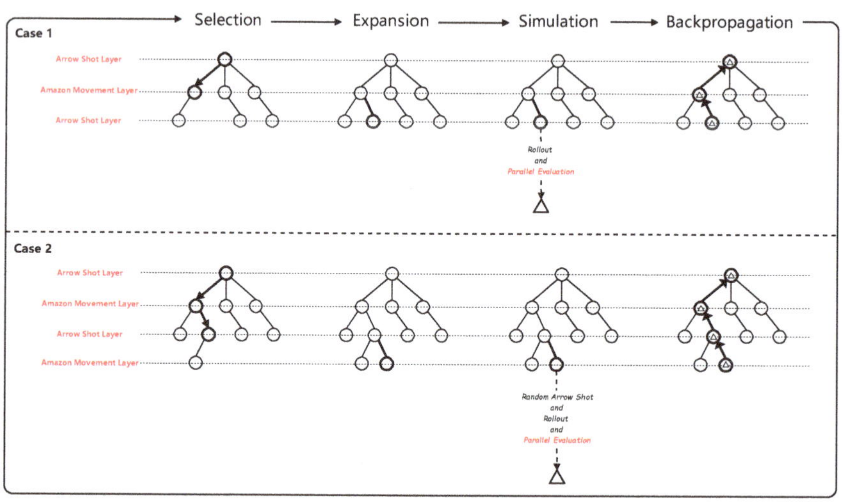

Figure 2. MCTS plus MG-PEO general framework.

As seen in Figure 2, due to the use of the Move Groups strategy, the algorithm operates under two scenarios during the simulation phase: if the current node is an Arrow Shot layer node, it executes Rollout and Parallel Evaluation; if the current node is an Amazon Movement layer node, it performs Random Arrow Shot, Rollout, and Parallel Evaluation.

The pseudo-code for the overall framework is described in Algorithm 1.

Algorithm 1: General Algorithm Framework

Input: s_0 (The current game State)
Output: Optimal decision
function MCTSSEARCH (s_0)
  create root node v_0 with state s_0
  while within the computational budget **do**
    $v_1 \leftarrow$ Selection (v_0)
    $v_2 \leftarrow$ Expansion (v_1, s_0)
    $\Delta \leftarrow$Simulation (v_2, s_0)

Backup (v_2,Δ)
return BESTCHILD(v_0)

3.2. Move Groups Strategy in Algorithm

The core idea of the Move Groups strategy is as follows: according to the rules, a node in the original search tree (Amazon Movement and Arrow Shot combined) is decomposed into two nodes (representing Amazon Movement and Arrow Shot, respectively). By utilizing the simulation phase of MCTS to assign value scores to an additional layer (the newly added layer), we can achieve the goals of pruning and saving time, based on the value scores of the extra layer (e.g., using the UCT strategy).

Specifically, when an extra layer node has not yet expanded its child nodes, its value score is initially infinite. Therefore, each extra layer node will first expand its child nodes once and employ a Shallow Rollout strategy to obtain an initial value score. Subsequently, we can select the extra layer node with the highest value score for further expansion and Rollout, until a particular extra layer node's child nodes are fully generated and the node is selected again. At this point, we can then derive the optimal decision from the child nodes, which is the core of early pruning. It should be noted that due to the dynamic MCTS backpropagation mechanism, the value scores of the extra layer nodes will dynamically change as their child nodes expand. Therefore, early pruning may also occur at the second, third, or other extra layer nodes. For details on the computation and updating of the value scores, please refer to Section 3.3. Since the complete step is a combination of two steps, namely, Amazon Movement and Arrow Shot, and the extra layer represents only one step, the total number of nodes in the extra layer must be less than the total number of nodes, thus enhancing the performance of early pruning in the Monte Carlo tree search algorithm.

However, the Move Groups strategy also increases the number of total tree nodes (for a complete one-step operation) due to the introduction of the extra layer, and if all nodes are expanded without pruning in advance, the extra overhead (expansion and evaluation) incurred by the nodes in the extra layer will negatively affect the algorithm, which will also lead to the fact that—in the worst-case scenario—the addition of the Move Groups strategy to the MCTS will perform slightly worse than the MCTS algorithm without the Move Groups policy. A complete theoretical analysis of the Move Groups policy is detailed in Section 4.1.

3.3. Parallel Evaluation Strategy in Algorithm

The core idea of the Parallel Evaluation strategy is that the time-consuming evaluation part of the MCTS simulation is processed in parallel optimization. It has been shown in the literature [35] that accelerating this labor-intensive evaluation function allows the Monte Carlo Tree Search algorithm to be iterated more frequently. This metric is very beneficial in compensating for the fact that the Move Groups strategy might fall into a local optimum (worst case); specifically, speeding up the evaluation function enables the Monte Carlo Tree Search to scale as quickly as possible, minimizing the impact of the worst-case scenario associated with the Move Groups strategy. The pseudo-code for the Parallel Evaluation part is as shown in Algorithm 2.

Algorithm 2: SituationEvaluation

Input: s_0 (The current Game State)
Output: Situation Evaluation Value
function SituationEvaluation(s_0)
$t_1, t_2, p_1, p_2, mobility \leftarrow$ ParallelEvaluationMetrics (s_0)
$Value = k1 * t1 + k2 * t2 + k3 * p1 + k4 * p2 + k5 * mobility$
return Value

Nodes undergo evaluation, and the resulting value scores guide node selection. Traditional Monte Carlo tree search algorithms typically choose the child node with the highest node score (winning rate) based on the current game state [36]. However, this selection method is not ideal, as it tends to prioritize immediate gains and can lead to local optima. To address this issue, this paper incorporates the "Shallow Rollout strategy" [37] and the "tree-based upper confidence interval" algorithm [19] to refine node selection. Specifically, the utilization value derived solely from decision-level nodes may be inaccurate. To enhance precision, a Shallow Rollout strategy is employed, simulating scenarios closer to the endgame. Additionally, the algorithm considers the magnitude of a node's exploratory value, which is elevated for nodes exhibiting high uncertainty and numerous future possibilities. In summary, the approach assesses both partial equilibrium utilization value and exploration value to facilitate more informed decision-making.

1. "Shallow Rollout Strategy": This means that the utility value is not calculated, not only based on the next move but also on the position of the game after randomly simulating the move several times. In this algorithm, we set the number of Rollouts to be two, and the depths to be 4 and 5. Specifically, after expanding the complete decision node (Amazon Movement plus Arrow Shot), we perform two Rollouts for the current situation. In each Rollout, we simulate two steps: the opponent's next decision (Amazon Movement plus Arrow Shot) and our subsequent decision (Amazon Movement plus Arrow Shot), to obtain a more forward-looking utility value. See pseudo-code Algorithm 3 for details. For the analysis of the relevant parameters, see Appendix A.
2. "Tree-based Upper Confidence Interval": As shown in Equation (8), the calculation formula of UCT consists of two components. The first term, X_i, represents the utility value of the information in the constructed search tree, and the second term represents the exploration value of the unvisited nodes. The constant C is used to adjust the proportion of the algorithm's trade-off between the two values. Note that the value of the root formula is infinite because of the presence of unreachable child nodes, which ensures that unreachable child nodes under the current node will be visited at least once.

$$UCT = X_i + C\sqrt{\frac{\ln N}{n_i}} \tag{8}$$

where X_i is the winning rate of the child node. N is the number of times the parent node is accessed. n_i is the number of times the child node is accessed. C is a constant ($\frac{1}{\sqrt{2}}$). Kocsis and Szepesvári [36] showed that the value satisfies the Hoeffding inequality with rewards in the range of $[0, 1]$.

Here, we can provide the complete pseudo-code as shown in Algorithm 3.

Algorithm 3: MCTS with the MG-PEO strategy

```
function Selection(v)
    while v is nonTerminal do
        if v is not fully expanded then
            return v
        else
            v ← BESTCHILD(v)
    return v
function Expansion(v,&s0)
    if v is an Amazon Movement Node then
        ch ← randomly create Arrow Shot Node
    else if v is an Arrow Shot Node
        ch ← randomly create the Amazon Movement Node
    s0 ← Update the state of the board
    return ch
function Simulation(v,s0)
```

```
    S ← s0
    //* depth = 4 and 5 (Independent order twice)
    S ← Rollout(S,depth)
    Δ ← SituationEvaluation(S)
    return Δ
function Rollout(S,depth)
    repeat
        if is Terminal (S) then
            pass
        if v is the Amazon Movement Node then
            arrow ← RandomArrow(S)
            S ← doAction(v,arrow)
            depth ← depth - 1
        else if v is the Arrow Shot Node then
            move ← parent of v
            S ← doAction(move,v)
            depth ← depth - 1
    until depth = 0 or gameover
    return S
function Backup(v,Δ)
    N(v) ← N(v) + 1
    Q(v) ← Q(v) + Δ(v, parent of v)
    v ← parent of v
function BESTCHILD(v)
    return argmax_{v' ∈ children of v} Q(v')/N(v') + c·sqrt(2 ln N(v) / N(v'))
```

4. MG-PEO Performance Analysis

In this section, we design two modules to analyze the MG-PEO strategy. First, we analyze the performance of the Move Groups strategy in Amazons. Second, we conduct an in-depth discussion on the performance improvement of the Parallel Evaluation mechanism in Amazons.

4.1. Performance of the Move Groups Strategy in Amazons

The effectiveness of a Monte Carlo tree search algorithm based on the law of large numbers depends largely on the number of situations it can search. The more situations the algorithm can search for, the easier it will be to find "tricks" that are usually hard to find and, thus, beat the opponent. In other words, the more computational the power, the more effective the Monte Carlo algorithm. Therefore, in order to objectively show the influence of the Move Groups strategy on the actual performance of the MCTS algorithm, we provide a new definition (winning convergence distance) to evaluate the performance of the algorithm.

Definition 1. ***Winning convergence distance.*** *This calculates the number of tree nodes expanded by the search tree, both in depth and breadth, from the current state (root node) to the winning state (game over). In general, the fewer new nodes the Monte Carlo tree needs to expand to achieve victory as soon as possible, the shorter the winning convergence distance.*

To visualize the winning convergence distance, we use the opening first step as an example. Since the number of nodes that can be generated from the first step to the winning state is immeasurable, we use the local optimal solution of the first step instead of the winning state, as shown in Figure 3.

Based on this, we can plot the Monte Carlo search tree with the Move Groups strategy added and the Monte Carlo search tree without the Move Groups strategy added, and compute the best-case and worst-case expanded node numbers, as shown in Figure 4 and Table 2.

Figure 3. The local optimal solution assumed in the first step of the opening. From left to right: initial state, after Amazon Movement, and after Arrow Shot.

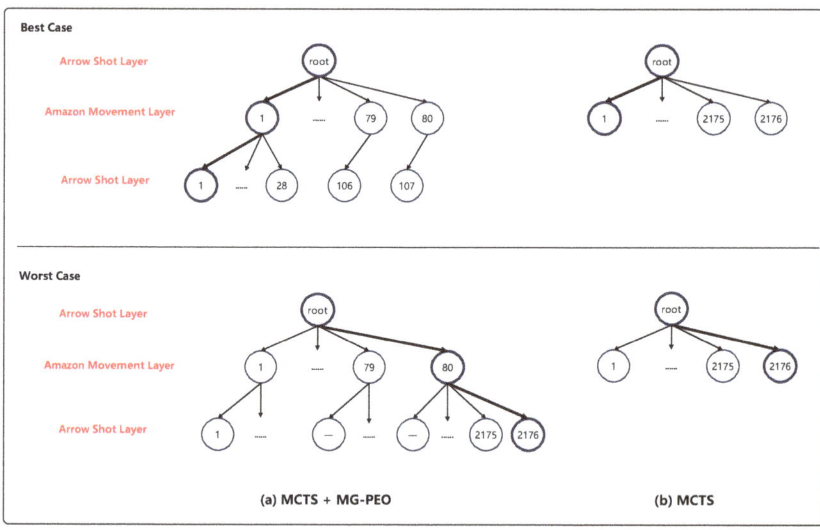

Figure 4. Plot of the winning convergence distance calculation. The number in the figure refers to the order in which the node is expanded at a certain layer.

Table 2. Winning convergence distance of two algorithms (unit: nodes).

Algorithm	Best Case	Worst Case
MCTS + MG-PEO	187	2256
MCTS	2176	2176

Red results indicate the best result in the same column.

In Figure 4 and Table 2, for the first step, the Monte Carlo tree search algorithm with the Move Groups strategy added needs to expand 80 Amazon Movement layer nodes first. Since the value score of an Amazon Movement layer node is infinite when it has not yet expanded its child nodes, each Amazon Movement layer node needs to further expand an Arrow Shot layer node to obtain an initial value score. Subsequently, we can select the Amazon Movement layer node with the highest value score for the next child node expansion. In the best case, the first Amazon Movement layer node has the highest value score. During the expansion of its subsequent Arrow Shot layer nodes, the value score of the parent node remains at the maximum observed across all Amazon Movement layer nodes; the other nodes in the Amazon Movement layer do not carry out the expansion of the next layer's nodes, which is a reflection of early pruning. Finally, the number of nodes expanded is 187. In the worst case, all possible nodes are fully expanded and traversed, resulting in a total of 2256 nodes being expanded.

The Monte Carlo tree search algorithm without the inclusion of the Move Groups strategy needs to select the node with the largest value score as the final decision after generating all possible nodes, regardless of the best or worst-case scenarios; resulting in a total of 2176 nodes being expanded.

In summary, we can conclude the following: in the best case, the winning convergence distance of the MCTS with the Move Groups strategy is significantly shorter than that of the traditional MCTS, while in the worst case, the winning convergence distance of the MCTS with the Move Groups strategy is slightly weaker than that of the traditional MCTS. This indicates that the Move Groups strategy has strong pruning and time-saving abilities, but at the same time, there are some shortcomings.

4.2. Performance of Parallel Evaluation Strategy

In this subsection, we delve into the number of threads required for the Parallel Evaluation mechanism, as well as the speedup ratio that multithreading can bring. Since the time consumption of the evaluation function mainly comes from the time from calculating each evaluation metric, the Parallel Evaluation part is essentially a multi-threaded calculation of evaluation metrics. The pseudo-code for the Parallel Evaluation metric function is shown in Algorithm 4.

Algorithm 4: Parallel Evaluation Metrics

```
Input: s0 (The current Game State)
Output: t1,t2,p1,p2,mobility
function ParallelEvaluationMetrics(s0)
    //* The calculation of Territory(t1, t2) and Position(p1, p2) metrics uses the same
        independent function four times, based on the King Move and QueenMove
        methods, which are calculated once for black and once for white.
    //* We optimize its external calls in parallel.
    Module1 = lambda (range)
        for the index in the range:
            color ← index/2
            type ← index%2
            CalTP(color,type)
    parallel_for(block_range(0,2),Module1)

    //* The Mobility(mobility) metric is calculated one function at a time, and the
        internal logic is to process each board position (GridSize = 100) independently.
    //* We optimize its inner loop processing logic in parallel.
    Module2 = lambda (range)
        for the index in the range:
            color ← index/2
            type ← index%2
            CalEveryBoardPosition()
    parallel_for(block_range(0,GridSize),Module2)
```

A. Discussion on the number of threads: Since the main metrics of the evaluation function include territory, position, and maneuverability metrics, values of the territory and position metrics can be calculated using a single function; however, as the calculations of these two metrics are related to the colors of the pieces and the calculation method (KingMove method and QueenMove method), four independent calculations are needed for the values of the territory and position metrics. The mobility indicator is calculated by a function that requires one independent calculation. The algorithm is optimized in parallel for the territory and position indicators, which theoretically require a total of four threads. For the maneuverability indicator, ten threads are theoretically needed for internal calculations related to the size of the board.

B. Exploration of the acceleration ratio that multi-threading can bring: In order to accurately explore the acceleration ratio, we counted the time consumed by the computation function of each evaluation metric, and the data are shown in Table 3.

Table 3. Module execution time and speed-up ratio.

Module	Serial Execution Time	Parallel Execution Time	Speed-Up Ratio
Module1	69 us	29 us	2.379
Mudule2	45 us	23 us	1.956
Whole Evaluation Function	114 us	54 us	2.111

As shown in Table 3, the calculation time for the optimized territory and position metrics achieved a 2.379-fold speedup, while the calculation time for the optimized mobility metric achieved a 1.956-fold speedup. The overall speedup ratio for the evaluation part was 2.111. In section A, we discussed the number of threads and noted that the theoretical speedup of parallelization should correspond to the number of threads. However, the time consumption of each module before and after optimization differed somewhat from the discussion in section A. We consider that the overhead of third-party parallel libraries[38] has consumed some computing resource performance. See Appendix B for details on the CPU usage analysis. Nevertheless, the parallel optimization mechanism reduced the time required to process the same tasks by 2.111 times, resulting in a significant performance improvement in practical applications.

5. Experiment and Results

In this section, in order to verify the effectiveness of the MG-PEO algorithm optimization strategy proposed in this paper, three experiments were designed: the first compares the relevant performance metrics of the MCTS algorithm with the MG-PEO strategy and the traditional MCTS algorithm, and a significance test is carried out on the comparison results. The second experiment focuses on assessing the magnitude of the effect of each optimization module of MG-PEO on MCTS, i.e., the ablation experiment. The third experiment is a generalized experimental analysis of the MG-PEO.

In addition, it is worth mentioning that the MG-PEO Amazons program proposed in this paper won first prize in the Amazons Competition at the 2023 China Collegiate Computer Games Championship & National Computer Games Tournament.

5.1. Experimental Environment Information

In order to ensure the reliability of the experimental results, we conducted all the experiments in a unified environment, and detailed information on the experimental environment settings is shown in Table 4.

Table 4. Experimental environment information.

Hardware and Constraints	Details
GPU	GeForce RTX 3070
CPU	Intel Core i7-11800H
Decision-Making time	5 s
Number of matches played by the same opponent	2
Number of sets per match	3
Experimental Matching Platform	SAU GAME Platform
Visual Studio Runtime Mode	[Release x64]

Against the same opponent, a total of six sets will be played, with three sets as the first player and three as the second player.

5.2. Quantitative and Qualitative Experiments

5.2.1. Winning Percentage Statistics and Analysis

In order to objectively and accurately assess the effectiveness of the MG-PEO algorithm optimization strategy, we selected the MCTS algorithm without Move-Groups optimization and without Parallel Evaluation optimization for comparison, and we played a total of 100 matches under the same conditions, with each match divided into 3 games each (first hand and second hand). Specifically, we chose 33 players who participated in a computer gaming competition and 17 players who open-sourced their rankings (ladder list) on the Botzone platform (https://www.botzone.org.cn/, accessed on 2 March 2024), totaling 50 opponents. Due to the requirement for third-party libraries, we locally exported the exe programs for all players and then conducted the games against each other on the SAU platform (http://computergames.caai.cn/platform/SAU_Game_Platform_2.1.0_r3.rar, accessed on 20 March 2024), and the results of the games are shown in Table 5. Detailed information on all the games can be found in Appendix C.

Table 5. The winning rate of the two algorithms.

Algorithm	Winning Percentage
MCTS	74%
MCTS + MG-PEO	97%

Red results indicate the best result in the same column.

In Table 5, the MCTS algorithm has a winning rate of 74% in Amazons Duel on the SAU matchmaking platform. In the same test environment, the MCTS algorithm with the MG-PEO strategy shows higher stability, and its winning rate in the Amazons Match on the SAU Matchmaking Platform reaches 97%. In summary, the MCTS algorithm with the MG-PEO strategy has more comprehensive and in-depth optimization when considering and utilizing strategies than the MCTS algorithm and, thus, shows a higher winning rate in this test scenario.

It is worth noting that—by observing the matches of the two algorithms—we found that the optimized MCTS algorithm often makes more accurate decisions than the unoptimized MCTS algorithm in some critical rounds. These key rounds often involve crucial positions for "encircle territory" or "block the opponent" strategies. Additionally, during the matches, we noticed that the optimized MCTS algorithm has a clear advantage over some traditional algorithms (such as Minimax and traditional MCTS). However, its performance is slightly lacking when competing against neural network programs trained with a large amount of game data. Nevertheless, this provides a direction for further improving the algorithm's performance in the next step.

5.2.2. Winning Convergence Distance Visualization and Analysis

In this sub-subsection, we count the number of match point rounds in which the algorithm's winning percentage assessment reaches 90% or more (the threshold for a solid win) in 100 games played by the two algorithms on the SAU platform, as a way to visualize the definition of the distance of convergence of a win, as well as to compare the strengths and weaknesses of the playing abilities of the two algorithms of the Amazons game. Here, we generally consider the outcome of a game to be clear when the algorithm evaluates a winning rate of 90% or more (barring low-level errors by the dominant side); such moments are considered to be match points and we believe that the earlier this occurs, the stronger the algorithms are. The average resulting data for the number of match point rounds for the two algorithms are shown in Table 6. See Appendix C for complete data:

Table 6. The average number of match point rounds in 100 matches where the win rate evaluation values of two algorithms exceed 90%.

Algorithm	Mean Value
MCTS	42.57
MCTS + MG-PEO	39.68

If the player loses, the match point rounds are taken as the maximum number of rounds, i.e., 47. Additionally, Red results indicate the best result in the same column.

As can be seen from Table 6, the average number of match point rounds required for the MCTS algorithm to reach the stable winning threshold (evaluation value over 90%) is 42.57 rounds. On the other hand, the MCTS algorithm with the MG-PEO strategy outperforms MCTS in terms of reaching the same stable winning threshold with an average of 39.68 rounds.

This indicates that the MCTS algorithm with the MG-PEO strategy converges faster than MCTS. It requires fewer average rounds than the traditional MCTS algorithm. The MCTS algorithm with the MG-PEO strategy uses the Move Groups strategy and the Parallel Evaluation strategy to optimize the strategy selection process of the MCTS algorithm so that it can find the best search paths in a shorter period of time and reach a stable winning state with a winning rate of more than 90% in advance.

In summary, the MCTS algorithm with the MG-PEO strategy has a shorter winning convergence distance than the traditional MCTS algorithm. It requires fewer rounds to achieve a higher winning rate and, thus, demonstrates superior playing ability.

5.2.3. Significance Test

In this subsection, we perform a significance test on the match point round count data, as counted in Section 5.2.2, to determine whether there is a significant difference between them. We conduct the tests at a significance level of 0.05. The complete match point round count data are detailed in Appendix C. First, we use the Shapiro–Wilk test to assume that both data sets obey a normal distribution. However, neither dataset conforms to a normal distribution. Based on this result, we use the Mann–Whitney U test to assume that there is no significant difference between the two groups of data. We then compare the distribution characteristics of the match point round data of the two algorithms. The detailed results are shown in Table 7.

Table 7. Significance of the test results.

Match Point Rounds Data	p-Value for Shapiro–Wilk Test (P_1)	p-Value for Mann–Whitney U Test (P_2)
MCTS	0.0002	1.16×10^{-8}
MCTS + MG-PEO	0.0013	

As a result of the Shapiro–Wilk test, both algorithms tested showed a P_1 value of less than 0.05 for the data on the number of match point rounds, leading us to reject the null hypothesis that the data for MCTS+MG-PEO and the data for MCTS both conform to a normal distribution. The results of the Mann–Whitney U test indicate that the P_2 value for the data on the number of match point rounds between the two algorithms is significantly smaller than 0.05, so we reject the original hypothesis. That is, there is a significant difference in the average number of winning steps between the two algorithms. Specifically, the average number of winning moves required by MCTS with the MG-PEO strategy is significantly less than that required by traditional MCTS against 100 players, suggesting that MCTS with the MG-PEO strategy outperforms traditional MCTS in terms of playing ability in Amazons.

5.3. Ablation Experiment

In this subsection, to evaluate the effectiveness of the Move Groups strategy and the Parallel Evaluation strategy in Amazons, we design two experiments: one that only employs the Move Groups strategy without using the Parallel Evaluation strategy, and another that only employs the Parallel Evaluation strategy without using the Move Groups strategy. The experimental results are shown in Table 8. On the one hand, the Move Groups strategy focuses on MCTS iterations within a limited time on the sub-nodes of more valuable additional-layer nodes by leveraging their value scores, thus avoiding the expansion of unimportant nodes. While the Move Groups strategy exhibits strong pruning capabilities, the value scores of additional-layer nodes dynamically change with the expansion of their sub-nodes due to the MCTS dynamic backpropagation update mechanism. Consequently, all nodes in the additional layer may be fully expanded and traversed multiple times (pruning has not occurred), potentially resulting in increased time spent compared to MCTS algorithms without the Move Groups strategy. On the other hand, because the proportion of the situation evaluation is limited, using only Parallel Evaluation optimization without adopting the Move Groups strategy offers limited performance improvement. Therefore, the combined optimization of employing both the Move Groups strategy and the Parallel Evaluation is effective and necessary.

Table 8. Ablation experiment analysis of the Move Groups strategy and Parallel Evaluation strategy.

Algorithm	Winning Percentage	Number of MCTS Iterations within 1s
MCTS	74%	2176
MCTS + PEO	89%	10,026
MCTS + MG	83%	5663
MCTS + MG-PEO	97%	45,536

The "Number of MCTS Iterations Within 1s" refers to the number of Monte Carlo tree search iterations conducted within one second. Under the Move Groups strategy, each MCTS iteration results in either an Amazon Movement node or an Arrow Shot node. Without using the Move Groups strategy, each MCTS iteration results in a complete decision node (Amazon Movement plus Arrow Shot). Additionally, Red results indicate the best result in the same column.

5.4. Generalization Analysis

In this subsection, we conducted a general analysis of the Move Groups strategy and the Parallel Evaluation strategy, discussing in depth their transferability to other board games.

1. Move Groups strategy: In some games, the branching factor can be very large, but many moves are similar. The Move Groups strategy creates an additional decision layer where all possible actions are grouped together, allowing us to handle the large branching factor of the game more efficiently. This strategy is beneficial for other games, such as Go [39] and the multi-armed bandit game with Move Groups [40]. We believe that this strategy is still worth exploring and investigating.
2. Parallel Evaluation strategy: The Parallel Evaluation strategy can provide effective acceleration, whether for simple rule-based games like Gomoku, more complex games like Chess and Go, or even modern innovative board games. Its core advantage lies in its ability to efficiently explore the decision tree, which is a common requirement in various board games.

6. Conclusions and Future Works

In this paper, we propose an efficient optimization of the Monte Carlo Tree Search algorithm for the Amazons game, which refines the Monte Carlo Tree Search capability through the Move Groups strategy. The Parallel Evaluation mechanism addresses the risk of the Move Groups strategy falling into a local optimum (these components are complementary to each other). The experimental results validate that the method proposed in this paper significantly improves the playing ability of the Amazons game.

Future research efforts are also included in our plans. First, to maximize the timesaving potential of the Move Groups strategy pruning, we hope to consider using more intelligent approaches (such as heuristic functions) to guide the pruning behavior of the Move Groups strategy. Secondly, the series of experiments in this paper demonstrate the powerful performance improvement capability of parallel optimization, so we plan to consider more parallel possibilities and more efficient parallel strategies in the future. Finally, we also hope that this algorithm can be further extended to solve more gameplaying problems.

Author Contributions: All authors contributed to the study's conception and design. Methodology, software, validation, investigation, data analysis, model verification, resources, data curation, visualization, writing—editing, and review: L.Z. and H.Z. Supervision, project administration, funding acquisition: Y.Z. All authors have read and agreed to the published version of the manuscript.

Funding: This research received no external funding.

Data Availability Statement: Part of the competition code used in this study is the publicly available open source code, which can be found at the following website: https://www.botzone.org.cn/, accessed on 2 March 2024.

Conflicts of Interest: The authors declare that they have no financial interests or personal relationships relevant to the content of this article's content.

Appendix A

In Appendix A, we discuss and analyze the effect of the depth of Rollout in the simulation phase on the algorithm's ability to play Amazons, and use the winning convergence distance metric (see Section 4.2 for details) to evaluate the playing ability. Shallow Rollout strategies can consider simulated positions closer to the endgame and more forward-looking games to compute more accurate position evaluation values, which can be used to better guide the node selection for MCTS. Therefore, it is crucial to balance the depth of Rollout; too shallow a depth will make the utilization value (winning rate) in the position evaluation formula less credible, while too deep a depth will lead to a single simulation iteration process that is too long, and the number of nodes expanded out in a finite period of time will become smaller, reducing the accuracy of the Monte Carlo tree search decision. We adjusted the Rollout depth value from 2 to 10 and found that the optimal value of Rollout depth is 4 or 5, as shown in Table A1.

Table A1. Parametric analysis of the Rollout depth.

Rollout Depth	1	2	3	4	5	6	7–10	4 and 5
Match Point Rounds	40.25	40.14	40.0	39.9	39.84	40.04	40.1	39.68

Red results indicate the best result in the same column.

In addition, we found in our experiments that Rollout twice (choosing 4 and 5 in-depth) works better than Rollout once (choosing only 4 or 5), i.e., the number of rounds at match points is smaller, the distance of convergence for winning is shorter, and the algorithm is more capable of playing Amazons.

Appendix B

Appendix B shows the detailed CPU usage of the algorithm with and without the Parallel Evaluation strategy. The monitoring environment is the performance profiler in Microsoft Visual Studio 2019, with the algorithm making only one decision, which takes 20 s. As shown in Figure A1, the top part of the image represents the CPU utilization, and the fluctuating part of the CPU utilization values corresponds to the algorithm's decision-making phase, while the remaining part corresponds to the input and output idle phases.

Figure A1. CPU utilization and top 5 modules occupying CPU resources under [Debug ×64] condition. The upper part shows the monitoring results of the algorithm executed sequentially, while the lower part shows the monitoring results of the algorithm executed in parallel.

From Figure A1, it is evident that the CPU utilization of the algorithm program in parallel execution is significantly higher than in sequential execution. When the algorithm program executes sequentially, both red-framed modules of the evaluation function are among the top 5 modules occupying the most CPU resources. This indicates that parallel optimization of the evaluation part is very necessary. During parallel execution of the algorithm program, the blue-framed third-party parallel library occupies a substantial amount of CPU resources. This indirectly indicates that the performance improvement after parallelization does not achieve the theoretical speedup due to significant resource consumption by external code and external calls.

Appendix C

Appendix C shows the complete game information, as well as the match point round count, as shown in Tables A2 and A3.

Table A2. Complete game information (MCTS plus MG-PEO).

ID	First Player	Second Player	Result	Match Point Rounds	Winner
1	Amazons based on Qt's QMainWindow framework	Divine Move (ours)	0:3	41	Divine Move (ours)
2	Divine Move (ours)	Amazons based on Qt's QMainWindow framework	3:0	39	Divine Move (ours)
3	Gomoku	Divine Move (ours)	0:3	39	Divine Move (ours)
4	Divine Move (ours)	Gomoku	3:0	36	Divine Move (ours)
5	Othello	Divine Move (ours)	0:3	35	Divine Move (ours)
6	Divine Move (ours)	Othello	3:0	33	Divine Move (ours)
7	God's Algorithm	Divine Move (ours)	0:3	43	Divine Move (ours)

Table A2. *Cont.*

ID	First Player	Second Player	Result	Match Point Rounds	Winner
8	Divine Move (ours)	God's Algorithm	3:0	42	Divine Move (ours)
9	Amazons Gaming System	Divine Move (ours)	0:3	39	Divine Move (ours)
10	Divine Move (ours)	Amazons Gaming System	3:0	37	Divine Move (ours)
11	Advance Little Queens	Divine Move (ours)	0:3	40	Divine Move (ours)
12	Divine Move (ours)	Advance Little Queens	3:0	37	Divine Move (ours)
13	Checkmate	Divine Move (ours)	0:3	41	Divine Move (ours)
14	Divine Move (ours)	Checkmate	3:0	38	Divine Move (ours)
15	Cliffhanger Amazons	Divine Move (ours)	0:3	40	Divine Move (ours)
16	Divine Move (ours)	Cliffhanger Amazons	3:0	37	Divine Move (ours)
17	Qi Kaide's Victory	Divine Move (ours)	0:3	41	Divine Move (ours)
18	Divine Move (ours)	Qi Kaide's Victory	3:0	36	Divine Move (ours)
19	Super Amazon	Divine Move (ours)	0:3	39	Divine Move (ours)
20	Divine Move (ours)	Super Amazon	3:0	36	Divine Move (ours)
21	God's Algorithm	Divine Move (ours)	0:3	41	Divine Move (ours)
22	Divine Move (ours)	God's Algorithm	3:0	37	Divine Move (ours)
23	Traveler Amazons	Divine Move (ours)	0:3	40	Divine Move (ours)
24	Divine Move (ours)	Traveler Amazons	3:0	35	Divine Move (ours)
25	Amazon Supreme Chess	Divine Move (ours)	0:3	41	Divine Move (ours)
26	Divine Move (ours)	Amazon Supreme Chess	3:0	39	Divine Move (ours)
27	Chess Troops Falling from Heaven	Divine Move (ours)	0:3	43	Divine Move (ours)
28	Divine Move (ours)	Chess Troops Falling from Heaven	3:0	41	Divine Move (ours)
29	Clove Amazons	Divine Move (ours)	0:3	40	Divine Move (ours)
30	Divine Move (ours)	Clove Amazons	3:0	37	Divine Move (ours)
31	Shao Guang's Amazons	Divine Move (ours)	0:3	43	Divine Move (ours)
32	Divine Move (ours)	Shao Guang's Amazons	3:0	39	Divine Move (ours)
33	AI plays chess	Divine Move (ours)	0:3	43	Divine Move (ours)
34	Divine Move (ours)	AI plays chess	3:0	39	Divine Move (ours)
35	Canopus One	Divine Move (ours)	0:3	39	Divine Move (ours)
36	Divine Move (ours)	Canopus One	3:0	35	Divine Move (ours)
37	Win the Opening Team	Divine Move (ours)	0:3	41	Divine Move (ours)
38	Divine Move (ours)	Win the Opening Team	3:0	39	Divine Move (ours)
39	Wukong Amazons	Divine Move (ours)	0:3	34	Divine Move (ours)
40	Divine Move (ours)	Wukong Amazons	3:0	30	Divine Move (ours)
41	Traveler Amazons	Divine Move (ours)	0:3	44	Divine Move (ours)
42	Divine Move (ours)	Traveler Amazons	3:0	40	Divine Move (ours)
43	Yue	Divine Move (ours)	0:3	41	Divine Move (ours)
44	Divine Move (ours)	Yue	3:0	40	Divine Move (ours)
45	Final Amazon	Divine Move (ours)	0:3	41	Divine Move (ours)
46	Divine Move (ours)	Final Amazon	3:0	38	Divine Move (ours)
47	Information University - Monte Carlo	Divine Move (ours)	1:2	42	Divine Move (ours)
48	Divine Move (ours)	Information University - Monte Carlo	3:0	40	Divine Move (ours)
49	Haha Hi	Divine Move (ours)	1:2	42	Divine Move (ours)
50	Divine Move (ours)	Haha Hi	3:0	39	Divine Move (ours)
51	Dragon Victory	Divine Move (ours)	0:3	41	Divine Move (ours)
52	Divine Move (ours)	Dragon Victory	3:0	37	Divine Move (ours)
53	Super Amazon	Divine Move (ours)	0:3	43	Divine Move (ours)
54	Divine Move (ours)	Super Amazon	3:0	38	Divine Move (ours)
55	Base Pairing Team	Divine Move (ours)	0:3	44	Divine Move (ours)
56	Divine Move (ours)	Base Pairing Team	3:0	41	Divine Move (ours)
57	Pass the Level	Divine Move (ours)	3:0	47	Pass the Level

Table A2. *Cont.*

ID	First Player	Second Player	Result	Match Point Rounds	Winner
58	Divine Move (ours)	Pass the Level	0:3	47	Pass the Level
59	Dalian Jiaotong University Amazons Team 1	Divine Move (ours)	0:3	41	Divine Move (ours)
60	Divine Move (ours)	Dalian Jiaotong University Amazons Team 1	3:0	39	Divine Move (ours)
61	Get Ashore	Divine Move (ours)	0:3	41	Divine Move (ours)
62	Divine Move (ours)	Get Ashore	3:0	40	Divine Move (ours)
63	Empty	Divine Move (ours)	0:3	44	Divine Move (ours)
64	Divine Move (ours)	Empty	3:0	41	Divine Move (ours)
65	Bull	Divine Move (ours)	0:3	42	Divine Move (ours)
66	Divine Move (ours)	Bull	3:0	40	Divine Move (ours)
67	Wukong Amazons	Divine Move (ours)	1:2	34	Divine Move (ours)
68	Divine Move (ours)	Wukong Amazons	3:0	31	Divine Move (ours)
69	Gangzi Fans Support Team	Divine Move (ours)	0:3	41	Divine Move (ours)
70	Divine Move (ours)	Gangzi Fans Support Team	3:0	39	Divine Move (ours)
71	Thai Pants Spicy	Divine Move (ours)	0:3	44	Divine Move (ours)
72	Divine Move (ours)	Thai Pants Spicy	3:0	41	Divine Move (ours)
73	Green Grass Cake	Divine Move (ours)	0:3	34	Divine Move (ours)
74	Divine Move (ours)	Green Grass Cake	3:0	30	Divine Move (ours)
75	Failed to Grab the Air and Didn't Grab the Plant Brain Hypoxia Team	Divine Move (ours)	0:3	40	Divine Move (ours)
76	Divine Move (ours)	Failed to Grab the Air and Didn't Grab the Plant Brain Hypoxia Team	3:0	37	Divine Move (ours)
77	DG	Divine Move (ours)	0:3	44	Divine Move (ours)
78	Divine Move (ours)	DG	3:0	39	Divine Move (ours)
79	Why is Tang Yang a God	Divine Move (ours)	0:3	42	Divine Move (ours)
80	Divine Move (ours)	Why is Tang Yang a God	3:0	39	Divine Move (ours)
81	Dream Team	Divine Move (ours)	0:3	43	Divine Move (ours)
82	Divine Move (ours)	Dream Team	3:0	39	Divine Move (ours)
83	Horse Face Skirt Daily and Easy to Wear	Divine Move (ours)	0:3	43	Divine Move (ours)
84	Divine Move (ours)	Horse Face Skirt Daily and Easy to Wear	3:0	40	Divine Move (ours)
85	Genshin Impact Expert	Divine Move (ours)	0:3	41	Divine Move (ours)
86	Divine Move (ours)	Genshin Impact Expert	3:0	37	Divine Move (ours)
87	Code Apprentice	Divine Move (ours)	0:3	42	Divine Move (ours)
88	Divine Move (ours)	Code Apprentice	3:0	41	Divine Move (ours)
89	Amazon Drift Notes	Divine Move (ours)	0:3	39	Divine Move (ours)
90	Divine Move (ours)	Amazon Drift Notes	3:0	37	Divine Move (ours)
91	Love Will Disappear, Right?	Divine Move (ours)	0:3	38	Divine Move (ours)
92	Divine Move (ours)	Love Will Disappear, Right?	3:0	33	Divine Move (ours)
93	Little Su and the Cat	Divine Move (ours)	0:3	43	Divine Move (ours)
94	Divine Move (ours)	Little Su and the Cat	3:0	42	Divine Move (ours)
95	Don't Want Marla	Divine Move (ours)	0:3	44	Divine Move (ours)
96	Divine Move (ours)	Don't Want Marla	3:0	43	Divine Move (ours)
97	Parameter Adjustment Team	Divine Move (ours)	0:3	44	Divine Move (ours)
98	Divine Move (ours)	Parameter Adjustment Team	3:0	41	Divine Move (ours)
99	AlphaAmazon	Divine Move (ours)	0:3	43	Divine Move (ours)
100	Divine Move (ours)	AlphaAmazon	3:0	42	Divine Move (ours)

Table A3. Complete game information (MCTS).

ID	First Player	Second Player	Result	Match Point Rounds	Winner
1	Amazons based on Qt's QMainWindow framework	MCTS (baseline)	1:2	43	MCTS (baseline)
2	MCTS (baseline)	Amazons based on Qt's QMainWindow framework	3:0	41	MCTS (baseline)
3	Gomoku	MCTS (baseline)	3:0	47	Gomoku
4	MCTS (baseline)	Gomoku	3:0	45	MCTS (baseline)
5	Othello	MCTS (baseline)	2:1	47	Othello
6	MCTS (baseline)	Othello	2:1	44	MCTS (baseline)
7	God's Algorithm	MCTS (baseline)	0:3	43	MCTS (baseline)
8	MCTS (baseline)	God's Algorithm	3:0	40	MCTS (baseline)
9	Amazons Gaming System	MCTS (baseline)	0:3	42	MCTS (baseline)
10	MCTS (baseline)	Amazons Gaming System	3:0	40	MCTS (baseline)
11	Advance Little Queens	MCTS (baseline)	3:0	47	Advance Little Queens
12	MCTS (baseline)	Advance Little Queens	3:0	43	MCTS (baseline)
13	Checkmate	MCTS (baseline)	2:1	47	Checkmate
14	MCTS (baseline)	Checkmate	3:0	40	MCTS (baseline)
15	Cliffhanger Amazons	MCTS (baseline)	3:0	47	Checkmate
16	MCTS (baseline)	Cliffhanger Amazons	3:0	44	MCTS (baseline)
17	Qi Kaide's Victory	MCTS (baseline)	0:3	44	MCTS (baseline)
18	MCTS (baseline)	Qi Kaide's Victory	3:0	41	MCTS (baseline)
19	Super Amazon	MCTS (baseline)	2:1	47	Super Amazon
20	MCTS (baseline)	Super Amazon	2:1	43	MCTS (baseline)
21	God's Algorithm	MCTS (baseline)	3:0	47	God's Algorithm
22	MCTS (baseline)	God's Algorithm	2:1	40	MCTS (baseline)
23	Traveler Amazons	MCTS (baseline)	2:1	47	Traveler Amazons
24	MCTS (baseline)	Traveler Amazons	3:0	42	MCTS (baseline)
25	Amazon Supreme Chess	MCTS (baseline)	0:3	40	MCTS (baseline)
26	MCTS (baseline)	Amazon Supreme Chess	3:0	41	MCTS (baseline)
27	Chess Troops Falling from Heaven	MCTS (baseline)	0:3	43	MCTS (baseline)
28	MCTS (baseline)	Chess Troops Falling from Heaven	3:0	39	MCTS (baseline)
29	Clove Amazons	MCTS (baseline)	0:3	44	MCTS (baseline)
30	MCTS (baseline)	Clove Amazons	3:0	40	MCTS (baseline)
31	Shao Guang's Amazons	MCTS (baseline)	1:2	43	MCTS (baseline)
32	MCTS (baseline)	Shao Guang's Amazons	3:0	40	MCTS (baseline)
33	AI plays chess	MCTS (baseline)	2:1	47	AI plays chess
34	MCTS (baseline)	AI plays chess	3:0	42	MCTS (baseline)
35	Canopus One	MCTS (baseline)	0:3	43	MCTS (baseline)
36	MCTS (baseline)	Canopus One	2:1	40	MCTS (baseline)
37	Win the Opening Team	MCTS (baseline)	3:0	47	Win the Opening Team
38	MCTS (baseline)	Win the Opening Team	3:0	44	MCTS (baseline)
39	Wukong Amazons	MCTS (baseline)	0:3	42	MCTS (baseline)
40	MCTS (baseline)	Wukong Amazons	3:0	39	MCTS (baseline)
41	Traveler Amazons	MCTS (baseline)	0:3	41	MCTS (baseline)
42	MCTS (baseline)	Traveler Amazons	3:0	36	MCTS (baseline)
43	Yue	MCTS (baseline)	0:3	44	MCTS (baseline)
44	MCTS (baseline)	Yue	3:0	41	MCTS (baseline)
45	Final Amazon	MCTS (baseline)	0:3	42	MCTS (baseline)
46	MCTS (baseline)	Final Amazon	3:0	37	MCTS (baseline)
47	Information University - Monte Carlo	MCTS (baseline)	3:0	47	Information University-Monte Carlo
48	MCTS (baseline)	Information University-Monte Carlo	0:3	47	Information University-Monte Carlo

Table A3. *Cont.*

ID	First Player	Second Player	Result	Match Point Rounds	Winner
49	Haha Hi	MCTS (baseline)	3:0	47	Haha Hi
50	MCTS (baseline)	Haha Hi	3:0	41	MCTS (baseline)
51	Dragon Victory	MCTS (baseline)	0:3	43	MCTS (baseline)
52	MCTS (baseline)	Dragon Victory	3:0	38	MCTS (baseline)
53	Super Amazon	MCTS (baseline)	0:3	41	MCTS (baseline)
54	MCTS (baseline)	Super Amazon	3:0	38	MCTS (baseline)
55	Base Pairing Team	MCTS (baseline)	3:0	45	Base Pairing Team
56	MCTS (baseline)	Base Pairing Team	0:3	42	Base Pairing Team
57	Pass the Level	MCTS (baseline)	3:0	47	Pass the Level
58	MCTS (baseline)	Pass the Level	0:3	47	Pass the Level
59	Dalian Jiaotong University Amazons Team 1	MCTS (baseline)	0:3	44	MCTS (baseline)
60	MCTS (baseline)	Dalian Jiaotong University Amazons Team 1	3:0	42	MCTS (baseline)
61	Get Ashore	MCTS (baseline)	3:0	47	Get Ashore
62	MCTS (baseline)	Get Ashore	0:3	47	Get Ashore
63	Empty	MCTS (baseline)	0:3	45	MCTS (baseline)
64	MCTS (baseline)	Empty	3:0	41	MCTS (baseline)
65	Bull	MCTS (baseline)	0:3	45	MCTS (baseline)
66	MCTS (baseline)	Bull	3:0	40	MCTS (baseline)
67	Wukong Amazons	MCTS (baseline)	2:1	47	Wukong Amazons
68	MCTS (baseline)	Wukong Amazons	3:0	39	MCTS (baseline)
69	Gangzi Fans Support Team	MCTS (baseline)	3:0	44	Gangzi Fans Support Team
70	MCTS (baseline)	Gangzi Fans Support Team	1:2	41	Gangzi Fans Support Team
71	Thai Pants Spicy	MCTS (baseline)	0:3	42	MCTS (baseline)
72	MCTS (baseline)	Thai Pants Spicy	3:0	40	MCTS (baseline)
73	Green Grass Cake	MCTS (baseline)	0:3	42	MCTS (baseline)
74	MCTS (baseline)	Green Grass Cake	3:0	37	MCTS (baseline)
75	Failed to Grab the Air and Didn't Grab the Plant Brain Hypoxia Team	MCTS (baseline)	0:3	41	MCTS (baseline)
76	MCTS (baseline)	Failed to Grab the Air and Didn't Grab the Plant Brain Hypoxia Team	3:0	40	MCTS (baseline)
77	DG	MCTS (baseline)	0:3	43	MCTS (baseline)
78	MCTS (baseline)	DG	3:0	39	MCTS (baseline)
79	Why is Tang Yang a God	MCTS (baseline)	2:1	47	Why is Tang Yang a God
80	MCTS (baseline)	Why is Tang Yang a God	3:0	44	MCTS (baseline)
81	Dream Team	MCTS (baseline)	0:3	43	MCTS (baseline)
82	MCTS (baseline)	Dream Team	3:0	44	MCTS (baseline)
83	Horse Face Skirt Daily and Easy to Wear	MCTS (baseline)	0:3	44	MCTS (baseline)
84	MCTS (baseline)	Horse Face Skirt Daily and Easy to Wear	3:0	40	MCTS (baseline)
85	Genshin Impact Expert	MCTS (baseline)	0:3	44	MCTS (baseline)
86	MCTS (baseline)	Genshin Impact Expert	3:0	39	MCTS (baseline)
87	Code Apprentice	MCTS (baseline)	0:3	42	MCTS (baseline)
88	MCTS (baseline)	Code Apprentice	3:0	40	MCTS (baseline)
89	Amazon Drift Notes	MCTS (baseline)	0:3	44	MCTS (baseline)
90	MCTS (baseline)	Amazon Drift Notes	3:0	42	MCTS (baseline)
91	Love Will Disappear, Right?	MCTS (baseline)	0:3	40	MCTS (baseline)
92	MCTS (baseline)	Love Will Disappear, Right?	3:0	38	MCTS (baseline)

Table A3. *Cont.*

ID	First Player	Second Player	Result	Match Point Rounds	Winner
93	Little Su and the Cat	MCTS (baseline)	0:3	44	MCTS (baseline)
94	MCTS (baseline)	Little Su and the Cat	3:0	40	MCTS (baseline)
95	Don't Want Marla	MCTS (baseline)	0:3	41	MCTS (baseline)
96	MCTS (baseline)	Don't Want Marla	3:0	37	MCTS (baseline)
97	Parameter Adjustment Team	MCTS (baseline)	0:3	42	MCTS (baseline)
98	MCTS (baseline)	Parameter Adjustment Team	3:0	39	MCTS (baseline)
99	AlphaAmazon	MCTS (baseline)	0:3	41	MCTS (baseline)
100	MCTS (baseline)	AlphaAmazon	0:3	47	AlphaAmazon

References

1. Li, R.; Gao, M. Amazons search algorithm design based on CNN model. *Digit. Technol. Appl.* **2022**, *40*, 164–166.
2. Guo, Q.; Li, S.; Bao, H. Research on evaluation function computer game of Amazon. *Comput. Eng. Appl.* **2012**, *48*, 50–54.
3. Guo, T.; Qiu, H.; Tong, B.; Wang, Y. Optimization and Comparison of Multiple Game Algorithms in Amazons. In Proceedings of the 2019 Chinese Control And Decision Conference (CCDC), Nanchang, China, 3–5 June 2019; pp. 6299–6304.
4. Quan, J.; Qiu, H.; Wang, Y.; Li, F.; Qiu, S. Application of UCT technologies for computer games of Amazon. In Proceedings of the 2016 Chinese Control and Decision Conference (CCDC), Yinchuan, China, 28–30 May 2016; pp. 6896–6899.
5. Ju, J.; Qiu, H.; Wang, F.; Wang, X.; Wang, Y. Research on Thread Optimization and Opening Library Based on Parallel PVS Algorithm in Amazons. In Proceedings of the 2021 33rd Chinese Control and Decision Conference (CCDC), Kunming, China, 28–30 May 2021; pp. 2207–2212.
6. Li, Z.; Ning, C.; Cao, J.; Li, Z. Amazons Based on UCT-PVS Hybrid Algorithm. In Proceedings of the 2021 33rd Chinese Control and Decision Conference (CCDC), Kunming, China, 28–30 May 2021; pp. 2179–2183.
7. Ding, M.; Bo, J.; Qi, Y.; Fu, Y.; Li, S. Design of Amazons Game System Based on Reinforcement Learning. In Proceedings of the 2019 Chinese Control And Decision Conference (CCDC), Nanchang, China, 3–5 June 2019; pp. 6337–6342.
8. Tong, B.; Qiu, H.; Guo, T.; Wang, Y. Research and Application of Parallel Computing of PVS Algorithm Based on Amazon Human-Machine Game. In Proceedings of the 2019 Chinese Control And Decision Conference (CCDC), Nanchang, China, 3–5 June 2019; pp. 6293–6298.
9. Chen, X.; Yang, L. Research on evaluation function in Amazons. *Comput. Knowl. Technol.* **2019**, *15*, 224–226.
10. Wang, C.; Ding, M. Interface design and implementation of personalized Amazons. *Intell. Comput. Appl.* **2017**, *7*, 78–80.
11. Zhang, L. Research on Amazons Game System Based on Minimax Search Algorithm. Master's Thesis, Northeast University, Shenyang, China, 2010.
12. Metropolis, N.; Ulam, S. The Monte Carlo Method. *J. Am. Stat. Assoc.* **1949**, *44*, 335–341. [CrossRef] [PubMed]
13. Coulom, R. Efficient Selectivity and Backup Operators in Monte-Carlo Tree Search. In Proceedings of the Computers and Games, Turin, Italy, 1–5 April 2007; pp. 72–83.
14. Gelly, S.; Kocsis, L.; Schoenauer, M.; Sebag, M.; Silver, D.; Szepesvári, C.; Teytaud, O. The grand challenge of computer Go: Monte Carlo tree search and extensions. *Commun. ACM* **2012**, *55*, 106–113. [CrossRef]
15. Gelly, S.; Silver, D. Monte-Carlo tree search and rapid action value estimation in computer Go. *Artif. Intell.* **2011**, *175*, 1856–1875. [CrossRef]
16. Vinyals, O.; Babuschkin, I.; Czarnecki, W.M.; Mathieu, M.; Dudzik, A.; Chung, J.; Choi, D.H.; Powell, R.; Ewalds, T.; Georgiev, P.; et al. Grandmaster level in StarCraft II using multi-agent reinforcement learning. *Nature* **2019**, *575*, 350–354. [CrossRef]
17. Silver, D.; Huang, A.; Maddison, C.J.; Guez, A.; Sifre, L.; van den Driessche, G.; Schrittwieser, J.; Antonoglou, I.; Panneershelvam, V.; Lanctot, M.; et al. Mastering the game of Go with deep neural networks and tree search. *Nature* **2016**, *529*, 484–489. [CrossRef]
18. Berner, C.; Brockman, G.; Chan, B.; Cheung, V.; Dębiak, P.; Dennison, C.; Farhi, D.; Fischer, Q.; Hashme, S.; Hesse, C.; et al. Dota 2 with Large Scale Deep Reinforcement Learning. *arXiv* **2019**, arXiv:1912.06680.
19. Browne, C.B.; Powley, E.; Whitehouse, D.; Lucas, S.M.; Cowling, P.I.; Rohlfshagen, P.; Tavener, S.; Perez, D.; Samothrakis, S.; Colton, S. A Survey of Monte Carlo Tree Search Methods. *IEEE Trans. Comput. Intell. AI Games* **2012**, *4*, 1–43. [CrossRef]
20. Kloetzer, J.; Iida, H.; Bouzy, B. The Monte-Carlo Approach in Amazons. In Proceedings of the Computer Games Workshop, Amsterdam, The Netherlands, 15–17 June 2007; pp. 185–192.
21. Shannon, C. E. Programming a computer for playing chess. *Lond. Edinb. Dublin Philos. Mag. J. Sci.* **1950**, *41*, 256–275. [CrossRef]
22. Chaslot, G.; Bakkes, S.; Szita, I.; Spronck, P. Monte-Carlo Tree Search: A New Framework for Game AI. In Proceedings of the AAAI Conference on Artificial Intelligence and Interactive Digital Entertainment, California, CA, USA, 22–24 October 2008; pp. 216–217.
23. Świechowski, M.; Godlewski, K.; Sawicki, B.; Mańdziuk, J. Monte Carlo Tree Search: A review of recent modifications and applications. *Artif. Intell. Rev.* **2023**, *56*, 2497–2562. [CrossRef]

24. Kloetzer, J. Monte-Carlo Opening Books for Amazons. In *Computers and Games: 7th International Conference (CG 2010), Kanazawa, Japan, September 24–26 2010, Revised Selected Papers 7*; Springer: Berlin/Heidelberg, Germany, 2011; pp. 124–135.
25. Song, J.; Müller, M. An Enhanced Solver for the Game of Amazons. *IEEE Trans. Comput. Intell. AI Games* **2014**, *7*, 16–27. [CrossRef]
26. Zhang, G.; Chen, X.; Chang, R.; Zhang, Y.; Wang, C.; Bai, L.; Wang, J.; Xu, C. Mastering the Game of Amazons Fast by Decoupling Network Learning. In Proceedings of the 2021 International Joint Conference on Neural Networks (IJCNN), Shenzhen, China, 18–22 July 2021; pp. 1–8.
27. de Koning, J. INVADER Prolongs Amazons Title. *ICGA J.* **2011**, *34*, 96. [CrossRef]
28. Kloetzer, J. INVADER Wins Amazons Tournament. *ICGA J.* **2009**, *32*, 112–113. [CrossRef]
29. Lorentz, R. Invader Wins Eighth Amazons Gold Medal. *ICGA J.* **2017**, *39*, 228–229. [CrossRef]
30. Guo, Q.; Li, S.; Bao, H. The Research of Searching Algorithm in Amazons Game. In Proceedings of the 2011 Chinese Control and Decision Conference (CCDC), Mianyang, China, 23–25 May 2011; pp. 1859–1862.
31. Li, X.; Hou, L.; Wu, L. UCT Algorithm in Amazons Human-Computer Games. In Proceedings of the 26th Chinese Control and Decision Conference (CCDC), Changsha, China, 31 May–2 June 2014; pp. 3358–3361.
32. Quan, J.; Qiu, H.; Wang, Y.; Li, Y.; Wang, X. Study the Performance of Search Algorithms in Amazons. In Proceedings of the 27th Chinese Control and Decision Conference (CCDC), Qingdao, China, 23–25 May 2015; pp. 5811–5813.
33. Lieberum, J. An Evaluation Function for the Game of Amazons. *Theor. Comput. Sci.* **2005**, *349*, 230–244. [CrossRef]
34. Chai, Z.; Fang, Z.; Zhu, J. Amazons Evaluation Optimization Strategy Based on PSO Algorithm. In Proceedings of the 2019 Chinese Control And Decision Conference (CCDC), Nanchang, China, 3–5 June 2019; pp. 6334–6336.
35. Sun, Y.; Yuan, D.; Gao, M.; Zhu, P. GPU Acceleration of Monte Carlo Tree Search Algorithm for Amazons and Its Evaluation Function. In Proceedings of the 2022 International Conference on Artificial Intelligence, Information Processing and Cloud Computing (AIIPCC), Kunming, China, 21–23 June 2022; pp. 434–440.
36. Kocsis, L.; Szepesvari, C.; Willemson, J. Improved Monte-Carlo Search. *Univ. Tartu Est. Tech. Rep.* **2006**, *1*, 1–22.
37. Finnsson, H.; Björnsson, Y. Game-tree properties and MCTS performance. *IJCAI* **2011**, *11*, 23–30.
38. Pheatt, C. Intel® threading building blocks. *J. Comput. Sci. Coll.* **2008**, *23*, 164–166.
39. Childs, B.E.; Brodeur, J.H.; Kocsis, L. Transpositions and move groups in monte carlo tree search. In Proceedings of the 2008 IEEE Symposium on Computational Intelligence and Games, Perth, Australia, 15–18 December 2008; pp. 389-395.
40. Van Eyck, G.; Müller, M. Revisiting move groups in monte-carlo tree search. In *Advances in Computer Games: 13th International Conference, ACG 2011, Tilburg, The Netherlands, 20–22 November 2011, Revised Selected Papers 13*; Springer: Berlin/Heidelberg, Germany, 2012; pp. 13–23.

algorithms

MDPI

Article

Imitating Human Go Players via Vision Transformer

Yu-Heng Hsieh, Chen-Chun Kao and Shyan-Ming Yuan *

Department of Computer Science, National Yang Ming Chiao Tung University, Hsinchu 30010, Taiwan; k28998989.cs11@nycu.edu.tw (Y.-H.H.); b311551147.cs11@nycu.edu.tw (C.-C.K.)
* Correspondence: smyuan@nycu.edu.tw

Abstract: Developing AI algorithms for the game of Go has long been a challenging task. While tools such as AlphaGo have revolutionized gameplay, their focus on maximizing win rates often leads to moves that are incomprehensible to human players, limiting their utility as training aids. This work introduces a novel approach to bridge this gap by leveraging a Vision Transformer (ViT) to develop an AI model that achieves professional-level play while mimicking human decision-making. Using a dataset from the KGS Go server, our ViT-based model achieves 51.49% accuracy in predicting expert moves with a simple feature set. Comparative analysis against CNN-based models highlights the ViT's superior performance in capturing patterns and replicating expert strategies. These findings establish ViTs as promising tools for enhancing Go training by aligning AI strategies with human intuition.

Keywords: Go; deep learning; Vision Transformer

1. Introduction

Developing algorithms for Go programs capable of human-level performance has long been considered an intractable challenge. This difficulty stems from the immense search space and the complex evaluation functions involved, where a single move can drastically influence the game's outcome. Traditional hand-crafted evaluation functions and rules have consistently fallen short of achieving even amateur-level gameplay. Consequently, the predominant approach over the decades has been to leverage deep learning models trained on expert gameplay records. These models, typically trained under a supervised learning paradigm, treat board positions as inputs and use the corresponding moves made by human experts as labels.

The groundbreaking success of AlphaGo has brought convolutional neural network (CNN)-based methods [1] to the forefront of Go-related tasks. By employing CNNs, AlphaGo not only defeated professional Go players but also demonstrated the viability of deep learning in mastering this intricate game. The successes of AlphaGo [2] and AlphaGo Zero [3] have encouraged Go players to use AI-powered software as training tools.

For instance, Figure 1 illustrates a fifth-line shoulder hit played by AlphaGo against professional ninth-dan player Lee Sedol. This move was described by commentators as "an unthinkable move" and "a mistake", as it defied conventional human Go intuition. Similarly, Figure 2 highlights another "mistake" by AlphaGo: selecting move A over move B, despite the latter being clearly superior from a human perspective, as it maximizes territory. This divergence arises because AlphaGo calculates win rates through a combination of neural networks and Monte Carlo Tree Search, which leads to a "thinking process" entirely different from human reasoning [4]. Other examples of non-human-like moves, such as slack moves played with no strategic intention other than prolonging the game, further emphasize the knowledge gap between humans and AI. Such moves contradict human intuition and experience, rendering them incomprehensible for players seeking to learn from the model.

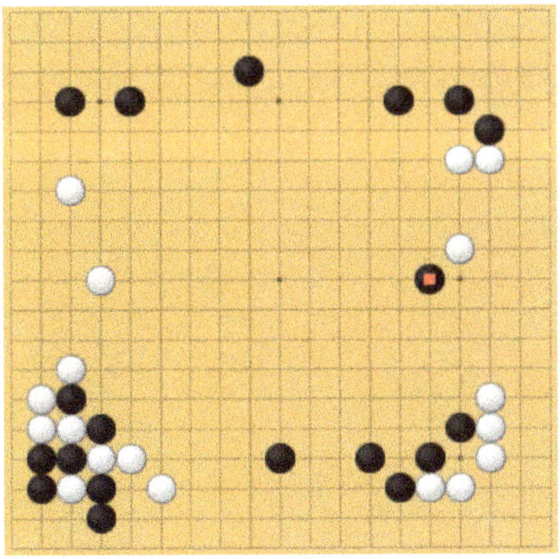

Figure 1. Game 2 between AlphaGo and Lee Sedol. AlphaGo played move 37 (marked by the red square) and gained a significant advantage from this move.

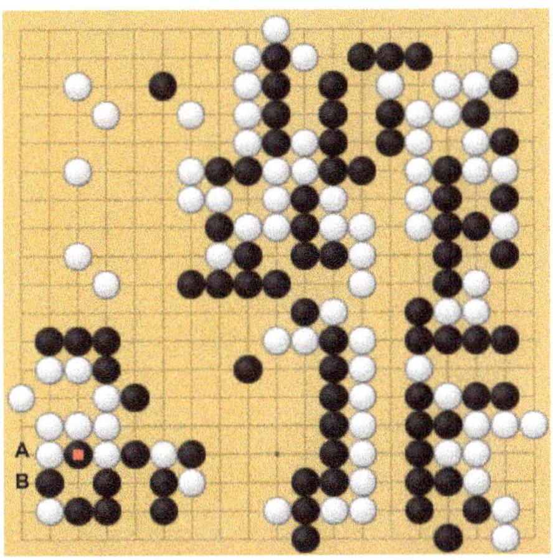

Figure 2. A "mistake" made by AlphaGo. This is game 1 between AlphaGo and Lee Sedol. After Lee Sedol played move 161 (marked by the red square), AlphaGo answered with move A, which is a "clear" mistake from a human perspective. Move B is obviously a better move than A.

The success of existing Go AI systems [2,3,5] lies in their use of self-play, where they play against themselves to maximize their win rate. This approach, however, leads to AI-generated moves that may not resemble human-like strategies, making them less suitable as a training tool. If players cannot understand the reasoning behind AI-generated moves, they are unlikely to replicate such strategies in human-versus-human competitions. Therefore, our study aims to develop a model capable of both formulating professional-level strategies and emulating human gameplay. This would allow Go players to engage with the AI as if they were playing against professional human opponents. Additionally, our model can serve as a post-game analysis tool to help players identify and correct mistakes made during the game.

While CNNs have delivered remarkable results in Go, they also exhibit notable limitations. Certain Go patterns, such as ladders and group life-and-death scenarios, involve long-range dependencies that require CNNs to be exceptionally deep. This increases network complexity and introduces challenges such as gradient vanishing or explosion.

Recent advances in Vision Transformers (ViTs) [6] suggest that Transformers can effectively handle computer vision tasks, often outperforming CNNs across multiple domains. The multi-head self-attention mechanism in ViTs is particularly adept at capturing long-range dependencies, making it well suited for addressing challenges in Go-related tasks.

In this study, we trained a ViT model on a dataset of game records from human experts. Our model achieved a top-one accuracy of 51.49% and a top-five accuracy of 83.12% using a simple feature set, surpassing a CNN-based model's top-one accuracy of 50.45%. In addition to conventional top-k accuracy metrics, we adopted extended top-k accuracy to account for equivalent moves—logically identical moves with different coordinates—addressing a unique evaluation challenge in Go.

This study makes several key contributions to the field of AI-driven Go training and gameplay:

1. **Application of Vision Transformers (ViTs) in Go**: We introduce a ViT-based model that captures long-range dependencies in Go and predicts future moves, providing deeper insights into game progression and improving gameplay understanding.
2. **Bridging AI and Human Intuition**: Our model emulates human decision-making, providing a more intuitive training tool for Go players to engage with the AI as if playing against a professional.
3. **Improved Top-one Accuracy Compared to Existing Studies:** By utilizing the ViT model, we achieved higher top-one accuracy compared to previous studies, demonstrating the superior capability of ViT in Go move prediction.

The remainder of this article is structured as follows: Section 2 reviews related work on applying deep learning models to Go, with a focus on CNNs, and introduces the background of ViT. Section 3 describes the dataset and the features used as model inputs. Section 4 presents the experimental setup, comparing the performance of ViT with that of two CNN-based models from prior studies on imitating human moves. Section 5 concludes the study and outlines potential directions for future work.

2. Background and Related Work

2.1. Deep Learning and Go

Deep learning has been applied across various fields, including time-series data prediction [7], medicine [8,9], and games [2,10–14]. In the domain of board games, winning strategies typically involve two main steps: evaluating the position and identifying the best move. However, designing a hand-crafted evaluation function for complex games such as Go is particularly challenging. To address this, researchers have utilized convolutional neural networks (CNNs) to learn directly from expert gameplay, bypassing the need for manual evaluation function design.

In 2003, Van Der Werf et al. [10] used hand-crafted features and proposed feature extraction methods such as the Eigenspace Separation Transform, combined with dimensional reduction, to train a multi-layer perceptron (MLP). They achieved 25% accuracy on professional games. Subsequent studies saw advancements with the adoption of CNNs. In 2008, Sutskever and Nair [11] used CNNs to mimic Go experts, employing previous moves and the current position as input. They achieved 34% accuracy for a single CNN model and 39.9% for an ensemble of CNNs. In 2014, Clark and Storkey [12] employed a more sophisticated feature set containing edge encoding and Ko constraints to train an eight-layer CNN, achieving 41.1% and 44.4% accuracy on two different Go datasets. In

2015, Maddison et al. [13] used a large feature set incorporating 36 feature planes, including the rank of the player and ladder patterns. They also used a deeper 12-layer CNN and achieved 55% accuracy. The work of AlphaGo [2] included a supervised learning stage to train the policy network using Go expert data. Their model used a much larger dataset with 48 feature planes and a 12-layer CNN, reaching 55.4% accuracy on the test set. These results highlighted the feasibility of applying CNNs to imitate human expert moves.

However, in Section 1, we pointed out the limitations of CNNs and aimed to demonstrate that Vision Transformers (ViTs) could outperform CNNs, making them a better candidate for imitating Go experts. We compared the performance of ViTs and CNNs on a dataset collected from the KGS Go server [15]. The models used were based on the same architecture as the policy network from AlphaGo [2] and the 12-layer CNN from Clark and Storkey [12]. The results indicated that ViT could predict more expert moves correctly on the test set.

2.2. Vision Transformer (ViT)

In 2017, the Transformer architecture was introduced by Vaswani et al. [16] to address challenges in natural language processing. Building on the success of Transformers and the self-attention mechanism, Dosovitskiy et al. [6] presented the Vision Transformer (ViT) for computer vision (Figure 3). ViT processes input images by first splitting them into patches. These patches are flattened, linearly projected into embedding vectors, and combined with learnable positional embeddings to encode spatial information. An additional class embedding is included, and these embeddings serve as inputs for the Transformer blocks. The final output is passed to an MLP head, which produces the classification result. This figure is adapted from Figure 1 of [6].

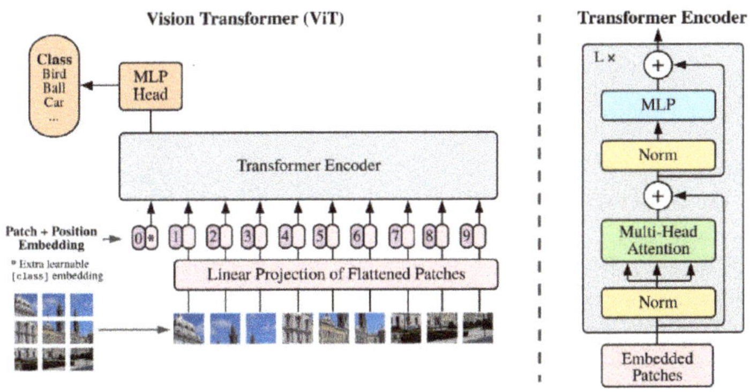

Figure 3. Model overview of the ViT.

The innovation of the ViT lies in its ability to effectively capture global context and long-range dependencies, outperforming CNNs that focus on local receptive fields. ViT treats image patches as tokens, akin to words in a sentence, enabling it to process the entire image simultaneously. After encoding spatial information through positional embeddings, ViT applies Transformer encoder blocks to perform self-attention operations on the patches. The MLP head at the last encoder block generates the final classification. A detailed explanation of the ViT architecture is provided in Section 3.

ViT has demonstrated state-of-the-art performance on multiple image classification benchmarks, often surpassing traditional CNNs. The success of ViT and its derivatives, such as the Swin Transformer [17], has inspired this study to explore the application of ViT in analyzing the game of Go.

The closest work to this study is that of Sagri et al. [18], in which EfficientFormer was used to play Go. However, their goal focused on maximizing the win rate rather than imitating human experts. Although their work applied Transformers to Go, the task itself differs from our approach. To the best of our knowledge, this is the first study to specifically focus on ViT in the context of Go with the goal of imitating human expert moves. We believe the results of this study can significantly contribute to the development of applications that mimic human Go experts, ultimately serving as valuable training tools.

3. Materials and Methods

3.1. Dataset

3.1.1. Dataset Formation

The dataset used in this study was collected from the KGS Go server, spanning from 2004 to 2019. To maintain a consistent level of gameplay quality, we excluded handicapped games and focused solely on matches involving players ranked between 4th dan and 9th dan. This decision was made to ensure that the model would learn from expert-level gameplay, as these ranks represent a high degree of skill and strategic depth, avoiding the potential noise or suboptimal moves that might arise from lower-ranked or handicapped games. The dataset provides a robust foundation for training a model aimed at imitating professional-level gameplay.

The dataset was divided into a training set and a holdout set, with the training set comprising 26,078,877 positions and the holdout set containing 1,376,321 positions. Each position captures a snapshot of the board at a specific point during a game, representing the arrangement of stones for both players. These positions serve as the input data for the model, enabling it to analyze and predict the next move based on the current board configuration.

One of the key properties of Go is its inherent symmetry. Due to the rules of the game, the information provided by each board position remains invariant under horizontal flips, vertical flips, and rotations. This characteristic, referred to as the symmetry property, allows significant data augmentation opportunities. In this study, we leveraged this property by applying all eight possible transformations to the board, including rotations of 90°, 180°, and 270°, as well as horizontal and vertical reflections, as shown in Figure 4. These transformations effectively expand the dataset while preserving the original strategic context of each position.

The labeling process for the dataset involved assigning a corresponding move to each board position. Specifically, the label for each position is the next move made by the human player in the game. This move is represented as a two-dimensional coordinate on the 19×19 Go board. To make the data compatible with the model, these coordinates are flattened into a one-hot vector of length 361, corresponding to all possible board positions (excluding the pass move). In this vector, the position where the move was played is marked with a value of 1, while all other positions are marked with 0. This one-hot encoding method provides a straightforward and efficient representation of the target variable, enabling the model to treat the task as a multi-class classification problem.

By focusing on expert-level gameplay and utilizing the symmetry property of Go, the dataset was designed to comprehensively reflect the strategic complexity and diversity of high-level matches. This approach ensures that the model is trained on data that closely mirror the patterns and decision-making processes of skilled human players.

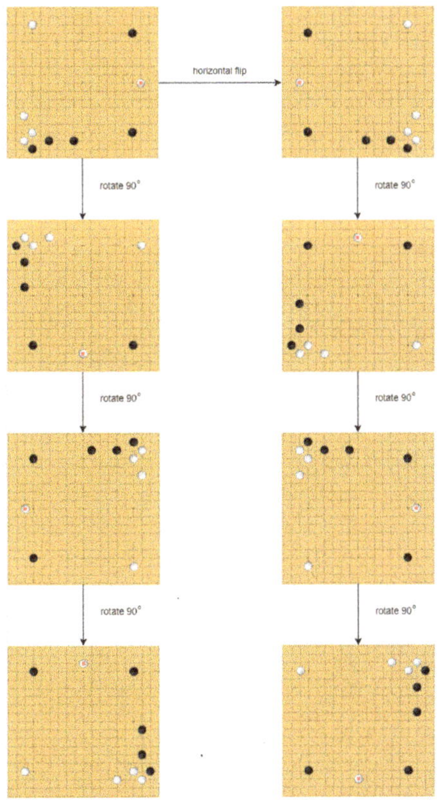

Figure 4. The symmetry property of Go. By the rules of Go, the eight positions in this figure are considered equivalent.

3.1.2. Feature Preprocessing

The feature set used for our model is extracted from raw board positions, as detailed in Table 1. These features are encoded using binary planes, where each plane corresponds to a specific aspect of the board configuration (e.g., black stones, white stones, liberties, etc.). This encoding process provides a comprehensive representation of the board state, enabling the model to learn meaningful patterns and strategies from the raw positions.

During both the training and inference phases, the features are initially stacked to form a tensor of shape $\mathbb{R}^{10\times19\times19}$, where 10 represents the number of feature planes and 19×19 corresponds to the dimensions of the Go board. To make the data compatible with the Vision Transformer (ViT), zero padding is then applied along the last two dimensions, resulting in an input tensor of shape $\mathbb{R}^{10\times21\times21}$. This padding step is essential because ViT requires the input to be divided into smaller patches, and the original board size of 19 does not evenly divide by the patch size, making it less ideal for the transformation process.

In the training phase, data augmentation techniques such as random flipping and rotation of the board positions are applied to further enhance the model's ability to generalize. By exploiting the inherent symmetry of Go positions, the model is exposed to a broader variety of board configurations, improving its robustness and helping it learn patterns that are invariant under these transformations. Additionally, during inference, the same symmetric property is leveraged to apply test-time augmentation, allowing the model to make more robust predictions by considering multiple transformed versions of the board.

Table 1. The features extracted from raw positions.

Feature	Shape	Description
Black	(1, 19, 19)	The positions of black stones are marked with 1. The rest are marked with 0.
White	(1, 19, 19)	The positions of white stones are marked with 1. The rest are marked with 0.
Invalid	(1, 19, 19)	The positions of invalid moves are marked with 1. The rest are marked with 0.
Turn	(1, 19, 19)	The entire plane is marked with 1 if it is black's turn to play or 0 if it is white's turn to play.
Ones	(1, 19, 19)	An entire plane is marked with 1.
Empty	(1, 19, 19)	The positions that are not occupied by a stone are marked with 1. The rest are marked with 0.
Recent moves	(4, 19, 19)	The features that store the most recent 4 moves. The ith plane of this feature stores the feature of the ith most recent move. The position of the move is marked with 1. The rest are marked with 0.

This approach not only helps in increasing the diversity of the training data but also ensures that the model is trained to recognize Go patterns that are consistent regardless of board orientation, leading to a more effective and generalizable model.

3.2. Vision Transformer for Go

In this work, we aim to demonstrate the capability of the Vision Transformer (ViT) to imitate the moves of human experts in the game of Go. This problem is formulated as a classification task, where each possible move on the board is treated as a distinct class. Given the 19×19 grid of the Go board, this results in a total of 361 possible classes, corresponding to all board positions, excluding the pass move. Each class represents a unique location on the board where a stone can be placed, and the model's goal is to predict the next move based on the current board configuration, mimicking the decisions made by expert players.

This section provides an overview of the key components involved in applying the Vision Transformer (ViT) to the task of imitating expert-level gameplay in Go. For a comprehensive theoretical background on the ViT, readers are encouraged to refer to [6,16]. Our methodology draws inspiration from [6], particularly for Equations (1) and (2), which outline the mathematical foundations of the ViT. These equations have been adapted to align with the specific requirements of our task, demonstrating how the ViT can be effectively applied to analyze board positions and predict the next move in Go.

An overview of our method is presented in Figure 5. In the ViT, the input features must be reshaped into a sequence of feature patches. The features from Table 1 have the shape $\mathbb{R}^{10\times19\times19}$, which cannot be reshaped directly because 19 is a prime number. Therefore, the features are first padded with zeros to form $\mathbb{R}^{10\times21\times21}$. We set the patch size to 7; accordingly, the features are broken down into 9 patches, each of shape 7×7. These patches are then flattened to form a sequence of 2D patches $p \in \mathbb{R}^{9\times(10\cdot7^2)}$. We use a learnable linear projection to project each patch into $\mathbb{R}^{768}$, resulting in projected patches $p_{proj} \in \mathbb{R}^{9\times768}$. After prepending an additional class token x_{class}, positional embeddings are added to incorporate spatial information, which is crucial for identifying long-range patterns on the board. The resulting tensor is used as input for the Transformer encoder, denoted by z_0. Formally, we define:

With the patch size set to 7, the padded features are divided into 9 patches, each of size 7×7. These patches are then flattened into a sequence of 2D patches represented as $p \in \mathbb{R}^{9\times(10\cdot7^2)}$. A learnable linear projection is applied to each patch, projecting the patches into a higher-dimensional space of $\mathbb{R}^{9\times 768}$. This step produces the projected patches $p_{proj} \in \mathbb{R}^{9\times 768}$, which are now suitable for processing by the ViT.

Before passing the patches into the Transformer encoder, an additional learnable class token x_{class} is prepended to the sequence. Positional embeddings are added to the sequence to encode spatial information, which is critical for recognizing long-range dependencies and patterns on the Go board. The resulting tensor, denoted as z_0, serves as the input to the Transformer encoder. Formally,

$$z_0 = [x_{class}; p_1L; p_2L \ldots; p_10L] + E_{pos},\ L \in \mathbb{R}^{(10\cdot 7^2)\times 768}, E_{pos} \in \mathbb{R}^{(10+1)\times 768} \quad (1)$$

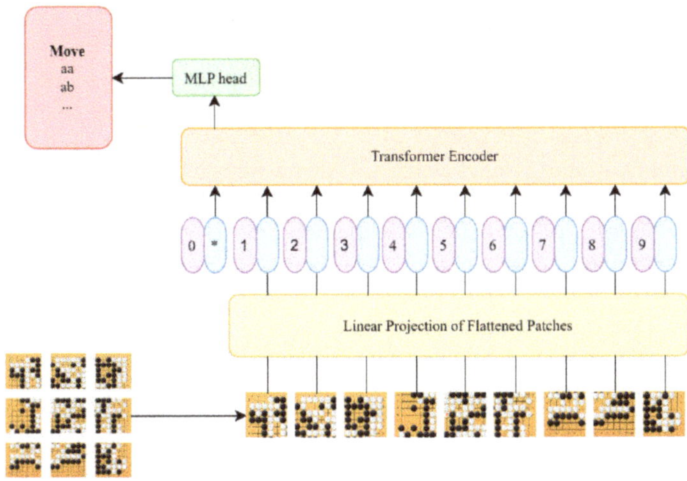

Figure 5. Vision Transformer for Go. It should be noted that the images of Go are for illustrative purposes. The actual data are the features from Table 1. The illustration of the figure was inspired by [6].

This formulation ensures that the input data are structured in a way that fully utilizes the ViT's capability to model the complex spatial and strategic relationships inherent in Go gameplay.

The Transformer encoder blocks used in our study are illustrated in Figure 3. To evaluate the impact of model depth on performance, we experimented with three different configurations of Vision Transformer (ViT) by varying the number of encoder blocks: 4, 8, and 12 blocks. Each encoder block comprises two key components: a multi-head attention (MA) module and a multi-layer perceptron (MLP) module. These components work together to model both local and global dependencies within the input data, enabling the network to capture the complex patterns inherent in Go gameplay.

The operations within each encoder block are described mathematically as follows:

1. **Multi-head Attention Module**:

The output of the multi-head attention module is computed as follows:

$$z'_l = MSA(LN(z_{l-1})) + z_{l-1},\ l = 1 \ldots L \quad (2)$$

Here, z_{l-1} is the input to the l-th encoder block, LN denotes layer normalization, and MSA represents the multi-head self-attention mechanism. The residual connection ($+z_{l-1}$) ensures stability during training by mitigating issues such as vanishing gradients.

2. **Multi-layer Perceptron Module**:

The output of the MLP module is calculated as follows:

$$z_l = MLP(LN(z'_l)) + z'_l,\ l = 1 \ldots L \tag{3}$$

where z'_l is the intermediate representation from the MA module, and the residual connection ($+z'_l$) further enhances training stability.

In this study, L is set to 4, 8, and 12 to compare the performance of Vision Transformer (ViT) models with varying depths. By experimenting with these different configurations, we aim to evaluate the trade-offs between model complexity and predictive accuracy in the task of mimicking expert-level Go gameplay.

After processing the input through all L encoder blocks, the output from the first embedding (corresponding to the class token) of the last encoder block undergoes layer normalization. This normalized representation serves as the basis for generating the final score for each possible move on the Go board.

These scores are then converted into a probability distribution over all potential moves using the softmax function. The softmax operation ensures that the scores are transformed into a normalized probability distribution, where the probabilities of all possible moves sum to 1. Mathematically, the softmax function is defined as follows:

$$softmax(z)_i = \frac{e^{z_j}}{\sum_{j=1}^{n} e^{z_j}} \tag{4}$$

where $z = [z_1, z_2, \ldots, z_n]$ represents the input logits, and $softmax(z)_i$ is the probability assigned to the i-th class (or move). Here, n corresponds to the total number of classes, which, in the context of a 19 × 19 Go board, is 361 (excluding the pass move).

This final probability distribution indicates the model's confidence for each possible move and is used to select the next move during inference, thereby enabling the model to imitate the decision-making process of expert Go players.

4. Experiments and Results

4.1. Experimental Settings

4.1.1. Training Settings for ViT

The model was trained on the training set for 80 epochs, and the results were evaluated on the holdout set after training. Each minibatch consisted of the trajectory of an entire game, where each data point represented a pair: a board position and the corresponding next move made by a human expert. Data points where the move was "pass" were discarded. Features extracted from the board position served as the input, while the move played was used as the ground truth label.

The Adam optimizer was employed for optimization, with an initial learning rate of 0.0001. Cross-entropy loss was used as the loss function. Different layers of the Vision Transformer (ViT) were trained, with each model requiring approximately 10 to 14 days to train on a single NVIDIA RTX 4070 GPU with 12 GB of memory.

4.1.2. Training Settings for CNNs

We also evaluated two additional models to compare the performance of the ViT with that of CNN-based architectures, using identical training and holdout sets. The comparison models included the policy network architecture from AlphaGo (Figure 6) and a 12-layer CNN adapted from [12] (Figure 7).

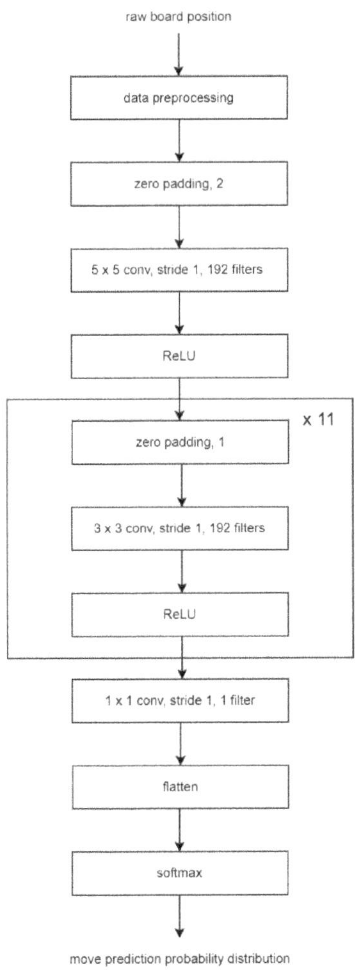

Figure 6. The policy network's architecture processes the raw board position through feature extraction, using the features specified in Table 1.

The **policy network** begins by padding input features with zeros to form a tensor of size $\mathbb{R}^{10\times23\times23}$ This tensor is processed through a sequence of convolutional layers, each followed by rectified linear unit (ReLU) activations. A final 1×1 convolutional layer, combined with flattening operations, converts the tensor into a vector of size $\mathbb{R}^{361}$. A softmax operation then derives the probability distribution of potential moves.

The **12-layer CNN** processes preprocessed input data structured as a tensor of size $\mathbb{R}^{10\times19\times19}$. A sequence of convolutional layers with ReLU activations is applied, and zero padding ensures that the tensor size remains $\mathbb{R}^{10\times19\times19}$. The final 1×1 convolutional layer outputs two $\mathbb{R}^{19\times19}$ tensors. Each tensor is flattened, and softmax operations are applied to produce the probability distributions for black and white moves, respectively.

In this study, these models are referred to as the "policy network" and the "12-layer CNN", and their performance is compared to that of the ViT.

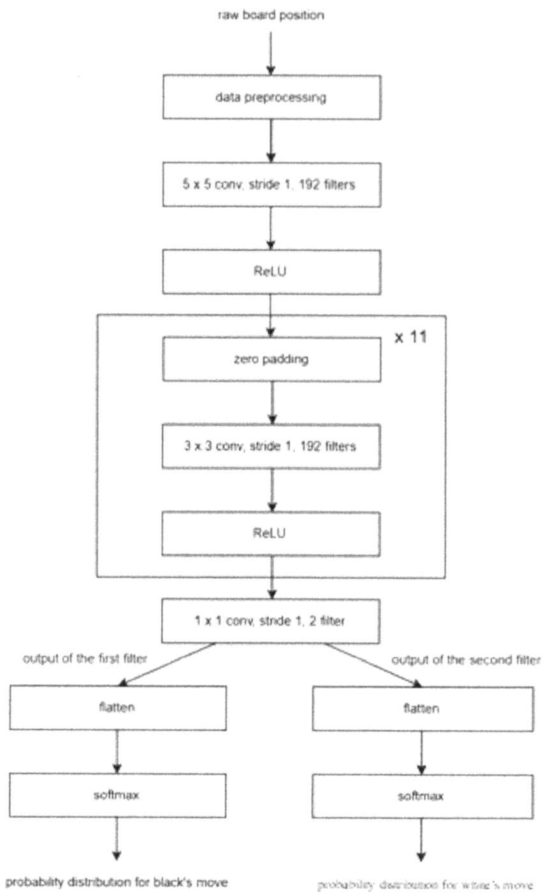

Figure 7. The 12-layer CNN for move prediction preprocesses the inputs by extracting the features listed in Table 1.

The two models share a similar CNN backbone structure, but their output layers are tailored to different objectives. The policy network employs a single output block that consolidates all information into a unified prediction. In contrast, the 12-layer CNN utilizes two separate output blocks, enabling it to handle game dynamics uniquely for each player. This distinction is significant, as it allows the 12-layer CNN to make more nuanced predictions by better capturing the complexities of player-specific strategies.

A significant architectural difference between the models lies in their input layers. The policy network uses the same comprehensive feature set as the ViT model, encom-passing various aspects of the game state, such as the current board configuration, previ-ous moves, and additional relevant features. In contrast, the 12-layer CNN excludes the "turn" feature from its input set, as detailed in Table 1 This exclusion required adjustments to the input layer to ensure the model could still effectively process the board state.

Both CNN-based models underwent the same rigorous training process. They were trained for 80 epochs, providing ample time for the models to learn from the training data. Stochastic Gradient Descent (SGD) was used as the optimization algorithm, with an initial learning rate of 0.003 that decayed by 50% every 16 epochs. Cross-entropy loss was employed as the loss function. Notably, the 12-layer CNN only updated parameters related to its output layer during training.

By comparing the performance of these two CNN-based models with the ViT approach, we aimed to gain deeper insights into how different deep learning architectures perform in the task of imitating human Go players. This comparative analysis is essential for identifying the model best suited for use as a training or analysis tool for Go players, ultimately contributing to their skill enhancement and understanding of the game.

4.1.3. Test-Time Augmentation

Test-time augmentation (TTA) is a technique employed to enhance the robustness and accuracy of model predictions during inference by generating multiple augmented samples from the test data. This approach mitigates the impact of individual transformations, providing a more reliable and consistent prediction. Go, with its symmetric board properties, is particularly well suited for TTA, as the board can be rotated and reflected in various ways without altering the fundamental nature of the game (Figure 8).

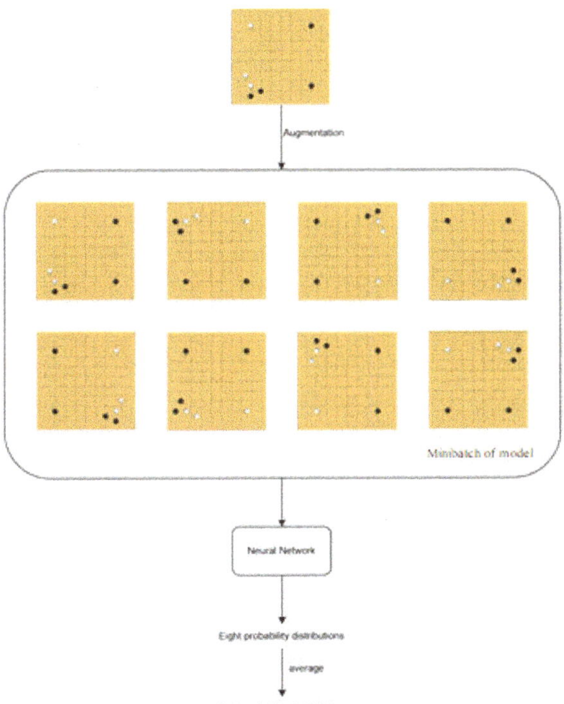

Figure 8. The process of test-time augmentation.

At inference time, each board position is augmented using its symmetric properties, generating eight symmetries through rotations and reflections. These symmetries are treated as a minibatch of inputs for the model. For each augmented position, the model computes a probability distribution by applying the softmax operation to its predictions. The resulting eight probability distributions are averaged to produce the final move probability distribution.

By leveraging TTA, the model's predictions become more stable and reliable, as they incorporate the game board's inherent symmetries. This process ensures that the model evaluates all symmetrical configurations, ultimately improving its predictive accuracy and robustness.

4.2. Performance Evaluation for Imitating Human Moves

4.2.1. Top-k Accuracy

To evaluate how well a model can imitate human players, we report both top-one and top-five accuracy. For a given board position, a prediction is considered correct for top-one accuracy if the model's highest-ranked move matches the human expert's move. For top-five accuracy, it is considered correct if the human expert's move is among the model's top five predicted moves. Formally, the top-k accuracy is defined as follows:

$$\text{Top-kAcc.} = \frac{1}{N}\sum_{i=1}^{N} I(y_i \in \text{Top-k}(\hat{x}_i)) \tag{5}$$

where the variables have the following meanings:

- N is the total number of instances in the dataset;
- y_i is the true label (human expert's move) for the i-th instance;
- $\hat{x}_i$ represents the predicted scores or probabilities for the i-th input;
- Top-k$(\hat{x}_i)$ is the set of k labels with the highest predicted scores or probabilities for the i-th instance;
- $I(\cdot)$ is the indicator function, returning 1 if the condition inside is true and 0 otherwise.

The results are summarized in Table 2, and test-time augmentation (TTA) leveraging the symmetric properties of Go was applied during evaluation. TTA is particularly effective for Go due to the game's symmetry, allowing the model to evaluate augmented versions of each position without additional training. This method significantly improved performance with no extra computational cost during training.

Table 2. The performance of ViT and CNNs is compared. We denote ViT with different layers as ViT/L = k, where k is the number of encoder blocks in the ViT.

Model	Symmetries	Top-1 Acc.	Top-5 Acc.
12-layer CNN	1	0.4911	0.8250
12-layer CNN	8	0.4921	0.8259
Policy network	1	0.4924	0.8134
Policy network	8	0.5045	0.8209
Vit/L = 4	1	0.4513	0.7674
Vit/L = 4	8	0.4726	0.7973
Vit/L = 8	1	0.4860	0.8031
Vit/L = 8	8	0.5050	0.8214
Vit/L = 12	1	0.4973	0.8154
Vit/L = 12	8	**0.5149**	**0.8312**

Our evaluation shows that ViT models, even with eight encoder blocks, outperform both CNN-based models in top-one and top-five accuracy after incorporating TTA. The best-performing model, ViT/L-12, achieved a top-one accuracy of 51.49%.

However, due to the computational cost, we limited our testing of ViT models to a maximum of 12 layers. As shown in Table 2, the results suggest that increasing the number of encoder blocks could further improve accuracy, indicating potential for even better performance with deeper models.

We compare our results with existing Go move prediction studies [19,20]. In [19], three different models were used: the Incep–Attention model, the Up–Down model, and an ensemble of the two models. Their top-one accuracy scores were 0.4074, 0.4420, and 0.4686, respectively. In [20], a mobile network was tested for Go move prediction, achieving a top-one accuracy of 0.4431. Compared to these studies, our approach demonstrates superior performance in top-one accuracy. However, it is worth noting that ViT, while achieving higher accuracy, has a larger number of parameters, potentially leading to higher computational requirements and an increased system load.

4.2.2. Extended Top-k Accuracy

In most studies, such as [2,12], only top-one accuracy is reported as a measure of a model's ability to mimic human experts. However, we argue that relying solely on top-*k* accuracy is insufficient for evaluating model performance, particularly in the context of Go.

In the opening stage of a Go game, there are often multiple logically equivalent moves according to the rules of the game. However, the ground truth typically contains only one of these moves. For instance, as illustrated in Figure 9, moves A and B are equivalent in terms of their impact on the game. If the ground truth labels move A as correct and the model predicts move B, it would be unjust to consider the prediction a failure, since both moves achieve the same strategic outcome.

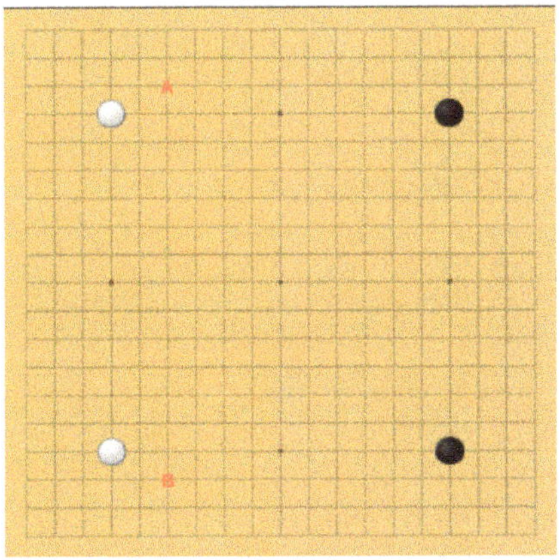

Figure 9. Black to play. Moves A and B are considered equivalent according to the rules.

An even more striking example is depicted in Figure 10, where eight moves are all logically equivalent. In this scenario, the model has only a one-eighth chance of being marked correct by top-one accuracy, despite all eight moves being equally valid. This limitation highlights the need for more nuanced evaluation metrics or alternative approaches that account for the equivalence of moves in certain game scenarios.

More formally, the extended top-k accuracy can be expressed by

$$\text{Extended Top-kAcc.} = \frac{1}{N}\sum_{i=1}^{N} II(y_i \in \bigcup_{y' \in Equiv(y_i)} \text{Top-k}(\hat{y}_i, y')) \tag{6}$$

where the variables have the following meanings:

- N is the total number of instances in the dataset;
- y_i is the true label for the i-th instance;
- y_i represents the predicted scores or probabilities for the i-th input;
- Top-k$(\hat{y}_i, y')$ represents the set of k labels with the highest predicted scores or probabilities for the i-th instance, considering label y';
- $Equiv(y_i)$ is the set of labels considered quivalent to the true label y_i;
- $II(\cdot)$ is the indicator function, which returns 1 if the condition inside is true and 0 otherwise.

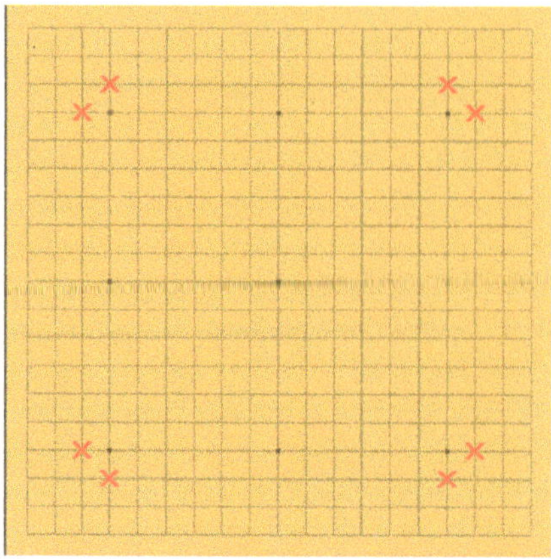

Figure 10. Black to play. All positions marked with an X are considered equivalent according to the rules.

The results regarding extended top-k accuracy are listed in Table 3. Performance evaluations based on top-k accuracy and extended top-k accuracy both showed that the ViT with eight encoder layers was sufficient for the task.

Table 3. The extended top-k accuracy of the ViT and CNNs is compared.

Model	Symmetries	Ext. Top-1 Acc.	Ext. Top-5 Acc.
12-layer CNN	1	0.4943	0.8274
12-layer CNN	8	0.4962	0.8272
Policy network	1	0.4930	0.8144
Policy network	8	0.5091	0.8237
Vit/L = 4	1	0.4533	0.7704
Vit/L = 4	8	0.4751	0.7993
Vit/L = 8	1	0.4892	0.8063
Vit/L = 8	8	0.5106	0.8278
Vit/L = 12	1	0.5013	0.8259
Vit/L = 12	8	**0.5187**	**0.8349**

4.2.3. Inference Time Analysis on Different Devices

In this section, we will discuss the model's inference time during the inference phase.

When learning to play Go, users may not always have access to high-performance computers. Many players might rely on lightweight devices to predict the next move. To evaluate the model's feasibility across different systems, we tested it on three devices: the GTX 1650, the RTX 3090, and the RTX 4090.

The results are illustrated in Figure 11, using a test dataset containing 1,376,321 positions. The total inference times were 280.23 s for the RTX 4090, 354.90 s for the RTX 3090, and 1523.62 s for the GTX 1650. These times correspond to an average inference time per position of 0.00021 s, 0.00026 s, and 0.0012 s, respectively.

These findings indicate that the model is computationally efficient and can be utilized effectively on lightweight devices equipped with a GPU.

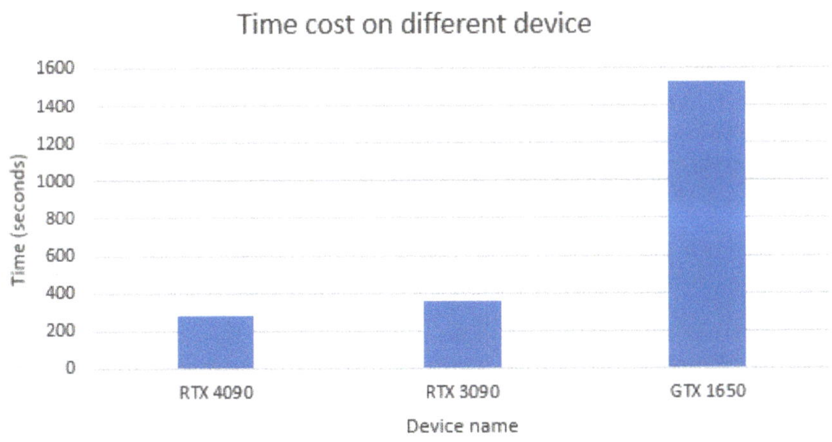

Figure 11. Time cost in different device.

5. Conclusions and Future Work

5.1. Conclusions

Building a model that achieves professional-level gameplay and also plays like humans is highly desirable in the Go community. In this study, we showcased the capability of the Vision Transformer (ViT) in this field. The ViT achieved 49.73% top-one accuracy without exploiting the symmetry property of the dataset from the KGS Go server and 51.49% top-one accuracy when exploiting the symmetry property using 12 encoder layers. These results demonstrate that the ViT can mimic expert moves better than CNN-based models.

We also proposed the extended top-k accuracy for evaluating model performance. To the best of our knowledge, all other research on imitating human Go players ignores the issue brought by the symmetric property and equivalent moves. The extended top-k accuracy was designed to address this problem, and we believe it can better evaluate the capability of models in imitating human experts. ViT achieved 50.13% extended top-one accuracy without test-time augmentation and 51.87% extended top-one accuracy with test-time augmentation using 12 encoder layers.

5.2. Future Work

During our experiments, as shown in Tables 2 and 3, we observed that adding more layers to the model provided room for improvement. Beyond this, exploring advanced Transformer-based architectures offers promising opportunities to enhance Go AI. For instance, the Swin Transformer, which has outperformed the ViT in computer vision tasks, could serve as a robust candidate for imitating human Go players. Its ability to capture long-range dependencies in game patterns suggests that it could potentially replace the backbone of win-oriented models such as AlphaGo, improving their ability to replicate human expertise more effectively.

In addition to the Swin Transformer, other Transformer-based models, such as the Data-efficient Image Transformer (DeiT) and Pyramid Vision Transformer (PVT), could also be integrated into Go AI frameworks to address specific challenges. The DeiT, with its knowledge distillation capabilities, is well suited for enhancing data efficiency and addressing data leakage issues, making it an ideal tool for mimicking rare playing styles and diversifying gameplay. Meanwhile, PVT, with its multi-scale feature extraction and Spatial Reduction Attention (SRA), excels in dense prediction tasks, making it a strong candidate for downstream applications requiring high-resolution processing, such as detailed Go strategy analysis.

By leveraging the unique strengths of these Transformer architectures, future research could optimize Go AI models for both high performance and human-like gameplay. This approach has the potential to revolutionize Go AI, providing more advanced tools for teaching, analyzing, and diversifying Go strategies.

Furthermore, our objective is to imitate the movements of professional Go players, using historical game data from a Go server as our dataset. In future research, we plan to utilize our predictive models to compete against professional Go players, further validating their effectiveness and refining their capabilities.

Author Contributions: Conceptualization, Y.-H.H., C.-C.K. and S.-M.Y.; methodology, Y.-H.H., C.-C.K. and S.-M.Y.; software, Y.-H.H. and C.-C.K.; validation, Y.-H.H., C.-C.K. and S.-M.Y.; formal analysis, Y.-H.H., C.-C.K. and S.-M.Y.; investigation, Y.-H.H., C.-C.K. and S.-M.Y.; resources, Y.-H.H., C.-C.K. and S.-M.Y.; data curation, Y.-H.H., C.-C.K. and S.-M.Y.; writing—original draft preparation, C.-C.K.; writing—review and editing, Y.-H.H.; visualization, C.-C.K.; supervision, S.-M.Y.; project administration, S.-M.Y. All authors have read and agreed to the published version of the manuscript.

Funding: This research received no funding.

Data Availability Statement: The dataset used in this paper is sourced from the KGS Go server, covering the period from 2004 to 2019. https://u-go.net/gamerecords/ (accessed on 25 February 2024). The code for our model has been uploaded to GitHub. Please refer to the following link: https://github.com/nctu-dcs-lab/ViT-Go (accessed on 25 February 2024).

Conflicts of Interest: The authors declare no conflicts of interest.

References

1. LeCun, Y.; Bottou, L.; Bengio, Y.; Haffner, P. Gradient-based learning applied to document recognition. *Proc. IEEE* **1998**, *86*, 2278–2324. [CrossRef]
2. Silver, D.; Huang, A.; Maddison, C.J.; Guez, A.; Sifre, L.; Van Den Driessche, G.; Schrittwieser, J.; Antonoglou, I.; Panneershelvam, V.; Lanctot, M.; et al. Mastering the game of Go with deep neural networks and tree search. *Nature* **2016**, *529*, 484–489. [CrossRef] [PubMed]
3. Silver, D.; Schrittwieser, J.; Simonyan, K.; Antonoglou, I.; Huang, A.; Guez, A.; Hubert, T.; Baker, L.; Lai, M.; Bolton, A.; et al. Mastering the game of go without human knowledge. *Nature* **2017**, *550*, 354–359. [CrossRef] [PubMed]
4. AlphaGo—The Movie | Full Award-Winning Documentary. Available online: https://www.youtube.com/watch?v=WXuK6gekU1Y (accessed on 1 July 2024).
5. Patankar, S.; Usakoyal, C.; Patil, P.; Raut, K. A Survey of Deep Reinforcement Learning in Game Playing. In Proceedings of the 2024 MIT Art, Design and Technology School of Computing International Conference (MITADTSoCiCon), Pune, India, 25–27 April 2024; IEEE: Piscataway, NJ, USA, 2024; pp. 1–5.
6. Dosovitskiy, A.; Beyer, L.; Kolesnikov, A.; Weissenborn, D.; Zhai, X.; Unterthiner, T.; Dehghani, M.; Minderer, M.; Heigold, G.; Gelly, S. An image is worth 16x16 words: Transformers for image recognition at scale. *arXiv* **2020**, arXiv:2010.11929.
7. Pellegrino, M.; Lombardo, G.; Adosoglou, G.; Cagnoni, S.; Pardalos, P.M.; Poggi, A. A Multi-Head LSTM Architecture for Bankruptcy Prediction with Time Series Accounting Data. *Future Internet* **2024**, *16*, 79. [CrossRef]
8. Saleh, S.N.; Elagamy, M.N.; Saleh, Y.N.; Osman, R.A. An Explainable Deep Learning-Enhanced IoMT Model for Effective Monitoring and Reduction of Maternal Mortality Risks. *Future Internet* **2024**, *16*, 411. [CrossRef]
9. Chen, S.-W.; Chen, J.-K.; Hsieh, Y.-H.; Chen, W.-H.; Liao, Y.-H.; Lin, Y.-C.; Chen, M.-C.; Tsai, C.-T.; Chai, J.-W.; Yuan, S.-M. Improving Patient Safety in the X-Ray Inspection Process with EfficientNet-Based Medical Assistance System. *Healthcare* **2023**, *11*, 2068. [CrossRef] [PubMed]
10. Van Der Werf, E.; Uiterwijk, J.W.; Postma, E.; Van Den Herik, J. Local move prediction in Go. In Proceedings of the Computers and Games: Third International Conference, CG 2002, Edmonton, AB, Canada, 25–27 July 2002; Revised Papers 3; Springer: Berlin, Germany, 2003; pp. 393–412.
11. Sutskever, I.; Nair, V. Mimicking go experts with convolutional neural networks. In Proceedings of the Artificial Neural Networks-ICANN 2008: 18th International Conference, Prague, Czech Republic, 3–6 September 2008; Proceedings, Part II 18; Springer: Berlin, Germany, 2008; pp. 101–110.
12. Clark, C.; Storkey, A. Teaching deep convolutional neural networks to play go. *arXiv* **2014**, arXiv:1412.3409.

13. Maddison, C.J.; Huang, A.; Sutskever, I.; Silver, D. Move evaluation in Go using deep convolutional neural networks. *arXiv* **2014**, arXiv:1412.6564.
14. Vinyals, O.; Babuschkin, I.; Czarnecki, W.M.; Mathieu, M.; Dudzik, A.; Chung, J.; Choi, D.H.; Powell, R.; Ewalds, T.; Georgiev, P.; et al. Grandmaster level in StarCraft II using multi-agent reinforcement learning. *Nature* **2019**, *575*, 350–354. [CrossRef] [PubMed]
15. KGS. KGS GO Server. Available online: https://u-go.net/gamerecords/ (accessed on 25 February 2024).
16. Vaswani, A.; Shazeer, N.; Parmar, N.; Uszkoreit, J.; Jones, L.; Gomez, A.N.; Kaiser, Ł.; Polosukhin, I. Attention is all you need. *arXiv* **2017**, arXiv:1706.03762.
17. Liu, Z.; Lin, Y.; Cao, Y.; Hu, H.; Wei, Y.; Zhang, Z.; Lin, S.; Guo, B. Swin transformer: Hierarchical vision transformer using shifted windows. In Proceedings of the IEEE/CVF International Conference on Computer Vision, Montreal, QC, Canada, 10–17 October 2021; pp. 10012–10022.
18. Sagri, A.; Cazenave, T.; Arjonilla, J.; Saffidine, A. Vision Transformers for Computer Go. In Proceedings of the International Conference on the Applications of Evolutionary Computation (Part of EvoStar), Aberystwyth, UK, 3–5 March 2024; Springer: Berlin, Germany, 2024; pp. 376–388.
19. Lin, Y.-C.; Huang, Y.-C. Streamlined Deep Learning Models for Move Prediction in Go-Game. *Electronics* **2024**, *13*, 3093. [CrossRef]
20. Cazenave, T. Mobile networks for computer Go. *IEEE Trans. Games* **2020**, *14*, 76–84. [CrossRef]

algorithms

MDPI

Article

Machine Learning for Decision Support and Automation in Games: A Study on Vehicle Optimal Path

Gonçalo Penelas [1], Luís Barbosa [1,2], Arsénio Reis [1,2], João Barroso [1,2] and Tiago Pinto [1,2,*]

[1] School of Science and Technology, University of Trás-os-Montes and Alto Douro, 5000-801 Vila Real, Portugal; al68536@alunos.utad.pt (G.P.); lfb@utad.pt (L.B.); ars@utad.pt (A.R.); jbarroso@utad.pt (J.B.)
[2] INESC-TEC UTAD Pole, 5000-801 Vila Real, Portugal
* Correspondence: tiagopinto@utad.pt

Abstract: In the field of gaming artificial intelligence, selecting the appropriate machine learning approach is essential for improving decision-making and automation. This paper examines the effectiveness of deep reinforcement learning (DRL) within interactive gaming environments, focusing on complex decision-making tasks. Utilizing the Unity engine, we conducted experiments to evaluate DRL methodologies in simulating realistic and adaptive agent behavior. A vehicle driving game is implemented, in which the goal is to reach a certain target within a small number of steps, while respecting the boundaries of the roads. Our study compares Proximal Policy Optimization (PPO) and Soft Actor–Critic (SAC) in terms of learning efficiency, decision-making accuracy, and adaptability. The results demonstrate that PPO successfully learns to reach the target, achieving higher and more stable cumulative rewards. Conversely, SAC struggles to reach the target, displaying significant variability and lower performance. These findings highlight the effectiveness of PPO in this context and indicate the need for further development, adaptation, and tuning of SAC. This research contributes to developing innovative approaches in how ML can improve how player agents adapt and react to their environments, thereby enhancing realism and dynamics in gaming experiences. Additionally, this work emphasizes the utility of using games to evolve such models, preparing them for real-world applications, namely in the field of vehicles' autonomous driving and optimal route calculation.

Keywords: artifical intelligence; machine learning; reinforcement learning; deep learning; deep reinforcement learning; Unity engine; ML-Agents Toolkit

1. Introduction

In the dynamic and rapidly evolving field of gaming artificial intelligence (AI), developing sophisticated autonomous agents has become a central goal, particularly in complex and interactive environments [1]. One of the most promising approaches to achieving advanced decision-making and automation in games involves deep reinforcement learning (DRL), a technique that merges the depth of deep learning (DL) with the goal-oriented capabilities of Reinforcement Learning (RL). These two conventional approaches are combined to overcome the limitations of RL in complex environments with large state spaces [2].

DRL-based algorithms deliver outstanding performance; however, the frequent need for evaluation significantly contributes to computational overload, resulting in notable decision delays and a decline in overall system performance [3]. The use of DRL in simulating autonomous driving within a game setting offers a unique opportunity to test and refine AI methodologies in an environment that mimics real-world dynamics. However, unlike standard toy problems often used in experimentation, the environment addressed in this paper simulates a real-world scenario with greater complexity and computational demands. This increased complexity enables a more rigorous evaluation of reinforcement learning algorithms like Proximal Policy Optimization (PPO) and Soft Actor–Critic (SAC), pushing them closer to real-world application limits. Through this, we aim to demonstrate whether these models are capable of addressing real-world problems or remain constrained to controlled research environments.

Unlike many recent studies, which focus primarily on theoretical DRL techniques and sensor integration [4], or explore different system architectures for autonomous driving [5], this work diverges by offering a simulation environment that closely approximates real-world conditions. While approaches like Model-Based Imitation Learning for Urban Driving (MILE) [6] represent steps toward reality, they utilize different methods and goals. Similarly, other works, such as the Performance Analysis of Deep Neural Network Controllers for Autonomous Driving using Nonlinear Model Predictive Control [7], focus on specific control strategies. In some cases, DRL has also been applied to trajectory planning problems, such as in the DRL-QiER framework, which combines DRL with quantum-inspired experience replay to optimize UAV mobility while minimizing communication outages [8]. Unlike DRL-QiER, which addresses UAV-specific challenges like airspace boundaries and wireless connectivity, this research focuses on terrestrial navigation with unique constraints, such as realistic motorcycle physics and complex terrain-based obstacles. In contrast, this research takes a more holistic approach by testing DRL techniques in a gaming environment that mirrors real-world driving dynamics. This allows for the evaluation of both decision-making efficiency and adaptability in a more realistic setting.

Although a significant design challenge for these scenarios is the transfer of learning, as the experience of playing a game differs greatly from driving a vehicle [9], this controlled setting allows for rapid experimentation and iteration, which is essential for advancing AI technologies and transferring learned lessons into real-world situations [10]. This study undertakes a comprehensive examination of DRL techniques to evaluate their effectiveness in improving the learning efficiency, decision-making accuracy, and adaptability of autonomous car agents in dynamic and potentially unpredictable gaming scenarios.

While DRL offers significant advantages to these scenarios, challenges remain in effectively learning from sparse, high-dimensional sensory inputs and ensuring safety and robustness in real-world driving scenarios. To address these challenges, increasing model complexity aims to enhance adaptability to intricate situations and improve generalization capacity. However, this approach also demands substantial volumes of high-quality training data, thereby increasing the complexity of the learning process and presenting additional hurdles in achieving efficient and effective training [11].

As the project progresses, we are introducing increasingly realistic and complex dynamics into the simulation environment. Currently, we are incorporating a detailed map based on the real-world geography of Vila Real, Portugal, which adds specificity and complexity to the terrain. Additionally, the simulation now features a motorcycle with more complex physics, requiring advanced handling of speed, balance, and motion. Obstacles such as terrain features and environmental challenges are being used as key constraints, pushing the DRL models to adapt to real-world driving conditions. This evolving complexity reflects the challenges faced in autonomous vehicle scenarios and drives further refinement of the models' scalability and adaptability in handling intricate environments. Moreover, through an extensive review of related work, which we summarize in Table 1, we did not find any projects that implemented DRL techniques within such a complex and realistic scenario. The combination of a detailed geographic map, realistic motorcycle physics, and the introduction of environmental obstacles sets this project apart, offering a unique challenge and opportunity for testing and advancing the capabilities of DRL models in real-world applications. A preview of the new environment, including the detailed map and enhanced physics features, is already being developed and will be provided later in this article to illustrate the complexity and realism achieved.

Table 1. Summary of Related Work.

Reference	Authors	Problem Addressed	Solving Method
[4]	Elallid et al. (2022)	Application of DRL techniques in autonomous driving, focusing on motion planning, decision-making, and vehicle control.	Integration of DRL with sensor technologies to enhance autonomous vehicle systems.
[5]	Bachute and Subhedar (2021)	Overview of autonomous driving system architectures and their components.	System-level architectural approaches, analyzing machine learning and deep learning algorithms.
[6]	Hu et al. (2022)	Urban driving tasks requiring imitation learning to navigate complex environments.	Implementation of Model-Based Imitation Learning (MILE) to improve urban driving scenarios.
[7]	Lee and Kang (2021)	Challenges in autonomous driving control strategies due to high computational demand.	Development of a data-driven deep neural network based on Nonlinear Model Predictive Control (NMPC).
[8]	Li and Aghvami (2022)	UAV trajectory planning under constraints like mobility and communication efficiency.	Use of DRL with Quantum-Inspired Experience Replay (DRL-QiER) for improved trajectory planning.

This work contributes to the existing body of research by providing insights and practical applications that can enhance real-world autonomous vehicle technology, offering a safe and cost-effective platform for testing complex AI-driven navigation strategies. By focusing on a vehicle navigating towards a target, this research not only enhances our understanding of how DRL can be applied to specific tasks in gaming but also contributes to the broader field of AI by demonstrating the potential of these techniques to develop agents that can learn and adapt in real-time. The findings indicate that DRL significantly improves the autonomy and realism of the vehicle's behavior, showcasing enhanced learning capabilities and more refined interaction dynamics within complex gaming environments. By exploring the application of DRL within the Unity engine to enhance the navigational abilities of a virtual vehicle, this work focuses on improving autonomous navigation to enable the vehicle to reach targets efficiently and adaptively. Subsequently, these findings can be applied and transposed to real application scenarios, such as the support of route and driving behavior definition for the electric motorbikes developed in the scope of the A-MoVeR project (see Funding and Acknowledgments sections).

Ultimately, this research aims to advance the development of innovative machine learning (ML) and AI approaches, potentially revolutionizing how autonomous systems adapt to and interact with their environment and other entities. This work also highlights the importance of using games as a means to develop and test AI models, preparing them for real-world applications and leading to more realistic and dynamic experiences in both gaming and practical scenarios.

This paper is structured in the following way. After this introduction, Section 2 provides an overview of the ML-Agents Toolkit used for training the agents, followed by detailed explanations of ML training methods, focusing on PPO and SAC. Section 3 details the practical project's structure, providing information about the environment, using the Unity engine, and the overview of the main objectives, with an emphasis on the current phase of simpler vehicle navigation, including the reward system and hyperparameters used. It also briefly outlines the three subsequent phases of the project, each progressively incorporating more realistic features. Finally, Section 4 presents the achieved results and evaluates the effectiveness of DRL techniques used in the defined scenarios.

2. Machine Learning Models

2.1. ML-Agents Toolkit

The Unity Machine Learning Agents Toolkit (ML-Agents Toolkit) is an open-source framework, provided by Unity Technologies [12], that converts games and simulations into environments for training intelligent agents. With an easy-to-use Python API, developers can train agents using techniques such as reinforcement learning, imitation learning, and neuroevolution. The toolkit offers PyTorch-based implementations of cutting-edge algorithms, facilitating the training of intelligent agents [13]. The primary training utility provided by the ML-Agents Toolkit is 'mlagents-learn'. This tool accepts numerous command-line options and utilizes a YAML configuration file containing all the necessary configurations and hyperparameters for training. The specific configurations and hyperparameters in this file can significantly impact training performance, always depending on the agents, environment, and the training method used [14].

2.2. Training Methods

Although the Unity ML-Agents Toolkit offers a specific range of training methods, it stills provides developers with both flexibility and efficiency in creating intelligent agents. The toolkit supports three primary training techniques, which can be utilized independently or in combination, to enhance the development process:

- **Behavioral Cloning (BC)**: This method, a form of imitation learning, involves the agent learning to replicate the actions that a demonstrator (human or not) would take in response to a given observed state [15].
- **Generative Adversarial Imitation Learning (GAIL)**: GAIL integrates imitation learning with reinforcement learning, enabling agents to learn from demonstrations with or without extrinsic rewards [13]. This direction attempts to imitate the expert behavior through direct policy optimization rather than learning the reward function first [16].
- **Reinforcement Learning (RL)**: This fundamental method involves training agents by interacting with the environment to maximize cumulative rewards [17]. RL can be implemented using PPO and SAC [13].

In closed-world environments, such as games, RL is applied with great success [18]. As it allows a software agent to take appropriate measures for a given environment to maximize the cumulative reward in a specific situation [19], agents do not learn from given examples but rather through interactive experiences with the environment [20]. So, among these methods, we will be focusing on PPO and SAC, which are two key reinforcement learning algorithms that play a significant role in the training process.

2.2.1. Proximal Policy Optimization

PPO is an on-policy optimization algorithm that employs a neural network to approximate an optimal function, mapping an agent's observations to the best possible actions in a given state. Integrated with frameworks such as TensorFlow, it interacts with Python processes to optimize step updates through a gradient descent framework. This method has shown to be more effective than traditional gradient descent, resulting in more stable and faster training processes [21]. It functions within an actor–critic framework, where the "actor" is responsible for selecting actions, and the "critic" evaluates them. This approach integrates current experiences with critiques to refine the policy, avoiding the large, destructive updates typical of traditional policy gradient methods. It accomplishes this by alternating between sampling data from environmental interactions and optimizing a clipped policy surrogate. The resulting balance of simplicity, computational efficiency, and effective sample utilization solidifies its position as a state-of-the-art method [22].

The core idea of PPO is to optimize a surrogate objective function while ensuring that the new policy does not deviate excessively from the old policy [23]. The key mathematical formula used in PPO is the objective function (1)

$$L^{\text{CLIP}}(\theta) = \hat{\mathbb{E}}_t\left[\min(r_t(\theta)\hat{A}_t, \text{clip}(r_t(\theta), 1-\epsilon, 1+\epsilon)\hat{A}_t)\right] \tag{1}$$

Here each component is defined as follows:

- θ represents the parameters of the policy (neural network) being optimized.
- $\hat{\mathbb{E}}_t$ denotes the empirical expectation over a finite batch of samples.
- $r_t(\theta)$ is the probability ratio between the new policy and the old policy, defined as

$$r_t(\theta) = \frac{\pi_\theta(a_t|s_t)}{\pi_{\theta_{\text{old}}}(a_t|s_t)} \tag{2}$$

  where $\pi_\theta(a_t|s_t)$ is the probability of taking action a_t given state s_t under the new policy, and $\pi_{\theta_{\text{old}}}(a_t|s_t)$ is the probability under the old policy.
- $\hat{A}_t$ is the advantage estimate at time step t, which measures how much better or worse the action a_t is compared to the expected action under the current policy.
- ϵ is a small hyperparameter that defines the clipping range.
- $\text{clip}(r_t(\theta), 1-\epsilon, 1+\epsilon)$ clips the probability ratio $r_t(\theta)$ to be within the range $[1-\epsilon, 1+\epsilon]$.

The objective function $L^{\text{CLIP}}(\theta)$ ensures that the new policy does not deviate significantly from the old policy by taking the minimum of the unclipped objective $r_t(\theta)\hat{A}_t$ and the clipped objective $\text{clip}(r_t(\theta), 1-\epsilon, 1+\epsilon)\hat{A}_t$. This conservative update helps maintain a balance between exploration and exploitation, leading to more stable and reliable learning [23,24].

In summary, the PPO objective function is designed to penalize large changes in the policy, ensuring smooth and stable policy updates while optimizing performance.

2.2.2. Soft Actor–Critic

SAC, unlike PPO, is an off-policy reinforcement learning algorithm. It can learn from experiences collected at any time in the past by storing them in an experience replay buffer, from which samples are randomly drawn during training. This approach significantly enhances sample efficiency, often requiring 5–10 times fewer samples than PPO to achieve comparable performance. However, SAC typically necessitates more model updates, making it well suited for environments where each step takes longer, around 0.1 s or more [13]. As an off-policy actor–critic algorithm based on the maximum entropy RL framework, SAC's training objective is to maximize both entropy and reward. This dual objective differentiates SAC from traditional actor–critic methods that solely focus on maximizing cumulative rewards. SAC modifies the objective function by incorporating the expected entropy of the policy, favoring stochastic policies and thus enhancing exploration [25,26].

The main objective functions of SAC are as follows:

1. Q-Function Update

The Q-function parameters are updated to minimize the soft Bellman residual:

$$J_Q(\theta) = \mathbb{E}_{(s_t,a_t)\sim\mathcal{D}}\left[\frac{1}{2}\left(Q_\theta(s_t,a_t) - \left(r(s_t,a_t) + \gamma\mathbb{E}_{s_{t+1}\sim p}[V_{\bar{\theta}}(s_{t+1})]\right)\right)^2\right] \tag{3}$$

In which, each component is defined as follows:

- $Q_\theta(s_t, a_t)$ is the Q-function parameterized by θ.
- $r(s_t, a_t)$ is the reward received after taking action a_t in state s_t.

- γ is the discount factor.
- $V_{\bar{\theta}}(s_{t+1})$ is the target value function.

2. *Value Function Update*

The value function is updated to minimize the difference between the Q-function and the expected value under the policy

$$J_V(\bar{\theta}) = \mathbb{E}_{s_t \sim \mathcal{D}}\left[\frac{1}{2}\left(V_{\bar{\theta}}(s_t) - \mathbb{E}_{a_t \sim \pi_\phi}\left[Q_\theta(s_t, a_t) - \log \pi_\phi(a_t|s_t)\right]\right)^2\right] \quad (4)$$

3. *Policy Update*

The policy parameters are updated to maximize the expected return while also maximizing the entropy to encourage exploration:

$$J_\pi(\phi) = \mathbb{E}_{s_t \sim \mathcal{D}, a_t \sim \pi_\phi}\left[\log \pi_\phi(a_t|s_t) - Q_\theta(s_t, a_t)\right] \quad (5)$$

Entropy Regularization

The entropy regularization term ensures that the policy does not become too deterministic:

$$\mathcal{H}(\pi(\cdot|s)) = -\mathbb{E}_{a \sim \pi}[\log \pi(a|s)] \quad (6)$$

Combining these components, the SAC algorithm alternates between updating the Q-function, the value function, and the policy using experience replay to sample batches of data. This approach enables SAC to achieve stable and efficient learning by maintaining a balance between exploration and exploitation [27–30].

3. Environment

The environment for our deep reinforcement learning study is designed to simulate a complex urban road network where an autonomous car must navigate effectively to reach a destination. The environment, built using the Unity engine, is structured as a grid of roads, resembling the layout of a well-organized city. Specifically, the design includes 6 parallel roads intersected by another 7 parallel roads, forming a grid that can be visualized as a table with rows and columns corresponding to these roads (Figure 1). This setup creates a total of 42 intersections where the roads meet, providing numerous possible paths and complex scenarios for the autonomous car to learn and navigate.

The project is structured to progress through several phases, each involving tests in various situations with different parameters. Currently, we are at a very early stage, with our primary focus on developing and refining the foundational aspects of our environment and testing the basic capabilities of our deep reinforcement learning models. At this initial phase, the environment remains quite simple, utilizing default parameters from the tutorials provided by the ML-Agents Toolkit. The phases will be described in the following subsections. Throughout all phases, the agent must prioritize paths that minimize the overall time to reach the targets. Hyperparameter tuning will be crucial for enhancing the performance of the models. The current phase of the project utilizes PPO and SAC to identify the most effective learning approach. The increasing complexity and evolution through the phases aim to develop a robust and adaptable autonomous navigation system, ensuring meticulous attention to detail and comprehensive scenario handling.

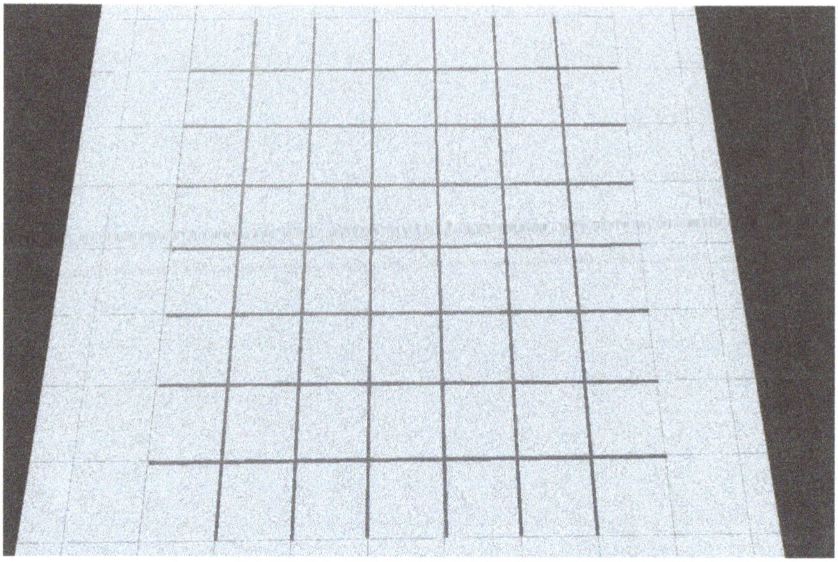

Figure 1. Above view of the map.

3.1. Unity Engine

The Unity engine [31], developed by Unity Technologies, is a leading platform for developing interactive, real-time 3D and 2D experiences. The engine offers an interactive simulation environment that provides a rich user experience [32]. Beyond their original purpose of video game development/designing, the versatility and robustness of modern game engines have extended their influence in designing realistic scenarios of various fields, making them invaluable across diverse sectors. Users who extend their design processes beyond gaming demonstrate the Unity engine's versatility as a comprehensive design tool applicable to various fields beyond game development [33]. Unity's workflow distinguishes itself from most other game development environments through its highly efficient visual process and broad cross-platform support, making it a favorite among developers [34].

3.2. Phase 1: Basic Navigation

In the first phase of our project, the objective is straightforward. The car only needs to reach the target, regardless of whether the target is on the road or not, by employing PPO and SAC.

To navigate the environment, the car is equipped with a 360-degree sensor that collects data from all directions, providing comprehensive situational awareness to the agent (Figure 2). This sensor setup ensures that the car can make informed decisions based on a full understanding of its surroundings.

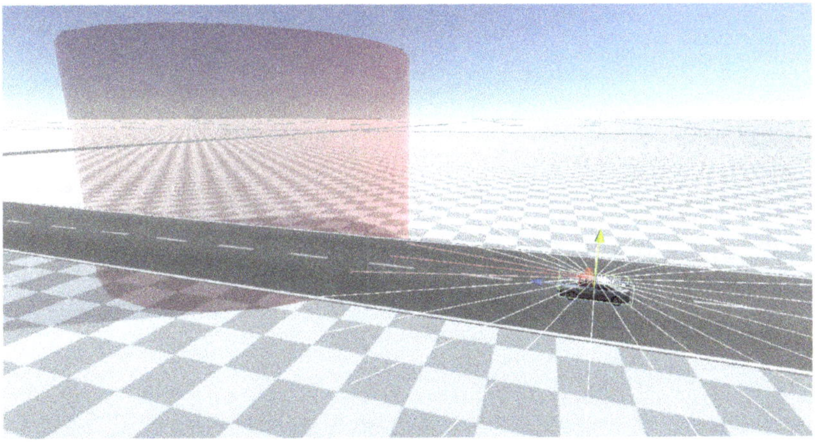

Figure 2. Target and agent side by side view.

3.2.1. Reward System

The reward structure in this phase is designed to encourage the car to reach the target efficiently. The car receives a significant reward when it reaches the target, which is registered as a collision with the target object, and receives an extra reward based on time efficiency. Additionally, incremental rewards are given as the car approaches the target, incentivizing it to move in the correct direction based on the angle to the target. Conversely, the car is penalized for actions that are counterproductive to reaching the target. These penalties include moving away from the target, significant backward movement, and taking too long to reach the target. The car also incurs a significant penalty when it reaches the environment's limits, indicated by a collision with the boundary.

1. Target Reaching Reward:

$$R_{target} = R_{base_t} + R_{time} \tag{7}$$

- R_{base_t}: Base reward for reaching the target.
- R_{time}: Extra reward based on time efficiency.

2. Proximity-Based Incremental Rewards:

$$R_{proximity} = R_{base_d} \times R_{angle} \tag{8}$$

- R_{base_d}: Base reward for approaching the target.
- R_{angle}: Reward based on the correct angle towards the target.

3. Penalties:

- *Moving Away from the Target:*

$$P_{away} = -P_{move\_away} \tag{9}$$

  - P_{move_away}: Penalty for moving away from the target.

- *Backward Movement:*

$$P_{backward} = -P_{backward\_move} \tag{10}$$

  - $P_{backward\_move}$: Penalty for significant backward movement.

- *Time Penalty:*

$$P_{time} = -P_{time\_elapsed} \tag{11}$$

- $P_{time\_elapsed}$: Penalty for taking too long.
- *Boundary Collision:*

$$P_{boundary} = -P_{boundary\_collision} \tag{12}$$

  - $P_{boundary\_collision}$: Penalty for colliding with the environment's boundary.

The reward structure is strategically designed to promote efficient and direct movement towards the target while discouraging deviations from this goal. The combination of significant target-reaching rewards, incremental proximity-based rewards, and penalties for counterproductive actions forms a comprehensive framework that guides the car towards optimal performance.

3.2.2. Hyperparameters

The hyperparameters are fine-tuned to optimize the performance of the autonomous car in reaching its target efficiently. These parameters are configured in a YAML file, provided by the ML-Agents' flexibility, which allows for easy modification and experimentation. In this initial phase the configurations used were based on the default ML-Agents hyperparameters, providing a solid foundation for further refinement [35,36]. Each hyperparameter is described and can be consulted in the documents provided by Unity Technologies [37], but there are some that require particular attention due to their significant impact on training performance, these are described below.

Shared Hyperparameters

The **learning rate** is the step size for gradient descent updates. A higher learning rate can speed up training but may cause instability, whereas a lower learning rate leads to more stable training but requires more iterations. The typical range for the learning rate is 1×10^{-5} to 1×10^{-3}, with a default value of 3×10^{-4}.

The **batch size** refers to the number of training samples per mini-batch. Larger batch sizes can provide more accurate gradient estimates but require more memory and computational power. The typical range for batch size is from 32 to 512, with default values being 64 for PPO and 256 for SAC.

The **gamma** parameter is the discount factor for future rewards. A higher gamma value puts more weight on future rewards, promoting long-term strategies. The typical range is from 0.8 to 0.995, with a default value of 0.99.

Proximal Policy Optimization (PPO)

For PPO, the **clip ratio** is a crucial parameter. It is used to clip the policy objective to prevent large updates, helping to maintain stable updates by limiting the extent to which the policy is changed in a single update. This parameter typically ranges from 0.1 to 0.3, with a default value of 0.2.

The number of **epochs** refers to how many times the learning algorithm will work through the entire training dataset. More epochs mean more thorough learning from the collected data but increase computational time. The typical range is from 3 to 10, with a default value of 10.

The **GAE lambda** is a smoothing parameter for Generalized Advantage Estimation (GAE). It balances bias and variance in advantage estimation, where higher values provide lower variance but higher bias. The typical range for GAE lambda is from 0.9 to 0.95, with a default value of 0.95.

The **entropy coefficient** is used for entropy regularization, encouraging exploration by adding an entropy term to the loss function. This prevents the policy from converging prematurely to suboptimal solutions. The entropy coefficient typically ranges from 0.01 to 0.1, with a default value of 0.01.

Soft Actor–Critic (SAC)

For SAC, the **tau** parameter is the interpolation parameter for the soft update of target network parameters. It affects the update speed of the target networks, balancing stability and responsiveness. The typical range for tau is from 0.005 to 0.05, with a default value of 0.005.

The **alpha** parameter is the entropy regularization coefficient, which determines the balance between exploration and exploitation. Higher values encourage more exploration, which can help in finding better policies but may also slow down convergence. The typical range for alpha is from 0.1 to 0.2, with a default value of 0.2.

The **target update interval** specifies the number of steps between target network updates. Frequent updates can make the training more responsive, while less frequent updates can enhance stability. The typical range is from 1 to 1000, with a default value of 1.

Finally, the **gradient steps** refer to the number of gradient steps performed after each environment step. More gradient steps can lead to better policy updates per interaction with the environment but also increase computational load. The typical range is from 1 to 4, with a default value of 1.

Selecting the appropriate hyperparameters is essential for the training's success. By understanding the roles and impacts of these hyperparameters, it is possible to achieve better performance in various environments. Beginning with the default values and adjusting as needed based on observed performance and stability is the recommended procedure to ensure effective and efficient training.

3.2.3. Implementation Overview

To provide a comprehensive understanding of the implementation, this section details the key steps involved in the car's decision-making and learning process. The following components form the core of our implementation: initialization, action selection, reward application, and environment interaction. The flowchart, Figure 3, illustrates the sequence of these steps, followed by pseudocode snippets that correspond to critical parts of the algorithm.

The flowchart highlights the following key steps:

- **Initialization**: Set up the environment, define hyperparameters, and initialize the agent (car) with its PPO or SAC algorithm (see Algorithm 1).
- **Action Loop**: For each episode, the agent senses its environment using the 360-degree sensor and selects an action based on the current policy (see Algorithm 2).
- **Environment Interaction**: The selected action is applied to the environment, and the agent moves according to the chosen action (see Algorithm 2).
- **Reward Calculation**: The reward function is evaluated based on the agent's new state, considering proximity to the target, penalties for undesirable actions, and the time taken (see Algorithm 3).
- **Policy Update**: Using the collected rewards and experiences, the agent updates its policy through gradient descent (see Algorithm 4).
- **Repeat**: The process repeats until the agent converges on an optimal policy or the training session ends (see Algorithm 5).

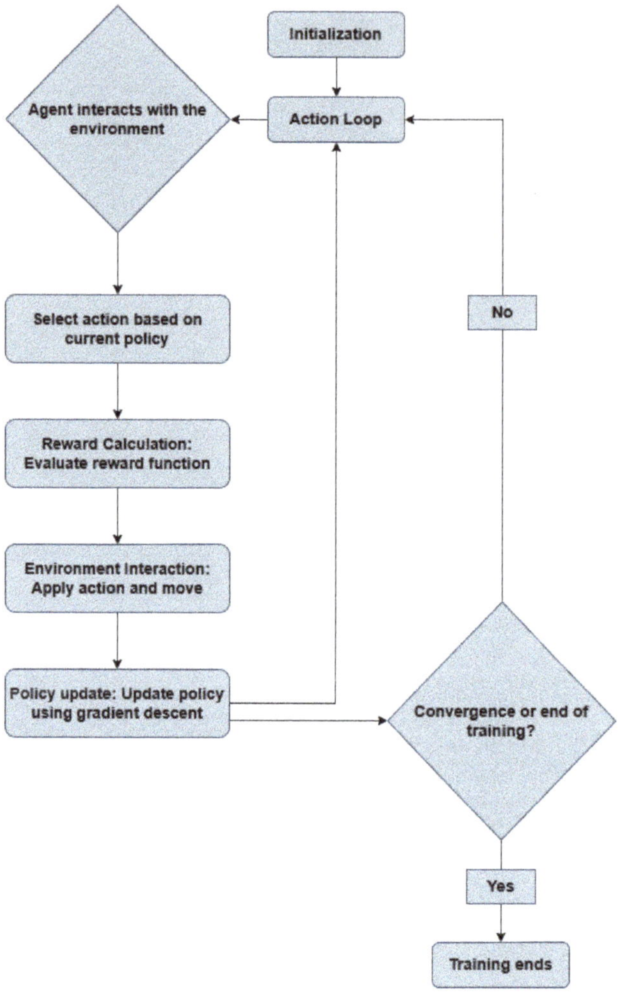

Figure 3. Flowchart of the implementation process.

Pseudocode Snippets

The following snippets correspond to the main components of the implementation, providing a structured representation of the logic described in the flowchart with a PPO example.

Algorithm 1 Initialization

Initialize environment: *env* ← Environment()
Initialize agent:
    agent ← Agent(algorithm = 'PPO',
    learning_rate = 3×10^{-4}, gamma = 0.99, batch_size = 64)
Initialize variables for tracking performance: *episode_rewards* ← []
for each episode from 1 to *max_episodes* **do**
    state ← *env.reset*() ▷ Reset environment for new episode
    total_reward ← 0
end for

Algorithm 2 Action Selection and Environment Interaction

```
while not done do
    action ← agent.select_action(state)                 ▷ Choose action using current policy
    next_state, reward, done ← env.step(action)          ▷ Apply action and get new state
    total_reward ← total_reward + reward                 ▷ Accumulate reward
    Store transition: agent.memory.add(state, action, reward, next_state, done)
    state ← next_state                                   ▷ Update state
end while
```

Algorithm 3 Reward Calculation

```
function CALCULATE_REWARD(state, action, target_position)
    if reached_target(state, target_position) then
        reward ← base_reward + time_bonus
    else if close_to_target(state, target_position) then
        reward ← proximity_reward × angle_reward
    else
        reward ← −penalty_for_bad_action(action)
    end if
    if hit_boundary(state) then
        reward ← reward − boundary_penalty
    end if
    return reward
end function
```

The reward function was designed to balance exploration and goal-oriented behavior, guiding the agent to navigate efficiently towards the target. Reaching the target yields a significant reward (`base_reward + time_bonus`), incentivizing success and efficient trajectories. Proximity rewards (`proximity_reward × angle_reward`) encourage steady progress while ensuring directional alignment.

Penalties discourage undesired behaviors, such as moving away from the target (`penalty_for_bad_action`) or hitting environment boundaries (`boundary_penalty`), reflecting real-world constraints. The modular design allows for easy adjustment of weights for different scenarios, ensuring flexibility and adaptability.

This function was iteratively refined during training to effectively incentivize desired behaviors, aligning with real-world applications.

Algorithm 4 Policy Update

```
if done then
    agent.update_policy()                ▷ Perform PPO updates using stored transitions
end if
Log episode results: episode_rewards.append(total_reward)
```

Algorithm 5 End of Training

```
After training, evaluate agent performance: evaluate_agent(agent, env)
```

3.3. Phase 2: Road-Bound Navigation

In the second phase, the complexity of the task increases as the car is required to reach the target while strictly adhering to the road. This phase introduces several enhancements to ensure the car remains on the designated path and navigates more effectively.

To achieve this, the integration of additional sensors into the car's system is envisaged. These include road-edge detectors, which help the car recognize and stay within the boundaries of the road. Moreover, lane-keeping sensors will be added to provide real-time feedback on lane position, enabling the car to make precise adjustments to its trajectory.

The reward and penalty system need to be significantly adjusted to promote road adherence. The car will receive rewards not only for reaching the target but also for maintaining its position on the road. Specifically, incremental rewards will be given for staying within lane boundaries and making smooth turns at intersections.

Penalizations will be imposed for deviations from the road, such as veering off the lane or crossing road edges. Additional penalties will be introduced for unsafe driving behaviors, including sharp turns, sudden stops, and rapid acceleration, which could indicate a loss of control. The car will also be penalized for any collisions with road boundaries or other objects, reinforcing the importance of safe and precise navigation.

3.4. Phase 3: Multi-Target Navigation

The third phase introduces the challenge of multi-target navigation, requiring the car to reach multiple targets sequentially while staying on the road. This phase significantly enhances the complexity of the task, necessitating advanced capabilities in route planning and dynamic path adjustments.

To accomplish this, the car's system will be upgraded with more sophisticated sensors and algorithms. These sensors will provide detailed information about the surroundings, enabling the car to plan its route more effectively.

Enhanced route planning capabilities will be implemented, allowing the car to dynamically adjust its path as it progresses towards each target. This involves the integration of real-time data processing and decision-making algorithms that can evaluate multiple routes and select the most efficient path. The car will also use predictive modeling to anticipate potential obstacles and traffic conditions, optimizing its navigation strategy.

The reward and penalty system will be further refined to account for the multi-target objective. Rewards will be given for reaching each target, with additional bonuses for efficiently transitioning between targets. Maintaining road adherence will continue to be rewarded, ensuring that the car navigates safely and reliably.

Penalizations will be introduced for missing targets, inefficient route choices, and any deviations from the road. The car will also be penalized for failing to reach targets within a reasonable time frame, encouraging prompt and efficient navigation. Collisions with road boundaries, obstacles, or other vehicles will incur significant penalties, reinforcing the importance of safe driving practices.

Moreover, this phase will simulate more complex urban environments with varied traffic patterns. The car must demonstrate the ability to navigate these scenarios while efficiently reaching multiple targets.

3.5. Phase 4: Obstacle-Aware Multi-Target Navigation

In the fourth and most complex phase, the car must navigate the road network, reach multiple targets, and avoid obstacles. This phase necessitates the introduction of advanced obstacle detection sensors and sophisticated decision-making capabilities to handle dynamic environments effectively.

To achieve this, the car will be equipped with a range of advanced sensors. These sensors will provide detailed, real-time data about the car's surroundings, enabling it to detect and avoid obstacles accurately.

The algorithms will be significantly enhanced to process this sensor data and make real-time decisions. The car will use advanced obstacle avoidance algorithms to navigate around obstacles while staying on the road and reaching multiple targets. This will involve predictive modeling to anticipate the movement of dynamic obstacles and adjust the car's path accordingly.

The reward and penalty system will be further refined to encourage safe and efficient navigation. Rewards will be given for successfully reaching each target, maintaining road adherence, and avoiding obstacles. Additional rewards will be provided for smooth navigation, efficient route planning, and prompt target acquisition.

Penalizations will be imposed for collisions with obstacles, deviating from the road, and inefficient navigation paths. The car will also be penalized for taking excessive time to reach targets or failing to avoid dynamic obstacles. These penalties will reinforce the importance of careful and efficient driving.

This phase will simulate highly dynamic and realistic urban environments. The car must demonstrate its ability to navigate these complex scenarios while maintaining high standards of safety and efficiency.

3.6. Preview of the New Environment

At this stage, the test environment incorporates a map modeled after the real-world geography of a section of Vila Real, Portugal (Figure 4). This environment provides a robust foundation for testing DRL models in a more realistic context, introducing geographical complexity that closely mirrors real-world scenarios.

Figure 4. Above view of the new environment map.

In addition to the map, we have introduced a new agent—a motorcycle instead of a car. This motorcycle is modeled after the real vehicle used in the A-MoVeR project (see Figure 5, where the virtual and real motorcycle are shown side by side). By implementing this specific vehicle, we have added a layer of complexity to the simulation, as the physics related to the motorcycle's movement are more intricate, requiring the agent to navigate with realistic speed, balance, and control. This step allows for a more accurate simulation of our real-world objectives, ensuring that the virtual tests are aligned with the physical performance of the A-MoVeR motorcycle (see Figure 6, where the motorcycle is navigating on the new environment).

(a) Real A-MoVeR motorcycle.

(b) Virtual A-MoVeR motorcycle

Figure 5. Real and virtual A-MoVeR motorcycle side by side.

Figure 6. Motorcycle navigating on the new environment.

Furthermore, in a more advanced phase of the project, various obstacles will be randomly distributed throughout the map, requiring the agent to learn how to overcome them. These obstacles will introduce additional challenges to the simulation, reflecting real-world conditions where vehicles must navigate through unpredictable environments. This evolution will further test the adaptability and learning efficiency of the DRL models, pushing them closer to real-world driving scenarios.

4. Results

4.1. Overview

Given the intrinsic differences in PPO and SAC complexity and update mechanisms, it is anticipated that SAC, which leverages memory from different steps to update its policy, should require a longer training period compared to PPO. However, this extended training time is expected to yield superior results, with SAC achieving optimal behavior more efficiently in terms of performance metrics. Conversely, PPO is expected to train more rapidly, but is projected to need a greater number of steps to reach optimal performance. This expectation arises from the inherent design of PPO, which focuses on simplicity and rapid iteration but may compromise on the speed of convergence to optimal behavior.

The results of these algorithms are analyzed using TensorBoard, provided by ML-Agents, which offers a comprehensive visualization of the training metrics. This analysis helps in understanding the convergence patterns, stability, and overall performance of the algorithms, allowing for a detailed comparison of their effectiveness in various scenarios.

4.2. Results Analysis

In the current phase of our project, where the objective is for the car to reach the target regardless of its position on or off the road, we have observed promising yet imperfect results. The car is generally successful in reaching the target with PPO, demonstrating its capability to learn and adapt effectively to the task. However, with SAC, the car rarely reaches the target, indicating significant challenges in its learning process.

The following analysis presents a comprehensive comparison of various metrics for PPO (represented in purple) and SAC (represented in orange). The actions in this experiment were implemented as continuous, and the training was conducted over 8 million steps. These visualizations provide valuable insights into the performance, stability, and learning efficiency of the two algorithms under the specified conditions. Additionally, Table 2 is presented, comparing key metrics between both algorithms.

- **Training Time**
  As anticipated, the training duration for PPO was 13.6 h, while SAC required a significantly longer training period of 1.541 days. This disparity in training times highlights the differences in the complexity and update mechanisms of the two algorithms.
- **Cumulative Reward Trend**
  The graph in Figure 7 illustrates the cumulative reward over time for PPO and SAC. The cumulative reward for PPO starts low but shows a consistent upward trend, stabilizing around a cumulative reward of 30 after approximately 3 million time steps. The curve is relatively smooth with some early fluctuations but becomes more stable as training progresses. In contrast, the cumulative reward for SAC starts low and initially rises but stabilizes at a much lower level compared to PPO. The SAC curve shows significant fluctuations throughout the training period, oscillating around −10 to 0 without a clear upward trend after the initial increase.

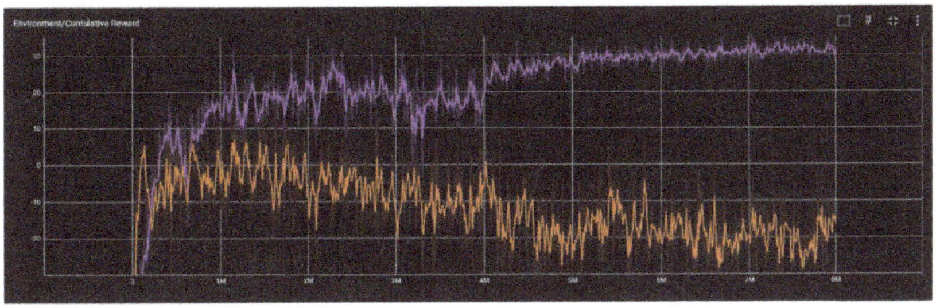

Figure 7. Cumulative reward over time for PPO (purple) and SAC (orange).

- **Learning Rate**
  Figure 8 shows the policy learning rate over time for both PPO and SAC. PPO starts with a higher learning rate that decreases more rapidly compared to SAC. This indicates a more aggressive learning approach initially, which then stabilizes as training progresses.

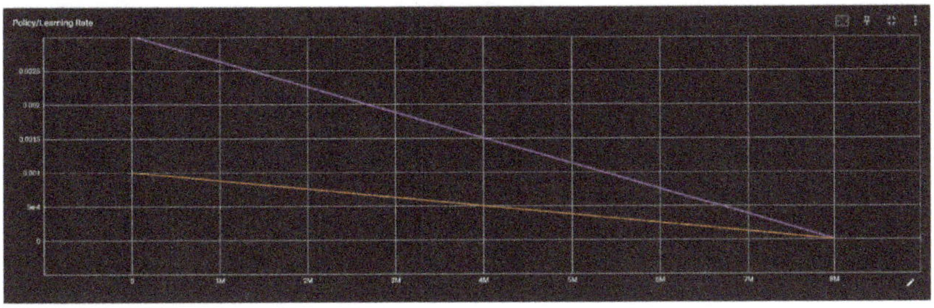

Figure 8. Policy learning rate over time for PPO (purple) and SAC (orange).

- **Policy Loss**
  The policy loss over time for both algorithms is shown in Figure 9. PPO maintains a consistently low policy loss throughout the training period, indicating stable policy updates. On the other hand, SAC exhibits a high and increasing policy loss, suggesting instability and inefficiency in policy updates.

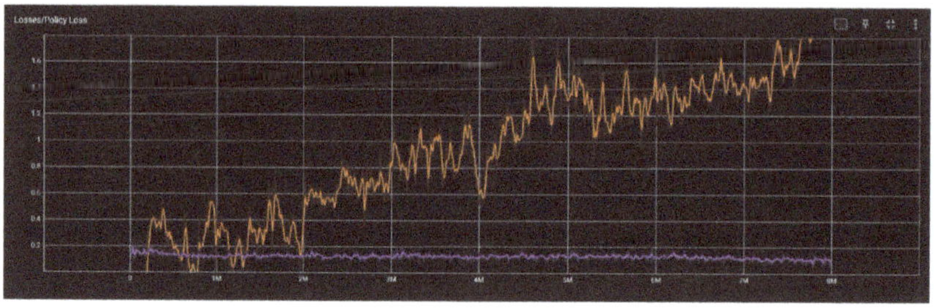

Figure 9. Policy loss over time for PPO (purple) and SAC (orange).

- **Cumulative Reward Distribution**
  Figures 10 and 11 present the cumulative reward distribution for PPO and SAC, respectively. PPO shows a more concentrated reward distribution towards higher rewards, while SAC's distribution is more spread out and centered around lower rewards.

Figure 10. Cumulative reward distribution for PPO.

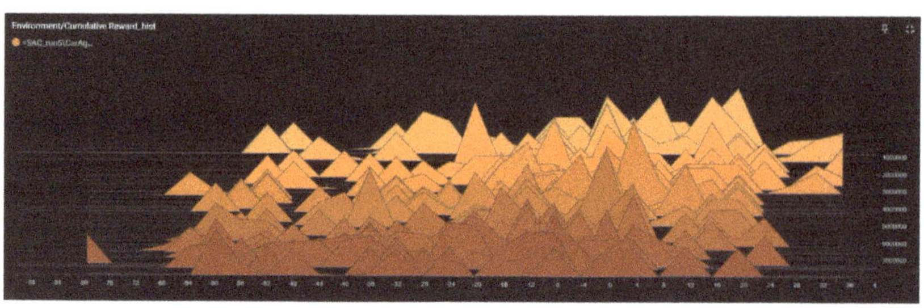

Figure 11. Cumulative reward distribution for SAC.

- **Value Loss**
  Figure 12 illustrates the value loss over time for both algorithms. PPO maintains a relatively low value loss with some fluctuations, whereas SAC shows a consistently low value loss, indicating different stability characteristics.

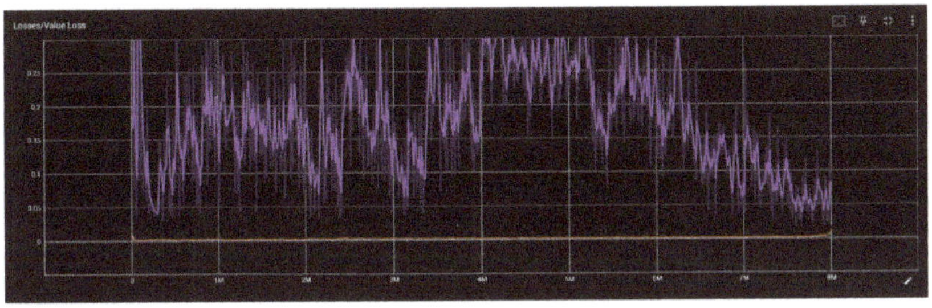

Figure 12. Value loss over time for PPO (purple) and SAC (orange).

- **Episode Length**
  The episode length over time is depicted in Figure 13. PPO shows a decreasing trend in episode length, stabilizing at a lower value, which suggests efficient learning and faster convergence to the target. SAC, however, maintains a relatively high and stable episode length, indicating inefficiency in learning to reach the target.

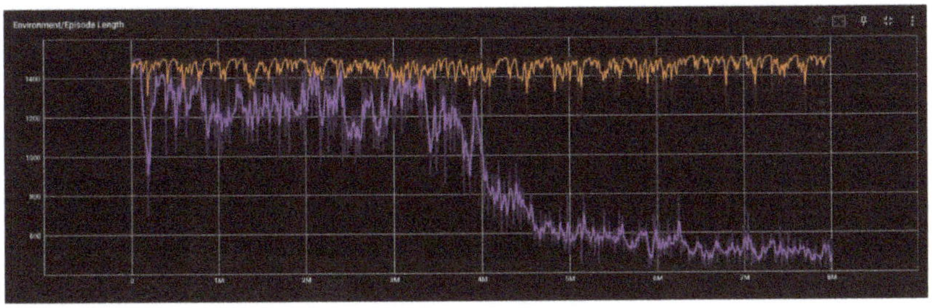

Figure 13. Episode length over time for PPO (purple) and SAC (orange).

Table 2. Comparison of PPO and SAC on Various Metrics.

Metric	PPO	SAC
Learning Rate (Initial - Final)	0.003–3.1 $\times$ 10^{-06}	0.001–6.3 $\times$ 10^{-07}
Policy Loss (Range)	0.06–0.2	−4.6–2.5
Cumulative Reward (Max)	37.4	18.9
Value Loss (Range)	0.02–1.4	0.0006–0.02
Episode Length (Range)	398.8–1499	1046–1499

The results suggest that PPO is more suitable for this environment or task, given its higher and more stable cumulative reward, as well as its faster training time. SAC, while trained for a longer period, did not perform as well, indicating the need for more fine-tuning or a different approach to parameter optimization. In summary, PPO outperforms SAC in terms of cumulative reward, stability, convergence, and training efficiency in this continuous action implementation scenario.

For future tuning, adjustments will be made to the parameters, observations, and other aspects of the training process. These changes aim to improve the performance and stability of both algorithms, with a focus on maximizing cumulative rewards and reducing variance.

5. Conclusions

This work demonstrates promising advances in the application of DRL for autonomous navigation within the Unity engine. Despite some imperfections, the car generally succeeds in reaching its target, highlighting the potential of DRL to enhance decision-making and adaptive behavior in dynamic gaming environments.

The initial phase of our project underscores the effectiveness of the Unity engine and ML-Agents Toolkit as a robust platform for testing and refining AI methodologies. These tools have provided a controlled yet dynamic environment that closely mimics real-world scenarios, facilitating rapid iteration and comprehensive analysis of DRL techniques. This foundational work sets the stage for future phases of the project, where increased complexity will further challenge and enhance the car's navigational capabilities.

Our results indicate that PPO has been successful in learning to reach the target, achieving higher and more stable cumulative rewards. In contrast, SAC has not been as successful, struggling to reach the target and showing significant variability in performance. This comparison highlights PPO's suitability for the current task and environment, with SAC requiring further fine-tuning and parameter optimization.

Beyond the gaming context, this research directly contributes to the A-MoVeR project, where we focus on optimizing route planning and energy management for autonomous motorcycles. The insights gained from simulation—such as efficient navigation strategies and handling real-world constraints—support the development of advanced decision-making models for route optimization and energy consumption prediction. These contributions align with the project's goals of providing effective logistical services for users.

Moving forward, the project will evolve through additional phases, each introducing more complex scenarios to push the boundaries of the car's learning and adaptability. Future tuning will involve adjustments to parameters, observations, and other aspects of the training process to improve the performance and stability of both algorithms. These changes aim to refine the reward system further, ensuring a balance between immediate rewards and the efficiency of reaching the target. Additionally, in future work, we will consider exploring and comparing other machine learning algorithms commonly used in similar fields, to further contextualize the performance and adaptability of PPO and SAC in these scenarios.

Overall, the results thus far affirm the potential of DRL in developing sophisticated, autonomous agents capable of real-time learning and adaptation. This research not only contributes to the field of gaming AI but also paves the way for broader applications of autonomous systems in real-world scenarios, enhancing their interaction dynamics and realism. The promising outcomes of this project highlight the importance of continued exploration and refinement of AI techniques, with the ultimate goal of revolutionizing autonomous systems' adaptability and efficiency in complex environments.

Author Contributions: Conceptualization, G.P. and T.P.; methodology, G.P.; software, G.P.; validation, L.B., A.R., J.B. and T.P.; formal analysis, T.P.; investigation, G.P.; data curation, G.P. and T.P.; writing—original draft preparation, G.P. and T.P.; writing—review and editing, G.P. and T.P.; supervision, L.B., A.R., J.B. and T.P.; project administration, L.B., A.R., J.B. and T.P.; funding acquisition, L.B., A.R., J.B. and T.P. All authors have read and agreed to the published version of the manuscript.

Funding: This study was developed under the project A-MoVeR—"Mobilizing Agenda for the Development of Products and Systems towards an Intelligent and Green Mobility", operation n.º 02/C05-i01.01/2022.PC646908627-00000069, approved under the terms of the call n.º 02/C05-i01/2022—Mobilizing Agendas for Business Innovation, financed by European funds provided to Portugal by the Recovery and Resilience Plan (RRP), in the scope of the European Recovery and Resilience Facility (RRF), framed in the Next Generation UE, for the period from 2021–2026.

Data Availability Statement: Data is contained within the article.

Conflicts of Interest: The authors declare no conflicts of interest.

Abbreviations

A-MoVeR	Mobilizing Agenda for the Development of Products and Systems
AI	Artificial Intelligence
DL	Deep Learning
DRL	Deep Reinforcement Learning
ML	Machine Learning
ML-Agents	Unity Machine Learning Agents Toolkit
PPO	Proximal Policy Optimization
RL	Reinforcement Learning
SAC	Soft Actor–Critic

References

1. Sun, B.; Zeng, Y.; Zhu, D. Dynamic task allocation in multi autonomous underwater vehicle confrontational games with multi-objective evaluation model and particle swarm optimization algorithm. *Appl. Soft Comput.* **2024**, *153*, 111295. [CrossRef]
2. Latif, S.; Cuayáhuitl, H.; Pervez, F.; Shamshad, F.; Ali, H.S.; Cambria, E. A survey on deep reinforcement learning for audio-based applications. *Artif. Intell. Rev.* **2022**, *56*, 2193–2240. [CrossRef]
3. Pang, G.; You, L.; Fu, L. An Efficient DRL-Based Link Adaptation for Cellular Networks with Low Overhead. In Proceedings of the 2024 IEEE Wireless Communications and Networking Conference (WCNC), Dubai, United Arab Emirates, 21–24 April 2024; pp. 1–6. [CrossRef]
4. Elallid, B.B.; Benamar, N.; Hafid, A.S.; Rachidi, T.; Mrani, N. A Comprehensive Survey on the Application of Deep and Reinforcement Learning Approaches in Autonomous Driving. *J. King Saud Univ.-Comput. Inf. Sci.* **2022**, *34*, 7366–7390. [CrossRef]
5. Bachute, M.R.; Subhedar, J.M. Autonomous Driving Architectures: Insights of Machine Learning and Deep Learning Algorithms. *Mach. Learn. Appl.* **2021**, *6*, 100164. [CrossRef]
6. Hu, A.; Corrado, G.; Griffiths, N.; Murez, Z.; Gurau, C.; Yeo, H.; Kendall, A.; Cipolla, R.; Shotton, J. Model-Based Imitation Learning for Urban Driving. In Proceedings of the Advances in Neural Information Processing Systems (NeurIPS), New Orleans, LA, USA, 28 November–9 December 2022. [CrossRef]
7. Lee, T.; Kang, Y. Performance Analysis of Deep Neural Network Controller for Autonomous Driving Learning from a Nonlinear Model Predictive Control Method. *Electronics* **2021**, *10*, 767. [CrossRef]
8. Li, Y.; Aghvami, A.H. Intelligent UAV Navigation: A DRL-QiER Solution. In Proceedings of the ICC 2022—IEEE International Conference on Communications, Seoul, Republic of Korea, 16–20 May 2022; pp. 419–424. [CrossRef]
9. Forneris, L.; Pighetti, A.; Lazzaroni, L.; Bellotti, F.; Capello, A.; Cossu, M.; Berta, R. Implementing Deep Reinforcement Learning (DRL)-based Driving Styles for Non-Player Vehicles. *Int. J. Serious Games* **2023**, *10*, 153–170. [CrossRef]
10. Yannakakis, G.N.; Togelius, J. *Artificial Intelligence and Games*, 1st ed.; Springer International Publishing: Cham, Switzerland, 2018. [CrossRef]
11. Chen, Y.; Ji, C.; Cai, Y.; Yan, T.; Su, B. Deep Reinforcement Learning in Autonomous Car Path Planning and Control: A Survey. *arXiv* **2024**, arXiv:2404.00340.
12. Wondering What Unity Is? Find Out Who We Are, Where We've Been and Where We're Going. Available online: https://unity.com/our-company (accessed on 29 November 2024).
13. Technologies, U. ML-Agents Overview—Unity ML-Agents Toolkit. 2024. Available online: https://unity-technologies.github.io/ml-agents/ML-Agents-Overview (accessed on 22 May 2024).
14. Unity-Technologies. Ml-Agents Documentation. 2024. Available online: https://github.com/Unity-Technologies/ml-agents/blob/develop/docs/Training-ML-Agents.md (accessed on 22 May 2024).
15. Pearce, T.; Zhu, J. Counter-Strike Deathmatch with Large-Scale Behavioural Cloning. In Proceedings of the 2022 IEEE Conference on Games (CoG), Beijing, China, 21–24 August 2022; pp. 104–111. [CrossRef]
16. Pham, D.T.; Tran, T.N.; Alam, S.; Duong, V.N. A Generative Adversarial Imitation Learning Approach for Realistic Aircraft Taxi-Speed Modeling. *IEEE Trans. Intell. Transp. Syst.* **2022**, *23*, 2509–2522. [CrossRef]
17. Hu, K.; Li, M.; Song, Z.; Xu, K.; Xia, Q.; Sun, N.; Zhou, P.; Xia, M. A review of research on reinforcement learning algorithms for multi-agents. *Neurocomputing* **2024**, *599*, 128068. [CrossRef]
18. Janiesch, C.; Zschech, P.; Heinrich, K. Machine learning and deep learning. *Electron. Mark.* **2021**, *31*, 685–695. [CrossRef]
19. Gupta, S.; Singal, G.; Garg, D. Deep Reinforcement Learning Techniques in Diversified Domains: A Survey. *Arch. Comput. Methods Eng.* **2021**, *28*, 4715–4754. [CrossRef]
20. Du, W.; Ding, S. A survey on multi-agent deep reinforcement learning: From the perspective of challenges and applications. *Artif. Intell. Rev.* **2021**, *54*, 3215–3238. [CrossRef]

21. Lukas, M.; Tomicic, I.; Bernik, A. Anticheat System Based on Reinforcement Learning Agents in Unity. *Information* **2022**, *13*, 173. [CrossRef]
22. Alagha, A.; Singh, S.; Mizouni, R.; Bentahar, J.; Otrok, H. Target localization using Multi-Agent Deep Reinforcement Learning with Proximal Policy Optimization. *Future Gener. Comput. Syst.* **2022**, *136*, 342–357. [CrossRef]
23. Liu, X.; Fotouhi, A.; Auger, D. Application of advanced tree search and proximal policy optimization on formula-E race strategy development. *Expert Syst. Appl.* **2022**, *197*, 116718. [CrossRef]
24. OpenAI. Proximal Policy Optimization—Spinning Up Documentation. 2020. Available online: https://spinningup.openai.com/en/latest/algorithms/ppo.html (accessed on 16 July 2024).
25. Wong, C.C., Chien, S.Y.; Feng, H.M.; Aoyama, H. Motion Planning for Dual-Arm Robot Based on Soft Actor-Critic. *IEEE Access* **2021**, *9*, 26871–26885. [CrossRef]
26. Kathirgamanathan, A.; Mangina, E.; Finn, D.P. Development of a Soft Actor Critic deep reinforcement learning approach for harnessing energy flexibility in a Large Office building. *Energy AI* **2021**, *5*, 100101. [CrossRef]
27. Haarnoja, T.; Zhou, A.; Abbeel, P.; Levine, S. Soft Actor-Critic: Off-Policy Maximum Entropy Deep Reinforcement Learning with a Stochastic Actor. *arXiv* **2018**, arXiv:1801.01290.
28. Haarnoja, T.; Zhou, A.; Hartikainen, K.; Tucker, G.; Ha, S.; Tan, J.; Kumar, V.; Zhu, H.; Gupta, A.; Abbeel, P.; et al. Soft Actor-Critic Algorithms and Applications. *arXiv* **2019**, arXiv:1812.05905.
29. OpenAI. Soft Actor-Critic—Spinning Up Documentation. 2020. Available online: https://spinningup.openai.com/en/latest/algorithms/sac.html (accessed on 16 July 2024).
30. Xu, D.; Cui, Y.; Ye, J.; Cha, S.W.; Li, A.; Zheng, C. A soft actor-critic-based energy management strategy for electric vehicles with hybrid energy storage systems. *J. Power Sources* **2022**, *524*, 231099. [CrossRef]
31. Technologies, U. Unity Real-Time Development Platform | 3D, 2D, VR & AR Engine. 2024. Available online: https://unity.com (accessed on 22 May 2024).
32. Singh, S.; Kaur, A. Game Development using Unity Game Engine. In Proceedings of the 2022 3rd International Conference on Computing, Analytics and Networks (ICAN), Rajpura, Punjab, India, 18–19 November 2022. [CrossRef]
33. Scheiding, R. Designing the Future? The Metaverse, NFTs, & the Future as Defined by Unity Users. *Games Cult.* **2023**, *18*, 804–820. [CrossRef]
34. Hocking, J. *Unity in Action*, 3rd ed.; Manning Publications: New York, NY, USA, 2022.
35. Unity-Technologies. Default PPO Training Configurations. 2024. Available online: https://github.com/Unity-Technologies/ml-agents/blob/develop/config/ppo/FoodCollector.yaml (accessed on 16 July 2024).
36. Unity-Technologies. Default SAC Training Configurations. 2024. Available online: https://github.com/Unity-Technologies/ml-agents/blob/develop/config/sac/FoodCollector.yaml (accessed on 16 July 2024).
37. Unity-Technologies. Ml-Agents Hyperparameters Documentation. 2024. Available online: https://github.com/Unity-Technologies/ml-agents/blob/develop/docs/Training-Configuration-File.md (accessed on 16 July 2024).

MDPI AG
Grosspeteranlage 5
4052 Basel
Switzerland
Tel.: +41 61 683 77 34

Algorithms Editorial Office
E-mail: algorithms@mdpi.com
www.mdpi.com/journal/algorithms

www.ingramcontent.com/pod-product-compliance
Lightning Source LLC
Chambersburg PA
CBHW041945260926
51850CB00018B/872
* 9 7 8 3 7 2 5 8 4 9 0 1 7 *